TOWARD A
THEORY OF
COGNITIVE
POETICS

TOWARD A THEORY OF COGNITIVE POETICS

REUVEN TSUR

sussex
ACADEMIC
PRESS
Brighton • Portland • Toronto

2 4 6 8 10 9 7 5 3 1

First published 2008 in Great Britain by
SUSSEX ACADEMIC PRESS
PO Box 139
Eastbourne BN24 9BP

Distributed in North America by
SUSSEX ACADEMIC PRESS
ISBS Publisher Services
920 NE 58th Ave #300, Portland, OR 97213, USA

British Library Cataloguing in Publication Data
A CIP catalogue record for this book is available from the British Library.

Library of Congress Cataloging-in-Publication Data
Tsur, Reuven.
 Toward a theory of cognitive poetics / Reuven Tsur. — Second, expanded and updated ed.
 p. cm.
 Includes bibliographical references and index.
 ISBN 978-1-84519-255-6 (h/c : alk. paper) —
 ISBN 978-1-84519-256-3 (pbk. : alk. paper)
 1. Poetics—Psychological aspects. 2. Cognitive grammar. I. Title.
P311.T73   2008
808.1—dc22

2007046043

Printed by TJ International, Padstow, Cornwall.
This book is printed on acid-free paper.

Contents

Preface to the First Edition vii

Preface to the Second Edition viii

Acknowledgments ix

A Note on Transliteration xi

General Assumptions

1. The Nature of Cognitive Poetics 1
2. Mental and Vocal Performance in Poetry Reading 29
3. Constructing a Stable World 43
4. Poetic Structure and Perceived Qualities 77

The Sound Stratum of Poetry

5. Rhyme Patterns, Gestalt Theory and Perceptual Forces 111
6. Metre and Rhythm 155
7. Delivery Style and Listener Response — an Empirical Study 181
8. Expressiveness and Musicality of Speech Sounds 209

The Units-of-Meaning Stratum

9. Semantic Representation and Information Processing 245
10. Literary Synaesthesia 283

The World Stratum

11. The Representative Anecdote: Human Contingency 295

Regulative Concepts

12. The Versatile Reader: Style as Open Concept 313
13. Style as Diagnosis and as Hypothesis
    Practical Application: The Ballad "Edward" 343
14. Archetypal Patterns 355

Poetry of Orientation & Disorientation

15.   Space Perception and Poetry of Orientation   385
16.   Poetry of Disorientation   405
17.   The Grotesque as an Aesthetic Mode   423

Poetry of Altered States of Consciousness

18.   Poetry and Altered States of Consciousness   451
19.   Obtrusive Rhythms and Emotive Crescendo   471
20.   The Divergent Passage and Ecstatic Poetry   495

Critics and Criticism

21.   The Implied Critic's Decision Style   511
22.   The Critic's Mental Dictionary   541

Cognitive Poetics and Cognitive Linguistics

23.   Lakoff's Roads Not Taken   577
24.   Deixis in Literature: What *Isn't* Cognitive Poetics?   595
25.   Comparing Approaches to Versification Style in *Cyrano de Bergerac*   623

References   641
Index   659

Preface
to the First Edition

The writing of a book that presumes to integrate one's theoretical work of twenty-five years or so is a frightening, though exciting, adventure. This book would have never been written were it not for the advice and support of two persons, Dr. Kees Michielsen of Elsevier Science Publishers, and Professor Jacob Mey of Odense University, to whom I wish to express my deepest gratitude. It was Dr. Michielsen who first suggested to me that I have reached a stage in my research into Cognitive Poetics in which I should attempt to integrate the various aspects of my work into a coherent whole. Professor Mey's advice proved to be crucial during two decisive stages of my endeavor. At the outset, it was he who advised me how to go about synthesizing my various writings published earlier; and while I was preparing the final version of this book, Professor Mey suggested a wealth of improvements. I felt in the course of our joint venture that it was, indeed, a co-operation with a kindred spirit.

I also wish to express my thanks to my colleagues at Tel Aviv University, Professor Zephyra Porath, and Ms. Ruthi Lavy, who read through the manuscript, made important comments and were always available for a stimulating discussion of the problems arising in the course of my work. Finally, I am indebted to the members of the Cognitive Poetics Workshop at the Katz Research Institute for Hebrew Literature, where for the past twelve years we have been discussing each others' works in progress; many of the ideas propounded here were discussed at this forum for the first time. For any remaining shortcomings, however, I alone take all the responsibility.

Preface
to the Second Edition

Since the first publication of this book many scholars adopted the term "Cognitive Poetics", and it is now widely used—in quite different senses. A colleague, one of the leading Cognitive Linguists, suggested that I publish a revised second edition, "taking into account the developments in Cognitive Poetics that occurred after the publication of your book". He suggested that I add to the present edition a few case studies comparing my analysis to some cognitive linguist's analysis of one issue each, so as to highlight the difference between our approaches. The last, new section of chapters contains three such studies, responding to three papers—by George Lakoff, Peter Stockwell, and Eve Sweetser.

A few years after the publication of the first edition I had, after twenty-five years of agonizing search, an enormous break-through in my instrumental research on the rhythmical performance of poetry. I published the results in my 1998 book: *Poetic Rhythm: Structure and Performance—An Empirical Study in Cognitive Poetics*. This is the only point on which I had to withdraw the position I put forward in the first edition of this book. So, in Chapter 6, "Metre and Rhythm", I replaced the discussion of the performance of Keats's "Bright star!" with a recent, more accurate analysis of the same recordings. I also added Chapter 7, "Delivery Style and Listener Response—An Empirical Study". This chapter goes two steps beyond the scope of the instrumental research reported in my book on poetic rhythm. It attempts to substantiate the inferences from the machine's output against the intuitions of flesh-and-blood listeners; and, thanks to recent software developments, I could manipulate recorded readings in accordance with the predictions of my theory, and observe the perceived differences. In Chapter 8, too, I inserted some instrumental stuff. I have also found on the web a compelling demonstration of the power of perceptual hypotheses in music perception, reinforcing my argument in Chapter 3, "Constructing a Stable World". The recordings analyzed are available online:
http://www.tau.ac.il/~tsurxx/SecondEditionSoundFiles/Toward2ndEd_SoundFiles.ht ml

Acknowledgments

Much of the research included in the present book has been published earlier. Since this book purports to *synthesize* my earlier work, it is sometimes difficult to tell the exact boundaries of the original publications. Chapter 1 includes pp. 5–28 of *What is Cognitive Poetics?*, 1983, The Katz Research Institute for Hebrew Literature; extensive extracts from "Horror Jokes, Black Humor, and Cognitive Poetics", *Humor 2–3:* 243–255, 1989; and brief extracts from *What Makes Sound Patterns Expressive?—The Poetic Mode of Speech Perception*, 1992, Durham: Duke University Press; and *On Metaphoring*, 1987, Israel Science Publishers. Chapter 2 is reproduced here with considerable changes from "Mental and Vocal Performance in Poetry Reading", *Literature and Psychology*, Proceedings of the Seventh International Conference on Literature and Psychology, Urbino, July 6–9, 1990, 149–159. My paper "Emotion, Emotional Qualities, and Poetry", *Psychocultural Review 2*, 1978: 165–180, has been distributed between chapters 3 and 4. The discussion of quotes 1–4 in Chapter 4 is reproduced here from *A Perception-Oriented Theory of Metre*, 1977, Tel Aviv: Tel Aviv University, The Porter Israeli Institute for Poetics and Semiotics (Papers on Poetics and Semiotics), pp. 180–185. A great part of Chapter 5 has been condensed from Chapters 2, 6, 8 of *A Perception-Oriented Theory of Metre*; and from "Articulateness and Requiredness in Iambic Verse", 1972, *Style* 6: 123–148. Chapter 6 has been condensed from Chapters 1, 2, 4, 5 of *A Perception-Oriented Theory of Metre*; and from "Contrast, Ambiguity, Double-Edgedness", *Poetics Today*, 6: 417–445; its last section has been reproduced from "Stress, Intonation, and Duration in Prose and Verse—Selected Issues in the Performance Dimension", 1985, *Eidos* II, 1–2: 5–8. Chapter 7 has been condensed from Chapters 1 and 2 of my book *What Makes Sound Patterns Expressive?—The Poetic Mode of Speech Perception*, 1992, Durham: Duke University Press, pp. 1–88. (by kind permission of Duke University Press). Chapter 8 has been condensed from Chapters 4 and 5 of *On Metaphoring*; and *Poetic Structure, Information-Processing and Perceived Effects*, 1983, The Katz Research Institute for Hebrew Literature. Chapter 9 is reproduced here from "Literary Synaesthesia: A Cognitive Approach", *Hebrew Linguistics* 28–29–30: LXXV–LXXVI, 1990, which is an abbreviated version of Chapter 12 of *On Metaphoring*. Extensive parts of Chapter 11 are adapted here from *Mediaeval Hebrew Poetry in a Double Perspective: The Versatile Reader and Hebrew Poetry in Spain*, 1987, University

Publishing Projects, pp. 7–54. A great part of Chapter 14 is extracted from Chapter 9 of *On Metaphoring*. Chapter 15 is reproduced here from Chapter 9 of *On Metaphoring*. The section "Oceanic Imagery in *Faust*: Ehrenzweig against Ehrenzweig" in Chapter 17 is reproduced here from "'Oceanic' Dedifferentiation and Poetic Metaphor", 1988, *Journal of Pragmatics* 12: 711–724. Chapter 18 includes much material from my *The Road to "Kubla Khan"*, 1987, Israel Science Publishers; *Hebrew Hypnotic Poetry*, 1988, The Katz Research Institute for Hebrew Literature; *Poetic Structure, Information-Processing and Perceived Effects*. My discussion of Snyder on Gray's "Elegy Written in a Country Churchyard" is reproduced here from *What Makes Sound Patterns Expressive? — The Poetic Mode of Speech Perception*, 1992, Durham: Duke University Press, pp. 45–47. The section "The Divergent Passage and Two Cognitive Mechanisms" in Chapter 19 is extracted from Chapters 7 and 8 of *A Perception-Oriented Theory of Metre*. Chapter 20 reproduces, with a few additions, two papers: "Two Critical Attitudes: Quest for Certitude and Negative Capability", *College English* 36, 1975: 776–788. Copyright 1975 by the National Council of Teachers of English. Reprinted with permission. "Levels of Information Processing in Reading Poetry", 1979, *Critical Inquiry*: 751–759. © by The University of Chicago. 0093–1896/79/ 0504–0009$01.58. Reprinted with permission. Chapter 21 includes *Critical Terms and Insight: The Mental Dictionary of "Critical Competence"*, 1983, The Katz Research Institute for Hebrew Literature; and pp. 28–36 from *What is Cognitive Poetics?* The discussions of Mediaeval Hebrew poetry are adapted from my Hebrew book *Mediaeval Hebrew Poetry in a Double Perspective: The Versatile Reader and Hebrew Poetry in Spain*. Chapter 23 is reprinted, with minor additions, from "Lakoff's Roads not Taken". *Pragmatics and Cognition* 7 (2000): 339–359. With kind permission by John Benjamins Publishing Company, Amsterdam/Philadelphia. www.benjamins.com

The following figures have been redrawn here, by permission of the original publishers:
* Rudolf Arnheim. *Art and Visual Perception: A Psychology of the Creative Eye*, figures from pages 1, 3, 57, 60, 39. Copyright © 1954 The Regents of the University of California. Reproduced as figure 1 in Chapter 2, figure 1 in Chapter 3, figures 1 and 2 in Chapter 5, and figure 1 in Chapter 6. * Figures 2, 3, and 4 (pp. 90–91) from *On the Experience of Time* by Robert E. Ornstein (Penguin Books, 1969), copyright © Robert E. Ornstein, 1969. Reproduced in Chapter 19, note 6. * Chapter 4, figure 1, from Köhler, Wolfgang; *The Task of **Gestalt** Psychology*. Copyright © 1969 by PUP. Reproduced by permission of Princeton University Press. * Chapter 8, figure 1, from Collins, A. M., and Quillian, M. R. (1969) "Retrieval Time from Semantic Memory". *Journal of Verbal Learning and Verbal Behavior*. 8: 240–247; reprinted by permission of the publisher and the authors. * Chapter 20, figures 1, 2, 3, and 4 are figures from *Human Information Processing: Individuals and Groups Functioning in Complex Social*

*Situation*s by Harold M. Schroder, Michael J. Driver, and Siegfried Streufert, copyright ©1967 by Holt, Rinehart and Winston, Inc., reprinted by permission of the publisher.

The author and publisher gratefully acknowledge the assistance and agreement of publishers and editors cited above. The publishers apologize for any errors or omissions in the above list and would be grateful to be notified of any corrections that should be incorporated in the next edition or reprint of this book.

A Note on Transliteration

I have given most Hebrew quotations in three versions: in the original, in a transliteration, and in a literal translation. There are considerable differences between Biblical, Mediaeval, and Modern Hebrew pronunciation; what is more, there are considerable differences between present-day speakers, according to their, or their parents', country of origin. In my transliteration, I have attempted to strike a kind of precarious consistency between Mediaeval Hebrew pronunciation, and my own idiolect of Israelese. In Biblical and Mediaeval Hebrew, the stops [b, g, d, k, p, t] each had an allophone, presumably fricative ([b̠, g̠, d̠, k̠, p̠, t̠]). In present-day spoken Hebrew, only [v, f, x] exist. In my transliteration, I have preserved only those fricatives that are used today. Nevertheless, I have preserved the distinction between [k] and [q], even though it is obliterated today. As for vowels, the distinction between ֫ and ֖ on the one hand, and ֺ and ֻ on the other, is not observed by present-day speakers; in accordance with this practice, I have transcribed the former two vowels as [a]; but, in accordance with Biblical Hebrew as well as my own idiolect, I have transcribed the latter pair as [e], and [ε], respectively. The *šwa mobile* ([ə]) has in Hebrew three allophones pronounced as [a], [ε], and [o]; since in Mediaeval Hebrew poetry, meter is based on a contrast between *šwa mobile* and full vowel, I have indicated these allophones in Mediaeval (but not in Modern) poetry as ǎ, ε̌, and ǒ.

TOWARD A THEORY OF COGNITIVE POETICS

CHAPTER 1

The Nature of Cognitive Poetics

Poetics and Cognitive Science

Like Molière's 'Bourgeois Nobleman', who discovered one day that all his life he had been speaking prose, I discovered in 1980 at the second annual conference of the Cognitive Science Association in New Haven that for the preceding ten years or so, most of my work in literary criticism and theory had been devoted to cognitive poetics.

As a review of the Twentieth Century critical scene may reveal, there are, on the one hand, impressionist critics who indulge in the **effects** of literary texts, but have difficulties in relating them to their **structures**. On the other hand, there are analytic and structuralist critics who excel in the **description** of the structure of literary texts, but it is not always clear what the human **significance** is of these texts, or how their perceived effects can be accounted for. Cognitive Poetics, as practiced in the present work, offers cognitive theories that systematically account for the relationship between the structure of literary texts and their perceived effects. By the same token, it discriminates which reported effects *may* legitimately be related to the structures in question, and which may not.

For my purpose, the term "poetics" may be defined as follows:

> The actual objects of poetics are the particular regularities that occur in literary texts and that determine the specific effects of poetry; in the final analysis—the human ability to produce poetic structures and understand their effect—that is, something which one might call *poetic competence.* (Bierwisch, 1970: 98–99)

Cognitive Poetics is an interdisciplinary approach to the study of literature employing the tools offered by cognitive science. "Cognitive science" is an umbrella term covering the various disciplines that investigate human information processing: cognitive psychology, psycholinguistics, artificial intelligence, and certain branches of linguistics, and of the philosophy of science. These explore the psychological processes involved in the acquisition, organization, and use of knowledge; in fact, in all information processing activities of the brain, ranging from the analysis of immediate stimuli to the organization of subjective experience. Cognitive Poetics explores the possible contributions of cognitive science to Poetics: it attempts to find out how poetic language and form, or the critic's decisions, are constrained and shaped by human information processing.

The present approach proposes to use cognitive theories to illuminate literature rather than use works of literature to illustrate cognitive theories. It emphasizes the particular and nice differences between cognitive processes in general and their unique exploitation for literary purposes; hence, its generalizations should be wide enough to be applicable to a great variety of literary works of art, while at the same time, they should provide means to make meaningful distinctions between, or within, specific works of literature. Such an approach requires the combination of the tools of cognitive science with those of the more traditional disciplines of literary criticism, literary history, linguistics, and aesthetics. An important task of cognitive poetics is to explore the possibilities and limitations of such combinations.

Such a conception of how poetic language or literary form is constrained and shaped by cognitive processes is not entirely new. We find a few exquisite though isolated examples already in Aristotle's *Poetics*. Consider the following passage from Chapter 7 of the *Poetics:*

> Again, a beautiful object, whether it be a picture of a living organism or any whole composed of parts, must not only have an orderly arrangement of parts, but must also be of a certain magnitude; for beauty depends on magnitude and order. Hence an exceedingly small picture cannot be beautiful; for the view of it is confused, the object being seen in an almost imperceptible moment of time. Nor, again, can one of vast size be beautiful; for as the eye cannot take it all in at once, the unity and sense of the whole is lost for the spectator; as for instance if there were a picture of a thousand miles long. [...]; so in the plot, a certain length is necessary and a length which can be easily embraced *by the memory.* [...] The limit as fixed by the nature of the drama itself is this: — *the greater the length, the more beautiful will the piece be by reason of its size, provided that the whole be perspicuous.* (Aristotle, 1951: 36; my italics)

Here beauty is defined both in the visual domain and the appreciation of drama in terms of the constraints of the cognitive apparatus; or, rather, by the opposing constraints of the cognitive apparatus constraining each other by determining the lower and upper limit. The inherent length of drama is regulated by the limitations of memory, rather than by the "water-clock". By contrast, in the novel, e.g., where the reader may freely turn the pages back and forth, size is *not* constrained by the limitations of memory; here, size is virtually unlimited, and the constraints of memory are exploited in other ways. While such insights are occasional in Aristotle's work, they constitute the central endeavor of Cognitive Poetics, which massively draws upon all available information from modern cognitive science.

Cognitive Poetics as practiced in the present study is trying to avoid a reductionist view of literary theory according to which all the "special sciences" can be reduced to "more basic sciences" and, eventually, to physics. "Psychological reductionism" writes Fodor (1979: 18) is "the doctrine that every psychological natural kind is, or is coextensive with, a neurological natural kind". By analogy, poetic reductionism would be the doctrine that every literary "natural" kind is, or is coextensive with, a psychological natural kind. A major assumption of the present cognitive approach is that literature does have important operational principles that cannot be exhausted in terms of cognitive science. To paraphrase Polányi (1967: 39), a complete cognitive (or phonetic, or phonological, or lexical) topography of a discourse would not tell us whether it is a literary discourse, and if so, how it works, and for what purpose. "We may call the control exercised by the organizational principle of a higher level on the particulars forming its lower level the principle of marginal control" (Polányi, 1967: 40). And Polányi continues:

> You can see, for example, how, in the hierarchy constituting speechmaking, successive working principles control the boundary left indeterminate on the next lower level. Voice production, which is the lowest level of speech, leaves largely open the combination of sounds into words, which is controlled by a vocabulary. Next, a vocabulary leaves largely open the combination of words into sentences, which is controlled by grammar. And so it goes. Moreover, each lower level imposes restrictions on the one above it, even as the laws of inanimate nature restrict the practicability of conceivable machines; and again, we may observe that a higher operation may fail when the next lower operation escapes from its control. (Ibid., 40–41)

To paraphrase Polányi (ibid.), the principles of literature may be said to govern the boundary conditions of a cognitive system—a set of conditions that is explicitly left undetermined by the laws of lower processes, physical, cognitive, and linguistic. If one knows what is the set of boundary conditions left undetermined, and by what laws of what "lower" processes, one may get a better understanding of the principles of literature that govern those boundary conditions. It is claimed that in this way Cognitive Poetics is capable of discerning and explaining significant literary phenomena which present insurmountable difficulties to other approaches.

The Purpose of Art and Cognitive Processes

Walter Pater (1951: 896) justified the existence of art thus: "Not the fruit of experience, but experience itself, is the end". "For art comes to you proposing frankly to give nothing but the highest quality to your moments as they pass, and simply for those moments' sake" (ibid., 897). Another illustrious ancestor of cognitive poetics stated the *raison d'être* of art as follows:

> The process of algebraization, the over-automatization of an object, permits the greatest economy of perceptive effort. Either objects are assigned

> only one feature—a number, for example—or else they function as though by formula and do not even appear in cognition [...]. Habituation devours works, cloths, furniture, one's wife, and the fear of war. "If the whole complex lives of many people go on unconsciously, then such lives are as if they had never been". And art exists that one may recover the sensation of life; it exists to make one feel things, to make the stone *stony*. The purpose of art is to impart the sensation of things as they are perceived and not as they are known. The technique of art is to make the object "unfamiliar", to make forms difficult, to increase the difficulty and length of perception because the process of perception is an aesthetic end in itself and must be prolonged. (Shklovsky, 1965: 12)

This passage is important for our discussion in several respects. In the first place, it shows what it is that art is better suited than anything else to do; and it also suggests that it is precisely this something that prevents human life from becoming meaningless. In the second place, it presents an instance of what cognitive poetics typically does. It indicates the way in which the human cognitive system typically functions in nonliterary experience, the way that "permits the greatest economy of perceptive effort". Finally it suggests that in order to achieve art's end, these normal cognitive processes must be disturbed, deformed, slowed down.

Shklovsky's paper is called "Art as Technique", and its main bulk is focused on a single device, that of making things "unfamiliar", intended to "impart the sensation of things as they are perceived and not as they are known", by prolonging the process of perception. Cognitive poetics examines a great variety of processes and investigates the ways in which they may be delayed by a great variety of devices other than the ones explored by Shklovsky. Systematic disturbance of the categorization process makes low-categorized information, as well as rich pre-categorial sensory information, available to consciousness.

One major assumption of cognitive poetics is that poetry exploits, for aesthetic purposes, cognitive (including linguistic) processes that were initially evolved for nonaesthetic purposes, just as in evolving linguistic ability, old cognitive and physiological mechanisms were turned to new ends. Such an assumption is more parsimonious than postulating independent aesthetic and/or linguistic mechanisms. Polányi's conception of "marginal control" and "emergence" is central to this assumption.

The reading of poetry involves the modification (or, sometimes, the deformation) of cognitive processes, and their adaptation for purposes for which they were not originally "devised". In certain extreme but central cases, this modification may become "organized violence against cognitive processes", to paraphrase the famous slogan of Russian Formalism. As will be emphasized time and again in the course of the present study, quite a few (but by no means all) central poetic effects are the result of some drastic interference with, or at least delay of, the regular course of cognitive processes, and the exploitation of its effects for aesthetic purposes. In other words, the cognitive correlates of poetic processes must be described in three respects: the normal cognitive processes; some kind of modification or disturbance of these processes; and their reorganization according to different principles.

Let me briefly illustrate this issue in semiotic terms. Every sign consists of a *signifiant* and a *signifié*. Humans, being sign-using animals, are inclined to move as rapidly as possible from the *signifiant* to the *signifié*, to extract as quickly as possible the information required for survival or adaptation. According to some semiotic conceptions of poetry, poetic texts require the reader to linger on the *signifiant* for a longer time than do nonpoetic texts, before moving on to the *signifié*. Strings of phonemes (that is, clusters of phonemes in syntagmatic combinations) are the *signifiants* of semantic clusters (called *meaning*) in verbal signs called *words*. Poetry imposes additional (paradigmatic) patterns on the phonological *signifiant,* called, e.g., meter, alliteration, rhyme. This is an aesthetic organizing principle (cf. "The poetic function projects the principle of equivalence from the axis of selection into the axis of combination"; Jakobson, 1960: 358). Thus, the aesthetic organization focuses more than is done usually on the string of phonemes, disrupting (or delaying at least) the automatic transition from the *signifiant* to the *signifié*. Such delay or disruption may reach different degrees of awareness; as will be suggested in chapter 4, important stylistic distinctions may be derived from such differences. In this respect, the semiotic conception of poetry becomes a specific instance of the wider conception propounded by Cognitive Poetics.

When we epitomize the response to poetry as organized violence against cognitive processes, we must understand, in the first place, those cognitive phenomena that are being "violated", or modified, as well as the *kinds* of violations we may expect to encounter in relation to poetry. In the second place, it is not enough to know that it is an "organized violence"; we must understand the principles of that organization. Furthermore, there also may be "organized violence" against cognitive processes according to different, non-aesthetic, principles. It will be suggested later in this chapter that the same cognitive processes are violated in the use of poetic language as in the tip-of-the-tongue (TOT) phenomenon (when one has a word at the tip of his tongue, and cannot recall it). However, the violence against this process is organized by aesthetic principles in the case of poetic language, whereas it is organized (and highly organized, at that) by psychopathological principles in the case of the TOT phenomenon (witness Freud's brilliant analysis of the case in which a young man was incapable of recalling the Latin word *aliquis* in a line from Virgil).

The principles of organization of this "violence" in poetic language lie in the domain of aesthetics and theoretical poetics. So, we shall encounter in the course of this study principles that may be familiar from those more traditional disciplines; the new insights—if any—that come from cognitive poetics are to be attributed to the application of aesthetic principles to the elements of cognitive processes. "Thus, each level is subject to dual control; first, by the laws that apply to its elements in themselves and second, by the laws that control the comprehensive entity formed by them" (Polányi, 1967: 36). In our case, the elements of cognitive processes underlying the response to poetry are controlled by the principles of cognitive science, and, at the same time, by the principles of aesthetics and theoretical poetics.

Coding and Recoding

Let us return now to Polányi's example of the principles of speech-making, and note, first, that the lowest item in this hierarchical organization, "voice-production", has two facets: the one explored by articulatory phonetics, and the one explored by acoustic phonetics. The point I wish to make is that speech sounds can be discussed on two organizational levels: as a stream of acoustic cues, and as a stream of phonetic units that are bundles of distinctive features.

Second, I wish to emphasize that the various levels of organization are not merely different levels (i.e., they are not a matter of simply putting segments together to form larger units), but have genuinely different principles of organization. These different principles are no mere freaks of nature; they are functionally determined, by the differing needs of communication, and by the limitations of the relevant mechanisms that shape and constrain them. To explain how this can be conceived, I wish to supplement Polányi's model by one put forward by Liberman and his co-researchers (1972), according to whom we are dealing with a series of conversions from one level of organization to another.

One might ask: Why do we need so many organizational principles for the various levels of language? The answer is that various levels of activities, with various constraints of the underlying mechanisms, are involved in communication. At the speech-end of the hierarchy, we have an acoustic signal *that is appropriate* for transmission, and a phonetic representation *that is appropriate* for storage in *short-term memory*. The "speech code" comprises conversion from one to the other. "The difference in information rate between the two levels of speech code is staggering. To transmit the signal in acoustic form and in high fidelity costs about 70,000 bits per second; for reasonable intelligibility we need about 40,000 bits per second. [...] We should suppose that a great deal of nervous tissue would have to be devoted to the storage of even relatively short stretches. By recoding into a phonetic representation, we reduce the cost to less than 40 bits per second, thus effecting a saving of 1,000 times" (Liberman et al., 1972). At the other end of the language-processing chain we find the semantic representation, the characteristics of which can be assumed to reflect properties of long-term memory.

Thus, Liberman and his associates identify five levels of streams of information (connected by four sets of grammatical rules): in addition to the two, acoustic and semantic, that we have already talked about, deep structure, surface structure and phonetic representation of generative grammars[1]. The information at every level has a different structure.

---

[1] The TG terminology and conceptual framework, or the exact number of parallel streams of information, are not essential to my argument. Certain parts of my argument could be put in Schank's terminology of an "interlingua", through which the machine can recognize that two utterances are synonymous or antonymous, can generate an indefinite number of paraphrases for the same text, or translations to an

Looking at the process from the speaker's view-point, we see, for example, that the semantic features must be replaced by phonological features in preparation for transmission. In this conversion, an utterance which is, at the semantic level, a single unit comprising many features of meaning becomes, phonologically, a number of units composed of a very few features, the phonologic units and features being in themselves meaningless. Again, the semantic representation of an utterance in coherent discourse will typically contain multiple references to the same topic. This amounts to a kind of redundancy which serves, perhaps, to protect the semantic representation from noise in long-term memory. In the acoustic representation, however, to preserve such repetitions would unduly prolong discourse. [...] We do not say *The man sings. The man married the girl. The girl is pretty,* but rather *The man who sings married the pretty girl.* The syntactic rules describe the ways in which such redundant references are deleted. At the acoustic and phonetic levels, *redundancy* of a very different kind may be desirable.

The omission of redundant semantic elements from the acoustic representation serves, however, a purpose that goes beyond saving the discourse from undue prolongation. It is also a connective device, which makes the discourse continuous with respect to a given noun. In terms of a well-known gestalt-rule, I would describe the principle underlying this device as follows: the shape of a clause must be weakened (i.e., made less explicit) in order to make it dependent on the whole discourse. The deletion of repetitions serves precisely this purpose of weakening the shapes of individual clauses. So, in what respect is the utterance "The man who sings married the pretty girl" inappropriate to the properties of long-term memory? Information must be stored in long-term memory in such a form that it should be available for new combinations and not only in the form in which it was first presented. The discontinuous sentences in "The man sings. The man married the girl. The girl is pretty", being self-contained, have stronger shapes and make the three chunks of information less dependent on the whole discourse, and thus more easily available for new combinations. Consequently, the same chunks of information are available also for the following (and many more) discourses: "The girl whom the man who sings married is pretty". The storing of information in discontinuous sentences, in which redundant references are not deleted, would appear to be a waste of mental storage space. However, this apparently wasteful storage, from which an indefinite number of con-

---

indefinite number of languages. Other parts of my arguments could conveniently be put in Fodor's more recent terms of "the modularity of the mind". What is essential for my argument is, that there are different streams of information with different principles of organization, for different purposes, and with clear steps of conversion between them, which can be disturbed or delayed for aesthetic purposes. I am using the TG terminology mainly because Liberman et al. are using it, and because it obviates the need to change my terminology at various stages of my argument.

tinuous discourses can be generated, is more efficient, on the one hand, than storing all that continuous discourse; on the other hand, it is also more efficient than extracting each time the information needed for the generation of new discourses from the original continuous discourse. "Computing memory is expensive, but long-term memory is cheap" (Fodor, 1979: 150).

Failure of Recoding

Liberman and his collaborators conceive of systems of versification as kinds of secondary codes. "For a literate society the function of verse is primarily esthetic, but for preliterate societies, verse is a means of transmitting verbal information of cultural importance with a minimum of paraphrase. The rules of verse are, in effect, an addition to phonology which requires that material not only should preserve the semantic values of the original, but should also conform to a specific, rule-determined, phonetic pattern" (Liberman et al., 1972). In terms of the premises of the present discussion, we can regard paraphrase, not as a result of forgetting, but rather as an essential correlate of the processes by which we normally communicate and remember. "If linguistic communications could only be stored in the form in which they were presented, we should presumably make inefficient use of our capacity for storage and retrieval; the information must be restructured if that which is communicated to us by language is to be well remembered" (ibid.). Now, it is precisely this process of successive restructurings or recodings that is interfered with by versification. In a sense, this increases our "capacity of retrieval" for the particular versified messages; but this is done at the price of patent interference with the cognitive economy of the system. So, we may regard versification as an instance of "organized violence" against cognitive processes.

Let us return, again, to Polányi's "principle of marginal control", and to my suggestion that literature has important operational principles that cannot be exhausted in terms of cognitive science. The lower-level processes, physical, physiological, and psychological, must be taken for granted, but normally need not be referred to in a literary analysis. As long as the system does not fail, they go unnoticed. As long as the processes of recodings go undisturbed, they may, indeed, be taken for granted. In Polányi's words, "we may observe that a higher operation may fail when the next lower operation escapes from its control". However, the failure of fast and complete recoding renders the lower operations not only observable; the failure itself may have a unique conscious quality. Such failures of the lower operations do not cause a complete breakdown of the system; the elements that become palpable by the failure are systematically exploited for aesthetic purposes, and so become proper elements in an aesthetic organization. To put it briefly: the discussion of cognitive processes becomes relevant to poetics, when the conscious quality of their failure is a crucial link in combinations with elements on another level of the message.

The chain of successive recodings can be delayed at other points, too—indeed, at all points; this delay, in turn, may or may not be exploited for aesthetic purposes.

Let us take just one more instance. Speech sounds do have a phonetic facet and an acoustic facet. The transition between the two involves complex recoding; that is, there is no one-to-one relationship between the phonetic unit and the acoustic cues. Since, however, we are usually not aware of acoustic cues, only of phonetic units, we may simply ignore the acoustic cues in our discussion of, e.g., expressive sound patterns in poetry, though we may rely on phonetic properties of the speech-sounds. Now, it has been found statistically that such liquids and nasals as /l/, /m/, are, in a variety of languages, positively correlated with tender poems and negatively with aggressive ones; whereas such voiceless stops as /t/, /k/, are positively correlated with aggressive poems, and negatively with tender ones (see Chapter 8). Phonetically, these groups of consonants are opposed along such dimensions as [±VOICED] and [±CONTINUOUS], and these dimensions may possibly account for some aspects of the "combinational potential" of these sounds. At first glance, it may have little poetic significance that these groups of consonants are also contrasted in their relative coding: liquids and nasals are relatively unencoded, whereas voiceless stops are highly encoded. In more familiar terms, this means that voiceless stops undergo more restructuring from acoustic cues to speech sounds than do liquids and nasals; in still more familiar terms, this means that there is little resemblance between the shape of the acoustic signal and the perceived shape of voiceless stops. In everyday speech, this need not interest us very much; this fact seems to be of no linguistic significance, and as such, of little poetic consequence.

Now, the correlation of liquids and nasals and of voiceless stops with tender and aggressive poems can be explained, precisely, in terms of a delay in recoding or restructuring, from acoustic cues to phonetic entities. Voiceless stops are perceived as unitary linguistic events, stripped of all pre-categorial sensory information. Here, the recoding process goes on with no interference. On the other hand, in relatively unencoded speech sounds, such as liquids and nasals, the recoding process can be "disturbed", so that some of the rich pre-categorial auditory information becomes available to consciousness. Emotional flexibility, an openness and responsiveness to rich pre-categorial information, is characteristic of tender feelings, whereas the lack of it characterizes aggression. Thus, liquids and nasals *may* have a *perceived quality* of tenderness, of emotional adaptability, or sensory richness, whereas voiceless stops may have a perceived quality of rigidity that may be positively correlated with aggression and negatively with tenderness.

Liberman and his collaborators suggest that there is a speech mode and a nonspeech mode of processing acoustic signals. The output of the latter is experienced in consciousness as music or natural noises; in the speech mode the output of the nonspeech mode is shut out from consciousness. I suggest that there may be a **poetic** mode as well, one that is similar to the speech mode in that it is focused on linguistic categories; but, at the same time, the output of the nonspeech mode, in the form of pre-categorial auditory information, becomes—however faintly—accessible to consciousness. From this point of view, voiceless stops are not to be conceived of as *mere* acoustic cues, completely restructured as phonetic categories, with no delay in recoding. This "no delay" is better regarded as a *marked* no delay, that is an instance opposed to vowels, liquids, and nasals, in which rich pre-categorial sensory information *can* be discerned.

Recoding De-Automatized
An Interaction View

Normally, the conversion from surface structure to deep structure and back is automatic and goes unnoticed. Some aesthetic effects crucially depend on a de-automatization of this conversion. Let us consider the following four dialogues:

(1)   — Mum, is Dad not ready to eat yet?
        — Shut up, I've just told you, he's not tender enough yet.

(2)   — Mum, is Dad not ready to eat yet?
        — Shut up, I've just told you, he's not finished with his work yet.

(3)   — Mum, is the chicken not ready to eat yet?
        — Shut up, I've just told you, it's not tender enough yet.

(4)   — Mum, is the chicken not ready to eat yet?
        — O.K., go and feed it.

A comparison between these four dialogues points up two kinds of relationships: first, between identical surface structures and different deep structures; second, between identical syntactic structures and different "scripts" derived from extralinguistic world knowledge. In addition, in (1), but not in the other three dialogues, we shall have to consider a relationship between these relationships and a certain aesthetic quality, variously described as *wit,* or *the grotesque.*

   To use a somewhat antiquated terminology, in all four dialogues, the first (interrogative) sentence is a transformation of the underlying 'kernel sentence' *"x is ready to eat"*. The mother's answers bring out in this surface shape two deep structures. In two of the sentences ((2), (4)), x is the 'deep subject' *(x eats y);* in the other two, it is the deep object *(y eats x).* However, the comparison between the four passages brings out the often overlooked fact that the interpretation of these questions depends not only on their deep structures, but also on some real-world knowledge. The various deep structures activate what we might call different *scripts*—extending somewhat the use of Schank and Abelson's term (1977). We cannot explain, with reference to deep structures only, why the default interpretation of "Dad is ready to eat" is *(x eats y),* whereas the default interpretation of "The chicken is ready to eat" is *(y eats x).* Passages (2) and (3) both activate the fairly trivial "family dinner" (or similar) script, whereas passage (1) activates some "cannibalism" script, which is much less trivial in a Western society (notice that in Schank and Abelson's usage, "nontrivial script" might be a contradiction in terms). The animal feeding script of

(4), too, would be less familiar in an urban society, whereas in a society in which it is familiar, it would be more difficult to account for the child's impatience.

What we have in (1) obviously belongs to the literary genre of 'horror jokes', a genre which crucially depends on a cognitive mechanism of mental sets shifting from a trivial "default script" automatically applied, to a script that has an element of horror in it, and so is less trivial. A **mental set** is the readiness to respond in a certain way. It is, obviously, an adaptation device of great survival value, and is required for handling any situation consistently. Of no less great survival value is the adaptation-device called **shift of mental sets.** This may be defined as the **shift** of one's readiness to respond in a certain way. It is required for handling *changing* situations in extra-linguistic reality. The use of these two (opposed) kinds of adaptation mechanisms may yield different kinds of pleasure. The *mental set* is a typical instance of gaining pleasure from the saving of mental energy. The *shift of mental sets* yields a kind of pleasure that is derived from the certainty that one's adaptation mechanisms function properly. *Wit* can now be described as the unique conscious quality of shifting mental sets, and the sense of *humor* as the ability to apply wit to difficult life situations, an ability that is usually regarded as a sign of mental health. In the light of the foregoing discussion, the reason for this would seem pretty obvious. The sense of humor, or the ability to apply wit to difficult life situations, is a sign of one's ability to shift one's mental sets in changing situations.[2] This shift of mental sets in (1) accounts for the witty or grotesque effect (grotesque effects will be discussed at some length later). In the present instance, the shift from one script to another presupposes a drastic interference with the automatic conversion from surface to deep structure. By the same token, we are prevented from forgetting the unique surface structure of the first sentence upon which the co-occurrence of the two deep structures crucially depends.

Here, then, the aesthetic effect arises from an interruption of the smooth working of the recoding process and the effects of this interruption on two further cognitive mechanisms: the automatic application of scripts to sentences, and the shift of mental set from a trivial default script to a nontrivial horror-script. So we see here both the *violence* against the recoding process and the interaction of the results of this violence with other cognitive mechanisms. These cognitive mechanisms *organize* those results in a way that is suited to achieve aesthetic effects.

A word must be said here about jokes as adaptive devices disrupted for aesthetic purposes. Jokes achieve their witty effect by inducing some marked shift of mental set, usually involving some changing situations. They are, then, an obvious case in which *an adaptive device is turned to aesthetic ends.* We should clearly distinguish between three aspects of the same process: changing situations, shift of mental sets,

---

[2] The position expounded here is consistent with Freudian theory too. "In assuming that the control of the ego over the discharge of energy is pleasurable in itself, we adopted one of the earliest, and frequently neglected, thoughts of Freud in this area; the suggestion that under certain conditions man may attempt to gain pleasure from the very activity of the psychic apparatus" (Kris, 1965: 63).

and wit as the unique conscious quality of the latter. In real life, it is the sequences of changing situations that constitute a problem for survival, and it is the ability to shift mental sets that has great survival value. Wit is, accordingly, merely a pleasurable "epiphenomenon", a conscious quality concomitant to the shift of mental sets which indicates to consciousness that the crucial adaptation mechanism is properly functioning, that is, that shift of mental sets *has* occurred. In jokes, however, the changing situations *per se* have little survival significance. Attention is shifted from them to the underlying cognitive mechanism, the shift of mental sets, and more pronouncedly, to its unique conscious quality, wit. This is how in jokes, *an adaptive device is turned to aesthetic ends:* attention is shifted from the changing situations and the adaptation mechanism handling them to the (pleasurable) conscious quality of their reliable functioning. A special relationship obtains here between the changing situation and the cognitive mechanism devised to cope with it (shift of mental sets). There is here no sequence of gradually fluctuating situations as in real life, but two discrete situations related only in a highly artificial manner, *via* the alternative meanings of one string of words. This state of affairs contributes two significant aspects to the joke. On the one hand, it may sharpen the incongruence between the successive situations to a degree that is unusual in consecutive real-life situations; on the other hand, the artificiality of the link facilitates the *turning* of the adaptive device *to aesthetic ends*. The shifting situations form no part of some credible, consistent reality, and attention is directed away from the *adaptive* aspect of the process to its *unique conscious quality,* that is, its perceived aesthetic quality: *wit.*

Semantic Representation

According to a prevalent—though by no means the only—present day-view of semantic representation, the meaning of words can be conceived of as of bundles of elements that are frequently referred to as "semantic features", or "meaning components", or "primitive concepts". Thus, the word *bachelor* can be analyzed into the following set of components: [+NOUN +COUNT +ANIMATE +HUMAN +ADULT +MALE −MARRIED]. The change of the sign of the last but one feature on this list to [−MALE] results in a meaning structure that can be realized in the surface word *spinster*. Deletion of the last feature in the above list results in a meaning structure that can be realized as the word *man*. If we delete the last feature on the above list and change the algebraic sign of the last but one feature, we get the meaning structure of *woman,* and so forth. This hierarchy of components forms the basis of the **hyponymic** organization of the vocabulary: *bachelor* is a hyponym (subordinate) of *man,* which in turn is a hyponym of *human,* which in turn is a hyponym of *animate things,* and so forth (conversely, *animate things* is a superordinate of *human,* and so forth).

Early research on this topic hoped to find a limited number of semantic primitives from which all the meanings of all the words in the world (or at least in a given language) could be derived, just as all the matter in the physical world used to be accounted for in terms of a small number of atoms. Now it is obvious that this is not the case, neither in semantics, nor in physics. Nevertheless, the advantage of this approach, viz., that it can account for our intuitions concerning significant meaning relationships, such as synonymy, antonymy, or hyponymy, remains in effect. Thus, for instance, it allows us to know that the sentences "John sold a book to Mary" and "Mary bought a book from John" are synonymous, since both *sold* and *bought* have in their meaning structure the primitive concepts [+CHANGE +HAVE] or, in Schank's notation, [+ATRANS]. This componential (or hyponymic) organization of the vocabulary can account for several cognitive processes. Thus, for instance, it is said to facilitate the process of word acquisition by infants.

> Although little is known about the details, it is generally assumed that the meanings of some words are easier to learn if the meanings of other words are already familiar. If this plausible assumption is true, the facilitation in learning may be mediated by these recurrent patterns of recurrent concepts. One might even speculate that while a word is learnt in terms of its relations to familiar patterns of primitive concepts [...] the time required to comprehend the word might be some function of the complexity of those relations, but that once the concept is a single cognitive chunk—once it is thoroughly overlearnt and automatic—such difference in processing time would disappear. (Miller, 1978: 97)

It will be readily recognized that what Miller is describing here is, in an important sense, the verbal equivalent of what Shklovsky described in the passage quoted earlier. Substitute "word meaning" for "object" in the following sentence, and you get a description that is almost a paraphrase of what happens to a word according to Miller, once it is mastered: "The process of 'algebraization', the over-automatization of an object, permits the greatest economy of perceptive effort". Even Shklovsky's phrase "objects are assigned only one proper feature" becomes most telling in this new context, when we substitute "words" for "objects". Consider, for instance, the following issues. When one says "That person is a bachelor", one usually asserts of that person only that he is unmarried, not that he is a human being, or an adult, or a male (although one *specifies,* by the same token, "that person" as adult and male). Similarly the negative: "That person is not a bachelor" negates only the lowest feature: saying "That person is not unmarried", while still specifying the person as adult and male. Assertion and negation appear to concern only a single—the lowest—feature of nouns.

Some further cognitive manipulations are typically focused on the lowest item in the list of features. Thus, in the word association game, according to Clark (1970: 276–277), the stimulus word *man* elicits *woman* 62 percent of the time (resulting from the change of the lowest feature [+MALE]), but elicits *boy* only 8 per cent of the time (resulting from the change of the lowest-but-one feature [+ADULT]); it elicits *girl* only 3 percent of the time (resulting from changing the two lowest features). Thus, *woman* is obviously the unmarked response to *man*, whereas *boy* and *girl* are marked to varying degrees.

Poetic language typically violates this cognitive organization of semantic representation in two opposite ways. Anti-grammatical rhyme activates, by way of opposition, precisely the highest features on the list, from the part-of-speech feature downwards.[3] Thus, the lowest features in the words concerned are activated by the syntactic structures of natural languages, whereas the highest features are activated by anti-grammatical rhyme, thus justifying in one sense Richards' dictum that "poetry is written with the fullest body of words". On the other hand, metaphors tend to delete all the higher features in the figurative term, and transfer the lowest feature(s) to the headword:

(5)   His wife is a gem.

Gem is a hyponym of *stone;* the former is differentiated from the latter by the opposing features [±PRECIOUS]. In the process of understanding, the understander transfers in this sentence [+PRECIOUS] to *his wife,* and deletes all the other, higher features, that conflict with the features of the proper term *(wife),* such as [+MINERAL −ANIMATE]. Our ability to understand novel metaphors seems to indicate that "the single chunk" which, according to Miller, words become when overlearned and automatic, is not final and irreversible; the processing of metaphors proceeds by taking this "single chunk" to its component pieces. The same process is indicated by the tip-of-the-tongue (TOT) phenomenon: according to a series of well controlled experiments (Brown, 1970), words can be conceived of as of bundles of sounds and semantic categories that are activated but prevented from "growing together" into a surface word in the TOT state.

Chomsky and his school treat semantic representation within a syntactic theory. Liberman and his colleagues, too, present their conception of coding and recoding (quoted above) within such a Chomskian frame of reference. Some later researchers, such as Roger Schank and Umberto Eco seem to believe, independently from each other, that linguistic creativity, the ability of human beings to produce and understand an indefinite number of utterances to which they have not been exposed before, can be accounted for in terms of semantic coding alone, without incorporating a syntactic component into the system. They prefer to incorporate the required information in the semantic coding of each word, as that word's "combinational potential".[4]

---

[3] "Anti-grammatical rhymes" (Jakobson's term) are rhymes that oppose words belonging to different parts of speech, as *sober~October* in Poe's "Ulalume", or even sets of morphemes that belong to different parts of speech, such as Pope's *in endless error hurl'd~and riddle of the worlld.* This issue is discussed in greater detail in Chapter 9.

[4] "Combinational potential" is anticipated in syntactic theories by Katz and Fodor's "selection-restriction features", or Weinreich's "transfer features". Being a mere secondary user of linguistics and psychology, I shall refrain from arbitrating in such controversies as the ones mentioned here or in footnotes 1, 5 and 6, and shall confine myself to pointing out what seems to be essential for my argument. Not infrequently, this "essential" turns out to be compatible with both positions.

What is more, Schank devised a semantic system of artificial intelligence ("conceptual dependency"), on the basis of which the machine can paraphrase stories, answer questions about them, summarize news items and translate them into a variety of languages. "Combinational potential" will be a key notion in the understanding of a variety of issues in the ensuing chapters, such as the relationship between the phonemic and semantic structure of a text in expressive sound pattern, the relationship between metric figures and the syntactic and semantic structures of verse lines and, last but not least, the application of the critical code.

As for the latter, one must distinguish a *first-order* language, applied to things and concepts in extra-linguistic reality, and a *second-order* language applied to first-order language (see Chapter 22). We shall have to assume that the critic has built up a second-order mental dictionary in ways that are not unlike our first-order mental dictionary, and deploys it in similar ways, with relation to unforeseen texts.

Cognitive Stability and Affect

Let us turn now to another central aspect of cognitive organization and its impact on poetry and poetics. It concerns the structure of "ordinary consciousness". As Ornstein (1975: 31–62) and some other cognitive psychologists maintain, ordinary consciousness is "a personal construction". Human beings are exposed to an incessant stream of incoming sensory information. If the organism had to cope with all this incoming information, it would be "flooded". But it has been mercifully equipped with an efficient data-reduction system. We are used to think of our sense organs as of a set of organs whose destination is *to let in* information, but, by the same token, its destination is also *to shut out* certain other kinds of information. Thus, our sense organs let in light and sound waves, but shut out radio, ultra-violet and infra-red waves.

> Sense organs and the brain serve to select the aspects of the environment which are more relevant for survival. Our ordinary consciousness is object-centered; it involves analysis, a separation of oneself from other objects and organisms. This selective, active, analytic construction enables us to achieve a relatively stable personal world in which we can differentiate objects and act upon them. The concepts of causality, linear time, and language are the essence of this mode. (Ornstein, 1975: 61) [5]

[5] The filter theory of consciousness, which goes back to Bergson at least and appears to be the majority view today in cognitive psychology, has been challenged by ecological psychologists, among them the convert Neisser:

> To pick one apple from a tree you need not filter out all the others; you just don't pick them. A theory of apple picking would have much to explain [...] but it would not have to specify a mechanism to keep unwanted apples our of your mouth. (Neisser, 1976: 85)

"Stability, constancy, consistency, differentiation" are among the key-words for the effects of cognitive organization. In the visual mode, for instance, from a stream of undifferentiated stimuli we differentiate a stable, consistent world (in Chapter 15 it will be illustrated how a stable physical world is constructed from a flux of changing retinal images). Whatever visual information can be organized into clear-cut shapes or well-defined objects, is emphasized, promoted, organized as "figures" that stand out clearly against some low-differentiated "ground". All other visual information is relegated to the mass of low-differentiated background. We can differentiate figures only at the price of dumping some information into an undifferentiated ground.

> Even changing events must exhibit some degree of consistency. "Linearity" is a convenient key-term in this respect. By linearity, I largely refer to the consciousness of events enduring in time, in sequence of cause and effects. Such linearity is essential in the development of an organized culture. It is necessary for planning into the future, for taking the lessons of past history into account. (Ornstein, 1975: 56)

Language, logic, and mathematics are among the most outstanding linear activities; a psychological atmosphere of patent purpose and a sense of control are among their chief characteristics. By virtue of such an organization we achieve cognitive stability, or perceptual constancy; without this, we could not be conscious of stable objects, which remain the same while we go away and come back again. Whenever we see a person from a different angle, or in a different lighting, we receive different visual information; were it not for perceptual constancy, we ought to perceive a different person each time (if we could perceive *persons* at all). Without highly sophisticated cognitive mechanisms for perceptual constancy, we could never perceive the same speech sounds in different phonetic environments, as those particular sounds; nor could we perceive the same utterance spoken by different speakers as the same utterance; nor even a single sustained vowel uttered by a male and a female speaker as the same vowel (see, e.g., Shankweiler et al., 1975). One particularly impressive demonstration of how the mechanisms of perceptual constancy work in speech perception was when I had opportunity to observe Nancy Spencer prepare stimuli for one of her experiments in the Haskins Laboratories. She recorded pairs of utterances such as

---

Such a conception is very attractive to me, and so is Neisser's claim that "there is no mechanism, process, or system that functions to reject these stimuli such that they would be perceived if it were to fail" (79). However, the processes of perceiving figure and ground relationships, or the findings that suggest the existence of a speech mode, a nonspeech mode, and a poetic mode seem to contradict this statement of Neisser's. At any rate, I believe that my argument does not stand or fail with the acceptance or nonacceptance of the filter theory. What is critical for my position is, that our rational activities organize as much available information as possible into clear categories, while intuition picks up information that escapes categorization.

(6)   Babies *may cry.*
(7)   In the Jewish bakery they *make rye*-bread.

She excised the italicized portion of (6) and spliced it onto (7), replacing its italicized portion. The results were fascinating: the word boundaries within the spliced sound sequence were perceived as required by the target sentence (7), and not as they were originally intended for the source sentence (6). Even more surprising, perhaps, is the fact that the glide /y/ had disappeared from the speech sound of (7); instead, one could discern some irrelevant inarticulate noise in the background that bore little resemblance to a speech sound.

Perceptual constancy and cognitive stability are vital indeed in human society and culture. If we could not expect other people to behave consistently over a considerable period of time, no human society could persist for even an hour. But vital as perceptual constancy and cognitive stability, in general, may be for our survival in the physical as well as in the social environment, we have bought it at a considerable price. We have bought our ability to perceive "figures" at the price of dumping some other information into the "ground", or "shutting it out" from the system altogether.

We do perceive some of this inconstant, pre-categorial, inarticulate information, however; the knowledge so gained is usually called *intuitive*. Intuitive knowledge so gained is indispensable for quick orientation, or for orientation in an ever-changing environment. In fact, as Bartlett indicated back in 1932, most of the complex cognitive activities, such as *perceiving* complex situations or *remembering* them, begin with an awareness of some such pre-categorial information. He calls this awareness "attitude", or "feeling", or "affect".

> An individual does not normally take such a situation detail by detail and meticulously build up the whole. In all ordinary instances he has an overmastering tendency simply to get a general impression of the whole; and, on the basis of this, he constructs the probable detail [...]. Ask the observer to characterize this general impression psychologically, and the word that is always cropping up is "attitude" [...]. The construction that is effected is the sort of construction that would justify the observer's "attitude". [...] It is [...], as I have often indicated, very largely a matter of feeling or affect. [...] When a subject is being asked to remember, very often the first thing that emerges is something of the nature of attitude, and its general effect is that of the justification of the attitude. (Bartlett, 1932: 206–207)[6]

6   Bartlett's (and subsequent researchers') conception of "constructing the probable detail" has been rejected by the Gibsons, according to whom the organism is to be thought of as attuned to properties of its environment that are objectively present, accurately specified, and veridically perceived. Neisser embraces the Gibsonian view, but finds it unsatisfying in certain respects. "Most obviously, it says nothing about what is in the perceiver's head. What kinds of cognitive structure does perception

This "general impression", "attitude", "feeling", or "affect" can be accounted for as having in one's processing space a considerable amount of pre-categorial information; we seem to be able to handle relatively large lumps of such information, make relatively crude but quick judgments about them, and extract no precise information. It gives the organism great flexibility and adaptability to ever-changing physical or mental environments. This pre-categorial information is fluid enough to fulfil a directive function; only after a fast and crude orientation it is used to construct or pick up—by way of perception *or* recall—the details of a situation consisting of hard and fast categories. What strikes one, indeed, is the fluidity and versatility of these judgments, their capability of keeping information in a state of flux and activity, without usurping the place of stable categories in consciousness.

D'Andrade (1980) speaks of these pre-categories as of an "information-holding system".

> Feelings and emotions tell how the world is, in a very vivid way, and often increase the activations of various action schemas, but permit delay so that planning, goal sequencing, reappraisal, and other complex procedures can occur. [...] They hold information in an active form, so that it doesn't go away, yet does not pre-empt everything else.

"Attitude", or "feeling", or "affect", thus described, are, then, a highly versatile device of information-holding, integration, orientation, and retrieval. They help us pick up bits and tittles of information, integrate them into a coherent whole, and adjust ourselves with relation to such information. One may surmise that the device was originally developed for fast and effective orientation in the physical environment and was later, in the course of evolution, adapted to the needs of mental adaptation on the one hand, and of other mental operations, such as retrieval from memory, on the other. One of the crucial uses of this mechanism is its use as a word-retrieval device. We have access to a huge reservoir of words in our long-term memory, from which we pick out with amazing ease and speed the words we are looking for. I submit that it is the mechanism just described that underlies this high-efficiency retrieval device. This is also indicated by the tip-of-the-tongue phenomenon, already mentioned several times. Here we can see the working of the word-retrieval device in slow motion. When we have a word at the tip of our tongue, we feel an "intensely active gap" in our consciousness, a gap which is vague and formless but, at the same time, has a uniquely definite conscious character. Any delay between the

---

require?" (Neisser, 1976: 19). He adopts, therefore, from Bartlett the notion of schemata as pre-existing structures and elaborates it as a central notion of his cognitive theory. For present purposes, we need not decide whether "attitudes" or "affects" are devices for "constructing the probable detail", or for the "direct pick-up of information", as long as we agree that they are devices for fast orientation that subsequently guide *either* the construction of the probable detail, *or* the pick-up of information (depending, probably, on the circumstances).

anticipation and picking out of words from semantic memory creates a state of un-fulfilled perceptual readiness, and the inner aspect of that active schema is an *affect* (this sentence is a paraphrase of Neisser's description of images; Neisser, 1976: 138).

One important function I claim for cognitive poetics is that it can bridge the ap-parently hopeless gap between human values and the stylistic and poetic devices that otherwise would be considered trivial from the human point of view. We have just touched upon the source of such a case. We have described a versatile device of ori-entation, whether for adaptation to the external world, or for picking out and re-trieving words from semantic memory. The two have in common a vague thing-free stream of information, used for fast and flexible orientation, which can be called an emotional quality. Thus, when the manipulation of words renders this fluid mass of information that serves as a retrieval device accessible to consciousness, the reader experiences in the text a feeling that is not unlike the experience of those directive devices the unique conscious quality of which we know as affects.

Values have been defined as devices that direct human activities, in the form of attitudes and affects as described above. The more permanent values of human soci-ety are abstractions from just such processes.

> One of the findings of anthropologists in their study of different cultures is that while performance of some procedures in every culture is a matter of option or convenience, the performance of most cultural procedures is mo-tivated by culturally learned "values". These values are a complex associa-tion of symbol and affect—that is, of representations of states of affairs as-sociated with feelings and emotions. [...] Most cultural representations fuse the ideational and affective components into a simple symbol. Thus, ordi-nary people say the stove is "hot", fusing together a representation of how things are with how we feel about them. (D'Andrade, 1980)

In many significant instances, as we shall see, poetry interferes with this fusion of ideational and affective components, loosening the relationship between the repre-sentation of how things are and how we feel about them. Sometimes it shifts atten-tion away from things altogether, or even effects what Ehrenzweig calls "thing de-struction".

To sum up, then, ordinary consciousness is a gradually evolving system that is selective and increasingly structured and differentiated. We pick up information rele-vant to our survival from a vast amount of information surrounding us. Some of this information is organized into hard and fast categories, clear-cut figures, stable objects, rational sequences. The rest is dumped into a low-differentiated mass of background. These categories, figures, objects, and sequences form the basis of sta-bility and rationality in our world. The capability of responding to rich pre-categorial information is usually called "intuition", and it is the basis of adaptability and fast orientation in fluid, changing circumstances. Analytic reason and intuition are, thus, complementary: each expands at the expense of the other. Our rational activities organize as much available information as possible into clear-cut categories; intuition relies on information that escapes categorization. The reliance on well-categorized information has the psychological atmosphere of control, certainty, and patent purpose; the reliance on pre-categorial information requires a capability of being in "uncertainties, mysteries, doubts, without irritable reaching after fact and reason" —in Keats' famous formulation—and yields adaptability and responsiveness.

High and Low Categorization

Those who represent ordinary consciousness as a personal construction do not imply that we can dispose of it at will; we are, as it were, imprisoned in our own construction. Our consciousness organizes the physical world into *things,* and we are nearly incapable of perceiving thing-free, pre-categorial information. Language is, by its very nature, conceptual, highly categorized. It is difficult to think of information we have no names for, and in our thinking we cannot go far beyond what we can speak about. On the other hand, when we attempt to communicate, e.g., our dreams, we discover that we can easily communicate the bare events of the dream, but not its affective burden. This is because we can communicate the *things* we dream about, as categorized in conceptual language; but not the rich pre-categorial information that infuses them. Thus, pre-categorial information has frequently a directive function: when we awake, we preserve a vague mood that influences our waking activities and decisions, even when we forget the things and events of the dream. One central assumption of cognitive poetics (shared with Romantic and Symbolist poetics) is that poetry attempts to overcome these limitations of human cognition. In poetry, then, as in all creative activities, there is an "essential tension" between a trend toward a higher than usual cognitive organization, and a "regression" to a relatively low cognitive organization. This is, of course, another way of saying that the response to poetry is "organized violence" against cognitive structures and processes. The cognitive organization of the environment into *things* dissolves into abstractions and *thing-free qualities.* This regression does not imply regression from human consciousness "to consciousness of the mollusc" (as Max Nordau, among others, disparaged synaesthesia). Poetic discourse is, perhaps, the most highly-structured discourse; the recourse to low-categorized information, which is experienced as affect, heightens one's responsiveness and flexibility in orientation. The cognitive organization of the world into things and concepts is synonymous, in an important sense, with differentiation. So, occasionally, I shall substitute "low-differentiated" for "low-categorized" information.

The varying relationships between highly-categorised and pre-categorial information may determine significant aspects of the various poetic styles. Thus, for instance, according to Cleanth Brooks, modern poetry as well as metaphysical poetry is characterized by the conspicuousness of such *attitudes* as irony, the instances of which are much less clearly categorized than explicit meanings. This is, of course, an amplification of both the representation of how things are, and of how we feel about them, in D'Andrade's words. In much Romantic and Symbolist poetry, on the other hand, low-categorized meanings can arouse the impression of being in the presence of the ineffable, the other-worldly, of getting a glimpse into some super-sensory, spiritual reality. On the semantic level, low-categorized information, or attitude, or affect, can be present in poetry as what Ehrenzweig (1965) called gestalt-free or thing-free qualities; as weak gestalts, or as meaning-components in words, or as abstractable from the things described. In this sense, abstract nouns may be "double-edged". On the one hand, they may refer to clear-cut concepts, and serve as *the* vehicle for rational thought; on the other hand, they may serve to isolate properties of things, and constitute gestalt-free or thing-free qualities; in this sense, they may serve as an efficient implement of thing destruction. In Chapter 15 I shall discuss the stylistic environments in which these contradictory aspects of this potential are realized. On the prosodic level, low-category information may be present as *diffuse* alliteration patterns, or metrical deviations that blur metric shapes (Tsur, 1977; 1998; 2003). Thus, when we describe those things in a poem, we have to have recourse to the terminology of traditional literary criticism.

In this way, the delay in the recoding from acoustic cues to phonetic representation, and the perception of rich pre-categorial auditory information in low-encoded speech sounds, as discussed above, is an instance of just this "essential tension" between high and low categorization.

Keats vs. Marlowe

The foregoing discussion may serve as a theoretical framework in which a description of texts, that uses the tools of traditional criticism, or linguistics, may assume special significance. Let us illustrate the points made above by comparing two poetic passages, the first from Keats's sonnet "On Seeing the Elgin Marbles", the second from Marlowe's tragedy "Tamburlaine".

(8)   Such dim-conceivèd glories of the brain
        Bring round the heart an indescribable feud ...

(9)   Nature that framed us of four elements,
        Warring within our breasts for regiment,
        Doth teach us all to have aspiring minds.

In spite of Tamburlaine's and Faustus' notorious craving for infinite things in Marlowe's tragedies, we may expect, from a common, sweeping generalization, Keats's poetry to be of a more romantic, more affective mood than Marlowe's poetry. It would be interesting to see whether and how the two passages bear out such pieces of "common knowledge".

The two passages have a considerable number of elements in common. Both refer, in a fairly direct way, to an undifferentiable feeling, in terms of a "gestalt-free" quality, by linguistic terms that are near-synonyms: a *war* "within our breasts", and a *feud* "round the heart", and its relation to what happens in our minds (or in the brain). For Keats, as a true Romantic, this is an intense passion at unique moments (one of his "many havens of intensity"); it is so intense that it cannot be sustained for a considerable period. For Marlowe, this feeling is rather a permanent disposition. Some readers report that they perceive a heightened affective quality in (8), as compared to (9). One possible explanation for this may rely on the different connotations of *warring* and *feud*. But far more significant seems to be the fact that whereas in Marlowe's passage it is the clearly differentiated "four elements" that are "warring within our breasts", Keats's "feud" around the heart is not only undifferentiated and gestalt-free, but *thing-free* too: in ordinary referential language we expect to be told the feud is taking place *between whom* or *what*. Moreover, the location *"round* the heart" is vaguer than *"in* the heart" would be. Thus, the more passionate impact of Keats's lines has to do with the fact that they are focused on violent actions, stripped of things that might carry them. Furthermore, although both metaphors seem to refer to some kind of emotional turbulence, Marlowe uses rhetorical devices to heighten its conscious "linear" quality, whereas Keats uses devices to mute, or obscure, this conscious quality. Marlowe's "warring within our breasts" is endowed with the psychological atmosphere of *patent purpose,* generated by the purposive ingredient in the words and phrases "for regiment", "teach", "aspiring minds", as well as by the conclusive nature of *all.*

Keats, on the other hand, emphasizes the undifferentiated character of the passion by the adjectives *"indescribable* feud", and *"dim*-conceivèd glories". I shall refrain from discussing all the aspects relevant to this comparison. I only want to discuss here the phrase

(10)   Glories of the brain.

The normal, "unmarked", syntactic structure of such constructions would be that concrete, "spatio-temporally continuous particulars" occur in the referring position (Strawson, 1967; see also below, Chapters 9, 18 and 24), as in

(11)   The brain has glories.
(12)   The brain is glorious.
(13)   The glorious brain

(By "spatio-temporally continuous particulars" Strawson means objects that are continuous in space, and if you go away and come back after ten minutes, an hour, a week, or a year they still have the same shape). Such more abstract or more general qualities as "glories" or "glorious" should occur as attributes or predicates, as in excerpts 11–13. In excerpt 10, the adjective is turned into an abstract noun which, in turn, is manipulated into the referring position instead the spatio-temporally continuous particular. (We may call such genitive phrases *nominalized predicates, thematised predicates* or *topicalised attributes).* They shift the focus of attention from "things as bundles of properties" to their "sensed properties", dissociated to some degree from the things. In the present context, this can be regarded as a kind of regression to a "pre-thing" state, it reinforces the thing-free quality encountered in *feud.*

This comparison of the two passages does not greatly differ from the usual techniques of close reading. Nonetheless, our discussion of consciousness and the categorization of information conveys several significant contributions. Theories of metaphor explore, typically, such issues as how to furnish the best possible paraphrase for a metaphor, how a variety of metaphors can be derived from one underlying metaphor, or how people understand novel metaphors. Here we have two metaphors that do not differ significantly in their meanings, but rather in their perceived effects. The cognitive frame of reference has contributed to an explanation of this difference: It has explained the relationship between certain linguistic structures and the "regression" to a low-category mode of perception; it has also explained, in turn, the relationship of such regression to the affective quality of the text, as well as to our cognitive characterization of poetry. We have also indicated how these relationships can be further pursued, so as to relate the texts to the effects of period and style, such as Classic/Romantic. One may, further, claim that it was the cognitive framework that suggested these linguistic tools for description; in a different frame of reference these descriptions would have appeared little more than trivial (see Chapter 22).[7]

Orientation and Disorientation

I have discussed affects and emotions as effective fast-orientation devices. Similar directive devices have been found in *wit* and *irony* (see above). The Grotesque is the co-occurrence of incompatible emotional tendencies, the most common of these being the co-occurrence of the laughable with some emotion such as the sublime, the pitiable, or the disgusting. Thomson (1972) speaks of "emotional disorientation" resulting from the conflicting emotional tendencies of the grotesque. I submit that here, too, "adaptive processes are disrupted". According to Burke (1957: 51–56), both laughter and horror or disgust are defense-mechanisms in the presence of a threat, the latter allowing the danger its authority, the former denying it. The grotesque is *the experiencing of emotional disorientation* when both defense-mechanisms are suddenly suspended (cf. Thomson, 1972: 58).

Now let us return to the horror joke in (1). The two situations underlying it require radically different, even opposing reactions, requiring a shift *from* readiness to respond to a trivial "default script" automatically applied, *to* a readiness to respond to a script that has an element of horror in it. This extreme shift of mental set accounts for the witty effect of this horror joke. Notice this, however. The horror element of the "cannibalism" script is typically experienced as extremely unpleasant. On the

---

[7] I have later incorporated this comparison of Keats and Marlowe in a comprehensive reading of Keats's sonnet (see Tsur, 2002).

other hand, as I have suggested above, wit as the unique conscious quality of shifting mental set is usually deemed pleasurable. The result is a conflict of opposite emotional tendencies, characterized by a sense of shock and emotional disorientation, typical of the grotesque. As a result, the joke's audience is exposed, stripped of its defenses, to a heightened awareness of a painful reality.

This emotional disorientation must be viewed in a wider perspective in poetry (to be discussed at some length in Chapters 16–17). I have treated orientation as an adaptive device turned to aesthetic ends. An unfulfilled readiness to pick up self-specifying information, so fundamental in orientation, may be the mechanism underlying the affective impact of certain Romantic descriptions. I have suggested that the mechanism involved may have a strong integrating effect on the environment in which it functions. The greater the degree of disintegration, the more pointed the effect of the mechanism of integration and orientation, up to a certain point. Beyond that point, the disintegrating environment escapes from the control of the orienting mechanism, and a *different kind* of coping procedure must be instantiated. For want of a better term, we might call this coping procedure *meta-awareness.* "Information about oneself, like all other information, can only be picked up by an appropriately tuned schema" (Neisser, 1976: 116). When something suddenly seems to go wrong, one has to check the tuning of one's own schemata. "Consciousness, according to Bartlett, enables an organism 'to turn around its own schemata'" (Miller and Johnson-Laird, 1976: 150). When the clashing emotional tendencies of the grotesque, of the metaphysical pun, or of the metaphysical conceit shock us out of tune with our environment, our own coping and linguistic mechanisms become perceptible to ourselves. The unique conscious quality of this moment is experienced as a sense of confusion and emotional disorientation. One of the major functions of poetry is to yield a heightened awareness. It may be the heightening of the awareness of the reality perceived, or of the cognitive mechanisms that enable us to perceive reality. The self-examination of cognitive mechanisms is still an investigation of reality; the investigation has merely lost its directness (cf. Pears, 1971: 31).

In the foregoing sections of the present chapter I have considered at some length two major adaptation devices: the shift of mental set (the unique conscious quality of which is *wit),* and the holding of rich pre-categorial, fluid information in an active state (the unique conscious quality of which is *attitude, feeling,* or *affect).* In Western literature, there are at least two major literary traditions, that of *wit* and of *serious emotion.* The approach put forward here is equally relevant to both traditions. What is more, it can explain how the two traditions are related to one another. Emotions are information kept in an active state; like wit, they are devices of adaptation to a changing reality. But whereas wit is focused, and consists in one sudden shift of mental set, emotions are diffuse and involve series of fine fluctuations. So, the present approach supplies the common ground against which the distinction between the two traditions can meaningfully be made. The present section thus lays the foundations for a distinction between two aesthetic modes in their own right, *Poetry of Orientation* and *Poetry of Disorientation.*

Poetry and Altered States of Consciousness

Earlier we have seen the significance of individuals' constructing an ordinary, personal consciousness. We have also seen that the response to poetry capitalizes on the disturbance or delay in the cognitive processes that constitute this consciousness. Ordinary consciousness is one of the greatest human achievements. However, this achievement is bought at the price of losing our ability to rely on some "lower" adaptive processes that are not controlled by "ordinary", conscious will. Our entire Western education teaches us to trust our reason and distrust, e.g., our emotions. *Altered states of consciousness* are mental states in which adult persons relinquish to some extent the control of "ordinary consciousness" which they have already acquired. By this, they achieve some relatively immediate exposure to reality, somewhat alleviating the rigid defenses built up by ordinary consciousness. In this, *altered states of consciousness* are not unlike exposure to the grotesque, to which they appear to be diagonally opposed in other respects.

Consequently, it will not be very surprising that, traditionally, certain poetic genres are closely associated with such *altered states of consciousness* as meditation, ecstasy, and hypnosis. It should be remarked, however, that it is almost impossible reliably to distinguish *between* these three states of consciousness in their poetic guise, whereas it may be quite profitable to distinguish between minor regressions from ordinary consciousness (discussed above), and the attempt to capture some "peak experience" or some altered state of consciousness by poetry. Although the borderline is blurred, the extremes seem clear and illuminating.

A major claim of some conventional as well as of Cognitive Poetics is that poetry yields a heightened consciousness. Some poetry heightens consciousness of the self's relationship to the surrounding space ("poetry of orientation"). Other poetry concerns heightened consciousness of an environment "run wild", which cannot be integrated any longer by regular "orientation-devices". Chapters 16–17 are devoted to the "Poetry of Disorientation" and discuss a variety of devices characteristic of disorientation, most notably the grotesque, the metaphysical conceit, and the sensuous metaphor. Chapters 18–20 discuss "Poetry and Altered States of Consciousness", and explore some ways in which a heightened consciousness may be gained of mental states that in one way or other escape the control of ordinary consciousness, most notably meditation, ecstatic and hypnotic poetry. (The phenomenon of Literary Synaesthesia, too, should belong here).

The Text, the Reader, the Critic

Let us return once more to the horror joke in (1). In discussing its effects, we have generated a scale of attitudes of mounting complexity: 1. mental set, that is, readiness to respond in a certain way; 2. shift of mental set; 3. conflicting emotional tendencies (emotional disorientation). Each later stage on this scale exacts greater cognitive complexity and readiness to face greater uncertainty than the preceding one. Consequently, there are persons who are capable of maintaining a consistent mental set, but feel threatened when required to shift mental sets; and there are, in turn, persons who feel capable of coping with shifting mental sets, but experience an exceptionally great threat when facing the sense of shock and emotional disorientation resulting from conflicting emotional tendencies. Finally, there are persons who not only feel well equipped to cope with shifting mental sets or the sense of shock and emotional disorientation resulting from conflicting emotional tendencies, but tend to experience these processes as pleasurable, since their very occurrence arouses confidence in them that their adaptive mechanisms function properly, when required. Thus, the notion of *"the* reader" ceases to be a unitary notion. We may expect to encounter readers of at least three degrees of readiness to face uncertainties and complexities.

Cognitive Poetics assumes, as do some more traditional approaches to poetry, that a text offers the reader aesthetically significant structures of aesthetically neutral materials. It is up to the reader to realize these structures more or less perfectly. In doing this, s/he deploys cognitive devices that are otherwise used for organizing *perceptual wholes* in our nonaesthetic environment (this issue will be pursued at considerable length in Chapter 3): again, cognitive devices developed for survival in a nonaesthetic environment are turned to aesthetic ends. The deployment of these cognitive devices is governed by the text's needs as well as by the reader's ability and readiness to deploy them: an ability and readiness which, in turn, are determined by certain psychological factors, such as cognitive complexity. The scale of attitudes of mounting complexity mentioned in the preceding paragraph, and the readiness of various readers to face the various degrees of complexity may serve as a model to this. At the beginning of the present chapter I claimed that cognitive poetics attempts to find out how poetic language or the critic's decisions are constrained and shaped by human information processing. The main bulk of the present chapter has been devoted to issues related to the constraining and shaping of poetic language. This last section briefly mentions some issues concerning critics' decisions. When I speak of performance by the critics, I shall rely on their application of the critical code and on their "decision style", as shaped and constrained by their "cognitive complexity".

As will be suggested in Chapters 3 and 13, stylistic categories and notions of genre have the character of perceptual hypotheses. How does the audience's familiarity with the conventions of the horror joke genre affect its response to a horror joke? We must distinguish here between social and literary conventions. The effect of (1), for instance, crucially depends upon the audience's familiarity with certain social conventions in Western society, according to which it is forbidden to eat human flesh, while it is customary in many families to wait for all its members to gather before starting to eat. Familiarity with the literary conventions of (1), on the other hand, is neither a necessary nor a sufficient condition for a successful response to (1). Suppose a naive audience of the horror joke. A person unfamiliar with its specific literary conventions responds to the trivial (family-dinner) situation in a certain way; the mother's answer induces him to change the situation to imagine a kitchen where Dad is boiling in the pot. As a result, he *will* change mental sets, and experience *wit* (provided that he is not prevented from this by his intolerance of conflicting emotional tendencies). Now suppose an audience *familiar* with the specific literary conventions of horror jokes. We might expect three kinds of response to the joke in (1) (which I have repeatedly encountered in any classroom where I "happened" to tell (1), without any warning). The majority of the audience will laugh at the end of the joke; a minority will laugh already at the end of the child's question, anticipating the shift of mental sets forced by the mother's answer, while some members of the audience will not find the story funny at all. Some of them will even indicate that they knew from the beginning that the child's question was to be understood in a situation in which Dad is boiling in the pot, and so no shift of mental sets took place. Hence, the answer to the question "How does the audience's familiarity with conventions affect its response to a horror joke?" depends on individual cognitive style. With persons who are highly tolerant of shifts of mental sets and of conflicting emotional tendencies familiarity with the specific conventions of horror jokes tends to *accelerate* the shift of mental sets; persons who are intolerant of shifts of mental sets and of conflicting emotional tendencies will tend to use their familiarity with the specific conventions of horror jokes to *prevent* the shift of mental sets from taking place: they may activate their readiness to respond to a horror situation, straight away at the end of the child's question, and the mother's answer will be in perfect harmony with it.

All this suggests that the mere application of the right critical tools to a text does not, in itself, guarantee acceptable results. In fact, as we have seen, the application of some critical tool to a text by different persons may yield even conflicting results. It is essential to realize that the application of critical tools (and its results) may be crucially influenced by the critic's cognitive complexity and decision style. This will be discussed at considerable length in Chapters 17 and 21.[8]

---

[8] Most frequently, critics speak of *"the* reader", or "the *competent* reader", or "the *qualified* reader", or "the *ideal* reader". In most cases, these phrases mean "a reader who complies with my theoretical analysis". Such a construal of *"the* reader" applies to the present work no less than to the work of I. A. Richards or Michael Riffaterre. In an attempt to balance this, in recent years I have done some empirical research into reader and listener response (see, e.g., Chapter 7 below, and the section *The Reader and Real Readers* in Tsur, 2006).

CHAPTER 2

Mental and Vocal Performance in Poetry Reading

As indicated in Chapter 1, Cognitive Poetics lays store by **perceived qualities** more than any other approach to poetry. One fundamental assumption of Cognitive Poetics is that one may account for the perceived quality of a text in terms of the text's structure and the reader's mental processes. A second assumption is that such an explanatory model should account—and in a systematic way—not only for some perceived effect, but also for alternative or even conflicting effects, when such effects are reported by various readers. It should be noted that the effects of poetic texts are not perceived in a way in which the effects of, say, touching an electric wire are perceived. The latter are perceived on mere exposure to the wires, whereas the former presuppose a certain kind of cooperation on the perceiver's part. Different perceived effects of the same piece of literature presuppose different kinds of cooperation. Perceptual qualities of texts arise only when they are performed in certain ways, that is, when the reader discriminates certain elements and realizes certain relationships between them. When readers discriminate other elements, or realize different relationships even between the same elements, one may expect that different perceived qualities will arise.

The word *performance* is used in three different but related senses in the domain we are discussing. The first sense is as it appears in the Chomskyan dichotomy *Competence ~ Performance,* the second one is what I shall call here *mental performance,* the third—*vocal performance,* as the phrase relates to the "performing arts". As Wellek and Warren (1956: 138–139) suggest in phenomenological terms, "the real poem must be conceived as a structure of norms, realized only partially in the actual experience of its many readers. Every single experience (reading, reciting, and so forth) is only an attempt—more or less successful and complete—to grasp this set of norms or standards". "The structure of a work of art has the character of a 'duty which I have to realize'. I shall always realize it imperfectly, but in spite of some incompleteness, a certain 'structure of determination' remains, just as in any other object of knowledge" (ibid., 141). Thus, the "structure of norms" is richer than its "realization", in the sense that only some of the alternative potential relationships are actualized, while the others are eliminated. On the other hand, and in another sense, the actualization is richer, in the sense that a work of art is "incomplete from the ontological point of view", and must be "filled in" with specific details.

When I speak of "Mental Performance", I refer to those alternative mental operations responsible for the alternative actual organizations of a text; it is through these operations that the alternative meanings and perceived effects arise. How does this "Mental Performance" relate to the Chomskyan dichotomy? I suggest that the term *Performance* is used in both cases in essentially the same sense: "Mental Performance" suggests 'the peculiar deployment of the reader's underlying structural knowledge in particular instances of reading'. "The reader's underlying structural knowledge" resides in the rules of his Linguistic and Poetic Competence; whereas their unique application in each instance belongs to the domain of performance, and need not be consistent from one person to another, or even from one reading to another by the same person of the same text. While the "duty which I have to realize" may remain the same, I may choose to realize it in different ways: from time to time I may prefer different incompletenesses. Such preferences may be affected by the reader's dissatisfaction with the kind of incompleteness of a preceding actualization, or by his personality style, momentary or more or less permanent moods and attitudes, perhaps even beliefs, both accidental and systematic. Perhaps some of these factors of "situational interference" may be defined in terms of their own competences; but are extraneous and incidental from the point of view of Linguistic and Poetic Competence.[1]

As to "vocal performance", this is the vocal realization of a poem's mental performance. In this sense, mental and vocal performance, as I use the term, are related to one another like the poem as a "system of norms" is to its mental performance. Here, again, vocal performance is a more concrete actualization and, by the same token, a less perfect approximation of the mental performance. Some potential relationships are again eliminated and some elements of the vocal medium, irrelevant to the mental performance to be actualized, become part of the final output. We are speaking of a chain of successive, increasingly concrete actualizations, each later actualization operating within the constraints of the preceding one. Substantial parts of Cognitive Poetics in general, and of the present book in particular, are devoted to the exploration of mental devices that may be utilized in alternative mental performances. The present chapter presents the general notions of *Mental and Vocal Performance* as a theoretical framework of the whole book, and mentions a selection of the mental operations involved, by briefly alluding to several case studies, elaborated at considerable length in the subsequent chapters.

Paraphrasing Arnheim, the realization of a poem involves the solution of a problem—namely, the creation of an organized whole (cf. Arnheim, 1957: 55). "Organized whole" is not a *given* fact, but rather an achievement by deploying certain cognitive strategies. It is hoped that the overall term "Mental Performance" can eventually be broken down into well-defined specific operations and that these operations can be integrated into one unified perception or experience. These

---

[1]   For *Linguistic* and *Poetic Competence* see Chapter 3. *Critical Competence* is discussed in Chapter 22; *Rhythmic Competence* is discussed in Chapters 6–7.

operations may include the discrimination of parts, their weighting relative to each other, and the realization of the relationship between them, to create an organized whole. To achieve this, differences between elements and structures may be "leveled" or "sharpened"; a series of items that constitute a cognitive 'overload' may be dealt with by the abstraction of common qualities generating some *category* or, alternatively, by 'dumping' such items into some undifferentiated background texture; and so forth. I assume that the reader has considerable freedom in the allocation of his representational and other mental resources, even within the rigorous constraints of the structure of a poem. Notice, however, my phrase "rigorous constraints": I am far from suggesting that "anything goes".

Relative Weighting

One kind of mental operations involved in mental performance (one that may give rise to alternative readings and perceived effects) concerns interpretation; it does not require to have recourse to specific cognitive mechanisms discussed in relation to my subsequent examples, but can usefully be treated in terms of analytic aesthetics and more or less traditional literary criticism. For the purposes of the present discussion, I will draw upon relatively short excerpts from my book on "Kubla Khan" (Tsur, 2006).

When one is engaged in an overview of a considerable number of more or less legitimate interpretations offered to a particular literary work of art, the question inevitably arises how a single poem can mean all those things, or even a part of them. Thus for instance, Schneider devotes the first chapter of her 1975 book to a consideration of the welter of interpretations to which Coleridge's major poems have been submitted. I shall have to confine myself to a relatively short quotation from it:

> Mr. Warren, Mr. Burke, Mr. Knight, Miss Bodkin, and the others cannot all be right (which does not, certainly, prove any one of them wrong). Their various symbolic interpretations of Coleridge's poems not only are not easily reconciled with one another on the basis of "different levels", but also impute quite different moods or emotional tones to the same poem. If *Christabel* is felt as the *Inferno,* it can scarcely also be felt as the moment of balance between good and evil. If *Kubla Khan* is the *Paradiso* of Dante, it is not easy to feel it also as exhibiting the conflict of heaven and hell or Coleridge's somewhat less than heavenly domestic life. To the confusion of these is added the voice of those other critics who maintain that [...] *Kubla Khan* is wholly without meaning of any kind. Though variety among critics is no doubt all to the good, one cannot help wondering a trifle about the present state of criticism when we find as little common ground as this among writers all very eminent, all brilliant and

persuasive in argument, and all engaged in describing the central effect of
the same poems. (Schneider, 1975: 16)

While I agree with Schneider on many occasions, this is one point on which I disagree with her. I accept completely Schneider's objection to the extravagancies of
symbolic interpretation; but I also believe that such a variety of interpretations as
she enumerates and many more *can* all be right, though some of them clearly *are*
wrong. The root of our disagreement is certainly in her phrase "all engaged in describing the central effect of the same poems", which is clearly an oversimplified
position. These critics are, indeed, "engaged in describing the central effect of the
same poems"; *but only following an interpretation.* As a matter of fact, these critics
are only marginally engaged in describing the central effect of these poems; what
they are doing, in the first place, is trying to elaborate interpretations. These interpretations are partial realizations of the poem as a system of norms, each of these
interpretations utilize a different subset of the norms, imputing different weights to
them relative to each other. As Morris Weitz (1972) has convincingly argued with
respect to the welter of *Hamlet*-interpretations, this is the most we can expect.

Let us consider, for instance, Schneider's misgivings: "If *Kubla Khan* is the
Paradiso of Dante, it is not easy to feel it also as exhibiting the conflict of heaven
and hell". How can two such incompatible interpretations refer to the same data in
the poem? The point is that the various critics *are not* dealing with the *same* data in
"Kubla Khan"; neither are they in *Hamlet* where, as Weitz (1972: 256) puts it, "the
data themselves are attributed ones, hypothesized by the critic".

The data accounted for in the various readings are determined by the relative
weight the critic bestows upon these data within the work of literature. Consider
this issue in "Kubla Khan". That the caverns are there and that they are opposed to
the *"sunny* pleasure-dome" is given in the poem; but that they are also opposed to
the mountain, or that this opposition reflects the conflict of heaven and hell, is
hypothesized by the critic. What is *the* theme of "Kubla Khan" cannot be directly
read off from from the data, it is a hypothesis, which the critic defends by further
hypotheses: from a specific hypothesis about "Kubla Khan" to a general one about
some more general patterns, such as the archetype of Paradise and Hades, or
"Coleridge's Divine Comedy", or romantic nature poetry, or the nature and structure
of ecstatic poetry. Now, the answer to the question to what degree are the caverns
considered "central, primary, most important" depends *inter alia* upon whether
"Kubla Khan is the *Paradiso* of Dante", or exhibits "the conflict of heaven and hell".
Consider Bodkin's characterization of caverns: "an essence of cold, darkness, and
stagnant air, from which imagination may fashion a place of punishment, the home
of the Evil One" (Bodkin, 1963: 101). Under the "conflict of heaven and hell"
reading, the aspects of caverns mentioned by Bodkin receive a considerable weight.
Both readings agree upon the centrality of Paradise in the overall pattern of the
poem, but in the former reading the poem is part of a wider pattern, along with two
more poems, viz., the pattern of "Coleridge's Divine Comedy". Under this pattern,

some cavern aspects suggested by Bodkin are necessarily toned down, and the opposition "a sunny pleasure-dome and caves of ice" suggests an overwhelming sense of wonder in the face of "a miracle of rare device", enhancing the directly felt pleasure in the description of the Paradise. This capability of "switching" from one set of aspects to another of the opposition corresponds to the ability suggested by Wittgenstein (1976: 214e) to "understand the request to pronounce the word 'till' and to mean it as a verb" (as opposed to, say, an adverb). It is this mental ability that underlies our capability of offering a variety of more or less legitimate interpretations of the same text. And this is a central aspect of what I have called "Mental Performance".

Leveling and Sharpening

A conspicuous cognitive device that effectively serves a wide variety of literary purposes, among them Mental Performance, is that of *Leveling-and-Sharpening*. When a stimulus pattern contains certain kinds of ambiguity (such as a slight deviation from some symmetrical pattern), simplification and strong shape may be achieved, according to Arnheim (1957: 57), "by changing a figure in which two structural patterns compete for dominance into another that shows clear dominance of one of them". This tendency is called "sharpening". The opposite tendency is called "leveling". "Leveling" attempts to minimize or even eliminate the unfitting detail. In the following design, both *a* and *d* deviate slightly from symmetrical patterns.

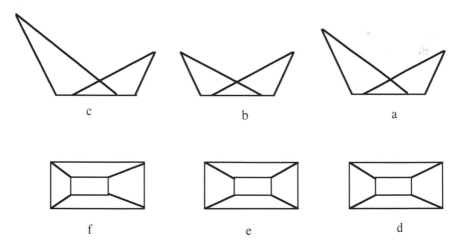

c   b   a

f   e   d

Figure 2.1 "Leveling" and "sharpening": When a stimulus pattern shows a slight deviation from some symmetrical pattern (as in *a* and *d*), subjects tend to restore symmetry (as in *b* and *e*), or exaggerate the asymmetry (as in *c* and *f*), so as to avoid ambiguity.

> When such figures are presented under conditions that keep the stimulus
> control weak enough to leave the observer with a margin of freedom, two
> types of reaction follow. Some persons perfect the symmetry of the model
> (*b, e*) whereas others exaggerate the asymmetry (*c, f*). (Arnheim, 1957: 57)

This mechanism has been most dramatically revealed in reader response, in an empirical study by Tsur, Glicksohn and Goodblatt (1990; 1991; see now Tsur, 2006:
115–141). This study is an attempt to obtain empirical evidence for the theoretical
analysis (presented in Chapter 5) of gestalt-qualities associated with varying rhyme-
patterns in one of Omar Khayyám's Rubáiyáth (with its *aaba* rhyme pattern, in
Edward FitzGerald's English translation) and two additional versions in which the
rhyme-pattern has been manipulated for experimental purposes *(aabb* and *aaaa). Let
us consider briefly this issue:

> (1)   Think, in this battered Caravanserai
>   Whose Portals are alternate Night and Day,
>   How Sultán after Sultán with his Pomp
>   Abode his destined Hour, and went his way.

From the analysis of our experimental results we came to the conclusion that relative to the (manipulated) *aabb* and *aaaa* versions, our respondents judged the (original) *aaba* version to be an *aabb manqué* on the one hand, and an *aaaa manqué* on the
other hand. In other words, the Rubáiyáth-form is rather irregular. Had the fourth
line of this quatrain rhymed with *pomp,* we would have had a stanza that could be
divided into two symmetrical halves; had the third line rhymed with *way,* we would
have had an equi-rhymed stanza. The Rubáiyáth-form falls short of both more regular shapes.

    This is a typical case that tends to elicit the cognitive mechanism of *Leveling-
and-Sharpening.* The reader may attempt to "level" the third line of the *aaba* stanza,
try to minimize its significance, in order to approximate the *aaaa* rhyme pattern.
Since the line *is* there, such an attempt would prove futile, however. "Sharpening",
by contrast, exaggerates the unfitting detail. That is exactly what happens in the
"archetypal" performance of the Rubáiyáth. Here, the return to the initial *aa* rhyme-
pattern after the deviating third line will arouse satisfaction in the reader. The greater
the disturbance experienced at the deviating line, the greater the gratification achieved
at the return to the initial rhyme-scheme. The reader may discover, then, that sharpening in this instance pays, and s/he may attempt to go as far as possible in this respect. Thus, the reader is left with a considerable margin of freedom in organizing
the stimulus-material.

    The term "Leveling-and-Sharpening" refers to a cognitive mechanism that can be
exploited in the service of a variety of wider issues. Its main effect is, as we have
seen, the elimination of ambiguity, uncertainty, and cognitive instability. Its description requires two dimensions at least, one in terms of the structure of the object

of perception or cognition; the other, in terms of the perceiving consciousness. The latter may depend on the perceiver's personality style, or on the degree s/he is equipped to handle ambiguous situations in a certain domain. George Klein (1951) established leveling-and-sharpening as a personality variable. Some people seem to have a permanent preference for achieving cognitive stability in their environment by leveling differences, others by sharpening them. This may have a major influence on systematic individual differences in response to literature, as well as in the crit- ics' deployment of their professional tools in their professional activities. Some of these assumptions have been substantiated in an experiment reported elsewhere (Tsur *et al.* 1990; 1991; Tsur, 2006: 115–141), where it was found that respondents to poetry who are low on a certain personality variable are inclined to handle structural ambiguities by leveling-and-sharpening, whereas respondents high on the same vari- able seem quite content with contemplating those structural ambiguities, without eliminating them. The experiments also show that familiarity with a certain domain of response may govern the application of this cognitive mechanism(Tsur *et al.* 1990). While psychology students are inclined to level certain differences in poetic structure (for the handling of which, presumably, they lack the tools), students of literature are inclined to sharpen them (precisely because they may be equipped with the required tools). One may conjecture that, in psychologically oriented tasks, the same students would manifest reverse tendencies.

Finally, there are the processes (mentioned in Chapter 13) by which highly effec- tive expressive resources are turned into conventions or ornaments. Leveling-and- sharpening may play an important role in these processes too. A conspicuous case in point may be the venerable thematic convention of "the contrarious passions in a lover". The most famous example is Petrarch's sonnet *"Pace non trovo"*, imitated and translated by poets throughout the Renaissance, among others by Wyatt:

(2)   I find no peace, and all my war is done,
       I fear and hope. I burn, and freeze like ice.
       I fly above the wind, yet cannot arise,
       And naught I have, and all the world I season. [...]
       Likewise displeathes me both death and life,
       And my delight is causer of this strife.

The same convention appears in Ronsard's original sonnet No. XII of his *Amours:*

(3)   J'espère et crains, je me tais et supplie,
       Or je suis glace, et ores un feu chaud,
       J'admire tout, et de rien ne me chaut,
       Je me délace, et puis je me relie.

Villon applied this convention outside love poetry, in his famous ballade:

(4)   Je meurs de seuf auprès de la fontaine,
        Chault comme feu, et tremble dents à dents;

This convention reflects two psychological phenomena: *ambivalence* and *sharpening*. *Ambivalence* is a state of conflicting attitudes or feelings, as when a mother causes pain to her child by vigorously pressing it to her bosom. According to Freud, much love is characterized by such ambivalence. *The Fontana Dictionary of Modern Thought* makes the following comment on literature in its *ambivalence* entry: "Whereas, in general, ambivalence is a potential source of undesirable stress [...], in a writer it is widely regarded as a source of strength and desirable tension, and in a fictional character as evidence of subtlety in his or her creator."

Complementary to this state of conflict, there is, according to Ehrenzweig (1965), a defense mechanism that, in a historical perspective, defends human culture against such tensions—even if "desirable".[2] The process of *sharpening* enhances in these poems the discordance between the conflicting attitudes, presenting them as clearly perceptible symmetrical opposites, thus taking out the potential source of undesirable stress, the uncertainty and the disquieting element from an unpleasantly ambiguous feeling. Since "ambivalence is a potential source of undesirable stress", readers of poetry may have sought for mental performances that reduce "undesirable stress", and may have discovered, independently from one another, that in certain poetic situations of considerable emotional strain, sharpening proves to be an exceptionally effective means to render those "contrarious passions" harmless. In this way, *one possible* mental performance of certain highly emotional, disquieting, ambivalent texts may have fossilized into a solid convention, reinforced through repeated social transmission.

Handling Cognitive Overload

According to the 'Limited Channel Capacity' hypothesis (see, e.g., Neisser, 1968), there is a rigid upper limit to the amount of information that an organism can process at any given time. When the information to be processed exceeds this limit, the organism may have recourse to a variety of cognitive strategies and devices. One possible way of handling an excess of information is to *recode* it in a more efficient manner, so as to require less processing space. Suppose you are requested to memorize the following series of numbers: 5 8 1 2 1 5 1 9 2 2 2 6, and requested to recall them one week later. In George Katona's experiment (reported by Brown, 1968), none of his subjects could recall them. Now, suppose, you are to learn the same

---

[2] This conjecture may gain further support from the typical presence (in all these instances) of another technique that is prone to take out the disquieting quality from a unique emotion: the 'catalogue technique' (this technique will be discussed at considerable length in Chapter 18). *Catalogue Verse* is a term "to describe lists of persons, places, things, or ideas which have a common denominator" *(The Princeton Encyclopedia of Poetry and Poetics).*

numbers along with their principle of organization: the difference between 5 and 8 is 3, between 8 and 12 is 4, between 12 and 15 is 3, between 15 and 19 is 4, and so on. Suppose, this principle is demonstrated to you by showing the numbers as follows:

Figure 2.2 Series of apparently random numbers are difficult to memorize. The same numbers are better memorized when their principle of organization is given prominence, alleviating cognitive overload.

"Subjects learning the series in this fashion could grasp it very quickly and, indeed, could quickly learn a much longer series organized according to the same principle. [...] Katona, furthermore, found that this second group retained the series after an interim of a week" (Brown, 1968: 72). This is one, rather artificial, instance of *recoding* information to reduce its load on one's mental processing space. In other cases, some more natural way of recoding might be more convenient, such as abstracting some common quality from a series of items, and organizing them in some more or less clearly definable *category*. In other cases again, an altogether different mental strategy may be required in order to alleviate cognitive overload. One of the best known instances concerns *perceptual* overload, when excessive perceptual information is dumped onto an undifferentiated ground, sometimes serving as background to a well-differentiated figure.

These latter two strategies are demonstrated at considerable length in Chapter 18, with respect to Whitman's catalogue technique. Earlier criticism of Whitman has distinguished between the "illustrative" and "meditative" functions of the Whitmanian catalogue. In Chapter 18 I suggest that underlying both the "meditative" function, and many other altered states of consciousness is a process involving "a succession of states each of which announces that which follows and contains that which precedes it. In reality no one begins or ends, but all extend into each other", to use Bergson's formulation (as quoted by Ehrenzweig, 1965: 35). One possible way, I suggest, that the illusion of a succession of states, all extending into each other, may arise in poetry is when the information conveyed by the succession of phrases of the catalogue constitutes a cognitive overload on the reader's processing space; in such a case, one might assume, the reader is compelled to handle this information by collapsing it into an undifferentiated mass. Below, Chapter 18, I consider alternative ways of explaining why certain poetic devices in certain mental performances do, in others do not cause cognitive overload. A chaotic over-differentiation resulting in cognitive overload is observed in relation to the use of synaesthetic metaphors in Baudelaire's "Correspondances", in Chapters 10 and 20.

Vocal Performance

Vocal Performance becomes relevant to my subject with respect to the rhythmic performance of poetry. Chapters 6 and 7 below discuss poetic rhythm. In my 1977 and 1998 books I came to the conclusion that—contrary to the claims of some metric theorists—there is no natural cut-off point between metricality and unmetricality in verse. This, however, does not imply that "anything goes". The distinction between an "acceptable" and "unacceptable" verse line can be drawn by reference to its being capable or incapable of a rhythmic performance. If correct, this insight reinforces the conception according to which significant stylistic distinctions between similar poetic structures can be made, depending on the kind of mental performances they require or afford. Whether a verse line is rhythmical or not depends on the reader's ability or willingness to perform it rhythmically. Different poets seem to have assumed different degrees of ability or willingness on their readers' part to perform their verses rhythmically. Milton seems to grant his readers an ability to perform certain lines that M. Halle and S. J. Keyser would not grant them; whereas Pope seems to deny his readers an ability to handle certain verse-lines that the Halle-Keyser (1971) theory would grant them. Jay Keyser (pers. com.) suggested to me, that such a criterion of acceptability presupposes a consistent theory of rhythmic performance. In a group of chapters of my 1977 book I have attempted to provide such a theory, based mainly on gestaltistic assumptions, occasionally supplemented by phonological and even phonetic descriptions. In my 1998 book and a series of additional articles (cf. Chapter 7 below) I submit recordings to instrumental investigation in an attempt to substantiate this theory empirically. The theory adopts from Wellek and Warren and later theorists the assumption that to account for poetic rhythm, one must distinguish metric pattern, stress pattern and pattern of performance. The first two of these patterns must be defined and assigned independently from each other. The third contains the solution of a perceptual problem presented by the first two. In principle, we have access to poetic rhythm only through some performance. The regular sequence of metric pattern exists in a reading as an expectation, as the reader's *metrical set*. When a stressed syllable occurs in a strong position, it *confirms* meter; when in a weak position, it *disconfirms* it.

In my use of the term in a context of poetic rhythm, *performance* refers to the set of conditions permitting the elements of both stress pattern and metric pattern to group into, and establish themselves as, perceptual units. The task of mental performance is to effect such groupings, whereas the task of vocal performance is somehow to convey them in the vocal medium, even when conflicting. Within the present theoretical framework, the conflicting patterns of meter and stress constitute the *structures of norms* to be realized by the reader. The mental grouping that enables this is *mental performance*. Alternative groupings of syllables in verse lines are allowed as long as they generate a set of conditions which allows the elements of both stress pattern and metric pattern to establish themselves as perceptual units. This process is governed by the gestalt-laws of perception. The syllables constituting the conflicting patterns must be grouped into as good shapes as the prevailing conditions permit; this, in turn, would save mental processing space, so that both conflicting patterns may establish themselves as perceptual units in the reader's perception. A small experiment reported in Chapter 6, below, suggests that experienced performers may be in basic agreement as for the mental grouping of syllables in some extreme instances of metric deviation, although this grouping may be effected by slightly different vocal resources. What is more, this grouping is in remarkable harmony with the predictions of the theory.

Thus, the conflicting sets of norms may be realized, albeit imperfectly, by some alternative patterns of grouping. This is their mental performance. These patterns of mental performance, in turn, can be actualized orally by some sub-group of a wide range of vocal devices: the manipulation of stress pattern, intonation contours, speed of utterance, and pauses (filled or unfilled). Any phonological element used for the grouping of syllables can be actualized by a variety of phonetic cues. To give just one example, linguistic stress, which is one of the major grouping agents, may be cued by pitch, duration, or amplitude (loudness)—usually by some mixture of them.

Thus, the various vocal resources appear as accidental concrete texture with respect to mental performance. And the alternative mental groupings appear to be imperfect concrete realizations of the conflicting sets of norms of stress and meter that, according to Wellek and Warren, constitute "the real poem".

Stratified System of Norms

I have been working within a theoretical model proposed by Wellek and Warren, according to which a poem is a stratified system of norms; this system is the potential cause of experience. Following Roman Ingarden who, in turn, employed the methods of Husserl's "Phenomenology", Wellek and Warren propose that the norms constituting the poem exist in the following strata:

> There is, first, the sound-stratum which is not, of course, to be confused with the actual sounding of the words, as our preceding argument must have shown. Still, this pattern is indispensable, as only on the basis of sound can the second stratum arise: the units of meaning. Every single word will have its meaning, will combine into units in the context, into syntagmas and sentence patterns. Out of this syntactic structure arises a third stratum, that of the objects represented, the "world" of the novelist, the characters, the setting. Ingarden adds two other strata which may not have to be distinguished as separable. The stratum of the "world" is seen from a particular viewpoint, which is not necessarily stated, but implied. An event presented in literature can be, for example, presented as "seen" or as "heard": even the same event, for example, the banging of a door; a character can be seen in its "inner" or "outer" characteristic traits. And finally, Ingarden speaks of a stratum of "metaphysical qualities" (the

sublime, the tragic, the terrible, the holy) of which art can give us contemplation. This stratum is not indispensable, and may be missing in some works of literature. Possibly the two last strata can be included in the "world", in the realm of represented objects. (Wellek and Warren, 1957: 139–140)

I strongly suspect that these "metaphysical qualities", in those instances at least which are most interesting from the literary point of view, are in fact *aesthetic qualities;* as such, they are to be discussed in Chapter 4.

With respect to this stratified system, the systematic study of literature is at its most rigorous when confined to a systematic exploration of one group of norms or one single stratum. Transition from one stratum to another, or the integration of the various strata for the sake of one common effect appears to defy systematic treatment, and all too frequently these phenomena are treated in an intuitive, pre-theoretical manner.[3] Cognitive Poetics as conceived in the present work assumes that such issues need not necessarily be treated in a pre-theoretical manner, but may be dealt with in certain less rigorous, though still systematic ways, in which predicates like 'make more plausible', 'lead us to expect that', or 'strongly suggest' apply.

As will be suggested in Chapter 4, the really significant aesthetic qualities typically belong to *wholes,* not to any of their parts, and emerge in unpredictable ways from the interaction of a variety of norms on a variety of strata. Accordingly, the present study proposes to explore some aspects of the various strata in their own right, but also will suggest how the interaction of the various strata to some common effect may be explored.[4]

---

[3] This state of affairs may dismay the positivists and factualists. It is, however, different in degree, not in kind, from the state of affairs in natural sciences. In his paper on theory construction, J. J. C. Smart points out that

> 'rigour' in the sense it is pursued in pure mathematics is not an ideal in applied mathematics (or physics). The conception of 'rigour' involved in physics is that whereby it makes sense to say 'rigorous enough'. (Smart, 1966: 237)

> Even if the steps within a theory are formalized, the important steps, which are those from the theory to the experimental facts, are of quite a different sort. [...] It is in this step from the theoretical to the empirical, and in the converse step from the empirical to the theoretical, that 'judgment' characteristically enters into science. (ibid., 238)

> [R]oughly speaking, we may say that within a theory or within the description of fact we are on one level of language, but when we step from the level of theory to the level of fact or vice versa, we are in a region where expressions like 'make more plausible', 'lead us to expect that', or 'strongly suggest' apply, but where the logical relations of implication and contradiction do not strictly apply. (ibid., 239).

[4] This interaction presents one of the more serious problems in the organization of the present book. Even when a chapter purports to explore certain single isolated element

The present book purports to give a comprehensive view of the poem as a stratified system of norms, the potential cause of experience. The first group of Chapters (1–4) is concerned with general assumptions; the next group of Chapters (5–8) will consider issues related to the sound stratum of poetry: meter, rhyme, stanza form, poetic rhythm and sound symbolism. It will be noticed that some of these issues, especially the two last-mentioned ones, can hardly be detached from the discussion of the units of meaning. The next group of chapters (9–10) will concern the units of meaning (only those chapters of the present book are reviewed here which are relevant to this model).

Theoretical models for the integration of the various strata are offered in Chapter 4. It is the elements on the sound stratum (regular or deviating meter), on the stratum of meaning units (abstract or concrete nouns, verbal or nominal style), and on the world stratum (objects that do or do not have a stable, characteristic visual shape) that determine the convergent or divergent structure of the poetic text and, eventually, the "emotional" or "witty" quality of the *whole*. Likewise, in the hierarchy of *signifiants* and *signifiés* that constitutes the poem, the attending from a *signifié* to its *signifiant* splits the focus of attention and may generate a witty quality.

Such an integrated whole is accessible only through some individual consciousness. Therefore, the perceived quality of the integrated whole depends to a considerable extent on effects reported by individuals. And as it may be expected, various individuals may report a wide range of perceived effects. Some of these differences are legitimate results of (legitimate) alternative mental performances, that is, of (legitimate) alternative realizations of the stratified system of norms. As such, the issue of different effects belongs among the issues discussed at the beginning of the present chapter. Some of these differences, however, are due to individual differences between the cognitive-styles of various readers and critics. Some of these cognitive styles seem more adaptable than others. It will be claimed that a cognitive style better suited for adaptive purposes is also better suited for aesthetic response; in both cases, the issue at stake is the capability of responding in a more or less adequate manner to some external stimuli, constrained by rules over which the individual has no control. Chapters 21 and 22 concern critical competence, the critical code, and the implied critic's decision-style. Chapters 23–25 are new: they respond to work done by Cognitive Linguists after the first publication of this book.

---

or norm in poetry, at *some* point it must be considered how it may interact with other elements and norms on other strata. But also, this is the best way to show what can be done with Cognitive Poetics that could not be done without it. As a result, certain issues will have to be discussed in a variety of chapters, not only in the place predetermined by the logical scheme of the present book.

CHAPTER 3

Constructing a Stable World

In Chapter 1, I have dwelled at some length on the issue of "ordinary consciousness" as a personal construct; in the present chapter I am going to elaborate on some aspects of this issue (following this process of construction step by step in certain areas), and on some of its implications for literature. For this discussion, I should single out two major issues that are, in fact, three: (1) constructing a stable world, in which certain things can be predicted from the available partial information; this crucially involves (2), the mental equipment for going beyond the information given; (3) the ability to handle streams of rapidly changing information. In this context we also should recall two opposite kinds of mental mechanisms briefly mentioned in Chapter 1: **Mental set** and **shift of mental sets. Mental set** is the readiness to respond in a certain way. It is, obviously, an adaptation device of great survival value. It is required for handling any situation consistently. Of no less great survival value is the adaptation device called **shift of mental sets.** This was defined as the **shift** of one's readiness to respond in a certain way; it is required for handling *changing* situations in extra-linguistic reality.

In Chapter 1, I argued at considerable length that Cognitive Poetics conceives of literary devices as of adaptation devices originally developed for survival in the physical and social environment, and eventually turned to aesthetic ends. The reader is referred to Chapter 1 for a discussion of the details of this development with regard to both **mental set** and **shift of mental sets.**

In the response to literature, one of the major principles that enable the reader to go beyond the information given in the text is what Culler calls **The Rule of Significance**. "The Rule of Significance" is, Culler suggests, the primary convention of literary competence: "read the poem as expressing a significant attitude to some problem concerning man and/or his relation to the universe" (Culler, 1975: 115). The rule requires the reader to perform semantic and thematic transformations until he *can* read the poem in such a way. These transformations are subject to the constraints that shape and constrain the cognitive processes of abstraction and symbolization. The most conspicuous constraint is the necessity of preserving the consistency of the physical-social-spiritual environment on the one hand, and the consistency of, e.g., a poetic text on the other. Another constraint imposes the deletion of the most specific features of any information added to the text, and continuation of the abstraction process "right to the end". In other words, all those specific features of the information added must be deleted which conflict with any explicit information in the text. As suggested in chapter 1, the witty character of a text arises from some sudden shift of mental sets. Its emotional quality arises from a series of continual shifts of mental sets on the one hand, and abstraction processes on the other. The process of abstraction, then, is a "double-edged" phenomenon: it is one of the most conspicuous tools by which intellectual processes construct a stable, consistent world; on the other hand, it is an effective means to hold information in an active form, so that it doesn't go away, yet does not preempt everything else. Thus, it makes a major contribution to our accomplishments, both intellectual and emotional, in handling of both the stable and the fluid element in our world. Frequent shifts of mental sets load the text with mental energy, and render the process flexible. A deviation from normal energy level, a flexible control of the adaptation processes, and the preservation of information in an active state are thus the essence of emotional processes.

Cognitive Growth

I would like to present some of the issues involved here from a developmental perspective, relying on Bruner's classical paper on "Cognitive Growth" (Bruner, 1973). Bruner claims that growth depends upon the mastery of techniques and cannot be understood without reference to such mastery. In this respect, he focuses on two matters: "The first has to do with the techniques or technologies that aid growing human beings to represent in a manageable way the recurrent features of the complex environments in which they live". He distinguishes three systems for processing information by which human beings construct models of their world: through action, through imagery, and through language. "A second concern is with integration, the means whereby acts are organized into higher-order ensembles, making possible the use of larger and larger units of information for the solution of particular problems" (ibid., 325). As will be seen, our discussions of these two kinds of processes may have a wide range of implications for Cognitive Poetics: some of these implications are seemingly incongruous among themselves; but this incongruence may be settled with reference to a hierarchic organization. Bruner gives the following summary of his discussion of the representational technologies:

> We have said that cognitive growth consists in part in the development of systems of representation as means for dealing with information. The growing child begins with a strong reliance upon learned action patterns to represent the world around him. In time, there is added to this technology a means of simultanizing regularities in experience into images that stand for events in the way that pictures do. To this is finally added a technology of translating experience into a symbol system that can be operated upon by rules of transformation that greatly increase the possible range of problem solving. One of the effects of this development, or possibly one of its causes, is the power for organizing acts of information processing

into more integrated and long-range problem-solving efforts. (Ibid., 345–346)

A symbol system represents things by design features that include remoteness and arbitrariness. A word neither points directly to its referent here and now, nor does it resemble it as a picture. The lexeme *Philadelphia* looks no more like the city so designated than does a nonsense. syllable (ibid., 328)

Bruner illustrates the transition from the stage of action-patterns representing the world to the stage of sensory-image representation by the following example: "The child is playing with a rattle in his crib. The rattle drops over the side. The child moves his clenched hand before his face, opens it, looks for the rattle. Not finding it there, he removes his hand, closed again, back to the edge of the crib, shakes it with movements like those he uses in shaking the rattle. Thereupon he moves his closed hand back toward his face, opens it, and looks. Again no rattle; and so he tries again. In several months, the child has benefited from experience to the degree that the rattle and action become separated. Whereas earlier he would not show signs of missing the rattle when it was removed unless he had begun reaching for it, now he cries and searches when the rattle is presented for a moment and hidden by a cover. He no longer repeats a movement to restore the rattle. In place of representation by action alone—where existence is defined by the compass of present action—it is now defined by an image that persists autonomously" (Bruner, 1973: 328).

Bruner illustrates the transition from the second to the third stage of representation by a wide range of illuminating experiments, of which we can touch here only upon a few. Some of these experiments are grouped around Piaget and Inhelder's classic "conservation" test. In this experiment, water is poured from one beaker to another; if the second beaker is thinner, children from four to seven will say "it has more to drink because the water is higher"; if the second beaker is wider, they will say it has less because the water is lower.

Françoise Frank tried to alter this behaviour in the following way. First she did the standard conservation test. In the next test, two beakers of different widths were hidden behind a screen, except for their top. "The experimenter pours the water from a standard beaker to a wider beaker. The child, without seeing the water, is asked which has more to drink, or do they have the same amount, the standard or the wider beaker. [...] In comparison with the unscreened pretest, there is a striking increase in correct equality judgments. Correct responses jump from 0 per cent to 50 per cent among the fours, from 20 per cent to 90 per cent among the fives, and from 50 per cent to 100 per cent among the sixes. With the screen present, most children justify their correct judgment by noting that 'It's the same water', or 'You only poured it'. Now the screen is removed. All the four-year-olds change their minds. The perceptual display overwhelms them and they decide that the wider beaker has less water. But virtually all of the five-year-olds (as well as all of the

sixes and all of the sevens) stick to their judgment, often invoking the difference between appearance and reality" (Bruner, ibid: 335–336). In a posttest with the screen
removed, the fours remain unaffected by their prior experience. With the fives, instead of 20% opting for conservation, as in the pretest, 70% do. With both sixes
and sevens, conservation increases from 50% to 90%. conservation

The three systems for processing information distinguished by Bruner, action,
imagery, and language, afford the child increasing flexibility and freedom to handle
information not present at the moment. This is the point that Bruner wished to
make by quoting these and other experiments. However, from the point of view of
Cognitive Poetics, we should make another, not less important point as well. The
three systems for processing information increasingly **lose contact with reality.**
"The process of algebraization" (mentioned in a passage by Shklovsky quoted in
Chapter 1) sets in. An increasing gap between the world "as it is" and "as it is
known" begins to develop, the handling of which may require the waste of considerable mental energy, and may be the source of maladaptive processes. "The purpose
of art is to impart the sensation of things as they are perceived and not as they are
known"—says Shklovsky. Ehrenzweig (1970: 135) speaks of "a creative ego
rhythm that swings between focussed gestalt and an oceanic undifferentiation", required for enabling one "to suspend the boundaries between self and not-self in order
to become more at home in the world of reality". "Freud saw in it only the basic religious experience. But it seems now that it belongs to all creativity" (ibid). One
important function of art and religion is, then, to reinstate contact with reality and,
in extreme instances, "to suspend the boundaries between self and not-self", by—
among other means—regression to lower (and more immediate) modes of the representation of reality.

This last mentioned experiment shows how the acquisition of verbal representation supersedes sensory representation, largely improving the child's intellectual
performance. By the same token, however, it lends dramatic support to the claim of
Aestheticist and Symbolist aesthetics that words (and our conceptual equipment)
step between us and the immediate experiencing of the world. In fact, the italicized
clause in the following sentence of Bruner's could have been taken from a treatise
on Aestheticist or Symbolist aesthetics:

> We know and respond to recurrent regularities in our environment by
> skilled and patterned acts, by conventionalized spatioqualitative imagery
> and selective perceptual organization, and through *linguistic encoding
> which,* as so many writers have remarked, *places a selective lattice between
> us and the physical environment.* (Bruner, op. cit., 327)

Thus, for instance, the great Hebrew poet Bialik writes in his essay "Veiling and
Revealing in Language": "For it is obvious that language with all its phrases does
not lead us into the innermost compartment, into the very essence of things; on the
contrary rather, it is precisely language that shields/partitions us from them"

(Bialik, 1954: 26). This seems to be the exact counterpart of Bruner's "lattice". Words and systems fall out of favor, Bialik says, not because they have lost their power to reveal, illuminate or eliminate the eternal unsettled questions, the "primordial chaos", but on the contrary, because they have been worn out, and are no longer capable of proper veiling and concealing (ibid., 29).

There is no way to escape from the use of words in poetry. Still, as Walter Pater put it in his essay on Giorgione (published in 1873), "all art aspires towards the condition of music". The reason for this belief was that "music possesses just that quality of suggestiveness that the Symbolists were looking for, and lacks just that element of precision which words necessarily possess and which the Symbolists wished to suppress" (Chadwick, 1971: 5). Symbolist poetry as well as varieties of mystic poetry attempt "to suspend the boundaries between self and not-self", by increasing the share of kinaesthetic and sensory imagery as compared to verbal representation (which, in the final resort, cannot be dispensed with in poetry). These issues will be discussed, in relation to poetry and altered states of consciousness, in Chapters 18–20. At present, I wish to mention only that in order to indicate such altered states of consciousness in poetry, regression to kinaesthetic and sensory imagery must be of a certain kind: viz., characterized by the absence of "focused gestalt". Symbolist and mystic poets attempt to penetrate "behind the surface of reality" (ibid., 5); but, in order to do so, they must first *reach* "the surface of reality" by loosening the "lattice of words between us and the physical environment"; and then loosening or destroying the representation of focused gestalts in it, as well as the focused gestalts of poetic form.

In other styles, however, regression need not be as drastic as that. According to Freudian theory, one possible source of pleasure (and a major one at that) consists in the regression to some earlier mode of functioning. This may be the case even where focused gestalts are involved. Many instances of wit in general—and of metaphysical wit in particular—may consist in exactly such regression. Let us explore one possible line of cognitive growth in this respect. Bruner summarizes an experiment of Olver's with children who are given words or pictures to sort into groups or to characterize in terms of how they are alike.

> The youngest children rely more heavily on perceptual attributes than do the others. As they grow older, grouping comes to depend increasingly upon the functional properties of things—but the transitional phase is worth some attention [...]. The first functional groupings are of an arbitrary type—what I or you can do to objects that render them alike [you can make noise with a newspaper by crumpling it and with a book by slamming it shut] rather than what is the conventional use or function to which objects can be put. [...] Gradually, with increasing maturity the child shifts to an appropriate and less egocentric form of using functional groupings. The shift from perceptual to functional groupings is accompanied by a corresponding shift in the syntactical structure of the groups formed.

> Complexive groupings [in which the various members are included in the class in accordance with a rule that does not account uniformly for the inclusion of all the members] steadily dwindle; superordinate groupings [in which one universal rule accounts for all the objects in the set] rise, until the latter almost replace the former in late adolescence. (Bruner, ibid., 343)

Now consider, in the light of this development, the following horror joke.

> (1) — Mrs. Jones, your husband has been overrun by the steam-roller.
> — Oh my God, I'm opening straight away.
> — Don't bother, we'll slip him under the door.

Most things said about horror jokes in Chapter 1 apply to this one, too. Here however the shift is not from a trivial situation to a horror situation, but rather from a very grave situation to a shocking one. The question that concerns us here is whether the shocking quality results merely from the men's insensitivity and violation of elementary politeness in such a grave human situation, or rather from their blatant violation of our adult cognitive accomplishments. In other words, why does it come to us as an utter surprise that the steam-roller may have flattened out its victim? Adult consciousness tends to categorize automatically the event under the superordinate concept "fatal accident". This is its *appropriate* function, its most important human significance. In other words, I am arguing that the default categorization of the event is not a matter of convention, but rather of the correct application of one of our most highly developed cognitive devices, for the purpose of best adaptation. For one thing, the men's answer is "arbitrarily functional": what you and I *can* do with a corpse overrun by the steam-roller. For another thing, the men's answer relies on perceptual attributes of the situation, rather than on its functional properties. In Freudian terms, pleasure is gained here by regression to an earlier mode of cognitive functioning, to the grouping of objects in accordance with their perceptual attributes and arbitrary functional properties. It is this fusion of pleasurable regression with the horrifying sight of the "flattened" corpse that generates the sense of shock and emotional disorientation. However, this "regression" is not to be considered as altogether maladaptive. In an important sense, it restores contact with physical reality, as things are, and not merely as they are known.

A similar, though less sensational, story can be told of "opening the door". In adult categorization, doors are there to allow certain kinds of communication when open, and to disallow them when closed. This would be their typical and appropriate functional use. In comparison to this, the fact that flat things *can* be slipped under them, may be regarded as an arbitrary functional property, though notes and letters *are* occasionally slipped under doors. Now further witty pleasure may be derived from the fact that these two instances of regression are fused in one single act. In other words, this information of considerable complexity is replaced by a single event of considerable simplicity, resulting in considerable saving of mental energy in handling it. This, too, according to Freudian theory is a major source of pleasure.

Let us consider now a poetic example. In one of the eleventh century Hebrew poet Yehuda Halevy's erotic poems the following two verse lines occur:

בָּךְ כָּל יְפִי – וְעוֹד מַה יִּתְרוֹן / בִּרְבִיד וְסַהֲרוֹן?

אַךְ יִמְנְעוּ לְחַבֵּק גָּרוֹן / וּנְשֹׁק לְצַוְּרוֹן!

bax kol yəfi — wə'od ma yitəron / birvid wəsahăron
ax yimnə'u ləhabbeq garon / un˘oq ləṣawwəron!

(2) You are endowed with all beauty so what's the good of necklace
and moon-shaped ornament
They only impede the embracing of the throat and the kissing
of the neck

These lines have some of the persuasive wit of Metaphysical Poetry, and contain a metaphysical conceit. Indeed, had Donne begun his dramatic speech in his *Elegy XIX* "To his Mistris Going to Bed" at an earlier stage of love-making, he may well have resorted to it. The appropriate functional grouping of "necklace and moon-shaped ornament" is with "things that adorn". The first line of the quotation relies on this grouping, by way of a hyperbolic twist: you are so beautiful that you need not (or even cannot) be adorned (made more beautiful) with jewels. The second line shifts to arbitrary functional grouping, with things that disturb love-making. Thus, again, adult cognitive habits are violated and, at the same time, attention is unexpectedly directed to certain neglected aspects of the physical environment.

A further aspect of the adaptational value of the conceit will become apparent if we return to Piaget's conservation test. Bruner reports an experiment by Nair who explores the arguments children use when they solve a conservation task correctly. Three kinds of arguments were set forth by the children to support their judgments, one perceptual, one having to do with action, and third, a "transformational" argument. "Of the children who thought the water was not equal in amount after pouring, 15 per cent used nonperceptual arguments to justify their judgment. Of those who recognized the equality of water, two thirds used nonperceptual arguments" (Bruner, 1968: 393). Now consider Donne's notorious compasses image which will be discussed at some length in Chapter 4. This metaphysical conceit develops consistently, with a false logic, a perceptual argument (the visual "behavior" of the compasses); at the same time, it develops consistently some genuine nonperceptual argument ("forbidding mourning"). As a result, it plays off an inadequate adaptive mechanism against an adequate one. In a developmental perspective, the conceit presents an opportunity to examine one's "outgrown", childish level of intellectual performance in the light of one's own adult level of functioning, which results in a feeling of relative freedom, superiority, and amusement.

Now we are turning to Bruner's second concern announced at the beginning of the present section, viz., with integration, "the means whereby acts are organized into higher-order ensembles, making possible the use of larger and larger units of information for the solution of particular problems". The literary implications of these cognitive technologies are quite different from the ones considered hitherto. They differ in two major respects. First, the poetic devices considered so far belong to micro-structure (texture); the issues to be considered belong to macro-structure. Second, the effects of the devices considered hitherto crucially depend on regression from some cognitive accomplishment; the literary mechanisms to be considered below make full use of the cognitive accomplishments concerned. We shall consider briefly two of the experiments mentioned by Bruner. One is by Mosher.

> He was concerned with strategies used by children from 6 to 11 for getting information in the game of Twenty Questions. They were to find out by yes–no questions what caused a car to go off the road and hit a tree. One may distinguish between connected constraint-locating questions ("Was it night-time?" followed up appropriately) and direct hypothesis-testing questions ("Did a bee fly in the window and sting the man on the eye and make him go off the road and hit the tree?"). From 6 to 11, more and more children use constraint-locating, connected questioning. (Bruner, ibid., 346)

The experimenters asked the children, after they have played their games, which of two questions they prefer—one of them a typical constraint-seeking question ("Was there anything wrong with the man?") and the other a typical direct test of a hypothesis ("Did the man have a heart attack?"). All the eleven-year-olds and all the eight-year-olds chose the constraint-seeking question, but only 29% of the six-year-olds did.

> When the older child receives a yes answer to his constraint-locating question, he most often follows up by asking another. When, on the rare occasion that a younger child asks a constraint question and it is answered yes, he almost invariably follows it up with a specific question to test a concrete hypothesis. The older child can accrete his information in a structure governed by consecutive inference. The younger child cannot. (Ibid., 346–347)

This experiment taps one of the most important mature cognitive abilities: *constraint-seeking*. This ability gives a person great flexibility and adaptability, especially in an environment about which little or nothing is known, in which highly generalized responses are required. This ability is contrasted to *specific questions to test a concrete hypothesis*. One of the basic assumptions of the present work is that abstract constraint-seeking behavior is the typical approach required in varieties of literary interpretation, or in the explication of metaphors. Thus, for instance, writing on similes and metaphors, George Miller (1979: 241) suggests: "Interpretation is not a search for a unique paraphrase of the implicit comparison, but rather a search for grounds that will constrain the basis of the comparison to a plausible set of alternatives". I am not concerned here with whether the comparison-view of metaphor is right or wrong. But I find this insight (like so many of Miller's insights) really stimulating. In a situation in which there may be an indefinite number of solutions, any "unique paraphrase" is likely to be totally arbitrary. So, if one wants to avoid arbitrariness, the best one may hope for is seeking *to reduce possible meanings* in a principled manner, through identifying constraints. To this end, "it is necessary to search the text and context for the author's grounds" (ibid.).

Now there is a curious fact in the domain of literary criticism. Whereas eleven-year-old and eight-year-old children usually reach a stage in their cognitive growth in which they tend to choose the constraint-seeking questions in the Twenty-Questions game, many adult literary critics, among them professors of literature, choose to relinquish this cognitive achievement: if their constraint question is answered yes, they "follow it up with a specific question to test a concrete hypothesis". They prefer a unique reason "to a plausible set of alternatives". When I was an undergraduate, our teacher in the first year Shakespeare course insisted that Ophelia was pregnant, Hamlet was the father of her child, and that is why eventually she committed suicide.

As for whether Ophelia's drowning was an accident or suicide, there are some quite plausible alternative suggestions in the play. According to the priest, "her death was doubtful"; according to the grave-diggers, "she drowned herself wittingly"; but the queen is the only one who gives a detailed account of her death, suggesting that it was an accident. So, far from knowing suicide for a fact, and since no further evidence is likely ever to turn up, one should at least stick to the priest's position, allowing for both alternatives.

As for the possible reasons for Ophelia's madness and/or suicide, we might ask a few constraint-locating questions, as in the game of Twenty Questions, and expect fairly dependable yes/no answers: "Were there any reasons to believe that Ophelia experienced some severe shock?", "Was there at anytime some affection between Hamlet and Ophelia?", "Did Hamlet treat Ophelia rudely?". It is on such a level of generality and explicit information that "the author's grounds" should be sought. But such more specific questions as "Did Ophelia have sexual intercourse with Hamlet?" or "Did she get pregnant by him?" or "Perhaps by Rosencrantz and Guildenstern?" should be left to the six-year-olds.

To be sure, an exponent of the pregnancy hypothesis can support it with further evidence: Does not Polonius explicitly warn Ophelia against Hamlet's intentions? Can we not find support in the sexual contents and overtones of Ophelia's speeches and songs in her condition of madness? Furthermore, it could be argued that a work of art is by its very nature ontologically incomplete, and that any interpretation *must* add information to the play from the outside, provided that such information is made plausible by some other available information, and does not contradict explicit information in the play. Such a conception of interpretations is perfectly acceptable to me. As I shall argue later, hypothesis testing is one of our most powerful tools of adaptation to reality, of "going beyond the information given" in extra-literary life. My main concern, however, is that the application of hypotheses should observe all the safeguards against maladaptive behavior. Here, of course, my opponent could argue: since you cannot know what is the correct answer, since you cannot know what the poet had in mind when writing a piece of literature, you cannot know either, whether *my* application of hypotheses will lead to a worse adaptation than *your* application.

I contend that good or bad adaptation is not determined by the specific results of the hypothesis-testing process, but by its general strategies. In real life, one *may* occasionally hit upon the right answer through maladaptive strategies, and miss the point through adequate strategies. But this seems the exception rather than the rule. In literary interpretation, by contrast, *this is all we have.* The only way we can know whether the results of some interpretation are admissible or not, is whether they were reached through adequate or inadequate cognitive strategies. What is adequate for deciding whether the amount of water remains the same when poured from one beaker to another, or for arriving at the correct answer in the game of Twenty Questions will also do for literary interpretation. This is so, even though (or even precisely because) in a work of literature one cannot arrive at *correct* answers, only at a *plausible* answer, and whenever anything is *plausible,* its opposite is *plausible* too (if it's plausible that it will rain tomorrow, it is also plausible that it won't; otherwise it would be *certain*).

So, let us consider another experiment, this time with adults, that provides massive evidence that constraint location leads to the finding of the correct answer, while search for supporting evidence prevents it. In a paper "On the Failure to Eliminate Hypotheses—A Second Look", P. C. Wason (1968) reports a series of experiments, in which the subjects were told that the series 2 4 6 conformed to a simple rule which they had to discover by generating successive series of their own. After each series they were told only whether their numbers conformed to the rule which was "numbers in increasing order of magnitude".

> Unlike most concept attainment tasks the point was not to see whether the subjects discovered the rule. The point was to see how they behaved when their hypotheses had been corroborated by confirming evidence. (Wason, 1968: 165)

> The task was intended to simulate the understanding of an event for which several superficial explanations are possible. Since the real explanation would be merely a concealed component in the superficial ones it will most frequently defy detection until the more obvious characteristics have

been varied. The analogy is not to creative thinking but to the search for simplicity, in the sense of minimal assumptions. [...] The correct rule cannot be proved but any incorrect hypothesis can be disproved. Moreover, an infinite number of series exemplifying any hypothesis can be generated. The subject cannot run out of numbers which confirm his hypotheses. (Ibid., 166)

The description "the understanding of an event for which several superficial explanations are possible" comes as near as possible to the description of the task in literary interpretation. Also the stipulation "The correct rule cannot be proved but any incorrect hypothesis can be disproved" is illuminating of literary interpretation. We also could paraphrase the last sentence as "The critic cannot run out of evidence which confirms his hypotheses"—and this would only slightly exaggerate the state of affairs in literary criticism.

The results of Wason's experiment are overwhelming. The more a subject was looking for confirming evidence, the more difficult it was for him or her to find the right answer. The more he/she was looking for disconfirming (that is, constraint-locating) evidence, the more quickly the answer was found. I shall give here only a short description of three of the protocols, at the two extremes of efficiency. In one protocol (Female aged 25), six series of numbers were generated before the correct rule was found; most series were intended to test a hypothesis that is different from the one confirmed. Only after the correct hypothesis was found, two additional series were generated to confirm it (9 minutes). Another protocol (Male aged 25), with essentially the same structure of hypotheses, took 10 minutes. At the other extreme, subject (Female aged 19) generates three series that confirm the same hypothesis, and makes a direct announcement of an incorrect hypothesis. Then she generates one series and announces another incorrect hypothesis. Then she generates another three series that confirm one (incorrect) hypothesis, and makes a direct announcement of it. Then she generates four series of numbers and gives up after 45 minutes.

Toward the end of his paper, Wason reports an experiment by Penrose, who attempted to generalize the problem in a pilot study by using as his task the inverted form of the Twenty Questions game.

In the ordinary game a person asks questions of increasing specificity in order to discover a particular object. In the inverted game a person thinks of a logical class which another person has to discover by finding out whether the object falls under it. Penrose selected the class of "living things" (analogous to numbers in increasing order of magnitude), and gave as the initial instance "a Siamese cat" (analogous to the series 2 4 6). The subjects (students) were instructed to keep a written record of both their instances and their hypotheses. They were told to announce the class only when they were highly confident they had discovered it.

Only three out of the ten subjects announced the correct class without announcing any incorrect ones. 47.1 per cent of their instances confirmed their hypotheses and 52.9 per cent disconfirmed them. On the other hand, 86.5 per cent of the instances generated by the remaining subjects confirmed their hypotheses and only 13.5 per cent disconfirmed them. All the instances generated by the successful subjects, which resulted in the refutation of a hypothesis, led to consistent changes of hypothesis. But among the unsuccessful subjects there were eleven cases in which hypotheses were retained although logically excluded by one or more instances. (Ibid., 171–172)

Wason ends his paper with the remark "These experiments demonstrate on a miniature scale, how dogmatic thinking and the refusal to entertain the possibility of alternatives can easily result in error". The possible relevance of dogmatism and other personality variables to the critical endeavor will be considered in Chapter 21. In the present context we are interested in one thing: that some cognitive strategies are more adequate, some less, to handle reality; and that an adequate interpretation makes use of the more adequate ones of those strategies.

At this point, we should go back to Bruner and consider yet one more experiment (by Potter) reported by him, in a study of the development of perceptual recognition.

Ordinary colored photographs of familiar scenes are presented to children between 6 and 12, the pictures coming gradually into focus. [...] Six-year-olds produce an abundance of hypotheses. But they rarely try to match new hypotheses to previous ones. "There is a big tower in the middle and a road over there and a big ice cream cone through the middle of the tower and a pumpkin on top". It is like a random collage. The 9-year-olds torrent of hypotheses, on the other hand, shows a sense of consistency about what is likely to appear with what. Things are in a context of likelihood, a frame of reference that demands internal consistency. Something is seen as a merry-go-round, and the child then restricts later hypotheses to the other things to be found in an amusement park. The adolescent operates under even more highly organized sequential constraints: He occasionally develops his initial hypotheses from what is implied by the properties of the picture, almost by intersection—"It is red and shiny and metallic: It must be a coffee-pot". Once such constraints are established, the order of hypotheses reflects even more the need to build up a consistent world of objects—even to the point of failing to recognize things that do not fit it. (Bruner, 1973: 347)

In twentieth-century literature, there are several corpuses in which the chain of events exhibits some illogicalities: plays of the Theatre of the Absurd, works by Beckett, stories by Kafka and Agnon, and many more. Some of these works rely in their effects precisely on the disruption of the cognitive mechanisms just considered, and result in an uneasy feeling of confusion, or even disorientation. This is their legitimate effect. Now, these disruptions are not entirely arbitrary, but conform with certain principles derived from the aesthetic conception of the work or literary style concerned (see, for instance, Chapters 16–17 below). Some critics who are incapable of facing this sense of confusion or disorientation, tend to look for certain allegorical or symbolic meanings, in order to mitigate this uneasy feeling. More frequently than not, however, such critics fail to observe a reasonable degree of consistency in the allegoric equivalences they establish. To achieve this "liberty", one widespread strategy of literary criticism is the atomization of the text: critics isolate small units from the whole narrative, and assign to them allegoric meanings independently from one another. Most typically, in such instances they do not attempt to observe the constraints of consistency, of "what is likely to appear with what". This appears to be precisely the purpose of this atomization exercise: one may dispel the atmosphere of uncertainty in a puzzling story by assigning *any* meaning to the units, with no need to bother about such nuisances as the constraints of consistency. As I shall argue below, it is typical of riddles to operate by a systematic suspension of the various constraints of consistency. In fact, such interpretations may turn a narrative into a series of riddles with the solutions provided by the critic. And where solutions are provided, they dispel the anxieties of uncertainties produced by certain literary texts.

We have followed at some length Bruner's presentation of the child's acquisition of the equipment required for handling information not present at the moment, and for the integration of larger chunks of reality; in short, the child's ability of abstract thinking. With this ability, the child constructs a world that stays stable for a considerable period, over considerable sections of space. Now this process of abstraction and the process of the shift of mental sets (mentioned earlier) seem contradictory. As a matter of fact, however, they depend on each other's activities. Bruner summarizes the attainment of the capability of abstraction by children in the course of their cognitive growth as follows:

> The child, in sum, is translating redundancy into a manipulable model of the environment that is governed by rules of implication. It is this model of the environment that permits him to go beyond the information before him. I would suggest that it is this new array of cognitive equipment that permits the child to transcend momentaneity, to integrate longer sequences of events. (Bruner, 1968: 405)

These cognitive abilities are required, of course, not only for the performance of such simple cognitive tasks as determining whether the amount of water has changed when poured from a tall and narrow beaker into a short and wide one. A cognitive model of a similar nature, only infinitely more sophisticated, is required for the handling of a complex social-spiritual reality that is in a constant flux. Such a cognitive model of the environment, which is very comprehensive, stable for a very long period of time, and governed by abstract implication rules is a prerequisite for a person to abandon himself without anxiety to shifts of mental sets. One must be assured that the world remains essentially the same, if one is to shift mental sets without apprehension, in accordance with the demands of a reality changing in its more concrete details. And conversely, only he who is capable of shifting his mental sets according to the demands of the changing reality, he who is capable of relinquishing cognitive categories created on the evidence of a small section of reality, is capable of constructing a cognitive model that is stable over a considerable period, without being compelled to ignore details of the constant flux on the more concrete levels. This "mission impossible" is accomplished through the construction of a hierarchic system of information processing, to be discussed at some length in Chapter 21.

The Nature of Emotion

We have closely followed Bruner's account of the child's cognitive growth, how the child acquires the ability to construct a stable reality, from one part of which valid inferences may be made to another. I have suggested, at the same time, that we also possess some rival mechanisms with which to handle a fluctuating or rapidly changing reality. One such typical mechanism is **wit**; another—**emotion.** There exists a tradition that views emotional processes as nonconceptual, as opposed to thought processes. This tradition seems extinct among today's psychologists; among literary critics, however, it seems to be very much alive to this very day. In the present section, I shall discuss at some length the nature of emotions, in what respects they are similar to conceptual thought, and in what respects they are not.

A glance at the collection of readings *The Nature of Emotion* (Arnold, 1968) may indicate that experimental and theoretical research in the last three decades or so tends to conceive of emotions as organized tendencies, as adjustment processes, as coping mechanisms. "Emotion is a tendency towards an object judged suitable, or away from an object judged unsuitable" (Arnold and Gasson, 1968: 203). Sometimes these tendencies are reinforced by glandular and muscular changes; but emotions may well occur without such bodily changes. Emotions cannot be located in any specific part of the body or of the neural system.

Emotions are not the opposite of thought processes (as sometimes assumed). On the contrary: no emotion can occur before at least two situation appraisals have taken place. Some authors insist on an additional distinction between intuitive and conscious appraisal, asserting that only the former may result in emotion: others do not care to make this distinction. Suppose I hear a sudden boom. My first response is a startle reflex. If the sound turns out to have been produced by a backfiring car, I need not refer to it anymore, and no emotion arises. If, however, it turns out to have been a shot aimed at me, I may experience *fear*. Before experiencing fear, I have to make two judgments, namely, I have to believe that I am in danger and I have to believe that I cannot properly handle the situation. Now suppose I am a teacher, and the boom comes from a naughty trick played by a student. In this case, I may believe, again, that I am (or my reputation is, or my lesson is) in danger. But this time I may have reason to believe that I am the stronger one. Thus, my response will be, most probably, *anger*. Similarly, a young singer before her debut may believe that her career may be at stake (i.e., in danger), and that she may not be able to cope with the situation. She may be *apprehensive*. At any rate, the individual does not experience emotion except in situations that are of significance to him.

It has been observed that sometimes, emotional response is inadequate in view of the objective situation. Some people interpret this to mean that our emotion interferes with our sober appraisal of the situation. Some psychologists seem to take the opposite view, however. It is our *cognitive appraisal* that leads to inadequate emotional response, as for instance by viewing a controversy as a matter of personal attack (see Arnheim, 1967: 307). As Lazarus (1968: 253–254) puts it, *"Appraisal does not imply awareness, good reality testing, or good adaptation. It implies only that thought processes are involved, not the kind of thought. A belief may be unwise, yet still be cognitive"* (Lazarus' italics)[1].

So far, emotion has been described as a response that does not greatly differ from other human responses. Many non-emotional states of mind may involve situation appraisals and adjustment to changing situations. Furthermore, no single differentiating feature of emotion has been found.

Duffy (1968: 139), an ardent exponent of the view described here says *"All* responses, not merely 'emotional' responses, occur as adjustments to stimulating conditions. *All* responses, not merely 'emotional' responses, occur at some particular *energy level. All* responses, like 'emotional' responses show *direction* toward a goal" (Duffy's italics). Still, everybody knows that there *is* a perceptual difference between emotional and non-emotional responses. We could speak about emotions more accurately not as a certain *kind* of response, but as a *set* of responses. The unique conscious quality attributed to emotions, says Duffy,

> may be said to represent the conscious counterpart of adjustive responses in *degree* rather than *kind* [...] Changes in energy level, in degree of organization of responses, and in conscious state occur in a continuum. There is no point on this continuum where a "non-emotional" degree of

[1]   *The Fontana Dictionary of Modern Thought* points out two different meanings of *Cognition*. "Originally the word distinguished the rational from the emotional and impulsive aspect of mental life. [...] The term is now used in Cognitive Psychology to refer to all information-processing activities of the brain, ranging from the analysis of immediate stimuli to the organization of subjective experience. [...]" Notice that Lazarus uses *cognitive* in the first sense, while it is used in the second sense in my phrase *Cognitive Poetics*.

> disorganization of response changes suddenly to an "emotional" degree of disorganization; and there is no point at which a "non-emotional" conscious state changes suddenly to an "emotional" one. These characteristics of experience and behavior show continuous variation rather than separation into hard and fast categories. Extremes of the continuum are readily identified as "emotion"; intermediate points offer difficulty in identification. For example, slight changes in energy level such as occur during "interest" or "boredom" usually leave the individual uncertain as to whether he is experiencing "emotion"; extreme changes, such as occur in "anger", are unequivocally identified. (Duffy, 1968: 138)

In the first place, then, emotion represents a marked change in the energy level. On the one hand, excitement, anger, joy, for example, involve greater mobilization of energy in the organism than our usual, non-emotional activities. On the other hand, sadness or melancholy may occur on a lower energy level. When the interpretation of the situation abruptly changes, the individual has to make quick adjustments. In such cases, violent changes of energy level may occur on all levels of mental as well as physiological activity. This involves that unique kind of sensation familiar to all of us as an emotional state of mind.

A change in the excitement level alone cannot be *the* differentiating feature of emotion; such a change can be brought about by drugs, too (Duffy). But it *can* be an important ingredient in emotion. Lazarus quotes a report on an experiment that emphasizes what he calls the "cognitive" antecedents of emotion. Epinephrine (a hormone connected with emotion, which typically results in marked evidence of arousal of the autonomic nervous system) was injected into subjects. Given precisely the same state of epinephrine-induced sympathetic activation, the experimenters were able, by cognitive manipulation, to produce in their subjects the very disparate states of euphoria and anger. However, in most life situations of emotional production (and this may be true, *mutatis mutandis,* of literature too) "there is no artificial booster given to ensure a high state of autonomic activation. The individual perceives and appraises a situation relevant to his welfare, and this appraisal is a crucial antecedent to the emotional reaction [...]. But the activation follows, it does not precede the cognition about the situation" (Lazarus, 1968: 260).

A second characteristic of emotion may be identified along the organization/disorganization continuum. It partially overlaps with the exclusiveness/ inclusiveness continuum. An emotional response is more inclusive than a purely rational one. It may be accompanied by "the appropriate muscular and glandular changes which are an integral part of emotional activity", in the words of Arnold and Gasson. "The evaluative judgment requires sensation, imagination and memory; it involves the intellect too [...]. The emotional situation involves the activity of many powers, often all the powers of the human being [...] all the functions working simultaneously" (Arnold and Gasson, 1968).

Reason, on the other hand, is exclusive. It is directed toward a goal and proceeds step by step in such a way that each later step follows from an earlier one. One difference between emotion and reason is, then, similar to that between a general trend (with occasional diverging tendencies) and a specific direction.

The extremes of this continuum may be described as more or less differentiated. The highly inclusive emotional response is spread over a large part of the organism and as such it tends to be more diffuse. Rational activities are more discriminating. The more distinctions one makes, the more differentiated one's activity is. Eliminating the irrelevant responses requires many and minute distinctions. Abstract thinking is highly differentiated.

Conceptual differentiation, definite direction, straightforward proceeding toward a goal imply a feeling of active control, of purposeful activity. Correspondingly, the inclusion of many impulses in a response may result in a sense of "disorganization", in a feeling of "loss of control" over the many activities involved. It is felt that the many activities and powers "break loose" and "overwhelm" the actively organizing mind. It may be marked with a feeling of passivity (hence the words *passion, agitated, excited* and the like would indicate both high energy level and being acted upon).

That emotion and thought are not two rigid, mutually exclusive categories, but rather two points on a spectrum with gradual shadings, will be readily seen if we examine the thought-end of this spectrum. J. P. Guilford distinguishes between divergent and convergent thinking abilities. Divergent-thinking activities "emphasize searching activities with freedom to go in different directions, if not necessary to do so in order to achieve an excellent performance. Convergent-thinking activities proceed toward one right answer, or one that is more or less clearly demanded by the information" (Guilford, 1970).

Convergent thinking proceeds toward a restricted answer or solution. If asked:

> "What is the opposite of high?" you would probably answer "Low". This is an example of convergent thinking. If asked "What is two times five plus four?" you would have no other alternative than to say "fourteen". But if you were asked to give a number of words that mean about the same as "low", you could produce several different responses, all satisfying the requirement, such as "depressed", "cheap", "degraded", and the like, and you would be correct. In this example we have an instance of divergent thinking. (Ibid., 180)

"Creative thinking" requires divergent-thinking ability. When confronted with a new problem in mathematics or geometry, no "sure" rules can be given how to solve it. The solution will come by *restructuring* the field in an unpredictable way, in a sudden flash of insight (see Köhler's discussion in the next chapter). The history of great scientific discoveries offers many examples in which a person directed great conscious effort to the solution of a problem over a long period. Paradoxically, the solution occurred in moments when the conscious control was relaxed, when the person was half asleep, taking a hot bath or the like. These sudden flashes of insight tend to be part of a certain sequence of events. They are preceded by a period of conscious effort directed to a specific goal. When the person has mastered all the relevant facts of the field, there is a need for "loosening" them, freely manipulating them, trying all sorts of recombination, transforming things one into another. This procedure is no mere trial and error. When the relevant facts fall into the pattern that constitutes the solution, they are suddenly recognized as such. The person cannot tell even what was the decisive step: it became part of the final pattern, and therefore, it usually cannot be remembered as an isolated step. There is good experimental evidence in favor of this conception of creative thinking (see Köhler, 1969; Maier, 1968).[2] This sudden "intuition", this lack of conscious control over the step leading to the goal are ingredients common to creative thinking and emotional response.

In this manner, creative thinking is one step along the exclusion/inclusion or organization/disorganization axis, in the direction of emotion. It is more adventurous; it requires us to relinquish the psychological atmosphere of certainty, the sense of control over our mental activities, to proceed towards one's goal in a less specific direction. We may, then, describe this continuum from emotion to reasoning as the divergence/convergence axis. (Convergent and divergent structures in poetry will be discussed at length in the next chapter).

[2]   See also Neisser (1968) "The Multiplicity of Thought":

> My thesis is that human thinking is a multiple activity. Awake or asleep, a number of more or less independent trains of thought usually coexist. Ordinarily, however, there is a "main sequence" in progress, dealing with some particular material in step-by-step fashion. The main sequence corresponds to the ordinary course of consciousness. It may or may not be directly influenced by the other processes going on simultaneously. The concurrent operations are not conscious, because consciousness is intrinsically single: one is aware of *a* train of thought, but not of details of several (316).

> For social as well as physical and physiological reasons, our *actions* have to display a certain degree of self-consistency. This demand is probably responsible for the original development of a "main sequence" within the multiplicity of thought (ibid.).

> No part alone is enough, no concatenation of parts. But if the analysis of the parts goes on simultaneously, along related sequences, there may come a moment when a higher-order operation [...] can combine them adaptively. In this situation, "insight" seems to involve building a novel hierarchy of existing processes. There is ample evidence already that the "components" of insightful behavior must be established in advance [...]. The present suggestion is that their *potential* existence is not enough: they must be *simultaneously* operative if a novel recombination is to emerge (320, all italics are Neisser's).

At the present stage of our argument, we must add an important corrective to our theory. Convergent mental activities are not necessarily uninvolved and selective. And, conversely, emotional responses, too, may proceed in a specific direction. In highly agitated states of mind, i.e., when activities are carried out on a high energy level, the many powers included in an emotional response may converge and act in a specific direction to attain a goal (see Duffy, 1968: 134–135). Convergent emotional qualities in poetry will be discussed at great length in Chapter 19 in relation to hypnotic and ecstatic poetry.

Hypotheses

In this section of the present chapter, I am going to consider at some length one of the most effective cognitive and intellectual tools for imposing unity and meaning upon apparently meaningless or unorganized information, as well as for going beyond it. One major assumption of cognitive poetics, I claimed in Chapter 1, is that poetry exploits for aesthetic purposes cognitive processes that initially evolved for nonaesthetic purposes. In Chapter 2, I paraphrased Arnheim to the effect that the realization of a poem involves the solution of a problem—namely, the creation of an organized whole. At the end of Chapter 1, I suggested that during the realization of poetic structures the reader deploys his cognitive devices used for organizing *perceptual wholes* in our nonaesthetic environment too. One of our most powerful cognitive tools for organizing both conceptual and perceptual wholes is the *hypothesis.*

According to *The American College Dictionary,* a **hypothesis** is "a proposition or set of propositions set forth as an explanation for the occurrence of some specified group of phenomena, either asserted merely as a provisional conjecture to guide investigation (**working hypothesis**) or accepted as highly probable in the light of established facts". In the present context it is essential to point out that a hypothesis imposes unity on incongruous phenomena. This is the most widely-held meaning of the term, and thus it is typically applied in the conceptual domain. As will be seen, this meaning is also extended to aesthetic theory in a rather specialized sense.

This term is widely used in the psychology of perception, too. Perceptions are accounted for in terms of a stimulus and a hypothesis. "Perceiving begins with an expectancy or hypothesis" (Bruner, 1951: 123). "Perceiving takes place in a 'tuned organism'" (ibid., 124). A hypothesis "may be regarded as a highly generalized state of readiness to respond selectively to classes of events in the environment" (ibid., 125). As a rule, we order structurally weak percepts with the help of hypotheses (ibid., 126–130). Let me illustrate this through a simple example adapted from Arnheim (1957: 39). "In an experiment familiar to all students of psychology, [...] Figure [3.1*a*] was reproduced as *b* when the subject had been told that an hourglass would appear briefly on the screen, whereas *c* resulted when the subject expected a table". In other words, "an expectancy or hypothesis" is aroused by the verbal instruction; and, under conditions that keep the stimulus control weak enough to leave the observer with a margin of freedom, this crucially influences perception and reproduction of the stimulus.

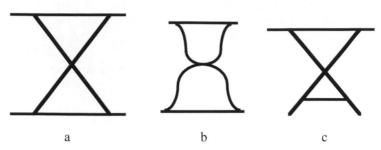

a   b   c

Figure 3.1   The force of perceptual hypotheses: design *a* was reproduced as *b* when the subject had been told that an hourglass would appear briefly on the screen, whereas *c* resulted when the subject expected a table.

Hypotheses are not always prompted by experimenters, not even in the psychological laboratory. In an experiment with Jewish and Catholic students, pairs of Jewish and Catholic symbols (verbal or pictorial) were presented simultaneously in a binocular, one to each eye. One of the findings of the experiment was that respondents had an inclination to perceive first the symbols of their own religious group (LoSciuto and Harley, 1970). This "highly generalized perceptual readiness" acquired through life experience is, in fact, a "perceptual hypothesis".

Such an experiment may give us an idea of the facility with which we apply perceptual hypotheses we don't even know we entertain *qua* perceptual hypotheses. It can explain why we respond selectively to one set of stimuli rather than to another. What we need, however, in order to account for our performance in aesthetic situations, is more complex: at least a demonstration that under different perceptual hypotheses we are capable of *seeing* the same stimulus material *as different meaningful wholes*. Such a demonstration was provided by a rather simple experiment by Roger Brown and Jean Berko.

In our experiment we used photographs of the actor Frois-Whitman "registering" various emotions. From the complete set we selected six pairs such that one member of each pair seemed to us to be a "cold" expression and the other "warm". We showed the first pair in the set to a subject and told him one picture showed emotion *A* and the other emotion *B*. On each subsequent pair the subject was asked to identify *A* and *B* and to tell us what characteristics of the faces guided his decision. It was a problem in category formation where the categories *A* and *B* were described as *kinds of emotions*. Other subjects were shown the same faces in the same order but they were told of one, "This is Mr. *A*" and of the other "This is Mr. *B*". Like the others, they were to identify *A* and *B* in each pair and name the attributes of the faces that guided their decisions. [...] The differences between the two groups of subjects are too large to require any tests of statistical significance. *Emotion* A was distinguished from *emotion* B in terms of expressive features like smiles and frowns. No subject mentioned any fixed features. *Mr.* A, on the other hand, was distinguished from *Mr.* B in terms of the nose, the ears, the hairline, etc. Almost every subject relied on such features even though these are pictures of the same man. It is not surprising that these subjects also made some use of expressive features since that is the correct hypothesis and expression can have criteriality for distinguishing one person from another. However, the expressive features were used less than the fixed features by this group. The subjects distinguishing *emotion* A from *emotion* B made twice as much use of expressive features as did the subjects distinguishing *Mr.* A from *Mr.* B. We have repeated this general design with other pictures and other subjects and there can be no doubt that referring a name to a super-ordinate affects the constitution of the referent category. (Brown, 1968: 218–219)

The perception of music, too, is governed by perceptual hypotheses. Let us turn now to a fascinating demonstration, by Diana Deutsch, that most dramatically demonstrates the importance of hypotheses in music perception. She took a well-known tune and distributed its notes haphazardly among three different octaves, retaining the correct notenames (C, D, E and so on). "Listen to the tune and try to guess its name", she says. "The task is surprisingly difficult!"[3] "The [second tune] is identical to the first one, except that now the tones are all in the same octave. You should have no difficulty in recognizing this tune. Once you know what to listen for, try the pattern of the [first tune] again—you might find it much easier to follow". In terms of the present discusssion, the second tune provides a hypothesis that organizes the first pattern into a coherent whole. By the same token, this experiment demonstrates the gestalt principle of **Proximity**. The nearer the notes to one another (in this case in pitch), it is easier to organize them into a coherent perceptual pattern.

In a similar way—I contend—we organize percepts offered by a poem into a (meaningful) hierarchic order. In the Brown–Berko experiment, the hypotheses were supplied explicitly by the experimenter; in the music experiment, by the second sound file. In perceiving a poem we use other hypotheses, such as style, genre, or archetype. These categories have been—I assume—acquired by past experience (archetypes, according to Jung, are innate) and one may apply them unconsciously or semi-consciously. In another ingeniously simple experiment, Roger Brown has shown that children of 3–5 years use abstract grammatical categories and make subtle distinctions between formal subclasses, having no difficulty in applying non-

---

3   The sound files are available online at:
http://www.tau.ac.il/~tsurxx/SecondEditionSoundFiles/Toward2ndEd_SoundFiles.html. They are derived from the website
http://www.philomel.com/musical_illusions/description.html#mysterious

sense words formed as particular nouns, mass nouns, and verbs to the correct class of objects or actions (ibid., 250–252). It would not be far-fetched to assume that educated adults may have acquired, by past experience, such categories as *romantic poem,* or *tragicomedy,* or *the death-and-rebirth archetypal pattern.*[4] This may suffice for my present argument; should the existence of a Jungian collective unconscious be proved, it may justify the attribution of additional strength to *certain* regulative concepts (such as archetypal patterns).

One may safely venture, then, a generalization that a necessary stage in enjoying a work of art (including literature) is the *perception* of the work. Perception involves distinction and organization and depends, among other things, on expectancies. Psychologists of perception call these expectancies *hypotheses.* In the aesthetic context I wish to point out the relevance of *hypotheses* in two domains: their relationship with **stylistic categories** and with **interpretation.**

"Stylistic categories", says Gombrich (1966: 100) "have the character of a hypothesis". James S. Ackerman asserts that "there is no objective correlative for our image of a style". We refer to style, because "the virtue of the concept of style is that by defining *relationships* it makes various kinds of order of what otherwise would be a vast continuum of self-sufficient products". "Style is a protection against chaos"; "our perceptual mechanisms cause us to interpret what we see in terms of what we know and expect" (Ackerman, 1957: 55).

> We create classes such as Impressionism, Baroque art, or Picasso's "Blue Period" on the assumption that a certain complex of elements common to a group of works is sufficiently stable, distinct, and relevant to justify characterizing it as a style. [...] This characterization of a style in terms of its stable factors is a hypothesis (and one which we must challenge constantly) that makes it possible to study change. (Ibid., 57)[5]

Defending an interpretation of a piece of art, or offering a procedure for such a defense clearly involves highly abstract, conscious, logical thinking, full with explicit inferences. Still, it is hard to avoid, in a feasible theory of interpretation, significant references to perceptual or other nonconceptual cognitive processes. Margolis, for instance, begins his paper on the logic of interpretation with reference to Wittgenstein's notion of "aspect-seeing", "aspect-blindness", "seeing as". There is, to be sure, a crucial difference between Wittgenstein's and Margolis' preoccupations. "Wittgenstein is speaking about getting someone to see something in a certain way; while here, the emphasis is rather on whether a certain way of seeing something is critically admissible" (Margolis, 1962: 110). It should be noted that Margolis is not concerned here only (or even not mainly) with the question whether

---

4   It will be discussed in Chapter 12 at considerable length how such categories are acquired.

5   The *structure* of hypotheses for the handling of period-style will be discussed in Chapter 12.

applying a certain set of propositions to something, is critically admissible, but rather whether a certain way of *seeing* something is. Margolis speaks of Catholicism, or Marxism, or the Freudian or Jungian analytical psychologies as of *myths*. These are powerful systems of ideas which, on the one hand, claim to be true about some important sector of the world. On the other hand, they are "perspectives", to which our habits of thinking and seeing are susceptible.

> A "myth", in the sense in which I am using the term, is a schema of the imagination which, independently of the scientific status of the propositions it may subtend, is capable of effectively organizing our way of viewing portions of the external world in accord with its distinctions. [...] We know a "myth" to be "objective" for criticism, though it may not be so for science, when the habits of thought and perception and imagination of normal persons are educable in its terms and when their responses to appropriate stimuli are generally predictable. (Ibid., 113)

In other words, such a "myth" can be *seen as* a scientific or *as* a perceptual hypothesis. It should be noted, however, that from this formulation also some conditions may be derived that may be necessary though not sufficient for deeming some way of "seeing as" as critically admissible as an interpretation. Thus, for instance, Faurisson's interpretation of Rimbaud's "Voyelles" as the blazoning of the female body may be deemed as critically inadmissible, since it is not such a schema of the imagination. Such a constraint must be postulated, even if one disputes its applicability to this specific instance, and even if one accepts Margolis' further comment:

> The imaginative schema (or "myth") that the critic uses need not be as elaborate and large-scale as the Freudian or Marxist or Catholic vision. It may be merely a formulable conviction about life that the artist may be supposed to have held, which, considered without regard to its own truth or falsity, adequacy or inadequacy, may, in the hands of the critic, enable us to impute a coherent design to a work otherwise defective or puzzling in this respect. (Ibid., 114)

Margolis' following comment may be seen to be in strict conformity with our conception of the actualizations of a poem by way of *general constraint location* rather than of supplying specific details: "The characteristic feature of critical interpretation that is philosophically most interesting is its tolerance of alternative and seemingly contrary hypotheses" (ibid., 116). In this respect, a critical interpretation is very much like a scientific hypothesis that typically asserts the *plausibility* rather than the *truth* of its statements. "Where the statements 'P is true' and 'Q is true' are contraries, the statements 'P is plausible' and 'Q is plausible' are not contraries" (ibid., 117).

Margolis' paper is called "The Logic of Interpretation", and it elaborates on the logical principles and steps involved in the application of an interpretive hypothesis to the individual work of art.[6] It also discusses at some length the similarities and differences between this procedure and the application of a scientific hypothesis to physical phenomena. In the investigation of physical phenomena, new evidence may be obtained that may decide which of two *plausible* hypotheses is *true*. "It must be admitted that, though they are always marginal to the main effort of science, considerations of plausibility are more nearly central to aesthetic criticism" (ibid., 116).

> There is, then, a characteristic rigor to critical interpretations, noticeably weaker than matters of fact ordinarily require. But, more important, the sort of rigor associated with determining matters of fact is flatly inappropriate in the circumstances in which interpretations are provided. (Ibid., 118)

As for the detailed process of applying hypotheses, we have already considered one crucial issue: looking for disconfirming evidence is at least as important as looking for confirming evidence. The other issue is what appears to be a "logical circle". Wellek and Warren speak of the "logical circle" in the application of hypotheses to such "regulative concepts" as *genres* and *period concepts*.

> The historian [...] must intuitively, though provisionally, grasp what is essential to the genre which is his concern, and then go to the origins of the genre, to verify or correct his hypothesis. Though the genre will appear in the history exemplified in the individual works, it will not be described by all traits of these individual works: we must conceive of genre as a "regulative" concept, some underlying pattern, a convention which is real, i.e., effective because it actually molds the writing of concrete works. [...] Exactly analogous problems are raised by a history of a period or movement. (Wellek and Warren, 1956: 252)

It is significant that this apparent "logical circle" in the conceptual application of hypotheses in aesthetics (and in science in general) is paralleled by an "information-confirming cycle" postulated by cognitive psychologists with reference to the perceptual application of hypotheses in everyday life (and where else). Bruner puts forward a three-steps model for such a cycle in perception. We shall not follow this model in its details. What concerns us here is his reflection *on* his model:

> The reader may object that our model of information-confirming cycle seems too saccadic, too jumpy, that perception seems to work more

---

6   The application of hypotheses as interpretations will be illustrated in Chapter 21, with reference to Goethe's "Erlkönig".

smoothly than our model indicates. There are two legitimate answers to this objection. The first is that only under well-practiced conditions of perceiving is the process so smooth. [...] But this rejoinder is trivial in the light of the second one. There need be no phenomenal resemblance, we would insist, between the feeling tone of a psychic process and the conceptual model used to predict or describe it. Nobody would seriously object today, for example, that the atomic theory of matter is an inadequate theory because matter, a rock for instance, does not look or feel like an amalgam of whirling atoms. (Bruner, 1951: 124)

Bruner's observation is even more significant for the discussion of aesthetic perception. Cognitive Poetics in particular, and much traditional poetics and criticism is concerned with a conceptual description of the process of aesthetic perception of specific works, or of certain types of poetic phenomena. Much energy has been spent on attempts to refute such endeavors, precisely with the kind of objections mentioned by Bruner. These are usually coupled with two additional arguments: by such conceptual analyses you destroy the aesthetic experience; and, usually presented as a question, "Do you think the author intended all that?". As for the latter, the absurdity of the question will be well brought out if one transfers it to another kind of artifact, e.g., "Do you think the carpenter intended that you apply Bruner's "information-confirming cycle" when you perceive his table?" So the right question appears to be "Do you think you ought to talk explicitly about all that?" Such a question may make sense in view of the objection that this may destroy the aesthetic experience or pleasure, and may be in place with reference to practical criticism. However, the practice may be justified by the contingencies of critical communication: it may be an efficient method of pointing out and justifying certain perceived effects, where other methods may have failed. So the question to be asked is, whether such a practice may destroy or enhance aesthetic experience or pleasure. I have no doubt whatever that, *if properly done,* it may enhance rather than destroy the aesthetic experience. Many thinkers have brought convincing arguments and evidence in favor of this position. I shall confine myself to only one, propounded by a psycho-analyst and a logician:

> Instruction, even though it is itself operative on a high ego level, may succeed in facilitating a relaxation of ego controls. Technical understanding may release energies otherwise employed in the reconstruction of the art works. (Kris and Kaplan, 1965: 256–257)

Communicative Competence & Riddles
In the present chapter we have been discussing the construction by ordinary consciousness of a tolerably predictable, stable world. One of the most important aspects of this stability concerns human communication systems. Some linguists,

psychologists, semioticians, and philosophers speak, in this context, of a social contract between the users of these systems: a "contract" that the "cooperative principle" will be observed, and that the systems will be used according to their rules and principles. There is a sense of stability and security, as long as all parties may be confident that the other parties, too, will stick to the contract. The term *Communicative Competence* is used "to cover a person's knowledge and ability to use all the semiotic systems available to him as a member of a given socio-cultural community. Linguistic Competence, or knowledge of the language-system, is therefore but one part of Communicative Competence" (Lyons, 1977: 573). Most important for our present inquiry, the other systems include *Literary* or *Poetic Competence, Rhythmic Competence* and *Critical Competence.*[7] Further on, Lyons speaks of what he proposes to describe as an ideal, 'omnicompetent' speaker of language, "where 'omnicompetence' implies, not only perfect mastery of the rules which determine the well-formedness of sentences, but also the ability to contextualize them" (ibid., 574).

As for Poetic Competence, in Chapter 1 I quoted Bierwisch:

> The actual objects of poetics are the particular regularities that occur in literary texts and that determine the specific effects of poetry; in the final analysis—the human ability to produce poetic structures and understand their effect—that is, something which one might call *poetic competence*. (1970: 98–99)

In Chapter 1, I alluded to the Russian Formalist doctrine according to which poetry is organized violence against language, and suggested that the response to poetry is organized violence against cognitive processes. It would be in strict conformity with our foregoing discussion (as it is also implied by the word "organized") to assume that in poetry there *are* constraints on the violence against language.

> They [the deviations—R.T.] achieve poetic effect only when the deviation has a specific regularity as its basis, when they stop being merely violations of the grammatical rules. This means that poetically effective deviations must be explainable in terms of rules of deviation which themselves specify the conditions and form of deviations. (Ibid., 110)

This brings us to an initial comparison and distinction between poems and riddles (which will be supplemented presently by an additional distinction). The effects of both poems and riddles are derived from deviations from, or violence against, ordinary language. But in riddles, in contrast to poems, these deviations and violations are either *ad hoc* and cannot be explained in terms of rules, or the rules of deviations themselves are thoroughly disguised, so that it is difficult to discover them. In most

---

7   "Rhythmic Competence" will be discussed in Chapters 6–7; "Critical Competence" will be discussed in Chapter 22.

instances, the latter appears to be the case; otherwise it would be impossible to solve the riddle. In other words, if in poetry we may expect mainly *additional* "rules of deviation", literary riddles are typically generated through the willing suspension of certain processes required by Linguistic and Poetic Competence; and in some instances, at least, it is hard to discover at which point of the hierarchy of rules the suspension occurs. Notwithstanding, riddles in literature must be considered within the terms of reference of aesthetic processes. In a moment we shall consider two instances, in which the riddle eventually succumbs to those processes and is turned into a different genre. I suggest that this phenomenon is no mere freak of literary history.

I propose to present some of the issues involved using Samson's riddle: "Out of the strong came something sweet" (*Judges,* 14:14). This is a good example of an unfair riddle. It refers to a specific event unknown to all but the person who propounds the riddle. Indeed, Samson himself claims: "If you had not ploughed with my heighfer, you would not have found out my riddle". In terms of our present theoretical framework, no amount of general constraint-location could lead to the solution of this particular riddle.

In the course of the centuries, however, what Culler calls "The Rule of Significance" (the primary convention of Literary Competence) was applied to this riddle in collective consciousness, that is, "Read the poem as expressing a significant attitude to some problem concerning man and/or his relation to the universe" (Culler, 1975: 115). Through the application of this convention, the Biblical verse referring to a specific, unusual event became a proverb in Hebrew: it assumed a highly general, abstract meaning: "out of something bad something good came out".[8] If one accepts another assumption of Culler's (ibid., 147) that "the function of genre conventions is to establish a contract between writer and reader so as to make certain relevant expectations", one may suggest that the proverb *qua* proverb instructs the reader to interpret the text as expressing a significant attitude to some *most general* problem concerning man and/or his relation to the universe. The process of abstraction from the proverb's figurative material must go all the way to the widest and most abstract generalizations. Going "all the way" in abstraction is a basic requirement of Literary Competence, if interpretation is to be constrained to a plausible set of meanings.

I tend to regard this process as evidence that even if the operation of the Rule of Significance is artificially suspended (as in the riddle), there is an inclination to apply it again, whenever a change in context enables it. In other words, I regard the application of the Rule of Significance as the natural *default* mode in literary contexts, as long as there is no good reason to suspend it. Another example of this process would be a poem like Petrarch's famous sonnet "Pace non trovo" (already mentioned in Chapter 2), the opening and closing lines of which I shall quote here again in Sir Thomas Wyatt's English translation:

---

8   The idea that this Biblical verse is a good example of a riddle turned into a proverb was suggested by the late Dan Pagis. The analysis is mine.

(3)   I find no peace, and all my war is done,
      I fear and hope. I burn, and freeze like ice.
      I fly above the wind, yet cannot arise,
      And naught I have, and all the world I season. [...]
            Likewise displeathes me both death and life,
            And my delight is causer of this strife.

Some scholars believe that this sonnet (and other, similar ones) grew out from a tradition of Provençal riddles, the solution of which is "love". *Love* denotes a general abstraction expressing a significant attitude. It is indeed easy to see, how a poem like this, consisting of a series of paradoxes, could serve as a riddle as well; but the qualified reader will have difficulty in suspending the Rule of Significance, and in refraining from emotionally responding to the abstraction throughout the reading, from the very beginning.

The regular mode of Poetic Competence consists, then, in the constant application of the Rule of Significance. From this point of view, the distinguishing mark of the riddle is that it instructs the respondent to disrupt the working of the linguistic rules he is accustomed to, as well as the Rule of Significance. The primal difficulty with the interpretation of riddles is that the respondent is inclined to apply the linguistic rules and the Rule of Significance to which he is accustomed; hence the default interpretation does not suit the riddle. The second difficulty is that after having discovered the need to disrupt the linguistic rules and the Rule of Significance, the respondent does not know at which interim stage he has to exit the normal interpretation process, in order to find the solution of the riddle. Let us briefly illustrate this through a riddle due to the eleventh century great Hebrew Poet, Yehuda Halevy:

יַעֲלַת הַחֵן תִּשְׁאָלֵנִי: / "אֶת מִי חָשַׁקְתָּ בִּצְבָאוֹת?"

וָאֹמַר לָהּ: "אִם לֹא תֵּדְעִי – / הָסִירִי הַשֵּׁשׁ מֵאוֹת!"

yaˤlat haḥen tiˀaleni / "ˀet mi haˇaqta biṣvaˀot?"
waˀomar la: "ˀim lo tedəˤi— / hasiri hašˇeš meˀot!"

(4)   The beautiful girl asks me: "Whom do you love among the
            gazelles?"
      I told her: "If you don't know, deduct/remove the six hundred".

The obvious meaning of the Hebrew phrase "ˇeš meˀot" is "six hundred", suggesting "deduct the six hundred" (from what)? However, the same sequence of graphemes may also suggest "Remove the six from (the Hebrew word) ˀot". As is well-known, the letters of the Hebrew alphabet also have a numerical value, *six* being assigned to the letter *waw*. The word *ʾott* is spelled *aleph-waw-taw*. Thus, after removing the letter *waw* from the word *ʾot,* we receive the word *ʾot,* that is, "you".

Here, the graphic sequence "šeš meʾot" signifies the phonological sequence [šeš meʾoθ]. The qualified reader passes automatically, without delay, from the graphic *signifiant* to the phonological sequence, which is the *signifié* with respect to the graphic sequence. At the same time, the phonological sequence is the *signifiant* with respect to the semantic *signifié,* namely, the number 600. The reader proceeds, again automatically and without delay, from the phonological *signifiant* to the semantic *signifié.* This tendency to automatic transition is reinforced by the verb *has-siri* ("deduct/remove"), which may designate a mathematical operation. Here, however, something seems to have gone wrong with the linguistic operation. The linguistic pattern required here is "deduct X from Y", whereas the text has only "deduct the X". The definite article, and the deviation from the proper linguistic pattern induces the reader experienced in reading poetry to apply the Rule of Significance, and to look for some general symbolic meaning that could be assigned to the number 600, and which, at the same time, might be regarded as an appropriate answer to the "beautiful girl's" question. If the reader is unsuccessful, s/he may understand that s/he has to deal with a riddle, that is, s/he understands that s/he must disrupt the chain of linguistic *signifiants* and *signifiés* described above, and suspend the application of the Rule of Significance. Then s/he goes back and searches for some link in this chain where it would suit the pattern "deduct the X from Y". Indeed, such a pattern is found in the phrase "remove the six from [the word] *ʾot"*. In order to render this formula meaningful, s/he must relinquish the earlier semantic *signifié* of the last word, and even its phonological *signifiant;* s/he must "attend back" to the graphic sequence, and to the numerical value of the letter *wav*w (6). After the removal of this letter from the graphic sequence *aleph-waw-taw (ʾot),* a new graphic sequence is generated that signifies a new phonological sequence [ʾat], the semantic *signifié* of which ("you") gives a reasonable answer to the girl's question.

When riddles are used in Mediaeval Hebrew Poetry as mannerist ornaments, they frequently go hand in hand with another kind of embellishment, the so-called "inlay language"[9] (Biblical allusion). The Israeli philosopher and literary critic, Eddy Zemach (1962: 12), arguing that "the Biblical world is the legitimate world" of the Mediaeval Hebrew poets, says among other things:

> If the poet says "brother of Aner", we must recall the Biblical phrase "Mamre the Amorite, brother of Eshcol and brother of Aner" *(Genesis,* 14:13), because the poet is alluding to a bunch of grapes for wine.[10] [...]
> If we read a verse-line "And the son of Avinoam came with mighty

9   "Inlay language" is a kind of literary allusion prevalent in Mediaeval Hebrew Poetry in which words and phrases taken from the Bible or other authoritative texts are used, frequently in an altered sense.

10   The proper noun *ʾɛškol* is an accidental homonym of the Hebrew common noun meaning "bunch [of grapes]".

waters", the poet requires us to call to mind [...] the original Biblical phrase and understand that he means "lightning" (alluding to Baraq the son of Avinoam from the Bible).[11]

These words require supplementing. Zemach illustrated his general argument by two examples that belong to a specific kind of "inlay language". The device mentioned fits exactly the above description of the riddle genre (but one should not infer from this that every instance, or most instances, of "inlay language" should be turned into riddles). The phrases "the brother of ʿAner" in a drinking song, or "the son of ʾAvinoʿam" in a nature description is perceived as meaningless. The application of the Rule of Significance (which governs the understanding of metaphors too) will soon lead to a dead end; then the reader may discover that he is dealing with a stylistic device of the riddle genre. In order to describe the linguistic-literary process whose disruption has generated these riddles, let us compare two verse-lines, one quoted above by Zemach, and another one quoted from a war poem by Shmuel Hannagid:

וּבָא בֶּן אֲבִינֹעַם בְּמַיִם כַּבִּירִים

uva ben ʾăvinoʿam bəmayim kabbirim.

(5)   And the son of Avinoam came with mighty waters

וַעֲשֵׂה לִי כְּמַעֲשֶׂךָ לְבָרָק וּדְבוֹרָה

waʿăse li kəmaʿsɛxa ləvaraq udəvora

(6)   And do to me as you did to Baraq and Debora

Both verses allude to Baraq and Debora's victory over Sis'era, recounted in *Judges,* 4–5. In (6), the reader encounters the graphic sequence *Baraq,* from which he automatically passes to the phonological sequence [baraq], from which he goes on, again, to Baraq, the person. Here he applies the Rule of Significance, and abstracts from Baraq's deeds the general abstraction "great victory" or the like; thus, Baraq's deeds serve as the vehicle for "great victory", the spiritual tenor of the verse line. After the event, the phonological sequence [baraq] too becomes active from the aesthetic point of view, *via* repetitive sound patterns commonly in use in all poetic

---

[11]   Here, again, the proper noun *Baraq* is an accidental homonym of the Hebrew common noun meaning "lightning".

periods (alliteration or paronomasia), through the first two words of the next line, "send a lightning" [bəroq baraq]:

בְּרֹק בָּרָק, אֱלֹהַי, וַתְּפִיצֵם

bəroq baraq, ʾɛ̆lohay, wahăfiṣem

(7)   Send a lightning, my God, and disperse them.

In the examples due to Zemach, the natural process is disrupted at a relatively early stage. The phonological sequence [baraq ben ʾăvinoʿam] or [ʾɛškol ʾăhi ʿaner] (or, in abbreviation, [ben ʾăvinoʿam] or [ʾăhi ʿaner] designate the persons known by these names. However, as we have said, in a drinking song or a nature description, the normal process fails to yield acceptable results. Nor can the application of the Rule of Significance help to settle the incongruence. At this point, the process must be disrupted. Instead of passing from the phonological *signifiant* to the semantic *signifié,* the reader must go to the phonological sequence of the *omitted* part of the proper name, which is an accidental homonym of a lexical word. From this phonological sequence, one must proceed to the semantic *signifié* of the lexical word (meaning "bunch of grapes", or "lightning").

We have examined the riddle with reference to the Rule of Significance, and in conjunction with allusion to Biblical phrases. The primary convention of Literary Competence, Culler suggests, is "The Rule of Significance". The riddle typically requires the willing suspension of "The Rule of Significance" (as well as of some rules of Linguistic Competence). Evidence for the supposition that such a suspension is hard to manage we find in the fact that there is a tendency to apply "The Rule of Significance" and turn the riddle into a proverb, or into paradoxical poetry. Further evidence for this supposition we find in the fact that varieties of mannerist and modernist literature exploit the suspension of "The Rule of Significance" for the arousal of a sense of confusion and emotional disorientation. In this respect, the riddle may be one of several devices of disorientation (along with sensuous metaphor and the absurd) in the service of mannerism and modernism, where "The Rule of Significance" must be suspended.

As we have seen, the relationship between riddle and poetry is quite complex. First, both are generated by deviations from the rules of Communicative Competence. Second, these deviations reflect different kinds of logic in the two. Third, riddles *may,* nonetheless, occur in certain types of mannerist poetry, as playful embellishment, when sufficiently conventionalized to lose their possible disorienting effect.

I wish briefly to consider two additional effects of the suspension of the rules of Communicative Competence—one in literature and one in literary criticism—with reference to the use of proper names. At the beginning of the present section, I suggested that in order to construct a predictable stable world, the semiotic codes available in a given socio-cultural community must properly be used; thus, a sense of stability and security is achieved. To what extent this is so, becomes palpable by the sense of discomfort when this principle is violated, as in Kafka's stories, in order to generate a nightmarish atmosphere of disorientation. Let us consider some characteristics of proper names. Referring to an object by a proper name is largely different from referring to it by a definite description. The traditional view, going back to John Stuart Mill, is that

> proper names do not have senses, they are meaningless marks; [...] whereas a definite description refers to an object only in virtue of the fact that it describes some *aspect* of that object, a proper name does not *describe* the object at all. To know that a definite description fits an object is to know a fact about that object; but to know its name is not so far to know any facts about it. (Searle, 1971: 234)

This conception is somewhat qualified by Searle. "The uniqueness and immense pragmatic convenience of proper names in our language lies precisely in the fact that they enable us to refer publicly to objects without being forced to raise issues and come to an agreement as to which descriptive characteristics constitute the identity of the object" (ibid., 140). "Definite descriptions [...] refer by providing an explicit description of the object. But proper names refer without providing such a description" (ibid., 141). Consequently, proper names can be used in the speech acts of *identifying reference* and of *calling,* but not in predication. Many proper names are derived from common nouns and phrases with full descriptive contents. This descriptive content, however, has degenerated, and proper names are applied irrespective of the descriptive contents of the common noun from which it is derived. A girl called *Grace* need not be graceful at all. Furthermore, when we call a boy *Gerald* or *Herbert,* we don't think of the etymological derivation of the names from Germanic "spear + rule", or from Old English "army + bright", respectively. This use of proper names can be changed in magic rites, not only in Amerindian tribes, but sometimes in modern urban society too. ∞*Hayyim* in Hebrew means "life"; but is also used as a proper name for males, irrespective of its dictionary meaning. However, when a former Israeli Interior Minister, a religious representative in the Knesset, Moshe Shapiro, was seriously injured, the name ∞*Hayyim* was added to his name as a middle name, saving his life (with some help from the doctors). He bore his middle name to the end of his life. This is a drastic deviation from the semiotic use of proper names. In the following passage from *The Castle,* Kafka indicates a different deviation from the proper semiotic use of proper names:

> 8. It was Frieda's great distinction, a distinction I'll be proud of to my dying day, that he used at least to call out her name, and that she could speak to him whenever she liked and was permitted the freedom of the peephole, but even to her he never talked. And the fact that he called her name didn't mean of necessity what one might think, he simply men-

tioned the name Frieda—who can tell what he was thinking of?—and that Frieda naturally came to him at once was her affair, and that she was admitted without let or hindrance was an act of grace on Klamm's part, but that he deliberately summoned her is more than one can maintain. [...] Klamm may perhaps call "Frieda" as before, that's possible, but she'll never again be admitted to his presence, a girl who has thrown herself away upon you. (*The Castle,* 52)

The effect of this passage is to deal a shock to the reader, to arouse an uncomfortable feeling in him, by shaking his simple faith in the contract guiding the observation of the cooperative principle in communication. Oddly enough, some other kinds of deviation from the normal semiotic use of proper names can be used by literary critics, precisely to alleviate the anxieties caused by a puzzling story which achieves its disorienting effect through a series of events, for the understanding of which no sufficient explicit clue is provided. As will be argued at length in Chapter 21, some critics, intolerant of ambiguous situations, are willing to go a long way to rid themselves of ignorance. One way to do so is to return to proper names their original descriptive meanings that can serve in predications, and try to reinterpret all the obscure events in the story in the light of these meanings. The descriptive content of names is then used as some oracle through which an omnipotent and authoritarian author, released from the constraints of the communicative contract, announces his arbitrary will. Such deciphering of the secret message concealed in proper names is usually not subjected to the constraints of consistency normally observed by nine-year-olds, according to the experiments reported by Bruner.[12] To provide just one such example, *Galia* is a widespread female name in modern Israel. This is the name of the heroïne of A. B. Yehoshua's puzzling, nightmarish story, "Galia's Wedding". The Hebrew critic Hillel Barzel, who has spent much effort in rendering such puzzling stories more comfortable, speaks of "the Divine Galia", splitting the name into two Hebrew words, *Gal + ya,* that is, "God's Wave" (or perhaps "God's Revelation").

The last few paragraphs have briefly explored the semiotic code governing the use of proper names. They suggested how Kafka occasionally deviates from this code, in order to generate a nightmarish atmosphere. On the other hand, we have found that certain critics deviate from this very semiotic code in other directions, in order to alleviate certain stories' (legitimate) nightmarish atmosphere, even where such an atmosphere is required by the genre.

Summary

The present chapter has taken a closer look at the skills of "ordinary consciousness" intended to construct a stable, rather predictable world. The first section followed the

---

[12]   There is, of course, legitimate allegory too, where the meaning of proper names *is* significant.

developmental process of the gradual acquisition of skills to handle information, present and absent; the second section discussed emotions as a mechanism to cope with rapidly changing information within the stable world; the third section examined *hypotheses* as a means for organizing information handled in scientific inquiry, in the process of perception, and in imposing unity on works of literature; the fourth and last section explored aspects of the Communicative Competence, mainly Linguistic and Poetic Competence.

We have explored in these sections how special literary effects can be achieved by deviating or regressing from certain cognitive accomplishments, mainly where micro-structures are concerned. Poets and theoreticians of certain poetic schools complain, in a rather impressionistic fashion, that words and concepts become partitions between reality and us. Our discussion has filled this impressionistic complaint with specific contents. By the same token, it has suggested how poetry may attempt to overcome this separation. On the other hand, we have found that where overall organization (macro-structure) is concerned, the same kinds of cognitive constraints must be applied by the reader and the critic as in the cognitive structures used to construct a predictable, stable world, in which one may go, in a fairly reliable and consistent manner, beyond the information given.

CHAPTER 4

Poetic Structure
and Perceived Qualities

Perceptual Qualities

At the beginning of Chapter 1, I attempted to locate Cognitive Poetics between analytic and impressionist criticism. The former, I suggested, excels in the description of the structure of literary texts, while the latter indulges in their perceived effects. Cognitive Poetics, I claim there, offers cognitive theories that systematically account for the relationship between the two. By the same token, it discriminates between reported effects which *may* legitimately be related to the structures in question, and those which may not.

Throughout the present book, I heavily rely on analytic critics and philosophers of various schools; I only occasionally and briefly mention critical impressionism. In the course of the present chapter, I shall quote a brief impressionist suggestion of an otherwise analytic critic (Oras), who has brilliant insights into the phonetic structure of poems. Oras' impressionist description of the text is preceded by illuminating prosodic descriptions, and is anything but counter-intuitive: he has recourse to an impressionist metaphor precisely because he seems to feel that something important remains to be said, and that his analytic tools are not well-suited to say this something. By this, Oras 'tunes' the reader's mind to what I consider to be the right wave-length for the appreciation of the piece of poetry concerned; however, he seems to be unable to relate it in a systematic manner to the poetic structure described. This is the point, I claim, where the theory expounded in the present work comes in most effectively: as I will show below, such metaphorical expressions *can* be related to the structure of the text in a *principled manner*. In later chapters, by contrast, I shall occasionally refer to Henri Peyre's discussions of French Symbolist poems, precisely as instances of impressionist criticism that miss the points, and whose inadequacies are exposed by the kind of principled discussion offered here.

Now, critical impressionism tends to be idiosyncratic, and has little to offer of public significance: at best, its pronouncements may be judged intuitively true, but cannot be shown to be related to the texts in a systematic way. By contrast, the cognitive approach proposed here explores, in the words of L.C. Knights, "how the mind works in certain *classes* of experience" (1948: 229, my italics); it assumes that it is precisely this working of the mind which shapes and constrains the perceived effects of literary works of art. The procedure outlined here may prove to be a first step in explaining how certain linguistic and poetic devices assume, eventually, human significance.

An analogy may throw light on the relation between structures, perceived effects, explanatory theories, and "how the mind works in certain *classes* of experience". Along the highways, one may sometimes see signs posted by the police:

Danger
Slippery Road

How do the police know that there is a *danger* of slipping at a certain place? This is less self-evident than would appear at first sight. Webster's *New Twentieth Century Dictionary* defines *danger* as "Liability to injury, pain, damage, or loss"; *slippery* is defined by the same dictionary as "causing or *liable* to cause sliding or slipping, as wet, waxed, or greasy surfaces"; the relevant meaning of *liable*, in turn, is defined there as "subject to the possibility of". Now, we know perfectly well, what an **actual** slipping is; but what is the **possibility of** slipping? And how do the police decide where there is a *possibility?* Do the police wait to see where cars slip, and wherever this happens, do they then decide that there is a "**possibility of** slipping" there? Do they also decide that there is no liability of slipping at places where no car has ever slipped before? These questions are analogous to the questions to be asked concerning the ways the critic decides on the possible perceived effects of a literary text.

The answer to all of the above questions seems to be that the police observe which are the places where cars frequently slip; they attempt to make generalizations as to the common characteristics of those places, such as the degree of the curve, the grade of the slope, the condition of the road, the speed of driving at which slippings occurred, and so forth. They then check these generalizations against certain more purely theoretical generalizations derived from geometry, trigonometry, and physics. Wherever the conditions for those generalizations hold true, the police will put up warning signs, even if no slipping ever occurred there; and conversely, they put no signs up at places where the road is straight, level, and in good repair, even if slippings occasionally *have* occurred there. The analogy is obvious: above, I quoted Wellek and Warren, according to whom the poem is a *potential* source of experience. Does the critic now decide that there is a *potential* perceived poetic effect wherever such an effect is reported by some reader? Or does he hold with Bierwisch that "poetics must explain just which structural qualities form the basis for definite effects"? In the latter case, the critic must exactly do what the police do: he must observe which are the texts where certain effects regularly are reported, attempt to make generalizations as for the common characteristics of those texts, and check these generalizations against certain more purely theoretical generalizations, derived from the various branches of literary theory, aesthetics, and cognitive science.

In the present section, I am going to explain the nature of perceived effects or perceptual qualities as I understand them. Perceptual qualities are *regional qualities.* That means that they cannot be accounted for in terms of cause and effect, or of means and ends, but in terms of parts and wholes. To explain the term *regional qualities,* we may (following Beardsley) consider each of its terms as part of a binary opposition: *local ~ regional* and *property ~ quality.* Cf.:

> An absolutely homogeneous part of the field is partless, and such a partless part may be called an *element* of the field. Analysis stops with the elements. [...] The white area inside the "O" in the word "local" is an element of this printed page, and its whiteness is therefore a local quality. But some complexes have qualities that are not qualities of their elements; the word "local" has five letters, but none of its letters does. [...] Let us call a property, or characteristic, that belongs to a complex but not to any of its parts a *regional property* of that complex. Notice that your having weight is *not* a regional property, in this sense, because your parts—arms and legs, for example—also have weight; but your property of weighing 150 pounds, if you do, *is* a regional property, for none of your parts weigh that much.

> Some regional properties can be perceived by the senses; some cannot. Your weighing 150 pounds is not directly perceivable—it has to be measured on a scale, or inferred in some other way—but your being heavy-set or thin *is* perceivable. In our description of aesthetic objects we are interested in the perceivable properties, for which we shall reserve the word "qualities". Thus, when I speak of regional qualities of a complex, I mean its perceptual regional properties. (Beardsley, 1958: 83)

It may be profitable for us to adapt an additional distinction from Beardsley notwithstanding the many unsettled questions concerning it, viz., that between *summative* and *emergent* regional properties (qualities).

> If two one pound weights are combined on a scale, the combination will have a weight of two pounds, which, by our definition, is a regional property. [...] On the other hand, the saltiness of sodium chlorid that is not present in its separate elements, or the wetness of H_2O when neither hydrogen nor oxygen is wet by itself, is not describable as a sum; something new and different seems to emerge from the combination. (Ibid., 83–84)

According to Beardsley, "perhaps the difference lies merely in the degree of surprisingness, and is not a fundamental difference at all"; at any rate, "in certain fields of science, emergence can be explained with reference to prevailing explanatory theories" (ibid.). In an important sense, the present book claims to proffer precisely such explanatory theories.

Another analytic philosopher, Frank Sibley (1962), speaks of *aesthetic qualities* (to be discussed at some length below). His claim is that "non-aesthetic features" never, by themselves, will generate sufficient conditions for aesthetic qualities to arise. These qualities can, then, be called "emergent regional qualities" *par excellence;* but the two categories are by no means co-extensive. The issue at stake is whether "explanatory theories" can ever take the place of exercising one's taste. Beardsley appears to avoid the question, while Sibley implies a negative answer. However, even when assuming a negative answer, "explanatory theories" may become indispensable for deciding which features typically *count toward* which qualities in poetry.

If the presence of "non-aesthetic features" never amounts to creating sufficient conditions for aesthetic qualities to emerge, how can we know what *are* the aesthetic qualities in a particular poem? Of special interest is the following passage from Sibley concerning aesthetic concepts.

> If we are not following rules and there are no conditions to appeal to, how are we to know when they are applicable? One very natural way to counter this question is to point out that some other sorts of concepts also are not condition-governed. We do not apply simple color-words by following rules or in accordance with principles. We see that the book is red by looking, just as we tell that the tea is sweet by tasting it. So too, it might be said, we just see (or fail to see) that things are delicate, balanced, and the like. (Sibley, 1962: 77)

Such a conception is familiar from other areas of poetic theory as well. Above, in the first chapter, I quoted a passage by Bierwisch, in which he suggests that "the actual objects of poetics are the regularities that occur in literary texts and that determine the specific effects of poetry". In the following passage, he further elaborates on the nature of the relationship between poetic structure, poetic effects, and poetics.

> Poetics must explain just which structural qualities form the basis for definite effects. It can and must explicate those consciously or unconsciously followed regularities that lead to the understanding of poetic structure and to a judgment of poeticality [...]; it must accept effects as given and determine the rules upon which they are founded. (Bierwisch, 1970: 108)

If "definite effects" in Bierwisch's passage can be taken to mean something like "aesthetic qualities", Sibley would presumably be shocked by the idea that anybody should attempt to determine the *rules* upon which these definite effects are founded. But these two theoreticians are in fundamental agreement on one crucial point: definite effects or aesthetic qualities cannot be *inferred* from the elements, but must be accepted as *given: only after the event* one may attempt to account for them.

This should not surprise us. As was pointed out in Chapter 2, and indeed will be repeated throughout the present book, perceived effects depend on perceptual organizations; poems being highly complex entities, the same material may give room for a variety of alternative perceptual organizations (mental performances). Only after the event can be known, what perceptual organization *has* been effected by the perceiver, and according to what perceptual rules. Furthermore, I conceive here of the reading of poetry as of one kind of creative thinking. And the state of affairs described here seems to apply not only to such highly evasive issues as aesthetic qualities, but to all creative thinking, even to rather simple problems in geometry, as the following example adapted from Köhler may indicate.

Imagine a circle with two perpendicular diameters drawn in (figure 1). Suppose I choose an arbitrary point *a* on its circumference, from which I draw two perpendiculars to the diameters, thus obtaining points *b* and *c*. Now I draw a line *l* between the points *b* and *c*. The question is what is the length of this line. It is not at all obvious how this question should be answered. Now, suppose I add the line *oa;* some people now immediately will find the answer. They seem to have restructured the information concerning points and perpendiculars into a rectangle. "The given line *l* is a diagonal of the given rectangle. [...] The second diagonal extends from the center of the circle to its circumference and is, therefore, the radius. Now, since the two diagonals of a rectangle are [...] always equally long, our line *l* must necessarily also have the length [...] of the radius. [...] In other words, once the material has been properly changed, we understand perfectly why the addition of the second diagonal gives us the required answer. This is what we call *insight* in thinking" (Köhler, 1969: 146–147).

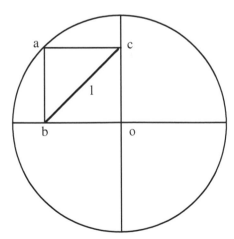

Figure 4.1   A problem for creative thinking: what is the length of the line *l* relative to the radius?

Insight is insight into relations that emerge when certain parts of a situation are inspected. [...] In the solution of a problem, I said, we suddenly become aware of new relations, but these new relations appear only after we have mentally changed, amplified, or restructured the given material. (Ibid., 152–153)

"But why [...] did we ever think of drawing new lines, and particularly that special line, the second diagonal?" (ibid., 153). No rules can be given for this thought activity in advance; as in the case of relating aesthetic qualities to poetic structures, it is only after the event that we can deploy all the geometrical rules (or poetic principles) we may know, in order to justify that restructuring of the material.

Bierwisch's passage quoted above gives no indication how we can know what "the specific effects of poetry" are, and what evidence is admissible. At any rate, his approach, just like Cognitive Poetics, reclaims the effects of poems from critical impressionism. It claims that effects can and should be dealt with by a systematic poetics. At the same time, it is a radical departure from that conception of "the Science of Literature" that regards only "objectively" describable structures as the legitimate objects of poetics. The quotations from Bierwisch suggest (although it is not borne out in the rest of his paper), that the effects of poetry—which, I assume, are not simply "given", but are reported (sometimes as conflicting) by a variety of readers—can be coded in such a way that they can be related to poetic structure in systematic, non-ad-hoc ways.

The foregoing discussion suggests, then, that a poetic analysis must typically consist of three steps: first, a structural description of the work, second, a description of the "given effect", and third, a cognitive explanation that relates the "given effect" in systematic ways to the description of the structure. This book will focus, mainly, on the third, most problematic of these steps, which (as will readily be seen) may nonetheless have quite interesting implications for the other two as well.

There are two approaches to this task of relating given effects to structural descriptions, usually complementing each other: a "top-down" and a "bottom-up" approach. The top-down approach begins with offering a model, or hypothesis, concerning some "mediating structure" that can systematically relate poetic structures to qualities which regularly have been attributed to them by readers and critics of various periods. The procedures involved are those involved in the confirmation (or falsification) of hypotheses, such as, for example, proposed by Smart (1966) or Margolis (1962). In order for the model (or hypothesis) to have "explanatory adequacy", it must not only be adequate to the description of the poetic structures and the "given effects"; it also must be adequate to independently established (or hypothesized) cognitive structures and processes relevant to the reading of poetry or the kind of effect concerned. This is how I understand Knights's phrase "how the mind works in certain *classes* of experience". Thus, for instance, I have discussed the divergent structure of emotions in the preceding chapter; below, I am going to propose a model of convergent and divergent mental processes that enables us to relate witty and emotional qualities to convergent and divergent poetic structures, as these qualities and structures have been regularly associated by critics of the past.

One important requirement of such models is that they should be able to accommodate incompatible effects reported by competent readers, assigning to them alternative routes within the same mediating structure (this issue is being treated in the present book under the heading of *mental performance*). Thus, the legitimacy of the models and of the reported effects become mutually dependent upon each other. A model is satisfactory when it can accommodate a considerable number of incompatible effects reported by competent readers; whereas a reported effect is legitimate when it can be accommodated by a model that has accommodated the majority of effects reported by competent readers, a competent reader being one who reports effects the majority of which turn out to be 'legitimate' on closer inspection. This is not a vicious circle; it can be, rather, regarded as an information-confirming cycle which yields increasingly accurate results.

The bottom-up approach is expounded at great length below (in Chapter 22); it begins with the application of critical terms, coded in certain ways, so that they may yield critical insight. For the purposes of the present chapter, 'insight' concerns the act of relating poetic qualities to poetic structures.

Necessary and Sufficient Conditions

In his discussion of aesthetic concepts used to refer to aesthetic quality, Sibley points out that necessary and sufficient conditions are not equally applicable to all concepts. At the one end, there are terms like "square", the application of which is governed by a set of necessary and sufficient conditions. At the other end, there are the 'aesthetic' or 'taste' concepts, such as *delicate, graceful, integrated, powerful, unified, vivid, dynamic,* for which neither necessary nor sufficient conditions are found. What we have are features that "at best count only *typically* or *characteristically* towards delicacy [...] that is, no group of them is ever logically sufficient" (Sibley, 1962: 69).

> One way of reinforcing this is to notice how features which are characteristically associated with one aesthetic term may also be similarly associated with other and rather different aesthetic terms. "Graceful" and "delicate" may be on the one hand sharply contrasted with terms like "violent", "grand", "fiery", "garish", or "massive". [...] But on the other hand "graceful" and "delicate" may also be contrasted with aesthetic terms which stand much closer to them, like "flaccid", "weakly", "washed out", "lanky", "anaemic", "wan", "insipid"; and the range of features characteristic of *these* qualities, pale color, slimness, lightness, lack of angularity and sharp contrast, is virtually identical with the range for "delicate" and "graceful". [...] Thus an object which is described very fully, but exclusively in terms of qualities characteristic of delicacy, may turn out on inspection to be not delicate at all but anaemic or insipid. (Ibid.)

In the remainder of this chapter I shall present two sets of perceptual qualities that can systematically be related to their respective sets of poetic structures, viz., *convergent* vs. *divergent* poetry, and *split* vs. *integrated* focus. In both cases, I shall focus on Milton's *Paradise Lost,* as compared to the work of one of his near-contemporaries, or even his own poetry. The dichotomies mentioned seem to be related to the foregoing theoretical considerations in rather complex ways. For instance, even when a theoretical model is offered in which one may predict, e.g., whether the emerging quality will be "emotional" or "witty", there still will be no way to predict, e.g., whether the emerging quality will be "witty" or "playful".

The distinction "convergent~divergent" is definitely not similar to that between "square~round"; nor does it exactly resemble the distinction between aesthetic concepts such as "delicate~insipid", or even "delicate~robust", though it may significantly be related to them in actual poems. In an important sense, it resembles certain distinctions within a third group of concepts such as "lazy~diligent", or "intelligent~unintelligent".

> Amongst these concepts to which attention has recently been paid are those for which no *necessary-and-sufficient* conditions can be provided, but for which there are a number of relevant features, A, B, C, D, E, such that the presence of some groups or combination of these features is *sufficient* for the application of the concept. The list of relevant features may be an open one; that is, given A, B, C, D, E, we may not wish to close off the possible relevance of other unlimited features beyond E. (Sibley, 1962: 66–67)

> [...] with concepts of this sort, although decisions may have to be made and judgment exercised, it is always possible to extract and state, from cases which have *already* clearly been decided, the sets of features or conditions which were regarded as sufficient in those cases. These relevant features which I am calling conditions are, it should be noted, features which, though not sufficient alone and needing to be combined with other similar features, nevertheless carry some weight and can count only in one direction [...] some group or set of them *is* sufficient fully to ensure or warrant the application of the term. An individual characterized by some of these features may not yet qualify to be called lazy or intelligent, and so on, beyond all question, but all that is needed is to add some further (indefinite) number of such characterizations and a point is reached where we have enough. [...] *We have left necessary-and-sufficient conditions behind, but we are still in the realm of sufficient conditions.* (Ibid.: 67–68, last italics mine)

Convergent and Divergent Poetry

Poems can be compared from the point of view of *convergence~divergence*. As for its structure, "convergent" style is marked by clear-cut shapes, both in content and structure; it is inclined towards definite directions and clear contrasts (prosodic or semantic); as for its perceptual quality, it is inclined towards an atmosphere of certainty, a quality of intellectual control. From the structural point of view, "divergent" style is marked by blurred shapes, both in content and structure; it exhibits general tendencies (rather than definite directions) and blurred contrasts (prosodic or semantic); from the point of view of perceptual quality, it is inclined towards an atmosphere of uncertainty, an emotional quality. Convergence appeals to the actively organizing mind, divergence to a more passively and flexibly receptive attitude. These perceptual qualities can systematically be related to their respective structures through gestalt-theory (cf. Meyer, 1956: 160–161, and Arnheim, 1957: 324–325), or through a theory of emotion. The two are not solid categories; the differences are of degree, shades are gradual, along a spectrum.

Chapter 2 elaborated Wellek's conception of a poem as a stratified system of norms. I have argued that the various norms on the various strata can be systematically explored independently of each other. The difficulty is to find some systematic way to integrate these norms into coherent wholes. I submit that the *convergence~divergence* dichotomy is a convenient tool for such an integration: the various elements, on the various strata, as well as their small-scale configurations, can be taken to count typically toward one or the other overall perceptual quality. In one style, the various linguistic elements *tend* to act in convergence, in another in divergence. These tendencies may be reinforced by aspects of the imagery: whether the things mentioned have solid characteristic shapes, or the nouns refer rather to "thing-free" abstractions and shapeless masses. Syntactic structure may also typically count toward one or the other overall quality: convergent poems tend to have a larger number of finite verbs, divergent ones a larger number of nouns and adjectives. Paratactic and hypotactic structure, too, may contribute to the respective overall qualities, but a discussion of the conditions under which they may do so, lies beyond the scope of the present work. As for repeated sound clusters, the difference of their perceptual qualities in the two styles is striking. In convergent style they tend to be salient, sometimes playful and witty; in divergent style, repeated sound clusters tend to fuse with the dispersed elements, heightening the emotional quality of the passage, perceived as *musicality*. Let me illustrate this distinction.

In his illuminating essay on the handling of sounds by Spenser and Milton, Ants Oras (1957) points out that alliterative sound patterns are more conspicuous in the former than in the latter poet, for two reasons: Milton uses sound patterns more sparingly and when he uses them, he tones them down. Oras discusses Milton's various muting techniques. But his explanation for one of his subtlest examples is not quite satisfactory. He quotes the following two passages from the two poets, in which there are, indeed, remarkable verbal likenesses.

(1)   For grief thereof, and divelish despite,
         From his infernall fournace forth he threw
         Huge flames, that dimmèd all the heavens light,

> Enrold in duskish smoke and brimstone blew ...
>
> *(Fairie Qvene* I, xi: 44)

(2)   At once as far as Angels ken he views
         The dismal situation strange and wilde:
         A dungeon horrible, on all sides round
         As one great Furnace flamed, yet from those flames
         No light, but rather darkness visible
         Served only to discover sights of woe ...

(Paradise Lost I: 59–64)

Oras picks out the following two sentences from the quoted passages: Spenser's "*F*rom his in*f*e*r*nall *fou*rnace *fo*rth he th*r*ew Huge *f*lames"[1], and Milton's "As one great *Fu*rnace *f*lamed, yet *fr*om those *f*lames", and remarks:

> They are deceptively alike. Yet there is at least one cardinal difference. This is the first case in *Paradise Lost* of alliterative accumulation on such a scale with sounds of such intensity, whereas Spenser has already been prodigal in filling lines with repeated consonants" (Oras 1957: 123).

Now, I really feel Spenser's alliteration as being more obtrusive, more conspicuous, than Milton's. But I cannot accept Oras' explanation. First, it is doubtful that this is the "first case" of "alliterative accumulation on such a scale" (see below my discussion of *Paradise Lost* I, 1–5). But even if true, this fact is irrelevant to our impression: the difference can be felt **in** the isolated passages, so the reasons should not be looked for **outside** them. One may partially improve on Oras' explanation by observing that in the italicized string of alliteration alone, there is one more item in Spenser's than in Milton's verse; in addition, the first line of the Spenser passage begins with *For grief thereof.* The different attitudes of the two poets to alliteration can be shown by a further observation. Milton, too, draws out his string of alliterations. Remembering that *v* is a voiced *f,* one may discover three of the consonants of *Furnace* (viz., *f, r, s*) in *Served* and *discover* in the last line. This may be counted as an additional technique of "toning down". But even all this is still only a small part of the story. Oras further remarks that in the Milton passage there is a "total impression of definite but finely graded design. What Milton has added, much as painters do by shading, is the dimension of depth". How true this sounds! It is hard to disprove Oras' statement; but that does not make it easier to prove it. In other words, this remark is critical impressionism at best. As suggested in the first paragraph of the present chapter, this is where Cognitive Poetics must step in, and offer some cognitive model that may relate Oras' roughly impressionist remark to

---

1   Notice, that in the phrase *infernall fournace* a cluster of three (not two) sounds is repeated, and that in *forth he threw* another cluster of two is repeated.

the structure of the text in a systematic, reasoned way. I submit that the present theoretical framework can effectively handle the issue under discussion. Suppose, for instance, that we can somehow show that there *is* more shading and depth in Milton's passage than in Spenser's: this may lend support to my claim that alliteration is less obtrusive, sounds less "witty", and indeed more musical, when it is embedded in a background of diffuse "shading". But what can "shading" mean, in the sense that there may be more of it in the Milton passage than in the Spenser passage?

I take "shading" to mean, as in painting, "a more or less thick texture of diffuse, blurred gestalts". And this is, precisely, wherein Milton's passage differs from Spenser's. Take, for instance, the rhythmic shape. As I have suggested, a phonetically weak shape, such as rhythmic ambiguity, may heighten the emotive appeal and decrease the pressure in the "psychological atmosphere of certainty and patent purpose". Let us consider the rhythmic structure of Spenser's passage:

(3)   For gríef theréof, and dívelish despíte,
      w   s   w s w   s w s   w s

      From his inférnall fóurnace fórth he thréw
      w   s   w s w   s   w   s   w   s

      Húge flámes, that dímmèd áll the héavens líght,
      w   s   w s   w   s   w s   w s

      Enróld in dúskish smóke and brímstóne bléw ...[2]
      w   s   w s   w   s   w   s   w   s

In this passage, there are no more than three instances in which stress pattern diverges from meter.[3] The least significant of those is the occurrence of the unstressed *his* in a strong position, in "From *his* infernall ...". More conspicuous is the unstressed syllable of the polysyllabic *dívelish* in a strong position (grouped backward). But what is felt most strongly is the additional stress (highlighted by the enjambement and the similar vowels in the consecutive syllables *threw / Huge)* in "he threw / Huge flames ...", 'neutralizing' the contrast between weak and strong position. By contrast, in general, the alliterations are highlighted by their converging with the lexically stressed syllables and with the strong positions of meter (except in "*d*ivelish *d*espite"). Now observe how blurred is the rhythmic shape of Milton's quotation:

---

2   The letters under the verse-lines indicate metrical **w**eak and **s**trong positions; the accents on the vowels indicate stressed syllables. In regular meter, stressed syllables occur in all strong positions, and only in strong positions. Thus, the present notation indicates metrical regularity and deviation at one and the same time (see below, Chapter 6).

3   As for the second stressed syllable of *brímstóne* in a weak position, I have elsewhere argued, that the most convergent solution for a compound with two consecutive stressed syllables in iambic metre is to begin in a strong position, whereas divergent poets like Milton prefer to begin such compounds in a weak position (cf. Tsur, 1977: 39–42; 1998: 176–191).

(4)   At ónce as fár as Ángels kén he viéws
w s   w   s w s   w   s   w   s

The dísmal situátion stránge and wílde:
w s   w   sw s   w   s   w   s

A dúngeon hórrible, on áll sídes róund
w s   w   s w s   w s   w   s

As óne gréat Fúrnace flámed, yet from thóse flámes
w s   w   s w   s   w   s   w   s

Nó líght, but ráther dárkness vísible
w s   w   s   w   s   s w s

Sérved ónly to discóver síghts of wóe …
w   s   w s w s w s   w   s

Counting the two possible emphatic stresses (on *thóse* and *Nó*), the ten deviances in this passage are the equivalent of 166 per hundred lines, which for Milton is not very bold. However, such unstressed syllables as *-ble* in strong positions, twice at the end of trisyllabics, have a marked weakening effect on the meter. *Visible* at the end of line 5 considerably weakens the gestalt of the whole line with its unstressed liquid for syllable-crest in the sensitive tenth position. Such groups as "on all sides round", "as one great furnace", "Served only", where no unstressed syllable in strong position precedes the syllable in a weak position, would be assimilated to the iambic cadence quite easily in end-stopped lines or couplets; their divergent pressure would be 'contained'. In a run-on context one is more easily tempted to assign full stress to the lexical words in weak positions. "Served" would not only 'soften' the onset of the line, but, being run-on from a line with an exceptionally blurred terminal, would give weight to a fluid, less than usually distinct shape. Impressionistically speaking, such a performance would render the passage 'plump' (that is, rather 'filled out', with no sharp outlines). The line quoted by Oras for its alliterations, as well as the preceding one, are among those that deviate most (the first line is one of the rare lines in Milton that are perfectly regular from the point of view of meter). The prominence of *from* in a strong position is reduced by its being an unstressed preposition, whereas the stressed words *great* and *those* occurring in weak positions, first, give prominence to syllables irrelevant to the alliteration and, second, weaken the rhythmic shape of the whole line. The way in which the two passages handle enjambement is instructive. A poem where the line always converges with the syntactic unit quite easily becomes rigid and 'jingling', and Spenser did resort to enjambement, though sparingly. Throughout *Paradise Lost,* enjambement is far more frequent than in *Fairie Qvene;* there is, however, a qualitative difference, too, corroborating the quantitative one. The enjambement in this quotation is rather unusually strained for *Fairie Qvene:* "he threw / Huge flames", especially when highlighted by assonance and deviation from meter. Notice, however, that in this case syntactic inversion strengthens the shape of the line-ending, first, by accentuating the straightforwardness of the action (especially since the foregrounded verbal particle indicates definite direction and unobstructed viewing); and second, by sharpening the contrast between strong position, stress, and alliteration (prominence) on the one hand, and unstressed syllable in weak position (non-prominence) on the other, in *fórth he thréw*. In a divergent poem, one might choose *he thréw fórth,* blurring the contrast not only between strong and weak positions by consecutive alliterating syllables and assigning an unstressed syllable to a strong position, but also between stress and nonstress *(threw* bears lexical stress, whereas *forth* bears the main stress of the collocation).

I have adopted Fowler's illuminating insight that "the smaller the grammatical unit concerned, the greater its resistance to being stretched over a metric boundary" (Fowler, 1966: 88). Yet, how smooth this passage from Spenser is, as compared with Milton's run-on sentences! As some psycholinguistic experiments bear witness, "sentences with a mild increase in predictive load are more difficult to remember" (P. Johnson-Laird, 1970). In our frame of reference this means that "predictive load" weakens gestalts, especially in run-on sentences. It may be "the last straw" that breaks the barrier of cognitive overload. The predictive load in Spenser's enjambement is as small as possible. After "he threw" one predicts a direct object, a prediction which is soon and amply fulfilled in "Huge flames". In Milton's passage, "on all sides round" is perceived as having divergent functions. It could be an attribute of "a dungeon horrible" (by the way, notice the concealed but strong alliteration: the first two consonants of "**du**ngeon" are repeated, in reverse order, in "rou**nd**"). Punctuation, however, instructs us to read "on all sides round" as an adverbial phrase predicting a verb. Thus, the line-ending is ambiguous: the reader must and must not halt here. The fulfillment of the prediction is delayed by the simile "as one great Furnace". The nouns demand a divergent alignment of the verb, diffusing its impact. "A dungeon ... flamed" / "Furnace flamed"; the surface subject is, of course, "dungeon", in which case the predictive load of the sentence is largely increased. Notice another difference: in Spenser, "fournace" precedes the run-on clause, so that at the line-terminal, "flames" is both syntactically and thematically predicted, whereas in Milton it is the grammatical category only that is predicted at the end of the line.

Thematically, *flamed* has no antecedent in Milton's passage; it is a blank prediction, so to speak. At the end of the next line "yet from those flames'' initiates a more sophisticated prediction pattern. The preposition *from* is not very likely to herald *served;* one would rather expect something like "from those flames / X emerged". Instead, we get the more complex and divergent formula, "Not X but Y", where Y is rewritten as an impressive oxymoron ("darkness visible"); this oxymoron, while changing the reader's expectations, still does not preclude the verb "emerged". The syntactic structure thus amplifies the psychological atmosphere of a **general tendency** and of **uncertainty** (as opposed to certainty and patent purpose). The wayward fulfillment of expectations increasingly focuses attention on the predicted *VP*. Here, however, a sudden shift—nay, a series of shifts—of emphasis further diffuses attention. Not only has a general, abstract verb *(served)* been substituted for the expected concrete motion-verb, but in its sense "was of use for" it shifts attention to the succeeding *NP,* for which a rank-shifted clause is substituted, in which, in turn, the *Verb* directs attention toward the succeeding *NP*. Thus, "sights of woe" generates an ostensible closure (which is further rendered deceptive by the appositive enumeration in the next line, "regions of sorrow, doleful shades, where peace ...", opening up a further, even more fluid movement).

Clear contrasts are of the very essence of strong shapes, of the psychological atmosphere of certainty and patent purpose. Contrastive elements are differently used in the imagery of the two passages. Spenser creates the contrast between *dimmed* and *light* in a fairly straightforward, logical manner. The flames thrown up by the Dragon are brighter than the light of Heaven, and present the latter as relatively dim. *Smokish dusk* is another straightforward means of dimming "all heavens light". The oxymoron "from those flames no light but rather darkness..." is less straightforward. The flames have all their frightening, torturing properties, but the light-aspect is eliminated (it would be a positive property). This is enhanced by the frightening properties of *Darkness*. "Darkness visible" may connote: a darkness so intense that it appears to be observed as some thick, visible (perhaps tangible) mass; so strong that even extremes change their very essence to their opposite; and/or: what to ordinary flesh-and-blood eyes appears as darkness, for Satan with his inverted scale of values serves as light; even visibility serves only to discover "dark" sights of woe; it is of little comfort. These divergent meanings are to be caught at once, blurring the conceptual meanings of *flames* and *darkness*.

As for the scenes described, Spenser directs the reader's eyes of the mind very differently from Milton—Spenser concentrates attention at one point: "His infernall fournace" refers to the dragon's mouth vomiting fire; "Huge flames", too, point in one direction. Milton makes a remarkable effort *not* to concentrate the reader's attention on any one point. The first line of the quotation sets the enormous perspectives of the scene. Milton could have made the second line more concrete, by writing something like "the dismal plains strange and wild" (though the view would have been still shapeless, diffuse). Having used an abstract noun ("Situation"), he further eliminates visible things, concentrating on the *quality* of the scene, enhanced by three adjectives connoting intensity. By the same token, the situation is individuated.

One normally associates a "dungeon" with narrow space and massive walls. Having established infinite perspectives, the physical attributes of the dungeon are eliminated and only its spiritual qualities linger on in the scenery (reinforcing the quality of "the dismal situation"). Similarly, the "walls" of the "great furnace" are in infinity, and the flames are dispersed "on all sides round', and not in the "center of the picture" as Oras suggests. It is these pervasive and intense thing-free qualities that are enhanced by the oxymoron "darkness visible / Served ... to discover". This is the thick texture of blurred shapes, the "shadings" in which Milton's sound patterns are diffused, adding "the dimension of depth," in Oras's words, generating 'soft' musicality rather than sharp, 'clicking' sound-plays.

Both styles may, as we have seen, make use of the same elements. The difference lies in their hierarchic arrangement. Even a fairly convergent poem, as Spenser's, may occasionally resort to typically divergent techniques, such as "he thréw / Húge flámes". Spenser, too, makes use of syntactic inversion (sometimes as marked as the occurrence in line 2), but Milton's inversions usually reach further, and are more effective. Spenser uses two finite verbs in four lines, Milton three in six lines; proportions are the same. But one of Spenser's verbs denotes visible motion in a specific direction. None of Milton's verbs denotes definite visible motion; *flamed* denotes an intense state, *viewed* and *served to discover* denote perception, suggesting a receptive attitude. Whatever ingredient of patent purpose and specific direction the last three verbs possess, is 'voided' by the syntactic manipulation of the focus of attention described earlier.

I have argued above that the distinction "convergent~divergent" is, in an important sense, similar to distinctions between such concepts as "lazy~diligent", or "intelligent~unintelligent". We must, however, point to two important respects in which the first opposition is unlike the other two. One source of the difference seems to be that the distinctions *lazy~diligent* or *intelligent~unintelligent* consist in an open set of potentially infinite number of behavioral variables; whereas a poem consists of a limited set of words (or, for that matter, of actual or imagined noises) which are necessarily the exponents of the entire hierarchy of features involved, at one and the same time. To put it plainly, the same string of phonemes that is the exponent of the words is also the exponent of the sentences, of the verse-line, of its metric and stress patterns (which may converge or diverge), of the stanza, of the figurative expressions, and so on.

Second, there are the "double-edged" phenomena. Those features that normally warrant the application of the term "divergent", may behave quite differently when occurring sporadically in a context of strong shapes. Consider a stressed syllable in a weak position; or a major syntactic boundary after the sixth, seventh, eighthz, or ninth positions; or a run-on sentence that begins after one of these positions. These are, precisely, the features which, when occurring in a sufficiently large number, warrant the application of the term "divergent". However, if they occur sporadically in a context of usually end-stopped lines, or in one of a series of emphatically closed couplets, they may count toward strong shapes. What seems to happen is that the end-stopped line, or couplet, strives to assert its strong shape in the reader's perception in front of incursion; it is, in fact, perceived as more vivid, more vigorous than it would be if there were no such incursion. If, however, there is a number of consecutive lines with run-on sentences that begin near the line-ending, and there is a number of stressed syllables in weak positions (combined, perhaps, with some more marked metric figures), there is an undefined point when the marked forms override the strong shapes which, suddenly, are perceived not as more vigorous, but as considerably weaker (see next chapter, excerpts 32–38).

Split and Integrated Focus

Poems also can be compared along the axis *split* and *integrated* focus. Dr. Johnson said of metaphysical wit that in it, the most heterogeneous elements are violently yoked together. I shall argue that every image yokes together heterogeneous elements. The difference between split and integrated focus lies not so much in the disparity of elements as in their different rhetorical manipulation. The same elements can occur in different hierarchic orders.

My use of the term *wit* combines the seventeenth century and the present day usage, at two different levels of description of the same text. In the latter usage, it refers to some regional quality such as 'sharpness', 'keenness' usually associated with cleverness and quickness of apprehension; in the former, it refers to poetic structures characterized by incongruities, by "the most heterogeneous elements violently yoked together". In this sense, one of the key terms is 'far-fetched'. My point here and, indeed, throughout the present book is that far-fetchedness is not necessarily determined by habit and convention. A far-fetched simile need not become natural through habit. The Neo-Classic distinction between 'true' and 'false' wit does not suggest, even in a historical perspective, that the kind of wit to which the reader is accustomed is 'true', while that kind to which he is not accustomed is 'false'. I claim that the two have different structures; this claim is borne out by the Neo-Classicists' discussions (see below).[4]

Divergent style may integrate the perception of discordant elements, generating what some critics call *soft focus*. On the other hand, when the various aspects of language converge along two lines, the focus is split (some critics call its perceptual quality *sharp focus),* usually generating wit or irony.

The focus of incongruous elements can be integrated, for instance, by subsuming them in a descriptive scheme, such as in a *chronographia* or *topographia,* in a landscape, a coherent situation, a sustained mythical image, a continuous epic or dramatic action, or by directing attention away from the figurative devices, to emotion, passion, or the like. On the other hand, focus can be split, to mention only a few possibilities, by a sudden leap from one universe of discourse to another, by "domesticating" a sublime theme, or by the unexpected introduction of a characteristic visual shape into a context of fluid, diffuse impressions, of vague, shapeless masses, thing-free qualities. One important device used to achieve a quality usually associated with metaphysical wit, is the *domestication* of great themes. According to Pope, "True Wit is Nature to Advantage dress'd". Metaphysical poets usually prefer to treat the sublime themes of poetry in terms of something less sublime, of everyday activities and niceties, precision being the antithesis of the sublime. Man-made instruments—instruments of precision, in particular—may have such "domesticating" effects, especially when unexpectedly introduced in an elevated or spiritual context.

---

4   As will be suggested in Chapter 9, anti-grammatic rhyme consists of heterogeneous semantic elements 'yoked' together. It will be suggested in Chapter 5 that in an environment of convergence and strong shapes, such rhymes usually have a 'witty' regional quality, 'witty' used in the sense of 'charaterized by sharpness usually associated with cleverness and quickness of apprehension'. This quickness can be accounted for by the properties of strong shapes.

Thus, what is bad Classicism, may be excellent Metaphysical poetry. To mention one outstanding example, "Longinus" in Chapter 17 of his *On the Sublime* says: "Wherefore a figure is at its best when the very fact that it is a figure escapes attention". This is true of the elevated kind of poetry (whether Classicist or Romantic) "Longinus" admired. By contrast, poems of the Mannerist type (Metaphysical, Modernistic, as well as Mediaeval Hebrew Poetry), achieve their witty effects by directing our attention back to the poetic figure (an extreme case of this would be what the Russian Formalists call "laying bare the device"). As a matter of fact, one can make illuminating generalizations on Mannerism at its best, if one bases oneself on the theoretical writings of the various kinds of Classicists. Consider the following passage from No. 62 of Joseph Addison's Spectator Papers:

> As *true Wit* generally consists in this Resemblance and Congruity of Ideas, *false Wit* chiefly consists in the Resemblance and Congruity of single Letters, as in Anagrams, Chronograms, Lipograms, and Acrosticks: Sometimes of Syllable, as in Ecchos and Doggerel Rhymes: Sometimes of Words, as in Punns and Quibbles; and sometimes of whole Sentences or Poems, cast into Figures of *Eggs, Axes* or *Altars* ... As *true Wit* consists in the Resemblance of Ideas, and *false Wit* in the Resemblance of Words, according to the foregoing Instances; there is another kind of Wit which consists Partly in the resemblance of Ideas, and partly in the Resemblance of Words; which for Distinction Sake I shall call *mixt Wit.* This Kind of Wit abounds in *Cowley,* more than in any Author that ever wrote.

> Mixt Wit is therefore a Composition of Punn and true Wit, and is more or less perfect as the Resemblance lies in the Ideas or in the Words.

Instead of "and is more or less perfect" we could read "and its focus is more or less integrated", so as to make the above quote fit perfectly into our scheme (turning, again, the normative into a descriptive distinction).

From the foregoing, an overall principle may be abstracted which, I submit, has considerable cognitive parsimony. Humans being sign-using animals, are inclined to *attend away* from the *signifiants* to the *signifiés.* The more attention is focused on a *signifié,* while the *signifiant* is only dimly perceived in the background, the more natural the expression is perceived to be. The distinctive quality of poetry is that attention is directed *back* to the *signifiant* to *some* extent. When attention is directed to the *signifiant* beyond a certain (operationally undefined) extent, the focus between *signifiant* and *signifié* is split, resulting in the witty quality that is characteristic of the various kinds of Mannerism. Ideas are signified by words which, in turn, are signified by strings of phonemes which, in turn, are signified by strings of letters. When one phonological *signfiant* is attached to two unrelated, or even incompatible *signifiés,* both relevant to the context, one cannot *attend away* from the *signifiant* to the *signifié;* that is why Addison considers "Punns" as *false Wit.* Other ways to draw attention *away* to the phonological *signfiant* are "Ecchos and Doggerel Rhymes". Attention may be further directed *away* to the graphemic *signfiant* by casting it "into Figures of *Eggs, Axes* or *Altars ...*", or the like. The language-user need not *learn* to appreciate the affect of these devices of directing attention *away* to *signifiants* at ever-increasing distances in a hierarchic system of *signifiants* and *signifiés;* the desired effect is the unique conscious quality produced by *going against his natural inclination.* What *does* require the acquisition of considerable skills is the ability to attend back from the *signifié* to the *signfiant;* but once acquired, the unique conscious quality of the process is experienced as the perceived quality of the text. This is what Morris Halle would call "Knowledge Unlearned and Untaught". This model would also accommodate "Longinus'" observation that "a figure is at its best when the very fact that it is a figure escapes attention". When you attend away from the figure to the meaning or the emotion suggested, focus is integrated, and the affect is natural; when you attend back to the figure, the vehicle of meaning, the focus of perception is split, and the perceived effect is witty.[5]

I wish to illustrate split and integrated focus by considering the way Donne and Milton handle the same poetic image, the image of the (twin) compasses. Donne, in his "Valediction forbidding Mourning" deals with a problem that "resembles ontological problems of the One and the Many", to use James Smith's phrasing: "Our two souls, therefore, which are one". I shall point out some of his devices that make the poem witty rather than emotional or sublime, that is, refer it to split focus: first, Donne treats the spiritual reality in terms of an instrument of precision, dwelling on exact details; second, in order to appreciate all the spiritual implications of the image, the reader must carefully *visualize* the details of the image:

> (5)   If they be two, they are two so
> As stiffe twin compasses are two,
> Thy soule, the fixt foot, makes no show
> To move, but doth if th'other doe.
>
> And though it in the centre sit,
> Yet when the other far doth rome,
> It leans and hearkens after it,
> And growes erect as that comes home.

Third, such words as *stiffe, move, leans,* and *growes erect* denote physical states and movements, but also may refer to states of mind. Thus, the same words refer to a physical description and to a mental description at one and the same time. In Addison's words, it achieves wit by the Resemblance of Words rather than by the Re-

---

5   My discussion of split and integrated focus here is quite different from, and complementary to, that in Chapters 1–3 of my book *On Metaphoring* (1987). Since the first publication of this book I have elaborated on "picture poetry" and "echo poetry" in Tsur 2002b; 2003: Chapter 8, "Visual and Auditory Ingenuities in Mystic Poetry".

semblance of Ideas, or, better, in addition to them. Fourth, the compasses serve as a good exemplar of the ontological problem of the one and the many; the other properties of compasses are irrelevant to the illustration of this idea. The texture irrelevant to the idea illustrated may serve to prevent the image from losing its reality, from becoming a "mere illustration of an idea", and so to preserve its *concrete identity*. Now, a variety of additional aspects of the compasses, "irrelevant texture" with respect to the original "illustration" of the "ontological problem", are successively exploited for illustrations of additional ideas related to the situation of departing lovers. Thus, the reader is prevented from attending away from the image-vehicle to the ideas illustrated; he is forced, time and again, to attend back to additional aspects of it. Thus, both the image-vehicle (the compasses) and the set of ideas illustrated (related to the departing lovers) "preserve their *warring identity*", in James Smith's words; each attempting to establish itself in the reader's perception as much as possible, thus amplifying the witty quality of the image. What is more, there is a frequent shift of mental sets from aspects of the image to the ideas illustrated (in accordance with what we have seen in Chapter 1, the unique conscious quality of shifts of mental sets is wit). The fact that these shifts of mental sets to and fro "happen" to fit in again and again in both sets, strongly amplifies the wit of the passage.

Fifth, the split focus of the passage is reinforced by the incompatible (or even conflicting) psychological atmospheres that characterize the two members of the simile: while the manipulation of a pair of compasses on the paper is perfectly unemotional, the speaker's valediction forbidding mourning is highly affectionate, to say the least (this may turn out to be a mild instance of the violation of Horace's decorum mentioned below, in Chapter 17, in relation to the grotesque).

Milton uses the compasses image very differently (VII. 224–231). He, too, introduces his instrument in a context of shapeless and sublime masses and abstractions. But unlike Donne, first, he does not "domesticate" the spiritual and the sublime, and second, makes the transition from visual shapes to shapeless entities as smooth as possible (and, certainly, not *vice versa*). The theme of Donne's poem is the lovers' souls and the compasses are a simile, constituting a *transfer* from the spiritual to the "domestic"; whereas in Milton, the theme is the Supreme Architect with his compasses. The compasses occupy a higher place in the hierarchy of Milton's poem than in Donne's. They are no "mere" figure of speech, the vehicle of a domesticated transfer; they are conceived as part of a sustained mythic image, really existent in the context of Creation-as-Architecture. Notice, first, that the shapeless masses are not presented in "warring" opposition to it, but subsumed under it. The shapelessness of Chaos is an extension of the Architect image, who gives shape to everything. Second, the description proceeds from the instrument to the sublime and shapeless, and not, as in Donne, from the spiritual and shapeless to the exact and domesticated instrument. Third, Milton's instrument is anything but "domesticated". He adapts it, well in advance, to its sublime task, so that the transition should not be abrupt:

(6)   Then stayed the fervid wheels, and in his hand
He took the *golden* compasses, prepared
In God's *eternal store,* to circumscribe
The universe and all created things. (VII. 224–227, my italics)

In line 228, attention is focused on the *exact* use of the compasses ("threatening" with the domestication of the Sublime Act):

(7)   One foot he centered, and the other turned...

But the design drawn by the golden compasses is not allowed to solidify into a definite circle (as in Donne). The second foot is lost in the vague and infinite and shapeless, or even matterless, so to speak:

(8)   One foot he centered, and the other turned
Round through the vast profundity obscure...[6]

Unlike *the Deep,* which may denote 'sea, Ocean', especially in the Miltonic vocabulary, its synonym, *profundity,* is a purely abstract noun. Its two epithets, *vast* and *obscure,* indicate vagueness, indistinctness, lack of understanding, immaterial qualities—as opposed to the exactitude of compasses and circumscription, which are related with the rational shapes of geometry. From lines 232 on, Milton elaborates on shapelessness as the background for Creation:

(9)   Thus God the heav'n created, thus the earth,
Matter unformed and *void. Darkness* profound
Cover'd *th'abyss*; but on the wat'ry *calm*
His brooding wings the *Spirit* of God *outspread,*
And vital *virtue* infused, and vital *warmth*
Throughout the *fluid mass...*   (VII. 232–237)

Notice my italics in the above passage, concentrating on shapeless matter and abstract nouns. Most illuminating is the transferred epithet in "wat'ry calm"; it substitutes an abstract noun for a concrete mass noun, *calm waters,* which itself denotes a shapeless substance. I shall return to this comparison at the beginning of Chapter 15. It will be found there that the two images appeal to different mechanisms of space perception, associated with analytic thinking and with holistic, emotionally-tinted perception, respectively.

"Longinus'" distinction between amplification and the sublime seems very much to the point of our discussion of Donne's and Milton's use of the compass-image:

---

6   Notice the diffuse perception of the sound clusters *n-t-r-d* in *centered, turned, round, profundity,* and *f-t* in *foot* and *profundity.*

> Now the definition given by the writers on rhetoric does not satisfy me. Amplification is, they say, discourse which invests the subject with grandeur. This definition, however, would surely apply in equal measure to sublimity and passion and figurative language, since they too invest the discourse with a certain degree of grandeur. The point of distinction between them seems to me to be that sublimity consists in elevation, while amplification embraces a multitude of details. Consequently, sublimity is often comprised in a single thought, while amplification is universally associated with a certain magnitude and abundance (Chapter 12).

Donne keeps returning to his compass-image, piling up similes one after the other, whereas Milton elaborates one single mythic image, itself of sublime dimensions. Thus, "Longinus" provides a small-scale model for the systematic relating of aesthetically significant effects to non-aesthetic verbal structures—relevant to, and consistent with, our detailed comparison of Donne's and Milton's use of the compass-image.

I have earlier suggested that the two types of style cannot be accounted for in a satisfactory manner merely with reference to the kinds of the material the poets used. We have found that Donne tended to treat the compass-image in a sharp split focus, as against Milton's soft integrated focus. Furthermore, one could profitably compare the strategies Milton himself uses in treating the same images in, say *Paradise Lost* and the Nativity Ode. In this way, one may make quite significant distinctions between almost "minimal pairs" of images, to which the phrase "other things being equal" can most specifically be applied. This also shows how quite unforeseen, evasively minute differences can fruitfully be handled by our present model as will be demonstrated in the following.

There is a wide range of sometimes incompatible definitions of the **Baroque**. As may be apparent by now, *Paradise Lost* complies with those definitions of the Baroque in which "divergent" structure and "integrated soft focus" are among the dominant stylistic principles. "Metaphysical", by contrast, applies to a style most conspicuously marked by "sharp split focus". Herbert Grierson included "On the Morning of Christ's Nativity" in his anthology of Metaphysical poets, making, by the same token, an implicit statement about its style. Helen Gardner, on the other hand, excluded this poem from *her* anthology, supporting her decision as follows: "I differ from Grierson in not including the 'Nativity Ode', a poem too epic in conception and style" (Gardner, 1972: 316). One should not, therefore, be too much surprised to find, e.g., that Milton treated the same images in slightly different manners, manipulating them in ways that in *Paradise Lost* typically count in the direction of integrated focus, and in the 'Nativity Ode' toward split focus. I shall confine my discussion to comparing one stanza of the Ode to parallels of its imagery in *Paradise Lost*. One may on first sight recognize no significant differences. Yet, the small "insignificant" differences gain significance by virtue of their contribution either to split or integrated focus. It would perhaps be more accurate to say that the slight differences between the two poems can be placed alongside a spectrum on which the device in *Paradise Lost* is nearer to the INTEGRATED end, whereas in the 'Nativity Ode' it is nearer to the SPLIT end.

> (10)   Such music (as 'tis said)
>   Before was never made,
>   But when of old the sons of morning sung,
>   While the Creator great
>   His constellations set,
>   And the well-balanced world on hinges hung,
>   And cast the dark foundations deep,
>   And bid the welt'ring waves their oozy channel keep.
>
> (lines 117–124)

The hanging of the well-balanced world recurs in *Paradise Lost:*

> (11)   [...] then founded, then conglobed
>   Like things to like, the rest to several place
>   Disparted and between spun out the air,
>   And earth self-balanced on her center hung. (VII. 239–242)

Hinges and harmonious sound occur together in

> (12)   [...] Heav'n opened wide
>   Her ever-during gates, harmonious sound
>   On golden hinges moving.   (VII. 205–207)

First, let me make some general observations: syntactically, one hypotactic sentence runs through this stanza of the Ode; the reader is required to follow, at the same time, both this complex sentence and a complex stanza form with lines of changing length. In *Paradise Lost,* on the other hand, the length of blank-verse lines is unchanged through hundreds of verses. The syntactic structure of the verses quoted in the present context from *Paradise Lost* is basically paratactic. This, in itself, can be insignificant. But these two structures can reinforce split and integrated focus, respectively. Hypotactic sentences running through stanzas with lines of changing length form, indeed, a structure much favored by metaphysical poets like Donne and Herbert; the reader seems to be "compelled" to split his attention between two consistent ways of proceeding.

Second, the parenthesis in line 117 of the Ode ("as 'tis said") seems to be a deliberate device of "domesticating" the sublime ("hearsay").

Third, a comparison of some images of the Ode with those of their Biblical source would show how Milton "distorted" the latter in the direction of the concrete and exact, limiting, as it were, their sublime imagination. "He stretches out the north over the void / and hangs the earth upon nothing. / He binds up the waters in his thick clouds […]" *(Job,* 26: 78). This description is exquisite for its delicate manipulation of shape-free and diffuse entities covering and supporting, so to speak, the earth. In the Nativity Ode, Milton presents the same elements with an emphasis on fixed shapes and stable positions. Instead of upon *nothing,* he hangs the earth on *hinges,* whereas in *Job,* paradoxically, the solid earth is firmly kept in its place by "airy nothing". Likewise, he "bid the welt'ring waves their oozy channel keep": in the Nativity Ode, the "welt'ring waves" are contained, nay securely canalized, in their solid channels. The sublime has been brought under control. This domestication of the "welt'ring waves" is apparent, not only as compared to "He binds up the waters", resulting in shapeless "thick clouds", but even when compared to "Let the waters under the heavens be gathered together into one place" *(Genesis,* 1: 9). "Be gathered together into one place" is vaguer than "their oozy channel keep".

In the present stanza of the Ode the first three lines give an account on a consistent level of discourse, of thing-free aural harmonies (with no reference to visual shapes). The rest of the stanza gives an account, also on a fairly consistent level of discourse, of things that have, primarily, a visual appeal and, usually, stable and characteristic visual shapes. The metaphorical possibilities on such consistent levels of discourse are rather restricted. The main effect of the passage comes, indeed, from the drastic shift from the shape-free aural appeal to the predominantly visual shapes which, inevitably, splits the focus.

In VII. 205–207 of *Paradise Lost,* the changes of level are more flexible. Also, the focus appears to be integrated, because the shifting levels are subsumed under one dominant, coherent image. The utterance begins on what Wimsatt calls "the substantive level": "Heav'n opened wide / Her ever-during gates". In the following, there is tension between two attributes of the opening gates, the less stable, less concretely defined, the one appealing to the sense of hearing ("harmonious sounds") on the one hand and, on the other, the more concrete (as compared to the "substantive level"), viz., the elaborate visual detail ("golden hinges"). Notice that the description might remain still meaningful—but the focus split—if the integrating over-all image were omitted:

(13)   […] Heav'n opened wide,
                    Harmonious sound on golden hinges moving.

The image could be even further domesticated, if "iron" were substituted for "golden.

A word must be said about how the diffuse and shapeless entities are united, brought together in an over-all visual image in lines VII. 239–242 of *Paradise Lost.* The verbs *founded* and *conglobed* refer to the act of taking shape and to stability. An important semantic ingredient of *conglobed* is "globe", one of the most perfect geometrical shapes. But this shape is not *contrasted* to diffuse matter as if we were dealing with two incompatible states. The verb's semantic ingredients include also the process of BECOMING, of transition from one state to another. Its object still suggests a multiplicity of entities upon which oneness is imposed: "conglobed / Like things to like". The rest of the lines 240–241 emphasize precisely the diffuseness of substance, even after having shapes imposed upon it.

I would like, further, to point out the difference between "And the well-balanced world on hinges hung", and "And earth self-balanced on her center hung". The former leaves nothing insecure. The world itself is *well*-balanced, and is hung on stable, solid hinges. (Here, some domesticating tension is derived from the abstract *world* being hung on concrete *hinges*). *Self*-balanced, on the other hand, implies lack of stable outward support. Here, the earth is kept in a state of rest; a state not due to some solid hinges, but to its placement in the center, that is, to invisible forces that counteract each other. This invisible support is enhanced, so to speak, by the underlying substance, the air "spun out" between the solid bodies. Even the word order corroborates the respective qualities of the two utterances: "And the well-balanced world", with the compound adjective preceding the noun, has the straightforwardness, the sense of security of rational discourse, while in "And earth self-balanced", though syntactically legitimate, the adjective following the noun has a quality of less certainty, of hesitating, of afterthought, so to speak. This hesitant quality, coupled with a caesura (which may or may not be observed) precisely after the fifth position, becomes an "icon", as it were, of the precarious balance of the earth.

Emotional Qualities in Poetry

Finally, I would like to bring together what I have said of the nature of emotions in the preceding, and of perceived qualities in the present chapter, with the *convergence ~ divergence* dichotomy in a discussion of the nature of emotional qualities in poetry.

When a piece of poetry is said to be sad, it does not necessarily mean that it makes *me* sad, just as a romantic quality in a poem or a symphony does not necessarily make *me* feel romantic. One may be perfectly consistent when asserting: "That sad piece of music (or literature) made me feel happy".

Hepburn makes a useful distinction between *experiencing* and *recognizing* an emotion. Accordingly, he distinguishes between two vocabularies, with "interestingly different 'logics'". Terms like "vivacious passage", and "lugubrious phrase", contain a clearer descriptive content than, say, "exciting passage", "thrilling section" and the like. The former expressions report on the detection of an emotional quality, the latter on the successful arousal of an emotion. But "it is oversimple to speak of two distinct vocabularies, for there are shadings, gradations, from one another" (Hepburn, 1968: 91–92). The recognition of an emotion leads quite frequently to arousal of an emotion of some kind, to some degree, although, as we have seen, the experienced emotion will not necessarily be the same as the recognized one.

Being a philosopher and not a literary critic, Hepburn maintains a high level of abstraction, and does not bother about such questions as "What do we perceive when we recognize emotion in a poem?", "What is the 'descriptive content' of emotion-words descriptive of?" I submit that it is precisely here that Cognitive Poetics and the theoretical framework elaborated in the present and the preceding chapter can offer meaningful answers. Let us consider the following two lines:

> (14)   That the wind came out of the cloud, chilling
>   And killing my Annabel Lee.

One striking property of these lines is the prominent sound repetition in *Chilling and killing*. The sound repetition *out-cloud* is less salient. Another striking point is that although the theme is the death of a little girl, the lines hardly sound sad. They sound rather witty or, at least, playful. The first explanation that one is inclined to offer is that the "punning" sound repetition makes the lines sound witty or playful. But does it? Let us consider the opening lines of *Paradise Lost:*

> (15)   Of Man's first disobedience, and the fruit
>   Of that forbidden tree, whose mortal taste
>   Brought death into our world, and all our woe,
>   With loss of Eden, till one greater Man
>   Restore us and regain the blissful seat,
>   Sing, Heav'nly Muse ...

This sounds anything but playful. But notice this: all the sounds of *forbidden* and of *Eden* are included in *disobedience,* in the same order. *Fruit* includes all the consonants of *tree* (repeated in the reverse order, in *mortal)* and two at least in *first.* The consonant-cluster *st* is repeated in *first, taste, restore, seat.* One could add the consonant cluster *loss* and *blissful* in lines 4 and 5, reinforcing the opposition between Fall and Redemption. Obviously, there is a greater number of sound repetitions in Milton, but they lend the passage some harmonious blend of backgrounded, *musical* rather than *witty* of *playful* quality. How can we account for this perceptual difference?

One difference is that the groups of sounds of *chilling and killing* are more concentrated; they are nearer in time to one another. A second difference is that in Poe, the repeated sounds are stringed, so to speak, in one direction, whereas in Milton, the various sound clusters are 'interwoven', yielding a diffuse 'texture', as it were, of various strings. Another difference is that in Poe's lines, the strong positions of the metric scheme coincide with the stressed syllables of the words. It is these converging patterns that are reinforced by the repeated sounds:

> (16)   chílling
>   s   w
>   And kílling my Ánnabel Lee
>   w   s   w   w s   w w   s

In Milton, lexical stress does not necessarily coincide with strong positions:

(17)   Of Mán's fírst disobédience, and the frúit
          w   s   w   s w s   w   s   w   s

Here, *first* occurs in a weak position; *dis-* and *and* in *s*trong ones. It is generally assumed nowadays by linguists that the decoding of speech involves both prediction of
what is to be said and a short-term memory storage of what has been said, until such
time as the meaning of the message has been cleared up (see, for instance, Frye,
1970: 48–50). Both parallel mechanisms are far more strained in Milton than in
Poe.[7]

In the latter's poem, even though "Chilling and killing" is syntactically subordinated to "came out", it is not "predicted" by the finite verb. The first part of (14),
"That the wind came out of the cloud", requires no further syntactic elaboration. The
rest of the quote runs to its end in a straightforward manner. The two transitive
verbs require a direct object and that is precisely what follows them, in the usual
order. Milton's passage, by contrast, puts a great strain on the reader's prediction and
short-term memory store. One must split, so to speak, one's attention. The poem
begins with a preposition, predicting a verb. The fulfillment of this prediction is
suspended until the beginning of line 6 *(Sing)*. While the reader proceeds in following up "this great argument" towards its logical conclusion, he must, at the
same time, *suspend* a part of his attention, in order to remember that at the beginning there was a loose end, demanding to be tied up. Compare the tone of Milton's
poem to the following transcription:

(18)   Heav'nly Muse! Sing
         Of Man's first disobedience, and the fruit
         Of that forbidden tree, whose mortal taste
         Brought death into our world, and all our woe...

This sounds somehow more *single-minded,* more *conclusive.* The various parallel
activities of our decoding apparatus more readily converge here. One may mitigate
the almost intolerable conclusiveness of the transcribed passage, by interpolating the
vocative between the verb and its indirect object, thus suspending, for a moment at
least, the flow of the utterance: "Sing, Heav'nly Muse, / Of Man's first disobedience, and the fruit...". The run-on phrases at the end of lines 1 and 2 of *Paradise
Lost* generate further divergence between the prosodic and the syntactic units.

The quotation from "Annabel Lee" represents a *conclusive* tone, achieved by an
emphatic convergence of parallel linguistic patterns. Repeated sounds, in such a context, are perceived as witty or playful. The passage from *Paradise Lost* represents a
suspensive tone, achieved by the divergence of parallel patterns, yielding a texture,

---

[7]   In other parts of Poe's poem, even in the immediately preceding lines, the predictive
        load of the sentence is rather great. The present statement should not, therefore, be
        automatically generalized to the whole poem, or to the bulk of Poe's poetry.

an *emotional* background to the "great argument" (see EXCURSUS, below, for the terms *conclusive* vs. *suspensive)*. The strings of repeated sounds are woven into the background texture, making the passage more musical. Such structures are sometimes reinforced on the semantic level of the poem. Thus, for instance, puns are usually considered as witty or playful. In his edition of Milton, Douglas Bush has pointed out two puns in the first two lines of *Paradise Lost:* "Fruit": both 'fruit' and 'result'; "Mortal": both 'human' and 'fatal'. Here, however, the divergent meanings are absorbed in the thick fabric of divergent strings. In "Annabel Lee", the playful quality is reinforced by the childish conception of the wind, described with so much exactitude: "The wind came out of the cloud" (and earlier in the poem, "A wind blew out of a cloud by night"). Furthermore, neither wind nor clouds have characteristic shapes. In nineteenth-century poetry, such words were most frequently used to suggest vague and divergent gestalt-free perception. Here, on the contrary, Poe uses *cloud* to signify a specific location, and the *wind* blows from this specific location in a specific direction (to Annabel Lee), at a specific time. This, too, as I hope to show presently, may be a characteristic of convergence.

Now, if we consider these two examples in the light of the theory of emotions expounded in the preceding chapter, we readily recognize Milton's divergent style as "emotional", because our emotional responses, too, are divergent. The emotional quality of the passage may not be derived from its contents. The passage comprises fragmentary allusions to events of mainly theological interest, a synopsis of "this great argument ... to justify the ways of God to men". And conversely, the two lines quoted from "Annabel Lee" are, in their contents, of immediate emotional interest. We do not recognize the event as sad, or painful, as we should have thought it was, because it is put forward in a convergent style. And our convergent mental activities are, usually, nearer to the non-emotional end of the scale. Thus, in the present case, the convergent structure overrides the sad event; instead of *reinforcing* each other, the two combine to yield a non-emotional (playful or witty) whole.

Summary

This chapter has explored the relationship between overall perceptual qualities of poetic passages and what both Beardsley and Sibley would call their perceptual conditions. These overall qualities are qualities of wholes, not of their parts, and emerge in complex, hardly predictable, or even unpredictable ways from their parts. In some cases, no necessary or sufficient conditions may be given for the application of the concepts describing the qualities; in other cases, there seem to be sufficient but no necessary conditions. In the latter, explanatory theories may be useful in accounting for the emergence of the regional qualities; in the former, they may, at best, help to determine which elements do typically count toward what overall qualities. In both types of cases, it is more profitable directly to experience the overall qualities, and to attempt only after the event to account for them with reference to explanatory theories and models. Cognitive Poetics typically offers cognitive theories and models to systematically relate aesthetic effects to structures of non-aesthetic elements. We have examined at considerable length two dichotomous pairs of structures, systematically related to their perceived effects: *convergent~divergent,* and *split~integrated* focus. Both pairs of structures are typically associated with the *witty~emotional* and related perceived qualities.

The categories *convergent~divergent* and *split~integrated* focus, with the respective spectra they constitute, have two conspicuous methodological advantages. First, they are general enough to be applicable to considerably different poems, even in vastly different cultures; at the same time, they are specific enough to allow us make meaningful distinctions between individual poems, between parts of the same poem, or between "minimal pairs" that may be "deceptively alike". At play are a wide range of metrical, linguistic, and thematic features at all ranks that in any poem count either toward, e.g., convergence or divergence. At the same time, features that may be absent from any given poem do not prevent its categorization as *convergent* or *divergent,* or its relative convergence or divergence from being compared to that of another poem. At the same time, unforeseen situations encountered for the first time also can be profitably handled by these distinctions. Second, these categories proffer a theoretical framework in which the interaction of metric style with other aspects of a poem may fruitfully be discussed. The respective "strong~weak" shapes of "convergent~divergent" style and of various stanza forms combine with "shape-bettering" and "shape-worsening" aspects of syntax, lexis, and imagery in inducing the spectrum of perceptual qualities described as "conclusive~suspensive". In other words, the perceptual qualities of a poem may be explained by reference to the unified perception of a human perceiver.

EXCURSUS
Conclusive and Suspensive Tone

Phrasal and Clausal Style

In the preceding section, I have confined myself as much as possible to the discussion of metric structures and syntactic predictions. But, as suggested there, the distinction **Conclusive and Suspensive Tone** requires the consideration of additional elements. I propose to do so in this excursus, making a few clarifications in terms of more or less traditional grammar.

Josephine Miles in her *Modes and Eras in English Poetry,* has shown ample statistical evidence that phrasal constructions prevail in a "sensuous" poetic tradition including Spenser, Milton, and Keats, while in Donne's more "cerebral" poetry, for instance, clausal constructions abound. Wordsworth, too, tends to prefer clausal constructions, as compared to Keats. Miles has established a positive statistical relationship between phrasal style and what she calls the "Sublime Poetry" of the 18th and 19th centuries.

The present excursus is devoted to an inquiry into such questions as "What are the respective poetic potentials of phrasal and clausal style?", and "Is there any logical connection between phrasal style and "Sublime Poetry" that could explain their co-occurrence?"

Let us begin our inquiry with a consideration of several quotations from Christine Brooke-Rose's *A Grammar of Metaphor,* and their implications for poetic theory. In Chapter 7 of her book, on "the genitive link" between metaphoric nouns, she writes among other things: "The relationship may be either one of essence or one of straight activity ...". And again,

> I have found that *of* can most successfully express the complete identity of the two linked nouns when the metaphor can very easily be turned into a verb: if love burns, it is a fire, if we give love, it is a gift, if death overshadows, it is a shade, etc. (1958: 155)

The present suggestion is that the relationships of essence and of straight activity will contribute to different poetic qualities.

In her Chapter 9, on the verb, the same author writes:

> The chief difference between the noun metaphor and the verb metaphor is one of explicitness. With the noun A called B more or less clearly according to the link. But the verb changes one noun into another by implication. And it does not explicitly 'replace' another action (ibid., 206).

Commenting on Konrad's *Étude sur la Métaphore,* Brooke-Rose writes:

> When we use a noun metaphorically, we make abstraction of certain attributes which it possesses, leaving out others which would not fit; for instance in "the roses of her cheeks", we think only of fragrance, pinkness and softness, not of thorns, leaves, yellowness or dark red. The metaphoric term, though a noun, becomes the bearer of one or more attributes and its value is approximately that of a substantive adjective. I would myself add that some of its attributes are often verbal, as in functional metaphor. The real point of Miss Konrad's analysis is much more interesting, though she seems hardly aware of it and does not develop it or apply it in criticism. [...] Whereas the noun is a complex of attributes, an action or attribute cannot be decomposed. Its full meaning depends on the noun with which it is used, and it can only be decomposed into species of itself, according to the noun with which it is associated: an elephant runs = runs heavily, a dancer runs = runs lightly.

Leaving adjectives aside for the moment, this means in fact two things. On the one hand, verbs are a more flexible element of language as far as meaning is concerned: that is, since they change their meaning slightly according to the noun with which they are used, they can also quickly extend their meaning and seem natural with each noun, so that an originally metaphoric use may rapidly cease to be metaphoric if the verb can be used in too many different senses with different nouns (ibid., 209).

Below, in Chapter 20, I will return to Konrad's theory of metaphor and its implications for cognitive poetics.

Conclusive and Suspensive Tone

Another distinction, that between **conclusive** and **suspensive** tone, may help us clarify the logical relationship between what Miles calls the "sublime poem", with its passionate tone, and the phrasal style she found characteristic of it.

First, I would point out that a *double entendre* is involved in the section's title terms. *To conclude* means in the present context (1) 'to bring [the utterance] to an end'; and (2) 'to determine; to make a decision [as to its meaning, to choose one out of several possible meanings]'. A straightforward logical argument is more *conclusive* in both senses than, say, an impressionistic description of a landscape. It will pursue to its logical end, proceed in a specific direction rather than linger on sensory details, and will prefer to define its terms as strictly as possible rather than use them ambiguously.

To suspend involves a corresponding *double entendre,* signifying (1) 'to stop for a time [the natural flow of information]'; (2) 'to keep [the meaning] undetermined'. A sentence with a long phrasal elaboration, especially when descriptive, will tend to be *suspensive* in both senses. Each additional phrase prolongs the sentence, delays its logical conclusion. Consequently, rival meanings of words and images will be eliminated, if at all, as late as possible. Inasmuch as such a construction admits of rival meanings, one of its possible effects is a so-called **soft focus**.

Suspensive quality *may* induce the reader, under certain circumstances, to linger on details in an attempt to make out which of the meanings are relevant. We have just seen that nouns tend to offer a greater number of attributes for metaphoric abstraction than verbs. Since phrasal style has, by definition, a greater proportion of nouns than has clausal style, it will, other things being equal, present a larger number of attributes for simultaneous contemplation than is offered by clausal style. The greater the number of attributes presented for simultaneous contemplation, the more blurred and fused they appear to perception. In other words, such noun metaphors will, other things being equal, tend to generate a low-differentiated perception, of a certain elusive emotional, or sublime, quality (such a hypothesis seems to be in harmony with Miles's statistical findings). In highly elaborate sentences, if the logical relationship between the phrases (and, sometimes, between the clauses as well) is not indicated clearly enough, they may weigh heavily on the reader's short-term memory; in such instances, he is inclined to group them into units of parallel entities, in order to facilitate perception and retention. Such groupings may foreground meaning components shared by the parallel entities which the reader abstracts as their common universals; such universals may appear to the reader as carrying the emotional or metaphoric load of these sentences.

When a sentence that is heavily loaded with phrases describes, say, a landscape or an object located in space and time, the effects mentioned above may be greatly intensified, owing to the fact that a spatio-temporally continuous visual object (1) has a greater number of sensory attributes that one can dwell upon than what would be the case, say, for an abstract argument; and (2) has no logical beginning, middle, and end, so as to render the description 'conclusive'.

Many visual objects have been described in very different ways; one most notable case is Achilles' shield and scepter as compared with the scepter of Agamemnon. In his *Laocoön,* Lessing comments on Homer's treatment of these objects. Below, I will reproduce a short excerpt from these comments, as quoted approvingly by Lukács. Lessing and Lukács agree that Homer does not *describe,* but *narrates:*

> Instead of a reproduction he gives us the history of the scepter: First, it is in the workshop of Hephaestus: then it glitters in the hands of Zeus; then it betokens the dignity of Hermes; now it is the baton of warlike Pelops; now the shepherd's staff of peace-loving Atreus, etc. [...] And again, when Achilles swears by *his* scepter to avenge the scorn shown him by Agamemnon, Homer gives us the history of this scepter. We see it still in leaf upon the mountains, the axe severs it from the trunk, pares it of leaves and bark and readies it to serve the judges of the people as token of their god-like office. (Lukács, 1962: 88)

The existence of such narrative presentations of the static visual objects does not controvert my argument; on the contrary, it is rather the case that the static visual objects are translated into something else, viz., into a narrative unfolding in time. The qualities I am concerned with here are of no interest to Lessing or Lukács; still, our discussion may throw some light on their distinction: Homer increased the conclusive tone of his text by turning the description into a narrative.

Some further grammatical observations based, partly, on Rulon Wells's paper "Nominal and Verbal Style" (1968) may be in order. We will see that phrasal structures are less conclusive than clausal ones, due, also, to some of the grammatical properties of verbs and nouns.

(1) "The finite verb has not only person but also number and [...] tense" (Wells, 1968: 218). This grants a greater precision to the expression (precision implying conclusiveness). Nominal style, on the other hand, makes room for ambiguity: "'At

the time of their arrival' has no one verbal counterpart, but two, 'when they arrived' and 'when they arrive'" (ibid.).

(2) "The nominal style in question also makes extensive use of compounds [...] These compounds are often inherently ambiguous" (ibid., 219–220). This observation is most apt with regard to, e.g., Keats's nominal style.

(3) To the above, I would add that clausal structures are more conclusive by virtue of a further difference between verbs and nouns. A transitive finite motion verb may establish a fairly clear logical relationship between a great number of phrases (e.g., between subject, direct and indirect objects, adverbs of time, place etc.). With an intransitive verb, or one which does not denote motion in space, the number of phrases naturally decreases; the number of phrases related to a noun is more limited, and their relationships are more ambiguous.

(4) The verb "to be" is half-way between nouns and verbs in this respect: "The feeling is sometimes expressed that the copula is not a true verb, since it has a purely logical function. On the other hand, it has person, tense, etc., like other verbs" (ibid., 214). It should be noticed that "the verb 'to be' can be omitted altogether. Omission of this verb is familiar in Greek and other languages when it functions as the copula, but the Sanscrit nominal style omits it even when it means "exists'" (ibid., 219; cf. also G. E. Moore's influential essay, "Is Existence a Predicate?" (1966)).

(5) In nominal style, "the number of distinct sentence patterns will decrease. Compound sentences (both with co-ordinating and subordinating conjunctions) tend to disappear, so that only simple (subject-predicate) sentences, more or less swollen by parentheses and modifiers, will be left" (ibid., 216), whereas "verbal style allows more diversity" (ibid., 217). Variety of stylistic resources thus may yield more vigor and vividness in literary expression.

(6) "The very fact that nominality is contrary to conversational style has its value" (ibid., 218).

As to conjunctions, the clearer the logical relationship between the parts of a sentence, the more conclusive it will appear to be. Conjunctions like *because, but* are less ambiguous, and therefore more conclusive than *and*. Aphorisms sometimes omit conjunctions (or even finite verbs) altogether; here, the logical relationship is so clear that one need not explicitly specify it (thus achieving brevity, which is a further possible requirement for conclusiveness).

The juxtaposition of linguistic units tends to heighten the rhythmic quality of an utterance and, by the same token, distract attention from clear logical relationships. In legal formulations, too, we often find a large number of parallel phrases; unlike in poetry, however, their logical relationship is marked with the utmost possible clarity.

Finally, I wish to make some remarks on sentential modes and the related verbal moods. **Questions** sometimes leave room for several possible interpretations and answers. This may enhance the suspensive tone. Rhetorical questions, on the other hand, imply mostly only one, indisputable answer. That is why they abound in highly conclusive texts (such as prophesies of God's coming wrath in the Bible). They imply an authoritative tone which leaves no room for alternatives.

The sentential mode of command (usually expressed by the imperative as well as by certain related exclamations) implies very frequently a tone of immediacy, an urgency, which does not leave the addressee time to reflect whether he should obey or not. The closer, of course, the command is to a request, the less urgent (and the less conclusive) its effect on the hearer will be. A sentence in the indicative, which is the unmarked verbal mood, tends to be, other things being equal, more conclusive than informative questions, but less conclusive than rhetorical questions. The negative is very frequently a categorical denial, but sometimes it implies a peculiar kind of ambiguity: it not only *negates* a thing, but also *presupposes* the existence of the thing negated. Linguists call this phenomenon the (regular, undefeasible) presupposition.[8]

---

[8]   The grammatical issues discussed in the present excursus could also be discussed in the context of the *units of meaning,* below.

CHAPTER 5

Rhyme Patterns, Gestalt Theory and Perceptual Forces

The sound stratum of poetry is a continuous embarrassment for many literary critics. While this stratum clearly is of the greatest literary significance, it is very difficult to say anything meaningful about its contribution to the *whole,* that can be defended in a systematic way. The reason is that we are dealing not with semantic, but with perceptual phenomena. Often, critics try to improvise some *ad hoc* semantic feature for the specific rhyme pattern; or produce some *ad hoc* metaphor describing the rhyme pattern or the stanza form or the metric pattern in question, showing that the same features or metaphors could be applied to the content (world stratum), too. I contend that the reluctance to explore the potentials of the sound stratum is not accidental, but has deep-seated reasons in human nature. In order to explain this, let us have a look at two cognitive experiments in sign perception:

> Fraisse (1969) exposed subjects to the visual form "O" in the context of other letters or, alternatively, in the context of geometrical forms. In the letter condition they were to respond orally "o", while in the forms condition they were to say "circle". Even after much practice, it always took longer to call the stimulus a "circle" than to call it an "o". This result reflects the general advantage which reading has over naming.
>
> Another good example of this advantage is the Stroop test (Jensen & Rohwer, 1966). In this test, color names (e.g., "yellow") are written in different-colored ink (e.g., blue). If the subject is required to read the word, he has little interference from the ink color, but if he is required to name the ink color, he has great difficulty because of interference from the color name. Again, this suggests that the relationship between a verbal stimulus and its name is much more direct than the description of a nonverbal stimulus in words. It is not clear why reading should be easier than naming in literate adults when, in fact, children learn to read after they learn many picture names (Posner, 1973: 26).

I wish to offer the following explanation (which is at some variance with Posner's). Signs consist of a sign vehicle, or *signifiant*, and a thing signified, or *signifié*. Humans are sign-using animals. Language and reading consist of a chain of *signifiants* and *signifiés:* the graphic *signifiant* points to the phonological *signifiés;* which, in turn, serves as the *signifiant* for the semantic *signifié.* The sign-using animal is programmed to get to the end of the chain of sign vehicles as quickly as possible, in order to realize its potential information value for survival. It takes considerable effort to stop and linger at some link at the chain of sign vehicles. In the two experiments reported by Posner, it was more difficult for the respondents to describe the *signifiant* than to "attend away" (in Polányi's term) from it to the *signifié.* As I insisted in Chapter 1, only for a very short time we remember the surface structure of messages received; we soon recode it into a semantic representation.

In everyday life, there is a tendency not to distinguish between the *signifiant* and the *signifié.* Poetic language, on the contrary, effects distinction between them to varying degrees (see in Chapter 22, Jakobson on "the function of poetry"). In non-literary language, the reader tends to "attend away" from the phonological *signifiant* to the semantic *signifié.* The sound patterns of poetry (meter, alliteration, rhyme and the like) force him to attend back to the sound stratum. Up to a certain point, a mild increase of the cognitive load on the perceptual apparatus caused by the reader's additional attention to these sound patterns is perceived as a more or less vague musical effect, usually of an emotional quality. Beyond that point, however, as suggested in Chapter 4, the focus becomes split, and the perceived quality may be 'witty'.

Gestalt Theory, Ink Blots & Poetic Qualities

The strings of sounds and their patterns are the only directly perceptible sensory information provided by language and poetry. It takes considerable tolerance of uncertainty to contemplate unclassified, 'meaningless' sensory information—actual or imagined. As will be argued in Chapter 16, in certain circumstances such contemplation may even arouse a sense of confusion, of emotional disorientation. The term 'meaningful', however, is ambiguous: one of its readings is nearer to 'referential', another to 'systematic'. 'Meaning' in the former sense gives more immediate gratification to one's quest for certitude than in the latter sense. Analytic criticism at its best would systematically explore, in isolation, one or the other aspect of the sound dimension of poetry. My conception (expounded in Chapter 4) of 'split' and 'integrated' focus, and of 'convergent' and 'divergent' poetry, provides models for the integration of the sound stratum with the other strata. What is more, it has provided tools for attributing some intense human qualities to such integrated wholes.

Cognitive Poetics assumes that one of the best ways to approach such issues is through gestalt theory. This is, in fact, the most comprehensive theory that accounts most consistently for the relationships between structures and perceptual qualities or emotional qualities. Its application in art criticism in general, and in literary theory in particular, is one of the most illuminating ways to relate structures with effects. Another approach that supports the gestaltist conception may be derived from the Rorschach ink blot test. As will be seen, there is furthermore some overlapping between gestalt theory and information theory with reference to the issues that concern us.

In several sections of the present chapter we are going to discuss the phonetic aspects of linguistic signs, and their grouping into perceptual structures by means of rhyming. The question arises what causes the phonetic aspects of those linguistic signs to be perceived as coherent entities with a proper shape and unity. Gestalt psychology has systematically investigated the possible answers to that question. The fundamental law of perception, the Law of *Prägnanz,* is commonly defined by gestalt psychologists as follows: "The psychological organization of any stimulus pattern will always be as good as the prevailing conditions allow", followed as a rule by a list of conditions for "good". "The general rule is that to the extent that stimuli possess similar features they form groups and are perceived as unified, co-herent, and stable structures" (Herrnstein-Smith, 1968: 41). The speech sounds of rhyming words most conspicuously possess such "similar features". In a footnote, Herrnstein-Smith adds:

> The "laws of organization", as formulated by Max Wertheimer, designate the conditions which maximize our tendency to respond to groups of indi-vidual stimuli as unified "percepts". These conditions include proximity and similarity. (ibid.)

In Chapter 4, I discussed convergent and divergent structures in poetry. These struc-tures can easily be translated to gestalt-language. Gestalt theory is preoccupied with strong and weak shapes, and with the perceptual "laws" that govern their perception. Convergent lines and specific directions may contribute to differentiated shapes. Di-vergent lines and general tendencies will rather yield ambiguous, undifferentiated, blurred shapes. "Shading" may be conceived of as of many divergent lines, each with a specific direction. Both according to gestalt theory and to the findings of Ror-schach, strong shapes are typically associated with rational qualities, weak shapes with emotional qualities. Colors as such have no shapes at all.

Arnheim has pointed out that it is shapes rather than colors that are used for writ-ing. Clearly differentiable shapes are more reliable for communication, even in small sizes (Arnheim, 1957: 323–324). In the Rorschach ink blot test, form re-sponses indicate an ability to exercise strong intellectual control, whereas the col-ored component is regarded as an affectively charged stimulus. A large number of color responses indicates emotional excitability. Rorschach discovered this empiri-cally; as to the bases of his deductions, he remarked himself that they were "quite insufficient to satisfy the demands of scientific logic" (Rorschach, 1951: 99). "Al-though much effort has been expended in experimental procedures designed to dis-prove this theory, it has been supported to a remarkable degree" (Alcock, 1963: 54).

Arnheim supplies some logical explanation, quoting Schachtel who has pointed out that the experience of color resembles that of affect or emotion. In both cases we tend to be passive receivers of stimulation. An emotion is not the product of the actively organizing mind. It merely presupposes a kind of openness, which, for example, a depressed person may not have. It strikes us as color does. Shape, on the contrary, seems to require a more active response. (Arnheim, 1957: 324–325)

Leonard B. Meyer, who applies gestalt theory to music, discusses strong and weak shapes and their perceived effects as follows: "Because good shape is intelligible in this sense, it creates a psychological atmosphere of certainty, security, and patent purpose, in which the listener feels a sense of control and power as well as a sense of specific tendency and definite direction" (Meyer, 1956: 160).

Where, on the other hand, there is chaotic overdifferentiation or primordial homogeneity, "the lack of distinct, tangible shapes and of well-articulated modes of progression is capable of arousing desires for, and expectations of, clarification and improvement" (ibid.); hence their emotional, non-conceptual quality. Both Meyer and Ehrenzweig throughout his (1965) book insist, each in their own way, that great art frequently presents a unique combination of strong and weak gestalts (or gestalt-free qualities).

The combination of strong gestalts with gestalt-free qualities is significant in the Rorschach test. This is particularly true of the Form/Diffusion (FK) score, for instance, which refers to a combination of good form perception with shading, when "the shading is used to present diffusion, darkness, or depth" (Alcock, 1963: 48). Scoring well on FK is a difficult achievement. It involves good form realization combined with shading organized to present an impression of perspective or other three-dimensional quality. It implies also an ability to exercise intellectual control when faced with stimuli that are commonly found to be disturbing, such as the light-dark amorphous shadings of the blots. It is as if the perceiver, in boldly organizing this shading as a vista, demonstrated that he can contemplate the powers of darkness with equanimity.

In Chapter 4, we have considered Donne's compasses image which, as I have insisted, demands the realization of its visual shape, while supporting a witty, non-emotional quality. In Milton's description of the Fallen Angel viewing the dismal situation (*Paradise Lost* I: 59–64), the very core of my analysis was based on the text's combination of good form perception with shading. The same is true of the description of the act of creation (VII. 224–227) quoted in the same chapter, where Milton starts out, again, with objects that have stable characteristic visual shapes, but are eventually superseded by infinite gestalt-free and thing-free qualities.

Rhyme Patterns

(1)   Hamlet
 Why, let the stricken deer go weep,
  The hart ungalled play;
 For some must watch, while some must sleep:
  So runs the world away! [...]

 For thou dost know, O Damon dear,
  This realm dismantled was
 Of Jove himself; and now reigns here
  A very, very—pajock.

    Horatio
 You might have rhymed.   (*Hamlet,* III. ii)

Horatio expresses a feeling of unease resulting from a sense of incompleteness, a desire for, and expectation of, clarification and improvement—to quote Meyer's words above. There is here an unfulfilled sense of what the gestaltists call *requiredness* (Köhler's term). "Requiredness is the demand that one part of the perceptual field may have on the other". Here there is a demand for *closing* the rhyme pattern. In the first stanza of Hamlet's poem, there is a feeling that the rhyme at the end of the fourth line most emphatically confirms an expectation, and closing it with a "click" achieves stability; it is this "click" and stability that is absent from the end of the second stanza. What the reader is conspicuously missing here is a sense of *closure*. The stronger the shape of the perceptual pattern, the stronger the *requiredness* of the missing element and, other things being equal, the stronger the closure if achieved. "Spatially or temporally perceived, a structure appears 'closed' when it is experienced as integral: coherent, complete, and stable" (Herrnstein-Smith, 1968: 2).

> Closure occurs when the concluding portion of a poem creates in the reader a sense of appropriate cessation. It announces and justifies the absence of further development; it reinforces the feeling of finality, completion and composure which we value in all works of art; and it gives ultimate unity and coherence to the reader's experience of the poem by providing a point from which all the preceding elements may be viewed comprehensively and their relations grasped as part of a significant design. (ibid., 36)

It should be noted that the (completed) rhyme pattern of the first stanza indicates the nature of the experience missing in the second stanza. However, the incompleteness of the second stanza would be felt even if it were not preceded by a more complete one. The expectation for completeness is generated by the second stanza on its own;

a comparison to the first stanza only *reinforces,* it does not generate this expectation.

In the following, I will explore some of the relevant gestalt principles. These principles were applied by Leonard B. Meyer and Rudolf Arnheim to music and the visual arts, respectively; by Barbara Herrnstein-Smith (1968) to poetic closure, and by Tsur (1977; 1998) to versification. Meyer speaks of the "Law of Good Continuation".

> A shape or pattern will, other things being equal, tend to be continued in its initial mode of operation. Thus, "to the factor of good continuation in purely spatial organization there corresponds the factor of the smooth curve of motion and continuous velocity in spatio-temporal organization". [...] Actually, of course, a line or motion does not perpetuate itself. It is only a series of lifeless stimuli. What happens is that the perception of a line or motion initiates a mental process, and it is this mental process which, following the mental line of least resistance, tends to be perpetuated and continued. (Meyer, 1956: 92)

Let us explore the application of these principles by considering the following passage, and comparing it to (1).

> (2)   In doubt his Mind and Body to prefer,
>   Born but to die, and reas'ning but to err;
>   Alike in ignorance, his reason such,
>   Whether he thinks too little or too much:
>   Chaos of Thought and Passion, all confus'd;
>   Still by himself abus'd, or disabus'd;
>   Created half to rise, and half to fall;
>   Great lord of all things, yet a prey to all;
>   Sole judge of Truth, in endless Error hurl'd:
>   The glory, jest and riddle of the world.
>   (Pope: "An Essay on Man", II. 9–18)

We may see here that the couplet (as a form) tends to be perceived as a percept that has considerable unity, owing to both the **similarity** of the rhyming line-endings and to their **proximity**. In terms of the "Law of Good Continuation", we expect after the first line a verse line that ends in a similar sound pattern, and this expectation *is* satisfied. In structural terms, there is only one structural principle in the couplet: that a first line rhymes with a second. As such, the couplet has a *simple* structure, simpler than those stanzas that have two or more structural principles. Such a strong shape creates, in Meyer's above formulation, "a psychological atmosphere of certainty, security, and patent purpose, in which the listener feels a sense of control and power as well as a sense of specific tendency and definite direction"—

it is perceived as having some intellectual or witty rather than emotional quality. Hence its relative abundance in witty poetry such as Pope's, or rationalist drama such as Racine's. I use here *witty* in the sense explained above (Chapter 4, note 4). As I claimed there, the regional quality of such rhymes is typically 'witty' in the sense of 'charaterized by sharpness usually associated with cleverness and quickness of apprehension'. This quickness can be accounted for by the properties of strong shapes discussed in the present paragraph: the "simpler" the shape, the "quicker" the response.

After the first couplet, the expectation for the same ending is thwarted; the "Law of Good Continuation", however, is not suspended, only shifted to a higher level of organization. From now on, the reader expects additional couplets to follow, and this expectation is amply confirmed. One ought, in fact, expect an endless succession of such couplets. In (2), by contrast, the reader may have, in spite of all, a feeling that he has reached the end of something, perhaps of a poetic passage. Whoever reads the isolated passage may feel that at its end there is not only a cessation but, in Barbara Herrnstein-Smith's words, a *proper* cessation. We have reached here a kind of *poetic closure;* in fact, what we encounter here is a rather effective closural device. "One of the most effective ways to indicate the conclusion of a poem generated by an indefinitely extensible principle is simply to modify that principle at the end of the poem" (Herrnstein-Smith, 1968: 53). In the present case, we are *not* looking at the end of a poem, but only of a short passage. Likewise, as is obvious, Pope has not modified the "indefinitely extensible principle" of the successive couplets. Still, the sense of closure is definitely there. The reason is that a superimposed, additional pattern has been modified. In every line of this succession of lines there is some dichotomy as "Mind and Body", or "Thought and Passion". In most instances this is sharpened into some antithesis, as in "Created half to rise, and half to fall", or "Great lord of all things, yet a prey to all". Sometimes the structure is even more sophisticated: the antithetical structures are sharpened into paradoxical phrasings; there are exactly two of such (symmetrical) clauses in a line, as in "Born but to die, and reas'ning but to err". In most of these lines, this symmetry is reinforced by a prosodic symmetry: the syntactic juncture coincides with the caesura (that is, in contrast to line 12, it occurs in the "region of balance" of the iambic pentameter line: after the fourth, fifth, or sixth position of the line). It is this binary structure that has been modified by the enumeration of *three* items in the last line: "The *glory, jest* and *riddle* of the world", indicating that the foregoing series has come to an end.

The quatrain, as, for instance, the first stanza in (1), with an alternating rhyme-scheme *(abab)* contains two pairs of rhymes. The members of each pair are **similar,** but their **proximity** is less than in the couplet. The quatrain has, in fact, two structural principles: that the first line rhymes with the third, and the second with the fourth. In (1), in addition (but not in (2)) the line lengths are different, too. The odd-numbered lines are eight syllables long, three of which can be further subdivided into two symmetrical hemistichs, that is, 4+4 syllables. In the third line, this symmetry is enhanced by the anaphoric repetition of *some must,* and the antithesis *watch ~ sleep,* in the two hemistichs. The even-numbered lines are six syllables long, that is, shorter than the odd-numbered lines, but longer than their hemistichs. This implies that neither at the line rank nor at the hemistich rank can the stanza be divided into units of equal length. Nevertheless, as indicated by the intuitive strength of closure at the end of the first stanza, and by the sense of frustration effected by the absence of closure at the end of the second stanza, this stanza shape is perceived as considerably strong. What is, then, the perceptual organization of such a stanza, so that it might warrant this intuitive experience of strong shape? The answer is "grouping": The reader groups perceptually together the first with the second line, and the third with the fourth. Symmetry is a device for making efficient use of our memory capacity. If a series of stimuli can be grouped into patterns of identical structures, only one structure needs to be remembered for all the patterns. Thus, the number of entities to be handled by the mental processes is reduced, and a complicated feeling "is replaced by a single feeling of greater intensity" (Peirce, quoted by Eco, 1979: 132). This may be one source of the "sense of control and power" typically associated with strong shapes.[1] In informational terms,

> We must recognize the importance of grouping or organizing the input sequence into units or chunks. Since the memory span is a fixed number of chunks, we can increase the number of bits of information that it contains simply by building larger and larger chunks, each chunk containing more information than before. (Miller, 1970: 43)

Likewise, we may organize, in certain circumstances, the stream of prosodic information into symmetrical units, "simply by building larger and larger chunks". In (1), for instance, we have to group together two rather dissimilar verse lines: one is eight syllables long, the other six syllables long; and the two lines do not rhyme with one another. In this way, however, the stanza is divided into two units of exactly the same structure: each contains a longer line followed by a shorter line; and an *a*-rhyme followed by a *b*-rhyme.

This brings us to a significant difference between these two poetic passages. The units of two lines are more thoroughly integrated into the larger unit in (1) than in (2); and in (2), the units of two stand out more clearly than in (1). In fact, in (2) it is only the effective closure at the end of the whole passage that organizes the couplets into a larger unit, after the event.

> The rule that governs the process is evident. The effect depends on the degree of simplicity of the whole as compared with the degree of simplicity of the parts. Greater simplicity of the whole makes for greater unity. The simpler the parts, the more clearly they tend to stand out as independent entities. (Arnheim, 1967: 61)

---

[1]   Another source may be the *balance* of the line: Gestalt theory conceives of symmetry as of the state of rest or balance due to the equal action of opposing perceptual forces.

On the whole, however, the simplicity of any part must be modified or weakened sufficiently to make the part dependent on, and therefore integrated with, its context. (ibid., 65)

The grouping together of two such dissimilar lines counts as such a weakening of the parts. In (2), the two lines long part is simple, and its lines tend clearly to stand out as independent entities; were it not for the closure, the whole would be rather loosely held together. The couplet, thus, is simple in an absolute sense: it has only one structural feature. The quatrain, by contrast, is simple in a relative sense: simplicity is achieved at a higher level, in spite of the lower level complexity, making the part dependent on, and therefore integrated with, its context.

At the beginning of the present chapter, I mentioned the critics' uneasiness with the need to handle issues related to sound patterns and rhyme schemes: "In many instances, critics try to improvise some *ad hoc* semantic feature for the specific rhyme pattern". I propose now an (admittedly unduly brief) consideration of such an instance, in order to see whether the gestalt tools proposed above can handle the same instance more adequately. Let us consider a few couplets from Pope (all italics are Pope's):

(3)   Our plentous Streams a various Race supply;
        The bright-ey'd Perch with Fins of *Tyrian* Dye,
        The silver Eel, in shining volume roll'd,
        The yellow Carp, in Scales bedrop'd with Gold,
        Swift Trouts, diversify'd with Crimson Stains,
        And Pikes, the Tyrants of the wat'ry Plains.
                                    ("Windsor Forest", 141–146)

(4)   Yet let not each gay *Turn* thy Rapture move,
        For Fools *Admire,* but Men of Sense *Approve.*
                                    ("An Essay on Criticism", 390–391)

(5)   Others for language all their care express,
        And value books, as Women *Men,* for *Dress.*
                                    ("An Essay on Criticism", 305–306)

(6)   He gathers Health from Herbs the Forest yields,
        And of their fragrant Physicks of the Fields.
                                    ("Windsor Forest", 241–142)

(7)   Such if there be, who loves so long, so well,
        Let him our sad, our tender story tell;
                                    ("Eloisa to Abelard", 363–364)

John A. Jones, in his book on Pope's couplet art, quotes (3), above, and makes the following comment on its third line:

> Because the participle "roll'd" is the rhyme word, the verb quality of "rolling" is emphasized rather than adjectival or substantive quality. "Shining volumes" is more effective coming before the rhyme "roll'd" than it would be after it, for it is the climactic rolling or writhing that is highlighted. We do not always think of volumes as round but here it means "coils"; and when "roll'd" describes "volumes", the eelish quality is heightened, as the reader can easily imagine, even if he has never landed an eel. (Jones, 1969: 74–75)

Consider the first sentence of this quotation from Jones. The word *because* suggests a logical, causal relationship between its two clauses. But is there? To justify such a statement, there must be some generalization that can be consistently maintained as, for instance, "When a participle occurs in the rhyme word, its verb quality is emphasized rather than adjectival or substantive quality". I am not aware of any such valid generalization. In fact, all the available grammatical and stylistic evidence suggests that the adjectival quality is emphasized in this epithet. Jones's interpretation, however, crucially seems to depend on the participle's "verb quality". Since, however, everybody feels that rhymes do something important to words, and so little is known about *what* they do to them, Jones quite safely resorts to the rhyme word to enlist it in the service of the "verb quality" construal of the participle. When words with certain meaning components are systematically manipulated into the rhyme, one can, perhaps, make a case for its significance; but even that cannot justify any generalization of *this* kind. Speech sounds are arbitrarily assigned to meanings in natural languages. Versification is, typically, an additional organization of the phonological component, irrespective of the meanings of the sounds. Whenever the critic claims that there is some interaction between sound and meaning, he must make explicit the principles on which he is relying. (As far as the present study is concerned, expressive sound patterns will be discussed in Chapter 8, the relationship between rhyme and meaning in chapter 9).

Syntactic inversion may be an effective foregrounding device, unless there are factors that tend to void it. In some cases, however, it may be reasonably supposed that the poet used his conventional right to syntactic inversion merely to make his words conform with meter and rhyme. In "shining volume roll'd", there may be room for just such 'reasonable supposition'. But, sometimes, there is more to it.

Consider the closing couplet of (2), above. The antithesis leaves little room for doubt that *Error* in the first line is a word of key importance. Although *hurl'd* contributes such components to the image as helplessness, passive endurance and inconstancy, its decisive component, physical transfer, has little relevance to the thought. *Hurl'd* constitutes a *virtuoso* rhyme with *world,* but this has been achieved at the double price of an "inelegant" syntactic inversion and manipulating the word of key importance out of the rhyme. Is it possible that a great master of poetic technique like Pope should be guilty of such incompetence? And how could we explain, then, that precisely this "incompetent" line constitutes one of the most famous couplets on which Pope's reputation as a major poet rests? An alternative explanation would be that the syntactic inversion, the *virtuoso* rhyme, and the manipulation of the key word out of the rhyme serve one common effect. As the casual collection of couplets in excerpts 4–7 may suggest, such inversions, manipulating words of little importance into the rhyme, are not uncommon in Pope. It will be noticed that in excerpts 4–6 the inversion occurs at the end of the first line of the couplet, whereas in (7) it occurs at the end of the second line. I shall argue that this is quite significant.

Consider (4). Here, "move" provides the finite verb and the idea of causation only; greater interest lies in the direct object *Rapture*, and even greater in the subject, *gay Turn*. In short, the syntactic inversion maneuvers precisely the nonemphatic verb into the rhyme. At the same time, the antithesis *fools* ~ *Men of Sense* focuses attention on the verbs *Admire* and *Approve*. These two verbs are near-synonyms in that they express a positive attitude; and they are near-antonyms in that they express uncritical enthusiasm and sound judgment, respectively. This semantic and rhetorical structure is the main source of this couplet's wit. The witty effect of the verb *Approve* is greatly enhanced here by its high degree of requiredness at this place. This verb is required here owing to its place in the rhyme pattern, in the antithesis and, as I shall argue below, in the segmentation of the line. So, in the light of the foregoing gestaltist discussion, one might suggest that the syntactic inversion at the end of the first line is functional: the structure of the first line is *weakened sufficiently to make the part dependent on, and therefore integrated with, its context.* In short, the weaker the ending of the first line, the stronger the structural closure perceived at the end of the couplet. As we shall see time and again, one of the most effective means of amplifying the closure of a piece of poetry, at various levels of organization, is to weaken the closure of the unit before, and thus make it more dependent on the whole.

Likewise, in excerpt (5) the inversion highlights the noun phrases *language* and *all their care;* the least emphatic member of the clause, the verb *express,* is again dislocated and placed into the rhyme. Great attention is focused, again, on *Dress* in the rhyme of the second line, by a variety of means: requiredness arising from segmentation, the rhetorical scheme (zeugma) and the convergence of two meanings in the word *Dress:* 'guise, appearance, adornment' and 'fine cloths'. A similar story can be told of the first line of excerpt (6), even though in the second line attention is not focused with such vigor on the rhyming word.

Contrary, then, to Jones's contention, in all these instances it is not the rhyme that effects the meaning of, and bestows emphasis on, the word that is manipulated into it, but rather the other way around: the relatively low semantic importance of the word manipulated into the line ending de-emphasizes the first rhyme. The process is governed by the gestalt principles discussed in the present chapter, and is intended to improve "the conditions which maximize our tendency to respond to groups of individual stimuli as unified 'percepts'".

We may observe a very different effect in excerpt (7), where the syntactic inversion occurs at the end of the second line. This couplet is perceived as "softer" than the instances discussed so far. This effect is achieved by a variety of means; but only the syntactic inversion at the end of the couplet concerns us here. "Eloisa to Abelard" is very different from Pope's other major poems. Here, the witty effect is replaced by a pervasive emotional tone, quite unusual in Pope. This emotional tone is supported by a relatively divergent structure. The drastic weakening of the closure at the *end* of the couplet is an effective means of weakening the overall gestalts within the rigid constraints of Pope's poetics.[2]

Let us turn now, with the above discussion of gestalts in mind, to the first stanza of the popular ballad "Edward":

> (8)   "Why dois your brand sae drap wi bluid,
> Edward, Edward,
> Why dois your brand sae drap wi bluid,
> And why so sad gang yee O?"
> "O I hae killed my hauke sae guid,
> Mither, mither,
> O I hae killed my hauke sae guid,
> And I had nae mair bot hee O."

It will be readily noticed that this stanza is heavily loaded with repetitions. These repetitions constitute a rigid formula repeated throughout the poem. Let us compare this stanza to its "gist" (by omitting the repetitive elements):

> (9)   "Why dois your brand sae drap wi bluid,
> And why so sad gang yee?"
> "O I hae killed my hauke sae guid,
> And I had nae mair bot hee."

Excerpt (9) conveys, roughly, the same semantic information as (8); but the impression it makes is quite different. The reason for this difference is to be looked for in the emotive overtones, and the overall gestalts of the stanza-forms. Both are effected by the presence or absence of the same words. The four-line stanza has a "good gestalt"; the grouping of its lines is symmetrical: there are two groups of identical structure, consisting of a tetrameter and a trimeter line each; the ends of the groups rhyme with each other. As in excerpt (1), the pairs of different-structured lines must be grouped together at the lower level, so that two groups of identical structure may

---

2   I have described the principles of Pope's prosody at some length elsewhere (Tsur, 1977: 42–45; 1998: 40–44).

be produced at the higher level. Excerpt (8), by contrast, has a very weak shape. This weakness can be expressed in the number of structural elements added to the structure of (9). The (odd-numbered) tetrameter lines of (9) are verbatim repeated in (8), the (even-numbered) trimeter lines are not. Between the two tokens of each tetrameter verse type, a dimeter line is enclosed, containing a repeated vocative. While the tetrameter and trimeter lines have an iambic character, the dimeter lines have a trochaic character.

As a result, the perceptual quality of the stanza in (9) is very different from that of the original: it has a more conclusive tone, a more 'straightforward' rhythm; it sounds sharper, somehow more measured. It has the psychological atmosphere of certainty, in which one feels a sense of control and definite direction. The original is more complex, its rhyme-scheme is less clearly perceived, it has a greater number of structural principles. As a perceptual corollary, it sounds 'softer', more suspensive in tone, and at the same time more colloquial, it is deprived of the psychological atmosphere of certainty, in which one feels a sense of control and definite direction.

We have been discussing the phonetic aspects of linguistic signs, and their grouping into perceptual structures by means of rhyming. We have been discussing the laws of organization that designate the conditions which maximize our tendency to respond to the phonetic aspects of those linguistic signs as coherent entities that have considerable shape and unity. Furthermore, we have been considering the effects of the "Law of *Prägnanz*" and of the "Law of Good Continuation". In addition, Meyer speaks of the "Law of Return", and of "Saturation".

The **"Law of Return"** is "the law that, other things being equal, it is better to return to any starting point whatsoever than not to return" (Meyer, 1956: 151). The "Law of Good Continuation" and the "Law of Return" impose different characteristics upon different strophic organizations, each of them being considered as "good" perceptual organization under the relevant law. Let us take as an example one of Omar Khayyám's Rubáiyáths, in Edward Fitzgerald's famous English version:

> (10) Think, in this battered Caravanserai
>   Whose Portals are alternate Night and Day,
>   How Sultán after Sultán with his Pomp
>   Abode his destined Hour, and went his way.

Let us try to distort the rhyme-scheme of this quatrain, as follows:

> (11) Think, in this battered Caravanserai
>   Whose Portals are alternate Night and Day,
>   How Sultán after Sultán did sojourn,
>   And went his way then — never to return.

Two different principles organize respectively Omar Khayyam's original Rubáiyáth and our alterated version. Excerpt (10) actualizes the "Law of Return". The third line deviates from the rhyme established in the first two lines; the fourth line returns to it. Excerpt (11) actualizes the "Law of Good Continuation". The first two lines of this quatrain constitute a "strong" shape: they are connected by a single rhyme, and constitute a symmetrical couplet that may be described by a single structural principle (the second line rhymes with the first). The couplet-pattern "perpetuates" itself, it recurs in the next two lines as well; and had the poem contained ten, or twenty, or one hundred lines, the same "Good Continuation" could have gone on, indefinitely, as it happens, indeed, in the poetry of such Neo-Classicists as Alexander Pope. In excerpt (10), according to the "Law of Good Continuation", a couplet to be completed is expected after the third line. In the isolated stanza, the Law of **Return** of the *aaba* rhyme-scheme comes as a surprise, and is perceptually justified only after the event. It should be noted as well that in excerpt (10) the return is **to a specific rhyme,** whereas in (11) **an abstract pattern** is repeated; the second couplet is based on a **different specific rhyme.**

It is also instructive to inspect the two versions from the point of view of **unity.** The Law of Return in (10) generates a tightly-closed and coherent unit. There is a feeling that the quatrain constitutes a single unit that is closed with a sharp "click". In accordance with the rule discussed above, viz., that the "effect depends on the degree of simplicity of the whole as compared with the degree of simplicity of the parts", in (11) the quatrain tends to decompose into its parts: two symmetrical sub-units, two couplets; and if the quatrain can be said to close with a "click", it is each of its two couplets that closes with such a "click".

The simplicity of the couplets is considerable in (11); what is more, they constitute a larger unit, divided into two parts with identical structures; as a result, they clearly stand out in perception, as two semi-independent units. This is not so in (10). Here, the smallest unit that may recur with regularity is the whole stanza. The third line, which is not part of any rhyme, is perceived in the quatrain as one that weakens the simplicity of the parts, and so increases their dependence on the whole.

How does the perceived effect differ in each of the two versions? Intuitively, the original version is wittier, more conclusive, than the transcribed version. The foregoing analysis may account for this perceptual difference. The key-term is **Poetic Closure.** Herrnstein-Smith distinguishes between structural and thematic closural devices. I have just considered an effective structural closural device in the original version; as for thematic closural devices, I shall have recourse in this chapter only to one viz., **closural allusion,** explained in the following two quotations: "The most casual survey of the concluding lines of any group of poems will reveal that in a considerable number of them there are words and phrases such as 'last', 'finished', 'end', 'rest', 'peace', or 'no more', which, while they do not refer to the conclusion of the poem itself, nevertheless signify termination or stability" (Herrnstein-Smith, 1968: 172). There is another, similar form of **closural allusion:** "references not to termination, finality, repose, or stability as such, but to events which, in our non-literary experiences, are associated with these qualities—events such as sleep, death, dusk, night, autumn, winter, descents, falls, leave-takings and home-comings" (ibid., 175–176).

If we now consider the two versions of Omar Khayyám's Rubáiyáth, we find in both two aspects of closural allusion: **going away,** and furthermore, going away as a metaphor for death. The source of the perceptual difference between the two versions is that in excerpt (10), the recurrence, the **return,** causes the poem to close with "a click", so as to impose maximum unity and coherence upon the reader's experiencing of the poem. Line 3 is perceived as disturbing the rhyme pattern; the return in line 4 to the established rhyme arouses a sense of gratification, of home-coming. This quality joins forces with the thematic element to render the closural allusion more effective. In excerpt (11), by contrast, the rhyming end of the fourth line generates a structural closure for the couplet only, disturbing, as a corollary, the perceptual integrity of the whole quatrain. Hence the wittier and more conclusive character of excerpt (10).

Let us consider now a second altered version of the same Rubáiyáth:

> (12)   Think, in this battered Caravanserai
> Whose Portals are alternate Night and Day,
> How Sultán after Sultán came to stay,
> Abode his destined Hour, and went his way.

When one element or one pattern is repeated without sufficient variation, says Meyer, there arises a feeling of **saturation.** "Our normal expectation is of progressive change and growth. A figure which is repeated over and over again arouses a strong expectation of change both because continuation is inhibited and because the figure is not allowed to reach completion" (Meyer, 1956: 135). And again, "If repetition is fairly exact and persistent, change rather than further repetition is expected, i.e., saturation sets in" (ibid,. 152). Herrnstein-Smith relates the emotive effect of saturation to boredom and fatigue (1968: 75).

When we contrast the impression made by excerpt (12) to that made by (10), there is a noticeable feeling of **saturation** arising from the four lines ending with the same rhyme. The source of unity in the two versions is of different kinds. The key-terms for the distinction between them are **grouping** and **differentiation.** The unchanging repetition of one rhyme in four or more lines is perceived as a homogeneous sequence, lacking sufficient differentiation. This kind of unity is relatively unstructured: its effect is mainly through accumulation. The original Rubáiyáth, with the initial symmetrical couplet-pattern, followed by the third, "deviant" line, while the fourth line "returns" to the rhyme established at the beginning, constitutes a coherent **structure,** imposing **unity** upon the sequence. We may adapt to the issue in hand Meyer's discussion of a slightly different issue:

> It is this creation of a larger rhythmic unit that gives the total phrase its over-all rhythmic form. For just as a series of beats which are equal both in

accent and duration will not give rise to an impression of rhythm (except in so far as the mind imposes its own arbitrary differentiation upon the stimuli) so, too, the smaller rhythmic groups will not give rise to larger patterns unless differentiation of accent or duration is present. (1956: 111)

There is no differentiation within the sequence of four lines ending in the same rhyme; any organization of the lines into groups originates either in the syntactic structure, or in the listener's mind imposing its own arbitrary differentiation upon them. In this respect, it is the third, "deviant" line in the Rubáiyáth that generates differences and distinctions, and through them—grouping and structure.[3]

The gestalt Laws discussed so far may explain some of the general differentiating features of the **sonnet**. And, more specifically, the Law of Good Continuation and the Law of Return may account for some of the differences between the Italian and the English sonnet. In our discussion of Omar Khayyám's Rubáiyáth, along with its various alterations, I have pointed out that these two laws impose different characteristics upon different strophic organizations, each of them being considered as "good" perceptual organization under the relevant law. With regard to the present issue, the organizing effect of the quatrain in the English sonnet is typically accounted for by the Law of Good Continuation, whereas the organizing effect of the quatrain that constitutes the octet of the Italian sonnet is typically accounted for by the Law of Return.

The English sonnet form comprises four units: three quatrains with an *abab* rhyme scheme each, followed by a couplet. Above, we have discussed this form at some length. At the higher level, it consists of two symmetrical groups of two lines, the second group constituting a "good continuation" of the first one. The second and third stanzas have the same structure, each constituting a "good continuation" of the preceding one. The concluding couplet seals the sonnet with an epigrammatic sharp ending that serves as a powerful closure, for two different reasons: first, it instantiates the principle I have quoted from Herrnstein-Smith: "One of the most effective ways to indicate the conclusion of a poem generated by an indefinitely extensible principle is simply to modify that principle at the end of the poem"; second, the couplet has a stronger shape than the quatrain. Sometimes the effectiveness of such a closure is further increased, and to a considerable degree, by weakening the closure of the last unit but one (we have encountered this device in Pope's couplet art). Consider the following sonnet by Michael Drayton:

(13)   *Farewell to Love*
Since there's no help, come let us kiss and part;
Nay I have done, you get no more of me;
And I am glad, yea, glad, with all my heart,
That thus so cleanly I myself can free;

---

[3]   Excerpts (10), (11), and (12) are discussed from an experimental point of view elsewhere (Tsur, Glicksohn, & Goodblatt, 1990; 1991; see now Tsur, 2006: 115–141).

Shake hands for ever, cancel all our vows,
And when we meet at any time again,
Be it not seen in either of our brows
That we one jot of former love retain.
Now at the last gasp of loves latest breath,
When his pulse failing, passion speechless lies,
When faith is kneeling by his bed of death,
And innocence is closing up his eyes,
      Now if thou would'st, when all have given him over,
      From death to life thou might'st him yet recover.

Ignoring important issues of segmentation in the poem, let us consider the effect of run-on sentences on the closure, or lack of closure, of the units. The first two lines are end-stopped. In the third and fourth line there is a mild enjambement, just enough to impose a slight weakening on the end of the third line, increasing the *requiredness* of the fourth line and, by the same token, the closure of the quatrain. In the second quatrain the same principle is repeated, but with a slight amplification. Only the first line of this quatrain is end-stopped, and the ensuing compound sentence expands over three lines strengthening, again, the closure of the quatrain. The next six lines have a peculiar structure. The function of the anaphoric *Now* at the beginning of the third quatrain and of the closing couplet is to tie together a series of subordinate clauses in the quatrain, and open up a subordinate clause of a different kind; each of these clauses heralding, with increasing vigor, the main clause of a very long and complex sentence. At the end of each line of the third quatrain, an adverbial (temporal) clause ends; thus, every line is clearly *articulated*, but the closure of the quatrain is considerably weakened by the compound sentence run on to the couplet. Thus, the couplet achieves a high degree of requiredness. Two short subordinate clauses in the first line of the couplet delay the main clause even further; and a mild inversion within the main clause further delays its subject and predicate. Thus, the ending of the stanza before the couplet and that of the first line of the couplet, as well as the first hemistich of the second line of the couplet are considerably weakened by syntactical means, enormously amplifying the force of the closure. This poignant closure lends exceptional force to the punch-line of the surprise ending.

The effects of some of the principles used in the last six lines of this sonnet (as pointed out here) are further amplified in the following sonnet by Keats:

(14)   When I have fears that I may cease to be
       Before my pen has gleaned my teeming brain,
       Before high-pilèd books, in charactery,
       Hold like rich garners the full-ripened grain;
       When I behold, upon the night's starred face
       Huge cloudy symbols of a high romance,

> And think that I may never live to trace
> Their shadows, with the magic hand of chance,
> And when I feel, fair creature of an hour!
> That I shall never look upon thee more,
> Never have relish in the faery power
> Of unreflecting love! — then on the shore
>   Of the wide world I stand alone, and think
>   Till love and fame to nothingness do sink.

I wish to point here out only two relevant issues. First, one complex sentence runs from the first word of the sonnet to its last. Each quatrain begins with the conjunction *When,* heralding a temporal clause, in fact a series of co-ordinate temporal clauses. By the same token, they herald the co-ordinate main clauses in the couplet. Second, also in this poem, we have a temporal adverb *(then)* referring back to the temporal conjunctions, the function of which, again, is to tie together a series of subordinate clauses in the quatrains with the clauses of the couplet. The ending of the last quatrain, however, is most drastically weakened by the fact that its last clause ends in the middle of line twelve, where the main clause of the couplet begins, with an adverb of place that cannot be related in any way to the preceding context. In this way, the shape of the third quatrain is weakened to an extreme degree; it is made dependent on, and integrated with its context. By the same token, the requiredness and closural force of the couplet is heightened to an unusual degree.

This device of beginning a main clause or independent clause situated in the final couplet with a "loose end" stretching back into the preceding twelfth line is not uncommon in Donne's "Holy Sonnets", as in the following two instances:

(15)   Let their flames retire,
         And burn me ô Lord, with a fiery zeal
         Of thee and thy house, which doth in eating heal.
                                        ("Holy Sonnet 5")

(16)   here on this lowly ground,
         Teach me how to repent; for that's as good
         As if thou'hadst seal'd my pardon, with thy blood.
                                        ("Holy Sonnet 7")

As I suggested above, the perceptual organization of the Italian sonnet's quatrains is governed by the Law of Return. Let us have a look at the octet of Keats's "On Sitting down to Read 'King Lear' Once Again":

(17)   O golden-tongued romance with serene lute!
         Fair-plumèd Syren, Queen of far-away!
         Leave melodizing on this wintry day,

Shut up thine olden pages, and be mute:
Adieu! for, once again, the fierce dispute
Betwixt damnation and impassioned clay
Must I burn through; once more humbly assay
The bitter-sweet of this Shakespearian fruit:

Here, too, we find a symmetrical organization, as well as a sense of satisfaction or relief when the symmetrical unit is completed. But here, the principle that governs the process is the Law of Return. The first line of this sonnet ends with the rhyme-word *lute*. Any expectation for a couplet, according to the Law of Good Continuation, will be refuted by the rhyme phrase *far-away;* and any expectation for "good continuation" of the *abab* kind is refuted again, by a second *b*-rhyme, *day.* Consequently, a feeling of relief is generated with the occurrence of the rhyme word *mute.* This sense of relief arises as a result of the "good return" to the first line, after a double refutation of the expectation of "good continuation". This stanza, too, may be divided into two symmetrical halves, but its second half is not a "good continuation" of its first half but rather its mirror-image. In this way, a more vigorous closure is obtained than in a stanza with alternating rhymes. This difference of effect can be described in another way, too. The alternating rhyme generates two halves of identical structure in the quatrain: their structure is relatively "simple", they tend to stand out clearly, as relatively independent entities. In the Italian sonnet's quatrain, by contrast, no parts of identical structures are generated; therefore, the whole quatrain tends to be perceived as relatively more unified, more stable. The "Law of Good Continuation" is operative when this structure is repeated in the second quatrain.

All this holds true of the isolated quatrains. But one of the important distinctive features of the Italian sonnet is, precisely, that slight syntactic deviations may totally change the perceptual grouping of lines. Let us have a passing look at the octet of Wordsworth's Westminster Bridge sonnet:

(18)   *Composed upon Westminster Bridge,*
              September 3, 1802
        Earth has not anything to show more fair:
        Dull would he be of soul who could pass by
        A sight so touching in its majesty:
        This City now doth, like a garment, wear
        The beauty of the morning; silent, bare,
        Ships, towers, domes, theatres, and temples lie
        Open unto the fields, and to the sky;
        All bright and glittering in the smokeless air.
        Never did sun more beautifully steep
        In his first splendour, valley, rock, or hill;
        Ne'er saw I, never felt, a calm so deep!

> The river glideth at his own sweet will:
> Dear God! the very houses seem asleep;
> And all that mighty heart is lying still!

Although this sonnet conforms with the severe rules of rhyming of the Italian sonnet, the syntactic grouping makes us perceive three couplets in the middle of the octet, such that the classical octet structure is "backgrounded". In Keats's Elgin-Marbles Sonnet (the first five lines of which are quoted in Chapter 15 as excerpt (9)), the rhyme pattern is even more complex: the first line of the second quatrain is emphatically grouped by syntax with the first quatrain:

(19)   My spirit is too weak—mortality
        Weighs heavily on me like unwilling sleep,
        And each imagined pinnacle and steep
        Of godlike hardship, tells me I must die
        Like a sick eagle looking at the sky.

As a result, the simple symmetrical patterns of the poem are blatantly violated by the rhyme. In the last six lines of the octet, two asymmetrical rhyme groups are obtained, in a most complex manner: *baa bba*—and all this, without violating the basic rhyme pattern of the octet. In other sonnets, the fifth line converges with an independent clause, thus being "ambiguous" with respect to perceptual grouping: it may be grouped with the preceding or the subsequent lines. In still other instances, a similar quatrain may be "straddled" between the two quatrains, thus: *ab baab ba.*

We may sum up, therefore, the potential inherent in the octet of the Italian sonnet as follows. In some instances, when syntactic organization supports it, the Law of Return governs the perceptual organization by quatrain, and generates a closure with a fairly vigorous "click". In other instances, when syntactic organization deviates only slightly from the needs of the quatrain, the tight grouping may easily fall apart and produce stable couplet patterns or, on the contrary, near-chaotic clusters of lines. In such instances, good gestalts of isolated lines or of groups of rhyming lines blur each other. The Italian sonnet's octet, then, carries both the potential of clear-cut, *"prägnant"* gestalt, and of "chaotic overdifferentiation", while the clear-cut, *"prägnant"* gestalt lurks in the background, and prevents the text from falling into utter chaos. In the former case, the strophic organization is apt to "punctuate" or emphasize the shape of the sequence of stimuli, thus organizing the stream of information into clear-cut shapes. In the latter case, the strophic organization is only dimly perceived, in the back of one's mind, and arouses a feeling that what is perceived as a chaotic mass of rhymed verse lines is characterized, in spite of all, by some more than usual order: "The *Hidden* Order of Art".

Let us consider now the perceptual structure of the sestet in the Italian sonnet. Some critics claim that the sestet increases the conciseness of expression, because two stanzas of four lines each are followed by two stanzas of three lines each. Such a claim appears somewhat naïve, since conciseness of expression cannot be determined by the number of prosodic units, but only by the amount of information per unit. The less predictable a certain unit, the greater the information it carries; the more predictable a unit, the smaller the information it carries; an obligatory element would carry no information at all (in English, for instance, every q is followed by a $u,$ the latter thus being completely predictable). The mere possibility of alternative rhyme patterns diminishes the predictability of some rhyme at a certain place in the sestet.

The sestet will contrast to the octet in an additional respect. The octet allows to organize lines by rhymes into symmetrical perceptual units. The octet may be divided into two identical quatrains, and each quatrain, in turn, may be divided into two symmetrical halves, whether this symmetry is based on "alternating" or "chiastic" rhymes. Even the "semi-stanza" is divided into two symmetrical halves of two lines (that do not rhyme with each other). By contrast, the basic unit of the sestet consists of three subunits that *ab ovo* cannot be divided into two symmetrical halves. Thus, whereas the smallest complete symmetrical unit in the octet is the quatrain, in the sestet, the smallest complete symmetrical unit is the combination of the two three-lines-long stanzas, whether their rhyme scheme is *ccd eed,* or *cde cde.* Furthermore, there are rhyme patterns in the sestet in which, eventually, the lines cannot be grouped into any symmetrical structure, as, for instance, *cdc dcd,* or *ccd ede.* Here, the perceiver must be content if no loose ends are left, and give up any claim to symmetry.

Consider now this *cdc dcd* structure in, e.g., the sestet of the Westminster-Bridge Sonnet. One alternative way to handle it would be to view its first four lines as a closed quatrain (*cdcd*). If so perceived, the last two lines compel the reader to "reopen" the already closed gestalt. Such an unsettling ending may induce the reader to perceptually restructure the sequence into groups of two lines (*cd*) which, in turn can be indefinitely repeated, yielding "good continuation" instead of frustrated closure. This would require to effect closure by different means. How does the poem suggest, then, that the indefinitely repeatable sequence *is* terminated? The last-but-one line introduces a strong closural element by the exclamation expressing a sudden recognition (as if the whole poem were meant to lead up to this recognition. But the next line suggests a continuing state that constitutes an anti-closure or even anticlimax. The ambiguity of "still" reinforces this effect: it may mean here "without motion, calm", or serve as a function word indicating the continuance of a condition.

For many poets, the sonnet form is a rigid mold, designed to impose a stable shape on whatever they may have to say. Alternatively, one might put it thus: in some poems the sonnet form is obvious, subsuming and organizing whatever complexities there may be at lower ranks. The ends of stanzas and, to a lesser extent, of lines, are usually reinforced by converging with some kind of syntactic juncture. In other poets such as Milton or some Romantics, this vigorous shape is notoriously "backgrounded". Milton was one of the first poets who, after a general flurry of "English Sonnets", returned to the Italian sonnet with its more strictly controlled rhyme-scheme. I have mentioned earlier that there was a potential ambiguity in the octet of this sonnet form, and Milton was one of the few poets who fully exploited it by the divergent grouping of lines through syntax. Milton, in fact, blurs not only the line terminals by run-on sentences, but also the boundaries between stanzas (quatrains or tercets), and even between the octet and the sestet.[4]

Perceptual Forces and Prosodic Boundaries

The term *Perceptual Force* is borrowed from gestalt psychology; the force is supposed to be inherent in both visual and aural perception. The existence of perceptual forces is most conspicuous in visual perception and this is the domain primarily explored by gestalt psychologists. At the beginning of his 1967 book, Arnheim demonstrates "the hidden structure of a square" by placing a black cardboard disk in various positions on a white square. Thus he "maps out" regions of tension and of balance. In figure 5.1, the disk lies slightly off the centre. "In looking at the disk we may find that it does not merely occupy a certain place but exhibits restlessness. This restlessness may be experienced as a tendency of the disk to get away from where it is placed or, more specifically, as a pull in a particular direction—for example, toward the center" (Arnheim, 1967: 2).

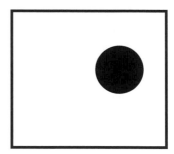

Figure 5.1   *Figure 5.2*

Psychologically, the pulls in the disk exist in the experience of any person who looks at it. Since these pulls have a point of attack, a direction and an intensity, they meet the conditions established by physicists for physical forces (ibid., 6).

---

[4]   I have elsewhere discussed at great length the unusual complexities of the sestet and the preceding enjambement in Milton's "On his Blindness" (Tsur, 1977: 203–207). Although this sonnet has the solid "skeleton" of an Italian sonnet, this structure is only vaguely discernible in the background, so to speak; it has the perceptual shape of ever-increasing fluidity, finally "dammed" by a strong closure (for a discussion of the perceptual mechanism underlying such structures, see below at the end of Chapter 20).

Although perceptual forces are not physical in the sense that gravity is, "there is no point in calling these forces 'illusions'. They are no more illusory than colors, which are attributed to the objects themselves, although they are actually nothing but the reactions of the nervous system to light of particular wave lengths" (ibid., 8).

The skeptical reader may object: "Let us grant that these 'perceptual forces' do exist in visual patterns (or even in musical patterns). But verbal expression may be quite different. It introduces referential meaning through an arbitrary system of linguistic structures. How can we know that your 'perceptual forces' survive in such a complex system, too?" It is difficult to give a conclusive answer to this objection. It is a most commendable and wise precaution in any inquiry not to take anything for granted. However, when pursued to the extreme, this principle may be crippling. Mentalist approaches to art are particularly vulnerable to such skepticism, since we know very little about the mental processes involved. Since in literary criticism it is hardly possible to go beyond the accumulation of unrelated facts without appealing, to some extent, to the critic's intuitive perceptions or to a theoretical framework, or to both, I shall make a brief attempt to meet the above objection by referring to psychological experiments by way of testing the notion of constituent or phrase structure of sentences, performed by Fodor, Bever and Garret at MIT.

> These researchers devised an ingenious technique for revealing the presence of phrase boundaries in the perception of sentences. The technique is based on the Gestalt assumption that a perceptual unit tends "to preserve its integrity by resisting interruptions" (Fodor and Bever, 1965: 415). In the experiment of Fodor and Bever, subjects listened to a sentence during which a click occurred, and immediately afterward were required to write down the sentence and indicate where the click had occurred. If a phrase is a perceptual unit, subjects should tend to hear a click which occurred during a phrase as having occurred between the phrases.
>
> One of their sentences was "That he was happy was evident from the way he smiled". This sentence has a major break between "happy" and "was". A click was placed at various positions in this sentence. [...] Each subject heard the sentence with only one click on it.
>
> Fodor and Bever found that subjects were most accurate in locating the click which occurred between the two major phrases of the sentence—i.e., between "happy" and "was" in the above example. Clicks occurring before this break tended to be displaced towards the right (i.e., into the break), and those occurring after the break towards the left (i.e., again into the break). Fodor and Bever conclude that their findings "appear to demonstrate that the major syntactic break plays an important role in determining the subjective location of noises perceived during speech", thus supporting the hypothesis that "the unit of speech perception corresponds to the constituent". One might call these results into question on the suspicion that the major syn-

tactic break is signalled by some acoustic means, such as pause. In additional research, however, Garret, Bever and Fodor (1966) have demonstrated that there are no clear acoustic cues that mark the breaks between constituent phrases. The most dramatic evidence of this surprising fact comes from an experiment comparing pairs of sentences such as:

(1)   As a result of their invention's *influence the company was given an award.*   *   *

(2)   The chairman whose methods still *influence the company was given an award.*   *   *

When subjects were asked where they hear the longest pause in the sentences, they report—as one might expect—that they hear a pause in (1) between "influence" and "the", and in (2) between "company" and "was". The perceived pause thus corresponds to the major constituent boundaries in the two sentences.

The ingenious part of the experiment comes next. The two sentences were recorded on tape, and the two italicized segments were interchanged. [...] *Subjects' perception of pause location, however, was unchanged.* The same was true of click displacement. As indicated by asterisks in the two sentences above, a click occurred either during "company" or "was". The perception of click location, however, was significantly different for the two sentences. The click in sentence (1) tended to be heard between "influence" and "the", and in (2) between "company" and "was". But remember the sentences were acoustically identical (Slobin, 1971: 25–26; italics in original).

To our present purpose, these results have two important implications: first, that perceptual forces do exist in a linguistic environment; second, perceptual forces in a linguistic environment are crucially influenced by the intruding event's coincidence with, or distance from, the boundary of the perceptual unit. In prosody, however, there is a further complication. One cannot elicit perceptual forces with the help of some extra-linguistic click. In poetry, the exponents of both the intruding and the disrupted events are words; the *same* words. To begin with a little-known phenomenon, in recent years I came across a perceptual force that pushes a minute-scale intruding event toward the boundary of a small-scale perceptual unit: "late peaking"—that is, when the peak of the intonation contour hits the vowel of a stressed syllable not in the middle, but between the middle and the end. This perceptual phenomenon is most effective in the oral performance of poetry (see Figure 6.2 next chapter).

The immediately observable exponents of all the perceptual units in poetry are, then, linguistic units. There are, however, two sets of organizational principles in poetry from which such perceptual units arise: one belongs to language, the other to versification. In one, we encounter a hierarchy of boundaries: sentence, clause, phrase, word and syllable; in the other, we encounter another hierarchy of boundaries: stanza, verse line, hemistich, and metric foot. When the major boundaries of the two sets coincide, there is a feeling of stability. When, however, they do not, the boundaries of perceptual units intrude upon each other, and perceptual forces of various intensities arise. Since, according to the gestalt assumption, a perceptual unit tends "to preserve its integrity by resisting interruptions", each one of the conflicting units will tend to reinforce itself in the reader's perception and, up to a certain point of complexity, their vividness will be heightened by the intrusion. Beyond that point, however, rather than *reinforcing* each other's shape, the two sets of perceptual units *blur* each other's shape until, eventually, a point of "cognitive overload" is reached, which the system handles by dumping the overload into an undifferentiated, gestalt-free mass. This is one way to describe the opposition between what some critics would call "sharp" and "soft focus". Furthermore, when the boundaries of the two sets of perceptual units intrude upon each other, certain, sometimes violent, perceptual forces arise: the intruding boundary is felt to be pushing toward the nearest boundary of the unit intruded upon. What is more, the nearer the intrusion to the boundary of a perceptual unit, the more strongly it "pushes" in the direction of the boundary. In the section "Articulateness and Requiredness" below, we shall have a closer look at such examples.

The majority of verse lines that contain eight positions or more are segmented into roughly two halves by a boundary called "caesura". I have elsewhere (Tsur, 1977: 66–67; 1998: 113–114) come to the conclusion that certain incompatible statements of various theoreticians concerning the nature of the caesura can easily be reconciled by suggesting that the conflicting statements refer to two indispensable yet clearly distinct aspects of the same phenomenon. "Caesura *organizes* in one respect and constitutes an *opposing term* in another respect". As gestalt psychologists have insisted time and again, segmentation may facilitate the perception of a complex whole. On the other hand, there is a "required sense of metrical impulsion across the break" (Levin, 1971: 185). The opposing term *intrudes,* and elicits a sense of *impulsion across* it. As Miller (1970) argued in a well-known paper, the span of immediate memory is fixed around the magical number seven, plus or minus two (Hayes found empirically that with "binary items the span is about nine, and [...] it drops to about five with monosyllabic English words"; ibid., 41). As I shall argue in the next chapter, the ability to perceive a verse line as a rhythmical unit crucially depends on one's ability to complete the unit before the traces of its beginning fade from immediate memory. So, one need not be surprised too much that prosodists have found that the longest verse line that can be perceived without segmentation as rhythmical is about ten positions long.[5] This can account for the fact that in twelve positions long lines there is an *obligatory* caesura after the sixth position.

---

[5]   *Position* is the smallest unit of versification, usually corresponding to a syllable in the linguistic dimension.

Some critics call every punctuation mark within a verse line a "caesura". According to the present conception, expounded at great length elsewhere (Tsur, 1977: 66–82; 1998: 113–139), ceasura is assigned by convention at, or around, the middle of the unit of versification; it is not a syntactic boundary. What is more, in perfect harmony with one of the central tenets of the present book, this convention reflects overwhelming perceptual needs which are the main object of the present chapter.[6] One need concerns, as I have just argued, a segmentation that is demanded for the perception of lines that, as a unit, exceed the span of immediate memory. The other concerns the part-whole relationship discussed above: "The simpler the parts, the more clearly they tend to stand out as independent entities"; in many instances, ceasura is the point where the two semi-independent parts meet. Syntactic boundaries *may* confirm caesura; in other instances, they may override it, generating tension.

The middle of an iambic tetrameter line is after the fourth position; that of the iambic hexameter line, after the sixth. Caesura is assigned to the middle not linguistically, but by convention or, possibly, by simplicity of perception. Consequently, in the first line of excerpt (20) there is a deliberate feeling that the word boundary after *point* confirms something, whereas in the second line there is a deliberate feeling that the absence of word boundary after the fourth position causes syntax to override something:

(20)   One single point in this belief
         From this organization sprung
                 (Shelley, "Peter Bell the Third", 569–570)

In both lines, this "something" is *caesura*. Such lines are well within the span of immediate memory. Segmentation is forced here upon the reader by the simplicity of the parts: the line falls into two equal halves (4 + 4 positions). Thus, the line is perceived as symmetrical and stable.

Now consider the following iambic hexameter lines:

(21)   A herd-abandoned deer struck by the hunter's dart
                 (Shelley, "Adonais", 296)
(22)   Which was like Cain's or Christ's—oh! that it should be so!
                 (ibid., 306)
(23)   The silence of the hart's accepted sacrifice (ibid., 315)
(24)   While thy cold embers choke the sordid hearth of shame (ibid.,
                 342)
(25)   The caruer Holme, the Maple seeldom inward sound
                 (Spenser, *Fairie Qvene,* I. i. 5.9)

---

6   In this sense, "caesura" refers to a versification boundary that may act in harmony with, or in opposition to, syntactic boundaries, generating interesting perceptual dynamics. In the other sense, merely a learned word is substituted for a commonsense everyday phrase, "punctuation mark".

Such lines require the observation of the caesura, if they are to be perceived as rhythmical units. In (21) and (22), syntactic boundaries of various degrees unambiguously confirm caesura. In (23), the caesura occurs in the middle of a possessive phrase, after *hart's*. If one observes a clear-cut break here, syntax becomes seriously distorted. One may, however, perform the line by prolonging *hart's*, not observing a stop after the word. (Remember the click experiment which proves that the boundary of a cognitive unit *can* be perceived, even if there is no acoustic indication of its existence). In this way, a feeling is generated that there is here a caesura as well as a "required sense of impulsion across the [non-existent] break". In (25), the caesura occurs in the middle of the word *Maple;* hence it is more difficult to perform the verse line as a rhythmical unit. Still, a performance of the kind suggested for (23) is conceivable. In the iambic hexameter, then, there are two reasons for the perception of a caesura: the subdivision forced by the simplicity of parts, and the need for the segmentation of a perceptual unit that exceeds the span of immediate memory. The verse line can be perceived as rhythmical only if both the syntactic and prosodic units are established as perceptual wholes. When the boundaries of the two coincide, this is easily done. When, however, the two occur at different points of the verse line, special techniques of mental and vocal performance (see Chapters 2 and 6–7) are required. In the absence of this performance, the verse line falls apart. When, however, such performance establishes them as perceptual units, each of the latter strives to reassert itself in the reader's perception, and impetuous perceptual forces may arise.

So far, we have considered verse lines whose number of positions is divisible by four. In iambic verse, such lines are divided by caesurae into segments that have exceptionally strong shapes. The resulting segments are similar in both length and structure: have the same number of positions (four or six); and each one begins with a weak position and ends with a strong position. This is not so in the iambic pentameter: many critics have intuitively observed that it has considerably greater integrity than either the iambic tetrameter or the iambic hexameter. I claim that the present discussion may account for this intuition. On the one hand, as I have suggested, the iambic pentameter is the longest line that can be perceived as a rhythmical unit without some kind of segmentation. On the other hand, it cannot be divided into segments of equal length and equal structure. Consider the following three lines (from sonnets by Milton, Keats and Shakespeare):

(26)   When I consider // how my light was spent
(27)   When I have fears // that I may cease to be
(28)   They that have power to hurt // and will do none

A major syntactic boundary divides each one of these lines at or near the middle. In (26), it divides the line into two segments of equal length: 5 + 5; their structure, however, is unequal: the first segment begins and ends with a weak position, whereas the second segment begins and ends with a strong position. In (27) and (28), on the other hand, the two segments have similar structures: both begin with a weak position and end with a strong one. Their lengths, however, are unequal: excerpt (27) divides into 4 + 6; (28) into 6 + 4.

The foregoing discussion leads to several conclusions. First, there is no single point in the iambic pentameter line which would divide it into two equal halves. If syntactic structure does not require segmentation, the line can be perceived as an un-segmented unit, as in the following line:

(29)   Oh that this too too solid flesh would melt

Second, rather than being limited to a single point, a caesura *region* occurs in ex-panding over positions IV, V, and VI. If a relatively high syntactic boundary occurs after one of these positions, it is perceived as confirming the caesura. That is, pre-cisely, what happens in excerpts 26–28. When more syntactic boundaries than one occur in this region, the highest boundary (or the one that is not lower than the adjacent ones) is perceived as confirming the caesura. Third, the phrase "perceived as confirming the caesura" has been carefully chosen. As I have suggested, a syntactic boundary does not create, only confirms the caesura: it is the verse line's perceptual structure that determines its place. Indeed, the iambic pentameter line's perceptual structure determines the fact that in it the caesura may occur after any one of three positions. Whenever the line's perceptual structure changes, the place of the caesura may shift from one position to another. Consider the following line:

(30)   Invoke thy aid to my advent'rous song.
            (*Paradise Lost* I, 13)

In this line, the caesura occurs after *aid* in position IV. Suppose however, that we add two more syllables to the verse line, turning it into an iambic hexameter, thus:

(31)   Invoke thy aid to my advent'rous song of praise.

If one continues to observe a caesura after *aid*, (31) is liable to fall apart. Here the caesura, in harmony with the perceptual needs of the iambic hexameter, is automati-cally shifted to after *my* in position VI, even though this happens in mid-phrase. Here, exactly as in (23), a feeling is generated of a caesura as well as a "sense of im-pulsion across the [non-existent] break".

Fourth, in (27) and (28), the caesura divides the line into two segments of similar structure but unequal length. According to this description, the caesura after position IV and after position VI ought to be of a similar nature. They are not, however. It is quite frequently felt that a caesura after position VI generates greater tension than after position IV. One of the most widely held assumptions in the cognitive research of language is that when two or more co-ordinate items follow one another, the longer member comes last. Paraphrasing Cooper and Ross (1965: 92), members which are easier to process (in this case, which are shorter) tend to occupy the first place(s), enabling the listener to handle the preliminary processing of this member, while new information is still presented to him by the speaker. "There is a general tendency for the weight of syntactic structure to occur late rather than earlier in the sentence, so as to avoid strain on a person's short-term memory in the course of constructing and interpreting sentences" (Leech, 1974: 197). This would suggest that a caesura after position IV is more natural, one after position VI more "marked". If this is true, we should expect caesurae to occur significantly more frequently after position IV than after position VI. And if I am right that caesura is a perceptual rather than a linguistic phenomenon, this should be so in a variety of (perhaps, all) languages, both in syllabotonic and non-syllabotonic poetry, as well as, *mutatis mutandis,* in music.

I have assigned the caesurae, according to a procedure described elsewhere (Tsur, 1977: 72–74; 1998: 116–118), in the first one hundred lines of Shakespeare's sonnets, *Paradise Lost,* "An Essay on Criticism", and the first one hundred decasyllabic lines in *Faerie Qvene* and "Adonais". The following table shows the number of lines in which caesurae occur after the fourth, fifth, or sixth position; "double" indicates lines in which two approximately equal major syntactic boundaries occur within the region of balance (which is not the same as indeterminacy). The difference between "total" and 100, in each poet, indicates the number of lines in which either syntax overrides caesura, or the assignment of caesura would have reflected personal inclination rather than an objectively assigned property of the line.

Table 5.1   The relative frequency of the placement of caesurae after positions IV, V, VI in five English poets

	Shakespeare	Milton	Pope	Spenser	Shelley
after IV	33	25	42	47	39
after V	32	24	32	18	15
after VI	14	23	9	27	18
double	1	1	6	=	1
total	80	73	89	92	73

All the poets examined have more lines in which the caesura occurs after the fourth position than after the sixth. Pope has almost five times as many, Shakespeare and Shelley only somewhat over twice as many, and Spenser somewhat less than twice as many. The exception in this context is Milton; there is no significant difference in the number of caesurae after positions IV, V and VI. We have to conclude, then, that the unmarked form is, beyond doubt, the caesura after position IV. In Chapter 4, I have distinguished between convergent and divergent poetry. We have found that in Milton's divergent poetry, contrasts were typically blurred (as, for instance, by stressed syllables in weak positions and unstressed ones in strong positions, and by divergent patterns of alliteration). Elsewhere (Tsur, 1977; 1998), I have shown that the divergent effect of Milton's poetry cannot be accounted for merely by the *number* of deviating stresses, but only by his having recourse to the marked options in a wide range of versification devices, of which stressed syllables in weak positions are only one and marked caesura appears to be another. By essentially the same procedure, I have assigned the caesurae to a random number of iambic pentameter lines by three Hebrew and two Hungarian poets (ibid., 82):

Table 5.2   The relative frequency of the placement of caesurae after positions IV, V, VI in three Hebrew and two Hungarian poets

	Shlonsky	Goldberg	Halkin	József	Tóth
after IV	54	123	13	28	30
after V	—	25	4	51	34
after VI	2	76	11	14	10
double	4	9	1	3	3
other	=	5	3	2	3
total	60	238	32	98	80

The same tendency is visible in some decasyllabic verse outside syllabotonic meter. In French syllabic poetry, decasyllabic lines are relatively rare. I have checked two of Villon's ballades (65 lines), and all the decasyllabic poems in Baudelaire's *Les Fleurs du Mal* (94 lines). The overwhelming majority of caesurae in these poems occurs after position IV (49 in Villon, and 64 in Baudelaire).

Articulateness and Requiredness

I have already briefly mentioned these two terms. In the present section, I propose to explore some of their further implications. *Articulateness* and *Requiredness* are two sides of the same coin; they are aspects of breaking up a whole into segments. When we speak of articulateness, we imply that a whole has been broken into parts, and that this facilitates perception of the whole. When we speak of Requiredness, we imply that each part is essential to the whole: when a part is missing, there is an acute feeling of incompleteness, of imbalance. Articulateness and requiredness depend on the relative strength of the whole. Requiredness is possible only where the whole is highly organized. If the integrity of the whole is not felt, deficiency cannot be felt either.

I mentioned above that according to the gestalt assumption, a perceptual unit tends "to preserve its integrity by resisting interruptions": each of two conflicting units will tend to reinforce itself in the reader's perception. The articulation of a perceptual unit suggests its interruption. Thus, articulation enhances requiredness in cases when the whole is strongly organized; at the same time, it also creates a need to reassert the integrity of this whole. The weaker the organization of the whole, the weaker the impact of requiredness. At the same time, the role played by articulation in perception increases and may become all-important. In a word, the smaller the relative strength of the whole, the more the emphasis shifts from the requiredness aspect of segmentation to its articulateness aspect.

Articulateness in poetry involves a *double entendre*. The word refers to both the idea of "clear, distinct", and the idea of "jointed". Pope is a highly articulate poet (in the sense that his long poems are segmented into well-shaped couplets and these again into lines and their subordinate iambic feet):

> (32)   Some foreign writers, some our own despise,
> The ancients only, or the moderns, prize.

The reader perceives here a distinct quality of wit, which seems to depend on the segmentation of the utterance. We do not perceive the whole as an undifferentiated lump of words, but break it up into small, easily perceptible units. There is a clearly defined couplet, which consists of clearly defined lines which are broken up into phrases. In the present example, the sentence converges with the couplet, the clauses reinforce the lines; in the first line, the break between the two phrases comes exactly at the middle. There is a similar break after the sixth syllable of the second line, but there is an additional, less expected break after the ninth syllable. At the same time, we can observe the requiredness of the last segment ("prize") in the second line, by trying to omit it. An exceptionally strong feeling of deficiency, of imbalance will follow.

"There is a rule", says Arnheim, "that the expression conveyed by any visual form will be only as clear-cut as the perceptual features that carry it" (Arnheim, 1957: 153). This seems true of poetic forms too and, certainly, of the sharp witty expression of the couplet in (32). But what happens in cases where the overall impression is not sharp and witty, but rather fuzzy and emotional? How can an utterance be both clear-cut and fuzzy? Let us take an example, which I shall later discuss in more detail. The following clause occurs in Shelley's "Ode to the West Wind": "...until thine azure sister of the Spring shall blow her clarion o'er the dreaming earth". This clause is rather long. The reader may wish to articulate it by breaking it up into several intonation contours while performing it. When articulated as prose, the boundary between the intonation contours is arbitrary, likely to vary from reading to reading, carrying as little significance as possible. When the overall articulation thus is ambiguous, the realization of the iambics is likewise doubtful. For poetic rhythm to arise, at least two levels of clear-cut shapes are required: a superordinate shape to be divided, and a series of subordinate shapes to divide into. When the text is broken up into lines, the grouping points are, so to speak, controlled by the text, and the reader can more easily realize the smaller-scale units, the iambic feet which, thus, further segment the utterance. The following is one possibility (adapted from Shelley):

> (33)   Until thine azure sister of the Spring
> Shall blow her clarion o'er the dreaming earth...

The superordinate shapes (the lines) are here unsegmented and, consequently, rigidly stable. Let us compare it to the version Shelley actually wrote:

(34)   until
      Thine azure sister of the Spring shall blow
      Her clarion o'er the dreaming earth ...

In both versions, the iambic metre is clearly actualized. Yet, notice that in (33), the reader is less aware of the separateness of the line and the clause; they converge to a large degree. By contrast, (34) is both fuzzier and more segmented: the clause is distributed between three lines, which are parts of two terzinas. The line-ending and the terzina-ending (after "until" and "blow") break up two of the three lines involved into smaller segments. At the same time, the run-on clause "blunts" the edges of the line and the terzina. Therefore, the iambic foot carries a greater burden of unification in (34). Thus, while our altered version creates a rigid mold in which the clause has to solidify, Shelley's own version is kept fluid. It retains some of its shapelessness (it threatens, so to speak, to escape back to chaos). The already fixed shapes (line, terzina) break up Shelley's version, but not at points where a rest is possible (after a conjunction, and between a verb and its idiomatically required direct object, respectively). The end of the clause breaks up the line, again at a point where rest is impossible. Articulation brings the utterance within the horizon of shape, close enough to make the reader *wish* for shape. But this shape is not stable enough: the reader still feels urged to reach some stable point of rest. Hence the feeling of fluidity.

When the syntactic unit (phrase, clause) does not converge with the line, it may, then, give rise to one of two opposite tendencies. The shape of the line may be blurred, or a tension between the syntactic and prosodic units may be generated. In the latter case, both syntactic and prosodic units "strive" to establish themselves in the reader's perception. So, in case of divergence, we may witness that the line is perceived as sharper than usual. If divergence goes beyond a certain point, the various shapes "lose control" and begin to fade into one another.

It would be to our advantage if we could say something more precise about the conditions in which the shapes tend to reinforce themselves and in which they tend to fade into one another. Let us consider a minimal pair, of a couplet from Pope's *The Rape of the Lock,* and an altered version with a different word order:

(35)   Now Lapdogs give themselves the rouzing Shake,
      And sleepless Lovers, just at Twelve, awake.

(36)   Now Lapdogs give themselves the rouzing Shake,
      And, just at Twelve, the sleepless Lovers wake.

The difference between the two versions seems rather slight. Still, (35) appears to be wittier. One of the salient reasons seems to be the difference in the place of the syntactic breaks. In (35), "And sleepless Lovers, just at Twelve" urgently *requires* completion. In Chapter 2, we have mentioned "leveling and sharpening". If figures that slightly deviate from symmetric patterns are presented under conditions that keep the stimulus control weak enough to leave the observer with a margin of freedom, some will perfect the symmetry of the model, whereas others will exaggerate the asymmetry so as to eliminate the uneasy feeling of ambiguity. The nearer to the end the break occurs, the greater our relief when the missing part is supplied. A break after the seventh, eighth, or ninth syllable generates increasingly greater tension, so that in (35), above, "awake" is highly required, and its occurrence is experienced as sudden relief—as wit. In the following couplet from the same poem, there is little that can account for the sharp wit of the second line, with the exception of the requiredness of the last phrase:

(37)   With earnest Eyes, with round unthinking Face,
         He first the Snuff-box open'd, then the Case.

Here the *requiredness* of the phrase, reinforced by the rhetoric scheme "first … then…", is due to the major syntactic break after position VII. This will be apparent if we compare Pope's to an antonymous phrase: "He first the Snuff-box closed, and then the Case"; or, to preserve the asyndeton, "He first the Snuff-box closed, at last the Case". Divergence of prosodic and syntactic units may exceed the single line. Enjambement is rather infrequent in Pope's poetry. But when he resorts to it, it serves to enhance the sharpness of the couplet rather than blunt it. Consider the following couplet, for instance:

(38)   For Spirits, freed from mortal Laws, with ease
         Assume what Sexes and what Shapes they please.

"With ease" is highly required to establish a strong line, with a sharp, closed shape. This line, however, achieves no closure. The clause runs on to the next line. Far from being blunted, the couplet "seeks" to establish and enhance itself. That is, distortion of symmetry and enjambement in the first line renders the second line of the couplet more required in order to yield a closed, stable shape. The closure of the couplet is reinforced by the parallelism and massive symmetry of the two phrases in the second line. In fact, we have got here a more extreme version of a closural principle earlier encountered. In excerpts (3), (4) and (5), above, we observed how Pope inverts word order in order to weaken the closure of the first line of the couplet, to make it more dependent on the whole and enhance the closure at the end of the couplet. Even more obviously we have observed in excerpts (14), (15) and (16) that the sentences may run on from the last quatrain to the couplet of a sonnet, to achieve a similar closural effect.

A major syntactic boundary near the beginning of a line generates usually tension *after* an enjambement. Compare, for instance, the tension generated by the boundary in the second line of excerpt (39), with the relative lack of tension after "Spirits" in excerpt (38):

> (39)   The Sprights in fiery Tergamants in Flame
>   Mount up, and take a Salamander's Name.

The incompleteness of syntax (the lack of verb) in the first line is apparently relevant to *requiredness* here. But note that tension diminishes when we alter the second line, without changing the first one:

> (40)   The Sprights in fiery Tergamants in Flame
>   Have mounted up, and take a Fairy's Name.

In the iambic tetrameter, too, the run-on sentence may generate tension when it stops before the fourth position (or, for that matter, when it breaks the line near the end). Compare the second line of the stanzas in excerpts (41) and (42), from Tennyson's *In Memoriam:*

> (41)   With trembling fingers did we weave
>   The holly round the Christmas hearth;
>   A rainy cloud possess'd the earth,
>   And sadly fell our Christmas-eve. (XXX)

> (42)   To-night ungather'd let us leave
>   This laurel, let this holly stand;
>   We live within the stranger's land,
>   And strangely falls our Christmas-eve. (CV)

Leaving rhymed verse behind, it is Browning whose blank verse sounds sharper and wittier than that of any other poet. I shall discuss here only one passage, from "Mr. Sludge, the Medium" (I have discussed some additional ones in Tsur, 1972):

> (43)   "D'ye think the sound, the nicely balanced man
>   "Like me"—(aside)—"like you yourself"—(aloud)
>   "He's stuff to make a 'medium'? Bless your soul,
>   "'Tis these hysteric, hybrid half-and-halfs,
>   "Equivocal, worthless vermine yield the fire! ...

The five lines contain only two, highly complex sentences. Yet, it should be noticed that the passage is exceedingly well articulated. At the end of each line a fairly defined phrase ends. The first line is the only one that ends with no punctuation mark or parenthesis. But a phrase of six syllables does little to resist a break after it; rather, the break helps to "articulate" the phrase. High tension, however, is generated in this case by the syntactic break after the two syllables "like me". The point seems to be that the line-endings are clear-cut, whereas the alternating phrases both break the lines up into pieces and reinforce their clear separateness as established units. The second line has everything needed for stable balance, with a break after the fourth syllable, reinforced by an antithesis ("aside-aloud"). The parentheses, however, stand out so markedly that the reader has no choice but to make significant breaks after the second, fourth, and eighth syllables, generating exceptionally high tension. In spite of this, reinforced by the symmetric balance, the line "withstands" pressure, exhibiting great strength of shape, so to speak, so that there should arise no ambiguous feeling whether the line is or is not a distinct unit. As a result, the shape of the poetic line is perceived more sharply than usual, and, at the same time, the alternating phrases make the passage sound more colloquial than usual. Browning not only breaks up his lines into as many phrases as possible but, more than that, he has a predilection for marking off the phrases from one another as clearly as possible. Vocatives, parentheses, and interjections are marked off by longer pauses and greater 'jumps' in intonation than, say, two adjacent parallel phrases. This sharpness of prosodic and syntactic shapes interacts with the irony of the contents, reinforcing the witty quality of each.

My next three examples are versions by three different authors of the same speech. One of the most memorable instances of Gloucester's villainy *(Richard III)* is the scene in which he gets rid of Lord Hastings:

> (44)   If? thou Protector of this damned Strumpet,
> Talk'st thou to me of Ifs: Thou art a Traytor,
> Off with his head; now, by Saint Paul I sweare,
> I will not dine, vntill I see the same.

The situation has its particular wit. It is reinforced by the "sharpness" of Richard's speech which, in turn, is a corollary of the rapid shift of diverse phrases, *without violating the integrity of the line.* Notice the isolated tense "If" at the beginning of the speech, quoted from Hastings' discourse, whereas the rest is Gloucester's direct speech. The rapid shift of levels of discourse appears here in the shift from "If" to direct speech and back to the quoted "Ifs", as well as in the rapid shift from the second person to the third person, varying the direction of his address ("thou Protector", "Off with his head", "now, by Saint *Paul* ", etc.). Thus Gloucester presents the various levels of discourse in sharp split focus.

Shakespeare actually amplifies here a technique which he found in Dolman's poem in *The Mirror for Magistrates:*

> (45)   Yf, traytor quod he? playest thou with yfs and ands?
> Ile on thy body avowe it with these hands.

Notice the isolated "Yf" followed by a short vocative ("traytor"), followed by a short parenthesis ("quod he"). The quoted "yfs" and "ands" not only diversify—intensify the subdivision of—the line. They give, at the same time, rise to a bold "antigrammatic" rhyme, by rhyming a conjunction (in the plural!) with a noun. So it strengthens the closure of the rhymed couplet—heightening its sense of unity.

It will be illuminating to compare this couplet of Dolman's to Sir Thomas More's prose account of the same incident.

> (46)   What quod the protectour thou seruest me I wene with iffs and andes, I tell the thei have so done, and that I will make good on thy body traitour.

Verbally, Dolman's account does not greatly differ from More's. Still, there seems to be a perceptual difference between them. Until now we have considered phrases deviating from the line which, breaking it up into smaller units, reassert, in fact, the perceptual integrity of the prosodic unit. The present comparison highlights the other side of the coin. We have seen how shifting phrases may enhance the prosodic unit. This time we may observe how the prosodic structure imposed on the phrases in Dolman's poem renders their shift far more emphatic than in More's prose account. We may add that in Browning, too, the prosodic infra-structure makes the shifting phrases—paradoxically enough—more salient and thus more colloquial.

So far we have considered lines in which requiredness and deviation led to the establishment of firm shapes. In cases where the syntactic structure opposed the prosodic unit (either line or couplet), the contrast eventually led to the enhancement of both the syntactic and the prosodic units. The clear-cut end of the line or of the couplet resisted, so to speak, the destructive tendencies of the divergent phrase structure and reinforced, in turn, the perception of the divergence. Thus, the focus of the reader's perception is *split* between the prosodic and syntactic strings. The perceptual quality of split focus is *sharpness* to varying degrees. We frequently found this quality reinforced by other aspects of the text, such as the ironic contents, the split and integrated focus, and the divergent and convergent quality (see above, in Chapter 4).

I have earlier suggested that if divergence goes beyond a certain point, the various shapes "lose control" and begin to fade into one another. When the field of perception is split into two, the effect may be sharp and witty. When divergence is spread over a wide range, outlines begin to become less clear, transitions become smoother, the poem presents a spectrum of gradual shadings. Such a blurred texture of divergent strings may have, as we have seen, strong emotive appeal. On the semantic level, this effect may be reinforced by some emotional contents and the lack of articulate visual shapes. I propose to call the resulting shadings conclusive and suspensive tone, respectively (see above, excursus to Chapter 4).

In suspensive tone, we may find the superimposition of syntactic upon prosodic units to happen in a manner similar to that observed in instances of conclusive tone.

Here, however, the subsequent units are sometimes not as clear-cut and closed; they exert no "counter-pressure" since the pressure bursts, so to speak, through the prosodic constraints. Underlying suspensive tone, there is usually a complex structure; it requires, therefore, more extensive discussion than the conclusive tone. Such a discussion should involve considerations concerning imagery, metric deviation, a distinction between verbal and nominal style, etc. I shall try to confine myself as much as possible to the discussion of the pentameter line and the run-on sentences. First, let us 'map out' the transition area from vigorous, conclusive couplets to a 'softer', suspensive tone, through a slight alteration of Shelley's text:

(47)   ...and fill
            With living hues and odours plain and hill.

This sounds not unlike Pope's couplets discussed above. The clause begins two positions before the end of the line. It requires strong closure; the next line supplies this, creating an 'airtight' couplet. This altered, and isolated quotation could, indeed, be mistaken for Neo-classic nature poetry. More correct quotation will change this impression and show the verses to be less conclusive:

(48)   ...and fill
            (Driving sweet buds like flocks to feed in air)
            With living hues and odours plain and hill.

Whereas the couplet is the most symmetrical stanza form and hence of the strongest shape, the *terzina* is asymmetric. It remains open, a "loose end" is left, insofar as the second line raises expectations for a rhyme which are fulfilled only in the next stanza. The next stanza leaves another "loose end", tied up in a third stanza, and so forth. The *terzina* has no "self-generated" end; there is no strong sense of stable closure in it. Consequently, it can be expected to exert less vigorous resistance to the pressure of enjambement. Thus, both the syntactic and prosodic units may be blurred rather than enhanced when tension arises. In this way, a completely different quality may be generated.

By beginning the clause after the eighth position of the pentameter line, Shelley's poem generates tension. Yet, unlike what is the case in Pope, this energy does not press against the constraints of a couplet. Our attention is not split between *two* sets reinforcing each other by way of contrast. By inserting the parenthesis, the second line of the *terzina* distorts and "diverts" the mutual pressure of the otherwise binary form. It also *suspends* the flow of the argument, interrupts the course of the syntactic unit between the verb and its complements, generating some additional tension. This, in a sense, may be perceived as the last straw that breaks the shapes, turning the 'bipolar' structure into a texture of gradual shadings, so to speak. So, instead of a *split* focus, we have a fuzzy, *soft* focus. Instead of an urgent straightforward rush to the conclusion of a witty couplet, the description becomes suspensive. The patent purpose, the pressure, has been 'transfigured' into intense and 'timeless' emotive appeal. Thus, the same device of enjambement may generate two different modes of poetry: either grouped around two poles, witty, or 'blurred' in the background, divergent, emotional.

Let us further experiment with Shelley's "Ode to the West Wind". If we let the sentences converge with the lines, their endings will be more clear-cut, even if we 'abolish' the rhymes. The reader is less aware of the separateness of line and phrase, and the poem loses some of its peculiar emotive impact, and sounds "flatter":

> (49)   Until thine azure sister of the Spring
> Shall blow her clarion o'er the dreaming earth
> Driving sweet buds like flocks to feed in air

As Shelley *did* write the poem, we have a fluid, fluctuating shape, sweeping from one line to another, from one *terzina* to another. The rhymes, for all their musicality, remain in the background. Only toward the end they come up against increasingly strong shapes:

> (50)   until
> Thine azure sister of the Spring shall blow
> Her clarion o'er the dreaming earth, and fill
> (Driving sweet buds like flocks to feed in air)
> With living hues and odours plain and hill:
> Wild Spirit, which art moving everywhere;
> Destroyer and preserver; hear, oh hear!

In Pope there is, usually, a syntactic stop at the end of every couplet (run-on couplets being the exception rather than the rule). In "Ode to the West Wind", by contrast, there is no significant syntactic stop between the first and the end of the twelfth line. In Pope, syntactic breaks *near* the extremes are rare (though we have focused attention precisely on these instances), whereas in Shelley's "Ode", the proportion is reversed. In its first part, for instance, there are seven major breaks after positions 1, 2, 3, 7, or 8 (in lines 2, 3, 5, 8, 10, and 13), and only three major breaks after positions 4 and 6 (in lines 1, 4, and 7). The device of breaking the lines near the extremes, when moderately used, reinforces the firmness of shape in Pope's couplets; when used abundantly, as in Shelley's "Ode", it makes for fluidity. In both cases, the technique heightens tension and energy. Towards the end of the first part, the "Ode" gradually solidifies into increasingly strong shapes; the last three lines are end-stopped; the couplet is vigorous and 'purposeful'; it is clearly 'joined' by a comma after *Spirit* and by the semi-colons. In this context, "hear, oh hear!" with its repeated verb stands out as a marked off unit; it appears to be required, thus strengthening the closure.[7]

Functional Interaction

So far I have discussed the gestalt organization of phonetic signifiers, their interaction with syntax, and the resulting perceptual forces. Only occasionally I have referred to their interaction with contents, even though there is a legitimate interest in these aspects for their own sake. This last section of the present chapter is devoted to a passage from *Paradise Lost;* it provides a detailed analysis of the significant interaction of the aspects discussed earlier with the poem's contents. We will take up the poem in mid-flow:

(51)   Him the Almighty Power
        Hurled headlong flaming from th'etherial sky
        With hideous ruin and combustion down
        To bottomless perdition, there to dwell
        In adamantine chains and penal fire,
        Who durst defy th'Omnipotent to arms.
                        (*Paradise Lost,* I: 44–49)

For one thing, this passage is not characteristic: its meter is far more regular than usual in Milton. This is, probably, functional, being related to the vigorous movement that is so conspicuous in the passage, not only by way of "telling", but also by way of "showing". Compare the use of the verb *hurl'd* in excerpt (51), to that in Pope's passage, quoted above as excerpt (2). In Pope's passage, the reader is *told* that Man is "in endless Error hurl'd"; in Milton's, he is *shown* the movement. The vigorous fall is felt, by many readers, as a perceptual quality of the passage, in spite of its scarcity of verbs. There are only three verbs in this passage, only two of them finite, and only one, "hurled", denotes physical motion. The exceptionally impetuous impact of the passage has not escaped the notice of the critics, who keep making great efforts to account for it. I submit that the theoretical equipment expounded in the present chapter can illuminate the issue. Let us make one more attempt to penetrate the structure of this passage, beginning our inquiry with a discussion by Donald Davie.

"Dramatic" is a poor word for this effect. One wants to speak of "muscularity", using "muscular", however, in a special sense. [...] The effect is kinetic. The placing of "Him", "down" and "to", in particular, gives us the il-

[7]   This passage as described above is a typical "divergent passage". Such a poetic passage is very complex, and its significant description must always be lengthy. Another typical divergent passage will be discussed below as 51, and Baudelaire's "Correspondances" in Chapter 20.

lusion as we read that our own muscles are tightened in panic as we experience in our own bodies a movement just as headlong and precipitate as the one described. We occupy in ourselves the gestalt of falling, just as we do before a good painting of the same event; it is hardly too much to say that the inversion of word order (object-subject-verb) has the same effect upon us as seeing the angel's head near the bottom of the painted canvas and his heels near the top. (Davie, 1960: 70–71)

Who would not agree that the enormous impact of this passage has to do with "the placing of 'Him', 'down' and 'to'", and with "the inversion of word order"? But it appears that Davie wishes to add something to his account, and to this end he introduces the analogy with painting, and gestalt, and the kinetic effect of "muscularity". Now, the problem with this explanation is that it is only an analogy, with many links missing, without which it cannot really be illuminating. Furthermore, it rather illegitimately combines the empathy-theory and gestalt-theory of art. Such gestaltist art critics as Rudolf Arnheim are inclined to dismiss as redundant the very assumption that the notion of motor mimicry is needed to account for our appreciation of any painting. As for my own approach, the minimum I would require is a more exact description of Milton's passage, and a way systematically to relate it to the reader's response, motor mimicry or other. For, if there is one thing this passage does extremely well, it is that in the disguise of psychology, it *tunes the reader's mind* to the effect of the description.

As for movement in painting, I have considered at some length Arnheim's conception of "perceptual forces", according to which our perceptual field is disturbed in a painting by certain shapes. It is the spectator's need to bring the field back into balance, into focal stability, that incites him to perceive it as pressing, or actually moving in the direction of some point where stability may be achieved. Imagine, for instance, that a painter like El Greco, undertake to paint the scene described by Milton; we might expect him to explore oblique directions, interfering with all conceivable symmetric arrangements and upsetting the stability of the painting's framework, as it were. This would render the downward movement impetuous indeed. Another difficulty with Davie's description directly concerns "the placing of 'Him', 'down' and 'to'". What is so extraordinary about that placing? Is it only the dislocation of "Him"? And if so, what is so peculiar about this dislocation? Obviously, the placing is governed by certain rules of perception and achieves its extraordinary impact by the interlocking of the latter with certain additional effects.

The first thing to notice is that the downward motion is part of a much larger scheme of movement. It is preceded by Satan's "upward" movement. The two are contrasted not only in direction, but also in cumulative impact of the one, as opposed to the suddenness, explicitness, and concentrated energy of the other. In lines 34–44, there are scattered expressions referring to Satan's ambition and pride, his "haughtiness": he is *"stirred up* with envy", "aspiring / To set himself in glory *above* his peers", "He trusted to have equaled the most *High*", *"Raised* impious war in Heaven". There is in Satan's vigorous *fall* some kind of moral as well as perceptual "justice": what goes up, must come down; and the longer the free fall, the greater the acceleration.

The main effect of the passage may be described by a phrase to which Donald Davie would hardly object, viz., "articulate energy". The energy draws upon the perceptual forces discussed above and, on the semantic level, upon contrasts and connotations of violence: "Almighty Power ... flaming ... hideous ruin ... penal fire ... durst defy th'Omnipotent to arms". *Headlong* means both "headforemost" and "hastily, impetuously". *Combustion* means both "burning" and "violent excitement, tumult". The opposition "from th'etherial sky ... to bottomless perdition" suggests tremendous energy.

I have used "articulate" in the sense of "jointed, separated into well-shaped pieces". Tension, on the other hand, arises from intrusion upon well-shaped sentences. So, on the syntactic level, the phrase "articulate energy" involves an oxymoron, a tension between two opposite tendencies. On the one hand, the energy is derived from dislocations, inversions, enjambements; it has a tumultuous, almost chaotic effect. On the other hand, the passage can be divided into well-shaped units, which prevent it from chaotically falling into pieces. The following sentence may be regarded as the core of the passage: "The Almighty Power hurled him down". It is this sentence that has been elaborated and has had its parts dislocated.

Dislocations and inversions have their peculiar dynamics. The greater the number of functions a dislocation fulfills, the more justified it seems; the further away a syntactic unit is removed, the greater the tension it generates (provided that it is not so far removed that the reader cannot relate it to its context); similarly, the smaller the unit, the more it resists dislocation. An inversion at the head of a passage may have a different function from one at its end: in the former case, it may herald what comes, highlighting, so to speak, the heralded part of the sentence; in the latter, it may reinforce a feeling of closure, of finality. Thus, the placing of *Him* differs from *there to dwell* (in line 47, instead of *to dwell there*) in three important respects. First, it has been moved much further away than *there*. Second, it opens up the movements, "heralding" what turns out to be a verb (of violent action). By contrast, the dislocation of *there,* signals what appears to be a (false) closing point; on a smaller scale, it also heralds a verb denoting permanent residence, as opposed to the impetuous movement denoted by the previous verb. Third, *Him* is a pronoun that bears emphatic stress here, but is manipulated into a weak position that is, in the present context, it intrudes upon an iambic foot in the middle, and initiates a perceptual force on a miniature scale. The inversion resulting in "there to dwell", by contrast, causes a metrically deviant phrase to conform with metric pattern, thus achieving "focal stability" at a crucial point of the line.

Him, in fact, is the smallest syntactic unit that could be dislocated. It is a monosyllabic word, usually unstressed and with a reduced vowel. How violently it resists dislocation will be seen, by way of contrast, if we alter the line, by changing a single phoneme, to *"whom* the Almighty Power hurled ...", leaving little trace of the high tension; or if we compare it with another dislocated unit, a complete clause, occupying a whole pentameter line (and involving no extra syntactic predictions): "Who durst defy th'Omnipotent to arms". The dislocation of this clause passes almost unnoticed. Yet, observe this: it is a relative clause, with no clear indication of its antecedent. The most plausible candidate is precisely *Him* at the beginning of the sentence ("Him, who durst" etc.). Assuming this is correct, the dislocation may generate the impression of a closed system, of a solid framework encompassing the rest of the passage. The possible impression is reinforced by the analogy of "the Almighty Power" and "th'Omnipotent to arms" in lines 44 and 49 (the latter, however, is again but a quasi-symmetry).

Now, consider the sentence "The Almighty Power Hurled him down": its span is 'pulled apart' in one direction by *him,* in the other by *down.* A particle like *down,* important as it is for the collocation, may be felt to be 'one item too much' in the environment of other short adverbials such as "headlong", or "flaming". Still, its omission could result in a feeling of absence. A lesser poet than Milton might have been forced into either position of incompetence (i.e., piling up adverbials, or omitting the one felt to be redundant). Milton turns the difficulty into a source of strength, by elaboration and dislocation: first, he omits "down" (solving the problem of 'redundancy'); then, having elaborated the clause with a series of longer prepositional phrases, he appends, so to speak, the missing word. In the wild commotion of the passage the reader has no time left to notice the absence of "down", but once he encounters the word, he suddenly realizes that this is what he had been expecting all along. The sentence is strenuously drawn apart between the extremes of two isolated monosyllabic adjuncts of the central verb.

The articulating power of the last (strong) position of a line may be enhanced through *requiredness;* this happens if the position is occupied by a monosyllable preceded by a polysyllable with its penultimate syllable stressed. In (51), four out of six lines have such an ending. The impact of "down" is strengthened by the fact that it is *required* in this sense, too. In other words, even if we could do without "down" from the idiomatic point of view, it is emphatically required from the metric point of view.

With "down", then, the reader comes to a point where, after a series of tensions and "frustrations", he first has the feeling of completeness, of closed shape. It is, then, this constant distortion and reinstatement of gestalts that may have impressed Donald Davie; some readers probably feel that it "gives us the illusion as we read that our own muscles are tightened in panic... We occupy in ourselves the gestalt of falling". This, however, is a secondary response, and by no means an essential or universal one. We can better account for the phenomenon in question by appealing to the reader's sense of distorted balance, followed by balance and relief when equilibrium is restored. Moreover, as I shall argue, this kind of structural manipulation is exploited to arouse in the reader a feeling not only of an *impetuous* falling but, also, of an *endless* falling. How can a text *show,* rather than merely *tell* its readers that a falling is endless indeed?

This process of the disturbance and reassertion of gestalts is further extended into the subsequent lines. With "down", the reader receives a strong feeling of closure; he also has the feeling that with it, he has reached the downmost point of the fall. However, as the absence of punctuation at the line-terminal may indicate, the syntactic unit is not yet necessarily over; the next line opens again the apparently closed gestalt which had been achieved so hard. It is not merely an additional item in the series of adverbials "headlong ... from th'etherial sky ... down ... to bottomless perdition...", but "down", until now regarded as a verbal particle, or a free adverb, is rankshifted to a preposition, changing its implication from 'the downmost point' to 'in a descending direction'; at the same time, "bottomless" informs us that there is no downmost point at all. "To bottomless perdition" opens up a new pentameter line that, in turn, requires its completion; the phrase overrides caesura and leaves a *required* stretch, three positions long. The sense of completeness is achieved with "there to dwell". We have seen above how this phrase reinforces a feeling of finality, of stop, of 'focal stability' both by the dislocation of "there" and the contrasting of "dwell" with "hurled". This finality, again, turns out to be illusory, and the gestalt is opened up by a run-on phrase "to dwell in adamantine chains". It is this sequence of stops, experienced and frustrated, that makes the reader experience an "endless fall".

In spite of this endless fall, however, the passage itself *must* stop somehow; what is more, it ought to have a "proper cessation". Line 48 is the first one in this passage that is really end-stopped. It enhances its sense of closure by two parallel phrases, separated by a 'marked' caesura: "In adamantine chains / and penal fire" (a segment of four positions at the end manifests *some* degree of requiredness). The critic, having cried "Wolf!" so many times, is required to provide some additional proof to make us 'believe' that the expanded clause and the series of *frustrated* closures have come indeed to an end. This proof is provided by a 'gratuitous' sequence: "Who durst defy th'Omnipotent to arms". "One of the most effective ways to indicate the conclusion of a poem generated by an indefinitely extensible principle is simply to modify that principle at the end of the poem", as Herrnstein-Smith has it. The sequence in question, beginning a new (dislocated) clause, convinces us that the previous "never-ending" clause is at last over; by reverting to the theme preceding the fall, it convinces us that the downward motion has come to an end; by converging with a pentameter line, it makes no further requirements for completion. This is the first and only line in our quotation that is run-on neither at its beginning nor at its end; moreover, it has an unmarked caesura (that is, after position IV). One of the effective devices that already have been used twice for "sabotaging" closure is reapplied in this line, this time for enhancing closure. Strictly speaking, the last phrase "to arms", has a fairly high degree of *requiredness*, since "Who durst defy th'Omnipotent" would make ample sense by itself, but would leave the line incomplete. By the addition of "to arms", not only the craving for completion is gratified, but the sense of *defy* has been implicitly changed from some general kind of opposition and impiety to the more specific "challenge to combat or contest", inherently requiring the complement "to arms".[8]

I wish to end this chapter with a methodological observation. The generally accepted method for handling perceived qualities is to assess empirically the response of flesh-and-blood readers (cf., e.g., Chapter 7 below). Here I have obviously proceeded in a different manner. Even though I have used the indicative mood (that represents the denoted act or state as an objective fact), I performed a very different kind of speech act. In Morris Weitz's (1962) terms, I made a "crucial recommendation" what to look for in a given piece of literature, and how to look at it. The afore-mentioned perceived qualities arise in a piece of literature, if at all, only if performed in a certain way. The gestalt laws of perception apply to all perception; but the qualities arise only in a certain mental performance. I made, then, suggestions as to a possible mental performance of the text. Then we may argue about two questions: whether this is a legitimate way to look at the text, and whether in such a performance the said qualities do indeed arise.

[8] I reproadueced this discussion, followed by a discussion of a recorded reading of this passage in my book on poetic rhythm (Tsur, 1998: 256–264).

CHAPTER 6

Meter and Rhythm

Rhythm is based on groups of *recurring* events of *different* kinds.[1] *Differentiation* in this formula is as important as *recurrence*. In the preceding chapter I quoted Meyer on this issue in music: "For just as a series of beats which are equal both in accent and duration will not give rise to an impression of rhythm (except in so far as the mind imposes its own arbitrary differentiation upon the stimuli) so, too, the smaller rhythmic groups will not give rise to larger patterns unless differentiation of accent or duration is present" (Meyer, 1956: 111).

I wish to mention here four versification systems that had a major impact on Western literatures: 1. Syllabic meter (predominant, e.g., in French and some other Romance languages) specifies the number of syllables in a verse line. 2. Tonic (accentual) meter (said to be predominant, e.g., in Biblical Hebrew verse) specifies the number of stresses in a verse line. 3. Quantitative meter (in classical Greek and Latin poetry, as well as in Mediaeval Arab and Hebrew poetry) specifies the order of longer and shorter events in a metric unit (foot), and the number of feet in a verse line. 4. Syllabotonic (syllabic accentual) meter (dominant in English poetry from, roughly, Chaucer to Yeats, and in some other modern languages, as in Russian, German, Hungarian, Hebrew) specifies both the number of syllables in a verse line, and the sequence of stressed and unstressed events in a foot. In fact, as I shall argue, it is the number of metrical positions rather than the number of syllables that are specified in syllabotonic verse.[2]

Notice the phrase "in a verse line", occurring in the description of all these versification systems. This is no mere convenience of formulation. Poetic rhythm must be specified by units at two ranks at least, between which there may be a part–whole relationship. The verse line (the unit above) is a *whole*, that is, a system that determines the character of its parts; whereas, as we have seen in the previous chapter, it is the relative simplicity of the parts that determines the strength and integrity of the whole. Poetic rhythm, then, is not just an endless series of recurrent events. If it is to be granted greater significance than the monotonous tick-tocking of a clock; this

---

[1] I have devoted to the Perception-Oriented Theory of Meter two book-length studies (Tsur, 1977; 1998) and several articles.

[2] In Chinese, which is a tone language (that is, makes use of musical pitches or movements in pitch to distinguish word meanings), there is a system based on alternations of level tones (Ping) and non-level or oblique tones (Ze) (I am told that this system has a duration aspect too).

"endless series" must be *articulated* into structured chunks amenable to the span of "immediate memory".

The Iambic Pentameter Line
and the Perception-Oriented Theory of Meter

The versification system in English poetry from Chaucer to Yeats is, as I have suggested, dominated by syllabotonic meter. The meter of the overwhelming majority of verse lines in this enormous corpus is the *iambic pentameter*, in which the foot consists of two events, with the second event of the foot stronger than the first, and in which there are five such feet in the verse line.

It will be readily seen that the vast majority of verse lines deviate from this abstract metric pattern to some extent or other. In what follows, we will be concerned with three questions of great importance. First, how does an experienced reader of poetry recognize a deviant verse line as, e.g., an iambic pentameter? Second, how does an experienced reader of poetry *handle* such a deviant line? And third, what are the perceived effects of such deviant verse lines?

In the archetypal iambic pentameter line, every even-numbered syllable is stressed, every odd-numbered syllable is unstressed. In the first 165 lines of *Paradise Lost,* however, there are no more than two such lines, one of them being excerpt (1), below. Let us consider briefly three consecutive lines *(Paradise Lost,* I: 59–61):

(1)   At ónce as fár as Ángels kén he viéws
     w s   w s w s   w   s w   s

(2)   The dísmal situátion stránge and wílde:
     w s   w s ws w   s   w   s

(3)   A dúngeon hórrible, on áll sídes róund
     w s   w s ws w s w   s

In excerpt (2), the first syllable of the word *situátion* is the fourth one in its line, that is, even-numbered; yet it is unstressed. In excerpt (3), by contrast, *sídes* is the ninth syllable, and should be unstressed; yet it is stressed. A fleeting view at any relatively short passage in *Paradise Lost* may reveal a wide range of deviances from the abstract meter, resulting in lines that have little resemblance to one another, meterwise. Why, then, should we call them by the common name "iambic pentameter"? One way to handle this problem is Robert Bridges' way who in his book on Milton's prosody provided a list of "allowable deviations". Such an approach is authoritarian in its conception. It accepts deviations from regularity on Milton's authority: it is allowable, because Milton used it. This, however, does not explain the source of Milton's metrical authority: why do centuries of readers treat Milton's verses not merely as "allowable", but as "Milton's miraculous organ voice"? Moreover, the common reader does not read poetry with a list of allowable deviations in hand. He *hears* when a deviation is allowable. What does he hear when he hears that some deviation *is* allowable?

This is where the Perception-Oriented Theory of Meter comes in. It adopts from Wellek and Warren the notion that to account for poetic rhythm, one must distinguish not one, but three patterns: metric pattern, stress pattern (prose rhythm), and pattern of performance. Morris Halle and Jay Keyser have reinvented the first two of Wellek and Warren's patterns, and propounded a brilliantly simple generative theory of meter, which can generate—they claim—all metrical verse lines, and only metrical verse lines. By internalizing the parsimonious rules of this theory—thus the argument goes—the reader can intuitively judge which is a metrical iambic pentameter line, and which is not. The great achievement of the Halle-Keyser Theory is that it provides clear-cut definitions and "correspondence rules". The fuzzy term *ictus* of traditional metrics was an indefinite mixture of metrical and linguistic prominence. Halle and Keyser's definions separate metrical strong and weak positions on the one hand, and linguistically stressed and unstressed syllables on the other; after which they provide "correspondence rules" for assigning the latter set to the former one.

Metric pattern consists of an abstract sequence of regularly alternating weak and strong positions, irrespective of the kind of syllables that occupy them. Stress pattern consists of a series of stressed and unstressed syllables; stress is assigned to a syllable by linguistic rules, irrespective of the metrical position that it may occupy. For metrical purposes, only a binary distinction is made, between syllables that do and those that do not bear lexical stress. Lexical stress is the stress that occurs in the most strongly stressed syllable of a lexical word. In English, for instance, lexical words are nouns, verbs, adjectives, and non-clitic adverbs. Pronouns, conjunctions, prepositions and auxiliary verbs bear no lexical stress. Native speakers of a language have strong intuitions concerning linguistic stress: it is part of their linguistic competence. In addition, Halle and Keyser proffer a theoretical construct: *stress maximum.* "When a stressed syllable is located between two unstressed syllables in the same syntactic constituent within a line of verse, this syllable is called a 'stress maximum'" (Halle and Keyser, 1971: 156). The syllable *gar-* in the phrase "a garden" is a stress maximum, whereas in "a big garden" the stress maximum is "neutralized by an adjacent stress".

In terms of these distinctions, excerpt (1) above can be described by the correspondence rule: "Stressed syllables occur in strong positions only, and in all strong positions". (2) can be described as "Stressed syllables occur in strong positions only, but not in all strong positions", whereas (3) can be described as "Stress maxima occur in strong positions only, but not in all strong positions". An unmetrical line is one in which a stress maximum occurs in a weak position. Excerpts (7)–(10) below contain lines that have, each, a stress maximum in the seventh (weak) position and are, thus, unmetrical under the Halle-Keyser theory. This constitutes a mounting scale of complexity; each later rule describes a verse structure that arouses greater tension than the earlier one.

Over the seventies, there seemed to be an almost concerted effort of prosodists all over the English speaking world to find counter-examples to the Halle-Keyser theory in order to refute it. What seems to have frightened these prosodists was, precisely, what I tend to regard its greatest asset: its rigouous thinking and clearly-defined terms and generative rules. Halle and Keyser themselves, together with their critics, have found in the vast corpus of iambic pentameter lines from Chaucer to Yeats a total of eleven counter-examples, that is, verse lines that would be judged as "unmetrical" under the latest version of the Halle-Keyser theory. This is quite an admirable result for the theory.

I have elsewhere discussed at great length the Halle-Keyser theory and its notion of "metricalness" (Tsur, 1977; 1998). Of all my arguments against the notion of metricalness, I shall repeat here only one, which I consider to be the most weighty one of them. In an Appendix to my *Perception-Oriented Theory of Meter* (1977, reprinted and expanded in 1998), I added to the existing list over forty instances of "unmetrical" lines from the poetry of such major English poets as Shakespeare, Milton, Keats, Shelley, and others; eighteen of these lines are from *Paradise Regained*. This poses three serious problems for the Halle-Keyser theory and its notion of metricalness. First, a sufficiently big number of "unmetrical" lines was obtained, to make the distribution of "violations" far from being random (I shall return to this issue in detail). Second, one must seriously question the utility of a notion of metricalness that legitimizes verse structures to which no poet ever has had recourse and, on the other hand, excludes verse structures that do occur, rarely though, in some of the greatest English poetry. Third, such a conception fails to make the proper distinction between verse lines and poetic styles that are on the approved side of the boundary of "metricalness", and those that are on the "wrong" side.

The Perception-Oriented Theory of Meter is a minor Copernican revolution, shifting the center of the prosodic universe from the "metricalness" of the verse line to the reader's ability or willingness to perform it rhythmically. One may arrange verse lines along scales of mounting complexity. The performer has at his disposal a wide range of performance devices, with the help of which he may render the deviant lines rhythmical. If he encounters some kind of deviation to which he has never been exposed before, he may resort to old devices, or invent new devices, exploiting the potential of his cognitive resources. The utmost limit of rhythmicality is determined by the reader's ability or willingness to perform the verse line rhythmically. Different poets seem to have drawn this utmost limit at different points on a variety of scales of mounting complexity. In other words, different poets assume in their readers different degrees of ability or willingness to perform a verse line rhythmically. Furthermore, one may expect every poet to strain this ability or willingness to some extent, and violate his own utmost limit of rhythmicality. But just as we may expect Pope to fix his utmost limit of rhythmicality at a lower point on the scales of mounting complexity than Milton, we also may expect that the former's violations of his own utmost limit of rhythmicality should be less bold in degree.

The theory adopts, then, from Wellek and Warren the notion that in order to account for poetic rhythm, one must distinguish three dimensions of the sound structure of poetry: metric pattern, stress pattern, and pattern of performance. It assumes that the first two of these patterns must be defined and assigned independently from each other, and that the third one is the solution of a perceptual problem presented by the first two. *Performance* refers to the set of conditions under which the stress pattern and metric pattern tend to group into, and establish themselves as, perceptual units. In lines of little complexity, performance tends to go unnoticed; statements about performance become increasingly necessary with increasing complexity of the line. Theoretically, however, performance is a dimension of lines of *any* complexity, whether read aloud or silently.

The regular sequence of metric pattern exists in a reading as an expectation, as the reader's *metrical set*. When a stressed syllable occurs in a **s**trong position, it *confirms* meter; when in a **w**eak position, it *disconfirms* it. A foot cannot be inverted, only its positions confirmed or disconfirmed. Thus, for instance, instead of an "inverted first foot" in the iambic meter I shall speak of a "stress displaced from the second to the first position". Now consider the following verse line:

4.   That fósters the dróop-héaded flówers áll.
     w   s   w   s   w   s   w   s   w   s

(Keats, "Ode on Melancholy", 13)

Dróop- in a weak position disconfirms meter; it frustrates our expectations for metrical regularity, staggering the reader's certainty of the established pattern. This uncertainty lasts, until meter is reasserted in the next strong position. The experienced reader will perform the line so as to preserve at least the memory of regular recurrence until meter is reasserted. The successive stressed syllables are perceived as emphatically grouped together. Now consider a more complex case:

(5)   Strrúng my ówn éars—I stróve hárd to escape
    w   s w   s   w   s   w   s w s

(Keats, "The Fall of Hyperion", 1, 127)

In this line, meter is confirmed in the fourth, sixth and tenth positions, and disconfirmed in the first, third and seventh positions. Metric pattern is asserted for the first time as late as the fourth position, where it has a coinciding downbeat with the stress pattern. Having disconfirmed or suspended meter over a stretch of three syllables, a "perceptual force" (see the preceding chapter) "pushing" toward the fourth position is experienced; when the fourth position is reached, a feeling of relief and certainty follows a feeling of suspense. The regular meter in such cases can be preserved in the reader's perception only if such a stretch of syllables is performed as a unit, as a stress-group.

Syntactically, *hard* in the seventh position is to be grouped with *strove* in the sixth. This seems to be required metrically too, since *hard* disconfirms the meter (and is "neutralized" by the preceding stress). It is, however, more difficult to *re-*

assert meter in advance, before the actual violation takes place. It demands some performance that enhances the memory of regular recurrence during the period of uncertainty. Some readers find it easier to group the last four syllables together emphatically and experience the relief and certainty in the tenth position, where the two groups, stress group and metric group, have a coinciding downbeat again (this is, for instance, how this line is performed by Richard Johnson on Argo PLP 1043).

(6)   Strúng my ówn éars—I stróve hárd to escápe
       w   s   w   s   w   s   w   s w   s

Such optional groupings are an important part of the *performance pattern*. I have called such a group a *stress valley*. It has an exceptionally strong shape: it is symmetrical and closed. It consists of two stresses embracing two slacks; or, it may be described as a shape the second half of which is the exact mirror image of its first half. In Chapters 2 and 5 I have discussed the Limited Channel Capacity hypothesis. According to this hypothesis, there is a rigid upper limit to the amount of information that an organism is able to process at any given time. When the information to be processed exceeds this limit, the organism may have recourse to a variety of cognitive strategies and devices. One possible way of handling an excess of information is to *recode* it in a more efficient manner, so as to require less processing space. A piecemeal treatment of metric deviation may generate such an excess of information. In (6), for instance, one must remember, in the sweep of the reading, that *hárd* is a stressed syllable, and that the position it occupies is weak; that *to* is an unstressed syllable, and that the position it occupies is strong; and that it should be the other way around. In terms of the Limited-Channel-Capacity hypothesis, a stress valley constitutes the *recoding* of some otherwise irregularly distributed stresses, so as to save the extra mental space needed for the realization of the divergent stress pattern and meter. Instead of loading the piecemeal information onto his memory, the reader *hears* the sequence of syllables as grouped into a closed, symmetrical, stable unit; and remembers, at the same time, the sequence of regularly alternating weak and strong positions.

    In the preceding chapter I have discussed gestalt principles of part–whole relationships. In order to understand the best perceptual organization of a line containing a stress valley in positions 7–10, another aspect must be considered. Simplicity of the whole resists subdivision; wholes containing irregularities may result in better perceptual organization when some part of them is isolated to some extent:

    The tendency to simplification will manifest itself in the way in which subdivision of patterns occurs. We know already that when a number of discrete units are given in the visual field, all or some of them may be seen as connected in such a way that the simplest possible organization results. The eight dots of Figure 6.1 will be seen as a circle or octagon *(a)* and not as two squares *(b)* or the combination of three units shown in *c;* the nine dots of *d* will split up into two main units—the circle plus the outsider. (Arnheim, 1957: 59)

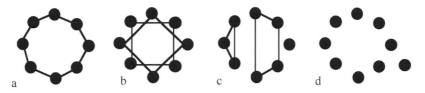

Figure 6.1   The eight dots will be seen as a circle or octagon *(a)* and not as two squares *(b)* or the combination of three units shown in *c;* the nine dots of *d* will split up into two main units—the circle plus the outsider .

The same principle is active in the perception of verse lines containing a stress valley. When the structure of the whole line becomes too complex, too irregular, subdivision may yield better shape; in the present instance, the stress valley deviating from the iambic pattern is perceptually isolated, yielding a more or less iambic chunk plus an isolated closed, symmetrical stress valley. In (6), perhaps the best perceptual organization may result when both at the beginning and at the end of the line a stress valley is isolated, resulting in a symmetrical, balanced structure.

The stress valley, with the concomitant mental processes indicated above, proves to be a very powerful tool for rhythmically performing a verse line in which there occur such extreme violations of meter as a *stress maximum in a weak position.* It had to be discovered, then, whether an experienced reader would perform a stress maximum in the seventh position, for instance, as part of a stress valley, or in some other pattern of performance. For this end, I asked five faculty members at the English department of the University of Sussex, to read aloud the following lines:

(7)   Buffet and scoffe, scorge, and crucifie mee!

(8)   Burnt after them to the bottomless pit

(9)   How many bards gild the lapses of time

(10) And with these words his temptation pursued

The readings were performed separately by the five readers, who had no advance knowledge of the stress valley hypothesis. They were asked to read the four lines *rhythmically,* so as to preserve the stress pattern of the words and as much of the meter as possible. After having read the lines, we discussed the readings, in order to make sure that *my description* fitted what the readers felt they had done.

I formulated two specific expectations: first, that the performance pattern would indicate a stress valley and second, that if excerpts (7)–(9) are performed with a closing stress valley, the readers would experience some extra difficulty with (10). The results left little room for doubt. The performances of four out of the five readers were strikingly similar (my discussion will refer only to these four readings). The fifth was somewhat ambiguous: it *could* be interpreted as a stress valley, but need not be. In the aftermath, the four were quite surprised, but *sure* that they had stressed the seventh syllable more strongly than they would have normally done (even though it was odd-numbered). The reason for this seems in harmony with our argument in the preceding chapter. Sharpening, that is, exaggerating the unfitting detail, generates a strong perceptual force pushing toward the end, by intruding upon the regular flow of the iambic stream. By the same token, it helps to segregate the symmetrical stress valley; and causes relief when the stress valley and the line ending have a coinciding downbeat. The four readers were also in agreement with one another that the last four syllables were performed *as a group,* closer in time to one another, and that the unstressed syllables in mid-group were performed somewhat more rapidly than usual.

My second expectation, too, was amply fulfilled. Three out of the four readers were puzzled by *temptation.* They had several tries before they found a satisfactory performance, amid such remarks as "It's funny" … "It's interesting" … "That's different" … "Are you sure Milton didn't stress *temp-* rather than *-ta-?*" The fourth reader performed the line in his "first go", but his solution was unmistakably the same as the one at which the others eventually arrived. All four solved the problem by a marked prolongation of *temp-* with a slight break after it. In the aftermath of the reading, they agreed that the difficulty lay in the need to *isolate* the last four syllables *as a group* (since the group begins in the middle of the word *temptation).*

Ad hoc explanations should always be the last refuge of the theoretician. Where a small number of counter-examples may call for *ad hoc* explanations, the discovery of a larger number may provide the basis for a more systematic explanation. Such a systematic explanation may gain enormously if the cognitive rationale behind it can be clearly brought out. Consider, for instance, excerpt (9). The first syllable of *lapses* constitutes a stress maximum in a weak position; according to the Halle-Keyser theory, this renders the line unmetrical. S. J. Keyser suggests that this "metrical lapse" is a kind of onomatopoeia, a metric pun. According to the conception of performance outlined above, and confirmed by the foregoing experiment, the four syllables of *lapses of time* can be performed rhythmically, by grouping them together. This renders the line acceptable, and the *ad hoc* explanation of "metric pun" becomes superfluous.

As I have mentioned above, in the "classical" papers on generative metrics from the years 1966–1971, a total of some eleven instances of stress maxima in weak positions are listed. Nine of them occur in the seventh position, two in the third. Some of them are "legitimized" by assigning "emphatic stress"; some are explained away by postulating an Italian influence of "double trochee", and one as a "metric pun". The number of the remaining instances is negligible indeed. This, however, changed with the addition of over forty instances of stress maxima in weak positions from major English texts. There are four positions in a pentameter line available for violation: 3, 5, 7, and 9 (in the first weak position of the line no stress maximum may occur, by definition). An even distribution of violations in weak positions would allocate some 11–12 in each position available for. There are, however, some 27–28 in the seventh position. It would be somewhat unreasonable to suppose that well over half the instances of "scribal errors", "poetic oversight", and "metric pun" should have occurred precisely in this position. About one third of the violations occur in the third position; and only a few, rather doubtful instances in positions 5 and 9.

In order to account for this uneven distribution of stress maxima in weak positions, one must assume that the line constitutes a *whole,* that is, a system that determines the character of its parts (that is, in the present instance, the character of its strong positions) and that some strong positions are stronger than others. Strong positions differ in their *grouping potential.* This difference can be observed with respect to both grouping by metric boundary and grouping by stress. In the preceding chapter we have established in the iambic pentameter line a hierarchy of metric boundaries governed by the laws of perception, with a decreasing grouping potential. The highest metric boundary is the line terminal, following the tenth position; next come the unmarked caesura (following the fourth position), and the marked caesura (following the sixth position); the lowest grouping potential is attributed to the second and eighth position, which are never followed by a metric boundary.

Using the number 2 to designate a boundary of greater weight than 1 (not necessarily *twice* as great), but smaller than 3, the number 1 to designate anything between "negative potential" and just "smaller than 2", we may assign the following potential of grouping to the various strong positions: X: 4; IV: 3; VI: 2; II & VIII: 1. One should expect the greatest number of stress maxima to occur in those weak positions in which they do least violence. Conversely, one should expect the smallest number of stress maxima to occur in those weak positions in which most violence is done to the meter. In this respect, we may well profit from the application of gestalt theory to rhythm in music:

> Whenever an accent is suppressed, [...] the mind, searching for focal stability of an accent with reference to which it can group weak beats, places particularly stress on the subsequent downbeat. Furthermore, the stronger the potential of the unrealized accent—the stronger it had been had it not been suppressed—the more effective the syncopation and the more forceful the impulse toward the next accent. (Cooper and Meyer, 1960: 103)

Now, a stress maximum in a weak position entails the suppression of the stresses in the adjoining strong positions. Consequently, the degree of violation by a stress maximum in a weak position may be expressed in terms of the adjacent strong positions in which the suppression of stress is entailed. Position numbers are designated by Roman numerals, their grouping potential by positive Arabic numbers; degrees of violation are designated by negative Arabic numbers.

11.   II   IV   VI   VIII   X
        1   3   2   1   4
                III   V   VII   IX
                −4   −5   −3   −5

Thus, we have established a scale of violations by stress maxima in weak positions (as the sum of the potential values of the unrealized adjacent stresses). According to our conception of metricalness expounded above, we should expect some poets (such as Pope) or some readers (such as Halle and Keyser) to draw the limit of metricalness so as to exclude all violations; others, by contrast, might include −3 and −4 but exclude −5 as unmetrical (e.g., Shakespeare and Milton); other poets, again, like Shelley and Keats, may even occasionally resort to −5. We should expect the greatest number of stress maxima in weak positions to occur in the seventh position, the next greatest in the third position, and so on. Which is, precisely, the case.

The exclusion of −5 as the greatest degree of violation is not a matter of pure arithmetics. The number refers to very real issues in metrical terms. A stress maximum in the ninth position means no confirmation of meter in the last, decisive position of the line (I have found, indeed, only stress maxima resulting from emphatic stress in the ninth position). A stress maximum in the fifth position entails the suppression of both grouping stresses and grouping boundaries, both in the fourth and the sixth positions: the very positions in which violation could be counteracted by grouping.[3]

Another aspect of this issue is the position in which "focal stability" is sought for. The stronger the grouping potential of a realized stress, the more forceful the impulse, the "bump" that it can absorb from the violating stress maxima. Conversely, if the degree of violation is greater than the grouping potential of the subsequent realized stress, the state resulting from the reinstatement of meter will be short of perfect equilibrium. There will be a further urge to reach focal stability in position IV or X. In the case of a stress maximum in a weak position, the mind must group not only "weak beats", but a whole stress valley beginning with a *violating stress.*

---

[3]   In Milton, I have found only one line in which a stress maximum may occur *either* in the fifth *or* in the seventh position; all the other examples of stress maxima in fifth positions were found in Keats and Shelley. Some of these cases involve verbs followed by prepositional phrases; considering the degree of violation involved, some readers may regard the prepositions as stressed verbal particles, neutralizing the stress maxima.

Combinational Potential and Double-Edgedness

In the present section, I shall examine a variety of metric structures from the perspectives of the distinctions made in the present and the preceding chapter. I shall try to show that this perspective provides the critic with powerful tools in a meaningful description of the interaction of meter with other poetic norms.

To praise a poem by saying: "How admirably the prosodic (or syntactic) structure suits the poetic quality of this poem!" is to miss the point. The poetic quality of a poem results not only from an interplay between prosodic and syntactic structures, but also from the poetic imagery, and so on. The same meter may interact in different poems with different elements, or even with the same elements in different hierarchies, but it will always "admirably" suit the quality of which it is a perceptual condition.

Instead of talking, therefore, of an overall quality in a poem that may be corroborated by meter or syntactic structure, one ought to speak of *combinational potential* of metrical, syntactical and thematic elements which may or may not be realized in one or another actual combination, yielding a variety of poetic qualities. Sometimes the combinational potential is intimately related to the perceived effects (or perceptual qualities) inherent in the various strata of the poem. In the following section, I shall attempt to describe some aspects of the typical combinational potential inherent in a variety of metric structures, for thus to achieve a better understanding of some of the ways in which meter helps to generate *qualities*. It will be noted that some metric structures are "double-(or multi-)edged", that is, they may act in two (or more) ways, depending on which aspects of their combinational potential are actualized. Thus, for instance, it will be suggested that iambic pentameter lines containing a number of polysyllables may tend to produce qualities as different as "a kind of metered academic language" and a "peculiar thrill of uncertainty", depending on which aspect of their combinational potential is actualized. Likewise, regular meter may tend to produce several different qualities, as ecstatic, intellectual or childish qualities, in accordance, again, with the particular potential that is actualized.[4] Here we have to repeat the slogan: "When Gestalt theory calls our attention to 'wholes', it is to the system that determines the character of its parts" (Brown, 1968: 71). Thus, in different wholes, the same metric structure may assume different characters. "Double-edgedness" must thus be distinguished from "ambiguity". The latter refers to the perceived effect of a metric unit, whereas the former refers to the perceived effects of the combinations into which it may enter.[5]

I have been treating a line of verse as a *perceptual field* in which *perceptual tensions* may arise, just as in any other stimulus pattern. The pattern, in turn, may interact with the *meaning* of the words whose sounds constitute the stimulus. Let us have a closer look at the line we have encountered in excerpt (7), one of the most extreme instances of divergent patterns in English verse, viz. Donne's

[4]   This issue will be discussed at length in chapter 19.
[5]   This distinction is further elaborated in Tsur, 1985 (see now Tsur, 2003: 167–197).

(12) Búffet and scóff, scórge, and crúcifie mée.
       w s w   s   w   s   w s w   s

In the first place, one may observe that three out of the five stressed syllables in this line occur in weak positions. The first is a usual instance of stress displaced to the first position (some critics call this a "trochaic inversion" at the line onset). There is nothing extraordinary in this. The third stress is "neutralized" by the preceding stress. The fourth, however, as we have seen, constitutes one of the gravest violations of meter: a stress maximum in a weak position.

We have already noticed some of the emphatic groupings the reader is required to make, if he wishes to maintain his "metrical set" against such a deviant stress pattern. Now we shall see a little more of this kind of grouping. In the present case, groupings will be made according to similarity of structure, similarity of ingredients, and similarity of position and proximity (these roughly correspond to the grouping principles established by gestalt psychologists). Take, for instance, the groups "Búffet and scóff ... crúcifie mée". They are similar in position ("balancing" the line at its extremes) and in structure: each of them constitutes a stress valley. In the first group, the stressed syllables are further grouped together by alliteration (*ff*), the part of speech they represent (imperative verb), and their meaning (painful treatment); the last group is tied together by one continuous phrase. So the two groups have "good shape"; they are symmetrical and "closed". This hierarchy of symmetries renders these groupings stable indeed.

We have here, then, a pattern superimposed upon the patterns of stress and meter. Without it, the line would fall into chaos. However, this grouping, too, is threatened with destruction by an additional, rival group: "scóff, scórge". This rival grouping is induced by the close proximity between the words, by the fact that they belong to the same part of speech, by their similarity in meaning, and by the repetition of the sound cluster *sco*. Even without these weighty reasons, *scórge*, a stressed syllable in a weak position, must be grouped with the adjacent stressed syllable. We have seen, indeed, that *scóff* is alliteratively grouped together with both the preceding and the subsequent verbs. The conflicting groupings render the word "ambiguous", not in the sense of "capable of two actualizations" (though one may well imagine various delivery styles for this line), but by the fact of its tenseness, thus enhancing the vague, uncertain, *emotional* quality of the line. As will be observed, the words of this line have tremendous emotive import and impetuous connotations of violence.

The divergent groups of stresses and the abstract metric groups of twos do have coinciding downbeats. It is at these points that the metric pattern may emphatically be reinstated. Between them, rhythm "trembles on the brink of chaos", "arousing desires for, and expectations of, clarification and improvement"—in Meyer's words (quoted in the preceding chapter). Thus, the points where the two patterns have coinciding downbeats, that is, in positions 4 and 10 (this, as we have seen, is no accident), become points of relief, so to speak, where meter is reconditioned, refreshed and renewed. In position 4, this is less conspicuous than in position 10, first because the "violation" of meter in the first position is conventional and relatively tame, and second because meter—far from being reconditioned here—demands the anticipation of (and compensation for) a violation in the next position before such a violation can actually take place. Hence the high tension and complexity at this point. Conversely, the clear reinstatement of meter, after a long series of infringements, occurs in the very last position of the line. The third and fourth stresses occur, precisely, in the "wrong" place. The third is "compensated" backward, the fourth, as we have said, is a stress maximum in the seventh (weak) position. This infringement inspires the reader with "awe, apprehension, and anxiety" that the utterance may escape back to chaos, "arousing powerful desires for, and expectations of, clarification and improvement". These desires and expectations are fulfilled, precisely, in the last position of the line, generating a strong feeling of closure. The line becomes well-shaped and, paradoxically, at the same time, near-chaotic. Hence its strong emotional impact.

Such a system, one that determines the character of its parts, takes up less "mental space" than do its components when unorganized in a *whole*. It is the additional grouping, then, that "makes room" for the perception of two or more rival patterns in counterpoint rather than in an unstructured "jumble". Furthermore, the character of any sequence of syllables in a line is determined by the system of groupings that constitute the line.

The feeling of uncertainty, of "anxiety", as it were, is particularly felt in the unstressed syllables of *crúcifie*. For their support, these syllables lean on that broken reed of a stress maximum in a weak position. They impart—on a miniature scale—something of the feeling of insecurity of a falling mountaineer who is uncertain whether his safety-rope has been properly secured. The last syllable of the group, however coinciding with the metric downbeat, brings a feeling of stability and relief. In the light of this analysis, the rhythmic pattern may appear to have an iconic impact in an essentially deviant use of *bottomless* by Milton and Shelley. In

13.   To bottomless^{2} perdition, there to dwell *(P.L. I. 47).*

bót- occurs in a strong position, followed by a sequence of three unstressed syllables before meter is reasserted. This, in itself, should not be regarded as very much out of the ordinary; it indicates, at any rate, that Milton, too, assigned stress to the first syllable of *bottomless*. Nevertheless, what can be described as the perceptual quality of "falling" and "anxiety" *is* there. By contrast, in the following three lines, *bót*- is a stress maximum in a weak position, adding momentum to the feeling of "anxiety":

(14)   Burnt after them to the bottomless^{7} pit *(P.L. VI. 866).*

(15)   With them from bliss to the bottomless^{7} deep *(P.R. I. 361).*

(16) And whelm on them to the bottomless void.[7]

(Prometheus Unbound, III. i. 76)

Considering the relative scarcity of stress maxima in weak positions, these examples from two major poets—whether independently arrived at, or copied by Shelley
from Milton—cannot be dismissed as insignificant. They are the more remarkable
since the poet (in excerpt (15)), by "to bottomless abyss" for example, could easily
have avoided the stress maximum in a weak position.

I have emphasized above that the pattern illustrated here may *appear* to have an
iconic impact, because what we have is not exactly iconic; it is more accurately
handled in terms of "combinational potential". The "falling" analogue is not part of
the metric pattern; it is merely a metaphor to suggest a peculiar psychological
atmosphere of insecurity and anxiety, which are perceptual qualities of the metric
shape under discussion. This metric shape is associated with a feeling of momentum
and craving for stability that may combine with any content and lend impetus to
such expressions as "crucifie mee", or

(17) Enduring thus the *retributive hour*[7]

(18) And with these words his temptation pursued[7]

The vague feeling of momentum, infirmity, and insecurity, along with a craving for
stability may become more constrained and assume a more definite character by
combining with certain meaning-components of such words as "bottomless". So
what appears to be an iconic quality of meter is, in fact, the result of the actualization of certain aspects of the combinational potential of the metric structure.

Strings of unstressed syllables in highly loaded contexts can be characterized as
follows: Active reassertion of the metric pattern occurs only in strong positions, by
stressed syllables, which suggests that if a stressed syllable is omitted there is some
uncertainty about whether the metric pattern has been duly preserved or not. Fowler
(1971: 193) has observed that strings containing such omissions tend to speed up
the verse. One reason for this is that among the acoustic cues for stress, we find duration of the syllable involved. A second reason, however, is that the uncertainty generates an urge to reach some point of stability as quickly as possible. In turn, this
"speeding up", while it lasts amplifies the feeling of instability. There is, then,
some mutual dependence between the prosodic structure and the overall quality of the
passage in which it occurs. The more emotively charged the passage, the more obtrusive the feeling of uncertainty carried by the strings of unstressed syllables. The
"weak shape" of these strings, in its turn, enhances the overall emotive quality of
the passage.

If the reader is willing to grant this much, he will probably become aware of
some further "delicacies" involved. Compare, for instance, the following lines:

(19) With them from bliss to the bot*tomless* deep
$$\overset{7}{}$$
(Paradise Regained, I. 361).

(20) Cast wanton eyes on the daugh*ters of* men (ibid., II. 180).

(21) And made him bow to the gods *of his* wives (ibid., 171).

The metric pattern of all three lines is violated by a stress maximum in the seventh position; furthermore, as the above ordering shows, they exhibit decreasing tension (or, for that matter, decreasing rate of speeding up) before their last position. If this is granted too, an explanation of the entire phenomenon readily offers itself: The violation generates an expectation—a looking *forward*—for the reaffirmation of meter. On the other hand, in polysyllabics like "bóttomless, crúcifie, dáughters", the unstressed syllables rely on the *preceding* stress, creating a split of direction. The more syllables "appended" to the stressed syllable of the polysyllabic, the longer the duration of this (additional) uncertainty (for an alternative explanation, see Tsur, 1977: 139).

I have dwelt at some length on instances in which strings of unstressed syllables occur in the vicinity of strong violation of meter. The reason is that—as I have suggested—the more loaded the verse, the more obtrusive the emotive quality of these strings. But, once alert to the affect, the reader can detect it in less deviant verse as well. Compare, for instance, the following lines:

(22) Lódged in his bréast as wéll might recomménd
(Paradise Regained., I. 301).
(23) My hárbor and my últimate repóse (ibid., III. 210).
(24) But áll subsísts by eleméntal strífe,
And Pássions are the élements of lífe
("An Essay on Man", I. 169–170).

The two unstressed syllables in *últimate* and *élements,* being grouped backward, generate a stronger feeling of uncertainty than in *recomménd* and *eleméntal,* where they are grouped forward. The overall effect of such backward grouping is a more moderate version of the backward grouping observed in excerpt (19). The line ends here with a phrase whose stress pattern confirms meter in position VI; a string of three unstressed syllables follows, which leaves the reader uncertain not only about the affirmation of meter, but also about the directions inherent in the line; finally, the metric pattern is triumphantly reinstated in the tenth position, sealing up the line with an emphatic closure. Or take another, unique, example:

25. And his vain importunity pursues *(Paradise Regained,* IV. 24).

There are two stress maxima in this line, in the third and sixth positions; the first stress maximum constitutes a grave violation of meter, the second its reinstatement. The two unstressed syllables *impor-* follow a stress maximum in a weak position, *–nity* follow a stress maximum in a strong position. Notwithstanding, a feeling of uncertainty appears to be stronger in *–nity* than in *impor–*, because, whereas the latter syllables look forward, the former look backward to the only stressed syllable of the same word for reassurance. Furthermore, the lack of confirmation in the eighth position requires an emphatic reinstatement of meter at the end of "–tunity pursues".

I have already mentioned that metric structures may be "double-edged". The "double-edgedness" of more than usually regular meter will be discussed in Chapter 19. In the remainder of the present section I shall explore the double-edgedness of verse lines that actualize fewer stresses than usual. Let us follow up one of Roger Fowler's brilliant insights in this respect:

> But the catch is that this blank verse style requires enormous technical skill [...]. From this point of view, lines like Wordsworth's *Unfolded transitory qualities...* are impressive feats of virtuosity. However, there is little point in admiring Wordsworth's technical achievement in lines like this: The long words do not stand out splendidly as do magnificent exotic proper names in Marlowe *(Usumcasane and Techelles both)* or in *Paradise Lost (In Vallombrosa, where th'Etrusian shades)*. In Wordsworth the polysyllables produce a kind of metered academic language, a continuous expository tone rather than points of spectacular decoration. The stress distinctions are levelled out, as we have seen, and the relationship with iambic verse appears tenuous until we realize that, even in this language of reduced accentual prominence, relatively heavy and relatively light stresses alternate regularly as the verse-design demands. The meter is "backgrounded" with great care so that it is quite unobtrusive but at the same time a stable faultless foundation. (Fowler, 1971: 194)

One is tempted to raise the question, "In what conditions do such lines have an 'academic', and in what conditions an 'exotic' tone"? In fact, when Marlowe uses no "exotic names" or "syntactic rhymes" (as pointed out by Fowler, ibid., 195), in *his* verse, too, polysyllables tend to produce "a kind of metered academic language, a continuous expository tone", as in

> (26) Our sóuls whose fáculties can comprehénd
> The wóndrous árchitecture of the wórld.

Here, too, "meter is 'backgrounded' with great care". The rule would seem to be this: "foreground" the language of a pentameter line that has only three stresses by *any means* — by repetitive schemes, such as "syntactic rhymes"; by "exotic names" as "Usumcasane" or "Vallombrosa"; or by displacing one of two stress maxima to a weak position, as in (25); alternatively, take the most common polysyllabic possible, heighten its "poetic impact" by repetition and polysyndeton, as in

(27) Tomorrow and tomorrow and tomorrow.

As a result, the sequences of unstressed syllables will have that peculiar thrill of uncertainty, that anxiety of "falling into an abyss". Of course, too much uncertainty may produce colloquial "slackness" of rhythm. Compare Yeats's line in excerpt (28) with Milton's notorious line in excerpt (29):

(28) Mónuments of unáging íntellect
(29) Immútable, immórtal, ínfinite.

In Milton's line, unlike in Yeats's, meter is confirmed in the second position. Moreover, the prominence of the first two strong positions is enhanced by the consonants *m — t* with an enclosed long back-vowel. The poetic load of (29) is reinforced by a "repetitive scheme": three adjectives are repeated, with a negative prefix, indicating [–HUMAN], that is *superhuman,* qualities—all legitimate citizens of the "grand style". In Yeats's style, there are no repetitive schemes, phonetic or syntactic; it consists of one continuous phrase. Rather removed from the "grand style", "unaging intellect" appears to be an all too human, rational, and "domesticated" version of "immutable, immortal, infinite".

The Cognitive Rationale of Rhythmical Performance

In the performance of poetry we may observe, roughly, three *delivery styles.* At one extreme, we find the sing-song of children chanting their nursery rhymes and the mechanical scansion of "freshmen", suppressing "prose rhythm"; at the other extreme, we find the prosaic rendering of readers "insensitive to rhythm", and of actors who wish to make poetic drama sound more "natural", by suppressing meter. In the middle, there is a complex *rhythmical* performance that avoids the suppression of either stress pattern or metric pattern. It is, however, plain that the human voice is incapable of performing both patterns at one and the same time. Our assumption all along the present chapter has been that it may be possible to do justice to the conflicting patterns by accommodating them in a third, superimposed pattern of performance. In the present short section I shall briefly suggest the cognitive rationale behind this assumption.

According to Neisser (1968) the human cognitive system is a multiple processing machine with limited channel capacity. The production and reception of speech is precisely such a multiple process. "Just as the speaker, in generating his message, is working on a number of different levels at the same time, so the listener in reconstructing it has to work on the same levels and, like the speaker, he works on them all at the same time. This means that, as the message is coming in, the listener is forming the morpheme string, reconstructing the word sequence and thus building up the sentence" (Frye, 1970: 49). It is important to note that this multilevel decoding of speech involves the use of two faculties: short-term memory and expectation. Utterances must be remembered in a certain way before they are understood in a satisfactory manner; at the same time, the listener anticipates what is going to be said. This enables the listener, simultaneously with his perception of the spoken utterance, to control and correct his decoding process. On the semantic level, metaphoric language may involve frustrations of expectations and contradictions to be settled. On the phonetic level, it involves the processing of prosodic information, which also relies on short-term memory and anticipation.

Two important aspects of *short-term memory* must be pointed out. As I have stressed in Chapter 1, we remember the surface structure of a sentence, with its actual syntactic structure and sound pattern only for a very short period. During this period, memory functions as an echo box, gradually fading out if there is no possibility of rehearsal. As soon as possible, we recode the sentence and it is its semantic representation that we remember. Conrad (1964) produced some experimental evidence that words are acoustically stored in short-term memory even when presented in visual form. If we are to attend to poetic rhythm too, everything possible must be done to prevent the acoustic memory trace from fading out before the rhythmic unit has been completed, or to complete the rhythmic unit before the acoustic memory-trace has faded out. This brings us to the second important aspect of short-term memory: its limitation. As I have emphasized in Chapters 2 and 5, the span of short-term memory is rigidly fixed around "the magical number 7 ± 2"—in George Miller's famous phrase. There is little possibility to extend the span of immediate memory beyond this. Thus, we can explain the fact that iambic pentameter lines are usually uttered on two or more breath-groups, whereas in everyday speech as many as ten or fifteen syllables can be pronounced on one single breath-group, with no difficulty. The imperative need to process the phonetic surface structure of poetic utterances also demands that they be segmented into units amenable to the span of immediate memory. This may also be another reason that the most frequent lines in English poetry are decasyllabic (iambic pentameters) whereas the longest line normally used in English, French, and several other modern languages is dodecasyllabic, with an obligatory caesura after the sixth syllable.

Since there is little possibility of extending the span of immediate memory by training, and since the number of parallel processes that may take place in one's "mental space" is restricted, the best way to increase one's "channel capacity", says Miller, is to *recode* the message in a more efficient way. Now, one of the *differentiae specificae* of poetic language is that there are strict limitations on the possibilities of recoding.

In most verse instances discussed in the present chapter, the stress pattern considerably diverges from the metric pattern. In such cases, the reader of poetry must rely on his metrical set. That is, whenever metric regularity is suspended, the reader may *echo,* so to speak, in his short-term memory, the regularly alternating underlying beats, even though they may have no trace in the acoustic signal. The reader may compensate, to some extent, for the absence of the metrical signal, by *antici- pating* the return of regular beats. All this is possible, if at all, for a very short pe- riod only, over a span of a very few "chunks". I said *if at all,* because the extra men- tal space required may not be available; besides, it takes a fairly experienced reader to perform such verse rhythmically.

Where should the extra space come from? As I have said, training can do little to extend the required mental space. But training *may* facilitate the recoding of the mes- sage. This, too, seems hardly useful in poetry reading. Still, there seem to be two ways of increasing the channel capacity, a "vertical" and a "horizontal" one.

Vertically, channel capacity can be increased by reducing the "noise level" of the message; or, what amounts to the same, the distinctive features by which phonemes are identified may be articulated more clearly (cf. Conrad, 1968). There is good ex- perimental evidence that in casual conversation, speakers and receivers of speech rely heavily on redundancies in the speech signal. Speakers may neglect to articulate properly all the phonemes they utter, and instead rely on the receiver's habitual pro- cess of forming and testing hypotheses concerning the contents of speech whenever the signal is insufficient. This procedure demands that one *remember* stretches of un- intelligible speech signal as long as 1000 msec., at the end of which time the signal may abruptly become intelligible (see Lieberman, 1967: 163–165). By increasing the number of dimensions along which phonemes are identified, that is, by clearly articulating the words, the listener may be spared some of the process of forming and testing hypotheses which, as the experiments described by Lieberman indicate, is a customary part of informal conversation. By the same token, the load on imme- diate memory is alleviated by a quicker coding of the sequence of words as meaning- ful.

Important aspects of the "horizontal" way of recoding have been discussed at length in the preceding and the present chapter. Mental space can be spared by clear articulation of stress groups and phrases; the breaking up of a sequence into clear-cut segments of 4, 5 or 6 chunks (syllables) facilitates perception. Furthermore, the shape of grouping may have bearing on the mental space occupied by the group. If it has a strong, *prägnant* gestalt, it is more easily perceived and remembered; by the same token, it also leaves more space for *echoing,* simultaneously, the metrical set where the regularly recurring beat must be suspended.

Prose vs. Verse—Stress, Intonation, Duration, and Articulation

The Perception-Oriented theory of meter, as I have said, constitutes a minor Coper- nican revolution, in that it shifts the center of the prosodic universe from the "metricalness" of the verse line to the reader's ability or willingness to perform the line rhythmically. Such a conception presupposes a theory of rhythmical perfor- mance; I have attempted to provide such a theory in Chapters 4–5 of an earlier book

(Tsur, 1977).[6] Some of the theory's basic assumptions were presented in the preceding section. In this last section of the present chapter, I am going to compare the handling of stress, intonation, duration and articulation in prose and verse.

Stress and intonation point up phonemic oppositions in prose language. Vowel duration indicates meaning oppositions in a few instances in English, as in such pairs of words as *fit* versus *feet*, or *dip* versus *deep*. But more frequently its function is emotive or rhythmic. In GH's "prosaic" reading of excerpt (33) the duration of *Bright* is 367 msec, in his "rhythmical" performance—550 msec. This makes no semantic, only rhythmic difference. Articulation suggests no meaning opposition. Our foregoing discussion of the cognitive rationale of rhythmical performance implies that in poetry articulation would be more careful than in prose.

In versification, the so-called "quantitative" meter is based on vowel or syllable duration; stress lies at the very roots of syllabotonic meter. Intonation becomes significant only when it must solve a problem posed by the conflict between prose rhythm and metric pattern, in order that a rhythmical performance of a deviant line may be generated. Apart from some possible emotive functions, intonation in prose language has three linguistic functions: (1) indicating the distinction between, for example, indicative, interrogative, and imperative sentences; (2) articulation of the speech stream into smaller perceptual units; (3) syntactic disambiguation. In poetic language, in addition, the function of intonation is to articulate the prosodic units as perceptual wholes. Consequently, it is a misconception—held, following Dr. Johnson, by some contemporary critics—that blank verse and *vers libre* are "often only verse for the eye". Just as the graphic arrangement on the page presents the lines as perceptual units to the eye, the intonation contours heard in the reading of poetry present the lines as perceptual units to the ear. Such contours are the result of the interaction of the intonation contours required by prose rhythm with those that articulate the line. It is assumed that the listener decodes these contours in terms of the intonation contours from whose interplay they arise. In fact, the main function of the graphic arrangement on the page is to give the reader instructions concerning the intonation contours appropriate to the lines. In what follows, I shall briefly examine some issues related to the effect of intonation upon rhythmical performance.

There is an acoustic interaction of intonation with stress in the displacement of stress from an even-numbered position to the preceding odd-numbered one.

> (30) Slíght is the Subject, but not so the Praise.
> w
>
> (31) And made him bow to the góds of his wives.
> w

6   A few years after the first edition of the present book I had an enormous breakthrough in the study of the rhythmical performance of poetry. In my 1998 book as well as a series of journal articles I reported research in which I submitted recorded readings to an instrumental investigation. Consequently, in the present chapter I replaced the original empirical analysis of excerpt 33 by a later, more accurate one. And I added Chapter 7, which may give a general idea of the nature of this research.

Loudness, duration, and fundamental frequency (in this order of increasing effective-ness) provide the acoustic cues for stress differences between syllables (Frye, 1958). The perceived stress of *Slíght* is cued by the relatively high pitch coincident with the onsets of line and syntactic unit. By contrast, the high pitch that contributes to the stress on *góds* occurs in the middle, rather than at the onset of a phrase and so the intonation contour that cues the remainder of the phrase is perceived as less natural. This may be one reason why traditional metrics allows "trochaic inversion" at line onsets and sometimes at the beginning of a sentence, but not in the middle.

It is sometimes pointed out that if one takes a piece of banal journalistic prose or a philosophical essay and sets it down on the page as a lyric poem, the words remain the same but their effect is substantially altered. The typographical arrangement produces a different kind of attention. The changes usually pointed out are both semantic and rhythmic. Writers of *vers libre* rely on their printers to call at-tention to what is called "cadence" or "rhythmic relation" (Culler, 1975). Consider, for example, the first sentence of Leibnitz's *Monadology* —"The monad of which we shall here speak is merely a simple substance, which enters into composites; simple, that is to say, without parts"—as rearranged by Monroe C. Beardsley (1958: 234):

(32) The monad
           Of which we shall here
                Speak
           Is merely a simple
      Substance,
      Which enters into composites;
      Simple,
           That is to say,
           Without parts.

I would argue that from the prosodic point of view, the typographic arrangement not only calls attention to cadence and rhythmic relations; it also affects them in some "mysterious ways" by calling up new intonational patterns. In a series of bril-liant experiments, C. I. Darwin and A. Donovan of Sussex University (1979, two papers and an unpublished demo tape) have shown that in sentences like "He turned up by ten talking of terrorism", subjects tend to hear equal time-intervals between the /t/ sounds in the stressed syllables, although they are objectively unequal. However, when they listen to a sequence of mechanical clicks that are acoustically similar, the same time intervals as between the /t/ sounds are perceived, as they should be, as unequal. When, finally, the clicks and the /t/ sounds in the text are carefully synchronized and sounded simultaneously, the intervals between the /t/

sounds are perceived as equal, whereas the intervals between the clicks are perceived as unequal.[7]

The tendency for perceptual isochrony works *within* intonation contours, but not *across* contour boundaries. When the text is broken up into verse lines, the graphic arrangement is realized in oral performance as intonation contours that are more numerous than in prose, as well as more clearly articulated or more strongly emphasized. It is quite plausible that the rhythmic character of a text broken up into verse lines is determined, *inter alia,* by our tendency to hear unequal time intervals as equal within the boundaries of each intonation contour.

Another factor that may affect rhythmic character concerns relative duration; it is implicit in the measurements of the "sound-recorders" at the beginning of the 20th century. Wallin found that "in artistically free declamation of English poetry, the ratio of length of short to long syllables is about 1:1.7; in English prose it is 1:1.5" (Schramm, 1935)[8]. It is doubtful that such a minute difference can be consciously perceived, but it is sufficient to make the listener feel that the stream of speech sounds has somehow become poetry for the ear and not only for the eye. Perhaps this difference is perceived as, simply, clearer articulation in poetry than in prose (as suggested in the preceding section).

I have made some predictions concerning grouping and over-articulation in the rhythmical performance of poetry, based on the hypotheses of limited channel capacity and of multiple information-processing discussed above. In order to test them, I had professors of literature record such verse lines as

(33)   Bright Star! would I were steadfast as thou art!,

both in a rhythmical and a prosaic way. It soon became clear that they had difficulties in performing the lines prosaically. In what follows we shall have a look at two performances of "Bright Star", excised from a "rhythmical" and a "prosaic" reading of excerpt (33) read by GH, professor of comparative literature (he was the only reader in my corpus who could produce rhythmical and sensibly prosaic readings of the same verse lines).

When I received my first initiation into the mysteries of speech research in 1980, I was told that neither grouping nor a clearer than usual articulation can be shown by the machine. One of the modest contributions of my recent work to instrumental phonetics may be that it has identified a few parameters that may indicate these perceptual qualities (the following analysis was done eighteen years after the recording, after having made those modest contributions). One of my consistently recur-

---

[7]   This difference between *t*s and clicks, amazing as they may seem, should not be too much surprising. It is in perfect harmony with the difference between the "speech mode" and the "non-speech mode" of aural perception, to be discussed in Chapter 8. The sound files for this experiment are available online at
http://www.tau.ac.il/~tsurxx/SecondEditionSoundFiles/SoundFiles.html.

[8]   My measurements suggest that such ratios may hold mainly in what I will call "convergent delivery style" in poetry reading.

ring findings is that certain phonetic features may contribute to a variety of perceived qualities at the same time. Duration, for instance, may contribute, among
other things, to stress perception and to an impression of over-articulation. Pitch
movement may contribute, at the same time, to stress perception and to continuation or discontinuation (this is exploited in excerpt (30), for instance). A pause
between words may indicate straightforward discontinuity; but, within a word before,
e.g., a word-final stop release, it is not at all perceived as a pause, but rather as a
clearer than usual articulation of the stop (and, by the same token, of the word
boundary). The degree of articulation of a word-final stop may depend, among other
things, on the presence or absence of a stop release; and if present, the release may
be longer or shorter, having more or less amplitude, and be preceded by a longer or
shorter pause (interpreted by the listener as the duration of the articulatory gesture).

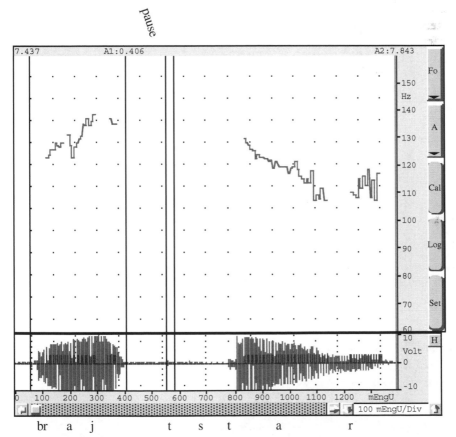

Figure 6.2   Wave plot and F$_0$ extract of "Bright Star!" in GH's "rhythmical" reading.[9]

---

[9]   The lower window presents the wave plot display which shows a plot of the wave amplitude (in volts) as a function of time (in milliseconds); the upper window presents a

Listening to the two readings gives the impression that the two words are relatively independent in the first reading, both heavily stressed, with a clearly articulated word boundary between them, yet continuous and closely grouped together. The two lexical words are equally stressed (thus deviating from the metric pattern); yet, the iambic lilt is somehow preserved in perception.[10] In the second reading, by contrast, the adjective is clearly subordinated to the following noun. At the same time, it is less well articulated, and the resulting impression is somehow more "prosaic".

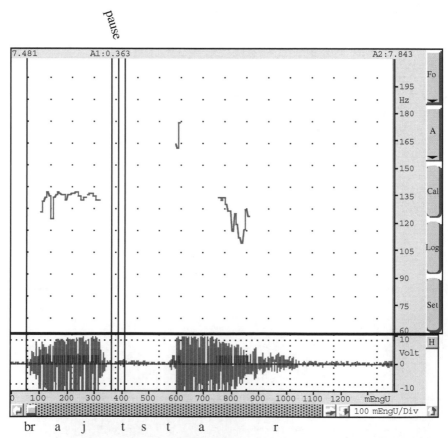

Figure 6.3   Wave plot and F$_0$ extract of "Bright Star!" in GH's "prosaic" reading.

---

fundamental frequency plot, which displays time on the horizontal axis and the estimated glottal frequency (F$_0$) in Hz on the vertical axis.

10   It would appear from this analysis that GH identifies "rhythmical performance" with what in Chapter 7 I will call "divergent delivery style"; that is, he sharpens the conflict between stressed syllables and weak positions, and then deploys the vocal devices predicted by the present study so as to reconcile the conflicting patterns in perception.

Some of the phonetic information reflected in the graphs may account for these impressions. There is no measurable pause between the two words in either reading. The duration of "Bright" and "Star" in Figure 6.2 is 550 msec and 844 msec respectively, as opposed to 367 msec and 641 msec in Figure 6.3. This may contribute to an impression that these words are more heavily stressed and more clearly articulated in the rhythmical than in the prosaic reading. The pitch contour on "Bright" is flat in Figure 6.3, and there is a leap from "Bright" to "Star" from 132.036 Hz to 175.000 Hz. This strongly suggests that the adjective is subordinated both in stress and intonation to the noun. The rising pitch contour on "Bright" in Figure 6.2 has a complex effect. First, it bestows considerable prominence on the adjective, releasing it, so to speak, from its subordination to the ensuing noun. At the same time, a rising sequence of sounds may have in music, as suggested by Cooper and Meyer (1960: 15), a strong "forward grouping" effect. What is more, by the same token it constitutes a "late peak" (Knowles, 1992). Normally, the highest point of the intonation contour is aligned with the middle of the syllabic crest. "Late peaking" occurs when the highest point "hits" the vowel later than its middle, or even on the following sonorant. In the present instance, the peak occurs at the second sound of the diphthong in "Bright". As I argued in Chapter 5, this tends to generate a forward-propelling "perceptual force". As we have seen, in Figure 6.3 the pitch contour subordinates "Bright" to "Star", whereas in Figure 6.2 it increases the prominence of "Bright". Rather than displaying an intonation leap between the two words, the falling curve on "Star" smoothly continues the rising curve on "Bright". Notwithstanding, the excessive duration and terminal contour of "Star" in Figure 6.2 takes care of its perceived stress.

Thus, the two words constitute in Figure 6.2 two distinct, equally prominent events, yet which are emphatically grouped together. The discreteness of the two words is enhanced by what Knowles (1991) calls "segmental discontinuity", generated by the over-articulation of the word-final /t/. In ordinary speech, the first word would be run into the next one, with no release of the word-final /t/. In both readings the /t/ is released. Though in Figure 6.3 the release has considerably greater amplitude, it is preceded by a 22 msec pause, whereas in Figure 6.2, the (weaker) release is preceded by a 131 msec (that is, six times longer) pause—interpreted by the listener as the duration of the sustained articulatory gesture.

GH had no advance knowledge of the hypotheses to be tested; but, if one may judge from the foregoing brief comparison, his notions of the difference between a rhythmical and a prosaic reading were very similar to the ones outlined above. In his rhythmical performance of the line he did not subordinate the adjective in the weak position to the ensuing noun as he did in what he considered the "prosaic" performance. On the contrary rather, he assigned a main stress to the lexical word in the first (weak) position, and then had recourse to vocal manipulations predicted above, grouping and over-articulation, so as to save the mental processing space required for the perception of the abstract metric pattern behind the immediately observable linguistic stress pattern. Why should a performer choose to overstress a stressed syllable in a weak position precisely in his "rhythmical" rather than in his "prosaic" performance? Because, as I will insist time and again, this allows him to enhance his aesthetic achievement: "the balance and reconcilement of opposite or discordant qualities" (see a more thorough discussion of these two readings in Tsur, 1998: 78–82; 321–326).[11]

To conclude. One cannot account for the rhythmic effect of complex instances of syllabotonic verse by the regular alternation of stressed and unstressed syllables. Nor can one account for this effect by relying on equal or proportional time intervals between stresses or "regions of strength". The explanation must be sought in one of two directions or their combination. On the one hand, one must assume an abstract scheme of mechanically alternating weak and strong positions that exists as a set of expectations in the reader's or listener's mind (the stress of prose rhythm may confirm or disconfirm these expectations) and induces pleasure when these expectations are reaffirmed after apparently having been thwarted.

On the other hand, one must assume the existence of a relatively large perceptual unit, the verse line, divided into smaller units consisting of sequences of stressed and unstressed syllables. The larger perceptual unit is articulated, in vocal realization, by its intonation contour, an element taken from "ordinary speech", which undergoes certain "distortions" in the rhythmic performance of poetry, preventing unrhymed and unmeasured verse from becoming "poetry for the eye" only. As long as the line is perceived as a whole, there is a tendency to perceive the smaller units as rhythmical. This last section has focused on the interaction of stress and intonation contours. What is perceived as rhythmic regularity based on the regular alternation of stressed and unstressed syllables must be explained, paradoxically enough, in terms of devices that increase the distinctness of the intonation contour—which, in turn, cues the integrity and unity of the perceptual unit.

[11] The sound files of these readings are available online at
http://www.tau.ac.il/~tsurxx/SecondEditionSoundFiles/SoundFiles.html.

CHAPTER 7

Delivery Style and Listener Response
An Empirical Study

In the preceding chapter I propounded a theory of meter including a theory of rhythmical performance of poetry. When I wanted to submit this theory to instrumental investigation, all the great gurus of instrumental phonetics told me that this was impossible, because the major part of poetic rhythm takes place in the mind, and only a small part of it is detectable in the vocal output. I decided to sidestep this problem by making certain predictions based on my theory as to the vocal manipulations required, and see whether performance instances judged rhythmical conform with these predictions. I made predictions in terms of relative stress, clear-cut articulation, gestalt grouping, and certain (musical) pitch-intervals. However, again, all the great gurus told me that none of these variables can be read off from the machine's output. It took me over twenty-five years of agonizing search to find a way to reformulate my research questions in terms that the machine could understand. These terms included continuity and discontinuity. My 1977 hypothesis was that conflicting patterns could be indicated by conflicting vocal cues (Tsur, 1977: 97, 103, 134). The breakthrough occurred when I found a way to treat a wide range of conflicting phenomena in terms of simultaneous continuity and discontinuity (this happened when I was exposed to the work of Gerry Knowles and Tom Barney at Lancaster University). These conflicting phenomena included run-on sentences, strings of consecutive stressed syllables, and even stress maximum in a weak position.[1]

This chapter goes one step beyond the scope of my earlier instrumental research: It attempts to substantiate the inferences from the machine's output against the intuitions of flesh-and-blood listeners. In other words, it is an empirical inquiry into the aesthetic event of the rhythmical performance of poetry. This event typically contains a reciter, a poetic text, and a listener (though the reciter himself may be the listener too). Poetic rhythm is accessible only through some kind of performance, vocalized or silent. Rhythmical performance is not a unitary phenomenon, one must distinguish between various delivery styles. This chapter aspires to give a fairly comprehensive description of the aesthetic event under discussion. A pilot

---

[1] The sound files of the readings discussed here are available online at
http://www.tau.ac.il/~tsurxx/SecondEditionSoundFiles/SoundFiles.html.
My instrumental research has been published in two books (Tsur, 1998; 2006), and a series of articles.

experiment suggests that apparently incompatible responses to the same delivery instance may result from the listeners' realisation of different subsets of aspects of the same event. They may, therefore, be meaningfully discussed and compared. My assumption is that rhythmical performance and delivery style are determined by the poem's metric structure, the performer's aesthetic conceptions and vocal resources, and the constraints of the cognitive system. I will concentrate on small-scale computer-aided analyses and comparisons of performances by leading British actors. Consequently, I will focus my discussion on two verse instances only: two recordings of two verse lines containing an enjambment from Keats's "Ode on a Grecian Urn", and four recordings of one line, the last line of Shakespeare's Sonnet 129, all from commercially-available recordings.

The Rhythmical Performance of Poetry

As I claimed in Chapter 6, an iambic pentameter line is supposed to consist of regularly alternating unstressed and stressed syllables. In the first one hundred sixty-five lines of *Paradise Lost* there are only two such lines. How do experienced readers of poetry recognize vastly different irregular stress patterns as iambic pentameter? Among the many attempts to answer this question, there is a venerable tradition of instrumental research as well. Since the early nineteen-twenties there has been instrumental research of poetry reading by the so-called "sound-recorders", in an attempt to discover some regularity. The greatest achievement of these researchers was that they refuted an obstinately persistent myth that there are equal or proportional time intervals between stressed syllables or regions of stress. But they had a naive conception of poetic rhythm: they thought they were measuring relationships that constitute the rhythm of a poem, whereas they were measuring some accidental performance of it. (Their work was summarised by Schramm (1935); see also Wimsatt and Beardsley (1959)). To avoid this problem, Wellek and Warren (1956, Chapter 13) proposed a model, according to which poetic rhythm has three "dimensions": an abstract versification pattern that consists of verse lines and regularly alternating weak and strong positions; a linguistic pattern that consists of syntactic units and irregularly alternating stressed and unstressed syllables; and a pattern of performance (generative metrists have reinvented the first two of them). In my conception, the rhythmical performance of poetry, just as the understanding of a metaphor, is a problem-solving activity: when the linguistic and versification patterns conflict, they are accommodated in a pattern of performance, such that both are perceptible simultaneously. Thus, the data measured by the instruments stop being accidental; they become functional. They are constrained by the solution of a problem posed by the conflicting patterns of the text on the one hand, and by the reciter's (and the audience's) phonetic competence and cognitive system on the other. They give information not about an arbitrary performance, but about the ways in which the conflicting patterns of language and versification can be reconciled and rendered acceptable. In an enjambment, for instance, the performer may convey both the verse line boundary and the run-on sentence as perceptual units, however strained, by having recourse to conflicting phonetic cues: cues of continuity and discontinuity simultaneously.

My recent work has been devoted to an instrumental study of the hitherto neglected performance dimension. My position regarding delivery style can be stated with reference to the "Performance" entry of *The New Princeton Encyclopedia of Poetry and Poetics* (1993: 893). "C. S. Lewis once identified two types of performers of metrical verse: 'Minstrels' (who recite in a wooden singsong voice, letting scansion override verse) and 'Actors' (who give a flamboyantly expressive recitation, ignoring meter altogether)". In the preceding chapter I stated the same distinction in somewhat differnt terms. In Wellek and Warren's terms, the Minstrel subdues the linguistic pattern (prose rhythm) and foregrounds the versification pattern; the Actor subdues the metric pattern in favour of the prose rhythm. My position is that there is a third "rhythmical performance", too, in which both metric pattern and linguistic stress pattern can be accommodated, such that both are established in the listener's perception.

Some reciters of poetry adopt one or another type of solution quite randomly; but some make a deliberate choice in adopting a consistent delivery style, whether consciously or unconsciouly. My attempt to compare two readings of the same text by the same actor reveals that during a long career an actor may change his aesthetic conception, perhaps unconsciously. Such a consistent change of conceptions may be detected even when looking into the minute details of the performances of one verse line. I personally believe that rhythmic complexities arising from conflicting patterns are there in order to realize them in vocal performance too. But in our cultural situation both the "actor's approach" and the "rhythmical performance" are considered legitimate. At any rate, my treatment of the issue will be mostly descriptive; but I will also explore how description may fade into evaluation.

My own way in empirical research is to collect judgments from students, colleagues or my research associates on whether the performer was successful in conveying the conflicting aspects of language and versification. And if possible, I try to compare alternative possiblities. Then I look for cues in the phonetic structures of the recordings, trying to find support for the intuitive judgments. In my present research I have also elicited responses through the internet medium.

In my instrumental research I have relied on two papers by Gerry Knowles (1991; 1992). In the first he investigated the nature of tone-groups. He explored the external discontinuities at the tone-group boundaries. These are temporal discontinuation (pause), pitch discontinuation (a sudden change in F_0—pitch, in plain English) and segmental discontinuation (that is, in normal speech the articulation of adjacent words is overlapping; when there is no overlap, it may count as discontinuity, even if there is no pause). Glottal stops in words beginning with a vowel, or word-final stop releases too may indicate segmental discontinuation[2]. This would be the most

---

[2]   Glottal stop is the speech sound inserted before "aim" when saying "I said 'an aim', not 'a name'". Stop release is the movement of one or more vocal organs in quitting the position for a speech sound. It is perceived as a "click". In the dictionary record-

evasive type of discontinuity. "The important distinction that seems to be emerging is between boundaries with or without pauses". In what follows, I shall explore how these correlates of tone-group boundaries can be exploited as conflicting cues for the perceptual accommodation of the conflicting patterns of speech and versification.

One of the most effective kinds of segmental discontinuity is the prolongation of a phoneme or of a syllable at the end of an utterance, arousing (very much like *fermata* in music) a sense of stability and lack of forward motion. While this is most useful in the kind of research I am engaged in, there is a big problem with this notion. There is no standard by which we can determine whether a phoneme or sequence of phonemes is longer or shorter than ought to be. Consequently, one must rely in this respect on one's intuitive judgment, or some roundabout reasoning about measurements and comparisons. In my recent work I have tried out two new methods: comparing the word in the poetic context to readings in the audio version of *Merriam-Webster's Collegiate Dictionary*; and instrumental manipulation of the phonetic structure of the words. In the above dictionary an audio pronunciation of the "citation form" of words is provided. Thus, the dictionary reading may serve as an objective standard (that is, without distortion of personal feelings or versification requirements), from which the artistic recital deviates. By instrumental manipulations I have inserted glottal stops or lengthened existing speech sounds in verse lines, listening to the rhythmic effect of the outcome.

A major forward-grouping agent in the rhythmic performance of divergent poetry is what called "late peaking". The peak of the pitch contour normally occurs in the middle of the syllabic crest; in some instances, however, it occurs late in the vowel, or even after it; and sometimes it occurs earlier than the middle. I have found in my corpus that late peaking generates an impetuous forward drive; in fact, the later the peaking, the more impetuous is the forward drive. This is also predicted by Gestalt theory (see my discussion of "perceptual forces" in Chapter 5).

Convergent and Divergent Delivery Styles

I suggested above that there is a "rhythmical performance", in which both metric pattern and linguistic stress pattern can be accommodated, such that both are established in the listener's perception. I intend to distinguish within the legitimate boundaries of "rhythmical performance" between "convergent" and "divergent deliv-

---

ing of "bright" there is an exceptionally salient stop release after /t/; in "brighten" there is none. Listen online to these two words, and then the isolated stop release.

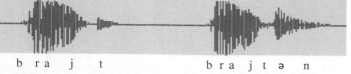

b   ra   j   t   b   ra   j   t   ə   n

http://www.tau.ac.il/~tsurxx/SecondEditionSoundFiles/SoundFiles.html

ery styles". Such convergence or divergence typically occurs between the metric and linguistic dimensions.

As I expounded in Chapter 6, my work is governed by the "limited-channel-capacity hypothesis" of human information processing. Most of the available mental space may be allocated to one sequence of information processing. In order to make parallel processes possible, they must be allocated mental processing space at the expense of the "main sequence". The need to perceive the linguistic and the versification dimensions at the same time requires some cognitive manipulation for saving mental processing space. Training cannot increase "channel capacity". But the amount of information processed may be increased by efficient coding. Consider the following joke: "How do you feel, in one word?" "Good". "And in two words?" "Not good". For our purpose, the point is that "not good" could be recoded in one word, as "bad". In the reading of poetry such semantic recoding is inadmissible. Neither words, nor their order can be changed in poetry. But there is a possibility for saving mental space by grouping and clearly articulating the speech units. Mental processing space may be saved by the grouping of shorter words into a larger perceptual unit on the one hand, or by the over-articulation of phonemes and of word boundaries on the other. Consider the phrases "peace talks" and "pea stalks". By clearly articulating the word boundaries, one may save mental processing space required to infer from the context which phrase is intended. The linguistic sequence requires continuity; the over-articulation of word boundaries generates discontinuity. The resulting spare processing space is required for the simultaneous perception of regularly alternating weak and strong positions that constitute the metrical set, and of the immediately-observable string of syllables where their stress pattern deviates from the versification pattern.

Performance of Enjambment

Poetic Rhythm consists, then, of three concurrent patterns: versification pattern, linguistic pattern and performance. Where the first two conflict, performance must offer an "elegant solution" to the problem. In a rhythmical performance, the conflicting linguistic and versification patterns are simultaneously perceptible. Enjambment consists in such a conflict: the line ending demands discontinuation in the flow of speech, the sentence running on from one line to the other requires continuation. The received view (formulated by Chatman) denies the possibility of a solution to such a problem:

> in performance, all ambiguities have to be resolved before or during delivery. Since the nature of performance is linear and temporal, sentences can only be read aloud once and must be given a specific intonational pattern. Hence in performance, the performer is forced to choose between alternative intonational patterns and their associated meanings. (The "Performance"

entry of *The New Princeton Encyclopedia of Poetry and Poetics,* 1993: 893; cf. Chatman, 1965; 1966)

I beg to differ on this matter. In my 1977 book I speculated that conflicting patterns can be indicated by conflicting vocal cues. In my 1998 book I demonstrated this in an instrumental research. Consider the following verse instance from Keats's "Ode on a Grecian Urn" in which the versification unit (the verse line) conflicts with the syntactic unit (the clause), that is, when the phrase or clause runs on from one line to the next one. Let us compare two recordings by two leading British actors, Douglas Hodge and Michael Sheen.

(1)   Sylvan historian, who canst thus express
       A flowery tale more sweetly than our rhyme...

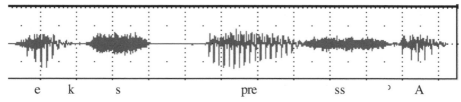

Figure 7.1   Wave plot of "express A" in Hodge's performance (ʾ indicates glottal stop)

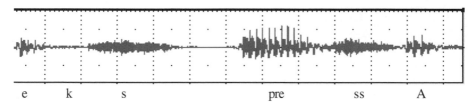

Figure 7.2   Wave plot of "express A" in Sheen's performance (no glottal stop)

The overwhelming majority of listeners made the judgment that Hodge offers an admirably rhythmical solution to the problem, by suggesting continuation and discontinuation at one and the same time at the end of the word "express", whereas in Sheen's reading "A" at the beginning of the next line is irritatingly continuous with "express". There is no measurable pause in either of the readings between the two words; and this takes care of syntactic continuity. Two significant differences between the two readings may account for the perceived difference between them. First, in Sheen's reading the /s/ of "express" is inseparably run into "A", whereas in Hodge's reading we may discern a glottal stop that perceptually separates the two words, indicated by a minute "lump" in the wave plot. Second, the syllable "press" in general, and the closing /s/ in particular, are considerably longer in Hodge's reading than in Sheen's.

How can we know that *these* are the variables that determine the effect? I cannot go here into the theoretical considerations. But I have reproduced in Sheen's reading the same perceived effect as in Hodge's reading by electronically manipulating it. I copied a section of Sheen's /s/ and repeatedly re-pasted it, prolonging the /s/. Then I copied from Hodge's reading the glottal stop and pasted it into Sheen's reading, before the "A". Again, the majority of listeners judged that in the doctored, but not the original, version conflicting cues for continuation and discontinuation are provided.[3]

In addition, Sheen overstresses *our*, violating the iambic cadence of the line. I made an attempt electronically to restore the iambic cadence without detracting from the emphatic effect. In manipulated version 2 I used the application Audacity to reduce the tempo of the word *rhyme*, lengthening it without affecting pitch, so as to make it break rhythmically even with the emphatic stress on *our*.

Gielgud vs. Gielgud

The rest of this chapter is focused on four delivery instances of a single verse line from a sonnet for which I had access to four recordings, two of which are by the same actor, sixteen years apart.[4] This allows me to consider significant differences between two delivery instances where certain other things are, still, equal—enabling me to set forth some of my distinctions with greater clarity and distinctness.

(2)   To shún the héaven that léads mén to this héll.
           w   s   w   s   w   s   w   s   w   s

Two structural difficulties are built into this verse line, for which the reciter must find an elegant solution. The three syllables "heaven that" must be assigned, in one way or another, to two metrical positions. And the sequence "leads men" poses a difficulty for prosodists who believe in metrical and unmetrical lines. Paul Kiparsky, for instance, claims that strings of consecutive stressed syllables must end in an even-numbered (strong) position. Strings that end in a weak (odd-numbered) position render the verse line "unmetrical". The reason is that the rightmost member in the

---

[3]   The theoretical framework and the comparison between Hodge's and Sheen's readings have been extracted from Tsur, 1998: Chapter 3. An extended version of the present section of this paper is available, with the sound files, online in Tsur 2000.

[4]   I am going to explore four readings of this verse line: by The Marlowe Society, Simon Callow, and two by Sir John Gielgud. Both of Gielgud's recordings are by Caedmon, in 1963 (the reading labelled "Gielgud 2") and 1979 ("Gielgud 1"). The discrepancy between the ordinal numbers and the order of recordings reflect my well-reasoned but mistaken assumption that the more complex aesthetic conception must be the later one.

string bears the greatest stress; it may not therefore—thus the argument goes—occur in a weak position. We will consider how Gielgud and other reciters handle the two difficulties in their readings.

In certain cases poets have licence to assign two syllables to one position, that is, where meter requires only one syllable. Traditional metrics solves the problem by "eliding" a vowel. Generative metrists rightly claim that this solution does not work in many instances. They have discovered certain phonetically-justifiable rules that would render such verse instances "metrical". A metrical position, they say, may be actualized by two syllables under the following conditions:

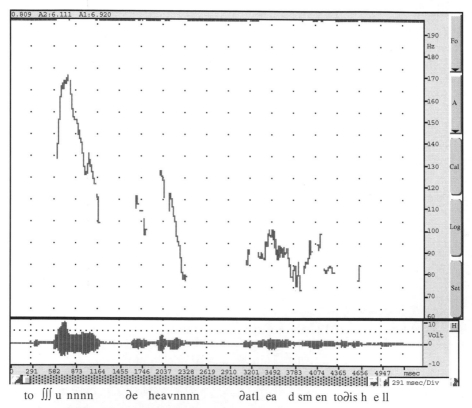

Figure 7.3   Wave plot and pitch extract of "To shun the heaven that leads men to this hell" Gielgud 1[5]

---

[5]   The lower window presents the wave plot display which shows a plot of the wave amplitude (in volts) on the vertical axis, as a function of time (in milliseconds) on the horizontal axis. The upper window presents a fundamental frequency plot, which displays time on the horizontal axis and the estimated glottal frequency (F_0 = pitch) in Hz on the vertical axis.

I. Where the syllables consist of two adjoining vowels, irrespective of word boundary, or where they are separated by a liquid or nasal or h or, from the early sixteenth century onwards, by a voiced fricative (cf. Halle and Keyser 1966, 209; Freeman 1969, 197–198).

II. "An unstressed or weakly stressed monosyllabic word may constitute a single metrical position with a preceding stressed or unstressed syllable" (Halle and Keyser 1966, 212).

There is a traditional stock of bisyllabic words which frequently occur in a single position, as "even, heaven, seven, power, tower, spirit, devil, evil," etc. Some of these words *cannot* be pronounced as a single syllable, even though the editor may omit one of the vowels, as in "heav'n". It will be observed that all these instances conform with Condition I. And so does "many a", which most frequently occupies two positions in iambic verse, instead three.

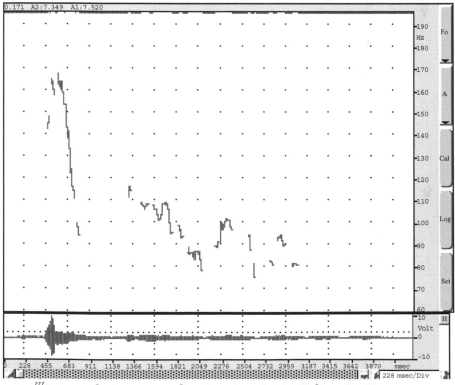

Figure 7.4 Wave plot and pitch extract of "To shun the heaven that leads men to this hell", Gielgud 2.

However, they "say nothing [...] about how this and similar lines are to be performed" (Halle and Keyser, 1966: 207). I claim that this licence is not a mere arbitrary "allowable deviation", nor a matter of mere internalisation of an abstract "rule". Certain pairs of syllables *may* constitute a single position precisely because they *can,* though need not, be performed in a certain way. The relevant phonemes: vowels, sonorants, *h,* and voiced fricatives, have a common feature of performance: continuity. The property shared by pairs of syllables like "heaven... I have... I am... devil... many a... tower... spirit" etc. is that there is no *abrupt stop consonant* between them and, except /h/, the transition between vowels has an element of periodicity. The transition from one vowel to another may be smoother, more fluent, without a clearly articulated boundary between the syllables; the boundary between the two vowels is fuzzy. I have suggested that in metrically complex lines there is sometimes a need for careful articulation in order for metrical positions to be perceived. In the present issue, the converse appears to be the case. If, e.g., "heaven" is emphatically articulated only at the end of the word, it will not indicate two metrical positions, although it is perceived as two syllables.

Examples from *Anthony and Cleopatra* and *Hamlet* suggest that there may be a third, altogether different kind of condition under which extrametrical syllables may occur in a line: when two syllables that are to be assigned to the same position are separated by a major syntactic boundary (usually at the caesura). In the line discussed here, the word "heaven" conforms with both Condition I and III. As we will see, a comparison of Gielgud's two readings suggests that there may be a substantial difference between them. Halle KeyserFreeman

When I first listened to these two performances by Gielgud, I tried to get an overall intuitive impression of the difference between them, rather than analyse it. I had an unexplained impression that Gielgud 2 is much more complex, artistically more sophisticated, rhythmically more satisfying. The best way to characterise my impression of Gielgud 1 was, perhaps, by punning on the English idioms "flat-out" and "flat out". The former is usually used as an intensive, that is, a modifier that has little meaning except to intensify the meaning it modifies; the latter suggests "in a blunt and direct manner". Later, when I compared the two readings' handling of the complexities of the verse line, this intuitive contrast was amply accounted for.

If you encounter the stretch of language "To shun the heaven that leads men to this hell" in a prose utterance, it may be uttered as a single unit, or will at most be segmented into two segments, the relative clause, and what precedes it. Both readings of Shakespeare's verse are parsed into more segments. Now when you look at the wave plots and pitch plots extracted from the two readings, an immediately-perceived difference becomes conspicuous. In Gielgud 1 there are two huge pauses (after "shun" and "heaven"). In the wave plot extracted from Gielgud 2 no such pauses are visible. Discontinuation is achieved here by means other than straightforward pauses.

Measurements concerning the word "heaven" may tell us much of the story (Table 1). In Gielgud's both readings /n/ is about 1.77 times longer than the combined duration of the preceding sounds. As I said earlier, there is no way to decide whether a given speech sound is longer or shorter than ought to be. Recently I began to use the electronic version of *The Merriam-Webster Collegiate Dictionary* as a standard for comparison. In this dictionary the words are not only printed, but also spoken by either a male or a female speaker. These recordings give the "citation form" of the words, with professional clearly-articulated pronunciation. The word "heaven" is spoken by the female speaker. Here the duration of /n/ is less than half of the combined duration of the preceding sounds. Obviously, in Gielgud's both readings the /n/ is exceptionally lengthened. I will argue that this difference has far-reaching rhythmic and aesthetic consequences.

Subjectively, the prolongation of /n/ is much more conspicuous in Gielgud 2 than in Gielgud 1. Indeed, it is insignificantly longer in Gielgud 2. But, as Table 7.1 shows, the two /n/s have roughly the same duration relative to the combined duration of the preceding speech sounds in the word. One important difference must be sought in the respective amplitude envelopes[6] of these /n/s. Consider Figure 7.5. In Gielgud 1, in the first three sounds of "heav'n" the amplitude curve juts out; the beginning of /n/ still has considerable amplitude (the second "hill" of the curve), but then the sound gradually fades away. In Gielgud 2 the amplitude level is relatively even: the first syllable does not jut out; and the curve on /n/ is higher than the bottom line, and does not fade away as in the other reading.

Table 7.1   Durations of the speech sounds of "heaven" in milliseconds (msec). Gielgud and The Marlowe Society elide the ə; the Dictionary and Callow do not. In Gielgud's readings /n/ is about 1.77 times longer than the combined duration of the preceding sounds. In the Dictionary and in Callow's reading the combined duration of the preceding sounds is over twice as long as that of /n/. In The Marlowe Society's reading /n/ is insignificantly longer than the combined duration of the preceding sounds.

	h	ɛ	v	ə	n	h+ɛ+v	ratio
Dictionary	44	106	55	95	137	300	0.456
Gielgud 1	100	89	80		478	269	1.776
Gielgud 2	142	77	59		492	278	1.769
Marlowe	111	81	78		203	197	1.030
Callow	53	78	62	83	133	276	0.481

The prolongation of /n/ has two quite different effects: it suggests what Gerry Knowles calls "segmental discontinuation"; and improves the articulation of the phoneme. Now the decaying amplitude in one reading lessens the effect of the articulation of /n/, whereas its sustained amplitude in the other reading strongly reinforces it. With reference to bisyllabic occupancy of metrical positions I suggested that if "heaven" is emphatically articulated only at the end of the word and underarticulated between the two syllables, it will not indicate two metrical positions, although it is perceived as two syllables. One would expect that the need to squeeze two syllables

---

6   "Amplitude" is the acoustic correlate of what appears to consciousness as "loudness", that is, the magnitude of the auditory sensation produced.

into one metrical position requires the reciter to elide the /ə / and shorten the /n/ as much as possible. Gielgud does elide the /ə /, but considerably lengthens the /n/; this is, precisely, what the present theory predicts: over- rather than underarticulation of the /n/. Listening to the two recordings confirms this speculation. The extrametrical syllable at the caesura is perceived as less disturbing in Gielgud 2 than in Gielgud 1. One of several reasons must be attributed to this overarticulation of the word-final /n/.

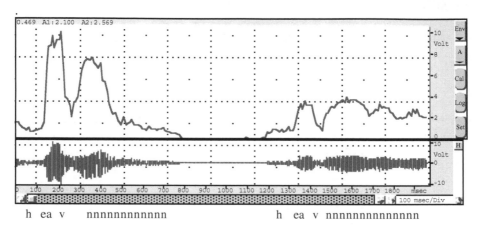

h   ea   v   nnnnnnnnnnnn   h   ea   v   nnnnnnnnnnnnnnn

Figure 7.5   Wave plot and amplitude envelope of "heav'n" in Gielgud 1 & Gielgud 2.

I have pointed out above another conspicuous difference between the two readings. In Gielgud 1 there is a huge 413-msec pause between "shun" and "the"; and an even longer, 503-msec pause between "heaven" and "that". Obviously, these function words are syntactically grouped forward, and the preceding pauses strongly underpin this forward-grouping. In Gielgud 2, by contrast, there is no measurable pause between these pairs of words. Notwithstanding this, one of my associates could hardly believe that there is no pause there in this reading. What is more, as Figure 7.4 shows, in Gielgud 2 the words "heaven" and "that" are uttered on one falling intonation contour, effectively grouping "that" backward rather than forward. It is the prolongation and overarticulation of the word-final /n/ that bears all the burden of generating discontinuity at the caesura.

    Perceptually, what happens here is quite sophisticated. We have got here conflicting cues for continuity and discontinuity. The shared intonation contour and the lack of pause groups the word "that" backward; the listener's syntactic knowledge and the sustained /n/ indicating a rest suggest a new start after "heaven". Consequently, a caesura and a "metrical impulse" across it are perceived at the same time. Levin (1971: 184–185) regards caesura as a metrical, not a linguistic fact. The line exerts pressure for completion upon which the caesura obtrudes. "If caesura is regarded as the syntactic pause or break, nothing is left to explain the required sense of metrical impulsion across that break" (185). I said above that in Gielgud 1, by contrast, I intuitively felt that the same syntactic juncture was thrust upon the reader "in a blunt and direct manner" and, at the same time, acted as a modifier that has little meaning except to intensify the meaning it modifies. This happens because the grouping cues cluster differently, displaying great redundancy. The beginning of a relative clause constitutes a major syntactic juncture. This is reinforced by an unusually long pause, and is further reinforced by the prolongation of the word-final /n/. It is this overarticulated syntactic juncture that confirms a prosodic event—a caesura. In terms of our initial stylistic distinction, in Gielgud 1 the cues act in convergence, in Gielgud 2 in divergence.

Let us go back to the three conditions suggested above under which a metrical position may be actualized by two syllables. The three syllables "heaven that" must be assigned to two metrical positions. This instance happens to conform with all three conditions, leaving the performer with a margin of freedom to choose. I have claimed that the three conditions imply different kinds of vocal performance. So far I treated the three kinds of vocal performance as more or less equal. But, as I said above, in Gielgud 2 the solution sounds somehow more acceptable than in Gielgud 1. The reason seems to be that the two readings realise different conditions. Gielgud 1 separates the syllables "-en" and "that" by a long pause, so that the two may be perceived as belonging to different units, preventing conflict (Condition III). I pointed out above that in Gielgud 1 the amplitude of /n/ gradually fades away, whereas in Gielgud 2 it is sustained (see Figure 7.5); owing to this, in the latter the /n/ is more salient and therefore more effective as a cue for discontinuation. This legitimises Gielgud 2 under Condition I. But this verse line can be legitimised under Condition II as well: "that" is an unstressed monosyllabic word with a reduced vowel. What kind of performance would this Condition require? In this reading, the word "that" is conspicuously underarticulated. As Figure 7.4 clearly shows, it is also emphatically grouped backward by two means: there is no measurable pause between the two words; and they are uttered on what Gerry Knowles calls an "internally defined" intonation curve. This is followed by "pitch discontinuation" (a sudden change in F_0). The pitch on "heaven" falls from 116.667 Hz to 97.566 Hz; then, on "that", further from 87.154 to 78.750Hz. Here the pitch curve changes direction and resets to 89.271 Hz, continuing upward to 102.558 Hz; then changing direction again, it descends to 97.137 Hz. .

Figure 7.6   Jastrow's "duck-rabbit" (from Wittgenstein, 1976: 194[e]).

The change of direction and the sudden leap of pitch indicate "pitch discontinuity", that is, a tone-group boundary. Thus, an exceptionally complex structure is generated: the three words "heaven that leads" are continuous, there is no measurable pause between them; "that" is grouped backward, but is part of the ensuing syntactic unit; at the same time, this stretch of words is parsed into three distinct units by powerful cues of discontinuity. Thus, the grouping of "that" becomes somewhat ambiguous. It is both preceded and followed by cues of discontinuity, and the perceiver has some freedom to group it either forward or backward, actualizing either Condition I or Condition II of bisyllabic occupancy. In either case, conspicuous discontinuity is generated, with a powerful impulse across it. However, as with Jastrow's notorious duck-rabbit, the two possibilities cannot be realised simultaneously. It is a matter of what Wittgenstein called "aspect switching". This possibility to switch from one solution to another will be more conspicuous if we realise that in The Marlowe Society's delivery instance there is only one possible solution. Here too "that" is grouped backward, but the /n/ is relatively short. Tone-group boundary is indicated only by the resetting pitch on "leads".

Two differences between the falling intonation contours on "heaven" seem to be quite obvious, one measurable, the other perceptual. First, in Gielgud 1 the falling intonation contour of "heaven" is much longer than in Gielgud 2: it begins at 127.457 Hz (much higher than the other reading), and falls to 77.915 Hz, slightly below the bottom line of "that" in the other reading. Second, concomitantly, the falling curve in Gielgud 1 arouses a feeling of "homecoming", whereas in Gielgud 2 there is a feeling that the curve fails to reach the point of rest, demanding completion. What is more, the /n/ is prolonged at this unsatisfactory point, generating a sense of arrest and a sense of impulsion across it at the same time. In Gielgud 1, by contrast, the "homecoming" of the falling intonation contour coincides with a major syntactic juncture, and the beginning of a longish pause. Exceptionally great stability is achieved.

Table 7.2   Durations of the speech sounds of "shun" in milliseconds (msecs). In the dictionary and in Callow's and The Marlowe Society's readings /n/ is shorter than the combined duration of the preceding sounds; in Gielgud's two readings it is longer.

	ʃ	ʌ	n	ʃ + ʌ
Dictionary	183	177	241	360
Gielgud 1	184	174	444	358
Gielgud 2	197	109	400	306
Marlowe	262	147	278	409
Callow	281	131	300	412

A similar story can be told, mutatis mutandis, about the sequence "shun the". In Gielgud 1 there is a longish pause between them (363 msec); in Gielgud 2 they are run one into the other. In both readings /n/ is considerably longer than the combined duration of the preceding sounds; in Gielgud 2 its relative duration is insignificantly longer than in Gielgud 1. In *The Merriam-Webster Colleagiate Dictionary,* by contrast, /n/ is considerably shorter. As after "heaven", after "shun" too Gielgud 1 resorts to redundant cues: the prolongation of /n/ reinforces discontinuity that is also signified by a longish pause; whereas in Gielgud 2 it indicates discontinuity where the two words are run one into another.

In Callow's and The Marlowe Society's readings (Figures 7.9–7.10), too, "shun" is run into "the". In the latter, intensity and the rising-falling intonation lend exceptional accent to "shun", but there is no discontinuity here. In the former, the 22-msec-longer /n/ and the falling terminal contour generate some discontinuity, placing it, in this respect, between Gielgud 2 and The Marlowe Society.

There are good prosodic and syntactic reasons (caesura and syntactic juncture) to indicate discontinuity after "heaven", with or without a pause. After "shun" it has neither syntactic, nor prosodic justification. It seems to be gratuitous—unless it has some rhetorical or paralinguistic justification. It is, perhaps, a prosodic mannerism.

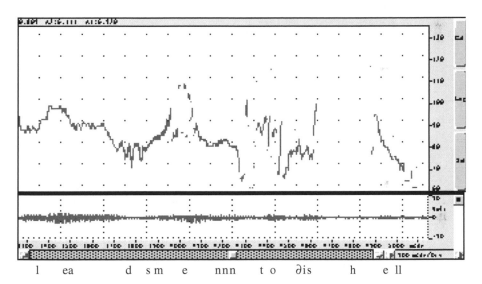

Figure 7.7   Wave plot and pitch extract of "leads men to this hell" (alternative method) Gielgud 1.

William Benson (2003, online) suggests that a single line of poetry can readily encompass one or two intonation units. One striking thing about Gielgud's two readings of this line is that he fragments the verse lines into at least three sentence fragments (sentence fragment is a word, phrase, or clause that usually has in speech the intonation of a sentence but lacks the grammatical structure usually found in the sentences of formal and especially written composition). This is a salient feature of poetry reading in general: stretches of speech are broken up into smaller than usual intonation units, so as to exert rigorous control over every syllable and metrical position. This may have emotive effects too. The pauses in Gielgud 1 may be perceived as a source of hesitancy, of lack of control. The reading in Gielgud 2 is divided into no fewer chunks, but by other means than pauses. Consequently, it is not perceived as hesitant; on the contrary rather, as a stretch of speech every bit of which is under strict control.

Toward the end of Figures 7.3 and 7.4 the pitch contour is poor or incomplete. In Gielgud 1 one clearly hears a rise of pitch on "men" after "leads". But in Figure 7.3 at this point the speech signal is so poor that the graph shows no trace of it. So, in Figures 7.7–7.8 I am providing some of the missing information by an alternative method of pitch extraction (autocorrelation).

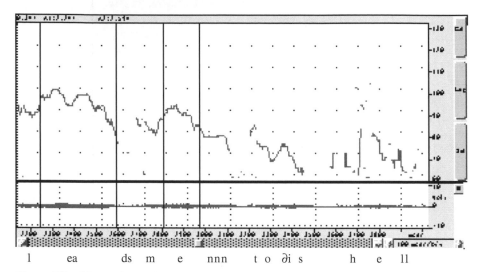

l   ea   ds   m   e   nnn   t o ∂i s   h   e   ll

Figure 7.8 Wave plot and pitch extract of "leads men to this hell" ("autocorrelation" method), Gielgud 2.

In Figure 7.7, the intonation contour clearly juts out on "men". Indeed, "men" bears greater stress than "leads"; but in this verse line, it is "men" that occurs in a weak position, infringing upon metric regularity. In the four readings under discussion we encounter three different ways of handling this problem. Callow grossly under-stresses "men", suppressing the stress pattern required by "prose rhythm". Gielgud 1, by contrast, duely stresses "men", infringing upon the stress pattern required by meter. Between these two extremes we find Gielgud 2 and The Marlowe Society. In Gielgud 1 the rising-falling pitch contour juts out on "men", cuing a stress that is stronger than the preceding one and, indeed, metric fluency is felt to be damaged. In Gielgud 2, by contrast, the intonation contour assigned to "men" is somewhat lower than that on "leads", but has similar shape. Thus, in this reading the stress of "men" is subordinated to that of "leads", satisfying the metric requirements. At the same time, the duration of "men" in Gielgud 2 is longer than in Gielgud 1, long enough to break somehow even with the stress on "leads". Thus it compensates for the lower pitch, just enough to satisfy the syntactic demand for a stressed syllable. The salient early peak on "men" effectively groups it with "leads" (in a strong position).

The same holds true, with the necessary changes, of Marlowe Society's reading. The perceptual process of "breaking even" by lengthening a weakly stressed syllable can be observed in action in my attempt to electronically lengthen "men" in Callow's reading (see below). Consider the relative durations of "men" in Table 7.3. In Gielgud 1 pitch contour cues stress, foregrounding its perceptual deviance; so, "men" is relatively short. In Gielgud 2 and The Marlowe Society's reading it is duration that takes care of relative stress. In Callow's reading "men" is shorter than in the other ones, and sharpens (rather than levels) the difference between the two consecutive stresses.

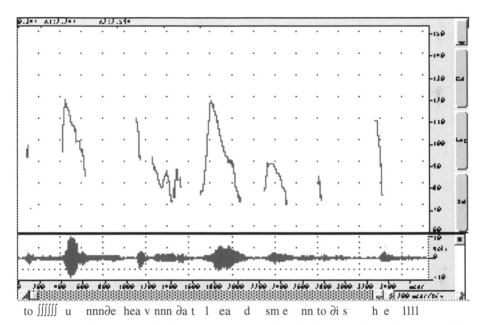

Figure 7.9   Wave plot and pitch extract of "To shun the heaven that leads men to this hell", Marlowe Society.

Table 7.3   Surprisingly, "men" is longish in the Dictionary. In Callow's reading it is the shortest of the four. In Gielgud 2 and The Marlowe Society's reading it is considerably longer than in Gielgud 1, compensating for the relatively low pitch of their intonation contour

	m	e	n	m + e	m + e + n
Dictionary	44	278	186	322	508
Gielgud 1	98	150	216	248	464
Gielgud 2	100	175	234	275	509
Marlowe	88	181	241	269	510
Callow	88	128	188	216	404

The present work assumes that clear-cut articulation saves mental processing space required for the simultaneous perception of the conflicting patterns of stress and meter. Rising-falling or steeply-falling intonation contours and relatively long speech sounds (as in "men" in Gielgud 2 and The Marlowe Society's reading) both contribute to such clear-cut articulation. I claim that artificial lengthening of the speech sounds of "men" in Callow's reading too (see below) improves articulation and contributes to the same effect.

Machine vs. Callow

I suggested above that the sequence "leads men" poses a difficulty for such generative metrists as Paul Kiparsky or Gilbert Youmans (Youmans 1989), who claim that strings of consecutive stressed syllables must end in an even-numbered (strong) position; strings that end in a weak (odd-numbered) position render the verse line "unmetrical". The reason is that the rightmost member in the string bears the greatest stress; it may not therefore occur in a weak position. Two of the four recordings solve this problem quite elegantly. Gielgud 2 (Figure 7.8) and The Marlowe Society (Figure 7.9) clearly articulate the boundaries of the two consecutive monosyllables by assigning them, each, a rising-and-falling intonation contour. This renders both consecutive syllables stressed, though with less perceived stress on "men" than on "leads". The clear articulation of these words allows to perceive the respective metrical positions as well. In Gielgud 1 too these words are assigned similar intonation contours; but that on "men" is somewhat higher, and the word is perceived as overstressed, disrupting to some extent the rhythmic flow. In Callow's recording we encounter serious trouble with these two words. "Leads" (in a strong position) bears strong stress cued by a rising-falling intonation contour; "men" is perceived as insufficiently stressed, in spite of the long-falling contour. Furthermore, as Figure 7.10 shows, the intonation contour of "leads" constitutes an exceptionally late peak. This has two perceptual corollaries: it increases the stress; and generates a forward-pushing "perceptual force", leaning on the insufficiently stressed "men" (in a weak position). As a result, the insufficient stressing of the latter is even more strongly felt. I had a methodological problem here: from the wave plot and pitch extract in Figure 7.10 I could not predict this rhythmic flaw. Measurements are of limited help here ("men" in this reading is considerably shorter than in the other readings or in the Dictionary). The fault was salient for my ears. When listening one after the other to the phrase "leads men" excised from the four readings, it is felt that, in three of them, "leads" exerts a "perceptual force" on "men"; whereas "men" strikes a delicate balance: it is sufficiently stressed to "withstand" this pressure, but is not stressed too much to infringe upon meter. In Callow's reading, the forward push on "leads" is amplified by late peaking; whereas the power of "men" to stand firm against the pressure is strongly reduced.

As I said above, measurements are of limited help in accounting for the rhythmic deficiency of Callow's reading. So I tried to see, by trial and error, what happens when certain elements are manipulated. Pitch, duration and amplitude (in this order of decreasing effectiveness) are variables that crucially influence perceived stress (Fry 1958). I can control only duration in a tolerably accurate manner; but in this respect, too, there are severe limitations. In such continuous consonants as /s/, /m/, /n/, /l/ I can copy a small portion and then paste it again and again into the signal, without considerably distorting speech. But when I come to do the same with vowels, pitch and vowel quality too may be effected, generating unnatural intonation contours and emotional qualities. As to "men", I had little difficulty to lengthen the /m/ and the /n/; but eventually I succeeded to lengthen the vowel between them too, with minimum distortion (there *is* some distortion: one of my informants commented that it "provides a false emotional emphasis to the line"). The reading labelled "Callow 2" is the doctored version. By lengthening the three speech sounds of "men", its ability to "exert force" in opposition to the thrust of "leads" is boosted. This is an ostensive way to support my argument, by changing features supposed to generate the quality under discussion, and exposing the resulting quality to the listening ear.

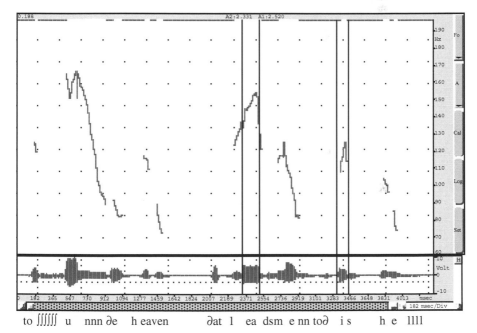

Figure 7.10   Wave plot and pitch extract of "To shun the heaven that leads men to this hell" , Callow 1.

There is a similar problem with the last two words. Presumably for rhetorical reasons, Callow assigns a strong emphatic stress to "this", disregarding the damage done to rhythm. Again, there is a late peak in "this", pressing forward, while the stress assigned to "hell" is insufficient to "withstand" this pressure. And again, the controlled lengthening of the last two speech sounds of "hell" by "copy-and-paste" caused it to stand firm against the thrust of the overstressed "this". Incidentally, the intonation contours generated in these specific instances do approximate the contours required to solve this rhythmic problem.

Flesh-and-Blood Listeners

A research like the present one must be guided by the researcher's intuitive perceptions regarding rhythmical and unrhythmical performances. At a certain point I had to ascertain whether other people had similar perceptions to mine. I needed informed informants. But also I had to request them to try to suspend their professional knowledge, and give as spontaneous and intuitive responses as possible. I made Gielgud's readings available on a webpage (later I added Callow's genuine and doctored versions), and asked some of my colleagues to respond to them. I also sent a request to the PSYART and Coglit lists. I received all in all five fairly detailed responses, from three literary theorists, one music theorist, and a practicing psychoanalyst who had written on Sonnet 129, as well as a brief interjected preference judgment. In such circumstances it is impossible to make a quantitative study, and I will have to weigh the answers from a qualitative point of view. It is difficult to compare answers to open-ended questions, when the various informants use different metaphors to describe their impressions. Moreover, as we shall see, the same informant may provide conflicting descriptions.

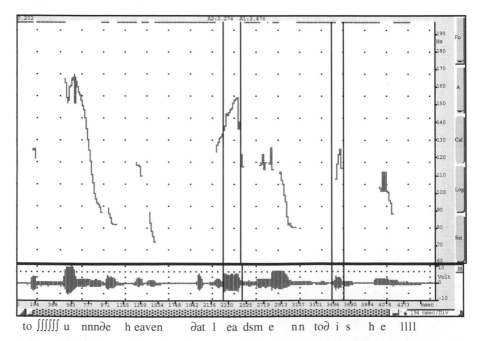

to ʃʃʃʃʃ u   nnnðe   h eaven   ðat l ea dsm e   nn toð i s   h e   llll

Figure 7.11   Wave plot and pitch extract of "To shun the heaven that leads men to this hell" , Callow 2.

All informants thought that both readings are within the boundaries of "rhythmical performance", though most informants thought that the first one is nearer to the minstrel's pole, the second one to the actor's pole. One informant made a more sophisticated judgment. Speaking of "the quavering voice on 'heaven' and 'leads'" in the second reading, he remarks: "I'm not sure, but that seems to push the first more toward the minstrel pole and the latter more toward the actor pole, but then the first version overstresses 'shun,' which seems 'actorly' to me. I suppose there are some ways in which each is minstrel-like and some ways in which each is actor-like".

All informants pointed out that the two readings had different rhythmic structures. The most accurate description of this difference runs as follows: "Overall, the rhythmical character of the first version is marked by the emphasis on and pauses after "shun" and "heaven," whereas the relative lack of pausing and the holding of the reverberations of final consonants so that they flow into the next word makes the second version more even and sonorant". Another respondent put it: "I suppose there are some ways in which each is minstrel-like and some ways in which each is actor-like. The readings [...] differ on the caesura and on the degree of stress. The stresses are more even in the second (which, I suppose, is a minstrel-like trait). In the first, 'shun' has a very strong stress; 'hell' somewhat less; 'heaven' and 'leads' less still. But they are similar in that the same words get stressed". These two passages, when juxtaposed, suggest that the respective convergent and divergent nature of the two readings is determined not so much by making the stress pattern conform with the metric pattern, but rather by their handling of segmentation. In reading 1 the pauses converge with the other cues for segmentation. In reading 2, by contrast, the "final consonants [...] flow into the next word", and segmentation is generated by conflicting cues. Most informants, however, can only report a general impression, and cannot point out such evasive details. Now consider "the stresses are more even in the second". As far as the "more even" stresses occur in strong positions, as the examples enumerated above, it is, indeed, "a minstrel-like trait". But when it is the consecutive stresses "leads men" that are more even, it is a paradigmatic "divergent" trait.

Another informant uses a simile: "The first is like a lullaby that 'lulls' the listener". Oddly enough, this is the person who felt that the first reading has "ominous rhythm" (see below). I don't consider this as sheer logical contradiction. I construe it, rather, as an expression used to describe a quality in the performance for which the writer had no technical term: that she felt a "convergent" quality in the delivery style. This conjecture is supported by her comment "Reading No. 1 approximates Style 1 [i.e., the Minstrel] (although I would not call it "wooden"!) Reading No. 2 approximates Style 2 [i.e., rhythmical performance]; clearly metrical, but an elision/syncopation that compresses the phrase for a slight rhetorical emphasis"

Most informants agreed that the first reading is more emotional. They differed, however, in their evaluation of this emotionality, as well as on its relation to other elements in the performance. Two of them spoke of "ominous rhythm" and "awesome emotional tone", respectively. They probably referred to the same perceived quality. In these comments, the emotional quality was implicitly judged as a "good-making" feature of the performance. One person, who happened to listen to the two readings (a hi-tech engineer) squarely declared that he definitely preferred number 2, because the other was "full of pathos". This person agrees, then, with the others as to the presence of the emotional quality, but makes an opposite value judgment. By the way, I happen to sympathise with his judgment.

The two informants who agree on this reading's "ominous" or "awesome" quality, attribute it to different sources. One attributes the awesome emotional tone to a "resonant" voice quality, and to fragmentation of the line by pauses. The other spoke of "ominous rhythm". But in the same sentence she also mentions the "rounded, velvety timbre of the first reading"; and later she uses the phrase "the more 'stilted' first version".[7] They both seem to refer, by their different terms, to fragmentation by pauses and to a surrounding aura of rich overtones. As to the source of the emotional quality, I tend to agree with the former informant. Resounding ("thundering") voice is regularly associated with emotions. Likewise, "the discontinuity of the first reading contributes to its awesome tone, because it inspires the listener with uncertainty. Concomitantly, it displays the moment-to-moment fluctuation of the living voice". So, one must distinguish between two mental acts: discerning the elements and perceived qualities of a verse line on the one hand, and, on the other, assuming a causal relationship between the two. Even if the source of the perceived qualities is displaced, the very discernment of elements and effects may still be sound.

Most informants preferred version 1. The reason for this preference is its more emotional quality. Though I was asking about "rhythmical performance", my informants could not keep it apart from the emotional element. As far as pauses are concerned, the same element is an exponent of both the rhythmic and emotional quality. But the "surrounding aura of rich overtones" (or "rounded, velvety timbre of the first reading") has everything to do with emotional qualities, and nothing with rhythmic qualities. The two informants who detected the "ominous" or "awesome" quality in reading 1 also concur in their preference for the first reading, and both continue with a "but". They seem to feel apologetic for not preferring the second reading, where the rhythmic solution is more conspicuous (e.g., "but have to admit"). In all these responses preference for emotional qualities slightly overrides the appreciation of rhythm. One informant, however, considers rhythm an outright obstacle: "I thought the rhythmic of number one was subsumed to the acting so that it might have easily gone unnoticed to my unpracticed ear. My attention was called to the rhythm of number two and it was somehow distracting and thereby detracting". This informant is the only one in the emerging sample who has no professional interest in poetic or musical rhythm. Indeed, he mentions his "unpracticed ear" with so many words. Yet,

---

[7]   I asked her what did she mean by "stilted". The dictionary defines "stilted" as "1. lacking fluency in being halting or unnatural in flow 2. pompous or unduly formal". She answered that she had meant only the first meaning, and in an objective, descriptive, non-evaluative sense. "Reading 1 may indeed be considered as referencing definition 2, but I was assessing only the 'rhythmical' aspects of the reading". The person who thought it was full of pathos would have agreed, presumably to the second meaning as well.

he noticed the more compelling rhythmic nature of number two; but for him rhythm is "somehow distracting and thereby detracting". Thus, on the descriptive level he seems to be in agreement with the earlier-mentioned two informants, but on the evaluative level they are diametrically opposed. This chapter, however, is about *the perception* of poetic rhythm, not about its *evaluation;* and what he perceives seems to be in harmony with my predictions.

One of the questions I asked was "Does the rhythmic structure of one or the other delivery instance interact in any way with the emotional tone of the line?". Figure 7.7 shows on "hell" a falling, classical terminal contour, appropriately indicating the end of an utterance (and of the poem). Two of my informants referred to this issue in almost identical terms. Both respondents discern this intonation contour, and offer similar interpretations. One suggests: "in reading 1, 'hell' marks the end of a long stepwise descent: as the lowest pitch, it functions therefore as a sonic metaphor, and the phrase mirrors the slow descent to hell that such abandonment to pleasure might occasion". The other is more cautious. She too regards it as a metaphor suggesting descent, but provides no specific details that cannot be substantiated or refuted. So, this may be regarded as an instance of what I elsewhere called "triple-encodedness" (Tsur, 2000; 2002). The same falling contour indicates the end of a syntactic unit (sentence), of a rhythmic unit (the line); at the same time, it is expressive of the long fall. Likewise, the pause after "heaven" indicates a (syntactic) clause ending, a (prosodic) caesura, and an emotional quality.[8]

I have earlier mentioned a comment that the first reading is like a lullaby that "lulls" the listener, and thus ironically points up the "heaven that leads to hell," whereas the compressed rhythm and rising tones of the second reading is all "nervous 'shunning'" with no "heavenly contrast". Here we encounter one of the widespread critical fallacies. The writer uses the term "lullaby" to designate a rhythmic quality, and then is carried away by her own expression, regarding it as ironical to the "heaven that leads to hell". Had she used, e.g., the term "obtrusive rhythm" instead "lullaby", no irony would have arisen. On the other hand, I am wondering how much of the description "the compressed rhythm and rising tones of the second reading is all nervous 'shunning'" refers, in fact, to what I was referring to in my analysis of the cues for continuity and discontinuity in the second reading. At this point, I should mention again a comment by another respondent: "The discontinuity of the first reading contributes to its awesome tone, because it inspires the listener with uncertainty. Concomitantly, it displays the moment-to-moment fluctuation of the living voice". In this respect, interaction appears to be genuine.

Another question I asked was "Can you point out specific problems in the verse line, and the vocal manipulations by which Gielgud solved or failed to solve them? " In my analysis I had pointed out two difficulties in this verse line: the three sylla-

---

[8]   Interestingly enough, these two informants seem to be in agreement in a number of responses: in being apologetic about preferring reading 1; in speaking of "awesome emotional tone" or "ominous rhythm"; and of "surrounding aura of rich overtones" or "rounded, velvety timbre". One is a literary theorist, the other a musicologist.

bles "heaven that" must be squeezed into two metrical positions, and the succession of stressed syllables "leads men" ends in a weak position. Only one respondent referred to both issues: the two readings "are similar in that the same words get stressed, and in both cases 'heaven' is shortened to a monosyllable. The result is that in both cases he makes the line a little more regular. Of course, he does not treat 'men to' as an iamb (which would be the sing-song version); in that sense, both are more actor-like". There is one more reference to each one of these issues, by different informants: "an elision/syncopation that compresses the phrase for a slight rhetorical emphasis"; and "The problem I see in the line is the falling of the main stress on 'men' on a W position. Metrically, this is balanced by 'leads' on the sixth position, which keeps it metrical according to the Halle–Keyser system".[9] As to elision, the computer makes it quite clear that in Gielgud's and The Marlowe Society's readings there is no schwa in "heaven", whereas in the dictionary and in Callow's reading there is one.

These three references to the two issues identify the problems and vaguely hint at the kind of solution, but I hoped also for acknowledging the differences in handling them. But that would, perhaps, be too much to ask. The present suggestion is that it is the performance that makes all the difference. If "men" receives its due linguistic stress, the verse line sounds unrhythmical; if it is unstressed, the iambic singsong is preserved, but the rhythm becomes childish. I claim that in the second reading Gielgud drastically lowers pitch, but compensates for this by lengthening "men". To have one's cake and eat it. In his first reading pitch juts out on "men" (see Figures 7.7–7.8).

The only response I received on the Callow manipulations was from this informant. "The emphasis on "men" [...] is balanced by that given to "leads" (in strong sixth position). The second version, in emphasizing "men" on the devil's note, for me throws off the rhythm (and provides a false emotional emphasis to the line)". Here, too, she implicitly invokes the Halle–Keyser theory ("is balanced by that given to 'leads'") to legitimise the deviant stress. To my great dismay, she perceives the first (genuine) reading as more rhythmical. I still feel that in Callow's genuine reading "men" is understressed, and just like in Gielgud's second reading, here too the lengthening of "men" strikes a precarious balance between stress and unstress. I plead, however, guilty of "providing a false emotional emphasis". The manipulation generated a "creaky" voice, which I could not avoid under the circumstances.[10]

---

9   This appears to be a conspicuous instance in which the informant's response reflects her theoretical knowledge rather than what she hears. She says that the deviation is acceptable because it conforms with the rules, not because it *sounds* acceptable.

10   Fortunately enough, there was a delay between the completion of this article and its first publication, during which I had access to the speech analyser "Praat". This application offers features for manipulating pitch and duration, yielding relatively natural results. This may avoid the "creaky" voice and provide less "false emotional emphasis" for the manipulated words in Callow's reading. I have manipulated only the duration, not the pitch of the words "men" and "hell", so as to leave all other things equal. Notwithstanding this, the change of speed *did* affect the voice quality of

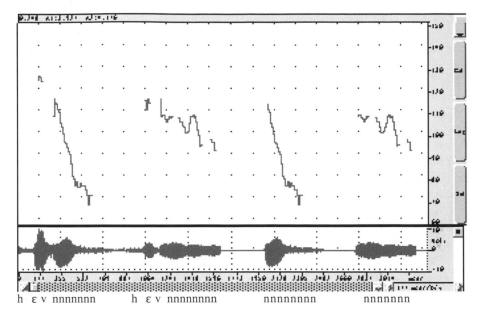

h ɛ v nnnnnnn   h ɛ v nnnnnnnn   nnnnnnnn   nnnnnnn

Figure 7.12   Wave plot and pitch extract of "heaven" in Gielgud 1 and Gielgud 2 with the respective excised /n/s. In Gielgud 1 /n/ has a falling, in Gielgud 2 a quavering contour.[11]

One informant gave his overall impression in an informal tone: "I didn't care for the caesura in the first version, but I didn't care for the quavering voice on 'heaven' and 'leads' in the second". I thought this overall impression may support some of my subtler analyses. He later expressly confirmed this. Here is what I wrote to him: "When you say "I didn't care for the caesura in the first version", I think you confirm my impression that the caesura is overarticulated by a syntactic juncture + long-falling intonation contour + a long pause + the exceptionally long /n/. I feel, therefore, that it is thrust on the reader "in a blunt and direct manner". When you say you "didn't care for the quavering voice on 'heaven' and 'leads' in the second", you draw attention to something I haven't noticed. In this reading there is no measurable pause at all, the function word "that" is grouped backward to "heaven" by intonation; so, it is the prolonged /n/ that carries all the burden of discontinuity. In absolute terms it is only slightly longer than the /n/ in the first reading; relative to the duration of the whole word, however, it is even insignificantly shorter. But in the first reading the amplitude gradually decays, whereas in the second it is sustained. Owing to this, the /n/ in the second reading is more salient (and therefore more effective in generating discontinuation). Now you have pointed out that the /n/ is

---

these words to some extent. Listen online to a version produced on a combination of two speech analysers, Praat and SoundScope (Callow 3).

[11] Listen to them online.

quavering too; this, in my opinion, increases its salience. At the same time it conveys an emotional quality which may be felt to be overdone, and therefore offensive". Again, this may be regarded as an instance of "triple-encodedness".

Finally, in Chapter 6 above (and in my 1977 book) I made my distinction between three delivery styles in somewhat different terms, as follows: "As for performance, we may observe, roughly, three 'delivery styles'. At one extreme we find the singsong of children chanting their nursery-rhymes and the mechanical scansion of 'freshmen', suppressing 'prose rhythm'; at the other extreme, we find the prosaic rendering of readers 'insensitive to rhythm', and of actors who wish to make poetic drama sound more 'natural', suppressing meter. In the middle, there is a complex *rhythmical* performance, that avoids the suppression of either stress pattern or metric pattern. It may be possible to do justice to the conflicting patterns by accommodating them in a third, superimposed pattern of performance". In my 1998 book I preferred to quote the *Princeton Encyclopedia* (1993) which, in turn, invokes C. S. Lewis. That was also the definition of "rhythmical performance" which I presented to my informants. Now I had to realise that though the two formulations refer to the same distinction, had I resorted to my first formulation, I may have obtained quite different results. The point is that in my original formulation I give a more purely rhythmical definition. Lewis' terms introduce the noisy elements "wooden" and "flamboyantly expressive". These elements had a negative and a positive effect on the results. On the one hand, they diverted the respondents' attention from the rhythmic structure to other aspects. On the other hand, they prompted comments on the emotional impact of the readings, and indications of the "triple-encodedness" of phonetic cues.

Some Methodological Conclusions

Analytic philosophy offers a meta-language required for handling such a welter of responses. Analytic philosophers as Beardsley (1958) and Margolis (1962) distinguish between descriptive, interpretive and evaluative statements. Sibley (1962) distinguishes aesthetic qualities in a work of art (referred to by "aesthetic concepts"), and nonaesthetic features that may "count toward" or "against" some aesthetic quality. Zemach (1976) points out that "aesthetic concepts" have both a descriptive and an evaluative component; the greater the share of the descriptive component, the smaller is that of the evaluative component, and vice versa. According to Beardsley, this evaluative component can be supported by reference to three General Canons of Evaluation: unity, complexity and some intense human quality. Another key expression would be "perceiving as" in the Wittgensteinean tradition. One may detect a resonant voice quality in a delivery instance, which may be perceived as an "emotional quality"; this, in turn, other things being equal, may be judged as a good-making feature of the aesthetic event, under the Canon of intense human quality. In describing this emotional quality, one may resort to aesthetic concepts that have more specific contents, such as "ominous" or "awesome". Other things, however, need not be equal. The term "full of pathos" too refers to some (perhaps the same) emotional quality, but has little specific descriptive contents and much evaluative contents. This term suggests that the aesthetic event does have an intense human quality, but little complexity or unity. According to Morris Weitz (1962), statements in aesthetic discourse are not factual statements, but crucial recommendations what to look for in aesthetic objects, and how to look at it.

English meter baffles scholarship. Renaissance poets who laid its foundations thought they were doing one thing but were, actually, doing another. All researchers are in agreement on one point: that this practice had admirable results. Prosodic research in the past four centuries attempted to discover the principles governing it. But all would-be explanations ran into compelling counterexamples. Most notably, Milton and Shelley, the poets most praised for their musicality, violated all the proposed rules. Wellek and Warren attempted to find method in this madness by breaking down the rhythmic process into three dimensions: prose rhythm, meter, and performance. In my recent work I have been engaged in an instrumental investigation of "rhythmical performance", of which I conceive as of a problem-solving activity. Conflicting patterns of prose rhythm and meter must be accommodated in a pattern of performance. I soon had to realise that "rhythmical performance" is not a unitary phenomenon: there are different legitimate delivery styles. In this chapter I set out to propound the linguistic, metric, phonetic and cognitive elements involved in the rhythmical performance of poetry, suggesting that in different delivery instances these elements may constitute different clusters, yielding different delivery styles. I started with C. S. Lewis' distinction between the minstrel and the actor, suggesting that between them one may locate "rhythmical performance". Within rhythmical performance I distinguished "Convergent" and "Divergent" delivery styles. The performance Gielgud 1 tends toward the former, Gielgud 2 toward the latter. In this chapter I have offered basic elements and general principles rather than a systematic exposition of specific delivery styles.

"Convergent" and "Divergent" poems on the one hand and "Convergent" and "Divergent" delivery styles on the other are by no means coextensive, though may reflect similar aesthetic conceptions. In Chapter 4 excerpts (1)–(2) we compared a piece of convergent poetry by Spenser to a comparable piece of divergent poetry by Milton. In these texts, similar linguistic and versification patterns act in convergence or divergence respectively. In the readings Gielgud 1 and Gielgud 2 the same poetic text (excerpt (2) above) is performed. Here it is the performer's vocal cues that act in convergence or divergence.

At a certain point I could not avoid ascertaining whether other listeners perceive the same aesthetic qualities as I do in the aesthetic events discussed. I had to look for informants whose professional training enabled them to understand that they were requested to respond to *certain aspects* of the aesthetic event. This involved me in another difficulty: such informants may be guided by their theoretical knowledge. So, I made efforts to prevent their responses to be affected either by their own theories or the experimenter's presumed expectations. I tried to elicit from my respondents responses as spontaneous as possible. The result was that only very few persons responded to my request; and those who responded provided responses that overlapped in some respects, but were at variance in others. In the last section of my article I tried to sort out what possible perceptions did those responses report, and what kinds of metalinguistic statements they were.

The aesthetic event of poetry recital is very complex. The responses I received suggest that in some instances my informants responded to different aspects of the same event. The event may be consistently and quite thoroughly described by the tools offered here. One must, however, realise that in a poll like the one reported here all the respondents will respond only to a small subset of aspects. Thus, even widely different responses may be consistent with one another. In the preceding section I made an attempt to point out how the different responses relate to the same underlying comprehensive description.

This procedure taught me the limitations of what I was doing. I cannot claim that my perceptions, which guided my investigation, are *the* correct ones, or are shared by most people. Nor were the perceptions reported by any of my respondents. But this does not mean that "anything goes". Some of my respondents, at least, did draw attention to some significant aspect of the aesthetic event, whether an aesthetic quality, or some set of features that generate it, or an evaluation of the resulting effect. The most I can do in these circumstances is to make a crucial recommendation as to what to look for in the rhythmical perfomance of poetry, and how to look at it.[12]

---

[12] The theory and instrumental approach outlined in the present chapter can be applied even to such extreme instances as stress maxima in weak positions (see Tsur, 1997; 1998: 195–219).

CHAPTER 8

Expressiveness and Musicality
of Speech Sounds

Musicality seems to be the most salient—if not *the* distinctive—property of poetry. The principles of musicality in verse have solidified in handbooks of versification into easily manageable rules. Unfortunately, however, such rules can hardly tell us the difference between, say, Milton's "miraculous organ voice" and the flatness of the verse by some of his imitators (cf. Tsur, 1977: 215–238). The problem is infinitely multiplied if we come to close readings of, say, French Symbolist poetry, where "mere" semantic analysis and semantic discussions appear sometimes ridiculously besides the point. When in such a plight, we find not infrequently that critics, students, or university professors are, on the one hand, wont to make some general comment on the poet's great mastery or on the impossibility to deal with the musicality of the poem; on the other hand, they may make some more specific statement on the quality of this or that sound, that would hardly hold water in a test of consistency. A random browsing through Henri Peyre's discussions of French Symbolist poems in Burnshaw's popular collection (1964) came up with the following crop. Baudelaire's "Harmonie du Soir" is "a masterpiece of musicality in poetry. [...] The music of words and rimes ingeniously interwoven cannot, of course, be adequately conveyed by a literal translation" (ibid., 14). "The three initial *v* sounds in line 1 are like piercing arrows of pain" (ibid., 15); in line 4, nonetheless, "the *v* and *l* sounds are subtly blended" (ibid). In Verlaine's "Clair de Lune", "the first stanza is filled with broad, calm, doleful *a* sounds" (ibid., 37), whereas in the sonnet "Le Vierge, le Vivace et le Bel Aujourd'hui", "Mallarmé's art stands at its highest. [...] All the rimes are in *i* or *ui,* a sound which has something of the angular sharpness of ice itself" (ibid., 55). Sometimes we hear comments on the "beautiful" sounds of a poem (more rarely on its "ugly" sounds) whereas, before the scientific impartiality of linguistic description all speech sounds are equal; nonetheless, for readers of poetry it is difficult to escape the feeling that some speech sounds are more equal than others. In what follows, I shall take up the notion that some speech sounds are more musical, more emotional, or more beautiful than others, and attempt to anchor my judgments in a system of phonological universals, in such a way that those judgments can be maintained more or less consistently.

Expressive Sound Patterns

Literary critics and ordinary readers usually have rather strong intuitions about the expressiveness of sound patterns in poetry. There is a vast literature on this subject; however, much of it is ad-hoc and arbitrary, or skeptical. "It is precisely critics interested in the meaning and idea-content of poetry", says Hrushovski (1968: 410), "that feel some kind of embarrassment toward the existence of sound organization, and attempt to enlist it in the service of the total interpretation. As against this approach there are critics and theoreticians who deny all in all the very existence of specific meanings attributable to specific sounds".

In what follows, I shall adopt Hrushovski's approach, according to which the various sounds of a language do have certain general potentials of meaningful impression (ibid., 412), and can be combined with meanings so that they impress the reader as if they expressed some specific meaning (ibid., 411). My claim is that these general potentials—which I shall refer to as "combinational potentials"—have firm intersubjective foundations on the acoustic, phonetic or phonological level of the sound structure of language. And I shall try to reveal some of their sources.

Hrushovski claims that much of the dispute whether or not sound can be expressive comes to a dead end, because the issue is treated as if it were one unitary phenomenon. "As a matter of fact, there are several kinds of relations between sound and meaning, and in each kind the problem is revealed in different forms" (ibid., 412). He discusses four kinds of such relations: a. Onomatopoeia; b. Expressive Sounds; c. Focusing Sound Patterns; d. Neutral Sound Patterns. Here I shall discuss only the first two of these. Hrushovski describes expressive sound pattern as follows:

> A sound combination is grasped as expressive of the tone, mood or some general quality of meaning. Here, an abstraction from the sound pattern (i.e. some kind of tone or "quality" of the sounds) is parallel to an abstraction from the meaning of the words (tone, mood etc.). (ibid., 444)

Traditional poetics has important things to say about how "tones, moods etc." are abstracted from the *meaning* of the words; but how are they abstracted from the speech sounds? The purpose of the present chapter can be described as an inquiry into some possible sources of the "tone" or "quality" of the sounds and the way these traits are grasped, as parallel to an abstraction from the meaning of the words (tone, mood, emotion, etc.). One important aspect of the issue is that sounds are what I call "double-edged"; that is, they may be "expressive" of vastly different, or even opposite, qualities. Thus, for instance, the sibilants /s/ and /ʃ/ may have a *hushing* quality in one context, and a *harsh* quality (to varying degrees) in some other. Thus, for instance, Hrushovski quotes Poe's line

(1)   And the silken, sad, uncertain rustling of each purple curtain

where the sibilants may be onomatopoetic, imitating the noises; or they may reinforce—or be expressive of—a quiet mood in Shakespeare's sonnet:

(2)   When to the sessions of sweet, silent thought
             I summon up remembrance of things past,
             I sigh the lack of many a thing I sought
             And with old woes new wail my dear time's waste.

My argument relies on the assumption that sounds are bundles of features, on the
acoustic, phonetic and phonological levels. The various features may have different
expressive potentials. The claim I shall elaborate in the course of this chapter is
that in different contexts, different potentials of the various features of the same
sounds may be realized. Thus, for instance, the sibilants /s/ and /ʃ/ may have at
some level of description features with noisy potentials as well as features with
hushing potentials; in Poe's line, the contents realize the former, in Shakespeare's
quatrain the latter. Moreover, speech sounds definitely do not have certain potentials, as a rewriting exercise performed by Hrushovski (1980: 44) may suggest:

> Now, if this is the case, would not any sound pattern do? Let us try to
> "rewrite" the Shakespearean lines using words similar in content:
>
>> When to the crux of crucial quiet thought
>> I crave and call remembrance of things past
>
> We have already created a very similar network of sounds, this time based
> on the repetition of *K*, strengthened by the cluster *K* + *R* (involving the
> original word "remembrance" too). Nevertheless, it seems that this sound
> pattern cannot possibly express silence, though "quiet thought" starts with
> *K* as "silent thought" starts with *S*. It is plausible that a reader will impute
> to this text something strong and harsh, reinforced by the sound pattern.
> The pivotal word may become "crux", though its counterpart "sessions"
> was subordinated to "sweet silent thought". One may generalize that, in a
> part of a text in which a sound pattern coexists with a number of semantic
> elements, the sound pattern may contribute to shifting the center of gravity
> from one direction of meaning to another.

Had the speech sounds no expressive potential of their own, the network of sounds
based on /k/ would have readily assumed the emotional quality of quietness, which
it doesn't. Here the sound tends to confer upon the text "something strong and
harsh", and "may contribute to shifting the center of gravity from one direction of
meaning to another" (e.g., from *quiet* to *crux*). However, this putative shifting of
the center of gravity became possible only through a regularization of metre in the
transcription: the two successive, alliterating stressed syllables in "sweet silent"

foreground these words and focus attention on their meanings. So let us amend the transcription to

(3)   When to the quorum of kind, quiet thought

also reinstating some of the legal connotations of the original text. But notice this: even though we are prevented now from shifting the center of gravity to some other "pivotal word", the /k/ sound retains its hard and strong quality, and by no means becomes expressive of some "kind, quiet" atmosphere originating in the meaning of the words. The sound pattern becomes either "neutral", or improper to the emotion expressed. As this exercise may suggest, speech sounds do have emotional potentials of their own, and one may not ascribe to them just any quality suggested by the meaning of the text.

In an attempt to test this suggestion, let us turn to Fónagy's paper on communication in poetry (1961), at the beginning of which statistical methods are applied to the expressive correspondence between mood and sound quality in poetry. This work is of particular interest for the present study, for two reasons at least. First, it does not investigate the relations of sounds with specific themes (as Peyre did), but with highly generic *moods:* "tender" and "aggressive". Second, it does not consider these moods in isolation, but as a pair of opposites whose mutual relations may be treated in terms of more/less rather than in absolute terms. The data Fónagy presents are illuminating and highly suggestive. In six especially tender and six especially aggressive poems by the Hungarian poet Sándor Pet˝fi,

> the majority of sounds occur with the same relative frequency in both groups. All the more striking is the fact that the frequency of certain sounds shows a significant difference in both groups. The phonemes /l/, /m/, and /n/ are definitely more frequent in tender-toned poems, whereas /k/, /t/, and /r/ predominate in those with aggressive tone. For some reason, precisely these sounds seem to be the most significantly correlated with aggression, either positively, or negatively. (ibid., 195)

The phonemes /m/ and /n/ have a similar negative correlation with aggression in poems by Hugo and Verlaine; /l/, too, is overwhelmingly tender for Verlaine, but not for Hugo. The voiceless stops /k/ and /t/ are significantly less frequent in tender poems by Pet˝fi, Verlaine and Hugo, and Rückert. So, this distribution is surely not language-dependent. It would be interesting to know to what extent, if at all, "double-edgedness" is responsible for the equal distribution of other sounds in both groups of poems, owing to conflicting features' canceling out each others' influence (I shall try to answer this question later on in this chapter). As for vowels, Fónagy mentions Macdermott who, through a statistical analysis of English poems, found that "dark vowels are more frequent in lines referring to dark colours, mystic obscurity, or slow and heavy movement, or depicting hatred and struggle" (ibid.,194).

From this summary, one might expect to find a greater frequency of dark vowels in aggressive poems than in tender ones. Fónagy's investigation of Pet˝fi's poetry reveals that this is indeed the case (for the other poets, he gives only the consonant distribution). Whereas the occurrence of the dark vowels in Standard Hungarian is 38.88%, in Pet˝fi's aggressive poems it was 44.38%, as against 36.73% in his tender poems. We obtain a reverse picture from the distribution of the light vowels. In Standard Hungarian their occurrence is 60.92%, whereas in Pet˝fi's tender poems it was 63.27%, against 55.62% in the aggressive poems. While these deviations from Standard Hungarian seem to be convincing enough, one might reasonably conjecture that the correlation between aggressive mood and dark vowels may be even more compelling. The problem is, however, that the results may have been "contaminated". A poem may have an especially tender mood, and still refer to dark colors (which, in turn, would have induced the poet to have recourse to words with dark vowels). The list of tender poems examined by Fónagy suggests that this indeed may be the case in his corpus. Two of the tender poems seem to have dark atmospheres (or themes, at least): "Borús, ködös ˝szi id˝" (Dark and Foggy Autumn Weather), and "Alkony" (Dusk). Statistical methods in poetics do not seem to be very successful in handling such multi-dimensional contrasts and correlations between moods and qualities.

Structuralist techniques make it possible to contrast several dimensions at one and the same time; these dimensions may evoke a considerable number of meaning and sound components, which, in turn, may combine in a variety of ways. Let us consider such a "minimal pair", thought up by Richards (1929: 220) for a somewhat different purpose. One of the many sacred cows Richards cheerfully slaughters in *Practical Criticism* is "the notion that poetic rhythm is independent of sense".

> It is easy, however, to show how much the rhythm we *ascribe* to words (and even their inherent rhythm's sounds) is influenced by our apprehension of their meanings. Compare, for example: —
>
>   Deep into a gloomy grot
> with
>   Peep into a roomy cot.

"Gloomy grot" and "roomy cot" are contrasted by, roughly, such semantic features as CONFINED ~ SPACIOUS; ILL-LIGHTED ~ BROAD DAYLIGHT; DISMAL ~ LIGHTSOME; SUBTERRANEAN ~ ON-THE-SURFACE; UNEARTHLY ~ EARTHLY; SERIOUS ~ EVERYDAY; SOMBER ~ LIGHT. *Deep* and *peep* are contrasted by such semantic features as (FAR) DOWNWARD ~ UPWARD ("to peep over"); GRAVE ~ FURTIVE; HEAVY ~ NIMBLE. Some of these contrasting pairs affect the rhythmic movement of these phrases (via, perhaps, our performance), resulting in a heavy slow cadence in the former and a light rhythm in the latter phrase (the heavy utterance of the former makes also use of the consonant clusters /gl/ and /gr/, whereas in the latter there are non-alliterative single consonants). Thus, performance only reinforces, in this case, a feeling of heaviness or lightness generated by the above features. But, owing largely to the act of contrasting, one also becomes aware, in the back of one's mind, of some interaction between semantic and phonetic features. Consider the stressed vowels shared by the contrasted words:

-eep	**-oomy**	**-ot**
long	long	short
high	high	middle
bright	dark	dark

In each of the two phrases, different vowel features may be utilized to enhance meaning; this is the source of the double-edgedness of the sounds. In *peep,* one tends to foreground the features [BRIGHT, HIGH], in *deep,* the feature [LONG] is interpreted perhaps as "(far) down". In *gloomy,* the feature [DARK] is emphasized, whereas in *roomy,* the features [LONG, HIGH] (i.e. spacious) are likely to be foregrounded.

Let us return to Fónagy's data concerning the distribution of consonants in tender and angry poems. As it was noted, the majority of consonants occur with about the same relative frequency in both groups of poems. I was wondering whether, in some cases at least, this equal distribution could not be attributed to the double-edgedness of certain sounds, that is, to their conflicting combinational potentials that cancel out each other's effects on statistics. There seems to be, indeed, some faint evidence to such mutual cancellation. The mean value of the frequency of /g/ in the tender poems of Hugo and Verlaine is 1.30%; in their aggressive poems, it was 1.21%, an insignificant difference, indeed. However, the individual numbers for the two poets seem to be rather significant. /g/ occurs over one and a half times more frequently in Verlaine's tender poems than in his angry ones (1.63: 1.07), whereas we find almost the reverse proportion in Hugo's poems: 0.96%in his tender poems, and 1.35% in his angry ones. Likewise, the frequency of /d/ in the tender poems of the two poets is 7.51%, whereas in their angry poems it is 7.94%. But taken individually, again, the same sound has opposite emotional tendencies for the two poets. For Verlaine it has a basically tender quality (10.11: 7.93), whereas for Hugo it has a basically aggressive quality (7.09: 5.76). For Pet"fi, both consonants are insignificantly more tender than angry.

Now, why is /k/ so hard and its repeated occurrence incompatible with an atmosphere of silence? And why are the voiced stops /d, g/ double-edged? Traditional acoustic phonetics may give us a clue. If we attempt to relate these voiced stops to their voiceless counterparts /t, k/, that were positively correlated with aggression, and to the sonorants /l, m/ that were negatively correlated with it, we find that /d, g/ resemble the first group in one respect, and the second group in another. As a preliminary, let us quote Fry's concise account (1970: 35–36):

Periodicity: The ear and the brain are quick to seize upon the difference between periodic and aperiodic sounds, between tones and noises, and can detect within very close limits the moment at which periodicity begins. In normal speech, all vowel sound, semi-vowels, liquids and nasals are periodic sounds, while noiseless consonants are aperiodic. Between these two classes, there are the voiced fricatives in which the ear recognizes an underlying periodicity, even though it is accompanied by aperiodic friction noise. In distinguishing between voiced and voiceless plosives, the exact moment at which periodicity begins is among the cues used by the listener. (Fry, 1970: 35)

Continuity: The distinction between continuous and interrupted sounds, for example between voiceless plosives and fricatives, depends upon this dimension. In English the /t/ sound is most commonly characterized by a short interruption of the flow of sound, followed by noise of short duration, while /s/ is a similar noise lasting considerably longer and without interruption. (ibid., 36)

Thus, the sequence **vowels, liquids & nasals, voiced fricatives, voiced stops, voiceless fricatives, voiceless stops** constitutes a scale of decreasing periodicity or sonority, in this order. The feature [±PERIODIC] is responsible for the opposition tone ~ noise, which is analogous, in a sense, to the opposition harmonious ~ not harmonious, or soft ~ hard. There are two additional relevant oppositions in the above scale: CONTINUOUS ~ ABRUPT, and ENCODED ~ UNENCODED. In chapter 1, I have already mentioned that the shape of perceived sounds is rarely similar to the shape of the acoustic information that carries it. This is *encodedness,* in fact, *a scale of relative encodedness* rather than a dichotomy, and one should bear in mind that even the least encoded speech sounds are very much encoded. The optimally tender sounds are periodic (voiced), continuous, and relatively unencoded; the optimally aggressive sounds are aperiodic (voiceless), abrupt, and highly encoded. In what follows, I shall try to account for these correlations. Now, it should be emphasized that two points (or even two areas) on this scale can be picked out and presented in opposition to each other as more or less aggressive; liquids and nasals are not inherently tender, or voiceless stops inherently aggressive. When we see in Fónagy's table (1961: 197) that a sound like /d/ or /g/ is aggressive for one poet and tender for another, even in the same language, this may suggest that Verlaine treated /d/ as an abrupt and encoded sound, and opposed it to continuous and relatively unencoded sounds, thereby subduing its voiced feature; whereas in /g/, on the contrary, he subdued the abrupt and encoded features, and opposed it to /k/ along the [±voiced] feature. Hugo did just the reverse. We must grant the poets a considerable degree of free choice, *within the constraints* of the sounds' combinational potentials. Hence the double-edged nature of these sounds.

The order of items on the above scale is not unambiguous, precisely because the various features vary independently from each other. We have ordered the items according to the periodicity feature. According to the continuity and encodedness features, voiceless fricatives ought to have preceded voiced stops. Since, however, what matters is that owing to these conflicting features the sounds are double-edged, and can be contrasted to the other sounds on each of these features separately, the exact order of these sounds in the middle of the scale seems insignificant. It should be noted, that /r/, although a periodic liquid, has outstanding aggressive potentials, especially in languages in which it is "rolled" or "intermittent". It is, actually, "double-edged": on the one hand, it is periodic, on the other, it is *multiply* interrupted.

Acoustic Coding

Perhaps the most intriguing characteristics of speech perception concern the problematic relationship between the perceived phonetic categories and the more or less rich, pre-categorial sensory information that is the carrier of such perception. In chapter 1, I claimed that verbal communication involves a series of conversions; at the hearer's end, it begins with an acoustic stream which he converts into strings of phonetic categories which, in turn, he converts into semantic units, and so forth. There is little structural resemblance between the acoustic information and the abstract phonetic categories; the former is thoroughly restructured, and excluded from consciousness. Very little, if at all, of the acoustic information remains available for direct introspection. Thus, for instance, we can tell from introspection, with some effort, that /s/ is "higher" than /ʃ/; but it is quite impossible to tell from introspection that the items in the sequence /ba, da, ga/ differ from one another only in the onset frequency of the second formant transition (for the meaning of these terms, see the next paragraph, and Figure 8.1).

There is no one to one relationship between the segments of perceived speech and the segments of the acoustic signal that carries it. As I have suggested in chapter 1, there is, between the two, a mediating step of "complex coding". Vowels consist of specific combinations of overtones, called formants. A formant is a concentration of acoustic energy within a restricted frequency region. With the help of a device called spectrograph (or sonograph), these concentrations of energy can be converted into patches of light and shade called spectrograms. In speech spectrograms, three or four formants can usually be detected. In the synthetic, hand-painted spectrograms of Figure 8.1, only the lowest two formants are represented. Formants are referred to by numbers: F_1, F_2, etc., the first being the lowest in frequency, the next the next higher, and so on (F_0 refers to the "baseline", the fundamental pitch).

A formant transition is a relatively rapid change in the position of the formant on the frequency scale. A device called pattern-playback converts hand-painted spectrograms into sound. This provides the basis for what has proven to be a convenient method of experimenting with the speech signal: it makes it possible to vary those parameters that were estimated to be of linguistic importance and subsequently test the result by listening to the vocal output. In Figure 8.1, the steady-state formants are, by their different positions on the frequency scale, the cues for the vowels /i/ and /u/. We can see that for these vowels there is a straightforward correspondence between acoustic and phonetic segments.

But consider now the voiced stop /d/. To isolate the acoustic cue for the segment, we should first notice the transition of the lower (first) formant. That transition is not specifically a cue for /d/; it rather tells the listener that the segment is one of the voiced stops, /b/, /d/, or /g/. [...] To produce /d/, instead of /b/, or /g/, we must add the transitions of the higher (second) formant, the parts of the pattern that are encircled by the [dotted] line (Liberman, 1970: 307–308).

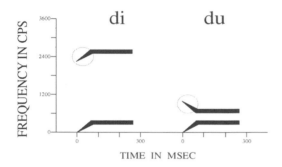

Figure 8.1 Simplified spectrographic patterns sufficient to produce the syllables [di] and [du].

If we play back only the circled parts of the pattern, we clearly hear what we would expect to, judging from the appearance of the formant transition: an upward glide in one case, and a rapidly falling whistle in the other. When the whole pattern is played back, we hear no glide or whistle, but the syllable /di/ or /du/. One and the same phoneme is prompted, then, by vastly different acoustic cues. In the case of /di/, the transition rises from approximately 2200 cps to 2600 cps; in /du/, it falls from about 1200 cps to 700 cps. Furthermore, there is no way to cut the patterns of Figure 8.1 so as to recover /d/ segments that can be substituted one for the other, or to obtain some piece that will produce /d/ alone. If we cut progressively into the syllable from the right-hand end, we hear /d/ plus either a vowel, or a nonspeech sound; at no point will we hear only /d/. "This is so, because the formant transition is, at every instant, providing information about two phonemes, the consonant and the vowel—that is, the phonemes are transmitted in parallel" (Liberman et al., 1967: 436). This is why the phenomenon in question is called *parallel transmission*.

In artificial laboratory conditions one can hear directly those glides and whistles. This may illustrate another distinctive characteristics of speech perception, called "categorial perception". I will quote Glucksberg and Danks's brief summary of the phenomenon (1975: 40–41).

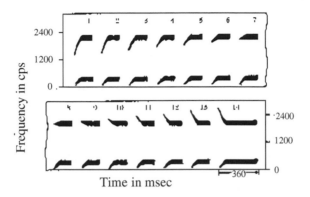

Figure 8.2 Hand-painted spectrograms of the syllables ba, da, ga. The ba–da–ga pitch continuum of F_2 is divided into 14 steps instead of three. The two parallel regions of black indicate regions of energy concentration, F_1 and F_2. Notice that the onset frequency of F_2 of da is higher than that of ba; and the onset frequency of F_2 of ga is higher than that of da.

In general, people can discriminate among a very large number of physical stimuli. For example, we can discriminate among approximately 1,200 different pitches, and among a wide variety of colors. We are also aware that such stimuli as pitches and colors vary continuously and smoothly along particular dimensions. Certain speech stimuli do not behave in this way [...]. Although the physical stimuli may vary continuously over a fairly wide range, we do not perceive this variation. Consider the continuous series of changes in the second formant of a simple English syllable, shown in Figure 8.2. These sound patterns produce the syllables [ba], [da], and [ga] when fed into a speech synthesizer. The first three syllables are heard as [ba], the next six as [da], and the last five as [ga]. People discriminate extremely well between these three "categories," but do not hear the differences within each category (Mattingly et al., 1971). The three [b]'s all sound the same, even though there is continuous change along a single dimension. Between stimuli 3 and 4, listeners perceive a shift from [b] to [d]. This difference is always perceived as quite distinct, even though it is physically no more different than the difference between stimuli 2 and 3 or between 4 and 5.

Onset frequency is the frequency from which a formant transition rises or falls. Parallel transmission and categorial perception may direct attention to some of the distinguishing marks of speech perception; they seem to indicate that we have a speech mode and a nonspeech mode of listening, which follow different paths in the neural system. I propose to illustrate the two series of sound stimuli from an unpublished demo tape by Terry Halwes. Listen (online) to the series in Figure 8.2, and see whether you can hear the change from /ba/ to /da/ to /ga/ occur suddenly. Now let us isolate the second formant transition, that piece of sound which differs across the series, and listen to just those sounds alone. Most people who listen to that series report hearing what we would expect, judging from the appearance of the formant transition: upward glides, and falling whistles displaying a gradual change from one to the next. The perception of the former series illustrates the speech mode, of the latter series—the nonspeech mode.

We seem to be tuned, normally, to the nonspeech mode; but as soon as the incoming stream of sounds gives the slightest indication that it may be carrying linguistic information, we automatically switch to the speech mode: we "attend away" *from* the acoustic signal *to* the combination of muscle movements that seem to have produced it (even in the case of hand-painted spectrograms); and *from* these elementary movements *away to* their joint purpose, the phoneme sequence. In certain circumstances, in what we might perhaps call the "poetic mode", some aspects of the formant structure of the acoustic signal may vaguely enter consciousness. As a result, people may have intuitions that certain vowel contrasts correspond to the BRIGHTNESS ~ DARKNESS contrast, some other to the HIGH ~ LOW contrast, or that certain consonants are "harder" than others. As a result, in turn, poets may use more frequently words that contain dark vowels, in lines referring to dark colors, mystic obscurity, or slow and heavy movement, or depicting hatred and struggle. At the reception end of the process, readers have vague intuitions that the sound patterns of these lines are somehow expressive of their atmosphere.

Notice that in the preceding paragraph I was talking of oppositions and not of specific qualities. I submit, in accordance with the structuralist conception, that it is more adequate to conceive of the back-front continuum as analogous in some way to the dark-light continuum, than attribute specific properties to the individual vowels. The same is true of "aggressive" and "tender" consonants. To this effect, Jakobson and Waugh (1979: 189) quote Gombrich with approval:

> The problem of synaesthetic equivalences will cease to look embarrassingly arbitrary if, hereto, we fix our attention not on likeness of elements but on structural relationships within a scale or a matrix. When we say that *i* is brighter than *u,* we find a surprising degree of general consent. If we are more careful still and say that the step from *u* to *i* is more like an upward step than a downward step, I think the majority will agree, whatever explanation each of us may be inclined to offer.

In other words, there need not be anything inherently dark or low in the vowel /u/, or inherently bright or high in the vowel /i/. Suffice it that the vowel continuum and the brightness continuum be perceived as somehow analogous to one another, and that the vowel /u/ and the value "dark" occupy similar positions on the respective continua. However, we have to explain yet, why the bright end of the brightness continuum is matched precisely with the front-extreme of the vowel continuum and not the other way around; or, likewise, why the high end of the height-continuum matches with the /i/-end of the vowel continuum rather than the other way around. My claim is, again, that certain perceptual aspects of the acoustic signal, irrelevant, in principle, to the speech mode, do enter consciousness, in spite of all.

There is some experimental evidence for the assumption that in certain instances pre-categorial acoustic information (from the nonspeech mode) does reach—subliminally though—awareness. Liberman et al. describe an experiment by T. Rand:

> To one ear he presented all the first formant, including the transitions, together with the steady-state parts of the second and third formants; when presented alone, these patterns sound vaguely like /da/. To the other ear, with proper time relationships carefully preserved, were presented the 50–msec second-formant and third-formant transitions; alone, these sound like [...] chirps [...]. But when these patterns were presented together—that is, dichotically—listeners clearly heard /ba/, /da/ or /ga/ (depending on the nature of the second-formant and third-formant transitions) in one ear and, simultaneously, nonspeech chirps in the other. Thus, it appears that the same acoustic events—the second-formant or third-formant transitions—can be processed simultaneously as speech and nonspeech. We should suppose, then, that the incoming signal goes indiscriminately to speech and nonspeech processors. If the speech processors succeed in extracting phonetic features, then the signal is speech; if they fail, the signal is processed only as nonspeech.

What is more, people appear to be capable of switching modes, by using different listening strategies. Fricative stimuli seem to be especially suited for the application of different strategies, such that they may be perceived fairly categorially in one situation but continuously in another (Repp, 1984: 287). Repp has investigated the possibility that with fricatives, for instance, little training would be necessary for acoustic discrimination of within-category differences. He employed an /s/–/ʃ/ continuum, followed by a vocalic context. The success of his procedure

> together with the introspections of the experienced listeners, suggested that the skill involved lay in perceptually segregating the noise from its vocalic context, which then made it possible to attend to its "pitch". Without this segregation, the phonetic percept was dominant. Once the auditory strategy

has been acquired, it is possible to switch back and forth between auditory and phonetic modes of listening, and it seems likely [...] that both strategies could be pursued simultaneously (or in very rapid succession) without any loss of accuracy. These results provide good evidence for the existence of two alternative modes of perception, phonetic and auditory—a distinction supported by much additional evidence (ibid., 307).

Repp's "auditory mode" does not abolish the distinction between the speech mode and the nonspeech mode. It merely provides evidence that even in the speech mode *some* pre-categorial sensory information is accessible, that is, that the poetic mode *is* possible.

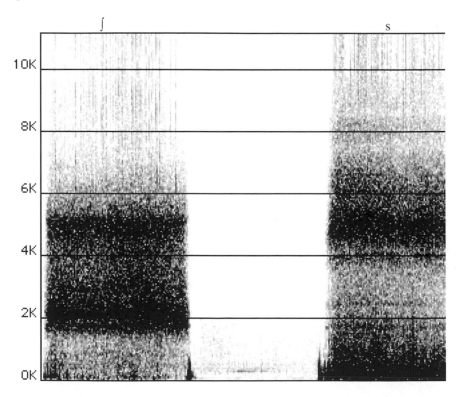

Figure 8.3 Sonograms of [ʃ] and [s], representing the first and second formant, and indicating why [s] is somehow "higher"

Above, I have presented Fónagy's findings concerning the distribution of speech sounds in aggressive and tender poems in a variety of languages. In chapter 1, I claimed that the emotional qualities associated with speech sounds arise from a delay in the recoding of the acoustic stream into the phonetic stream. As I also suggested, some speech sounds are more highly encoded than others (i. e., the pre-categorial sensory information is less available to consciousness). Now, the correlation of liquids and nasals, on the one hand, and of voiceless stops on the other, with tender and aggressive poems, respectively, can be explained, precisely, in terms of a delay in recoding or restructuring from acoustic cues to phonetic entities. Voiceless stops are perceived as unitary linguistic events, stripped of all pre-categorial sensory information. Here, the recoding process goes on with no interference. On the other hand, in relatively unencoded speech sounds, such as liquids and nasals, the recoding process can be "disturbed", so that some of the rich pre-categorial auditory information becomes available to consciousness. Emotional flexibility, an openness and responsiveness to rich pre-categorial information, is characteristic of tender feelings, whereas the lack of it characterizes aggression. Thus, liquids and nasals may have a perceived quality of tenderness, of emotional adaptability and sensory richness, whereas voiceless stops may have a perceived quality of rigidity that may be positively correlated with aggression, and negatively with tenderness.

Now we may be able to explain two rather puzzling issues concerning the emotional characteristics of speech sounds, which we have already encountered above: the consistent emotional difference between periodic and aperiodic consonants, and the double-edgedness of the sibilants. It seems to be well established that [±PERIODIC] is analogous with [±TENDER], coupling the positive with the positive and the negative with the negative values of the two dichotomies. How should we account for this analogy? To say that aperiodic sounds are noises, or that periodic sounds are musical whereas aperiodic sounds are harsh, may be true enough, but it explains nothing: it merely restates the issue.

Periodic sounds have been described (May and Repp, 1982: 145) as "the recurrence of signal portions with similar structure", whereas aperiodic stimuli have a "randomly changing waveform", that "may have more idiosyncratic features to be remembered". The recurring signal portions with similar structures may arouse in the perceiver a relatively relaxed kind of attentiveness (there will be no surprises, one may expect the same waveform to recur). Thus, periodic sounds are experienced as smoothly flowing. The randomly changing waveforms of aperiodic sounds, with their "idiosyncratic features", are experienced as disorder, as a disruption of the "relaxed kind of attentiveness". Thus, aperiodic sounds are experienced as harsh, strident, turbulent, and the like.

Now we have reached a point where we may attempt to account for the notorious double-edgedness of the sibilants. On the one hand, sound patterns based on /s, ʹ/ may serve as sound imitations of natural noises of varying volumes (varying from the rustling of curtains to the roar of the sea); on the other hand, these sounds may have a tender, hushing quality. This double-edgedness seems to be derived from the phenomenon observed above that with regard to these consonants we have alternative cognitive strategies available, to direct our attention to the linguistic category or to the auditory information that carries it. The tender or hushing quality of /s, ʹ/ may have to do with their feature [+CONTINUOUS] and with their being of the few consonants that need little restructuring in the course of phonetic decoding of the signal, enabling the perceiver to attend to some rich, inarticulate sensory information, typically correlated, as I have suggested, with tenderness. Their "noisy" quality springs from the aperiodic nature of this sensory information. The feature [– VOICED] will be interpreted in the "strident" context as *lack* of sonority, richness or smoothness; in the "hushing" context it may be interpreted as having an onomatopoetic element, the imitation of whispering.

Onomatopoeia—The Constraints of Semiotic Systems

There is a parable by Izmailov about the cuckoo who tells her neighbours in the province about the wonderful song of the nightingale she heard in a far-away country. She learned this song, and is willing to reproduce it for the benefit of her neighbours. They all are eager to hear that marvellous song, so the cuckoo starts singing: "kukuk, kukuk, kukuk". The moral of the parable is that that's what happens to bad translators of poetry. My thesis in this section is that Izmailov does an injustice to the cuckoo (not to some translators). When you translate from one semiotic system to another, you are constrained by the options of the target system. The cuckoo had no choice but to use cuckoo-language for the translation. The question is whether she utilized those options of cuckoo-language that are nearest to the nightingale's song. After all, Izmailov himself committed exactly the same kind of inadequacy he attributes to the cuckoo. The bird emits neither the speech sound [k] nor [u]; it uses no speech sounds at all. But a poet (any poet) in human language is constrained by the phoneme system of his language; he can translate the cuckoo's song only to those speech sounds. His translation will be judged adaquate if he chooses those speech sounds that are most similar in their effect to the cuckoo's call.

The issue at stake is the translation of perceived qualities from reality to some semiotic system, or from one semiotic system to another (in fact, the cuckoo's call too is a semiotic system). The precision of translation depends on how fine-grained are the sign-units of the target system. If the target system is sufficiently fine-grained and its nearest options are chosen to represent a source phenomenon, it may evoke a perception that the two are "equivalent". I propose to present the problem through a well-known linguistic-literary phenomenon: onomatopoeia. Onomatopoeia is the imitation of natural sounds by speech sounds. There is an open set of infinite noises in the world. But most alphabets contain only twenty-something letters that convey in any language a closed system of about fifty (up to a maximum of 100) speech sounds. Nevertheless, we tend to accept many instances of onomatopoeia as quite adequate phonetic equivalents of the natural noises. How can language imitate, with such a limited number of speech sounds an infinite number of natural noises? Take the bird called "cuckoo". The cuckoo's name is said to have an onomatopoeic origin: it is said to imitate the sound the bird makes, and the bird is said to emit the sound [kukuk]. As I suggested, the bird emits neither the speech sound [k] nor [u]; it uses no speech sounds at all. It emits two continuous sounds with a characteristic pitch interval between them, roughly a minor third. These sounds are continuous, have a steady-state pitch and an abrupt onset. I have hypothesized that the overtone structure of the steady-state sound is nearest to the formant structure of a rounded back vowel, and the formant transitions indicating a [k] before an [u]. That is why the name of this bird contains the sound sequence [ku] in so many languages.[1] In human language, European languages at least, pitch intervals are part of the intonation system, not of the lexicon. Consequently, the pitch interval characteristic of the cuckoo's call is not included in the bird's name (the lexicon is not sufficiently "fine-grained" for the pitch interval).

In order to test the above hypotheses, I took the European cuckoo's song (from a tape issued by the Israeli Nature Conservation Association) and submitted it to an instrumental analysis, comparing it to three cardinal vowels, the phonetic [i], [a] and [u] (included in the speech analyser package "SoundScope"). There is plenty of background noise in the cuckoo recording, and I could not obtain a usable spectrogram. But my application offers an option to extract formants of the speech sounds by a different ("LPC based") method. A comparison between the first two "formants" of the cuckoo's call and the cardinal vowels yielded illuminating results (see Figure 8.4).

---

[1]　My evidence for this generalization is anecdotal. It is true for German, English, French, Hungarian and Hebrew cuckoos (these are the languages with which I am familiar; judging from Izmailov's parable, this is the case in Russian too). I am not in a position to collect the information from African or Amer-Indian languages. In the cuckoo's case there may be some proved mutual influence among these languages. But then we must explain why, when the name is not of onomatopoeic origin, there is little influence between them. English "nightingale", for instance, resembles only its German counterpart ("Nachtigall"); in French it is "rossignol", in Hungarian "fülemüle", in Hebrew "zamir".

After having written the foregoing comment, I happened to meet a young Chinese woman from Beigin, and asked her what was the Chinese word for "cuckoo". She said it was [pu-ku]. The [k] sounded very deep down the throat; and there was a falling-rising tone on the second syllable, that had nothing to do with the characteristic interval of the cuckoo song. I am indebted to Sinologist Lihi Laor, who told me that in Chinese the [±VOICED] opposition doesn't exist, only the [±ASPIRATED] opposition. My impression that it was a deep [k] indicates that it is an unaspirated [k]. In fact, both plosives are unvoiced and unaspirated. To her great surprise, her native speaker colleagues of various Chinese dialects all came up with exactly the same word. One might further speculate that the deep [k] may corroborate my co-articulation hypothesis; the unaspirated plosives may corroborate my abruptness hypothesis. The falling-rising tone on [ku] suggests that even Chinese cannot lexicalize the minor third interval; it is the linguistic constraints that determine the tone. My colleague Zvika Serper tells me that in Japanese the word for cuckoo is semantically (rather than phonetically) based: Hatodokei = dove + clock. Its call, however, is phonetically based: poppoo = kuku (which, too, repeats a voiceless plosive, each token followed by a rounded backvowel). In an online English to Japanese dictionary the English word "cuckoo" turned up "kokyu" and "kakkou". Available: http://www.freedict.com/onldict/onldict.php
I lack, however, information about the phonological constraints of these languages that might, perhaps, account for the differences between their respective words for [kuku].

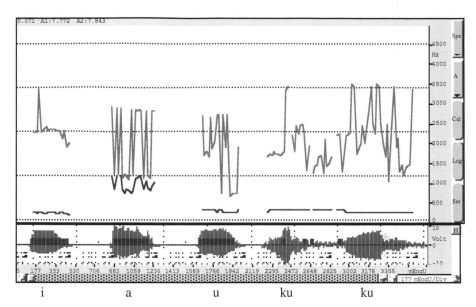

Figure 8.4 The upper window presents the first and second formant of the cuckoo's song and of the phonetic vowels i–a–u; the lower window presents their wave form.

In the upper window of Figure 8.4, the first formant of [i], [u], and [kuku] form straightish horizontal lines between 0 and 500 Hz; the first formant of [a] crinkles around 1000 Hz, slightly touching the second formant. The first "formant" of the cuckoo's call looks very much like that of the [i] and the [u] both in shape and frequency range (though more perfectly horizontal), and very much unlike that of the [a]. The second "formant" of the cuckoo's song is less regular than that of the [a] and the [u], but displays similar tendencies and is smeared over a roughly similar (but somewhat higher) pitch range. Thus, in harmony with my hypothesis, the overtone structure of the cuckoo's song displays greater resemblance to the [u] than to the other two cardinal vowels. My second expectation, however, has been bluntly refuted: there is no part in the cuckoo's song that sounds like [k]; we hear something more like [huhu]. Nor is there any sign of [k] in the computer's output. Before tackling this problem, let us have a look at the pitch contours extracted from the recordings of the cuckoo's song and the cardinal vowels (Figure 8.5).

The first observation to be made is that the two couldn't be pasted in the same window: the fundamental frequency of the cuckoo's call is about 5–6 times (!) higher than that of the vowels spoken by a male speaker. It reaches up to almost 780 Hz, and reaches down to exactly 580 Hz, whereas the vowels' intonation contours in figure 8.5 reach up to about 135 Hz, and down to about 95 Hz (the typical male voice range is specified in the application as 80–150 Hz; the typical female range as 120–280 Hz). The remarkable thing to notice is that in spite of this enormous difference of pitch, the cuckoo's call and the vowel [u] are perceived as equally "dark". This happens because the perceived "darkness" is determined not by their fundamental pitch, but by their overtone structure, which we have found to be similar.

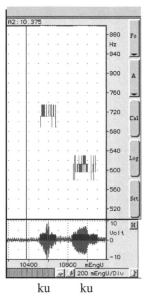
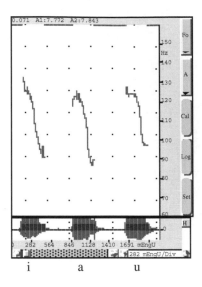

Figure 8.5   The upper windows present the pitch contours of the cuckoo's song and of the phonetic vowels i–a–u spoken by a male; the lower windows presents their wave form.

I have said that pitch countour does not belong to the lexicon of human speech, but to its intonation system. But, as figure 8.5 indicates, the pitch contours of the cuckoo's call and those of the spoken vowels tend to be very dissimilar. The intonation contour of an isolated vowel tends to move over a considerable pitch range, and the perceived pitch of such a vowel is usually unpredictable. The cuckoo's song, by contrast, abruptly begins at a steady-state perceived pitch. I submit that this is the abruptness we perceive at the onset of the cuckoo's song, indicated by an abrupt voiceless plosive in human onomatopoeia. The voiceless plosive contributes to the perceived similarity only the abstract quality ABRUPTNESS. Thus, the cuckoo's abrupt pitch onset is not translated in human lexicon to a similar abrupt pitch onset (and cannot be lexicalized as such), but to an abruptly articulated consonant, which has nothing to do with pitch. Now there are at least three voiceless plosives in human language, [p], [t] and [k]. Why is it that precisely the [k] is perceived in so many languages as suitable to reproduce the cuckoo's song, and not the other ones? There are two possible answers to this question. First, phonetically, [p] and [t] are "diffuse" consonants, [k] is characterised as "compact", that is, more abrupt. Second, there is the problem of co-articulation: [u] is a backvowel, and as such it is more easily co-articulated with the velar [k] than with the dental [t] or the bilabial [p]. To understand better the nature of this co-articulation, the reader is invited to pronounce the words "kill" and "call". He will notice that in the latter, before the back vowel, the [k] is pronounced at a much lower point of the vocal track.

I have spoken above of degrees of encodedness. While in the [s–ʃ] distinction respondents can tell by conscious introspection that the former is somehow higher than the latter, in the [ba, da, ga] series, they can't tell that all the difference between them is a rise in the onset frequency of the second formant transition (see Figures 8.2 and 8.6). However, when asked to order these nonsense syllables in the order of their relative "metallicness", they (1) don't say they don't know what I am talking about, and (2) they tend to judge [ba] as the least metallic of the three, and after some hesitation, to judge [ga] as the most metallic of them. In such issues I don't usually look for a straightforward structural resemblance between [ga] and "metallicness", but rather proceed in three steps: (1) I collect empirical evidence for intuitions of respondents; (2) concerning these intuitions, try to determine what phonetic scale is perceived as analogous to what nonphonetic scale (e.g., [i–u] is analogous to both "high-low" and "bright-dark"); and (3) attempt to explain why precisely the "high" and "bright" poles are matched with the phonetic [i]-pole rather than the other way around.

Now, as to the analogy between the [ba, da, ga] series and the [±METALLIC] spectrum, I was rather stammering at the third stage, and it was Gaver's paper that gave me the systematic clue for an explanation: "The sounds made by vibrating wood decay quickly, with low frequencies lasting longer than high ones, whereas the sounds made by vibrating metal decay slowly, with high-frequency showing less damping than low ones. In addition, metal sounds have partials [=overtones—R.T.] with well-defined frequency peaks, whereas wooden sound partials are smeared over frequency space" (pp. 293–294). Even if the sound structure of vibrating metals is quite unlike the sound structure of the voiced plosive [g], this might be sufficient to warrant the matching of the [ga]-pole of the phonetic sequence, with the "metallic"-pole of the [±METALLIC] spectrum. Now this matching may be reinforced by the opposition "well-defined frequency peaks" ~ "smeared over frequency space", which may be perceived as corresponding to the COMPACT ~ DIFFUSE opposition in the traditional phonetics domain, characterising [g] ~ [b, d]. Again, these may be different kinds of compactness and diffuseness, but sufficient to suggest the matching of the [+METALLIC]-pole of one scale with the [ga]-pole rather than the [ba]-pole of the other.

There is nothing metallic in the velum, the place of articulation of the [k]. It is the acoustic features pointed out in the preceding paragraph that render [k] more metallic than [p] or [t]. This can explain why we hear the clock tick-tocking rather than, e.g., tip-topping. The [k] is better suited than the [p] or the [t] to imitate the metallic click of the clock.

We have explained two crucial things about onomatopoeia: first, that behind the rigid categories of speech sounds one can discern some rich pre-categorial sound information that may resemble natural sounds in one way or other; and it is possible to acquire auditory strategies to switch back and forth between auditory and phonetic modes of listening; and second, that certain natural noises have more common features with one speech sound than with some others.

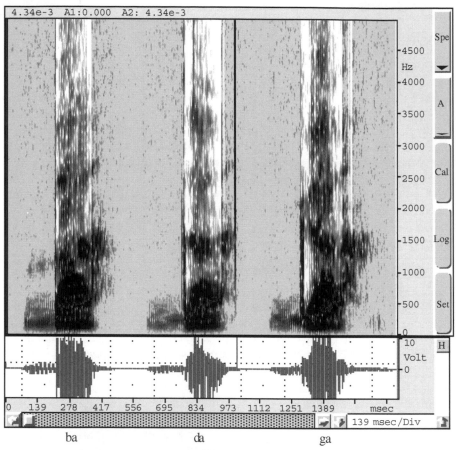

Figure 8.6   Spectrograms of the syllables ba, da, ga, in natural speech.

But we have still not explained two additional findings which, in fact, appear to be two sides of the same coin. First, we have said that there is an infinity of natural noises, but only about 50–100 speech sounds in any given language. And second, we have found that the same speech sound [k] may imitate some metallic noises, or indicate an abrupt onset (not necessarily metallic) of the word that imitates the natural sound "ku-ku". These two issues are intimately related. Every speech sound is a bundle of features. In different contexts we may attend to different features of the same sound. When the context changes from, say, *kuku* to, say, *ticktock,* we attend away from one feature (abruptness) to another (metallicness). I claim that this ability to attend away from one feature to another is similar to what Wittgenstein called "aspect switching". In this way, the closed and limited system of the speech sounds of a language may offer an indefinite number of features to be exploitated for the imitation of natural sounds.

Relevant features can be multiplied indefinitely, and one may discover unexpected phonetic or phonological features. Let us consider a minimal pair that can illustrate this. In Hebrew, *mətaktek* means "ticktocking"; we attend to the repeated voiceless plosives and perceive the word as onomatopoeic. *Mətaktak*, by contrast, means "sweetish". In Hebrew, the repetition of the last syllable's consonantal frame is lexicalized, suggesting "somewhat (sweet)". A wide range of such "moderate" adjectives can be derived in this way from "main-entry" adjectives: *hamatsmats* (sourish) from *hamuts* (sour), *adamdam* (reddish) from *adom* (red), *yərakrak* (greenish) from *yarok* (green), and so forth. Hebrew slang even derives *gəvarbar* (somewhat man) from gɛvɛr [man]. The meaning directs our attention to this redoubling of the syllable, and we attend away from the acoustic features of the specific consonants.

Finally, we may observe that in different contexts different potentials of the voiceless plosive /k/ may be actualized. In some poetic contexts it may contribute, as we have seen, to the expression of an aggressive mood; in some contexts it may imitate metallic noises as in "click" and "tick-tock"; and in some contexts, as in "kuku" it may suggest an abrupt onset.

Front vs. Back Vowels

Let us turn now to a thought-experiment, based on a set of real experiments at the Haskins Laboratories, back in the early fifties. The aim of this thought-experiment is to offer an explanation for the intuition that back vowels are "darker" and "lower" than front vowels. It will be suggested that certain physical qualities of the acoustic signal enter consciousness, in spite of the speech mode, when we perceive back vowels as dark and low and front vowels as bright and high. These associations seem to have a general, culture-independent validity. The search for an explanation for this is summarized by Jakobson and Waugh (1979: 188–194).

Consider the widespread intuition expressed by Gombrich, that the step from /u/ to /i/ is more like an upward step than a downward step. In an important sense, each of these two vowels can be uttered on any fundamental pitch. Yet, in another, no less important sense, the two vowels are exactly of the same height. This will be also apparent if we look again at Figure 8.1. The first formants of the two vowels are of exactly of the same frequency (250 cps). If, on the other hand, we look at the frequency of the second formants, we find that the second formant of /i/ is of a much higher frequency than that of /u/ (2900 vs. 700 cps).

Now, what about the correspondence of the dark–bright continuum to the /u/–/i/ continuum? Let us grant that these two continua should be made analogous to one another. Why should the /i/-pole be matched precisely with the "bright"-pole, and not the other way around? In what acoustic features that are relevant to the opposition DARK ~ BRIGHT are the back vowels opposed to the front vowels? Let us have yet another look at Figure 8.1. We might say, of course, that the significantly higher second formant bestows some luster upon the front vowels. This assumption is corroborated by what happens if we play back the spectrograms after reducing the intensity of the higher formant of most front vowels and some middle vowels. "Small attenuations of the higher formant caused the vowel to acquire a quality that can best be described as 'dull'" (Delattre et al., 1952: 204).

But a much more interesting side to the story emerges—one having considerable psychological consequences. Figure 8.1 is representative of the formant structures of back vowels and front vowels. In the former, the two formants are significantly closer to one another than in the latter. Delattre and his colleagues produced good experimental evidence that vowels whose first and second formants are closer together are perceived in a different manner from those whose formants are wider apart. Roughly, we might say, the human ear effectively fuses the two formants when they are close enough, whereas it seems to perceive them as fairly differentiated when they are sufficiently apart. The ear averages the first and second formant frequencies of the back vowels, whereas the first two formants of the front vowels stand out clearly in our subliminal perception. For the vowels where the first two formants are relatively close together, one can find reasonably good one-formant equivalents that occupy an intermediate position between the first and second formant of the two-formant vowel (nearer to the lower formant). It is difficult to find one-formant equivalents for the front vowels, in which the two formants are rather far apart.

In other words, the first two formants of the front vowels stand so clearly apart that they cannot be averaged. This assumption is corroborated by the effect of reductions in the intensity of the lower formant of the back vowels, which caused a change in color toward the respective adjacent vowel. "We should suppose, then, that reducing the intensity of the lower formant [...] would have the effect of increasing the higher formant's relative contribution to the 'mean' and would thus effectively raise the mean formant" (ibid., 203). When, however, the intensity of the lower formant was reduced in the front vowels, "the vowel color was replaced by a nonvowel sound [..]. In no case did a reduction in the intensity of the lower formant cause a clear *shift* in vowel color" (ibid). With arbitrarily chosen two-formant patterns (which did not sound like vowels) "the two formants of the nonvowel pattern, however close together they may be, did not fuse into a single sound, but tended rather to be heard as two-component chords" (ibid., 206).

We might conclude, then, that in the case of the fused formants of the back vowels, as well as in the averaged one-formant versions, the ear reanalyzes, as it were, a less differentiated acoustic signal in terms of the frequencies that appear to have been fused inside it.

How does all this bear on the analogy of the vowel continuum with the brightness continuum? The acoustic signal of the back vowels is of relatively low differentiation. The ear receives from the two formants an impression that is sufficiently indistinguishable from that which would be heard from one formant placed somewhere in between. I submit, then, that relatively low differentiation and relative darkness are similar phenomenally to a sufficient degree to warrant the matching of the back vowel extreme of the vowel continuum with the dark extreme of the brightness continuum. *Indistinguishable* is the key word. It is, then, some perceptual quality of the acoustic signal that sometimes intrudes, so to speak, into the speech mode, creating the poetic mode.

A further step is still required to complete our thought-experiment. As we have seen, a relatively low differentiation in vowel perception is naturally matched with darkness, when the two continua are perceived as analogous. When back vowels are frequent in verse lines that refer to dark colors, the dark potential of the vowels is realized by combination with the dark elements of the meaning. Readers may have an intuition that the sound is somehow "an echo of the sense", or that the sounds are somehow "expressive" of the sense. It would appear that it is the conventionally established metaphorical relationship between darkness and "mystic obscurity", or such emotions as hatred, that is mediating between vowel color and such meaning components. In the light of the foregoing analysis, however, I wish to suggest that the relatively undifferentiated perceptions associated with the back vowels may be *directly related to* the lowly differentiated perception associated with "mystic obscurities", and that there is no need for a mediating metaphorical concept. Likewise, in the light of my analysis of emotions and emotional qualities (Chapter 3), low differentiation is a characteristic of emotional (as opposed to rational) qualities. Low differentiation combined with a high energy level can be an important ingredient in such emotions and emotional qualities as anger or hatred. Thus, when back vowels are frequent in verse lines depicting hatred or struggle, they may be perceived, again, as expressive, with no need, again, for a mediating metaphorical concept. The foregoing analysis of the structural relationship between back vowels, darkness, mystic obscurity, and hatred or struggle may be regarded as further reinforcement of one of the basic tenets of the present study: that "past experience" is insufficient as an explanation for certain metaphorical intuitions; that some metaphorical relationships originate in processes that are deeper than cultural conditioning; and that certain culturally conditioned metaphorical conventions are results rather than causes: they came to reflect, through repeated cultural transmission, certain underlying cognitive processes.

It has been suggested to us that we might conduct a "real" experiment to find out whether subjects who perceive back vowels as darker than front vowels, do indeed perceive them also as more complex. So, we have conducted an experiment[2] in which subjects were requested to characterize /u/ and /i/ with four pairs of antonymous adjectives that are directly applicable to the pre-categorical sensory information.

---

[2] This part of the research was jointly conducted with Yehosheba Bentov, Ruth Lavy, and Hanna Lock.

Subjects. Subjects were 120 students at the Seminar Hakkibbutsim Teachers' Training College, who were asked by their teacher to stay after class to take an experimental test.

Stimuli. The test material consisted of a sheet with the vowels /i/ and /u/ (in two different contexts) printed in Hebrew, and a list of eight pairs of antonymous adjectives. The test was a forced-choice test: subjects were requested to characterize each vowel by the more suitable member of each pair. In the first, null-context, the vowels were printed in isolation; in the other, they were part of the nonsense syllables /pit/ and /put/. The test was administered to sixty subjects in each of the contexts. Initially, the two contexts were planned as a pilot test, in order to allow us choose the condition that would yield the more significant results. As will be seen below, the differences between the two conditions were insignificant; however, the *direction* and *consistency* of the difference was found to be rather significant. Two groups of pairs of adjectives were used. Four pairs *(dark ~ bright, far ~ near, big ~ small, low ~ high)* refer to perceived qualities that have been regularly and quite consistently associated with these vowels. Four other pairs *(thick ~ thin, differentiated ~ undifferentiated, spacious ~ dense, simple ~ complicated)* were the test adjectives; they were chosen as pairs of adjectives that could characterize the perceived quality of the acoustic information, as discussed above.

The set-up of the experiments was chosen, mainly, to get around a problem of communication with the subjects. If one explains clearly what kind of intuition one is looking for, one may interfere with the subjects' spontaneous response; and if one refrains from such explanation, one cannot be sufficiently sure that the responses reflect the *kind* of perceived qualities one is interested in. This was the reason for the inclusion of the first four pairs of adjectives: they could, on the one hand, specify to some extent for the subjects the kind of task they were expected to perform on the test-items; and on the other, they could indicate to the experimenter whether the task *was* understood by the subjects.

In the second group four pairs of adjectives were similarly included. This was done because of the uncertainty concerning which pair would describe for the subjects the perceived quality of the acoustic information least ambiguously. The possibility of such an ambiguity was confirmed, unexpectedly enough, in relation to the pair of adjectives *low ~ high*. in the first group (see below). For this reason, the present test was initially intended as a pilot test, to help us choose the appropriate pair of adjectives. The results, however, were surprisingly unambiguous (in the expected direction) with respect to all four test pairs of adjectives.

A few comments on the adjective pairs used follow here. The Hebrew adjectives for *thick ~ thin* do not have the ambiguity of the English adjectives. *Samikh* means "thick" as in the phrases "thick syrup" and "thick smoke"; *dalil* (meaning "sparse" or "diluted") is perceived as its proper antonym. *Meruwaḥ* in the third pair is ambiguous, meaning "spacious" or "wide open"; the chance that it might be taken to refer to the articulatory gesture rather than to the acoustic correlates existed; its antonym, however, clearly denotes "dense, crowded, compact". There was a suspicion that the pair *differentiated ~ undifferentiated* might be unfamiliar to the subjects in the sense expected here. Finally, the adjectives *simple ~ complicated* are too abstract, and so it might be doubtful whether the subjects would apply them to the sensory qualities of the acoustic correlates of the vowels, or to some other aspects. Hence, it was expected that the adjectives *thick ~ thin* would best reflect the subjects' intuitions concerning the sensory qualities of the vowels.

Very significantly, all pairs of adjectives except one were attributed more frequently in the expected way than the other way around. The only pair that showed a tendency opposite to expectation was *high ~ low*. This seems rather odd, since the intuition that the step from /u/ to /i/ is more like an upward step than like a downward step is fairly consistent. Two factors seem to have influenced these deviant results. First, there is the fact that the relevant Hebrew adjectives are ambiguous, meaning either *high ~ low,* or *tall ~ short;* actually, this fact was brought out by the unexpected results. Second, the occurrence of this adjective pair after the pairs *big ~ small* and *far ~ near* may have influenced subjects to construe it as referring to relative size rather than relative pitch.

Results   The results are given in table 8.1.

Table 8.1 Notice that the majority of subjects characterize /i/ as "lighter, nearer, smaller, thinner, more differentiated, more spacious and simpler" than /u/.

phoneme	dark	light	n.r.	far	near	n.r.	big	small	n.r.	low	high	n.r.
/i/	6	53	1	14	45	1	6	51	3	33	25	2
/pit/	14	46	–	20	40	–	17	43	–	36	23	1
/u/	53	6	1	46	14	–	52	7	1	26	31	3
/put/	46	14	–	40	20	–	43	17	–	23	36	1

phoneme	thick	thin	n.r.	undif.	dif.	n.r.	dense	spac.	n.r.	simp.	comp.	n.r.
/i/	9	49	2	21	37	2	18	39	3	51	8	1
/pit/	13	47	–	26	33	1	25	35	–	50	9	1
/u/	50	9	1	37	22	1	39	19	2	8	51	1
/put/	47	13	–	33	26	1	35	25	–	9	50	1

When we compare the results for the /i/ ~ /u/ pair with the results for the /pit/ ~ /put/ pair, we find exactly the same general tendency: the numbers for each particular pair are similar, only the "dominant" attribution is insignificantly lower for /pit/ ~ /put/, whereas the "recessive" attribution is correspondingly higher. The relation between the two curves can be seen in figure 8.7.

Results like these can be explained in terms of Rakerd's (1984) finding that "vowels in consonantal context are more linguistically perceived than are isolated vowels". In other words, the perception of vowels in consonantal context is more

categorial, whereas in isolated vowels more pre-categorial information can be perceived; alternatively, the underlying sensory information, by virtue of which a
vowel is typically associated with certain perceptual qualities, varies from one consonantal context to another, owing to "parallel transmission", that is, owing to "the
fact that a talker often co-articulates the neighboring segments of an utterance (that
is, overlaps their respective productions) such that the acoustic signal is jointly influenced by those segments" (Rakerd, 1984: 123).

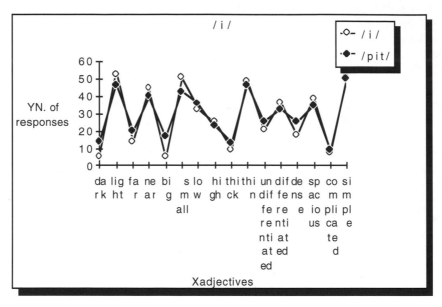

Figure 8.7   Notice that in the *pit*-curve the peaks and ebbs are consistently nearer to
one another than in the *i*-curve.

We have been seeking experimental support for certain speculations in cognitive
poetics, namely, first, that in many cases the perceptual qualities associated with
certain speech sounds can be accounted for by assuming that in the "poetic mode",
some of the rich pre-categorial sensory information underlying the speech sound
does reach consciousness; and second, that the perception of rounded back-vowels as
"darker" than the unrounded front-vowels can be accounted for by the fact that F_1
and F_2 of back vowels are less differentiated, closer together, than the same
formants of the front vowels. Our findings are thoroughly consistent with these
hypotheses. It is, however, questionable whether they constitute sufficient proof for
them. Consequently, the validity of our "proof" crucially depends on the extent to
which our findings fit into other related facts and findings.

Musicality in Verse and Phonological Universals

Roman Jakobson's remarkable little book (1968), *Child Language, Aphasia, and Phonological Universals,* first published in German in 1941, established a dynamic model, built on structuralist phonology, that appears to have considerable psychological reality. As I shall claim below, this phonological model can account for a variety of literary phenomena. It presents the reader with certain universal laws of phonological dynamics, as abstracted from the order in which children master speech, from the reversed order in which aphatics lose speech, and from the same laws of "solidarity" for both phenomena, as it is known from the languages all over the world (the property later was to be termed "markedness"). Just as there are no cases in which the use of, say, the vowel /y/ (ü) has been acquired before /u/, or /u/ lost before /y/, no language has been found in which the vowel /y/ exists but not /u/, or the vowel /ø/ (ö) but not /o/.

The dynamics underlying Jakobson's model involve a series of splits of the undifferentiated mass of sounds into contrasts realized by the speaker. A remarkable thing about the way children learn to speak is that in a pre-language phase of babbling, each child provides ample evidence that he may have at his disposal all the sounds existing in all the languages of the world. Afterwards, suddenly, he forgets, as it seems, his whole repertoire and, as the first step to speech, he learns to make distinction between consonants and vowels. This contrast appears in its sharpest manifestation possible, i.e., when the child starts saying /pa/. /p/ is a voiceless consonant, pronounced with a maximum closure of the lips, /a/ is a vowel (voiced by its very nature), pronounced with a maximum opening of the lips. The next two oppositions of consonants the child acquires are ORAL ~ NASAL and LABIAL ~ DENTAL, usually in this order (hence the basic vocabulary of children in many languages, *papa, mama, tata, nana;* "by the repetition of the same syllable, children signal that their phonation is not babbling, but a verbal message" [Jakobson and Waugh, 1979: 196]. Subsequently, the vowels split in two directions, along the /a/ ~ /u/ line (WIDE ~ NARROW), and the /u/ ~ /i/ line (ROUNDED ~ UNROUNDED). The former split has been felt to involve a perceptual contrast between CHROMATIC ~ ACHROMATIC, the latter one between dark and light vowels.

Of unusually great interest are some of Jakobson's observations on the differentiation between denotative and expressive use of speech sounds. While the child proceeds with mastering the "arbitrary linguistic signs", selecting and contrasting sounds that are "inseparably linked to the sign nature of language", he constantly resorts to the other sounds, still unmastered, for sound gestures (interjections and onomatopoeia). Children use certain sounds for onomatopoetic functions, "while they continue to replace them in their remaining vocabulary". If this distinction is not realized by linguists, they see only great confusion in the process of children's acquisition of speech. "Sound gestures, which tend to form a layer apart even in the language of the adult, appear to seek out those sounds which are inadmissible in a given language" (Jakobson, 1968: 25–26). Nasal vowels are of the latest acquisitions of the child, and are rare in the world's languages. Indeed, "nasalization is especially charged with emotion in the child" (ibid., 72). "The oral stop, on the other hand, carries either less emotion or no emotion at all, and is not used for complaining, but for 'drawing attention, dismissing, refusing', and as a calmer, more apathetic designation, and thereby signals the real transition from emotional expression to symbolic language" (ibid., 75).

One of the virtues of a good developmental model is that it can also give insight into the nature of regressions. The nature of regressions to be discussed here can also be accounted for within the general framework of psychoanalytic theory; but Jakobson's cognitive model is able to describe and predict their specific details. This, of course, is an enormous advantage for the practical critic. In order to understand the aesthetic relevance of these regressions, it is enough to note that poetry has to do with pleasure on the one hand, and with the expression of emotions on the other.

As I have mentioned earlier (above, Chapter 3), one of the possible sources of pleasure in human beings, according to psychoanalytic theory, is the regression to a level of functioning characteristic of an earlier age. According to Kris and Gombrich (1965), the scribbling style of caricature involves regression to the infantile pleasure in exploring articulate motor activities, just as punning and nonsense talk involve regression to prelanguage babbling. It would be quite plausible to suggest that the phonetic aspects of poetry afford similar pleasure in the exploration of meaningless sounds, a pleasure which is realized in a publicly respectable medium. Similarly, Ehrenzweig (1965) asserts that in painting and music there are articulate gestalts appealing to our "surface mind", and inarticulate, thing-free scribblings and sounds, appealing to our "depth mind". Now we may add with Jakobson that in child language, there are two distinct uses of sound: **referential**, which is nonemotional, and **expressive**, making use of sounds which are not yet utilized for the "arbitrary linguistic signs". In poetic language, we have both at one and the same time. Sounds are combined into words by a "syntagmatic" relationship (Jakobson, 1968: 70), "forming entities of linguistic value" (ibid., 25). At the same time, there is a nonreferential combination of sounds, based on repetition, forming reference-free— *thing-free,* so to speak—qualities, exploiting not so much differentiated *contrasting features,* as similarities. In the general practice of literary critics it is sometimes only pointed out that these repetitions are there. In Chapter 4, I have shown how these poetic repetitions may *converge* or *diverge* to constitute some compact sound pattern or generate a diffuse, thing-free sound texture, and thus contribute to the witty or emotional quality of a poem. In the present chapter I am proposing another set of distinctions derived from Jakobson's model for the description of sound effects in poetry.

The following problem arises in connection with regression to infantile pleasure in sounds: can we distinguish *mere* regression to infantile pleasure from a *structured* regression? Before answering this question, let us consider first some instances of "mere" regression.

> Thus we find [...] a considerable number of babbling words in the vocabu-
> lary of all languages taken over from the "nursery language". It has been
> established repeatedly that a child in full control of his language can sud-
> denly take pleasure in reverting to the role of a baby. [...] And Gabelentz
> has pointed out that courting lovers quite frequently talk in child language
> [...]. (ibid., 16–17)

And again, Jakobson mentions "the coquettish, precious love-language of Russian
peasant women in Northeast Siberia", consisting in replacing a /j/ for a liquid; "this
so-called 'sweet-talk' is a deliberate infantilism" (ibid). All these are, clearly, examples of regressions of various degrees to a less differentiated use of phonemes. Some
of the cases suggest, as well, that they have been loaded with varying degrees of
emotional charge. One can, however, attach no poetic value to these regressions.

Indeed, poetic value can be attributed, in general, only to "structured" regression,
and not to mere "deliberate infantilism". Structuring, in turn, depends in one way or
other upon "good gestalts". Regression to some undifferentiated world is "mere infantilism", whereas underlying artistic pleasure we may find regression to some undifferentiated perception **by way of perceiving differentiated or intensive gestalts.**
Good gestalts, or referential meaning, satisfy the "Platonic Censor" in us, so that it
refrains from suppressing "offensive", undifferentiated or irrational information.

When discussing the relationship between poetic language and regression to a
more infantile use of speech sounds, several distinctions are required. The first distinction concerns the **kind** of regression. It may be a regression to the emotive,
nonreferential use of speech sounds, or to a phonological system that is less differentiated than that of adult language. Both kinds of regression have been discussed
above. The first kind of regression is, as we have said, characteristic of poetic language, supplying the "respectable, publicly acceptable excuse" for nonreferential use
of the sound strings, an excuse that is based on referential use of the same sounds.
The second kind of regression (to a more primitive phonological system) is, in general, not characteristic of poetic language. Therefore, typically, it may be considered
as no more than what Jakobson called "deliberate infantilism", even though it **may**
occur in literature as the mimesis of infantile, or as coquettish speech.

Our second distinction will be between "mere infantilism" and regression to a relatively primitive phonological system when it is merely an optional extra, additional to the sign nature of language. In other words, regression to a relatively primitive phonological system assumes poetic value, when it occurs simultaneously
with the syntagmatic, or with the referential use of speech sounds, but forms no unambiguous part of it.

Our next distinction is made **within** the first kind of regression, the one characteristic of poetic language. The parallel, nonreferential sound clusters, perceived by way
of, and in addition to, their referential, and syntagmatic combination, may be either
convergent or **divergent.** I have discussed this distinction at considerable length in

Chapter 4 (see also my discussion in Chapter 20 of divergent sound patterns in the second stanza of Baudelaire's "Correspondances").

One may present the foregoing distinctions in figure 8.

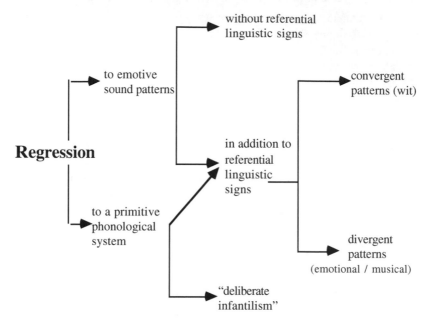

Figure 8.8   Phonological regression and sound patterns in poetry.

Many impressionistic comments have been made on the sound texture in language and in poetry. Some of them have been accepted, for generations, as indisputable truths. One of the aims of Cognitive Poetics is—as I indicated in Chapter 1—to claim back as large areas of criticism as possible from arbitrary impressionism; at the same time, it endeavors to render the reader's impression a legitimate and integral part of criticism. This twofold aim I try to realize in the present study, too. Poetics, says Bierwisch (1970: 108), "must accept effects as given and determine the rules upon which they are founded". In what follows, I shall use phonetic and phonological generalizations in an attempt to determine the rules upon which certain impressionistic generalizations, founded upon some widespread beliefs concerning the "aesthetic" quality of speech sounds, are founded.

My first example refers to an effect, for whose very existence the chief evidence is anecdotal only. This anecdotal evidence, however, is so persistent and consistent that it seems to be worth the effort to try to account for it. Certain speech sounds are considered more "beautiful", more "musical" than others. Some other sounds, on the contrary, are deemed especially "ugly" or "unmusical". The French language, for instance, is felt to be especially musical, thanks to its abundance of nasal vowels, and its absence of affricates (such as /ts/ and /pf/), which are quite conspicuous in German, for instance.

In addition to the feeling that nasal sounds are beautiful whereas affricates are especially ugly, the notion that exceptional beauty is to be found in the sound sequence -*eur* is found to occur among the French. A French girl, for example, (with an M.A. in English and French literature) assured me on a certain occasion, that the word *couleur* contributes very much to the beauty of Baudelaire's "Correspondances". In saying so, she prolonged -*eur* with all her French charm. All this, of course, amounts to sheer critical impressionism. I asked her, what about the sound of *puanteur* (stink)? Is it as beautiful as *couleur?* Obviously, the sound, at best, may "*seem* an echo of the sense", but it has no aesthetic or referential value of its own. Yet, despite one's better judgment, one is inclined to believe that in some cases –*eur* and -*on* do have a different, possibly higher, aesthetic or expressive potential; though, again, it sounds to me as though such cases are more salient, or more frequent, in Baudelaire's or Verlaine's poetry than in Boileau's or La Fontaine's. Can such an arbitrary suggestion be somehow justified? I propose here a tentative explanation (which is in need of extensive examination). The evaluative terms "beautiful" and "ugly" when applied to sounds, can be translated into descriptive terms, and even located along some more or less objective or intersubjective scale. Two sets of considerations discussed so far are relevant here: first, the order of acquisition of the phoneme, and second, some acoustic cues for their perception; namely, the distinctions I have made above, along the [PERIODICITY] and [CONTINUITY] axes.

The order of acquisition of phonemes has been extensively discussed in the present chapter. The latest acquisitions have a double character. On the one hand, they appear to constitute the highest linguistic layer, the most rational accessories of referential language (and the first to dissolve in aphasia). On the other hand, if one considers the acquired phonological system in its entirety, the last acquisitions had served for the longest time exclusively as gestures (onomatopoeia and interjections). In the last phases of speech-learning (and the first stages of aphasia), they may be used as "especially charged with emotion" when used as sound gestures while, at the same time, being unavailable for making up "arbitrary linguistic signs". As for the anecdotal "beautiful" sounds, such as the nasal vowels and the syllable –*eur* mentioned above, the phonemes /ø/, /r/, and the nasal vowels are (as predicted by the model) among the latest acquisitions of children in languages in which they occur; and, according to Jakobson, relatively rare in the world's languages. A similar story can be told of the especially "ugly" sounds. The affricates /pf/ and /ts/ are rare in the languages of the world, and are among the latest acquisitions by children if these sounds occur in their mother tongue: they can be acquired only after the acquisition of the respective oppositions /p/ ~ /f/ and /t/ ~ /s/. They frequently serve for expressing disgust, contempt or disapproval; some French find them, indeed, extremely displeasing in foreign languages and poems.

It would appear, that the impressionistic-subjective distinction concerning the "beauty" of some speech sounds and the "ugliness" of some others can be translated into two pairs of objective or intersubjective opposites. In the first place, the latest acquisitions *may* assume greater emotional or aesthetic intensity than earlier ones, for "better" or "worse". In the second place, within the late acquisitions, continuous and periodic sounds are "beautiful", whereas the interrupted, aperiodic sounds are "ugly".

It is difficult to contrive a test to verify or refute such a speculative assertion. At any rate, it seems to me that if the above speculations are tolerably well founded, this postulate must be taken into account not only when French poetry is compared to, e.g., Hebrew or Hungarian poetry, but also when different styles within French poetry are compared. Thus, for instance, I have assumed that a Classicist such as Boileau should resort to nasal vowels in rhymes less frequently than Symbolists like Baudelaire or Verlaine, whose poetry "strives" to achieve the state of music. My findings seem to confirm this assumption. In the first one hundred lines of Boileau's *L'Art Poétique* I have found seven couplets with nasal vowels in their rhymes; in the forty lines of Baudelaire's "Au Lecteur" (the introductory poem of *Les Fleurs du Mal*) I have found also seven rhyme-pairs that contain nasal vowels (14% as against 35%; exactly two and a half times as many).[3] However, nothing short of a large-scale investigation can be reliable.

It seems, then, that the subjective "ugly" affricates and "beautiful" nasal vowels and the sound sequence *–eur* can be translated into the objective oppositions [±CONTINUOUS] and [±PERIODIC]—an opposition that is most strongly perceived in phonemes of late acquisition. The later acquisitions *may* have greater emotional impact than the earlier ones. Generally, neither in everyday, nor in literary language is this difference perceptible. The referential meaning, and even some of the more outstanding phonetic aspects "usurp" the reader's attention, so that such subtle oppositions are subdued, or completely ignored. These phenomena can contribute—if at all—to poetry only when the reader is able (to use Keats's phrase) "to make up his mind about nothing—to let the mind be a thoroughfare for all thoughts", sensations and impressions, "without any irritable reaching after fact and reason" or articulate shapes; in short, in impressionistic, divergent, gestalt-free poetry, such as the second stanza of Baudelaire's "Correspondances" (to be discussed at length in Chapter 20), or Verlaine's notorious "Chanson d'Automne".

In Baudelaire's "Au Lecteur" there is, then, a considerably greater proportion of nasal-vowel rhymes than in Boileau's *L'Art Poétique*. In order to keep things in their appropriate proportions, I wish to remark that the nasal vowels in this poem are perceived as far less active than, say, in Baudelaire's "Correspondances", or Verlaine's "Chanson d'Automne". One conspicuous reason for this seems to be that the materials handled by this poem are far from thing-free and gestalt-free. A consider-

---

[3] This distribution is, of course, not fixed throughout Baudelaire's poetry. In the next few poems, in "Bénédiction" and "Les Phares" the percentage is somewhat lower, whereas in the sonnet "Correspondances" there are three rhyme-pairs involving nasal vowels (almost 43%). But in all cases, the percentage is considerably higher than in Boileau's poem.

able part of the imagery is based on things that have stable characteristic visual shapes. The basic attitude of the poem is to *persuade,* so it exhibits the psychological atmosphere of definite direction and patent purpose. As a result, the cognitive system *is* under the control of good gestalts on several levels, and the sounds that are potentially charged with emotions are felt to be perceived as abstract categories rather than auditory information. As this example may indicate, the Symbolist poets seem to have had a predilection for emotionally active speech sounds in prominent positions. However, in this poem the potential sensuous and emotional activity of the sounds in question is kept down, because they are placed in a context of things, and shapes, and a psychological atmosphere of definite direction, patent purpose and a sense of control.

Finally, rather than examining at length, e.g., Verlaine's notorious "Chanson d'Automne" (which I have done elsewhere, Tsur 1992), I propose to consider here another instance of the exploitation of nasal vowels, where, in addition, the crucial problem of sound and image arises in a most conspicuous way: a stanza from the Hungarian poet, Mihály Babits's "Sad Poem".

(4)   Barangoló, borongó,
        Ki bamba bún borong,
        Borzongó bús bolyongó
        Baráttalan bolond.

        (A straying, gloomy [person],
        Brooding over stolid sorrow,
        A shuddering, mournful, roaming,
        Friendless fool.)

This stanza became famous for its alliterations: ten of its eleven words begin with a *b.* This is achieved without violating the natural word order (or, for that matter, the rhyme pattern or the iambic meter). While in Verlaine's poem, one may make a good case for onomatopoeia or for an expressive sound pattern, many readers have difficulties in their attempt to account for the strong emotional impact of the sound effect in the above stanza. Fónagy (1971: 169) writes of this poem: "According to the results of experiments made with Hungarian readers, within this context [...], the voiced stop suggested mainly two images: nine readers out of twenty heard a bell sounding or saw a solitary bell-tower, while six others were reminded of the mournful sound of funeral drums". We have got no indication of the literary sophistication of Fónagy's subjects; nor do we know what was the exact question to which these answers were given. At any rate, I don't think this is the most rewarding way to handle the sound effect of this stanza. Neither the bells nor the funeral-drums are mentioned in any way in this stanza or anywhere else in this poem. These subjects' responses have introduced irrelevant images, "noisy" elements into the stanza which, I submit, only distract attention from the real sources of its patent emotional effect.

In the first place, it would appear that the dominant emotional effect in the sound-stratum is set by the overwhelming abundance of nasal backvowels (rather than by alliterating voiced stops). As I shall try to show, the bell or drum images, too, are more likely to be suggested by the nasal backvowels than by the voiced stops. The voiced stops seem to have here, at most, a corroborating effect.

It would appear that the theory propounded in the present chapter is able to supply a more straightforward explanation of the emotional impact of the sound effect of this stanza. It seems to draw upon the cumulative effect of several factors. First, we have got here an intensive set of nonreferential sound patterns superimposed upon the arbitrary, referential linguistic signs. This, as we have suggested earlier, may have a marked emotional effect. Second, nasal vowels are relatively rare in the world's languages, and are of the infants' latest acquisitions within the vowel system of those languages in which they occur. From this follows that these sounds serve in babbling until a relatively late stage and are especially loaded with emotion; they are especially prone to serve as sound gestures in emotive sound patterns or onoma-topoeia. Third, all vowels, as well as the sonorants /l, r, m, n/ (which are in relative abundance in this stanza), are continuous, periodic, low encoded speech sounds, and thus tend to contribute, in the proper circumstances, to the perceived effect of some tender emotion. It is in this phonetic context that the periodic aspects of the [+VOICED] feature of the voiced stop /b/ and the voiced fricative /z/ are also empha-sized. Fourth, backvowels, whose F_1 and F_2 are not easily differentiated, may, in the proper thematic circumstances, add a dark tint to the tender emotional quality of a poem.

Being immensely aware of the emotional impact of the sound structure of this stanza, subjects may have had recourse to the relatively crude tools which were at their disposal. They seem to have been biased by an inadequate theory of sound effects. Having subliminally perceived, beyond the phonetic categories, some rich pre-categorial, periodic information, they projected a musical instrument (bell or drum) onto the scene of the stanza, so as to establish some onomatopoetic relation-ship between the sound structure of the stanza and the sounds of the musical instru-ments. These instruments, in turn, are conceived of as part of a stereotypically mournful situation (a funeral), the mournfulness of which is felt to reinforce the sadness of the stanza. My claim is that the theory propounded here may account for the emotional effect, felt by many readers to exist in the sound structure of this stanza, in a way that is systematic as well as more parsimonious in that it does not have to rely on the introduction of more or less arbitrary images into the poem.

Finally, in my discussion of onomatopoeia above I argue that when you trans-late from one semiotic system to another, you are constrained by the options of the target system. Now I will invoke this principle to illuminate Jakobon's claims from another angle, by adducing an example of how affricates may be utilized for sound gestures and onomatopoeia. Affricates are late acquisitions and abrupt. Ger-man [pf] is acquired only after the acquisition of the plosive [p] and the fricative [f]. English and Hebrew infants stop short of acquiring this sound. German, Hebrew and

Hungarian [ts] is acquired only after the acquisition of the plosive [t] and the fricative [s]. In German there is an interjection "pfuj", expressing disgust (imitating a gesture of the lips, as though "spitting"). In Hebrew and English, this bilabial affricate does not exist; so, these languages are confined to the nearest bilabials, for the same sound gesture: in Hebrew "fuya"; in English "fie". The dental affricate [ts] does exist in Hebrew (acquired after [t] and [s]); indeed, a stand-alone [ts] occasionally serves in informal Hebrew to express displeasure.

Spitting is a gesture of the lips serving to expel harmful food and other unwanted substances. So it became a gesture expressive of disgust. In human language, such an eliminating gesture is frequently imitated by some word beginning with a bilabial phoneme. According to Jakobson, later aquisitions (such as affricates) have greater expressive potential than earlier acquisitions (such as plosives or fricatives). Thus German, whose phonological system contains the affricate [pf] is fine-grained enough to use an interjection that is most effective in expressing disgust [pfuj]. The word "pfeifen" (to whistle, to pipe), by contrast, directs attention to a different aspect of the same lip gesture: the lips are used to produce the whistling sound, or to blow the instrument. English and Hebrew phonology is less fine-grained in this respect (the affricate [pf] does not exist in them); so, they can only approximate it: are forced to have recourse to some bilabial that is an earlier acquisition. Thus, for instance, the English word akin to "pfeifen" is "pipe" -- involving two bilabial plosives. The Hebrew word corresponding to "whistle", "lətsaftsef", is a most interesting case of choosing the nearest option which a semiotic system can offer. [f] is a bilabial fricative; no affricate is available in Hebrew at this place of articulation, but the distinctive feature [+AFFRICATE] occurs in the other consonant, [ts]. Reduplication of the syllable in the word "lətsaftsef" relates it to the transition from the child's babbling stage to the arbitrary use of verbal signs. I have quoted earlier Jakobson and Waugh to the effect that "by the repetition of the same syllable, children signal that their phonation is not babbling but a verbal message". Victoria Fromkin (1973: 110–117) pointed out that in "slips of the tongue" sometimes distinctive features exchange places, or move from one speech sound to another. Elsewhere (Tsur, 2003) I illustrated this by the example of a young Hebrew poet who inadvertently substituted the Hebrew word "məfagrim" (mentally retarded) for "məvakrim" (critics). In this instance, the features [+ VOICED] and [–VOICED] changed places: the [v] in "məvakrim" is a voiced [f]; whereas the [k] is a voiceless [g]. Such slips of the tongue indicate that transfer of the feature [+AFFRICATE] in "lətsaftsef" from the bilabial to the preceding consonant *may* have psychological reality, and is no mere academic exercise.

CHAPTER 9

Semantic Representation
and Information Processing

In the present chapter, I am going to explore the representation and encoding of the units of meaning, and the implications of these processes for poetic language. When I speak of *units of meaning,* I mean *mainly,* but not *only,* "linguistic units". In attempting to account for the metaphoric competence of human beings, it is hard to draw the demarcation line between semantic knowledge and world knowledge. In what follows, I am going to propose a cognitive theory and a description of the semantic structure of figurative language and of rhyme, to be supplemented by some indications of world-knowledge structure.

Since the structure of figurative language relies heavily on metaphor, the first question that arises is that of a theory of metaphor. In my assumption, such a theory must satisfy four requirements of "adequacy":

- to give a structural description of metaphors;
- to explain how human beings understand novel metaphors;
- to explain the relationship between this process and the process by which human beings produce and understand novel pieces of literal discourse;
- to explain the relationship between these processes and the perceived effects of metaphors.

The semantic information processing model underlying this work is a hierarchic model of "meaning components", or "features", or "semantic primitives". With the help of such models, various researchers have explained how young children acquire the lexicon of their mother tongue, how adults understand synonymic and antonymic relationships. With the help of such a model, H. H. Clark (1970) accounted for his findings in word associations and Fillmore (1971) for the difference between explicit statements and presuppositions in predication. A similar conception underlies Schank's methods (1973 and later) in artificial intelligence, with the help of which the computer program produces and understands sentences to which it has never been exposed. The ability of human beings to produce and understand novel metaphors is not explained by the "invention" of novel meanings, or by "multiplying" lexical entries in one's "mental dictionary", but by assuming that the logical contradiction between the terms of the metaphor causes to delete certain meaning components and to emphasize others. These meaning components, as suggested above, are not acquired for the specific purpose of understanding metaphors, but underlie other cognitive processes as well. In Chapter 1, I have already anticipated some of my main arguments concerning semantic representation in the present chapter. I have presented there two models of hierarchic organization, one of semantic features, and one called "hyponymy". I have argued there that one may attempt to account with the help of such models for linguistic intuitions concerning synonymy, antonymy, as well as for the performance of humans in word association. In the present chapter, I shall discuss how such hierarchies can account for intuitions concerning the meanings and perceived qualities of metaphors, as well as the perceived qualities of rhymes.

According to the present conception, figurative language is based on those models of information-processing. This theory rejects the approach that relies on "conventional meanings" in an attempt to account for the ability of human beings to understand metaphors. Rather it assumes that far from solving it, 'convention' amplifies the problem and transfers it from one place to another. For, in this case, we have to explain how the conventional metaphor was understood for the first time, and in addition, how it became conventional.

Markedness

How do we intuitively prefer one construal of a metaphor to another? Alternatively, how do we reject certain, rather plausible, construals of metaphors? Let me emphasize at the outset that I have no magic formula which would help one discover which one of two plausible construals of one metaphor is *the* correct one. At best, we may hope to find some procedure to determine which one of two construals of a metaphor is more plausible, more "natural", and assume that he who prefers the less natural construal, must give good reasons for not having recourse to the more natural one, whereas he who prefers the more natural construal need not vindicate his not having had recourse to the less natural one. In other words, as in so many domains of inquiry, we must look for our salvation (partial at least) in the notion of 'markedness', a term resorted to frequently in recent years by structuralists. Of two opposites, the unmarked term is the one that is neutral with respect to a certain opposition. The term "marked" implies an awareness of not having resorted to some other possible term. This point can be illustrated by the story about the Jewish Robinson Crusoe, who on his solitary island builds a dining room where he eats; a bedroom, where he sleeps; a kitchen, where he cooks his meals; a synagogue, where he prays and another synagogue in which he does *not* pray, on principle. The moment we become aware of the synagogue in which he does *not* pray, the synagogue in which he *does* pray becomes marked: his praying in it is not a matter of course any more. The clauses *where he eats, where he sleeps, where he cooks his meals, where he prays* sound as mere tautological descriptions of their respective buildings. The existence of a synagogue in which he does *not* pray turns the phrase *where he prays* into more meaningful, after the event. This is the case with alternative interpretations of metaphors, too. The marked interpretation requires good reasons for being preferred to the unmarked one. "As a matter of course", one must choose the "natural", unmarked interpretation.[1]

Cancellation vs. Multiplication

I propose to consider how new meanings are attributed to words in metaphoric expressions. Let us have a look at the following two sentences:

(1)   The sun is a ball of fire.
(2)   The boy next door is a ball of fire.

The addressee will have no difficulty in finding in his/her mental dictionary the relevant lexical meanings of *ball* and *fire* required for the understanding of (1). On the other hand, he is quite unlikely to find there the lexical meanings required for the understanding of (2). He seems to lack the appropriate lexical entries: the expression is metaphorical.

Cohen (1979) presents two prevalent rival methods by which such meanings as those of the words *ball of fire* in (2) may be handled. The first one is to **multiply lexical entries**, to add *ball of fire$_2$* to one's mental dictionary. The alternative method is to derive the new metaphoric meaning from the original lexical entry, by **canceling semantic features**. The method of **multiplication** is not parsimonious, since it requires an indefinite number of entries in one's mental dictionary, and does not reveal where these entries come from, when they are needed. The method of **cancellation**, on the other hand, derives—according to the changing circumstances—an indefinite number of new meanings from a finite number of existing entries.

> Scientific inquiry tends to make more progress if it avoids unnecessary multiplications of entities, and it is this Ockhamian policy that the method of cancellation pursues. If we could formulate the principles controlling feature-cancellation in the composition of sentence meanings we would gain a powerful, general insight into the semantics of natural languages [...]. The method of multiplication merely records what meanings exist, without explaining how they are generated. It lists elements but does not explore relations. (ibid., 69)

What is, then, the relationship between *ball of fire$_1$* and *ball of fire$_2$*? First of all we must remark that there may also be *ball of fire$_3$*, and so on, endlessly. What are the metaphoric meanings depends, among other things, upon the situation which the expression refers to: whether we know that the boy next door is a small mischievous brat, who has inexhaustible energy, moves quickly, appears unexpectedly and sows

---

[1]   It should be noted that sometimes the binary opposition [±MARKED] is but a section of the scale "more/less marked".

destruction on all sides; or that he is roly-poly, (that is, small, roundish, and fat) and has red hair. Accordingly, we may offer two paraphrases at least to (2):

(3)   The boy next door is a mischief-doer with inexhaustible energy.
(4)   The boy next door is roly-poly, and has red hair.

An interesting thing should be noticed about these two paraphrases. While people usually admit both paraphrases as legitimate and plausible, most tend to prefer (3) to (4) as a paraphrase for (2). We have here, then, according to the multiplication method, three lexical entries for one expression, with no need to relate them to one another. According to the foregoing conception, by contrast, we shall have to account for a series of problems related to the relation between them. First, what is the relation between the literal and the metaphoric meanings? Second, what is the relationship between the metaphoric meanings themselves? Third, how can a person who knows the literal meaning understand the metaphoric meanings? Fourth, why is there a tendency to prefer excerpt (3) to (4) as a paraphrase for (2)?

One may answer the first and third questions together, because the key to both answers is **feature-cancellation**. *Ball* is a noun that refers to an inanimate physical object. It is opposed to other inanimate physical objects in that all points on its external surface are at an equal distance from its center. As a result of this shape, one of the empirical features of the ball is that only one point of its external surface is in contact with the surface on which it rests; it can therefore move in any direction with minimal friction. *Fire* is a noun that refers to the combination of phenomena that accompany burning: heat, light, intense red color. Fire is the source of immense energy, and consumes quickly everything it touches. *The boy next door* in (2) cancels in *ball of fire* all those features that are incompatible with it, first and foremost, such "high" features as [+PHYSICAL OBJECT, −ANIMATE, −HUMAN], so that only some of the concrete empirical features are left. According to (3), the feature canceled in *ball* is [+SPHERIC SHAPE]; the feature retained is [SWIFT MOVEMENT IN ALL DIRECTIONS]. In *fire,* the features [+LIGHT] and [+INTENSE RED] are cancelled, while the features [+IMMENSE ENERGY] or [+HEAT] (=temperament) are retained. These features are transferred to the subject *The boy next door* as his physical or mental properties. According to (4), some of these processes are reversed. In *ball,* the feature [+SWIFT MOVEMENT] is canceled, and the feature [+SPHERIC SHAPE] is retained. In *fire* all the features are canceled except for [+INTENSE RED].

In order to answer the second and fourth questions, one must distinguish, following Brooke-Rose (1958: 155), "functional metaphors" (*A* is called *B* by virtue of what it does), and "sensuous metaphors" (*A* is called *B* by virtue of what it looks like or, less frequently, by virtue of what it sounds, smells, feels, or tastes like). In terms of (3), *a ball of fire* in (2) is a functional metaphor; in terms of (4), it is a sensuous metaphor. There seems to be in human nature an inclination to prefer functional to sensuous metaphors. One of the assumptions of cognitive poetics is that in relation to poetic language, cognitive mechanisms initially acquired for survival in man's physical and social environment have been turned to aesthetic ends. For the purpose of survival, it is less important to know what an object looks like than to know what it can do. This seems to be the reason for the cognitive tendency first to notice the functional elements in a figurative construction and only when this fails to account for the metaphor, to notice—if at all—the sensuous elements. In certain styles, of course, poets may capitalize on this preference, in an attempt to achieve effects of markedness, by having recourse to sensuous metaphors. It is worth noting in this context that students, and even professors, of literature seem to be reluctant to construe metaphors as sensuous, and seek to impute some "functional" construal upon sensuous metaphors (see *infra*, Chapter 16). Furthermore, similes and metaphors based on stable and characteristic visual shapes tend to arouse a feeling of wit, of unnaturalness, because even where there is a great visual resemblance, as long as there is no complete identity, the resemblance will foreground the details in which B differs from A (cf. Chapters 4 and 15).

In my discussion of the features of *ball*, I emphasized the features in which the ball *differs* from other inanimate physical objects. We are up against a hierarchic organization of the features of objects, such as [+NOUN +COUNT +COMMON +CONCRETE −ANIMATE +GEOMETRIC SOLID +SPHERIC SHAPE (#ball)]. In this case, *ball* is perceived as a member in a "contrast set": the ball is unique in that it is opposed in certain features to other solid objects, as cube, conus, etc. It may, of course, be a member in other contrast sets as well, as in "toys", or, as in this specific case, in an ad-hoc category: "shapes which fire may assume". At any rate, for the purpose of our discussion, one thing is important: when a word is used in a figurative sense, it is based on some feature by which the object *differs* from other members of its contrast set. There will be an intuitive inclination to construe the figurative expression based on features that distinguish the object from its contrast set, rather than on the shared features. A figurative expression that compels us to skip the distinctive features and to found the meaning on the shared features, is generally perceived as marked, unnatural, witty.

Consider the following:

> (5) Mary has the feet of a gazelle: not as nimble, not as graceful, but as hairy.

The question that arises here is whether we have here a deviation from an accidental bound expression, or an interference with habits of semantic information processing. The question is, therefore, whether such instances of wit become possible only by deviating from a relatively small number of bound expressions, where the meaning of a metaphor or a simile is determined by some arbitrary convention, or rather, whether the reader is capable of perceiving this kind of wit also in instances that are founded on expressions which he has encountered for the first time. The present work assumes that the most significant conventions are transmitted (or determined in each individual case, as a result of psychological needs) on the level of *cognitive structures* rather than on the level of specific expressions. Moreover, the cognitive structures can explain why precisely these specific expressions rather than others become bound. **Hairiness** is a property common to gazelles and most wild animals—in fact, to most mammals, whereas the nimbleness and gracefulness of feet are among the properties that distinguish gazelles from other wild animals. Wit becomes possible here, because the speaker may expect his audience to interpret his utterance on the basis of what distinguishes, stereotypically, gazelles' feet from other wild animals' or from other mammals' feet, whereas the metaphor in (5) is based on a feature that is shared by gazelles' and other mammals' feet. One might, of course, argue, that gracefulness and nimbleness are the figurative values of a "gazelle's feet" by convention. However, as I have suggested in the introduction to this chapter, in this way we only amplify the problem and transfer it from one place to another.

Culler (1975: 180–181), in his discussion of the poetics of the lyrics, writes: "Metaphor is a combination of two synecdoches: it moves from a whole to one of its parts to another whole which contains that part, or from a member to a general class and then back again to another member of that class". He gives the following example of the transfer "member → class→ member":

(6)   oak → tall things→ any tall person or object.

There is, however, a snag in Culler's definition. It would allow one to use *oak* as a metaphor not only for some tall person or object, but also for "birch" or "pine", *via* the class "tree". One must, therefore, emphasize: the metaphor is typically based not just on any class to which *oak* happens to belong, but on a class defined by some property in which oaks differ from other trees. Consider, for instance, the following statement:

(7)   John is an oak.

Here, all the features of *oak* are canceled, except for the features that typically distinguish oaks from other trees: [+TALL +STRONG]. These features are transferred to John.

Here I cannot go into a discussion of the logical status of meaning components (or semantic features). Nor shall I get involved in such arguments as whether all meanings can be exhausted by semantic components, whether one must distinguish between "markers" and "distinguishers", and so forth. Nor shall I go into the question whether the number of "semantic primitives" with which all the nuances of meaning can be expressed does not reach, eventually, the number of words in the lexicon. In this respect, I adopt Janet Dean Fodor's view, that the purpose of abstracting semantic components is to reveal meanings and relationships between meanings, rather than reduce the scope of the lexicon (Fodor, 1980: 147). My business here is, indeed, to reveal meanings and, mainly, relationships between meanings; that is why I may safely ignore all those controversial issues.

The feature cancellation method may, then, explain how we understand new metaphors, or how conventional metaphors may have been understood by their first addressees. Furthermore, it may also account for the mechanism by which the conventional 'symbolic' meanings of *oak* or *gazelle's feet* have improved their chances to prevail, by natural selection, in the course of repeated social transmission. On the other hand, the critic who appeals to conventional symbolism in order to account for the meanings of figurative expressions, tacitly relies on the multiplication method, and his reasoning suffers from all its shortcomings.

This mode of explanation has an additional shortcoming. In the first section of this chapter I suggested in passing that emotional and witty effects are derived from an increased activity of the cognitive mechanisms; the psychologists call this increase a *shift of mental sets*. The derivation of new meanings from the old meanings of words is just such an increased activity of cognitive mechanisms. The critic who accounts for the meanings of figurative expressions by relying on conventional symbolism, that is, who treats the symbolic meanings of words as if they were separate lexical entries, cancels the very literariness of figurative expressions (see my critique of Lakoff in chapter 23).

General Terms vs. 'Spatio-Temporal Continuity'

A further step in our argument is necessary in order to eliminate counter-examples of the following sort:

(8)   He is an oak—he has an acorn on his nose.
(9)   There are roses in her cheeks—with thorns.

The effect of these examples is witty (i.e., marked), because it is more natural to understand "He is an oak" as 'He is tall and strong' than as 'He has acorns'. Likewise, it is quite natural to transfer 'pinkness' or 'softness' from "roses" to "cheeks", but not "thorns". The witty effect results from the fact that listeners are tuned, as a matter of course, to interpreting the expression in the natural way, whereas the speaker in excerpts (8) and (9) points out other meanings, no less natural from the empirical point of view, but less natural from the psychological point of view. The oak is distinguished from other trees in having acorns, among other things; one of the distinguishing marks of roses is their having thorns. Consequently, the status of 'having acorns' is similar to that of 'tall and strong', and that of 'having thorns' to that of 'pink and soft'. This time, too, the explanation goes far beyond 'convention'. One could argue that just as *gazelle-feet* are a conventional symbol of grace and nimbleness rather than of hairiness, so the *oak* is a conventional symbol of tallness and strength, rather than of having acorns; and the rose, as an attribute of a woman's cheek, a conventional symbol of softness and of a certain color, rather than of having thorns. More specifically, the preference of "grace and nimbleness" to "hairiness" as the symbolic significance of *gazelle-feet;* of "tall and strong" to "having acorns" as the symbolic significance of *oak;* and of "pink and soft" to "having thorns" as the symbolic significance of *roses* all reflect some basic psycholinguistic process.

The rule followed by the speakers of language can be extracted from an important paper by Strawson (1967). Although its main issue is a different one, this paper is a gold mine of distinctions that may contribute to the understanding of the nature of figurative language. Strawson's interest is focused on the logical distinction between *singular terms* and *general terms* in predicative position.

In order to elucidate the difference between these two terms, not as hard and fast categories, but as relative categories that nevertheless enable a clear (and even creative) application in predication, Strawson analyses the following example: Betty is a better date than Sally. Betty is willing and pretty, and Sally, too, is willing and pretty. But, in addition, Betty is witty, whereas Sally is not. Strawson builds on this story a series of entities consisting of three stages: (a) "Betty;" (b) "pretty" (or "prettiness"—from this point of view, there is no difference between adjectives and abstract nouns); (c) "qualities desirable in a date".

> But what is the general nature of such a series, what is it about its terms and their relations that confers upon them these further relations, these claims to relative referential and predicative positions? Well, it will scarcely be denied that "Betty" is used typically to designate a spatio-temporally continuous particular. And it will scarcely be denied that the meaning of "pretty" is such that it may be said to *group* such particulars in accordance with a certain kind of principle. [...] Now, consider such a term as (c) "desirable in a date". This term has a grouping function, too. It does not directly group particulars; it groups ways such as term (b)'s way, of *grouping particulars*. (Strawson, 1967: 82–83)

Strawson is careful to distinguish between grouping in this sense and in another sense.

> Now, in a certain sense, "Betty" may be said to group particulars too: a particular arm, leg, face, even a particular action, might all be truthfully ascribed to Betty. But obviously the principle on which "Betty" groups particulars like arms and legs is quite a different sort of principle from the principle on which "pretty" groups particulars like Betty and Sally. [...] These likenesses and unlikenesses are registered [...] in the philosophical usage which permits us to say that Betty is a case or instance of prettiness, and prettiness a case or instance of a quality desirable in a date but forbids us to say that Betty's left arm or anything else is a case or instance of Betty. (ibid., 82–83)

There is, then, a distinction between "being a particular part of" (or "element in" etc.) and "being a particular instance of".

> What makes it correct to count a star as a bit of the Plough or an arm or a leg as a bit of Betty has at least to do with their spatio-temporal relation to

other bits of the Plough or of Betty in a way in which what makes it correct to count something as an instance of gold has nothing to do with its spatio-temporal relations to other instances of gold. (ibid., 83)

If we return now to 'having acorns' as opposed to 'tall and strong' as attributes of *oak,* we may say that *acorn* is a spatio-temporally continuous particular, and is *a part of* the oak. The same is true of the thorns of the rose, whereas 'tall and strong' and 'soft and pink' are qualities that group particulars with one another. A metaphor the third term of which is a spatio-temporally continuous particular is perceived as less natural than a metaphor whose third term is a general quality that groups together particulars between which no spatio-temporal continuity exists. Cohen (1979), who proposes a theory of metaphor that is not unlike the one offered here, gives the following example.

(10)   Jane has the face of a wild rose.

He comments: "Though a woman's face may share the colour of a wild rose blossom, or even have a similar shape, it certainly lacks other empirical properties associated with wild roses such as their spiky stems" (ibid., 70). Cohen tries to discover what features are *deleted* in metaphoric expressions, and his answer is "empirical properties". But he has no answer to the question why those empirical features, rather than others, are deleted. Consider

(11)   Jane has the face of a wild rose—full of thorns.

This figure is based on items that are spatio-temporally continuous with the rose; the thorns constitute a spatio-temporal continuity making properties that 'have grown together' into objects that have stable and characteristic visual shapes. In order to receive the general quality 'spikiness', a quality of the same conceptual grouping as 'softness', 'pinkness', one must move away from "rose" to its parts; these are related, but not identical entities. Now notice this: it makes little sense in this context to ask "what features are *not* transferred from *wild rose"*; one must rather ask "what quality is generated when a spatio-temporally continuous element is transferred?", and the answer is: "Unnatural, witty hence marked".

I have further utilized Strawson's model to account for some exceptionally forceful figurative constructions of "the ABSTRACT of the CONCRETE" form ("thematized predicate"), in texts which attempt to communicate the ineffable (see my discussion of Whitman's meditative catalogue in Chapter 18, and of lowly-differentiated emotional qualities in Chapter 24).

Subject and Predicate

There are various scales of markedness that may account for stylistic intuitions in relation to metaphors. In addition to the possible sources of markedness considered so far, I shall consider one more, similar one. Let us have a look at a casual selection of trivial metaphors, excerpts (12)–(15), representing mere concoctions of more or less accidental nouns.

(12)   The table is a mountain.
(13)   The mountain is a table.
(14)   The beast of burden is a carrousel.
(15)   The carrousel is a beast of burden.
(16)   John's wife is a gem.
(17)   The rock died.

Mountain and *table* have a common superordinate: "inanimate things". However, as one may expect from the foregoing discussions, their metaphoric collocation is achieved on different grounds. Both in excerpt (12) and (13), some of the most concrete features—that is, the lowest ones on the list—are activated. Actually, *mountain* and *table* differ in most of their features, and only a minority of their features can be conceived of as common. Many properties of *mountain* are incompatible with the properties of *table*. The meaningful combination of these two words becomes possible as a result of the deletion of the incompatible features from the **metaphoric member** of the expression; the features that are not deleted are foregrounded and transferred to the non-metaphoric member as qualifiers.

Now let us point out, first, that when *mountain* is the metaphoric member, the common feature is different than when *table* is the metaphoric member; and, second, that in both (12) and (13), there is a natural inclination to take the predicate noun to be the metaphorical member, and to understand the subject noun literally. In (12), there is a natural inclination to delete from *mountain* all the features that are incompatible with *table,* and to characterize "the table" as "big" or "high". In (13), there is a tendency to delete from *table* all the features that are incompatible with *mountain,* and characterize "the mountain" as "having a flat top". The same is true of the next two sentences. There is here, too, a tendency to delete the "superfluous" features from, precisely, the predicate noun, that is, to regard the predicate noun rather than the subject noun as metaphorical, whether we wish to characterize, in (14), the "beast of burden" as something that keeps going around for a long time, or we wish to characterize, in (15), the "merry-go-round" as something that is capable of exerting great efforts.

I submit, therefore, that in metaphors of the form SUBJECT PREDICATE the natural inclination is to take the predicate rather than the subject to be the metaphorical term; this will be the unmarked construal, wherever such a construal may go both ways. Now, let us consider (16). The natural inclination is to construe this sentence as "John's wife is pretty, precious, rare"; and this will be the unmarked construal. Notice, however, that the same sentence may be construed differently. The deep structure of "wife" contains "marry (x, y)", marriage being one kind of human link, one that differs from other kinds of human links by its exclusive and enduring nature, sharing affection, or the like. We may, therefore, construe (16) as "John's link to a gem is of an enduring and exclusive nature, characterized by strong affection". Here, the redundant features are deleted from the subject phrase, and the resulting construal is perceived as fairly unnatural. This is the marked construal.

It would have been more natural to express this idea in a reverse order.

(18)   The gem is John's wife.

Three comments seem to be required here. First, the conventional application of *gem* to "woman" corroborates the inclination to regard the predicate phrase as the metaphorical term in (16). Second, convention is not all-powerful: when in (18), *gem* occurs in the subject-phrase, the power of the convention is considerably weakened. Even when *gem* occurs in the predicate position, the power of convention can be overridden, but this will be experienced as unnatural: the metaphor will be marked. Third, external support—thematic, for instance—may facilitate the acceptance of a marked construal; compare, for instance, (16) to a sentence with an identical structure:

(19)   Harpagon's wife is a treasure-box.

Now, consider (17):

(17)   The rock died.

According to the subject-predicate criterion, the feature to be deleted is [±ALIVE] in *died* (rather than [−ANIMATE] in *rock*). The resulting meaning is "the rock decayed" or "the rock ceased to exist". This meaning, however, appears somewhat strained (unnatural), a quality that can be accounted for with the help of another parameter we have already discussed. *Die* means [+[CHANGE from [+ALIVE] to [−ALIVE]]. The feature [−ANIMATE] in *rock* requires the deletion of the feature [±ALIVE] from *die*. Now, "being alive" is a kind of (that is, a hyponym of) "being in a sound condition" or of "existing", so it is a higher feature that becomes the carrier of the meaning of the verb; thus: [+CHANGE from [+SOUND] to [−SOUND]] or [+[CHANGE from [+EXIST] to [−EXIST]], realized in the surface predicates "decay" and "cease to exist", respectively. The intuition that the expression is strained is derived from the fact that the conflict of features deletes the lowest feature of the verb, and so compels a marked construal. Now, consider such a paraphrase as "the rock crumbled away". Here, there would be no construal of metaphor, but rather an interpretation, supplementing feature deletion with feature addition, semantic information processing with inference based on world knowledge.

There is, of course, an alternative, marked way of construing (17), by deleting the feature [−ANIMATE] in *rock* and transferring to it the features [+ANIMATE +HUMAN +ALIVE] from *die*. Thus, the meaning that results will be: 'the firm person died'. This construal exploits a semantic-syntactic structure that is used in language for non-metaphoric expressions as well, such as

(20)   Before I first met her, my wife had been a librarian.

The phrase *my wife* is derived here from the phrase "X is my wife", where *my wife* is in the predicate position; the sentence can be paraphrased as "The woman who is at present my wife was in the past (before I first met her) a librarian". Similarly, in (17), the phrase "The rock" is derived from the phrase, "X is a rock", where the metaphoric expression is in the predicate position, and so is consistent with the generalization that it is the predicate term of a metaphoric expression that tends to be understood as figurative. Accordingly, (17) can be paraphrased as "The person who was a rock died".

The reason for the afore-mentioned figurative asymmetry goes back to the logical asymmetry of the subject phrase and the predicate phrase in a sentence. As we have seen, Strawson (1967) discusses singular terms in subject position and general terms in predicative position. Strawson's most important innovation in this respect consists in the fact that he turned these absolute categories into relative ones. We have seen how with the help of relatively simple distinctions one may distinguish: (a) spatio-temporally continuous particulars; (b) properties of spatio-temporally continuous particulars; and (c) properties of properties (and so on). In this way, what Strawson achieved was more than eliminating descriptions that are "inaccurate, unclear or both" (71).

Strawson's proposal has considerable generative power as well. For my purpose, at any rate, it is important that the *relatively singular term* must occur in the subject position; and that for the correct application of this distinction, the speaker (or the philosopher) need not master a complex system of taxonomy. If I say

(21)   The captain is angry,

the term that denotes a spatio-temporally continuous particular occurs in the subject position, whereas the general term, "is angry", is the predicate. Both terms apply to the same referent, but in different senses. Both give a general characterization of the referent, one as "captain" (X is a captain), the other as "angry" (X is angry); but the subject phrase has an additional function: to attach the discourse to a particular referent. Thus, Strawson is speaking of a "general characterization", performed both by the subject phrase and the predicate phrase, and of a "particular attachment", performed by the subject phrase only. These are the means to specify *general types* of situations, things, events, etc., on the one hand, and, on the other, to attach these general specifications to *particular cases,* to indicate their particular incidence in the world.

Some theories of metaphor that were prevalent in the first half of the twentieth century may have given the impression that metaphoric expressions need not have a referent. Astonishing as it may appear, metaphors, too, **refer** to *something* (real or imaginary), though sometimes it may be difficult to discover what this something is. Language users are conditioned to identify the referent through the subject phrase.

Consequently, it is increasingly essential to minimize semantic changes in the subject phrase as the difficulty in 'decoding' a metaphor increases. And, conversely, the assignment of a concrete noun in a predicative position activates the addressee's inclination to generalize; this may be one of the reasons that it pays to place the figurative expressions in the predicative position. Consider

(22)   He is a Cicero.
(23)   He is a Napoleon.
(24)   He is a Paganini.

Such sentences tend to activate the addressee's readiness to generalize. Notice, however, that again these generalizations do not rely on the general items in the hierarchic organization of the meaning components. These sentences do not mean "He is a Roman (a Frenchman, an Italian)", or "He is a human" or "He is animate", and so forth. The generalizations are derived from the lowest features by which Cicero, Napoleon, or Paganini differ from their fellow humans, from their countrymen, or from other orators, generals, or violinists: "He is a brilliant orator, an ambitious general who became a dictator, a violin-virtuoso".

The Full Richness of Categories

In the foregoing, I have presented a theory of markedness in figurative language. We have found several variables on which markedness can be based: hierarchic organization of features, the dichotomy *functional ~ sensuous* metaphor, the presence or absence of spatio-temporally continuous entities, and location of the figurative member of the metaphor in the subject or the predicate.

In fact, the theory exploits two aspects of the hierarchic conception of semantic features or meaning components: for markedness, and for figurative creativity. New meanings are derived from old meanings by way of feature deletion; and the marked or unmarked effect is determined by the place of the retained features in the hierarchy. 'Unmarked' meanings are generated by making use of information at the most specific level of the hierarchy, whereas 'marked' meanings skip the most specific level of information and make use of relatively 'high' features; the specific information remains 'redundant'. We have seen that the redundancy of specific information may generate a marked effect. The generation of metaphors (in distinction from the generation of similes, for instance) is based on a mechanism of canceling higher features and also some of the specific features of words.

The foregoing conception of componential analysis assumes that categories may be defined with the help of a minimum number of features; and therefore, it fails to account for the way cognitive systems handle the complex categories of extra-linguistic reality. The cognitive functioning of human beings (and certainly their metaphoric creativity) is based on the knowledge of the full richness of categories. Consequently, we must supplement our foregoing model in three theoretical directions: Rosch's and Mervis' theory of *good examples,* Collins and Quillian's model of *semantic memory,* and the LNR group's (named after Lindsay, Norman, and Rumelhart) notion of *cognitive schemata* (or Schank's notion of *script).*

Rosch and Mervis developed a theory of *good examples.* This theory enables one to predict, according to principles that seem to be universal, what will be considered as a less or more typical example of a category. It emphasizes the configuration of features within categories. Two (possibly universal) principles determine the relative goodness of an example: the principle of family resemblance and that of contrast sets. "According to the family resemblance principle, the better examples are those that have larger numbers of attributes that are widely shared with other category members. [...] Correspondingly, the poorer category members are those that have fewer attributes shared with other category members" (Mervis, 1980: 287). "According to the contrast set principle, the good examples of a category are those that have few (if any) attributes that are commonly present in members of other similar categories" (ibid.). This conception has, on the one hand, far-reaching consequences for the relative naturalness of a figurative expression. On the other hand, this theory makes it possible to predict the configuration of specific features of the good representatives of a category. The features that carry the figurative meanings after the deletion of some other features will be selected from these specific features. Let us consider the category *furniture.*

> The best examples of the category furniture—chairs (dining) tables, and couches—all have rigid frames (assuming for the moment that beanbag chairs are not really chairs), all serve as support for objects (either people or things), and are all fairly large. [...] However, when one begins to consider the poorer examples, exceptions to each of the attributes shared by the good examples will almost always be found. Thus [...], such items as floor pillows, and rugs do not have rigid frames. Things like lamps do not serve as support for other objects, and things like stacking tables, vases and many floor pillows are quite small. (ibid., 286)

Let us consider now the following line, by the great Hebrew poet Alterman:

רַק הָרַעַם גּוֹרֵר אֵי־שָׁם רָהִיטִים

raq hara'am gorer ˀey-ˇam rahitim

(25)   Only the thunder is dragging furniture somewhere.

The sound produced by the thunder is inarticulate and random, and comes from "above", as if the upstairs neighbor dragged his furniture around. It is obvious that this requires imagining some "good examples" of *furniture,* that is, pieces of furniture that "have rigid frames" and "are fairly large", and not, for instance, carpets, curtains, or lamps. But even if we change the predicate, so as to suit some less good examples of *furniture,* metaphors like "Only the night spreads black furniture" for "Only the night spreads black curtains", or "Only the stars light up glimmering furniture" for "Only the stars light up glimmering lamps" will sound odd. The generic categories resemble always, in their figurative use, their best examples. If the text explicitly mentions some poor example in a figurative espression, such a simile or metaphor turns out highly **marked.** Baudelaire's famous sonnet "Correspondances" provides an illuminating instance:

26.   Vaste comme la nuit et comme la clarté.
                   (Vast as the night and as the light)

This simile makes somehow *light* equal *night* in an indirect manner and generates a powerful, though implicit oxymoron. The simile being "somehow" unsatisfactory, its oxymoron directs attention away from the simile to the fact that both night and light are treated in the lines as "vast". It is quite obvious that *night* is indefinitely, or even infinitely, vast; and the same can be true of *light* as a thing-free and gestalt-free quality. Still, the simile appears to be unsatisfactory. The reason seems to be that, although indefinitely vast, *night* is a poor example of vastness. This can be accounted for by the principles of family resemblance and of contrast set. The attributes of *night,* such as **darkness,** are not necessarily shared with other members of the category *vast things;* at the same time, it is shared with a considerable number of things that are *not* members of this category.

Let us turn now to the Collins and Quillian (1969) model of *semantic memory.* At this point, one has to distinguish between, on the one had, *features* arranged in a hyponymic scale, in which each lower category is included in the category above, and, on the other, (empirical) *properties.* Such a distinction is quite problematic from the point of view of logic; but it may help to reveal certain significant relationships between meanings, and we shall have to pursue this issue at some length. Let us consider again the meaning of the word *ball* as discussed above. The skeleton of this meaning is a hierarchy of distinctive features: [+NOUN +COUNT +COMMON +CONCRETE −ANIMATE +GEOMETRIC SOLID +SPHERIC SHAPE (#ball)]. As a matter of fact, we are up against a 'hyponymic' scale: each later category is included in the preceding one. Such a hierarchic conception of distinctive features assumes that one may define categories by the smallest number of features; however, such a definition cannot give a satisfactory account of how the cognitive system handles the complex categories of reality. The cognitive functioning of humans (and, certainly, their metaphoric creativeness) must be based on a knowledge of the full richness of categories. One must, therefore, supplement the minimum set of distinctive features by a maximum of information concerning empirical properties. Thus, for instance, the sphere differs from all other geometrical bodies by the fact that every point on its surface is at equal distance from its center point. As a result of this distinctive shape, the ball has a series of empirical properties, such as, for instance, that at any given time only one point on its external surface is in contact with the surface upon which it is placed; it may, therefore, move with minimum friction in all directions, that is, with maximum ease. Whatever its logical status, this distinction between hyponymic relationships and empirical properties does have psychological reality: according to experiments by Collins and Quillian, it takes less time to verify such statements as "A canary is a bird", or "A bird is an animal" than such statements as "A canary is yellow", or "A canary can fly".

To assume the necessity of having "a knowledge of the full richness of categories" is to face the problem of the parsimonious storage of information required for an open set of empirical properties. Collins and Quillian presented a hierarchic model, in which the category *canary* is represented as a sub-category of *bird* and the category *bird* as a subcategory of *animal*. The fact that animals can breathe is not separately stored for each kind of animal, but at the animal level only. The fact that birds have wings, for instance, is stored at the *bird* level, whereas yellow color and the ability to sing are stored at the *canary* level (see Figure 9.1). Accordingly, the time required to verify such statements as "A canary can breathe", "A canary can fly", and "A canary can sing" is gradually decreasing.

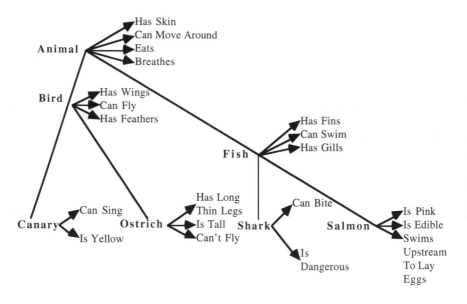

Figure 9.1 Section from Collins and Quillian's (1969) Model of Semantic Memory Hyponyms and Properties.

There have been difficulties in replicating the experiments by Collins and Quillian. This may be due to the fact that some of the subjects in these experiments relied in their responses on the cognitive organization presented here, and some others on their personal acquaintance with some specific canary, whose capability of breathing, flying and singing could be directly observed. However, in cases in which the cognitive functioning of humans must choose between the reliance on some general cognitive structure and some casual personal experience, we have quite good reasons to suppose that there is a clear (though by no means absolute) tendency to prefer the former to the latter.[2] This tendency seems to be even stronger in relation to figurative language.

Now consider the following simile of Wordsworth's:

(27)   The holy Time is quiet as a nun.

Dorothy Mack (1975: 224) may have had this verse line in mind when suggesting an example for her claim that one must have recourse to some of the most outstanding properties of the object that serves as a simile. One may say

(28)   as quiet as a nun,

but hardly

(29)   as nervous as a nun.

Nuns are frequently associated with quietness: quietness, not nervousness, is part of the stereotype of a nun. One must, however, supplement Mack's suggestion with the trite observation that the moment we think that nuns are human beings, we agree that they can be nervous. In order to render the simile in (29) meaningful, says Mack, the situation requires some further specification, such as

(30)   as nervous as a pregnant nun at Mass.

In the above terms, the meaning of *nun* may be analysed into the following list of features: [+NOUN +COUNT +COMMON +CONCRETE +ANIMATE +HUMAN +ADULT −MALE +SOCIAL ROLE (#nun)]. Following Collins and Quillian, one may assume that the empirical properties of nuns are stored in long-term memory at the various levels of this hierarchy, and thus are accessible to consciousness with varying degrees of ease. Thus, for instance, at the level [#nun] such properties are stored as "is unmarried, is quiet, prays much, looks like a penguin". At the level [−Male], such properties are stored as "could become pregnant". At the level [+Human], such properties are stored as "can be nervous". At the level [+Animate], such properties are stored as "has skin, can breathe", and so forth.

---

2   Consider the following riddle. In a car accident a man was killed and his son seriously injured. In the hospital they called in a famous surgeon to operate on him. The famous surgeon said: I can't operate on this child, because he is my son. Who was the speaker? There is some evidence that even female surgeons tend to say at first "His father", and then be confused when reminded that the father was killed. In our feminist age this my have changed.

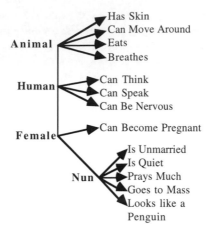

Figure 9.2   Further Articulation of Collins and Quillian's Model.

On the model of the experiments of Collins and Quillian with *canary,* we may assume that it will take less time for subjects to verify such statements as "A nun is
unmarried" than "A nun can become pregnant"; less time to verify "A nun can be
quiet" than "A nun can be nervous" (unless one is well acquainted with a specific
nun, who is recalled as having been nervous and/or pregnant). In conjecturing this, I
am relying on the assumption that we begin our search of long-term memory at the
most specific level ([#nun]), and from there proceed to the less specific levels of the
hierarchy ([−MALE +HUMAN +ANIMATE]) and scan the properties stored at each
level; all of which takes time. From the cognitive point of view, such search-time
is translated into a feeling of relative markedness. Consequently, the default situation in which we shall imagine a nun will more resemble an "unmarried, quiet nun
praying at Mass" than a "nervous, pregnant nun, fainting at Mass". The latter situation, though not impossible, is marked with respect to the former. The discarding of
the default situation and the sudden shift to the marked situation are usually perceived as "comic" or "witty", or "ironical". Indeed, when I summarize Mack's arguments in my lectures on figurative language, there is usually a grin in the
classroom when I quote (30). One might add, furthermore, that all the distinctive
information conveyed by *as a nun* in (29) is irrelevant to the simile, and is therefore
redundant and generates a marked simile (see figure 9.2).

Finally, consider the following line by the Hebrew imagist poet Shlonsky:

וְוָהָאֶבֶן תִּנְשֹׁף – כְּמוֹ חַי וְצוֹמֵחַ

wəhaʾeven tinˇof—kəmo ḥay wəṣomeaḥ

(31)   And the stone is breathing like animate and growing things.

It requires an unmarked construal. Had he written "And the stone is breathing like a canary", the simile would have been marked, for two related reasons: the features that distinguish canaries from birds, and birds from animals, are irrelevant to the simile; therefore *canary,* though itself animate, is not a very good example of breathing things.

Scripts (Schemata)

Linguistic knowledge is, then, insufficient for language use and, certainly, for the use of figurative language. One must incorporate in one's model world knowledge as well. In the preceding section, we have taken the first steps in this direction. In Chapter 1, with reference to examples (1)–(4) I have illuminated another aspect in which world knowledge comes into verbal discourse. I have suggested there, that verbal structures undergo considerable changes of meaning, by being placed in different situations, or scripts, or schemata. Such cognitive researchers as Schank or Rumelhart came early in their semantic research to the insight that the only way out of the linguistic dead end was to make a quantum leap from the semantic structure of words to the structure of *scripts* or *schemata,* in which the words occur.

According to Schank's conception, the task of the SCRIPT is to supplement (rather than replace) the conceptual analysis of words. Rumelhart (1979: 85–86), demonstrates the limitations of the semantic approach of componential analysis by the following frame of sentence:

(32)   X raised his hand and stopped the car.

If we substitute the phrase the *policeman* for *X,* the most likely account perhaps for this event will be, Rumelhart suggests, "one involving a traffic cop who is signalling to a driver to stop his car. Note that this brings under consideration a number of concepts that are not mentioned in the sentence itself. For example, this interpretation requires that the car has a driver and that the policeman stopped the car by signaling with his hand to the driver, who then most likely puts his foot on the brake of the car causing it finally to halt". If, however, we substitute *Superman* for *X,* we shall have to understand that the car was stopped with no intentional cooperation on the driver's part. There is no possibility to account for this difference between the two sentences by relying on the different semantic make-ups of the two nouns. We must assume, instead, that the phrase *the policeman* instantiates the POLICEMAN SCRIPT, whereas the word *Superman* instantiates the SUPERMAN SCRIPT.

The important question is, then, how do we reconstruct the situation from an isolated expression, in the absence of all other information concerning the overall context; in other words, the question is, how do we infer from what is explicitly said to the details of the situation referred to by the utterance. Linguists and psychologists have become much aware of this problem, mainly as a result of work done in artificial intelligence.

Artificial intelligence is the computer simulation of flesh-and-blood people's cognitive functioning. One of the differences between a regular computer program and an artificial intelligence program is as follows: suppose we feed into the computer the sentence

(33)   John went to the cinema yesterday,

and ask the computer such questions as "Did John enter the theater?", or "Did he buy a ticket?", or "Did he see a picture?". An ordinary computer program would answer "No", since all it knows is that John went *to* the cinema. Whereas an artificial intelligence program would answer to these questions "Very likely, yes". If we may infer from this example as for the cognitive functioning of flesh-and-blood people, we ought to learn from it two things: first, that we complete automatically the situation, so as to render the discourse meaningful; second, that inferences don't have the status of facts, only of hypotheses, of "default options", so to speak. Thus, for instance, there is no logical contradiction in a statement like

(34)   John went to the cinema yesterday, but all the tickets were sold.

If inferences had the status of **facts**, we would have faced a logical contradiction here. Had (33) not suggested the default option that John bought a ticket, went in and saw a picture, the word *but* would have been redundant in (34).

Human beings have intuitions, with the help of which they may make inferences from what is explicitly stated to what is implicit in the situation. Computers have no intuitions. It would appear, however, that a solution to the problem of how inferences are made by computers from the explicit to the implicit, may also explain how the intuitions of flesh-and-blood people may work in such instances. The Yale group of researchers in artificial intelligence (see, e.g., Schank and Abelson, 1977) attacked this pragmatic problem by having recourse to SCRIPTS. Thus, for instance, the expression *went to the cinema* instantiates the SCRIPT of GOING TO THE CINEMA, which includes as default stages such actions as "going to …, buying a ticket, going in, and seeing a picture". The FANCY RESTAURANT SCRIPT, for instance, includes such a default string of actions as "guest enters; the hostess seats him; the waiter hands him the menu card; the guest orders food; the waiter serves the food ordered; guest consumes food; guest pays; guest gives tip; guest leaves". Thus, for instance, if the following story is fed into the computer,

(35)   John entered a fancy restaurant, ordered steak and chips, left a large
         tip and went out,

the artificial intelligence program will assume, **by default**, that all the stages of the script took place. Consequently, if it is asked questions like "Was John seated by the hostess?", or "Did the waiter serve him the food he ordered?", the program will answer "Very likely", or "Possibly, yes", or the like. On the other hand, such a sequence of events does not exclude a sequel like

> (36)   The waiter wondered: "Why did he give me such a large tip? I refused to serve him, because he was not dressed according to the decorum of the place".

Moreover, a similar beginning may develop quite differently—thus for instance:

> (37)   John entered a fancy restaurant, took out a machine-gun, and announced: "This is a robbery".

In this case, the first verb phrase instantiates the FANCY RESTAURANT SCRIPT; the second verb phrase eliminates it and instantiates the ARMED ROBBERY SCRIPT. On the human level, the substitution of one script for another is experienced as surprise or wit.

Schank and his colleagues assume that the intuitions of flesh-and-blood human beings in dealing with situations work in a similar fashion, based on similar SCRIPTs. Indeed, the LNR group in cognitive psychology, at the University of California, San Diego, spoke of cognitive SCHEMATA in the minds of human beings, in a sense very similar to SCRIPTs:

> Having selected and verified that some configuration of schemata offers a sufficient account for the situation, it is said to be understood. As I use the term, a "schema" is taken to be an abstract representation of a generalized concept or situation, and a schema is said "to account for a situation" whenever that situation can be taken as an instance of the general class of concepts represented by the schema. (Rumelhart, 1979: 85)

> As the sentences are read, schemata are activated, evaluated, and refined or discarded. (ibid., 87)

The test whether a story has some underlying SCRIPT is the **definite article test**. If we feel, intuitively, that *the* may be added to nouns with no antecedent occurrence, it strongly suggests that they refer to objects that are typically associated with a SCRIPT. Consider the following beginning of a story:

> (38)   John entered a fancy restaurant, *the* hostess seated him, *the* waiter handed him *the* menu-card … and so forth.

Such a usage of the definite article indicates that there is a SCRIPT underlying our discourse on fancy restaurants. One way to test the psychological reality of linguistic or pragmatic devices is to consider the effects of ignoring them. Thus, for instance, suppose the story in (38) began rather as

> (39)   John entered a fancy restaurant, *a* hostess seated him, *a* waiter handed him *a* menu-card ... and so forth.

Such a beginning could be used as a literary device of alienation, of "making strange", to indicate, from John's point of view, that he has never been in a fancy restaurant before; or, in the foregoing terminology, he has not yet acquired the FANCY RESTAURANT SCRIPT. Hence, we may assume that people normally do have intuitions concerning such a SCRIPT.

What follows now is a short exploration of how people apply scripts to isolated expressions; why do they prefer one script rather than another to deal with an expression to which they are exposed for the first time. Let us begin our discussion with a Talmudic saying:

> (40)   She who conceived in the bath-tub (Ḥagiga 15. 1).

This clause is ambiguous, as is revealed by the following two paraphrases:

> (41)   She had sexual intercourse in the bath-tub and became pregnant.
> (42)   She bathed in the bath-tub and conceived by the sperm that was in the water.

Asked how they understood the Talmudic expression in (40), acquaintances of mine, not versed in the Talmud, answered: "In itself, in the absence of any general context, I understand: 'conceived—not by way of normal sexual intercourse' but by some sperm that was in the water". It would appear, that my informants preferred intuitively sentence (42) to (41) as a paraphrase for (40). In order to find out how widespread this intuition may be, I improvised an experiment with a casual group of students at the Department of Hebrew Literature, Tel Aviv University, whom I asked to write down what they understood by (40). In addition to explicit formulations, I considered as a preference for (42) those responses in which water played an active part in conceiving; as well as responses that suggested the absence of sexual intercourse (the Virgin Mary, for instance). In this respect, there were two versions: there were those who accepted conceiving by water in the bath-tub as a possible fact, and those who regarded it as an attempt to hide the truth concerning (forbidden) sexual relations. But for our purposes, both are considered as a preference for (42). The answers have generally confirmed the existence of an intuitive tendency to prefer (42) to (41) as a paraphrase for (40). Out of 15 written responses, six contained no information that could settle on one paraphrase or other ("I have no idea"; "It seems, the meaning is metaphoric"; or, for instance, the informant who misheard *nitʿawra* for *nitʿabra* [that is, "became blind" for "conceived"], etc.). Six responses were founded—as explained above—on (42); three responses explicitly said "had sexual intercourse in the bath-tub". It is interesting to compare the relative lengths of the responses. The three responses founded on (41) were short and straightforward. Most of the responses founded on (42) were rather long, containing several clauses. One may infer from this that to some of the informants it was not very clear how one possibly could conceive by the water; yet, in spite of this, they preferred such an interpretation. Further random remarks made after the test revealed additional factors that may have influenced the answers. One of the students remarked that there had been a motion picture in which the heroine had sexual intercourse in the bath-tub. Another student mentioned a well-known Hebrew song about "Hannale, who did not know" how she became pregnant. One of the students said she had intended to give something like (42) as a paraphrase, but since she could find no scientific explanation for that, eventually she wrote (41). I have found among my oral informants too, that a familiarity with the joke presented below in (44) may have influenced some of the answers.

The question to be asked is: Why do people prefer paraphrase (42) to paraphrase (41)? One could conduct an illuminating study by itself of the explanations which some of the informants volunteered to give. Thus, for instance, some of them explained, that it is uncommon to have sexual intercourse in the bath-tub, so they preferred interpretation (42). However, it does not seem to be more common to conceive by sperm in the water. Moreover, consider the following expression, for instance:

(43)   She who conceived on the airplane.

The place indicated here is not more frequent as a place for sexual intercourse than the bath-tub. Nevertheless, the only interpretation usually offered is conceiving by way of ordinary intercourse. Another explanation sometimes offered was that it is the familiarity with the Talmudic source that determines the preference of paraphrase (42). Underlying such explanations we may find a conception of "Homo Loquens" as a creature whose responses all have been determined by conditioned reflexes— something which is unacceptable to the present cognitive approach. In order to eliminate this possibility, I have asked my informants who answered in writing, to state whether they knew the expression before. All of them stated "I did not know the expression before".

The first thing we can learn from the relation of (40) to its two paraphrases is that it is not enough to rely on a string of words in order to determine the meaning of a discourse. Discourse receives one of its several meanings only when it is perceived as part of a "plot". In this respect, some distinguish "sentence meaning" from "utterer's meaning" (e.g., Grice). The question is, then, why are we inclined to invent, when presented with (40), the plot suggested by (42) rather than the plot suggested by (41).

People have very strong intuitions as for the preference of certain meanings to others; and in the course of current communication, we may rely on a considerable degree of uniformity as for the meanings preferred by our interlocutors. Otherwise, the following joke would have been considerably less effective than it is:

(44)   A medical student asks the Professor whether one may get syphilis in the toilet. The answer is: "One may, but it is uncomfortable".

It appears, that the meaning attributed automatically—in the absence of further specification—to utterances like

(45)   She conceived in the bath-tub.
(46)   He got syphilis in the toilet.

is the meaning that implies "not by way of ordinary intercourse". Whereas for utterances like

(47)   She conceived on the airplane.
(48)   He got syphilis on the airplane.

the interpretation offered automatically implies "by way of ordinary intercourse". The conventional way of grammarians to handle this problem of the two meanings is to distinguish two meanings of the prepositional phrases *in the bath-tub* and *in the toilet:* they may refer either to the place or to the instrument related to the action. But this does not account for the intuitive preference of speakers for one meaning or the other, out of the context. In fact, any attempt to explain in a consistent manner this cognitive behavior of people by relying only on a semantic or syntactic analysis of the string of words is doomed to failure. At the same time, an understanding of the semantic character of the verbs involved may improve our understanding of the phenomenon. It seems to me that one factor that is perceived here is the semantic difference between the verbs. *Conceived* is a verb that denotes a change of state as a result of some action denoted by another verb. It would appear that, when talking of some result, it is less important to know the circumstances of the action that caused that result (unless, of course, one may point out some direct connection between the special circumstances and the resulting state[3]). Let us compare the following two utterances:

(49)   He ate at the drawing studio.
(50)   He had his fill at the drawing studio.

One may, again, detect some strangeness in (50), but not in (49). In (50), the adverbial adjunct of place appears to be superfluous. Especially when long-term results are concerned, the exact time, place, or circumstances are regarded as unimportant.

---

[3]   An example of such "special circumstances" would be the sentence "He got AIDS in Africa", aids being widespread in Africa.

What is, then, the role of the prepositional phrases *in the bath-tub* and *in the toilet* in sentences (45) and (46)? Do they refer merely to the place in which the event takes place, or to the instrument that has some decisive role in bringing about the event? How does the intuition of people work, who prefer the instrument-meaning, as in (45) and (46), to the place-meaning, as in (47) and (48)? It would appear that the solution should be given in terms of the instantiation of SCRIPTS. *Conception* has not a specific script of its own; it is typically associated with the SEXUAL IN-TERCOURSE SCRIPT. That is why (41) is a possible paraphrase of (40): the verb *conceived* instantiates (as a default option) the whole SCRIPT. In such a case, *in the bath-tub* may serve as the specification of the place where the event took place. Since *in the bath-tub* conveys information that is redundant in a sense, the respondent may discard the whole SCRIPT and triy the BATH-TUB SCRIPT. The ingredient "not by way of normal sexual intercourse" in the responses of some of my informants is derived from the discarding of the SEXUAL INTERCOURSE SCRIPT, which is the default script for conception. Subsequently, the respondent tries the BATH-TUB SCRIPT. Hence the *water* ingredient even in those responses which could not hit on the "sperm in the water" as the cause of conception, as in the following response of a (female) student: "A woman who became pregnant in the bath-tub, or something that has swollen and its dimensions have swollen as a result of its being placed in the bath-tub, that is, swollen by water". And if the respondent succeeds in finding some connection between conception and the main features of the bath-tub script, s/he may attribute to (40) some meaning such that (42) is one of its possible paraphrases.

Now, when the prepositional phrase *on the airplane* in (47) and (48) instantiates the AIRPLANE SCRIPT, it furnishes no information that might account, "not by way of normal sexual intercourse", for the facts of conception or infection. Consequently, the respondent feels compelled to instantiate again the SEXUAL INTERCOURSE SCRIPT, and to remain with the redundant information that creates the effect of **markedness**.

Coming back now to the joke conveyed by (44), it is based—with the necessary changes—on a sentence that is very much like (40), with two paraphrases akin to (41) and (42). Here, too, the prepositional phrase conveys redundant information; here, too, the SEXUAL INTERCOURSE SCRIPT is instantiated and discarded; and here too, the prepositional phrase offers a script that may account for the infection "not by way of normal sexual intercourse". That is how the "audience" of the joke interprets the medical student's question. The professor's answer, on the other hand, reverts to the script in which the information conveyed by the prepositional phrase is perceived as redundant. Thus, a witty effect is achieved, in several ways, and at one and the same time. First, a series of shifts of mental sets takes place, "back and forth"; witty effects are based on shifts of mental sets. Second, the process settles eventually on a meaning that has already been considered and discarded as containing some redundant information; and that redundant information too may be the source of a comic effect. Third, the same redundant information is exploited to convey a meaning that is opposite to the explicit meaning: "One may, but it is uncomfortable" is to be understood as "One may not (in the sense you have in mind)". Fourth, in this way the professor displays an attitude of freedom, superiority, and amusement, whereas the "audience" of the joke perceives itself as being caught up in a fixed pattern of semantic information processing; this is the archetypal situation of irony

I have mentioned above, in relation to (32), the importance attributed by Rumelhart to COGNITIVE SCHEMATA (or SCRIPTS) with respect to literal meaning. He claims that componential analysis alone cannot account for our ability to produce and understand literal utterances which we have not heard before. The meaning of the sentence "X raised his hand and stopped the car" will not depend only on the meaning components of the words substituted for X *(Policeman* or *Superman),* but also on the SCRIPT or COGNITIVE SCHEMA which they instantiate. From this, however, Rumelhart jumps to the conclusion, that the feature deletion theory of metaphor is inadequate. A look at his counter-examples will suggest that here, too, we have feature-cancellation; but the act of cancellation has been transferred from the word-level to the script-level, assuming that scripts or cognitive schemata, too, are made up of sets of meaning components or semantic features. This is suggested, in fact, by Rumelhart's own discussion of the utterance

(51)   Encyclopedias are gold mines.

Rumelhart comments on this utterance:

> According to the schema theory of comprehension suggested above, the task for the comprehender is to find a schema within which this utterance is coherent. Here we have a case of predication, the process of interpretation presumably involves applying the schemata suggested by the predicate term to the subject term. [...] In this case, we find that the "gold mine" schema fits only partially, although certain of the primary characteristics of gold mines can be shown to be true of encyclopedias (such as the characteristic of containing something of value—if only you look for it), other characteristics (such as being underground) do not hold. I suspect that it is the unevenness of account—certain primary feature of the gold mine schema fit very well, others not at all—that leads to the metaphorical flavor of statements such as this. (Rumelhart, 1979: 90)

Clearly this analysis points up two, not only one, aspects of the use of schemata in the understanding of metaphoric expressions. On the one hand, it imputes coherence to metaphorical expressions, just as to literal ones. On the other hand, it points up exactly the same kind of cognitive operations, with respect to schemata, that we have identified with respect to words in metaphoric expressions, viz., the cancellation of part of the features that constitute the word, and the transference of the remaining features to the topic of the metaphor.

At this stage of my argument, I propose briefly to consider a literary metaphor by the Hebrew poet Alterman, drawing together my claims concerning the use of scripts in the explication of metaphors and those concerning the markedness of metaphors that skip the most specific features in the hierarchy.

פֹּה אוֹרְזִים, יָפָתִי, אֶת שְׂרִידֵי הַבִּינָה,
כֶּאֱרֹז צַוְּרוֹנִים וּנְיָרוֹת לִבְרִיחָה.

po ʾorzim, yafati, ʾɛt sride habbina,
kɛʾɛroz ṣawwronim unyarot livriḥa.

(52)   Here, my beauty, the remnants of wits are packed,
        As collars and papers are packed for fleeing.

What kind of insightful comment on the *packing of the remnants of wits* can we derive from the *packing of collars and papers,* or on "the remnants of wits" from *packing* ? Do the simile or the metaphor thus stated illustrate, or modify, or interact with, the topic? Do we understand now better in any way how the remnants of wits are packed? It might be more illuminating to treat the second line as if it activated the cognitive schema of "flight". "Flight" and "losing one's wits" are analogous in that in both one loses his sense of control, in the social or mental sense. We may assume that one of the default stages of the "flight"-script is a hasty and almost indiscriminate packing of belongings. Collars may be considered, in connection with the flight-script, either as of the most trivial possessions, or of the remnants of lost status; and the packing of collars—as a desperate attempt to save its last "crumbles" at least. But packing is irrelevant to "losing one's wits". Hence, "the packing of the remnants of wits" suggests the pulling-together, tightening, strengthening of all that has been left of one's wits, as a last fixed point, or last refuge, while losing the sense of stability, certitude, and control. Alternatively, *packing* is perceived as an instance of the category "pulling-together and tightening". The specific physical action involved in packing is irrelevant to pulling together one's wits. Consequently, the metaphor compels one to skip the concrete and specific information conveyed by the verb, and hence is perceived as marked. Moreover, the simile "As collars and papers are packed" reinforces precisely that concrete and specific information conveyed by the verb, which is irrelevant to the metaphor. Part of the witty (or modernistic) effect of these lines is derived from the fact that the specific "packing" which instantiates the cognitive schema of flight, is redundant: it is irrelevant precisely to those features for the foregrounding of which the cognitive schema has been activated (such as "desperate attempt at hasty rescue"). It is even more conspicuous that all the information conveyed by "collars and papers" is irrelevant to the object of description: "losing one's wits".

Symbolization, Abstraction, Allusion

In the present chapter, I have discussed at considerable length the derivation of new meanings from old meanings by feature deletion; I have considered this issue both with reference to single words and to scripts (or schemata). In Chapter 3, above, I discussed at considerable length the process by which children gradually acquire the conceptual apparatus for "going beyond the information given" and for preserving the stability of reality; I have pointed out that these techniques could be exploited for literary purposes in two opposite ways. On the one hand, special literary effects can be achieved by *deviating* or *regressing* from certain cognitive accomplishments, mainly where micro-structures are concerned. On the other hand, as we have found, where overall organization (macro-structure) is concerned, the *same kinds of cognitive constraints* must be applied by the reader and the critic as in the cognitive structures used to construct a predictable, stable world, in which one may go, in a fairly reliable and consistent manner, beyond the information given. In the present section, I am going to draw together all these threads in a conception of the literary symbol. In the present context, too, two opposite directions of feature deletion must be considered. When the figurative process affects micro-structure, all the higher features are to be deleted, and only some of the lower features retained. When the figurative process affects macro-structure, feature deletion begins at the bottom, until a 'sufficiently' abstract structure is obtained. This is, in fact, how some cognitive psychologists describe the process of concept attainment (e.g., Kreitler and Kreitler, 1972: 304). To explore just how much is this "sufficient" is the business of the present section.

One of the aims of interpretation is to state the theme of a literary work of art. The scripts or schemata discussed above are frequently just such *themes*. Symbolic interpretations may be obtained, when specific features of the ostensible theme of a work are deleted.

> [Abstraction] is generally viewed as a high-level cognitive process which consists in the removal of features that characterize only the individual or particular phenomenon. Its product is a concept that includes those features which are common to a class of particular objects or events. [...] [T]he ignoring of some features in the course of abstraction always results in an increased emphasis on the remaining features and that these remaining features form a concept which invokes both the particular case and the class (Kreitler and Kreitler, 1972: 302).

In this manner, a wider theme is obtained. Alternatively, symbolic interpretation is frequently generated by introducing a further theme from extra-literary reality, from some other verbal expression, or from some myth. In these instances, the ostensible theme of the work and the imported theme have a wide range of shared features at the higher levels. The lower-level features must be deleted from the "imported" theme, so as to avoid conflict of features.

One rather widespread way to introduce such external themes to literary works of art is literary allusion. Literary allusion is the simultaneous activation of two texts (cf. Ben-Porat, 1976). Thus, two themes or situations are simultaneously in the focus of attention. Those features in the "imported" theme or situation are deleted, which are incompatible with the explicit features of the theme or situation in the target-text. By the same token, the remaining features are foregrounded and transferred to the "importing" work. This, however, is not the only, nor even the most important function of allusion in a work of literature. Quite frequently, the text alluded to may serve as a point of departure for a shift of semantic and/or mental sets, resulting in wit or irony. In a love sonnet written by the aging Victor Hugo to the young and beautiful Judith Gautier both functions are patent. The sonnet ends with a powerful Metaphysical conceit:

(53)   Nous sommes tous les deux voisins du ciel, madame,
         Puisque vous êtes belle et puisque je suis vieux.

         (We both are neighbors of heaven, madam,
         Because you are beautiful, and I am old).

The speaker and the addressee are "neighbors of heaven" in different senses: Hugo because he is old, and is soon to die and go to heaven; Judith, because she is endowed with "heavenly" beauty. The two *clichés,* with their different senses, mean the same on the literal level, and are incompatible in their implications. By using the first person plural, "we both are neighbors of heaven", the two expressions are developed so literally that both their meanings must be intended. This lends a turn of metaphysical wit to the expression. This witty turn is reinforced by the allusion in the sonnet's title: "Ave, Dea; moriturus te salutat" (Hail Goddess, the one who is about to die salutes you). The meaning of this text is simultaneously activated with the gladiators' "Ave Caesar, morituri te salutant" (Hail Caesar, the ones who are about to die salute you). This allusion functions on two different levels: on the verbal level it foregrounds an extreme shift of semantic and mental sets. The gladiators' *morituri* suggests "the ones who are to be killed in a most brutal way for your (senseless) pleasure"; whereas Hugo's *moriturus* suggests "the one who is about to die of old age". The gladiators' *te salutant* suggests "are disgraced in all possible manners"; Hugo's *te salutat* suggests "loves you". On the situational level, it performs exactly the kind of feature deletion discussed so far. All the physical actions of killing are deleted from the gladiator script; only such highly general features are retained as 'disgrace', and 'desperate and agonizing helplessness'. The features of disgrace and cruelty may join the Petrarcan element in the lady's description as "goddess" and having "heavenly beauty".

In the remainder of the present section, I am going to examine one instance of literary allusion, with reference to abstraction, feature deletion, and symbolization, as it is handled by two different critics. Many critics have remarked in one way or another that Coleridge's "Kubla Khan" is a poem about poetry. I propose to investigate their different ways of making that remark. Let us begin with Watson's (1973: 227–228) statement:

> "Kubla Khan", then, is not just about poetry: it is about two kinds of poem. One of them is there in the first thirty-six lines of the poem; and though the other is nowhere to be found, we are told what it would do to the reader and what it would do to the poet.

Watson does not offer this as a *hypothesis,* but as an indisputable *fact:*

> What is "Kubla Khan" about? This is, or ought to be, an established fact of criticism: "Kubla Khan" is a poem about poetry. [...] Anyone who objects that there is not a word about poetry in it should be sent at once to the conclusion and asked, even if he has never read any Plato, what in English poetry this is like:
>
>> Weave a circle round him thrice,
>> And close your eyes with holy dread,
>> For he on honey-dew has fed,
>> And drunk the milk of Paradise.
>
> There are dozens of parallels in Renaissance English to this account of poetic inspiration, all based—though rarely at first hand—on Plato's view of poetic madness in the *Ion* or the *Phaedrus*. Shakespeare's banter about "the poet's eye, in a fine frenzy rolling" in *A Midsummer Night's Dream* is perhaps the most famous. The "flashing eyes" and "floating hair" of Coleridge's poem belong to a poet in the fury of creation. Verbal resemblances to the text of Plato itself confirm that the last paragraph of the poem is a prolonged Platonic allusion. Socrates, in the *Ion,* compares lyric poets to "Bacchic maidens who draw *milk and honey* from the rivers when under the influence of Dionysus" and adds that poets "gather their strains from *honeyed fountains* out of the gardens and dells of the Muses [...]" Ion himself, describing the effects of poetic recitation, confesses that "when I speak of horrors, my hair stands on end [...]" The very phrase "holy dread" is Platonic (*Laws* 671 D). (Watson, 1973: 226)

The parallel between Plato and Coleridge's passage is convincing enough. But does this prove, beyond Watson's rhetoric, that "Kubla Khan" is indeed a poem about poetry? Let us have a look at Schneider's discussion of the same issue:

> Essentially, the picture is but the ancient conventional description of the poet with his "eye in a fine frenzy rolling". This conception was old even in Plato's day, and practically every detail used by Coleridge was a commonplace in it. The description derived a good deal from the accounts of

persons possessed by the god in Dionysus worship and the Orphic cults—
flashing eyes and streaming hair, as well as honey, milk, magic, holiness,
and dread (Schneider, 1975: 245).

Then comes a long quotation from *Ion,* including the passages quoted by Watson.
Then Schneider concludes:

> Coleridge's inspiration, music, holiness inspiring awe, milk and honey,
> are all explicitly here; and the flashing eyes and floating hair are implicit in
> the "Corybantian revellers" and "Bacchic maidens". (ibid., 246)

The differences between Schneider's and Watson's positions are very small, but
rather significant. Schneider extends the poet's "fine frenzy" to "persons possessed
by the god in Dionysus worship and the Orphic cults"; that is, she regards it as a
more specific instance of ecstasy, inspiration, possession. In her concluding
paragraph, she mentions such abstractions as "inspiration, music, holiness inspiring
awe", but no *poetic* inspiration. Both Schneider and Watson go outside the text for
the substantiation of their interpretation, and both go to the same texts. But Schneider, firstly, widens the scope of her external sources, and views within it Plato and
Shakespeare *in proportion.* Secondly, from them she abstracts a higher abstraction
which, by the same token, does not contain elements that conflict with what is
explicitly stated in the poem. In other words, she resorts to the abstraction process,
whose "product is a concept that includes those features which are common to a
class of particular objects or events". Watson, on the contrary, fails to transcend and
depart from the immediate and perceptual characteristics of Plato's description of the
poet, and insists on his presence in the last lines of the poem. In such allusions,
only the most general abstractions should be imported into the poem; from the
more specific levels of abstraction, only those meaning components from the
source-text (Plato) should be transferred (if at all) that do not conflict with the more
specific components in the target-text ("Kubla Khan").

Let us supplement these two pieces of criticism with a third one, which does
identify "Kubla Khan" with poetic creation, but without appealing to Plato and
Shakespeare. It is most illuminating to see what happens in Humphrey House's paper with regard to the above. It should be contrasted to Watson's confident dictum
not only in its contents, but also in its tone. He states: "For 'Kubla Khan' is a
poem about the act of poetic creation, about the 'ecstasy in imaginative fulfilment'"
(House, 1973: 201). This sentence is far from achieving the precision of academic
writing; by the same token, it seems to aim at a precision required for capturing
evasive intuitions. It suggests one thing, and then adds, as a casual afterthought, a
correction, as it were, that appears to be more precise. At any rate, the phrases
"poetic creation" and "the ecstasy in imaginative fulfilment" are far from being synonymous. But it is perhaps an indirect indication of House's great sensitivity to
"subtle and minimal cues" and to their balance and proportion, instances of which
abound in his Clark lectures on Coleridge. In this context, what could be regarded as

House's "academic ineptness" is, in fact, a means for capturing his evasive intuitions, and as such, a kind of indirect evidence of his negative capability. "Ecstasy in imaginative fulfilment" is a more general term than "poetic creation", in the sense that "poetic creation" is a specific case of "imaginative fulfillment". Thus the more general term can, under a certain interpretation, describe Kubla Khan's building enterprise as well.

Spiritual Space

The foregoing theory may throw some new light on previous, well-established discussions of poetic metaphor. Thus, for instance, Wilson Knight's (and others') reconstruction of the "spiritual space" of Shakespeare's plays from the latter's recurrent imagery can be further articulated in terms of the present work. The lowest components of the images are usually active in the immediate context of the scene. The higher features are activated only when they recur in several images that are dissimilar on the lower level. Thus, for instance, to illustrate my point very briefly, in *Julius Caesar,* says Knight (1965: 34), "the flash of *metals* illumines the action" (my italics—R.T.). *Metals,* upon which Knight bases his interpretation, are relatively high on the list of features; they are embodied in the various references to daggers and swords, to crowns, gold, drachmas, Plutus' mine, an ass bearing gold, and so forth; the feature [+METAL] is only activated through accumulation and mutual reinforcement in the various concrete items. Thus, if Knight is right, the lowest features of Shakespeare's figurative language are used for communication as described above with relation to "unmarked" metaphors; the higher features are exploited for the generation of the play's "spiritual atmosphere". Consider the following lines:

> (54)   Nor stony tower, nor walls of beaten brass,
> Nor airless dungeon, nor strong links of iron,
> Can be retentive to the strength of spirit.
>
> (*Julius Caesar,* I. iii. 93–95)

Here, in the immediate context, *brass* and *iron* are grouped with materials and constructions that are exemplary for passive strength and impenetrability; with gold and lead, they are grouped as metals, but not as especially hard.

In Chapter 14, I am going to discuss the nature of recurring imagery in drama in general, and in Goethe's *Faust* in particular. The present conception may further articulate the picture there, where I discuss the opposite scene-terms in the Evening scene, in Gretchen's "small, neatly kept room". The same setting is perceived differently by Faust and Gretchen. Thus, for instance, Gretchen's room is praised by the enamored Faust as "How all about a sense impresses/ of quiet, order and content!" But when Gretchen enters, she feels "It is so close, so sultry, here! *(She opens a window)"*. Faust, on entering, invokes the twilight "O welcome, twilight soft and sweet", whereas Gretchen enters, a few minutes later, "carrying a lamp". The concrete features in this description and imagery refer to the concrete situation: some time has passed, and it has become darker. But for the sensitive Gretchen, her room is felt to be at once dark, sultry, and close: she has some elementary sensations relevant to the immediate scene, which on a higher level may be described as 'adverse to life', and are related to the death and rebirth themes of the play.

Rhyme and Meaning

In his paper "One Relationship between Rhyme and Reason", Wimsatt (1964) points out the difference between Chaucer's rhymes and Pope's. Chaucer's are "tame" rhymes, in which the same parts of speech are used in closely parallel functions, as in

> (55)   And he was clad in cote and hood of green.
>   A sheef of pecock arwes, bright and kene,
>   Under his belt he bar full thriftily,
>   Wel coude he dresse his takel yemanly ...

Not so Pope, who achieves his witty effects, among other means, by rhyming, e.g., nouns with verbs, verbs with adverbs, in different syntactic positions, as in

> (56)   Blessed with each talent and each art to please,
>   And born to write, converse, and live with ease,
>   Should such a man, too fond to rule alone,
>   Bear like a Turke, no brother near the throne ...

Such rhymes are perceived as *vigorous*. *Tame* and *vigorous* describe the perceived effects of these rhymes. The remark that vigorous rhymes involve different parts of speech describes their structure. The vigorous effect of "anti-grammatical" rhymes (Roman Jakobson's term) can be explained in terms of the semantic information-processing model expounded above. In Chapter 1, I briefly summarized Clark's research on word association. His findings can be accounted for by assuming that the responses obtained are produced according to the simplicity-of-production rule: "Perform the least change on the lowest feature, with the restriction that the result must correspond to an English word [...] Unsuccessful applications of simpler rules therefore force people to use more and more complex rules" (Clark, 1970: 280–281). Eventually, this amounts to the principle of exerting minimum effort. Anti-grammatical rhymes are produced contrary to the simplicity-of-production rule: 'Change as many features as possible, as high on the list as possible',[4] resulting in the assertion of maximum effort—hence its *vigorous* effect.

---

[4]   I have elsewhere (Tsur, 1983b) discussed at much greater length this conception of rhyme and semantic information-processing.

The semantic structure of the rhymes in (56) is, then, anti-grammatical; its perceived effect is vigorous and witty. It will be noticed that the rhymes in the overwhelming majority of Pope's couplets quoted throughout Chapter 5 are like that. In (57), however, the perceived effect is quite different. Here the rhymes enhance a certain "thing-free" atmosphere, and an intense, vague feeling rather than sharp wit:

> (57)   Here, where the world is quiet;   *Adj.*
>   Here, where all trouble seems   *V + 3rd pers. sing.*
>   Dead winds' and spent waves' riot   *N –plural*
>   In doubtful dreams of dreams;   *N +plural*
>   I watch the green field growing …*

In Chapter 4, I have distinguished between convergent and divergent structures in poetry, with their respective witty and emotional perceived qualities. (57) has a wide range of "divergent" elements. To mention only a few: one single compound sentence runs through the first five lines, overriding the closure of the symmetrical quatrain as well as its division into two symmetrical halves; *Dead* and *waves* in line 3, and *field* in line 5 are stressed syllables in weak positions, creating strings of two and three consecutive stressed syllables, blurring metric shape; the phrase structure too is very complex in line 3; on the semantic level, no entities that have stable characteristic visual shapes are mentioned in the quotation; the anaphoric *Here, where* in the first and second line arouses expectation that these two lines should be somehow parallel—instead, the first line parallels, syntactically, lines 2–4. Rhymes can, then, have not only different structures, with their respective "vigorous" and "tame" perceived effects; they also may be part of different types of *hyper-systems,* and infuse their respective witty and emotional perceived effects with some elusive kind of energy. My claim will be that the same semantic model that explains the perceived effects of the rhyme's *hypo-structure* also explains its contribution to the effect of *hyper-structure* (the last three italicized terms are taken from Eco, 1976).

Meaning as Oppositions & Degrees of Articulation

At the heart of componential analysis is the notion that semantic components reveal themselves in analogies among words. The method involves three steps, with the investigator's intuition important at each step:

> (1) Select a domain of words that all seem interrelated;
> (2) Form analogies among the words in the domain;
> (3) Identify the semantic components on the basis of analogies.
>   (Clark & Clark, 1977: 416)

Meaning, however, also implies opposition, based on those analogies.

Why should the sememe «dog» be opposed, let us say, to «cat», or to «kangaroo»? One suddenly realizes that this last question is the same as was posed by Jakobson [...] when asking why one phoneme should be opposed to another. In fact the definition of a phoneme as a minimal oppositional entity has to give way to a more analytical definition: a phoneme is a bundle of more analytical distinctive features, and the system of positions and oppositions is directly concerned with these features and not with the phoneme, which is only the result of a network of presences and absences of these features.

The same internal network of mutually opposed features should also rule the differences between two sememes. (Eco, 1976: 84)

We have considered a variety of verbal functions: knowing the meanings of words and the differences between them, Clark's version of the word-association game, and the response to anti-grammatical rhyme. All three are ruled by "the same internal network of mutually opposed features", which may or may not have a hierarchical structure. Whenever there is a hierarchical structure, ordinary linguistic competence tends to make use, for informative purposes, of the lowest features, whereas anti-grammatical rhyme tends to be effective in opposing relatively high features.

The foregoing description may help us to characterize what kind of a sign anti-grammatical rhyme is. If our description is adequate, the meaning units that constitute an anti-grammatical rhyme become an "internal network of mutually opposed features" in the fullest sense of the word. The "lower" features of the words are activated by their "informative" use in the syntagmatic linguistic strings; the "higher" features of the words are differentiated and activated by their opposition to higher features in their "rhyme-fellows"; they help to define one another more clearly. The members of anti-grammatical rhymes, therefore, can be characterized as being more than usually well-articulated; that is to say, grammatical and anti-grammatical rhymes are contrasted in their degree of articulation. There is in anti-grammatical rhyme some sort of an "inverted double articulation" (cf. Martinet, 1962). Its syntagmatic combination (first articulation) is on the phonological level, with a second articulation setting up as pertinent features the network of meaning components.

There is a gestalt rule that the expression conveyed by any form will be only as clear-cut as the perceptual features that carry it (cf. above, chapter 5). Consequently, the expression conveyed by poems abounding in anti-grammatical rhymes will be perceived, *ceteris paribus,* as more clear-cut than those abounding in grammatical rhymes.

If we accept the commonplace that language is the material (or one of the materials) of poetry, then this super-articulateness of anti-grammatic rhyme is not without aesthetic interest, in the light of the following comment by Eco:

Modern aesthetics would say that aesthetic enjoyment brings into play even microstructures of the material from which it is made. Which is true enough, except that a semiotic definition of these microstructures must go on to say that they represent the pertinent elements of a further segmentation of the material in question, thus suggesting the possibility of a more *Basic Form* of the expression. Aesthetics is not only concerned with hypersystems such as the various connotations that the work of art conveys above and beyond its immediate communicative appearance; it is also concerned with a whole series of hypostructures. (Eco, 1976: 265; Eco's italics)

Of particular interest for this conception of articulateness is Eco's discussion (ibid., 132), in a non-aesthetic context, of Peirces notion of "abduction" (or "hypothetic inference") and its emotional correlate, in which a "complicated feeling [...] is replaced by a single feeling of greater intensity". "Hypothesis substitutes, for a complicated tangle of predicates attached to one subject, a single conception [...]", Peirce says. "Thus the various sounds made by the instruments of an orchestra strike upon the ear, and the result is a peculiar musical emotion, quite different from the sounds themselves". Eco comments on this:

> If this interpretive movement stopped at the enjoyment of such an imprecise emotion, there would be neither abduction, nor anything else relevant to our present purposes. But the hypothetical movement is fulfilled when a new sense (a new combinational quality) is assigned to every sound, inasmuch as they compose the new contextual meaning of the musical piece. (ibid)

This suits, *mutatis mutandis,* admirably the particular structure and feeling of antigrammatical rhyme, which enables to see each "rhyme fellow" as a complicated tangle of features and as a single concept at one and the same time. By virtue of the oppositions, a new sense (a new combinational quality) is replacing, in antigrammatical rhyme, "a complicated feeling by a single feeling of greater intensity".

I have claimed that the same semantic model that explains the perceived effect of the rhyme's hypostructure also explains its contribution to the respective effects of the differing hyperstructures. There appears to be a considerable phenomenological difference between the effects of anti-grammatical rhyme in convergent and divergent contexts. One 'parsimonious' way to describe this effect would be that whatever the dominant perceptual quality of the poem, witty, emotional, or atmospherical, antigrammatical rhyme enhances it, infuses it so to speak with additional energy.

By now, however, we have conjectured enough about the mediating structure involved to be able to give a more specific account of how this energy yields different effects in different contexts. We have conceived of anti-grammatical rhymes as the "internal network of mutually opposed predicates" or features which is more than usually well articulated (its components are well defined and perceptible as more or less separated). As a result, the rhyming word is perceived as a single concept and as a complicated tangle of features at one and the same time. The separate components are conceived in a convergent context as packed more tightly together, thus increasing the number of the converging elements. Emotional and atmospherical effects are usually related with the respective degrees of moderately and highly diffuse textures. In such a context, the same separate elements appear to mingle in the background texture, to 'saturate' it, and thus to heighten its intensity or 'chroma'.

> "The function of poetry", wrote Jakobson in 1933, "is to point out that the sign is not identical with its referent; [...] along with the awareness of the identity of the sign and the referent [...] we need the consciousness of the inadequacy of this identity". (Erlich, 1965: 181)

Such a conception of poetry assigns a peculiar place to anti-grammatic rhyme. The oppositional activation of features higher on the list brings into foreground the meaning components of the words that constitute the rhyme; these components, as a rule, are not immediately associated with reference, and therefore not "automatically" identified with the referents. The "irrelevant features" render the sign-vehicle partially independent from the referent.

Poetic discourse, then, whether convergent and compact or divergent and fuzzy, is semantically better articulated than prosaic discourse. Both figurative language and rhyme increase the opposition and differentiation of meaning components—metaphor and simile at the lower end of the scale, symbol and anti-grammatical rhyme at the higher end.

CHAPTER 10

Literary Synaesthesia

The present chapter attempts to explore the nature of individual synaesthetic transfers, their perceived qualities, their wider aesthetic purpose as well as their contribution to their more immediate context in the poem as a whole. It also wants to offer tools that may account for the critics' intuitions concerning the perceived qualities of synaesthetic transfers.

The term *synaesthesia* suggests the joining of sensations derived from different sensory domains. One must distinguish between the joining of sense *impressions* derived from the various sensory domains, and the joining of *terms* derived from the *vocabularies* of the various sensory domains. The former concerns synaesthesia as a psychological phenomenon; the latter is *Verbal Synaesthesia. Literary Synaesthesia,* then, is the exploitation of verbal synaesthaesia for specific literary effects, of which the present chapter discusses: emotional and witty. In Romantic poetry and in 19th century Symbolism, Literary Synaesthesia typically contributes to some undifferentiated emotional quality, some "vague, dreamy, or uncanny hallucinatory moods", or some strange, magical experience or heightened mystery. In some varieties of mannerist poetry, as in some modernist and 17th century Metaphysical poetry, this typically makes for a witty quality. Literary synaesthesia is typically concerned with verbal constructs and not with "dual perceptions". When we use a synaesthetic metaphor, it is its *terms* that are derived from two sensory domains; the reality referred to may be evasive, undifferentiated, or "ineffable", even "supersensuous", but it need not necessarily belong to two different sensory domains.

Many writers on synaesthesia have been preoccupied with such questions as which synaesthetic metaphors are to be credited with the description of a "genuine", which ones merely of a "feigned", experience. W. B. Stanford (1942), for instance, collected a considerable number of synaesthetic metaphors, and pronounced his verdict on whether they reflected some genuine experience of the poet or some "concocted" experience. His intuitions are sensitive, but he seems incapable of accounting for them in any consistent, systematic manner. Most of his reasons are *ad hoc*, and rely on circumstantial evidence. As in the chapter on meter, concerning this issue, too, I shall perform a small "Copernican" revolution: rather than trying to reconstruct the poet's experience that gave rise to the metaphor, I shall attempt to offer tools that may account, as systematically as possible, for the *critics'* intuition in responding to the metaphor. The cognitive approach advocated in the present work assumes that sincerity, far from being a "biographical fact", is a perceptual quality of the poem or of the metaphor as a whole, *irrespective of what the poet actually felt when writing the poem.* The major assumption of the present work is that one may account in a fairly consistent manner for people's intuitions concerning the "genuineness" of synaesthetic transfers. Synaesthesia tends to sharpen the logical contradiction between the incompatible terms of a metaphor. Focusing one's attention on its incompatible terms generates a perceived effect of **wit**. Hence the "concocted" character of many of the inter-sense (or *cross-modal)* transfers. A low-differentiated emotional quality is perceived only when the incompatible terms appear to be smoothly **fused,** as when the reader **attends away** from the incompatible terms to some overwhelming passion, or to some thing-free and gestalt-free quality, arousing the intuition that the given synaesthetic metaphor reflects *genuine* experience. The effect of such a gestalt-free vision may be greatly enhanced in some situation defined "here-and-now", in which the perceiving consciousness is to locate itself in relation to its environment, very much in the manner of spatial orientation (cf. Chapters 15 and 24). And conversely, the presence of good shapes in the sound-stratum of the poem, or of objects with stable characteristic visual shapes in its world-stratum may impede the smooth fusion of the incompatible terms into a synaesthetic whole, and generate some witty quality.

I am going to consider six issues that affect the perceived **genuineness** or **ingenuity** of synaesthetic metaphors: the first is related with the opposition between focused gestalt and "undifferentiatedness", the second with highly and less differentiated sensory domains; the third concerns one's orientation-mechanism in a situation defined *here-and-now;* the fourth the introduction of opposite emotional tendencies, the fifth handles the multiple relationships between the incompatible terms of the metaphor. The sixth issue is related to the problem of "chaotic overdifferentiation".

The key-term to the first two issues is [±DIFFERENTIATION]. Ehrenzweig (1970: 135), who combines gestalt-psychology with psychoanalysis to explore art, speaks of "a creative ego rhythm that swings between focussed gestalt and an oceanic undifferentiation".[1] A cognitive explanation of this rhythm would point out that hard and fast categories (that eventually amount to *cognitive stability)* are indispensable for such elementary abilities as to recognize a person or a place as the same person or place on different encounters, or a series of vastly different sound-stimuli emitted by different speakers as the same word. But this cognitive stability is bought at the price of relinquishing subtle and minimal pre-categorial cues perceptible only by intuition, which are equally indispensable for survival.

One of man's greatest achievements is his cognitive differentiation. This accomplishment, however, plays the tyrant to him: the less differentiated processes become less accessible to him and less reliable. Ehrenzweig implies that religion and art are among the means that may yield some heightened consciousness of these less differentiated processes. Synaesthesia consist in regression to a state in which the various sensory domains are less than usually differentiated from one another.

---

1   In some of his publications, Ehrenzweig uses the term *undifferentiation,* in some, *dedifferentiation.* The former term suggests a state, the latter a process.

What is more, it imposes the dominance of the less differentiated sensory domains upon the more differentiated ones. Such sensory domains as touch, heat and weight can make fewer kinds of distinctions than, say, the senses of sight and hearing. They can also less reliably discriminate among the various degrees of the sensory attributes present in their respective domains. It is difficult even to differentiate between these three sensory domains, which are treated by many as a single sensory domain.

Another major source of the intuition that a given synaesthetic metaphor reflects *genuine* experience has been explored by Ullmann (1945, 1957). He investigated *statistical tendencies* and claimed that his statistical investigations "will give no information concerning any single transfer, but may say something about the general movement and dynamics of the processes" (Ullmann, 1957: 276). I shall claim, however, that knowing "something about the general movement and dynamics of the processes" may give us valuable insights into intuitions concerning single transfers as well.

Ullmann examined the intersense transfers in the poetry of twelve nineteenth-century poets in three languages, English, French and Hungarian. The direction of the transfers was checked. According to his findings, "transfers tend to mount from the lower to the higher reaches of the sensorium, from the less differentiated sensations to the more differentiated ones, and not vice versa" (Ullmann, 1957: 280).

> It is in strict conformity with the first tendency that the touch, the lowest level of the sensorium, should be the main purveyor of transfers. Though it is only one of six possible sources, it looms large in all twelve poets analysed. (ibid., 282)

The predominant destination, however, turned out, surprisingly, to be not the sense of sight, but the sense of sound, the second highest in the hierarchy. Ullmann interprets this as follows:

> Visual terminology is incomparably richer than its auditional counterpart, and has also far more similes and images at its command. Of the two sensory domains at the top end of the scale, sound stands more in need of external support than light, form or colour. (ibid., 283)

This explanation is not very convincing. Poverty of terminology is not the only (or even the main) reason for using metaphors in poetry. A principle of the Biblical "pauper's ewe" seems at work here. The richer the sensory domain, the more it "borrows", the poorer the domain, the more it "lends". As for the relative scarcity of the visual domain in Ullmann's findings, I argue that it is **visual shapes** that hinder intersense transfer. As Dombi's explorations of Hungarian impressionism may suggest, when attention is focused on **colors,** the visual sense does become the predominant destination in synaesthesia.

According to Ullmann's own data, it is precisely touch, the lowest level of senso-rium (with the poorest vocabulary) that is the main purveyor of transfers. For this, the reason seems that speaking of the more differentiated sensory domain in terms of a less differentiated one is a powerful means for achieving undifferentiatedness. Lan-guage being a highly categorized conceptual system, it would appear to be impossi-ble to talk about undifferentiated, pre-categorial sensory or emotional information. If this were true, such phrases as *verbal art,* or *mystic poetry* would have been a con-tradiction in terms. We know that this is not the case. One of the major assump-tions of the present work is that poetry in general, and figurative language in partic-ular, consist of a permanent pursuit after finding ways to overcome the tyranny of highly differentiated linguistic categories. Talking about sounds and colors in terms of the tactile or thermal vocabularies may convey just such an impression of their undifferentiated, pre-categorial sensory aspects.

Romantic poetry, perhaps more than any other trend, cultivates the "spontaneous overflow of powerful feeling". The tendency established by Ullmann in Romantic poetry seems to reflect some deep-seated cognitive structure that may serve as a ba-sis for distinguishing between *marked* and *unmarked* intersense transfers: when you speak of the "higher", more differentiated sense in terms of the "lower", less differen-tiated sense (that is, when you transfer *upwards*), it is the *unmarked* transfer. When you speak of the "lower", less differentiated sense in terms of the "higher", more dif-ferentiated sense (that is, you transfer *downwards),* it is the *marked* transfer. In the present context we should mention two universal features of markedness. First, the frequency of marked forms in a certain group of linguistic devices is smaller than, or equal to, but not higher than that of the unmarked forms. Second, the marked forms are perceived as less natural than the unmarked forms. This may well account for the fact that downward transfers are usually felt to be less smoothly integrated than up-ward transfers. This generalization is very frequently born out by the perceived qual-ity of individual transfers.

From the foregoing, one might predict that phrases like *soft sounds*, *warm sounds, soft colors, warm colors* would be judged as more natural than, e.g., *loud touch, loud temperature, green touch, green temperature*, or *minor-scale touch* or *variegated temperature*. In this respect, the idiomatic colloquial phrases seem to have taken forms that fit well with the natural constraints of the human mind.[2]

At this point I wish to consider a pair of examples by Keats, upon which most of the foregoing distinctions and generalizations may be focused.

---

[2]   In a series of well-controlled experiments, Yeshayahu Shen found that Hebrew-speaking subjects judge novel synaesthetic expressions that conform with Ull-mann's "panchronistic tendencies" as more natural and meaningful than those which run counter to it. This bias tends to override even linguistic conventions. He found similar tendencies in experiments with Indonesian subjects. These findings may indicate that the origins of these preferences are cognitive rather than gram-matical, pragmatic (e.g., conventionality) or cultural conditioning.

(1)   And taste the music of that vision pale.

(Keats, *Isabella*: XLIX)

(2)   The same bright face I tasted in my sleep

(Keats, *Endymion*, I: 895)

Some evasive *mood,* some uncanny atmosphere, is suggested in (1). It is generated with the help of the double intersense transfer, both in the expected direction, **upward**, that is, it speaks of *vision* in terms of *music*; and of *music*, in turn, in terms of *taste*. It should be noticed that though *vision* belongs to the visual vocabulary, it is a thing-free quality, detached from any stable, characteristic visual shape. *Vision,* in distinction from *sight*, refers not only to what is seen, but also to an impassioned state of mind with uncanny connotations. The paleness of the vision may be associated with the paleness of the dead, or of Isabella, or of the moonlit scene. This multiple relationship enhances the *vagueness* of the description. *Music* connotes a pleasant fusion of sounds, expanding toward the perceiving self; the transfer to a lower sense, *taste,* enhances the indistinctness of the fused sensations. The powerful fusion of the discordant senses heightens the discharge of emotions, eliminating the contradictory sensuous ingredients, leaving the reader with the *feel* of a supersensuous, mysterious atmosphere.

As for (2), Ullmann finds that it is a strange phrase (1957: 287). I have suggested above that intersense transfer is more capable of splitting the focus of perception than ordinary metaphor. To elicit an emotional rather than witty response requires fusion of the sensory information into a 'soft focus'. Well-defined shapes tend to resist this fusion, whereas thing-free qualities promote it. In the foregoing two examples, "The same bright face I tasted" and "And taste the music of that vision pale" there is an "upward" transfer, from tasting to seeing, and as such, both ought to be perceived as "smooth" and "natural". The characteristic shape of *face,* however, appears to be an obstacle to *tasting*. That seems the source of the "strangeness" of the expression.

Recently, Ramachandran and Hubbard (2001: 28), who believe that synaesthesia result from electric overflow or short circuit between neighboring brain centers, attempted to give a neurological account of this kind of metaphors. They hypothesised that if there is cross-wiring between adjoining brain regions, "between primary gustatory cortex and adjoining hand and face regions of primary somatosensory cortex, the result might be a person who 'tastes shapes'". What can we learn from this about the literary effect of excerpt 2? Not very much. Suppose we became convinced that Ramachandran and Hubbard's hypothesis applied to 's brain. We would account by it for the genesis of the figure, not its literary effect. It would not change Ullmann's impression that "it is a strange phrase", that is, that tasting an object with a stable characteristic visual shape yields a marked synaesthetic metaphor, with all the stylistic implications of this. Genetic explanations are guided by principles that are different from those guiding aesthetic explanations.

With this problem in mind, I had a look at Cytowic's (2003) book *The Man Who Tasted Shapes*. To Cytowic's surprise, the phenomenon had nothing to do with visual shapes. "'This a mental image you see?' I asked. 'No, no,' he stressed 'I don't see anything. I don't imagine anything. I *feel* it in my hands as if it were in front of me'" (65). Later Cytowic summed up: "His sensations were elementary things, like hard and soft; a smooth, rough, or squashy texture; warm or cool surfaces" (67). Moreover, in the passage "Oh, dear," he said, slurping a spoonful, "there aren't enough points on the chicken" (3), Cytowic's informant doesn't speak of shapes in terms of taste (as "tasting shapes" would imply), but of tastes in terms of the sense of touch. In fact, *The Man who Palpated Tastes* would be a more appropriate title for this book. This, then, turned out to be a touch→taste association, in perfect compliance with Ullmann's panchronistic tendencies, as well as with my claim that stable visual shapes resist smooth synaesthesia. So, tasting a face, *pace* Ramachandran and Hubbard, would not comply with the synaesthetic perceptions of Cytowic's informant either. It would appear that Ramachandran and Hubbard's speculations were prompted by the misnomer of Citowic's book.

In a similar way one might explain why the problem of Homer's sincerity in using "lily-voiced cicadas" so much troubled W.B. Stanford. If the connotation *white* of the lilies is relevant here, it is a downward transfer, and has some strangeness about it. If, as Stanford suggests, "apparently what was suggested to his mind, by the smooth, liquid voice of the insects, was the silky cool texture of the lily" (Stanford, 1942: 30), it would be a touch→sound (and temperature→sound) transfer, that of the highest frequency. If it is a smell→sound transfer, though one of the rarest in Ullmann's texts, it is still an upward one. Why, then, is its "sincerity" so doubtful? Obviously, because "lily" is too concrete an object for intersense transfer, and its definite shape is not very likely to dissolve into a gestalt-free quality. Stanford supports the *sincerity* of this synaesthetic metaphor by the more "obvious sincerity" of three other ones in Homer: *woolly screaming, dry sound,* and *parched sound* (ibid., 29–30). Now this kind of argument is fallacious. Supposing that we *can* argue about the relative sincerity of metaphoric transfers, we still need not accept that *all* the metaphors of a poet are uniformly sincere or insincere. Homer *could be* sincere in writing *woolly screams* and insincere in writing *lily-voiced cicadas*. If, however, we make our judgments, relying on the criteria expounded above, we should note, first of all, that the "more obviously sincere" transfers are, in the first place, gestalt-free entities that, unlike *lily,* lack characteristic visual shapes. Second, we have here touch→sound transfers, which are obviously the most frequent kind of transfer according to Ullmann's findings. In certain contexts, *woolly screams* may be construed as a **transferred epithet**, that is, as "the screaming of some woolly [animal]". But even so, the transferred-epithet construal may serve as a realistic motivation for some real intersense transfer, in which such tactile predicates as *soft* and *thick* are abstracted from *woolly* and applied to the sound texture.

Stanford himself handles Homer's touch→sound transfers in a very different way. "These four are all descriptions of things heard in terms of physical texture or touch—some slight evidence for the tradition that Homer [...] was blind" (ibid., 30). Now, the panchronistic tendencies discovered by Ullmann compel us to come to one of two conclusions. Either that all Romantic poets who had recourse to synaesthetic metaphor were blind, or that these tendencies reflected some different psychological mechanism. It would appear that the second conclusion may account for a greater number of facts known about poems and poets.

My own position in this respect is that literary synaesthesia cannot be defended or attacked on grounds of sincerity; that sincerity is an impression, a perceptual quality of a text, not necessarily a biographical fact—at any rate, it is difficult or impossible to trace it as such. It can be best dealt with as a corollary of the poem's rhetorical appeal. Stanford's article offers several extremely instructive examples of synaesthetic transfers, as well as examples of his own reaction to them. As we have seen, Stanford is mainly engaged in the genetic explanation of the transfers. The problem of sincerity troubles him more than anything else. Quotations from Herbert and Crashaw "seem sincere", on circumstantial evidence, unlike a quotation from Donne, which is "a concoction, not a description of an experience" (ibid., 27–28). "Hopkins' imagery is guaranteed by his recorded experiences". Consequently, "the fact that he, a poet of sheer sincerity and an abhorrer of rhetoric, could speak of a sound as being 'orange' is some evidence that Oscar Wilde was not merely being ingenious when he described music as 'scarlet'" (29).

Stanford was a very perceptive reader of poetry, and had some fine insights into the perceived qualities of synaesthetic metaphors. However, he assumed that sincerity is a biographical fact in extraliterary reality. As I have suggested, the cognitive approach advocated in the present work assumes that sincerity, far from being a "biographical fact", is a perceptual quality of the poem or of the metaphor as a whole, *irrespective of what the poet actually felt when writing the poem.* Instead of hunting down the alleged biographical facts in extraliterary reality, cognitive poetics proposes to explain the reader's (or the critic's) intuition who perceives a certain quality in a poem or a metaphor. I shall try, then, some of Stanford's fine insights against the nonintentionalistic frame of reference expounded in the present study. First, let us consider Jules Romain's two verse lines (quoted by Stanford, 1942: 28)

(3)   Le lac sonnait midi d'un tel coup de lumière
        Que l'eau même semblait une forme de feu ...

which Stanford presents as an instance of true synaesthetic metaphors, i.e., direct and literal descriptions of actual (and often unusual) experiences, as opposed to "ingenious presentations of not very extraordinary concepts".

Consider, then, Stanford's phrase "actual experience"; if he means by it *sincere experience*, it is hardly possible to discuss it. If, however, one is to understand this as an *immediate, concrete* situation rather than a *general* concept, one can make out an arguable case for his position: in Jules Romain's lines, there seems to be an immediately perceived, concrete landscape. How does this affect the impression formulated by Stanford? I have alluded above to the view that language and other "linear" activities typically appear to consciousness as compact and logical, whereas such global processes as intuitions, emotions, mystic experiences as well as spatial orientation appear as diffuse. Poetry is a constant struggle to overcome the tyranny of conceptual language, and convey vague, diffuse qualities with the help of words. One conspicuous technique is to get the reader to imagine some concrete landscape, in which information is diffuse, not focused, and which, *via* the orientation mechanism, activates the emotional mode of information-processing (see below, Chapters 15 and 24). Discussing general concepts (even such concepts as *intuition*) requires, in Arnheim's term, "an actively organizing mind". Actual insight, on the other hand, requires a receptive attitude, an openness—not to preconceived concepts, but to evanescent, shapeless impressions, in a concrete situation. In the two lines by Jules Romain, there is a particular landscape, at a particular time. *"Coup de lumière"* conveys a notion of ampleness, as well as fleeting suddenness. These qualities mutually reinforce each other with similar qualities connoted by *sonnait*. *Feu* in the next line amplifies *lumière*, adding to the visual and auditory the lower thermal sensation. The identification of water with fire heightens the intensities of the interplay of senses; this oxymoron is mitigated by *semblait*, and integrated by the possible verisimilitude of a nature image, so that the reader's reason is "not too much shocked by it". It should be noticed, in addition, that although a concrete landscape has been indicated, not one of the seven nouns denotes an object that has a characteristic, differentiated visual shape. This may heighten the impact of an intense, thing-free quality perceived in a concrete landscape.

Now let us consider the second sentence of Stanford's paper and briefly comment on the short examples piled up in it. Synaesthesia, he says,

> has been developed to an extreme by Miss Sitwell who writes of a "rustling sun", "shrill leaves", the "busy chatter of heat", and describes how

> The light is braying like an ass

and

> The morning light creaks down again

> (ibid., 26)

Stanford's formulation appears to suggest that he considers Edith Sitwell's synaesthetic metaphors as facetious, or unnatural, or witty or, in more recent terminology, marked. What is it that makes her synaesthesia so "extreme"? The short answer is that in all of them, the undifferentiated fusion of senses is impeded in one of the ways discussed in the present chapter. In "rustling sun" and "shrill leaves", the epithet is drawn from the auditory, the noun from the visual domain; thus, it is an upward transfer, and as such it ought to be "natural". However, the nouns denote solid objects with stable visual shapes. "The light is braying like an ass" and "The morning light creaks down again", too, transfer from the auditory to the visual domain, and *light* denotes a thing-free and gestalt-free quality; but the fusion is impeded by the introduction of opposite emotional tendencies, *light* indicating some positive, *braying like an ass*—some negative emotional attitude. The same conflicting tendencies may characterize the attribution of "creaks down" to "the morning light". In the "busy chatter of heat", the transfer goes downward from the auditory to the thermal sense and splits the focus of perception; and it is further domesticated by the adjective "busy". In this downward transfer considerable tension arises between the differentiated notion *chatter* and undifferentiated notion *heat.* Stanford quotes the following lines from Donne's Elegy IV (*The Perfume*)

(4)   A loud perfume, which at my entrance cryed,
       Ev'n at thy father's nose.,

and suggests, that it is "a concoction, not a description of an experience" (ibid., 27–28). In terms of the present study, the witty quality of Donne's *loud perfume* is due, first and foremost, to the downward, sound→scent transfer. As we might expect from Ullmann's panchronistic tendencies, *loud perfumes* should be perceived as less natural than, say, *loud colours.* But the "incompatibility" of the epithet with the noun is further emphasized by a second term drawn from the auditory domain *(cryed),* forcing the reader to focus attention on the more highly differentiated sensory domain. Moreover, although *perfume* denotes a thing-free and gestalt-free *diffuse* entity, it is **focused,** in Donne's verse, "Ev'n at thy father's nose".

The nature of *loud perfume* will be illuminated from an unexpected angle, if we compare it to an antonymous phrase. Dombi (1974: 37) quotes the phrase *néma illat* ("mute scent") from an unnamed Hungarian impressionist poet. One might expect it to have a similar quality to that of *loud perfume.* It hasn't, however. It sounds much more "natural", much less witty, much more "experiential". There appear to be three reasons for this. First, *mute*—although derived from a high, differentiated sensory domain—implies the **absence** of the [auditory] gradient indicated by it, and thus emphasizes precisely the lack of perceptibility, the lack of differentiation of the scent. Second (in the isolated quotation, at least), the diffuse scent has *not* been *focused* (as in Donne's poem) around someone's nose. Third but not least, Donne's metaphor merely translates "one sense impression into the terms of another sense", pointing up a single ingredient relevant in *loud,* that could just as well be paraphrased as *strong;* whereas *mute scent,* under the construal suggested above, generates a multiple relationship between its terms, suggesting both the presence and the absence of the sensory stimulus. In this way, this metaphor approaches a more complex conception of synaesthesia that enables "the poet to combine the power of several sense impressions into one collective impression"—in Erika Erhardt-Siebolt's formulation (1932).

Finally, Richard H. Fogle has gathered an impressive collection of quotations in his paper "Synaesthetic Imagery in Keats" (1964). Though unaware of the tendencies established by Ullmann, most of his examples, naturally, conform with them. He, however, is arrested by the following "startling synaesthetic image from *Endymion*":

(5)   [...] lost in pleasure at her feet he sinks,
       Touching with *dazzled lips her starlight hands*.
                                        (Keats, *Endymion*, IV, 418–19)

Fogle aptly remarks: "There is a trace of 'wit' of conscious ingenuity which lends to the image a certain flavor of modernity" (Fogle, 1964: 43), but says nothing that might account for its wit and "flavor of modernity". It is two of the principles discussed in the present chapter that can account for this impression. First, we have here a sight→touch transfer, a transfer that runs contrary to the panchronistic tendencies; second, the synaesthetic transfer involves here two solid "objects", *lips* and *hands*.

When in *A Midsummer Night's Dream* Shakespeare parodies synaesthetic metaphor, he violates precisely the two principles discussed here in order to achieve a ludicrous effect:

(6)   Pyr. I see a voice; now will I to the chink,
       To spy an I can hear my Thisby's face.

"I see a voice" is a downward transfer; and the upward transfer "hear my Thisby's face" involves a stable characteristic visual shape. The ludicrous effect is reinforced by the mechanical interchange of the verbs "see" and "hear"—something mechanical encrusted on the living.

Notwithstanding our foregoing discussion, in certain circumstances downward synaesthetic transfer *is* acceptable as "smooth, natural, genuine". To explain this, let us briefly review some of our basic generalizations. Synaesthetic transfer is perceived as "smooth, natural, genuine", first, when we speak of the more differentiated sense in terms of the less differentiated sense, in an attempt to capture those aspects of physical and psychological reality that are too little differentiated for a highly differentiated conceptual language; second, when both terms of the metaphor refer to thing-free and gestalt-free qualities. The effect of these conditions may be strongly reinforced when those thing-free and gestalt-free qualities occur in the vast perspectives of a "concrete situation", defined "here and now", in which the orientation mechanism may be supposed to function, processing information diffusely and readily integrating many inputs at once. We have found that both downward transfers and strong shapes are hostile to the "smooth, natural, genuine" fusion of senses in synaesthesia. As I have suggested, the two transfers are related *via* the notion [±DIFFERENTIATION]. Downward transfer means to talk about the lesser differentiated sense in terms of the more highly differentiated one; whereas **shape** may be regarded as a kind of stylistic "mean" lying between the extremes of chaotic overdifferentiation and primordial homogeneity (cf. Meyer, 1957: 161). Likewise, consciousness and rationality are *differentiated,* just as emotional and unconscious processes are undifferentiated.

We may find, quite frequently, that in Impressionist and Symbolist poetry downward transfer may be perceived as "smooth" and suggesting some "genuine mood", when its differentiating effect becomes part of, and is intensified by, some kind of "chaotic overdifferentiation" (reinforced, more often than not, by the activity of the orientation mechanism, in a concrete situation defined "here and now"). Now it should be noticed that—paradoxically enough—the fine distinctions of synaesthesia, too, may typically lead to overdifferentiation. When the Hungarian Impressionist poet Árpád Tóth says

(7)   És felzokog egy *felhorzsolt illaton,*
        Mely vesztett édent éreztet vele.

        (He breaks into sobbing on a *bruised scent,*
        Which arouses in him a feel of lost Eden),

he suggests some barely noticeable aspect of the scent; and it is precisely this undifferentiated quality that may remind one of sensations and experiences hardly accessible to consciousness or introspection. "The synaesthetical attribute *bruised* represents the aching mood of remembrance with the materialization of the past scent" (Dombi, 1974: 40). "Aching" is too strong a word here. The Hungarian past participle *felhorzsolt* suggests abrasion, bruising caused by almost smooth rubbing or friction. The meaning components "fine texture" and "friction" are more salient in it than "pain" of any sort. Our basic level perception of the world is typically based on much "grosser" percepts. A universe that is perceived through a multitude of such fine undifferentiated sensations is experienced as suffering from "chaotic overdifferentiation". There arises some kind of "perceptual overload", which the cognitive system handles by fusing the "overwhelming" amount of information in some continuous, low differentiated mass, very much in the way it "dumps" in the background, in painting and music, all the information that exceeds its handling capacity (see above, Chapter 2). Impressionist and Symbolist poetry not infrequently resort to downward transfers in a context that generates precisely such chaos and overdifferentiation. In Chapter 20, I shall discuss at great length Baudelaire's "Correspondances". Among other things, I shall claim there that owing to the various techniques of "thing-destruction" and synaesthesia, we have in that poem an overdifferentiated chaotic universe that cannot be disturbed, only corroborated, by downward transfers.

A happy state of chaotic fusion of senses in the author's early childhood is described in the first chapter of the autobiographical novel *Saphiah* (Aftergrowth) by the great Hebrew Romantic poet, Bialik. From this chaotic fusion of senses, no stable world has yet been constructed by personal consciousness:

> (8)   At times I heard the silence and saw the voices, because my senses knew no limits and boundaries yet, and entered into each other's domains. The sound drew along the sight, the sight the sound, and the scent—both.

In such a "chaotic" state of fusion, it is quite insignificant whether the less differentiated senses draw along the more differentiated ones, or *vice versa*. The immense "intuitive" effect of this description is reinforced by two further elements: that the sensations or percepts are mentioned here apart from the objects or events of which they are attributes; and that they are preceded by an oxymoron *(I heard the silence)*.

The present chapter has pointed out a "double-edged" quality of synaesthetic metaphors. In some instances, they are perceived as "witty", in some others as expressing the experiencing of some ineffable reality. Some critics speak in the latter case of a genuine experience, whereas in the former case they call it a concoction of an experience, or the like. Usually, they have difficulties in accounting for such verdicts, and their utterances have the appearance of arbitrariness. The present chapter has attempted to introduce method into this "madness". First, it shifted the focus of attention from the author's experience, as inaccessible to the critic, to the reader's intuitions. Second, it substituted descriptive for evaluative terms. Third, it attempted to show that these descriptive terms can quite consistently capture the differences between synaesthetic metaphors judged genuine, respectively concocted. Finally, it attempted to show that these distinctions conform with some of the more general assumptions of Cognitive Poetics; sometimes they even rely on some of the cognitive mechanisms discussed in the other chapters of the present book.[3]

---

[3]   For more details, see the chapter of the same title in my book *On Metaphoring* (Tsur, 1987 b).

CHAPTER 11

The Representative Anecdote:
Human Contingency

If the sound stratum is the most amenable to systematic exploration by Cognitive Poetics, what Wellek and Warren call "the world stratum" is least amenable to it. The world consists of an infinite number of kinds of elements, which may occur in predictable or unpredictable combinations. In the present chapter, I shall make an attempt to offer a *model* of the world with the help of which, imperfect and tentative as it may be, one may make some significant and systematic distinctions of aesthetic interest. In the subsequent chapters, poetic styles and systematic distinctions between them will be discussed time and again. In these chapters, styles will be discussed as **regulative concepts,** as principles that organize in certain typical ways the poetic norms on the various strata of Wellek and Warren's model of a poem (presented in Chapter 2). However, poetic style does not imply **organization** only, but also the focusing of attention on, or "the efficient overstressing of", certain sections of reality. So, if this aspect of poetic style, too, is to be handled in a systematic way, some model of reality must be presented. This will be done in the present brief chapter.

In Chapter 1, I had recourse to Victor Shklovsky (1965: 12) and Walter Pater (1951: 896) in an exposition of the purpose of art. "If the whole complex lives of many people", Shklovsky quotes Tolstoy, "go on unconsciously, then such lives are as if they had never been". Thus, the reason that "art exists [is] that one may recover the sensation of life [...]. The purpose of art is to impart the sensation of things as they are perceived and not as they are known". Pater contends that "art comes to you proposing frankly to give nothing but the highest quality to your moments as they pass". Toward the end of Chapter 1, I state, in harmony with this view: "A major claim of some conventional as well as of Cognitive Poetics is that poetry yields an heightened consciousness". In conformity with his aestheticist conception, Pater completes his dictum by "and simply for those moments' sake". The cognitive perspective adopted here (not to mention Tolstoy's view of art) oblige us to say something about the wider situation in which "the sensation of life" occurs. While the bulk of the present book is devoted to issues concerning cognitive processes in their relationship to the structural phenomena and perceptual qualities of literature, by contrast, the present, relatively brief, chapter is devoted to an existential situation: the kind of situation in which a heightened consciousness arises. We shall also attempt to follow up some of the more significant aesthetic implications of this existential situation. On the one hand, we shall use it to distinguish between a variety of style-types: Romantic vs. Metaphysical, and these two vs. Modern Absurd Literature. On the other hand, it will be considered how this conception may account for a certain, typically Romantic, imagery.

What we are here after is quite complex. It must be, on the one hand, significantly relevant to a great variety of (if not *most* or *all*) works of art, or at least of literature. On the other hand, it must do justice to the significant differences between them. There is a great danger—witness the work of many literary critics and theorists—that such an "existential situation" tends to reduce all literature or all art to a single "essence". However, what I am pursuing here is to elucidate the nature of individual works of literature, of genres, of styles, both in their individuality and their relationship to one another. I have referred, on several occasions, in the present study to Burke's distinction between a "proportionalizing" and an "essentializing" (or "reductionist") strategy of analysis. What we need is a technique that *reduces* the complex situation to a highly generalized situation that may be relevant to the analysis of a wide range of works, genres, styles; and still does not lose sight of the *proportions* between the elements that constitute their structures, and thus can do justice to them in their "uniqueness", that is, can account for the differences between them as well. To this end, I propose to adapt Burke's notion of the "representative anecdote".

> Men seek for vocabularies that will be faithful *reflections* of reality. To this end, they must develop vocabularies that are *selections* of reality. And any selection of reality must, in certain circumstances, function as a *deflection* of reality. Insofar as the vocabulary meets the needs of reflection, we can say that it has the necessary scope. In its selectivity it is reduction. Its scope and reduction become a deflection when the given terminology, or calculus, is not suited to the subject matter which it is designed to calculate. (Burke, 1962: 59)

Burke calls such selections of reality *representative anecdotes*. Hyman (1955: 329, 335) suggests the term *key metaphor* for them. At various times, Burke used different key metaphors ("Note the progress of his key metaphors Man as Declaimer in *Counter-Statement,* to Man as Artist in *Permanence and Change,* Man as Gesturer in *Attitudes Toward History,* and Man as Warrior in *The Philosophy of Literary Form*" [Hyman, 1955: 332] and, eventually, the key metaphor of "drama" or "dramatism" in *A Grammar of Motives* [ibid., 335]). Burke calls the first section of *The Philosophy of Literary Form* "Situations and Strategies". On the first page he begins by distinguishing between these two notions:

So I should propose an initial working distinction between "strategies" and "situations", whereby we think of poetry (I use the term to include any work of critical or imaginative cast) as the adopting of various strategies for the encompassing of situations. These strategies size up the situations, name their structure and outstanding ingredients, and name them in a way that contains an attitude towards them. [...] Consider a proverb, for instance. Think of the endless variety of situations, distinct in their particularities, which this proverb may "size up", or attitudinally name. (Burke, 1957: 4)

Such a conception of "representative anecdotes" is strikingly similar to D'Andrade's conception of values as "a complex association of symbol and affect—that is, of representations of states of affairs associated with feelings and emotions" quoted in Chapter 1.

In Chapter 14 I shall apply to archetypal patterns Kenneth Burke's image of hub-and-spokes from his slogan "the Ritual Drama as 'Hub'". I suggest that it may fruitfully be applied to "representative anecdotes" as well. Not as the *sole* hub, but *one possible* hub out of several ones. I propose to take the representative anecdote as "'hub', with all other aspects of human action treated as spokes radiating from this hub". As will be seen, a variety of literary styles may be regarded as "the 'efficient' overstressing of one or another of the ingredients" found in the underlying *representative anecdote*. The image of hub-and-spokes suggests a "proportionalizing", nonreductionist approach. Nonetheless, one must supplement it with the conception of the literary work, genre and style as stratified systems of norms, as put forward in Chapters 2 and 12, so as to keep them in their right proportions.

The Representative Anecdote: Man as Prisoner

In order to obtain a *representative anecdote* sufficiently wide to cover a *condition humaine* underlying a wide variety of historical and cultural situations from which artistic styles and genres may have cropped, I am turning to a conception originally expounded in theology, which I have found very useful for my purpose. I contend that the *representative anecdote* proposed below may point up significant relationships between such remote literary styles as Romantic poetry and Metaphysical poetry, both in their devotional and secular aspects, and some varieties of modernistic literature (e.g., Absurd Drama or Kafka). My *representative anecdote* is the archetypal situation in which, according to Gordon D. Kaufman, people use "God-talk", that is, language in which such terms as *God*, or *the gods, angels, demons, the other world*, and so on, occur. "Such speech appears within the context of man's sense of limitation, finitude, guilt, and sin, on the one hand, and his question about the meaning or value or significance of himself, his life, and his world, on the other" (Kaufman, 1972: 46). Such questions seem to be strongly relevant to literature in most cultural periods, even if it is not of the religious kind at all.

> In this respect the idea of God functions as a *limiting concept,* that is, a concept that does not primarily have content in its own right drawn directly out of a specific experience, but refers to that which we do *not* know but which is the ultimate limit of all our experiences. [...] It must be observed that we [...] are also involved in a certain duality here, between what is in fact concretely experienced, and the limit(s) of all experience and knowledge. (ibid., 47–48)[1]

What literary movements as different as Metaphysical poetry, Romantic poetry and Absurd drama or literature of extreme situations (as, e.g., Kafka) have in common is a feeling of human limitedness, being confined to the "here and now"; but against this common background of shared feeling illuminating distinctions can be made. Kaufman's formulation may help us to make two sets of distinctions. First, between Metaphysical and Romantic poetry on the one hand, and certain versions of modernistic literature (Absurd Drama, for instance), on the other; and second, between the two poetic styles, Romantic and Metaphysical, themselves. One important feature of the *absurd,* for instance, is the sense of human limitation "heightened, to any limit heightened", in a world in which "God is dead". Whereas for the Absurd drama any attempt to transcend this world is utterly futile, Romantic and Metaphysical poetry set themselves to *transcend* the limit. Most conspicuous and intriguing from the point of view of Cognitive Poetics is the observation that both Romantic and Metaphysical poetry are typically set in a concrete situation sharply defined *here and now.* Kaufman's conception of the nature of the ultimate and the immediate limit is illuminating here.

> For the awareness of finitude is not purely conceptual or hypothetical; it is an awareness of *my actual being* as here (in this time and place) rather than there, as restricted in this particular concrete way [...]. It is the awareness of *my being limited* that we are here dealing with and thus in some sense an actual "encounter" with that which *limits me.* (ibid., 54)

It seems to be this *my being limited here and now* that mystics of all ages and religions attempt to transcend. How do we experience the Ultimate Limit? Kaufman makes the following suggestion (which is at variance with some of the existentialist literature):

---

[1]   Kaufman carefully emphasizes that his paper "is concerned with the question of the *meaning* rather than the *truth* of statements containing the word 'God'. No attempt will be made here to prove either that God does or does not exist, that is, that the word 'God' does or does not actually relate to a reality. Questions of that sort can be faced only if we already know what we mean when we use the word 'God'" (ibid., 44–45). In a recent book on religious and mystic poetry (Tsur, 2003) I have "returned" Kaufman's model to its theological context.

All that we ever experience directly are particular events of suffering, death (of others), joy, peace, and so forth. It is only in *reflection upon these* and the attempts to *understand ourselves in the light of these happenings* that we become aware of our limitedness on all sides. Along with this awareness of our being hemmed in, powerful emotions of terror, despair, revulsion, anxiety, and the like, are often—perhaps always—generated, and this total intellectual-emotional complex may then be called the "experience of finitude" or awareness of the "boundary situation" or something of the sort. But it must be observed that this experience of radical contingency is not an *immediate* awareness of restriction, as when one butts one's head against a stone wall; it depends rather upon a generalization from such occasional immediate experience of limitation to the total situation of the self. [...] Thus, the so-called experience of finitude or contingency, however powerful the emotions that accompany and deepen and reinforce it, has an intellectual root, and it is possible only because man is a reflective being. (ibid., 52–53)

This description of "the so-called experience of finitude or contingency" may indicate, within the framework of a situation sharply defined here and now, the distinction between Romantic and Metaphysical poetry. We have said that what these two poetic styles have in common with Theatre of the Absurd is a feeling of human limitedness, being confined to the "here and now". However, unlike the Theatre of the Absurd, Romantic and Metaphysical Poetry assume that there *is* some other world that enables the transcendence of our limited world.

As for the distinction between Metaphysical and Romantic poetry, it is not merely a difference between their respective presentations of "here" and "there", but also, and more important for our purpose, a difference in the emphasis given to their relative weight. Metaphysical poetry typically focuses attention upon the "total intellectual-emotional complex", the "powerful emotions [of terror, despair, revulsion, anxiety, and the like]" *and,* at the same time, upon the "intellectual root" of the experience.[2] Metaphysical Poetry typically focuses attention upon the afore-said emotional and intellectual processes, while also giving some indication of the attempt to transcend the ultimate limit. Romantic poetry, in turn, typically *attends away from* these processes *to* the attempt to transcend the ultimate limit. At the same time, much of Romanticism's culture-pessimism draws upon this "awareness of our being hemmed in". Furthermore, just as the "generalization from such occasional immediate experience of limitation to the total situation of the self" may account for the structure of the typical Metaphysical reasoning, it may also account for the structure of the typical Romantic nature imagery, which consists in a nature description that

[2]   That may be one of the things implied by Sir Herbert Grierson (1965) when he characterizes Metaphysical Poetry as "a strain of passionate paradoxical reasoning". The point appears to be that both passion and reasoning are separately amplified up to a point when they are not in harmony with one another any more.

is at once a real situation and the vehicle of a metaphor pointing to some more general idea, or some supersensory reality.[3] The two styles differ in the extent of the presence and explicitness of their inferences. While in Metaphysical poetry the reader is aware of complex inferences during the transition from the image upon which his awareness is focused, in Romantic poetry the transition occurs with the immediateness of perception.

Of considerable literary interest we may find the following distinction, also due to Kaufman:

> The self's awareness of being restricted on all sides, rendering problematic the very meaning of existence, gives rise to the question: *What* is it that in this way hems us in? How is this *ultimate* Limit, of which we are aware in the "experience of finitude", to be conceived? There appear to be four fundamental types of limiting experience, and these supply models with the aid of which the ultimate Limit can be conceived. The first two are relatively simple: (a) selves experience external *physical* limitation and restriction upon the activities through the resistance of material objects over and against them; (b) they experience from within the *organic* limitation of their own powers, especially in illness, weakness, failure, and exhaustion. The other two are somewhat more complex: (c) they experience the external *personal* limitation of other selves engaged in activities and programs running counter to their own—the clash of wills, decisions, and purposes—but precisely because matters of volition and intention are subjective, this experience is neither simply internal, nor external, but is interpersonal and social; (d) they experience the *normative* constraints and restrictions upon them, expressed in such distinctions as true-false, real-illusory, good-bad, right-wrong, beautiful-ugly, which distinctions, though felt subjectively and from within, appear to the self not to be its own spontaneous creations but to impinge upon it with categorical demands and claims. (ibid., 56)

Based on these limiting experiences, Kaufman puts forward in this and the next chapter of his book two models of transcendence (and of God): the *interpersonal* and the *teleological*. The former assumes that "insofar as our knowledge of another self emerges within the process of communication, we are here encountering a reality which is, strictly speaking, beyond the reach and observation of our senses, which, therefore, must be understood in contrast to objects of ordinary sensory perception" (ibid., 74). The latter proceeds from the assumption that "a self is able to formulate objectives, to set them as goals to be realized, and then to organize his life in such a way as to move toward and often to realize them" (ibid., 75). These two models of

---

[3]   In this case, and in contrast to Metaphysical poetry, there are efforts to keep the situation, the generalization, and the passion abstracted in harmony with one another. This is one way to indicate the nature of the "integrated focus" discussed in chapter 4.

transcendence lead to quite diverse theological conceptions. The interpersonal model leads to personalistic notions of ultimate reality, whereas

> If one makes teleological transcendence the model, one is led toward a theology of *being*. The ultimate reality will be understood as the good "which moves [all other things but is] itself unmoved". All finite reality will be viewed as necessarily grounded in this ultimate reality, and as, in turn, striving toward it (ibid., 77).

One can briefly illustrate this distinction *via* the following verse by the eleventh-century Hebrew poet, Ibn Gabirol, in which both conceptions are manifest in a peculiar way:

וְהוּא נִכְסָף לְשׁוּמוֹ יֵשׁ כְּמוֹ יֵשׁ / כְּמוֹ חוֹשֵׁק אֲשֶׁר נִכְסָף לְדוֹדוֹ

wəhu nixsaf ləsumo yeˇ kəmo yeˇ / kəmo hoˇeq ʾăˇɛr nixsaf lədodo

(1)   And it is yearning to turn into existence from quasi-existence
      like a lover who is yearning for his belovèd

This verse line is the sixth one in a short philosophical poem ("I love thee with the love of a man to his only one"), the Arabic gloss on which says: "And he had, further, an answer to someone who asked him about the nature of existence". One of the putative meanings of the first hemistich in this verse line is: "Matter is aspiring to pass from an imperfect mode of existence to a perfect mode of existence". The first hemistich conveys, then, the "teleological model", the "theology of *being*", whereas the second hemistich conveys a model based on interpersonal love. The two models are stitched together in this verse by the verb *yearning*. This verb has two outstanding meaning components: [+PURPOSEFUL] and [+INTENSE EMOTION]. According to Kaufman's analysis, moving or striving toward some objective is of the essence of the "teleological model"; the component [+INTENSE EMOTION] is less relevant to this model. The simile in the second hemistich, by contrast, serves to accentuate precisely this component. Thus, the verse focuses attention precisely on the *stitch* between the two theological models of Ultimate Reality. Hence the sense of **splitting the focus of attention** (cf. above, Chapter 4), of **metaphysical wit.**

Much (but not all) devotional poetry is based on interpersonal models of transcendence (and of God). Much of mystic poetry, and much of Romanticism's craving for the infinite, is based on the kind of teleological transcendence suggested by Kaufman. Some of the relevant issues will be touched upon in later chapters on Archetypal Patterns (Chapter 14) and on Altered States of Consciousness (chapters 18–20).

The foregoing exposition is necessarily sketchy. In what follows, I shall make a short comment on an absurd play; then I shall compare a piece of Romantic to a piece of Metaphysical poetry and, finally, I shall illustrate the foregoing conception with reference to romantic imagery at considerable length. The absurd play is Beckett's *Waiting for Godot,* which we shall consider at some length in Chapter 21. The two tramps in the play are in a situation of human limitedness at its extreme. The only thing they are capable of doing to improve their situation is *wait for Godot,* who might satisfy some of their basic needs, such as food and shelter, and perhaps would not beat them; but Godot postpones his arrival evening after evening. Even when they *voice* experiences concerning "the *normative* constraints and restrictions", or concerning the destiny of man and his place in the universe, it is merely a parody of such talk, to which they resort only to "pass" the time, which otherwise would be standing still, meaninglessly. The two tramps sum up such a dialogue as follows:

> 2. Estragon: That wasn't such a bad little canter.
>   Vladimir: Yes, but now we'll have to find something else (p. 42).

Comparing Two Passages:
Romantic and Metaphysical

I propose to demonstrate certain aspects of the distinction between Romantic and Metaphysical poetry by drawing together my discussion of human limitation in the present chapter, and of space perception in Chapter 15, below. This I will do by way of comparing two short passages due to two great Hebrew poets; the first passage is from Tchernikhovsky's idyll "Circumcision", the other from Alterman's lyric poem "Rainy Boulevard" (translations are my own). Excerpt (3) is part of a long description of a Jewish Rabbi and a Cossack coachman travelling through the Russian *steppe.*

> (3)   And the traveller felt like
>   Letting his powerful voice be heard, going from one sea to the other,
>   Filling the space of the air with the wild, lonely voices,
>   So that the swans among the reeds and the wolves in the desolate
>   lands hear them
>   And respond from the lakeshore, howling from their hollows of dust
>   And the caller feel releaved, for sensing a sign of life in the distance.
>   (Tchernikhovsky: "Circumcision")

> (4)   Behold the glass—its name is more lucid than our names;
>   Who will pass through the freeze of its reflection?
>   At its threshold, as at the threshold of our soul,

The noise becomes separated from the light.
(Alterman: "Rainy Boulevard")

For a fruitful comparison of these two passages, we must anticipate our argument in Chapter 15, below. The ground for the comparison is to be sought in the distinction between the senses and the attempt to overcome their limitations. As to (3), I will draw upon Kant's discussion of "aesthetic estimation", also quoted in Chapter 15 (Kant, 1969). "Aesthetic estimation" is a mental activity in which "the imagination tries to comprehend or encompass the whole representation in one single intuition" (Beardsley, 1966: 218). From the point of view of the egocentric observer, the *steppe,* as well as the human history and prehistory that took place on the *steppe,* expand, in "Circumcision", beyond the scope of the observer's perception, and so they are perceived as "boundless"—thrown together, so to speak, with infinity. The emotional effect of this experiencing of what Kant calls an "absolute magnitude", is the *sublime.*

However, the epic narrator does not confine himself here to the effect of transcending the limits of our perception, or imagination, as this effect emerges in the description of objects that are "absolutely great" in their existence in space and time. Many romantic poets distinguish between a *visible,* and an *invisible* world; the latter extending *beyond the ultimate limits* of what is accessible to our senses. Any attempt directly to describe the invisible world would be regarded as transferring the "otherworldly" to *this* side of these limits. In order to arouse the feeling of having intuited the world beyond the ultimate limits of the senses, the epic narrator summons up the essential differences between the senses, so as to indicate the perception of nature's "invisible" beings. *Seeing* is the most "rational" of our senses: it is the most differentiated sense, and it is the only sense with which we may perceive spatio-temporally continuous objects, that is, objects that have stable shapes, that do not change in time, and that are separate from other objects. Sound, on the other hand, is thing-free energy, with no stable visual shape. Consequently, "filling the space of the air with the wild, lonely voices" means in the present context 'filling all the visible space with most intensely perceived thing-free energy'. The gap between the visual and auditory senses is conspicuous in the present passage in that the swans and the wolves are hidden from the eyes by the "reeds", or by the "hollows of dust", and, what is more important, by "the distance". Only their voices are perceptible to the senses; and these voices are thing-free entities, that is, they are free of spatio-temporal continuity.

When the cognitive system functions properly in everyday life, the various senses *cooperate* as though they were synchronized; one is unaware of any possible difference between them. The two passages discussed in the present section are similar in that both present us with physical conditions in which the "synchronicity" of the visual and of the auditory senses is disrupted: in the former passage by the enormous distances, in the latter by the glass and its unique properties: viz., that it lets the light waves through, but not the sound waves. Furthermore, the glass is transparent, as if there were nothing there; but it is a physical obstacle, obstructing one from passing through it ("Who will pass through the freeze of its reflection?").

However, the difference between the two texts, too, can be neatly delineated against this common ground. Basing our comparison on the disruption of the "synchronicity" of the visual and the auditory senses, the two images may be contrasted in five relevant respects.

First, the perception of the *steppe* strains the power of the senses to the utmost, thus arousing the immediate feeling of an "ultimate" limit. By contrast, the glass presents a rather trivial obstacle, which under normal circumstances can be avoided—for instance, by opening the window, or changing one's place. A limit such as this can be made to *represent* the ultimate limit by way of some additional intellectual activity, viz., by abstraction or analogy. This is one of the sources of the contrast that is perceived as an effect of the two passages. In excerpt (3), the disruption of the synchronicity of the senses is registered as a natural disruption indicating man's final limitation, which one may sense in an intuitive, immediate fashion. In excerpt (4), by contrast, the disruption of the synchronicity of the senses is perceived as artificially contrived and quite easily to be gotten rid off. Paraphrasing Burke's (1957: 52) distinction between the sublime and the ridiculous, the first excerpt allows, the second refuses the obstruction its authority. As a result, the latter passage is perceived as witty.

Second, when cognitive mechanisms function in their natural mode, we tend (in Polányi's term) to "attend away" from them, to the *objects* of cognitive processing; we perceive the activity as fluent and natural. In Alterman's poem, attention is focused on the very act of separating the noise from the light, whereas in Tchernikhovsky's, one is expected to attend away from the act of separating the senses to what is being perceived by the separate senses.

Third, different kinds of cognitive mechanisms are activated in the two passages. The emphatic dissociation of the senses requires a high degree of conscious, intellectual effort, in contrast to, e.g., the child's naïve, undifferentiated perception. As suggested above, Alterman's description is focused on the dissociation of the senses, whereas Tchernikhovsky's description centers around one's self-perception in relation to one's environment and the overall directions of the surrounding space. By this technique, he activates our orientation mechanisms, which typically involve a fast and diffuse integration of input from a variety of sensory sources; a mode of functioning such as this is characteristical of emotional processes (see below, Chapter 15).

Fourth, an additional contrast between the perceived effects of the two passages results from the control of point of view: whether or not the information is smoothly integrated in the description. In excerpt (3), Tchernikhovsky subsumes the whole description in a consistent situation, viewed from a consistent point of view; there are no contradictions among its components. As a result, the description is perceived in a soft, integrated focus (see above, Chapter 4). By contrast, in excerpt (4), Alterman examines the various physical properties of the glass one after the other:

lucidity, solid resistance ("freeze"), transparence to light but not to sound. Alterman enumerates these properties in succession, generalizing from them individually, the various generalizations being relevant to man's place in the universe and to his relationship to the surrounding objects. The various generalizations are not necessarily compatible with one another, and their subsumption under a coherent situation is certainly not required, or even possible. Consequently, the description is perceived in a sharp, split focus.

Fifth, Alterman uses a number of additional verbal devices so as to further sharpen the split focus of perception. In the first line, lucidity is transferred, by way of metonymy, from the glass to its name, which, in turn, is compared to the lucidity of our own names. An opaque expression results, causing delay in the understanding of the image. The phrase "the freeze of its reflection" contains, in my translation, an ambiguity not present in the Hebrew original: *reflection* translates here a Hebrew noun derived from a verb meaning 'think, ponder, meditate'; but the other meaning of the English noun, the casting back of light or images, is very much relevant to the present context. The genitive link between *freeze* and *reflection* is illustrative and arbitrary at one and the same time. On the one hand, the reflection is transparent like the glass; on the other hand, it is unlike the glass in that it is not solid. Consequently, the freeze simultaneously illustrates and contradicts the reflection. However, all this is true only as long as we consider the phrase in its isolation. When we examine it in the wider context of the whole stanza, we become aware of a strange inversion: not the reflection, but the glass is the object of description. It is the reflection, the thought, that serves to characterize the *freeze of the glass*. In other words, precisely the psychological process, the thing *beyond the limits* of direct inspection, serves as an illustration of the physical object that *is* accessible to direct inspection, rather than the other way around. This inversion intensifies the witty quality of the description.

Contingency and Transcendence in the Imagery of *Faust*

In the present section, I propose to work out at some length that part of my model which refers to Romantic poetry. My paradigmatic case will be *Faust Part One*. I shall attempt to show that far from being confined to the idea-content of the play, this conception may significantly account also for substantial parts of its imagery. And the same could be said of a great variety of Romantic works, in a variety of languages.

Faust I is very much preoccupied with the ultimate limitation of man, and attempts to transcend it. Both the *interpersonal* and the *teleological* models (in fact, all four fundamental types of limiting experience) are explored. Faust's encounter with the Earth Spirit in his study is an attempt to experience ultimate reality in the personalistic mode. In the following passage, we find Faust's cravings for what might be called *teleological transcendence*. Man is not only limited, as all created things, by gravitation; he has not been endowed, like birds, with the capability of flying.

This *physical* limitation, reinforced by the immediate *physical* limitation of Faust's "low, dark room, scarce habitable", of "the pressing weight of roof and gable", serves as a vividly sensed metaphor for the Ultimate Limit to be transcended.

> (5)   O full and splendid Moon, whom I
>   Have, from this desk, seen climb the sky
>   So many a midnight,—would thy glow
>   For the last time beheld my woe!
>   Ever thine eye, most mournful friend,
>   O'er books and papers saw me bend;
>   But would that I, on mountains grand,
>   Amid thy blessèd light could stand,
>   With spirits through mountain-caverns hover,
>   Float in thy twilight the meadows over,
>   And, freed from the fumes of lore that swathe me,
>   To health in thy dewy fountains bathe me.
>   Ah, me! this dungeon still I see!
>   This drear, accursèd masonry,
>   Where even the welcome daylight strains
>   But duskly through the painted panes.
>   Hemmed in by many a toppling heap
>   Of books worm-eaten, gray with dust,
>   Which to the vaulted ceiling creep,
>   Amidst them smoky papers thrust,—
>   With glasses, boxes, round me stacked,
>   And instruments together hurled,
>   Ancestral lumber stuffed and packed—
>   That is my world: and what a world!
> (386–409)[4]

It is quite suggestive that both Kaufman in his theological work and Bayard Taylor in his translation of *Faust* use the key-term *hemmed in*. The basic opposition here is between sitting in some dark, confined, smoky space, and between hovering in space that is unlimited both in the vertical and the horizontal dimension (this is what is suggested here by *mountains grand,* and *float the meadows over*), in the fresh air, in the moonlight. Books, utensils, household goods, have only one effect in this respect: to confine more and more the enclosing space. Romantic Nature poetry regards the physical objects of Nature, as a rule, as double-edged objects: on the one hand, they separate man from the Ultimate Reality which is there, beyond; on the other hand, they *are* in direct contact with that Ultimate Reality, and thus also serve as a connecting link. The physical objects of the actual scene are man-made, and only one aspect is emphasized in them: constraining man.

---

[4]   All the translations from *Faust* are by Bayard Taylor.

It will also be noticed that the imagery quoted here at length could be quoted, no less plausibly, as imagery of the DEATH AND REBIRTH ARCHETYPE (v. below, Chapter 14). This is to suggest that the oppositions DEATH ~ REBIRTH and ULTIMATE LIMIT ~ TRANSCENDENCE are somehow akin in the play. One might say that the "spokes" of the "hub", the abstract emotional pattern, "radiate" to the alternating states involved in the more concrete DEATH AND REBIRTH ARCHETYPE, and further on to the alternating modes of existence, so to speak, of ultimate limitation and of transcending it. Hence the element of "the pressing weight of roof and gable", and the elements of standing "on mountains grand, amid [the moon's] blesséd light", and floating "in [its] twilight the meadows over".

One of the "four fundamental types of limiting experience", mentioned above, was that selves "experience from within the *organic* limitation of their own powers". Romanticism directs much effort to the transcendence of this limitation. One of the mental states eagerly sought by the Romanticists was a state of increased vital powers, at the time of communion with some unlimited entity (e.g., infinity), canceling the limits between self and not-self,[5] and gaining some significant insight, or vision of totality. One of the most significant metaphors for such an "experiencing of totality" is associated with immersion in fresh water, as in "to health in thy dewy fountains bathe me", or in some abstract quality, as in the last line of the following passage:

> (6)　(*He opens the Book and perceives the sign of the Macrocosm*).
> 　　Ha! what a sudden rapture leaps from this
> 　　I view, through all my senses swiftly flowing!
> 　　I feel a youthful, holy, vital bliss
> 　　In every vein and fibre newly glowing.
> 　　Was it a God who traced this sign,
> 　　With calm across my tumult stealing,
> 　　My troubled heart to joy unsealing,
> 　　With impulse, mystic and divine,
> 　　The powers of Nature here, around my path, revealing?
> 　　Am I a God?—so clear mine eyes!
> 　　In these pure features I behold
> 　　Creative Nature to my soul unfold.
> 　　What says the sage, now I first recognize:
> 　　"The spirit-world no closures fasten;
> 　　Thy mind is shut, thy heart is dead:
> 　　Disciple, up! untiring, hasten

---

[5]　In the Freudian terms used in chapter 14, this would amount to "oceanic dedifferentiation". I have discussed its implications for figurative language in Tsur, 1987b, 177–190, reprinted as Tsur, 1988, and Tsur, 1989.

to bathe thy breast in morning-red!"[6]
$$(431-446)$$

We have here the rise of vital forces within the self: "I feel a youthful, holy, vital bliss / in every vein and fibre newly glowing"; and it is crucially related with the total immersion in an abstract quality "to bathe thy breast in morning-red!", yielding a kind of feeling of experiencing totality.

One might suggest that *insight* is achieved when one is capable of seeing in a flash the multiplicity of loosely related *parts* as *one tightly organized whole.* If so, the sequel of this passage conveys, precisely, such an *insight;* this is reinforced, on the "mythological" level, by imagery suggesting that Faust is *seeing into* the workings of the invisible forces of nature (overcoming his natural limitations in this respect).

(7)   (*He contemplates the sign.*)
How each the Whole its substance gives,
Each in the other works and lives!
Like heavenly forces rising and descending,
Their golden urns reciprocally lending,
With wings that winnow sweet blessing
From Heaven through Earth I see them pressing,
Filling the All with harmony unceasing.
$$(447-453)$$

Kaufman's paper is called "Transcendence without Mythology". He quotes Bultmann's definition of "mythology", put forward for the purposes of his "demythologizing" program: "the use of imagery to express the otherwordly in terms of this world and the divine in terms of human life, the other side in terms of this side" (Kaufman, 1972: 43). It is quite clear that Goethe uses plenty of imagery "to express the other side in terms of this side". Nevertheless, it would appear, our "demythologizing" exercise may be quite useful, yielding an insight into the purpose of imagery in *Faust,* as well as into significant relationships of romantic ecstatic poetry to other kinds of literature.

It is assumed here that we are dealing here with a *Romantic* poem; and that the kind of existential situation (representative anecdote) underlying it may illuminate its imagery, as well as help to understand some of its significant relationships with works that belong to other styles, some of which are quite remote in nature. This use of imagery will be taken up again when discussing archetypal patterns and, once more, when discussing ecstatic poetry.

---

[6]   I shall return to the last four lines of this quotation in Chapter 18.

"The Womb" As Representative Anecdote

Our short discussion of *Waiting for Godot* drew attention to a possible, important aspect of human contingency: **need for shelter.** "God" is not a "limiting experience" only, but a "stronghold", too. Thus, once introduced, opposite potentials of "walls" as imagery can be exploited at one and the same time, or successively: walls may obstruct from going beyond, but may also protect; small rooms may restrict and confine, but may also provide shelter. Thus, our attitude toward them may be basically ambivalent.

In cognitive terms one might suggest that Freud and his followers "encoded" this information constituting ambivalence into the spatial image of "the Womb". As this formulation of mine indicates, I am going to treat the Freudian issue in a very unorthodox way. Psychoanalytic literature has devoted much attention to the growth of the self, beginning with the foetus' state in the womb, and usually ending with the emotional separation of the child from his parents. In a classical paper on this topic, Ferenczi (1925) speaks of the development of the sense of reality. The foetus' state in the womb is the prototype of a long series of recurring situations. In this state, the mother's body supplies all the foetus' needs for food, liquids, oxygen, and protection from the outside world. The foetus fills all the available space, makes no distinction between "subject" and "object", and has no knowledge of reality. In this state, the "pleasure principle" has overall dominance; the "reality principle" does not exist. As the foetus grows, enclosure and protection become confinement and restriction. From this perspective, birth is a (traumatic) transition to a less protective (but also less restrictive) state of existence. Further growth results in a series of such transitions to states of ever-decreasing protection. The earlier the stage, the more integrated a person with his background; the later the stage—the more separated he feels. By the same token, from stage to stage, there is a growing "abyss" between "subject" and "object", and a gradual increase of the share of the reality principle, at the expense of the pleasure principle.

It follows from the foregoing discussion that the same setting of enclosure that in *Faust* is perceived as restricting and confining, may also be perceived as a protection to which the perceiving consciousness is desperately clinging. Sometimes, one and the same poet may use the same setting for these opposite purposes, sometimes in one and the same poem, sometimes in different but related poems.

I propose briefly to consider here a group of two such poems by the great Hebrew Romantic poet, Ḥayyim Naḥman Bialik. Let us have a look at the first and fourth stanzas of his poem "Alone", in a plain English prose translation.

(8)   All were carried away by the wind [spirit], all were swept away by
                                                    the Light,
       A new song [poetry] made the morning of their lives rejoice;
       And I, young of birds, have been forgotten

Under the wings of the ˇəkhina.[7]

"Being under the wings of the ˇəkhina" is an idiomatic expression in Hebrew, meaning "being faithful to Jewish religion". However, the metaphor "young of birds" in the preceding line realizes the idiom, suggesting a mother bird, protecting her chick under her wings. But this protection easily becomes hindering ("As if hedging my way with her broken wing", in the fifth stanza). In the first line, the referent of the subject *all* is not clear: whether it is all the brood of the young bird, or all the companions of a young man (in which case, "young of birds" must be understood metaphorically). This ambiguity is only reinforced by the ambiguity of the Hebrew noun *ruah,* which may mean either "wind" (in this case it would refer to young birds), or "spirit", that is, "the spirit of a new age" (in this case it would refer to young people). Likewise, *Light* in its literal sense would corroborate the reading "young birds', whereas in a figurative sense, meaning "Enlightenment", it would corroborate the meaning "young people" carried away by the spirit of a new age. The Hebrew word ˇira may mean either "song" or "poetry"; in the former case it may refer to an environment of birds; in the latter case, to the environment of a new cultural age. The fourth stanza of this poem reads:

(9)   And when my heart yearned to the window, to the light,
       And when it was too narrow for me under her wing,
       She hid her face against my shoulder, and her tear
       Dropped on the page of my Talmud-book.

In this stanza we come up against the imagery familiar from *Faust*. There is the confinement in the inside; and beyond the window, there is the (unattainable) "outside" with the light, toward which the speaker can only yearn. The child is sitting in the *beth midra* ˇ, the traditional Jewish school for higher education. We have got here a triple crisis, of three different scopes. First, the child is sitting all day long in the darkish room studying the Talmud, and is longing to go out and play in the sunlight. Second, he is the last one left in the *beth midra* ˇ, and he too would like to go outside, to another cultural and social environment. In this sense, the *beth midra* ˇ is a cultural institution, and stands for a way of life as well as for a stage in the nation's history. Third, in between these two scopes there is the "family" scope, the image of the mother bird, wailing that all her young flew out, and this last chick, too, is longing to fly away. In the second stanza, it is explicitly written: "She felt anxious for me, her only son". In fact, what we have got here is the archetypal womb experience as "'hub', with all other aspects of *human* action treated as spokes radiating from this hub". The experiencing consciousness is protected, but it also feels restricted in its human potentials, and wants to get to the unrestricted "out", to the light. This occurs within the scope of the person's daily routine in studying the

---

7   ˇəkhina is, in Jewish theology, a female representation of God on earth.

Talmud; within the scope of his individual development, when he feels restricted "under his mother's wings"; and within the scope of the nation's history, which is at a turning point of cultural, religious, and social crisis.

The same setting recurs in another one of Bialik's *beth midra˘* poems, "Before the Bookcase". Here, the speaker tells about a terrible stormy night, with the lonely, "last of the last" boys who sees the "permanent candle" die away. Here the small light is inside, while the storm and the dark night reign outside. Here the light, the "permanent candle", stands for Jewish tradition; but also is the only source of light in the stormy night. Very much is said in this poem that would be relevant to our present discussion. But I wish to focus attention only on one short passage.

> (10)   I saw my stronghold breaking down [...]
>   Only the flame of my candle is still dying,
>   Moving to and fro, leaping its leap of death,
>   And suddenly the window was broken, all light went out,
>   And I, helpless chick, was thrown out of the nest,
>   In the domain of night and its darkness.

This is a sudden and violent transition from a sheltered state to a state open to the storm, as traumatic as birth. And although physically it is the storm that *breaks into* the room, the event is perceived as if the experiencing consciousness were *forced out* of the shelter. What is more, one of the main themes of the poem is that the speaker, as an adult, *can* return to the physical place, but he cannot experience the reintegration with the physical and spiritual space from which he was "expelled"; he cannot overcome the abyss between subject and object. Here, again, the expulsion from the shelter seems to apply to three levels of experience: losing the relative comfort of light and warmth of the closed room, growing up, and leaving the relative safety of traditional culture and religion.

Summary

This chapter attempts to handle in a systematic way what Wellek and Warren call "the world stratum" of the poem. In order to account for a basic human situation, it has presented two "representative anecdotes", both of which claim some universal validity on non-literary grounds. There is considerable overlap between the two. Both present Man in an enclosure which protects and restricts him at one and the same time, and which he longs to transcend. When he is outside this enclosure, he is again in an ambivalent situation: he has gained relative freedom, but at the price of losing relative protection. In one case, he is a prisoner, in the other, an exile. In both cases, he longs to "transcend" the boundary, to get into the other, "inaccessible" world.

There are two basic constraints on such a "representative anecdote". On the one hand, it must be complex enough to encode the complexities of the basic *condition humaine;* on the other hand, it must be general enough to generalize across a vast variety of human situations, and afford meaningful distinctions between them. It should be noticed that although one of my "representative anecdotes" originates in a Freudian notion, my approach to it is vastly different from that of some of Freud's followers. I do not claim that the womb-situation is *"the* meaning" of a vast variety of real life situations, to which they can be reduced. I don't even claim, though I don't deny it either, that the chronological precedence of the womb-situation is the real reason of the emotional appeal of the other situations, which it underlies; in other words, living creatures seek shelter not only because they were expelled from the relative comfort of the womb, but also because shelters provide protection against dangers and unpleasant experiences in the immediate present. My point is, that this "representative anecdote" is so effective precisely because the womb image encodes most efficiently those ingredients of great emotive appeal, a configuration of which recurs in a wide range of possible human situations.[8] Finally, consider the purpose of the exercise. The "representative anecdote" is *not* offered here in order to show that all, or most, or much literature can be reduced to a common essence, but in order to make meaningful and systematic distinctions between literary styles; that is, to show that various poetic styles attempt to cope with the same kind of underlying human situation, but by different means: viz., by efficiently overstressing various sectors of its.

---

[8] In chapter 14, there will be a suggestion how this womb image may be utilized in archetypal criticism, and what its constraints are.

CHAPTER 12

The Versatile Reader:
Style as Open Concept

In Chapter 3 we used the concept of period style (and of genre) as a hypothesis, both in the conceptual and the perceptual sense of the term. A hypothesis may be a set of propositions formulated to guide investigation, or a kind of mental attitude—what Bruner called "perceptual readiness". Wellek and Warren speak of period styles (and genres) as of "Regulative Concepts". The present chapter investigates the nature and structure of these hypotheses (regulative concepts), and the ways in which cognitive systems acquire and handle them.

From observation we know that there are readers who can handle a great variety of poetic styles with relative ease and considerable adequacy, on rather slight exposure to them. This reader will be called "The Versatile Reader". It must be assumed that the Versatile Reader has coded the various poetic styles in a way that is more efficient than memorizing long lists of specific conventions for each poetic style. A process of gradual differentiation, effected through sets of contrastive features, must be assumed—from a general notion of poetry, through *types* of styles, to increasingly *specific* styles. It is suggested here that the expressive effects of poetic structures that constitute the various styles and style-types need not be *learnt:* they are the unique, conscious qualities of the activities of adaptation devices, originally acquired for nonliterary purposes, but now turned to aesthetic ends.

In order to understand the nature of certain kinds of poetic styles, an opposite, 'fossilizing tendency', too, must be realized: the process by which poetic devices of great expressive force are turned into 'harmless ornament'. Finally, the question of the Versatile Reader's historical self and his ability to handle literatures of other historical periods must be raised. (This will be done in a brief Coda to the chapter).

Essences and Layers

(1)   [Taking an onion, he strips it skin by skin]
        What an incredible number of layers!
        Don't we get to the heart of it soon?
                [He pulls the whole onion to pieces]

No, I'm damned if we do. Right down to the centre
There's nothing but layers—smaller and smaller…
Nature is witty.
                    (Ibsen, *Peer Gynt*, trans. Peter Watts, p. 191)

What do we mean when we say we understand a poem? Part of the understanding has to do with *style*. On hearing a piece of baroque, or classical, or romantic music, a trained listener—and not necessarily a professional musician—can ascribe its quality, with a fair chance of correctness, to its style. The same is frequently true of a piece of poetry. We feel there is, in a baroque poem, a quality different from a Renaissance or a Romantic poem to which we respond. How can we get to this quality peculiar to each style? Should we, like Peer Gynt, peel the poem layer after layer hoping that its essence is hiding there somewhere at the core? (Rabbi Naḥman of Braslaw is reported to have said that you peel and peel the onion layer after layer; finally, however, you still are left with something: with the tears in your eyes). Or should we say with Arnheim that "there is no reason to imitate Molière's doctoral candidate who explained the sleep-inducing effect of opium by a *virtus dormitiva*"? (Arnheim, 1967: 316).

Nineteenth century cultural historians—Germans in particular—assumed a *Zeitgeist* lurking at the core of cultural periods and/or artistic styles. Some twentieth century critics are critical of these assumptions (see e.g. Gombrich, 1969). Kenneth Burke (1957: 221–250), in his paper "Freud and the Analysis of Poetry" makes a distinction between an "essentializing" and a "proportionalizing" strategy in critical activities. In my various writings, I have adopted the "proportionalizing" strategy; here too, instead of assuming a *virtus romantica*, or virtues latent in other period-styles, I shall put forward a "proportionalizing" theory of structural elements. Throughout the present book I have conceived of the poem as a stratified system of norms (cf. Chapter 2). If you peel the poem layer after layer, you will have, eventually, nothing in your hands (*pace* Rabbi Naḥman; but then again, he was talking about eyes). The peculiar quality does not reside *at the core*, but in the various layers *put together*.

Likewise, one may conceive of literary genres, and of stylistic periods, as of stratified systems of norms. Poems (as well as periods) may be contrasted in each specific norm on each stratum of the system. Thus, when we find intuitively that Donne's seventeenth-century English divine poems, for instance, greatly differ from Ibn Gabirol's eleventh-century Hebrew divine poems—though both Metaphysical— the difference of language should be considered as rather trivial. We should, rather, look for the source of this difference in the contrasts of the specific conventions on the various strata of the system. Oppositions in minute, though significant details, such as in the metric system (e.g., quantitative or syllabo-tonic) or a peculiar vocabulary, may crucially effect our stylistic intuitions concerning the *whole*, even though we may be incapable of pointing out the source of these intuitions. This should not be very surprising.

From experimental results we can derive the law that the change in total complexes is more exactly perceived than any change in their parts. The more organized, extensive and closed these complexes are and the more important the part is for the whole, the more accurate will be the judgment of JND [just noticeable differences]. Methodological difficulties have prevented thus far the study of JNDs in feeling. Even primitive awareness reacts more accurately on the basis of emotional sensitivity than by means of part functions. It has been observed over and over that the smallest changes in experience are felt emotionally long before the change can be exactly described. (Krueger, 1968: 100–101)

Works of literature and, especially, poems are just such "organized, extensive and closed complexes", in which the part is most important for the whole. In other words, the conception presented here can explain why we so frequently have strong intuitions concerning perceived differences between varieties included in the same stylistic category, without being able to put our finger on the source of those intuitions.

Is There Such a Thing as *Romanticism?*

From Lovejoy's essay "On the Discrimination of Romanticisms" (1961) one may draw two diametrically opposed conclusions. The issue at stake is whether one is looking for common features only, or for differences as well. One possible conclusion is that, since 'Romanticism' refers to things involving fundamentally different or opposed elements, the best thing to do is to abandon the term altogether (or to use it in the plural, which amounts to the same denial of meaning). Now, consider a geometrical term like *parallelogram*. All parallelograms have *a priori* one important feature in common: two pairs of parallel sides. Notwithstanding this, the term does not refer to one single object, but to at least four different kinds— rectangles and rhomboïds, equilaterals and non-equilaterals. Any two of these have different or even incompatible attributes. As for the various romanticisms, on the other hand—as Lovejoy rightly insists—"there may be some common denominator of them all; but if so, it has never yet been clearly exhibited, and its presence is not to be assumed *a priori*" (Lovejoy, 1961: 236). The problem with Lovejoy's argument is however, that he seems to acknowledge only *a priori*, no *a posteriori* definitions. He expects the term *Romanticism* to be capable of a definition that is similar to the definition of the geometrical term *parallelogram*.

The alternative conclusion from Lovejoy's essay is that in discussing a literary period, one should proceed, as in geometry, by a twofold procedure: one must delimit an area—in geometry *a priori*, by definition, in literary criticism *a posteriori*, by what Wittgenstein called an "open concept"—and, at the same time, one should discriminate entities. One should differentiate between literary and other uses of language; and, within literature, between romantic and other styles of poetry; between various romanticisms within Romanticism; and, eventually, between individual poems. One may safely assume that there are significantly different elements in any two poems within the boundaries of any romanticism as discriminated by Lovejoy. In other words, one cannot rely on any single "discrimination", but rather on a hierarchy of discriminations, which by no means should ignore differences between individual poems.

Let us compare, for a minute, three well-known English poems, usually associated with romanticism: "Michael" and "Daffodils" by Wordsworth, and "Ode on a Grecian Urn" by Keats. Are they similar in any important respect? The first two are similar in an affectionate attitude to nature, or to people close to nature. A definition based on this common feature would, however, exclude the third poem. The last two, again, have in common an ecstatic response to an unusual sight. A definition based on this common feature, again, would exclude the first poem. On the other hand, if we take features shared by all three, such as iambic meter, we shall have exceeded by far the boundaries of Romanticism. Lovejoy's solution to the problem is well-known: we should not speak of Romanticism, but of Romanticisms. René Wellek, however, takes issues with this conception and insists that we should talk of Romanticism in the singular, and rejects all in all Lovejoy's solution. He argues that there is a remarkable degree of unity in European Romanticism (Wellek, 1965: 160 ff.). Not only that there are some persistent elements such as "imagination for view of poetry, nature for view of the world and symbol and myth for poetic style" (ibid., 161), but there is also a "profound coherence and mutual implication between the Romantic views of nature, imagination and symbol" (ibid., 197).

In what follows, I shall neither try to arbitrate between these two great authorities, nor to reconcile them. I shall, rather, put forward a Wittgensteinian view of period style in general and of Romanticism in particular; while assimilating certain elements from both the above authors' views, my proposal throws the whole issue into a different perspective. I should like to begin with an observation of Pears's on *naming* in general; an observation which applies to the naming of period styles as well:

> An analogy will help us to deal with this new form of difficulty. Naming is like electing the sort of member who makes a difference to a club. Strictly we cannot say without qualification to what club he was elected, since it was one club before he was elected and another club after he was elected. (Pears, 1966: 57–58)

"The meaning is the use" is Wittgenstein's famous slogan, and it applies to period styles as well as to "games" or to "the tools in a tool box". You cannot find any common attribute shared by all "tools" or "games", except for "family resemblances". Wittgenstein discusses at some length the various activities called "games". You may find many similarities between many pairs of them, but no "essence" that is common to all games. "And the result of this examination is: we see a complicated network of similarities overlapping and crisscrossing: sometimes overall similarities, sometimes similarities of details" (Wittgenstein, 1976: § 66). He calls such concepts as "tools" or "games" *open concepts*. Morris Weitz has profitably transferred the term "open concept" to the domain of aesthetic enquiry. He contends that *Art*, or literary genres like *Novel*, are open concepts (which Lakoff, 1987, rechristens 'fuzzy concepts'). People use them without defining their exact meaning, and they find themselves in agreement with regard to a broad area of "overlapping definitions".

> But the basic resemblance between these concepts is their open texture. In elucidating them, certain (paradigm) cases can be given, about which there can be no question as to their being correctly described as "art" or "game", but no exhaustive set of cases can be given. I can list some cases and some conditions under which I can apply correctly the concept of art but I cannot list all of them, for the all-important reason that unforeseeable or novel conditions are always forthcoming or envisageable. (Weitz, 1962: 53–54)

> A concept is open if its conditions of application are amendable or corrigible; that is, if a situation or case can be imagined or secured which would call for some sort of *decision* on our part to extend the use of the concept to cover this, or to close the concept and invent a new one to deal with the new case and its new property. (ibid., 54)

The term *Romanticism* denotes an open concept, similarly to terms like *art, novel* and *game*, and many more; and if we ban it, we have to ban the other ones too. Or, alternatively, we have to legitimize *Romanticism* too. Weitz illustrates this open character of "art" by examples drawn from one of its subconcepts.

> Consider questions like "Is Dos Passos' *U.S* a novel?", "Is V. Woolf's *To the Lighthouse* a novel?", "Is Joyce's *Finnegans Wake* a novel?". On the traditional view, these are construed as factual problems to be answered yes or no in accordance with the presence or absence of defining properties. But certainly this is not how any of these questions is answered. [...] what is at stake is not factual analysis concerning necessary and sufficient properties but a decision as to whether the work under examination is similar in certain respects to other works already called "novels", and consequently warrants the extension of the concept to cover the new case. (ibid., 54)

I submit that period-terms, too, refer to open concepts. Viewed from this angle, the points of disagreement between Wellek and Lovejoy suddenly vanish. Both could sloganize their starting point as "The meaning is the use". Both examine actual uses of the term *Romanticism*, scrutinize the recurring elements in various uses and point out discrepancies. As for Lovejoy, he has almost defined, at the end of his essay, what an open concept is—in Wittgenstein's sense (though hardly intentionally). But he draws a conclusion that is diametrically opposed to Wittgenstein's position toward open concepts. In the following passage, one could replace "Romanticism" by "game":

> We have, then, observed and compared [...] three "Romanticisms". In the first and second we have found certain common elements, but still more significant oppositions; in the second and third we have found certain other elements, but likewise significant oppositions. But between the first and the third the common elements are very scanty. (Lovejoy, 1961: 251–252)

The following passage by Wellek, on the other hand, overlaps with another part of Weitz's argument, but is still short of a conception of open concept:

> We shall rather try to show that there is a growing area of agreement and even convergence among the definitions or, more modestly, descriptions of romanticism as they have been attempted by responsible scholars in recent decades in several countries. (Wellek, 1965: 203)

Take now the following instance: Lovejoy shows that Warton's Romanticism was different from Friedrich Schlegel's, whereas Wellek insists that this "proves only that Joseph Warton was an early naturalistic preromanticist". That is to say, Joseph Warton cannot serve as a counterexample to any definition of Romanticism, because he belongs to a different category: "early naturalistic preromanticism". Thus, the definition of Romanticism becomes, in Beryl Lake's term (1967), *irrefutable* (cf. my discussion of the definition of the "grotesque" in Chapter 17, below). According to Weitz's approach, this is a situation which calls for "some sort of *decision* on our part to extend the use of the concept to cover this, or to close the concept and invent a new one to deal with the new case and its new property"; or, as Wittgenstein succinctly put it: "We draw a boundary—for a special purpose" (§ 69). To take another case, in some histories of English literature, Blake is categorized as a "pre-romanticist", in some as a "romanticist". This may be a situation in which not one, but two decisions are to be made; first, whether to open a concept for "Pre-Romanticism", or to include some of the poets in question in the concept "Romanticism" and some in that of "Classicism"; and second, where to draw the boundary between the concepts (e.g., with respect to Blake). As to the first decision, Daiches, for instance, unlike Wellek, or Legouis and Cazamian (1935), does not consider "Pre-Romanticism" as a useful category at all: "It does not help to label poets like Gray (still less, Blake) "pre-romantic", for that suggests that there was a single movement developing in a straight line and those who came later were more thoroughly in the movement than those who preceded them" (1968: 857).

With regard to the second decision, as between "hills" and "mountains", there is no natural cut-off point between Romanticism and Pre-Romanticism, or Classicism, and the boundary must be drawn in an arbitrary manner, with respect to the special purpose of the specific discussion in hand.[1]

Morris Weitz called his article "The Role of Theory in Aesthetics". In its last paragraphs, he deals with the use of rival definitions of art. "The value of each of the theories", he says, "resides in its attempt to state and to justify certain criteria which are either neglected or distorted by previous theories" (1962: 58).

> Thus, the role of theory is not to define anything but to use the definitional form, almost epigrammatically, to pin-point a crucial recommendation to turn our attention once again [to this or that element in the work]. (ibid., 59)

It seems, then, that "Michael", "Daffodils", and "Ode on a Grecian Urn" have no essence in common, and that they are called romantic by virtue of their being placed in the same blurred area of open concept, called "Romanticism". Such a conception of period style in general, and of Romanticism in particular, illuminating as it is, seems to be still unsatisfactory. It is hard to accept that Romanticism should have no internal structure, however loose, and that the "core" of the concept should be determined by an accidentally chosen paradigmatic example, by virtue of mere consensus. One cannot help thinking that consensus as to poem X being an example of romantic poetry is not enough; poem X must be a *good* example. Cognitive psychologists such as Rosch and Mervis have put forward a theory of "good examples" (to which I have already referred in Chapter 9, in relation to metaphor, and semantic representation). There seem to be two cognitive principles by which consensus can be reached, not only as to what is an example of "fruit", or "bird", or "furniture", but also as to what is a *good example* of these categories. The two principles are "the principle of family resemblance" (derived, as we may guess, from Wittgenstein), and "the principle of contrast set". A good example of a category will be the one that has the features shared by most (though not necessarily all) examples of the category; and among these features those will rank high that emphasize the greatest contrast between this and neighboring categories. We have conceived of individual poems, of period styles, as well as of genres, as of "stratified systems of norms". Any two styles will be contrasted in a great number of norms, on all strata perhaps; and the boundary will be drawn for the special purposes of the specific discussion, in an arbitrary manner (I shall illustrate this point somewhat later). I have earlier quoted Wellek's argument that there is a remarkable degree of unity in Euro-

---

[1]   Indeed, Legouis and Cazamian (1935) discuss Warton in their chapter on "The Pre-Romantic Period". Blake is the last poet discussed in this chapter. By contrast, in Daiches' *A Critical History of English Literature,* Blake is the first poet discussed under Romanticism; Gray is said to belong to an earlier age by both literary histories, described as late Classicism.

pean Romanticism, with some persistent elements such as "imagination for view of poetry, nature for view of the world and symbol and myth for poetic style". These elements (and some additional ones) will not be shared by every romantic poem. But they will be shared by all the *good* examples of romantic poetry. By the same token, they will emphasize the contrast between themselves and the good examples of, say, classicism or mannerism. Furthermore, the good examples of, e.g., Romanticism are more likely to belong to certain poetic genres than to others. The reason is that poems, genres, period-styles, all being stratified systems of the same kinds of norms, may typically share a great number of norms on several strata. Thus, for instance, a good example of romantic poetry will rely on imagination, and will cherish nature and use it as a symbol, in an attempt to get a glimpse into an invisible, more real reality than that of "the light of common day". We may expect, therefore, that some of the *best examples* of romantic poetry will belong to a mixture of nature poetry and of the genres of meditative or ecstatic poetry. This may also explain what Wellek may have meant by the suggestion that there is also a "profound coherence and mutual implication between the romantic views of nature, imagination and symbol".

According to the "principle of contrast set", we may expect romanticism to exhibit certain features that are contrasted to rationalism. Thus we have, indeed, *imagination*, which is the use of the total of psychical powers, *emotions, the irrational* (primitive psychical powers); likewise we have *ecstasy*, involving the activation of the total of psychical powers at high energy levels. Since rationalism emphasizes the use of man's highly differentiated mental faculties, the *undifferentiated perceptions* of the child or of natural man will be reasonably contrasted to it.

There is, in the literature, an overpowering number of observations on "the common structures and essences of works produced in a certain period". While I cannot possibly do justice to all of them, still I wish to mention at least in this context a neglected idea of Gombrich's, namely, that the unity of a style consists, sometimes, not in what the works cherish, but in what they try to shun; to such negative qualities we refer by "terms of exclusion" (Gombrich, 1966: 88). "It is no accident, I believe, that various terms for non-classical styles turn out to be such terms of exclusion" (ibid., 89). This conception can easily be translated into the above-mentioned "principle of contrast set".

In view of Cognitive Poetics' preoccupation with ordinary consciousness as a personal construct (see Chapters 1 and 3, above), and with the relationships of poetry with "altered states of consciousness" (see Chapters 18–20, below), I shall shift the focus of my discussion from *rationalism* to *consciousness*, of which I consider "*modern*", *mature, awake consciousness* to be the most concentrated form. Let us consider, then, this notion in some of its antithetic relations as presented in Figure 1; we shall find that even such "terms of exclusion" may imply some positive values. Each of these "antitheses" to Mature Consciousness (although not quite consistent with one another), frequently serves the romantic poets to escape from the tortures of "the light of common day", from the tyranny of the here-and-now.

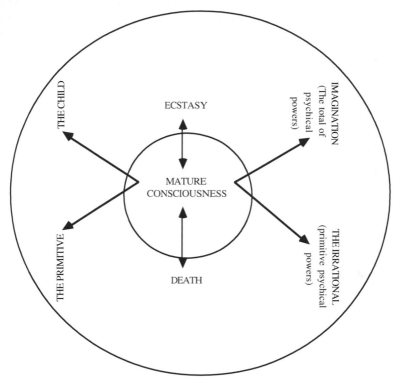

Figure 12.1   Romanticism as a term of exclusion: Aspects of Romanticism as oppositions to Rationalism.

I intend to pay special attention to the extremes DEATH~ECSTASY in Figure 1. They have one quality in common: the absence of ordinary consciousness. On the other hand, they are diametrically opposed in that death is a state of *complete lack* of human activity, while ecstasy is a state of extremely intense psychic experience. Thus, avoiding the normal middle, i.e. MATURE CONSCIOUSNESS, the poem is apt to express the mystic oxymoron and ecstasy, while at the same time, any description of death or nothingness *may* connote lack of consciousness. In the best of romantic poetry, we find sometimes that inactivity through death is counterbalanced by some intense activity, or immense sublimity (connoting intensity).

Thus we find that in some of Keats's poems ecstasy is achieved by using death-imagery in a context of intense passion. Consider the endings of some of the sonnets in which Keats achieves his "many havens of intensity".

(2)   ...then on the shore
               Of the wide world I stand alone and think
               Till Love and Fame to nothingness do sink.

                                   (Keats, "When I have fears")

(3)   Still, still to hear her tender-taken breath,
       And so live ever—or else swoon to death.
                           (Keats, "Bright Star")

(4)   Love, Fame and Beauty are intense indeed,
       But death intenser; Death is Life's high meed.
                           (Keats, "Why did I laugh?")

In Wordsworth's "Daffodils", ecstasy occurs in a context of "but little thought", "in vacant or in pensive mood" (this issue will be discussed at greater length in Chapter 19). Wordsworth's "Michael" or the "leech-gatherer" of "Resolution and Independence", or "The Solitary Reaper" may be situated at another edge of the excluded middle, that of natural man; at another edge of the scheme we might locate Wordsworth's child, the "best philosopher".

On Contrasting Stylistic Periods

In the preceding section, we have conceived of individual poems, of period styles, as well as of genres, as of "stratified systems of norms". I suggested there that any two styles will be contrasted in a great number of norms, on all strata perhaps; and the boundaries will be drawn for the special purposes of the specific discussion, in an arbitrary manner. I had earlier quoted Krueger, according to whom it has been observed over and over again that "in total complexes", the smallest changes in experience are felt emotionally long before the change can be exactly described. "Even primitive awareness reacts more accurately on the basis of emotional sensitivity than by means of part functions". That is why we tend to perceive the contrast between organized wholes, rather than between the individual strata or norms. I wish to illustrate this point by referring to an on-going debate in Hebrew Literary History concerning the question, "At which point did Modern Hebrew Literature begin?" I claim that the present conceptual framework can give a more accurate answer than the ones traditionally offered. One might surmise that one source of the traditional difficulty was in the perceptual phenomenon discussed by Krueger, owing to which people tended to look for the "essence" of "total complexes", rather than meddle with "just noticeable differences" in a variety of norms, at a number of strata. Like Peer Gynt, they were looking for the internal essence of the onion, instead of considering its unique quality to be perceived in the whole, in the many layers put together. For a short exposition of the dispute, I am going to present it as summarized by the late Professor Halkin:

Lachover (and others with him) begins to count the beginning of Modern Hebrew Literature with Rabbi Moshe Ḥayyim Luzzatto. In his opinion, whoever considers literature as artistic creation whose main justification is the artistic-aesthetic pleasure aroused in the reader rather than its pragmatic-social aspects, must pin-point the beginning of Modern Hebrew Literature with Luzzatto. Luzzatto was the first one to open the gate for artistic-aesthetic writing in Hebrew in his poetry, and mainly in his book *Educated Language.*

Klauzner rejects this view. He claims that although Luzzatto writes sometimes works that appear to be Belles Lettres, his work is actually engaged precisely in those domains in which traditional religious literature was engaged, witness his Kabbalistic and Moral books. (Halkin, 1984: 32–33)

Both historians have isolated a single "essence" to characterize the "real nature" of Luzzatto's work. The question is, apparently, which is the "right" criterion to determine the poet's place in the history of literature—assuming, of course, that the two criteria are sufficiently supported. However, according to Lachover's criterion, one ought to put the beginning of Modern Hebrew literature in eleventh century secular poetry, since it "considers literature as artistic creation whose main justification is the artistic-aesthetic pleasure aroused in the reader". On the other hand, in Klauzner's view, Modern Hebrew Literature must not be defined by its aesthetic conception either, but by its contents: this is a *littérature engagée*, which treats "Israel's real problems in that period—problems of society, education, religion, etc." I submit, then, that the difference between Luzzatto and later poets is not that the former treats problems of religion and the latter not, but that they treat different problems of religion, from different world views. Furthermore, Mediaeval and Modern Hebrew Literature do not differ in having or not having an aesthetic purpose but, first, in the different character of their aesthetic conceptions and second, in the different relationship between the aesthetic conception and the other elements in the poetic works.

There is a less influential view, proposed by Eisig Silberschlag in the *Princeton Encyclopedia of Poetry and Poetics*, who is critical of Lachover's and Klauzner's position:

Modern Hebrew Literature does not begin, as standard textbooks indicate with Moses Hayyim Luzzatto or Moses Mendelssohn. No such terminus a quo can possibly be accepted for a multitude of writings which appear not in one country but in numerous lands. Modern Hebrew literature has its beginnings in various countries at different times: in Italy in the 16th, in Holland in the 17th, in Germany in the 18th, in Poland and Russia in the 19th century. A convenient starting point for Modern Hebrew literature is 1492: the date of the Jewish exile from Spain. (Silberschlag, 1974: 341)

Silberschlag too, however, does not seem to object to the kind of criteria proposed by Lachover and Klauzner, for every individual country.

The "hard core" which Lachover and Klauzner thought to have discovered at the heart of the onion, suddenly vanishes, then, between their fingers. The basic assumption of the present work is that the real "essence" of an onion, of a poem, of a genre, or of a literary period resides in the unique combination of its various layers. One may detect this "essence" only via the perceived effect of the whole. Thus, the only way to account for intuitions concerning differences between literary styles seems to be possible by reference to the various elements from which they arise.

Wellek and Warren (1956: 129) propose to replace the old distinction between form and contents: "It would be better to rechristen all the aesthetically indifferent elements 'materials', while the manner in which they acquire aesthetic efficacy may be called 'structure'. [...] 'Structure' is a concept including both content and form so far as they are organized for aesthetic purposes". According to Krueger, such a "structure" will be emotionally experienced more immediately than any one of its parts. In Polányi's formulation, we attend away from the individual materials (which we can know only intellectually, or by "tacit knowledge") to the perceived effect of the whole, which is the source of the unity of the poetic object. This distinction between materials and structures, supplemented by Krueger's and Polányi's observations may explain how intuitions work in general with respect to the attribution of a poem or some corpus of poems to some stylistic category.

When contrasting Mediaeval Hebrew poetry with Modern Hebrew poetry, one must contrast, then, the poems, or the styles, in as many norms, on as many strata as possible. The contrasts of the various norms and strata are independent variables, so that change in one of them does not necessarily entail change in the others. Genres, as I have already insisted, are stratified systems of norms. They make use of norms on the various strata—prosodic, thematic; there are figurative-rhetorical norms, there is the norm called 'point of view'; sometimes also metaphysical qualities are involved, such as the sublime or the tragic. Mediaeval Hebrew poetry is different from Modern Hebrew poetry in its genres: the former adopted the genres prevalent in Mediaeval Arabic poetry, whereas the latter adopted genres prevalent in Western European literature. In the prosodic domain, the former has recourse to a quantitative meter based on the alternation of schwas and vowels, or to a syllabic metre in which schwas do not count; whereas the poetry of the Hebrew Enlightenment (roughly, from 1800 on) uses syllabic meter. In Mediaeval Hebrew poetry strophic forms derived from Arabic poetry are prominent, as is the monotonous "equi-rhyme", repeating the same sound-ending over tens or hundreds of lines. Moreover, there is a link between the metric systems and the rhyming systems: the "equi-rhymed" poems are usually based on the afore-mentioned quantitative meter, whereas the strophic poems on syllabic metre. In the poetry of the Hebrew Enlightenment, strophic forms derived from Western European poetry are prominent. It is interesting to notice that the "equi-rhymed" poems based on quantitative meter are usually felt to be the paradigmatic Mediaeval poem, and not the strophic poems based on syllabic meter. The reason appears to be related to "the principle of contrast set": Hebrew Enlightenment poetry, too, is typically strophic with syllabic meter. In the lexical domain, the distinction is somewhat more difficult. Both Mediaeval and Enlightenment poetry draw their vocabulary typically from the Bible; this requires more delicate distinctions, upon which I cannot dwell here. I shall only mention that in Mediaeval poetry the great variety of morphological models is conspicuous and goes far beyond the semantic needs. This is not an isolated phenomenon: it is related to the severe prosodic demands in the domain of meter as well as of rhyme. In the domain of figurative language, Mediaeval poetry is marked by an abundance of ornaments, as compared to its relative functionality in Enlightenment poetry. The distinction between the two styles in respect of figurative language could be further articulated. Klauzner's foregoing observations suggest, at least, a distinction between the two styles in their themes and idea contents (which belong to the represented world). But, in putting forward a contrast between works "actually engaged in those domains in which traditional religious literature was engaged" and those engaged in "Israel's real problems in the 19th century—problems of society, education, religion, etc.", he ignores that part of secular poetry that is irrelevant to this opposition.

Consequently, the paradigm of Mediaeval Hebrew poetry will be defined with reference to the combination of its various materials: its typical themes; its generic models drawn from Arabic literature; the meter of schwas-and-vowels; the abundance of rhetorical ornaments; its typical vocabulary. The paradigm of Enlightenment poetry will be defined with reference to the combination of its various materials: its typical themes; its generic models drawn from European literature; the syllabic meter; the functionality of its figurative language; its typical vocabulary. The intuitive distinction between the Enlightenment poetry and the one preceding it is, then, rather elusive. It is based on the perceived quality of the whole, rather than of one or another detail. In Polányi's terms, we may have only tacit knowledge of the particulars that constitute the whole (Polányi, 1967: 10).

Moreover, there is no fool-proof criterion for attributing all of Luzzatto's work to either Modern or Mediaeval literature. In this respect, as we have seen, both Lachover and Klauzner make arbitrary claims that require the distortion of literary reality. When we rely, as proposed here, on a stratified system of oppositions for an intuitive distinction between Modern Hebrew literature and the literature preceding it, it becomes conspicuous that no such unambiguous and consistent distinction can be made. In his allegorical plays, for instance, Luzzatto adopts Western European Baroque drama as a generic model. But for meter, he adopts one of the quantitative schwa-and-vowels meters, prevalent in Mediaeval poetry. At the same time, Luzzatto abandoned the "inlay" language, that used to fill the verse lines of Mediaeval poets with Biblical phrases—usually with a twist in their meanings (cf. Chapter 3 n. 8). The problem becomes more acute (if indeed it is a problem) with Dante's contemporary, the Hebrew poet Immanuel of Rome (preceding Luzzatto by 400 years). This poet used to present in his Cantos certain issues twice: once in rhymed prose that followed certain Arabic models, and once in a sonnet, following Dante's model of the Italian sonnet (he wrote also sonnets in Italian). The meter of these sonnets was, again, the Mediaeval schwa-and-vowels meter, while the rhyming words and figurative language were nearly identical with the ones in the rhymed-prose version.

This section has validated, then, two of the afore-mentioned claims: that period style, like a single poem or genre, is a stratified system of norms; and that, furthermore, it is an open concept. As between hills and mountains, there is no natural boundary between two stylistic periods: we draw it to a purpose, in an arbitrary manner.

Some Empirical Evidence

So far, it has been assumed that readers indeed have significant and reliable intuitions concerning the styles of literary works, such as Mannerist, Classicist, Romantic. I have myself adhered to this assumption for about three decades on theoretical grounds, without having satisfactory empirical evidence for it. Recently, however, I came across a study that provided just such evidence, even in a version that is stronger than required for my argument. While the study in question has nothing to say about the structural considerations propounded above, it convincingly demonstrates that stylistic categories can be quite reliably recognized not only within the poetic medium, but even across the various artistic media; and not only by highly trained, but also by artistically naive people. "What began as a simple effort to demonstrate that even the most common cross-media styles are not apparent to aesthetically naive observers ended up as an investigation of how such people are in fact quite able to perceive both cross-media styles and period styles" (Hasenfus, Martindale, & Birnbaum, 1983: 842).

> The sensitivity of artistically naive people to cross-media styles (baroque, neoclassic, and romantic) and to period styles (works composed by artists born during the same epoch) in four media (painting, poetry, music, and architecture) was assessed. In two studies, adult subjects tended spontaneously to sort stimuli according to both cross-media styles and period styles. In a third study, nursery school children were shown to be able to sort pictures of paintings and architectural façades on the basis of cross-media styles. Other experiments using rating scales again demonstrated that artistically naive adults are sensitive to both cross-media styles and period styles even when they are not implicitly urged to disregard medium. These and other studies using rating scales suggested that the bases for discrimination of both cross-media styles and period styles are the dimensions of realistic versus unrealistic and of overall arousal potential. (ibid., 841; abstract)

While my analysis above assumed a considerable sophistication in people from the artistic point of view, the study by Hasenfus *et al.* assessed the performance of artistically naive adults and of nursery school children. The rating scales used gave no information concerning the structural discriminations of the observers. Above, I have quoted Krueger saying that "Even primitive awareness reacts more accurately on the basis of emotional sensitivity than by means of part functions". At least one basis for discrimination by the artistically naive adults and nursery school children of the experiment was the "overall arousal potential of the works", presumably reflecting "part functions" in highly organized, extensive, and closed "total complexes".

The Versatile Reader and Historical Perspective

The present book has been discussing literature in two perspectives. First, it has discussed specific poems at considerable length, analyzed them as the result of the interaction of the idea contents, figurative language, genre, prosody, as objects that have not only meaning, but also perceived effect. Second, it has discussed the qualifications required from the reader to realize the poems. These qualifications include, on the one hand, those kinds of knowledge that in recent years have been called by theoreticians *Poetic Competence*; on the other hand, they include the reader's ability to utilize, for the realization of the poem, cognitive processes that had originally been developed for survival in extra-literary reality. A reader who has acquired these qualifications will be called in what follows *The Versatile Reader*. The remainder of this chapter will be devoted to *The Versatile Reader* and the ways in which he handles the literature of remote as well as of recent historical periods. By the same token, it will explore a number of issues concerning the nature of cultural styles and our awareness of them.

A short survey of the contemporary cultural scene may serve to illuminate the issue. "This is the first century", says Empson (1968: 340), "which has tried to appreciate all art works that ever were, anywhere; and [...] this [...] was bound to produce a kind of traffic jam". One crucial aspect of this "traffic jam" concerns the amount of "past experience" and the "underlying knowledge" of poetic conventions to be assumed in the Versatile Reader, a reader who is able to respond more or less adequately to a wide range of poetic styles. The average high-school student in Israel, for instance, is required to respond to Biblical literature, Homer, Greek Tragedy, Mediaeval Hebrew poetry, Shakespeare, Racine, Romantic poetry, some Nineteenth-Century novels—French and Russian—some modern Hebrew poetry and fiction, Kafka, Beckett, some American and Oriental literature, and so on. Some of these kids do remarkably well. Psychologically—not epistemologically—speaking, there may be some reluctance to concede that such a Versatile Reader "knows" long lists of specific conventions relevant to the poetic styles and genres. This might constitute too heavy a burden on his memory, and might well restrict the responsivity of his consciousness. Since the versatile reader seems to be endowed with some kind of creativity, some more efficient mechanism must be postulated, with the help of which he may "process" meaningfully certain poetic conventions to which he never has been exposed before.

There seem to be two possible approaches to the Versatile Reader's handling of poetic conventions. One approach would credit him with the knowledge of long lists of specific conventions; an alternative approach would credit him with a very high degree of flexibility and creativity, and assume him to be capable of assimilating all the conventions he either already knows, or will discover in the course of his reading. The history of this opposition between the two approaches has yet to be written. Let me mention only a relatively recent controversy that between the "Chicago Critics", and the "Coleridgean" tradition of criticism, as reflected in Wimsatt's criticism of the Chicago School.

> One of the central Chicago doctrines maintains that every poem ought to be seen as belonging to a specific kind, species, or genre of poems (tragic, comic, lyric, didactic) and ought to be treated according to the "causes" which determine this specific kind. A poem should be treated as an instance not of poetry in general but of a specific kind of poetry. (Wimsatt, 1954: 52–53)

> Literary critics in the Coleridgean tradition, if I understand them, have been Occamites with regard to literary entities and specific values. "Let not the categories be multiplied. We will defend the essential concept of a poem, a work of verbal art, and insist that it applies always differently to an indefinite number of individual instances. The name of the species (tragic, comic, lyric) will be neutral descriptive terms of great utility but not different aesthetic essences and no points of reference for different definable rules". (ibid., 54)

What should be considered as "the essential concept of a poem, a work of verbal art"? For our present purpose, a most plausible candidate offers itself in Chapter XIV of Coleridge's *Biographia Literaria*, where Coleridge characterizes Imagination as "the balance or reconcilement of opposite or discordant qualities". Following this conception, Cleanth Brooks asserts that "there is a sense in which paradox is the language appropriate and inevitable to poetry" (Brooks, 1968: 1). But, in addition, one *must* also *explicitly* "insist that it applies always differently to an indefinite number of individual instances".

Such a "universal theory of poetry" (to paraphrase a Chomskyan expression) may be useful in laying the foundation for a generative conception of *The Versatile Reader*. It would offer an account of the "essential concept of a poem"; the conventions of the individual period-styles and genres need include only the specific rules and contents of a genre or some period-style which differentiate it from other genres or period-styles. In this way, we may avoid both "the critical monism" of which Ronald Crane, leader of the Chicago School, accused Brooks, *and* the Chicago critics' "pluralism" involving separate systems which, according to Wimsatt (1954: 43), "are represented mainly as parallels or analogues, using separate vocabularies for separate purposes and not translatable into one another except with great distortion".

This version of Wimsatt's "Coleridgean Critic" relies on an epistemological model of gradual differentiation. It seems to be in harmony, in a significant way, both with our above conception of perceiving period styles, and with processes of gradual differentiation in various areas of cognitive growth. It seems to fit, as well, the actual process of real readers' acquiring their versatility. Thus, our model may have what may be described by another Chomskyan term as "explanatory adequacy".

One of the main lessons of the present theory is that poetics is not just a casual collection of arbitrary conventions. Most of the more abstract conventions and many of the immediately observable elements have come, in the process of repeated social transmission, to take forms which are well fitted to the natural capacities and constraints of the human brain. The individual can respond in a roughly appropriate manner to many of these conventions even when exposed to them for the first few times, since their poetic effects depend to a considerable extent upon the exploitation of cognitive structures and processes that have been evolved for the needs of survival, for the purpose of man's adaptation to his physical and social environment.

All this does not imply, however, that we may safely ignore poetic conventions as some of the (Coleridgean) New Critics did. The better a reader versed in the conventions of a given type of poetry, the more perceptive he may become, that is, the better he may become in identifying and picking up the units to be processed in a given poem. They are used as cognitive schemata, hypotheses, for the pick-up of information from poems. Furthermore, as the writings of some of the New Critics may attest, the penalty for ignoring conventions is ending up with a uniform body of, say, *paradoxical* poems (as the "essential concept of a poem"), in which one can hardly tell whether there is any systematic difference between Shakespeare's *Macbeth*, Donne's "The Canonization", Milton's "L'Allegro" and "Il Penseroso", Herrick's "Corinna's Going A-Maying", Pope's "The Rape of the Lock", Gray's "Elegy written in a Country Church-Yard", Wordsworth's Immortality Ode, Keats's "Ode on a Grecian Urn", Tennyson's "Tears, Idle Tears", and Yeats's "Among School-Children" (Brooks, 1968).

Poetry *is* the reconcilement of opposite or discordant qualities. But in different types of poetry, systematically different kinds of opposite elements are reconciled in systematically different ways. The Versatile Reader, even if he is not acquainted in advance with these different kinds of discordant elements and ways of reconciliation, may discover some of them (and respond to them in the course of reading), by contrasting poems of different types. Thus, conventions *are* relevant to a moderate Coleridgean system, as "neutral descriptive terms of great utility"; for the Versatile Reader it is sufficient to use them within a top-down system, as distinctive features or contrastive devices that differentiate systematically between different kinds of poems. Conventions and configurations of conventions can be intuitively discovered in the course of reading a newly encountered poem, but only to the extent to which they differentiate it from already familiar groups of poems. The task of the teacher or the literary critic remains, then, to point out to the reader whether these newly encountered differentiating elements are there as individual characteristics of a specific work, or as part of a system of conventions. In the latter case, the reader learns what he already knows.

This conception of a hierarchic model of conventions, realized by way of contrasting stylistic categories to other, neighboring categories, relies on a cognitive mechanism that has *not* been acquired specifically for the purposes of literary response; indeed, we are confronting one of the basic mechanisms by which the cognitive system chooses the "good example" of the various categories, that is, *the principle of contrast set* (see above, this chapter, and cf. Chapter 9, Mervis' discussion of the theory of "good example").

The cognitive structure and processes and their exploitation for aesthetic purposes, as discussed throughout the present book, combined with all the knowledge acquired for specifically literary purposes as well as that acquired for extra-literary purposes of survival, are indispensable, but still insufficient, for an explanation of the performance of the Versatile Reader. As I will be arguing at considerable length in Chapter 21, such a performance also requires a certain cognitive style, viz., what I have called, in Keats's term, *negative capability*, "that is when man is capable of being in uncertainties, mysteries, doubts, without any irritable reaching after fact & reason" (letter to his brothers, 21 December, 1817). This "negative capability", in turn, presupposes (maybe even consists in) a complex cognitive structure, characterized neither by rigidly fixed rules, nor by an absence of rules, but by a greater number of conflicting rules on the lower levels of information processing which may be accommodated by rules on a higher level (cf. Chapter 21). It is within such an overall structure that the cognitive processes discussed throughout the present work can account for the performance of the Versatile Reader. .

Romantic, Metaphysical, and *Précieux* Poetry

In the foregoing, I have presented, following Cleanth Brooks (who, again, followed Coleridge), a possible candidate for the "essential concept of a poem": "the reconcilement of opposite or discordant qualities". I have also suggested that such a definition in itself is insufficient: in different types of poetry, systematically different kinds of opposite elements are reconciled in systematically different ways. The Versatile Reader, even if he is not acquainted in advance with these different kinds of discordant elements and ways of reconciliation, may discover some of them (and respond to them in the course of reading), by contrasting poems of different types.

This relationship between poetic style on the one hand, and the kinds of oppositions and kinds of reconciliation on the other, is central to the issue at hand. Of the many possible combinations, I wish to examine here only one, but one that constitutes one of the most crucial stages of the process of cognitive differentiation mentioned above; I have in mind the changing relationships between paradoxical contents and paradoxical phrasing. Of the four logical possibilities of combination there are three that are of interest here: paradoxical contents and non-paradoxical phrasing; paradoxical contents and paradoxical phrasing; non-paradoxical contents and paradoxical phrasing. Accordingly, we obtain three paradigms of poetry, most typically represented by Romantic, Metaphysical, and *Précieux*[2] poetry, respectively.

Let us begin our discussion with one of the most widely-quoted definitions of Metaphysical poetry (originally due to James Smith (Smith, 1933)), in Odette de Mourgues's succinct formulation:

> Mr. J. C. Smith has shown how poetry handling ontological problems will possess the note of tension and strain which Professor Grierson finds in the metaphysical poets and calls "the strain of passionate paradoxical reasoning". "Problems of this kind are not infinite in number and variety" says Mr. Smith. They are variations on the essential problem of the many and the one; they are problems of time, space and eternity ... (Mourgues, 1953: 8)

However, as we shall see in a moment, a considerable part of Romantic poetry at its best deals with the very same ontological problems, "of the many and the one, of time, space, and eternity". Consequently, the thematic side of this definition must be supplemented by the definition of the typical Metaphysical Conceit:

> The elements of the conceit must be such that they can enter into a solid union and at the same time preserve their warring identity. (ibid., 9)

But how does Romantic poetry handle these "variations on the essential problem of the many and the one, the problems of time, space and eternity"? Descriptions of apparently infinite space in Romantic poetry serve quite frequently as metaphor for infinite time, thus revealed in space perceived "here and now". "By following their instinctive love of visible things", says Bowra (1961: 273), the romantic poets "could find themselves in the presence of what they called 'eternity'". In poems like Shelley's "Ozymandias", the translucence of eternity through the visible world is reinforced by an additional metonymic device: the sand is simultaneously a metonymic expression for the "boundless" desert and for the destructive force of infinite time. Consider the concluding lines of the poem:

(5)   "My name is Ozymandias, King of Kings:
         Look at my works, ye mighty, and despair!"
         Nothing behind remains. Round the decay

---

2   I have taken this term from Mourgues, 1953.

> Of that colossal wreck, boundless and bare,
> The lone and level sands stretch far away.

Ozymandias' bragging words must be understood, then, simultaneously, in two different contexts, played off one against the other: the context of his presumably impressive buildings, and the context of "The lone and level sands [that] stretch far away". Thus, the poetic passage connects abstractions like "time", "transience", to the concrete description via a concrete metonymy, "sand". In such descriptions, the integration of concrete and abstract elements is at its maximum, and the reader is not aware of the conflict between them. Consequently, we are dealing here with poetry in which paradoxical content is presented in a non-paradoxical phrasing (what I have called in Chapter 4 *integrated focus*).

Metaphysical and *Précieux* poetry are opposed to Romantic poetry by virtue of their paradoxical phrasing (what I have called *split focus*); at the same time, they are opposed to one another by virtue of the nature of reality referred to by the paradoxical phrasing. Both seventeenth century English Metaphysical poetry and eleventh century Hebrew Metaphysical poetry confront, quite frequently, a paradoxical mode of existence, whereas in *Précieux* poetry, the paradoxical phrasing refers to some non-paradoxical mode of existence. Both seventeenth century English poetry— Metaphysical and *Précieux* alike—and eleventh century Hebrew poetry in Spain developed against a background of rhetorical-ornamental poetry, and have ample recourse to paradoxical phrasings. Poetry, in which the paradox resides in the figurative vehicle only, but not in the tenor, is *Précieux*; poetry, in which the paradox resides both in the vehicle and the tenor, is Metaphysical.

The following verse is from a divine poem by Shlomo Ibn Gabirol:

מְרוֹמוֹת לֹא יְכִילוּךְ לְשִׁבְתָּךְ / וְאוּלָם יֵשׁ מְקוֹמְךָ תּוֹךְ שְׂעִפִּי

> məromot lo yəxiluxa ləˇivtax
> wəʾulam yeˇ məqomxa tox səʿippi

(6)   The Skies cannot contain Thee to sit there
        but Thou hast a place in my thoughts

This expression refers to one of the paradoxical attributes of God, who is greater than anything we can imagine, but at the same time resides in the smallest things as well. By the same token, Man, too, is possibly presented as great and small at one and the same time. Thus, this paradoxical phrasing refers to some paradoxical modes of existence. Or, consider the following epigram by the eleventh century Hebrew poet, Yehuda Halevy:

עַבְדֵי זְמָן עַבְדֵי עֲבָדִים הֵם / עֶבֶד אֲדֹנָי הוּא לְבַד חָפְשִׁי

ʿavdey zəman ʿavdey ʿăvadim hem / ʿɛvɛd ʾădonay hu ləvad ḥofˇi

(7)   The slaves of time are slaves of slaves
           the slave of God alone is free

The paradoxical phrasing in the second hemistich refers to a paradoxical conception of reality, which is one of the central paradoxes of the monotheistic religions. We may encounter the same paradox in Donne's Holy Sonnet 14:

(8)   for I
           Except you enthrall mee, never shall be free

It is illuminating to compare the two versions of this paradox. On the one hand, both sharpen the generalization, Yehuda Halevy by *alone*, Donne by *Except ... never*. On the other hand, in Donne's poem there is an underlying dramatic situation, pointed out by Pierre Legouis as well as by Wilie Sypher as a central device in Metaphysical poetry in general and in Donne's poetry in particular (the "dramatic device"), and which, according to Helen Gardner, may make the difference between epigram and metaphysical conceit. Yehuda Halevy, by contrast to Donne, leaves his paradox on the level of a generalized epigram;[3] he, however, combines his paradox with another typical metaphysical device, the pun. The genitive phrase "slave of slaves" is, in fact, ambiguous in Hebrew. It may be construed as a superlative, as "of the lowest slaves", as in "a slave of slaves shall he be to his brothers" (Genesis 9: 25), or as a plain possessive, "a slaves' slave"; and, significantly enough, both meanings fit into the context, in different ways. The first meaning sharpens as far as possible the contradiction between *slaves* and *free*; the second meaning adds a rational motivation, as it were, to the irrational statement: "the slave of God... is free", relative to those who are slaves to the slaves of God.

Now consider the following ornamental use of paradox, in a drinking-poem by Moshe Ibn Ezra

אֵשׁ קָדְחוּ אוּרָיו וְלֹא נֻפַּחוּ / תּוֹךְ מִזְרְקֵי בָרָד וְהִתְלַקָּחוּ

ʾeˇ qadəḥu ʾuraw wəlo nuppaḥu / tox mizrəqey barad wəhitlaqqaḥu

(9)   The flames of fire were kindled unblown
           in fountains of hail which caught fire

---

[3]   This is *not* a difference between the specific period-styles, nor between individual poets, but between poems. Notice, that in the quotation from Ibn Gabirol's poem, the dramatic device prevails.

This paradoxical expression can easily be settled, when it is realized that it refers to some reality that is not paradoxical: the wine is in crystal goblets. The wine has some properties in common with fire (redness, heat); and both hail and goblets consist of transparent crystals. But the reader utilizes them only for identifying the possible (highly conventionalized) referent.

As a final, less obvious instance I wish to consider a pair of examples from English poetry of the sixteenth and seventeenth centuries. In Shakespeare's *A Midsummer Night's Dream*, III. ii., Helena utters the following sequence of lines:

> (10)   So we grew together,
> Like to a double cherry, seeming parted;
> But yet a union in partition,
> Two lovely berries moulded on one stem;
> So, with two seeming bodies, but one heart,
> Two of the first, like coats in heraldry,
> Due but to one, and crownéd with one crest.

This sequence is part of a longer catalog. In a term proposed in Chapters 2 and 18 with reference to Whitman, it is an "illustrative catalog": it illustrates "the ontological problem of the one and the many". As suggested in those chapters, the cognitive system saves mental processing space in the handling of such catalogues by recoding them in a more efficient way: it abstracts one category ("the ontological problem of the one and the many") from the items that are similar and disregards (or, at least, decreases the weight of) the irrelevant concrete texture, which is different in every item. Thus, the elements of these images lose their "warring identity". The same ontological problem is presented by Donne's famous compasses image, discussed in Chapters 4 and 15:

> (11)   If they be two, they are two so
> As stiffe twin compasses are two,
> Thy soule, the fixt foot, makes no show
> To move, but doth if th'other doe.
>
> And though it in the centre sit,
> Yet when the other far doth rome,
> It leans and hearkens after it,
> And growes erect as that comes home.

In Chapter 4, I make, among others, the following comment. The compasses serve as a good example of the ontological problem of the one and the many; the other properties of a compass are irrelevant to the illustration of this idea. The texture which is irrelevant to the idea illustrated may serve to prevent the image from losing its reality, from becoming a "mere illustration of an idea"; hence to preserve its

concrete identity. Now, a variety of additional aspects of the compasses, all representing "irrelevant texture" with respect to the original "illustration" of the "ontological problem", are successively exploited for illustrations of additional ideas related to the situation of departing lovers. Thus, the reader is prevented from attending away from the image-vehicle to the ideas illustrated; he is forced, time and
again, to attend back to additional aspects of it. In this way, both the image-vehicle
(the compasses) and the set of ideas illustrated (related to the departing lovers) "preserve their *warring identity*", in James Smith's words; each attempting to establish
itself in the reader's perception as much as possible, thus heightening the witty
quality of the image. In terms of the present discussion, the two passages can be regarded as various treatments of the same kind of paradox: Donne's image is the prototypical metaphysical image; Shakespeare's Renaissance catalogue is a first step in
the direction of the *précieux*.

One ought to remark, finally, that unlike what is the case in seventeenth century
English poetry, in Mediaeval Hebrew poetry this difference between *Précieux* and
Metaphysical poetry is not one between the individual styles of poets, but a difference between genres. In divine and philosophical poetry, paradoxical phrasing usually refers to some paradoxical reality, whereas in drinking songs, for instance, the
paradoxical phrasing usually refers, rather playfully, to some non-paradoxical reality.

The foregoing discussion would suggest that the Versatile Reader is capable of
making significant distinctions between three stylistic paradigms in vastly different
periods, languages, and cultures, provided that he can abstract and apply two pairs of
opposites and their creative combinations: [+PARADOXICAL] ~ [–PARADOXI-
CAL]—applied to the pair **phrasing ~ mode of existence.** As soon as the reader
becomes aware of these possibilities, he can perform the various combinations and
experience their respective stylistic quality, even if he is exposed for the first time
to this specific instance of poetry.

The question is now to be raised whether the different varieties of Mediaeval Hebrew poetry, of sixteenth and seventeenth century European poetry and the various
kinds of modernistic poetry can be subsumed (in spite of their individual differences)
under one major literary concept. I think this is the case, and that the concept in
question is that of **Mannerism**. The objection can be made that in doing this, we
are slurring crucial differences between them. I claim that the opposite is the case
and will try to make my point in the next section as follows. First, by asserting
that the various styles all are varieties of Mannerism, I am rendering them comparable to one another. Second, and by the same token, I am rendering them con-
trastable to one another in meaningful respects.

Mannerist, Metaphysical, *Précieux*

It is difficult to draw the border between the three terms in the title of the present
section; hence, many critics use them interchangeably. The terms have this in

common that they compel the reader to focus attention on the individual figures of speech rather than on the composition of the whole. For each one of these terms, we can find a critic who would use it for the whole range of possibilities covered by the three terms. On the other hand, there are critics who make efforts to define and restrict the application of each of the three terms. Many critics use the term *Mannerism* in a pejorative sense, to refer to a style marked by an excess of ornaments and frequent repetition of a limited number of stylistic devices, whether functionally required or not. This links the term with *Précieux*. On the other hand, at least one important theoretician uses it in a very different sense:

> Thus, mannerism has two modes, technical and psychological. Behind the technical ingenuities of mannerist style there usually is a personal unrest, a complex psychology that agitates the form and the phrase. (Sypher, 1955: 116)

Sypher's usage links the term *Mannerism* with *Metaphysical*. I use the term *Metaphysical* when the "personal unrest", the "complex psychology" of Mannerism are emphasized by a variety of densely packed technical devices. When a term is needed to refer to the whole area, *Précieux* as well as *Metaphysical*, I resort to *Mannerism*. This section will attempt to show how the term *Mannerism* covers all those areas of poetic conception.

In Chapter 16, we shall see the cognitive functions fulfilled by such typical metaphysical devices as the metaphysical pun and conceit, and we shall use these functions in an effort to explain the effects of those devices on the readers. In *Précieux* poetry we may encounter the same kinds of devices, but with strongly reduced effect. In what follows, I propose to consider at some length a process of great cognitive interest, that tends to *reduce* the expressive force of highly affective devices: one of the assumptions of cognitive poetics is that *précieux* devices are highly affective devices in which cognitive activity has fossilized. This is the source of ornamental art.[4]

"There is in the human mind a strong reluctance", says Wilson Knight (1965: XI), "to face, with full consciousness, the products of poetic genius". A similar conception was put forward by Anton Ehrenzweig (1965) in relation to music and the visual arts. Ehrenzweig elaborates at great length on the defense mechanisms with the help of which human society protects itself against the expressive force of artistic devices and turns them into style, that is, harmless ornament. Gombrich's 1963 position (see below) is, largely, in harmony with Ehrenzweig's conclusions. I shall attempt to apply here briefly Ehrenzweig's conception to ornament in poetry, modified by Wylie Sypher's conception. Ehrenzweig speaks of three stages of the

---

[4]   In chapter 2, I have traced in some detail the putative process by which ambivalent emotions may have been "sharpened" into series of paradoxes, taking out the "undesirable stress" from them, while solidifying into the frozen convention of "contrarious passions in the lover".

development of artistic devices: The first one is a stage when artistic devices are perceived subliminally, so that they can strongly affect what he calls the "depth mind". The more emphatic these devices, the stronger their emotional appeal, provided that they don't become consciously perceptible. When they become semi-consciously perceptible, they are considered to be in bad taste, cheaply emotional. This is the second stage. At the third stage, these devices are turned into ornaments, with drastically reduced emotional appeal. As long as the "inarticulate" glissandos and vibratos of singers and the great masters of the violin are not consciously audible, they have a strong and valued emotional appeal. When second-rate singers and violinists exaggerate them so that they become semi-consciously audible, such devices are considered "offensive", or "in bad taste". In the third stage, this offensive emotional force is eliminated, when these devices of ambiguous status are "sharpened" into fully conscious, but rigid and lifeless ornaments. A fourth stage may be added: this is when such "dead" ornaments are revived through poetic manipulation. In Chapter 13, we shall see how such highly expressive devices as repetition and the vocative are turned into *style* in the popular ballad "Edward"; there we shall also see, how the restricted formula of these fossilized devices is revived again, and exploited as a major expressive resource.

When we come now to whole works and to period-styles, we may realize that Ehrenzweig's three stages roughly correspond to three out of the four stages of Renaissance Style, according to Sypher (1955: 6): A provisional formulation (Renaissance), a disintegration (Mannerism) and what Sypher calls "academic codification". We might suggest that in the first stage, that of the "provisional formulation", the art-consumer (reader, listener, spectator) tends to attend away from the individual devices to the architecture of the whole, whereas in the second stage he is forced to attend back to the devices that supply "cheap" or "easy effects", immediate satisfaction, with possible serious damage to the architectural structure of the whole. In Melchiori's phrasing (1966: 138), "the total effect is frequently lost sight of, or is reached through accumulation rather than through a harmonious disposition of structural parts", whereas "details are worked out with a goldsmith's care". In fact, this is exactly what happens in the third stage: one "technique" of ornamental style to prevent the reader from facing the expressive resources of poetry is to multiply them and thus cancel their uniqueness and take out the disturbing element from them. "A danger of the system lies in the fact that, in manneristic epochs, the ornatus is piled on indiscriminately and meaninglessly. In rhetoric itself, then, lies concealed one of the seeds of Mannerism. It produces a luxuriant growth in Latin Middle Ages" (Curtius, 1973: 274).

A possible (extreme) means for creating what may be regarded as "cheap or easy effects" is the use of jewellery, or of sophisticated perfumes as metaphoric vehicles. This we find, typically, in the Mediaeval poetic genre devoted to the triple theme of drinking, love, and the description of the garden in which these activities take place. Pagis (1970: 257), in his study of the poetics of Mediaeval Hebrew secular poetry, says: "The poet neglects many details of reality; on the other hand, he brings up typical details whose metaphoric presentation suggests the luxuries of a refined culture: the odour of blossoming is like rare perfumes, the wine is like a ruby set in crystal; flowers, too, resemble a variety of gems, the whole garden itself is like rich embroidery or jewels of pure flattened gold". Artistic pleasure typically arises when some emotional or perceptual tension is replaced, or rather resolved, by some structure that induces a feeling of stability. Jewels, rare perfumes, rich embroideries, "gold to airy thinness beat" are paradigms of pleasurable sensations with no need to undergo first the experience of perceptual or emotional tensions. This explanation can be supplemented by one of Gombrich's comments (1963: 15). "For what else is gold but the glittering, sunlike metal that never ages or fades? Or what else are jewels but gaily sparkling stones which do not break? There was a time [...] when riches, economic wealth, could thus feast the eye, when the miser could enjoy the sparkle of his hoard, instead of having to admire balance sheets. The fact that wealth can no longer be seen, that it no longer provides direct visual gratifications, belongs with the many dissociations of value from immediate experience, which is the price we pay for our complex civilization". The question cognitive poetics asks in relation to such instances is: "What is the typical effect achieved by such a convention in the poetry of gardens?" The answer seems to lie in the foregoing generalizations about the turning of expressive resources into "easy effects" and ornaments, by yielding directly imagined "visual gratification".

In divine poetry, there are similar, illuminating cases. The mystic experience reflected in much of Jewish spiritual literature hides many extremely dangerous adventures. One may remove these troubling elements from expressive resources, by turning them into frozen style. One of the most effective expressive resources is repetition. In much poetry, said to be derived from so-called *merkava* mysticism, this repetition degenerated into rigid formulas repeated in an enormous number of lines, where only one word or phrase is replaced from line to line, in a fixed place, in an alphabetical order. If, as information theory states, the amount of information an expression carries increases in proportion with its unexpectedness, such poetic structures are voided of all expressive force. In Christian sacred texts, too, the fossils of similar processes can be detected. Gombrich (1984: 294) makes a comment that seems to be pertinent: "If a legal text follows certain formulas, a few words will suffice for recognition, and if the text is a litany or chant [...] the repeated words will be wholly redundant. What is more interesting is the relation between stringencies and redundancy".

Against this background, I shall attempt to reinterpret my foregoing discussion of types of paradox, interpreting them as two stages in the evolution of one and the same literary device. This device is sometimes used for the heightened effectiveness, to express the threatening intricacy of reality; sometimes as a mere ornament for achieving "easy effects". We have found that in Moshe Ibn Ezra's drinking-poem the paradoxical expression can easily be resolved, when it is realized that it refers to some reality that is not paradoxical: the wine is in crystal goblets. As I have suggested, the wine does have some properties in common with fire (redness, heat); and both hail and goblets consist of transparent crystals. But these shared properties are kept inactive in the reader's consciousness: he utilizes them only for identifying the possible (highly conventionalized) referent. In this way, the potentially expressive resource becomes a frozen convention.

By contrast, the verse from Shlomo Ibn Gabirol's divine poem, quoted above, refers to one of the paradoxical attributes of God. If Ibn Ezra's paradox was a "surface paradox", and can be associated with a *précieux* style, Ibn Gabirol's paradox is a "paradox of depth", and can be associated with a metaphysical style of poetry: it refers to a paradoxical mode of existence. In the first instance, the reader may easily escape the uncertainties and anxieties of a paradoxical existence; in the latter, he must remain in it and experience the cognitive tension that heightens the artistic effect.

Coda: Historical Perspective and Individual Consciousness

In order to account for the Versatile Reader's performance, some additional issues must be considered, such as whether we can approach remote literatures of the past in a meaningful way, or whether such attempts are doomed to failure. My position is that such questions are quite similar to questions of approaching a single poem of the past or of the present; and are not unlike the questions concerning the ways we handle our extra-literary reality. Such questions and their respective answers, I suggest, are not so much different in kind, as in details.

I have been working throughout the present work with Wellek and Warren's conception of the mode of existence of a literary work of art, according to which a poem is a stratified system of norms, to be realized only partially in any individual reading. According to the same authors, period styles and literary genres, too, are stratified systems of norms and, I should add, the same epistemological and cognitive issues are raised by the problems of their realizations in the acts of knowing. However, as Kant's microscope analogy (see below) as well as Wittgenstein's criticism of it may suggest, these issues go far beyond the perception and the understanding of literature, and concern the very foundations of our existence.

I shall attempt to approach the issue through E. D. Hirsch's presentation of the metaphysical dimension of Heidegger's and his adherents' historicism.

> An interpreter must therefore learn to live with his historical self just as Freud would have him live with his subliminal self, not by trying to negate it, which is impossible, but by consciously making the best of it. (Hirsch, 1972: 251)

According to Hirsch, the historicists draw from the Freudian analogy the conclusion that "interpreters make the best of our historicity not by reconstructing an alien world from our texts but by interpreting them within our own world and make them speak to us"—a position that is, Hirsch says, "skeptical and dogmatic at once". Sufficiently misunderstood, however, this analogy may lead to an altogether different, or even opposite, position. The interpreter must learn to live with his historical self, by becoming conscious of it, just as Freud would have him become conscious of his subliminal self. The more we know about our own subliminal or historical self, the more effectively we can distinguish it from the others. Extremely vicious disturbances may arise when one is not sufficiently conscious of one's own historical or subliminal self, when these selves interfere with one's ability to discriminate one's own self from the objects of one's cognition. The first step to remedy this is to become conscious of such interferences, and eliminate their effect. In other words, rather than succumbing to one's historical self, one must eliminate its harmful effect by becoming conscious of it.

In fact, the present book assumes that any knowledge of the poetry and poetics of the Hebrew Middle Ages, for instance, may improve our understanding of their spirit; nevertheless, this is not a sufficient (perhaps not even a necessary) condition. Whoever believes that he can "accurately reconstruct past meanings", or the spirit of a past age by mere acquisition of information in ever-increasing amounts, deceives himself (this, of course, is not to give legitimacy to ignorance). We shall see in Chapter 17, with reference to "Ibn Gabirol's Grotesque Disease", the difficulties encountered by the greatest scholar of Mediaeval Hebrew Poetry, when confronted with poems that describe the most repellent symptoms of this disease by using similes that suggest beauty and pleasantness.[5] Here, the key for responding to these poems is not in the learning of additional items of the poetic conventions of the period, but in the reader's becoming aware of the nature of his own responses.

The notion of what Hirsch elsewhere has called "the fallacy of homogeneous past" may be of some service. An awareness that in the present there is a great variety of attitudes toward possible poetic effects, may induce an awareness that the past is not homogeneous either. By becoming aware of one's own intolerance of ambiguity or of emotional disorientation, and of possible kinds of poetry in the present and the past, one may eventually grant the legitimacy of the grotesque effect in Ibn Gabirol's poems about his illness. In short, in order to respond properly to this kind of poetry, the critic or scholar ought both to acquire additional differentiation, additional knowledge about possible structures and effects in present and past poetry, and acquire more understanding of the nature of his own responses, so that he may reduce their potentially harmful interference.

We are inescapably imprisoned in the Seven Towers of our consciousness: a consciousness that has been shaped here and now, and which no amount of knowledge will let us break out of: all knowledge will reach us through the distorting prism of our here-and-now self. The only way to "neutralize" this distorting effect is

---

5   Ibn Gabirol seems to have suffered from a repulsive dermatological disease. In his poetry he "heightened, to any degree heightened" (to use Hopkins' phrase) the description of the symptoms, by using grotesque imagery. Schirmann consulted present-day doctors with the poems, and eventually came up with the diagnosis that the poet suffered from tuberculosis of the skin. Needless to say, I am less than happy with such a treatment of poems.

to discern the peculiar kind of distortion through which we, as individual consciousnesses, perceive present-day reality or the poetry of recent or remote ages. My discussions of the implied critic's decision style are, in fact, aimed at this goal.

Finally, I should briefly consider this issue in the perspective of David Pears's criticism of the old Kantian microscope analogy in his introductory remarks on Kant's and Wittgenstein's critical philosophy.

> If a scientist became convinced that what he saw through his microscope was an effect of a flaw in the lens, he would start all over again. But the analogy is imperfect at the essential point. A microscope yields one set of observations, whereas what comes through the lens of the mind is the totality of human experience. So in this case there is no possibility of sidestepping and no independent check, and the very idea, that this lens might be flawed, seems to be empty. (Pears, 1971: 30–31)

At some varience with Pears's implications, my point is that we do not build worlds of individual fantasies under the pretext of reading a poem or entering the world of a different cultural period. We try to make sure that the perceived poems or cultural periods are sufficiently similar, so as to afford meaningful discussions between a great variety of perceivers. This can be done only if we find out as much as possible about our shared tools and strategies of perception, as well as about the peculiar biases of our individual lenses that seem to be responsible for individual differences in perception. I submit that my discussions of "Mental Performance" in Chapter 2 and of "The Implied Critic's Decision Style" in Chapter 21 are major steps in this direction.

CHAPTER 13

Style as Diagnosis and as Hypothesis Practical Application: The Ballad "Edward"

**Stylistic and Psychological
Syndromes in Literary Criticism**

The foregoing chapters were organized around theoretical issues; specific texts were discussed rather briefly, by way of illustration. By contrast, the present chapter is focused on one single poem the Scotch folk ballad "Edward", applying to it notions developed in the preceding chapters. The chapter addresses a wide variety of issues, most of them mentioned in the preceding chapters, but some of them anticipating later chapters. In chapter 3, "Constructing a Stable World", I have suggested that stylistic categories like period style, genre, or archetype have the nature of a hypothesis or "regulative concept"; in Chapter 12, "The Versatile Reader—Style As Open Concept", I have elaborated on the structures of such hypotheses or "regulative concepts". In Chapter 3 I also stressed, with Margolis, that interpretations, too, have the nature of hypotheses. In the present chapter, I am exploring, at considerable length, issues concerning the application of such hypotheses in particular instances, with reference to the ballad "Edward". In both Chapter 3 and the present chapter, I also allude to Ehrenzweig's conception according to which individual readers as well as society tend to apply defense mechanisms to artistic devices of great expressive force, turning them into "ornament". I am also invoking Wilson Knight, who says that "There is in the human mind a strong reluctance to face, with full consciousness, the products of poetic genius". This issue is intimately related to that of the "Implied Critic's Decision Style", discussed in Chapter 21, and also referred to in Chapter 17. These and related issues will be also explored here with reference to the same ballad.

The present chapter is an inquiry into the question "How does extra-literary, or aesthetically indifferent information become of aesthetic interest"; or, more specifically, "What is the use of postulating a psychological or of a stylistic syndrome[1] in

---

[1] I use *syndrome* in the sense of "a Pattern of characteristic symptoms occurring together".

the course of literary interpretation?" By the same token, it is an inquiry into the question "How do some readers prevent aesthetically indifferent information from assuming aesthetic interest?" The psychological syndrome will be typically represented by the term "the Oedipus complex"; the stylistic syndrome by that of "the ballad genre". Both will be discussed in relation to the popular ballad "Edward". It will be noticed that in such a formulation, a concept which belongs to the traditional notion of "content" and one which belongs to the traditional notion of "form" are treated on a par. It will perhaps also be apparent that I have adopted a rival pair of terms, proposed by Wellek and Warren:

> It would be better to rechristen all aesthetically indifferent elements "materials", while the manner in which they acquire aesthetic efficacy may be called "structure". This distinction is by no means a simple renaming of the old pair, content and form. It cuts right across the old boundary lines. "Materials" include elements formerly considered part of content, and parts formerly considered formal. Structure is a concept including both content and form so far as they are organized for aesthetic purposes. (Wellek and Warren, 1956: 129)

Diagnosis and Hypothesis

The statements "Poem X is a ballad" or "Protagonist Y suffers from an Oedipus complex" are ambiguous, according to—roughly speaking—whether it is a conclusion or a point of departure in our discussion; in other words, whether we are interested in the syndrome as diagnosis or as hypothesis. A diagnosis boils down all available evidence to *one* conclusion. A hypothesis is a mental scheme which helps to find and organize as much data as possible.

At the symposium *Perception—An Approach to Personality* held in 1949-1950 at the University of Texas (Blake and Ramsey eds., 1951) many of the papers that were presented reinforced the impression that there is a persistent preoccupation in the interpretation of perception and personality with the struggle to achieve definiteness and environmental stability, that is, to avoid ignorance and ambiguity. In this context, psychologists distinguish between flexible and rigid attitudes, as determined by a person's tolerance or intolerance of ambiguity. 'Rigid' persons, who do not tolerate ambiguous situations "have in effect to relieve their anxiety by having rapid closure in cognitive and perceptual reactions as well as in emotional and social spheres" (Miller, 1951: 263).

> This is a way in which some organisms handle the problem of ignorance by coming to a conclusion—any conclusion—in order to avoid the anxiety that would otherwise arise. (ibid.)

In this light, we may consider the systematic ambiguity of assertions concerning psychological and stylistic syndromes, e.g., "Poem X is a ballad", or "Protagonist Y suffers from an Oedipus complex". As diagnoses the reassertions entail 'rapid closure'. They achieve certainty by *exclusion:* exclusion of ambiguous elements in the poem and, in parallel, exclusion of complex, ambiguous "cognitive and perceptual reactions" in the emotional sphere.

Pigeonholing gives certainty, but no insight into, or sensitive response to, a poem. As hypotheses, "Poem X is a ballad" or "Protagonist Y has an Oedipus complex" allow us the freedom "to live in uncertainties, mysteries, doubts, without any irritable reaching for facts and reasons"; they enable the reader to suspend or delay closure. By attributing a poem to a certain style category, or a protagonist to a certain psychological category, we avail ourselves of a set of norms (a "syndrome"), held consciously or unconsciously. In the course of reading, one perceives more clearly those elements in the poem which conform with the set of norms; having partially dispelled ignorance, one may delay 'closure' and master 'deviating' elements, too. Thus, ignorance is eliminated by *inclusion:* inclusion of ambiguous elements in the poem and, possibly, inclusion of complex, ambiguous 'cognitive and perceptual reactions' in the emotional sphere. If closure is sufficiently delayed, a complex interplay between the hypothesis and the poem may take place. The reader gives priority in perception to those elements which conform with his hypothesis, while he 'adapts' to it some of the 'deviating' elements, possibly perceived 'subliminally', organizing them into a hierarchy. If there are too many elements that disconfirm the hypothesis, the reader may 'amend' his set of expected norms—which, in turn, amends his perception of the poem.

Here, too, pigeonholing gives certainty, but no insight into, or sensitive response to, a poem. This can be conveniently explained in terms of the cognitive mechanisms assumed by structuralist poetics to underlie the use of rhetorical figures.

> The repertoire of rhetorical figures serves as a set of instructions which readers can apply when they encounter a problem in the text, though in some cases it is not so much the operations that are important as the reassurance that what seems odd is perfectly acceptable since it is figurative expression of some kind and therefore capable of being understood. If one knows that hyperbole, litotes, zeugma, syllepsis, oxymoron, paradox and irony are possible, one will not be surprised to find words or phrases that must be dealt with in the ways that these figures suggest. (Culler, 1975: 181)

Paradoxically enough, this passage gives us a cue not only to how "the repertoire of rhetorical figures" gives insight, but also to how "pigeonholing gives certainty, but no insight". The crucial clause seems to be "not so much the operations that are important as the reassurance". However, "instructions" and "reassurance" are not—or should not be taken to be two independent factors, as implied by this clause. "Reassurance" should not be considered as a goal in itself, but rather as a psychological pre-condition under which the instructions *can* be carried out. Pigeon-holing results, when readers or critics are content with the "reassurance that what seems odd is perfectly acceptable since it is figurative expression", or a convention of a genre, or a symptom of a psychological syndrome, but have no thought of getting (or performing) any further instructions. For these readers, the performing of instructions could, "at best", lead to the final "reassurance that what seems odd is perfectly acceptable"; "at worst", it might "unnecessarily" complicate things or even lead to new ambiguities. So why bother?

Conventional Style and Individual Expression in "Edward"

Anton Ehrenzweig (1965), in his sometimes speculative but always illuminating book on the psychology of music and of the visual arts, puts forward the view that, in order to avoid the more "dangerous", expressive elements of an artistic work, we tend to suppress expressive features by formalizing them—we turn them into *style* ("style-as-diagnosis", one might add). He illustrates his contention by examples from erotic symbolism in primitive art and from various stages of the evolution of Western music. This view is coupled with another characteristic of unpenetrating reading: when we recognize *the* style of an artistic work, i.e., the features it has in common with other, comparable works, we tend to be less discriminating, less keen in perceiving the differences, the infinitesimal traits which, indeed, are the deviation from style; in George Klein's term, we tend to "level" out the differences between the unique works. In such cases, explication of the poem may be of decisive importance.

Thus, for instance, we have been told that some characteristics of the ballad style are *repetition* (often merely decorative) and *ellipsis* (often quite easily completed). When we ask "What does *this* repetition or *that* ellipsis contribute to the ballad?", we often are given the *diagnosis* "It is a characteristic of ballad style", or that "it contributes to the balladic atmosphere". Whenever there is threefold repetition, one may quite surely expect to be told that "it contributes to the popular-ballad-style".

Now, I would by no means deny that repetition does contribute to the balladic character of the ballad. I would even admit that these characteristics add a certain charm, *naïveté,* to the ballad. Still, I want to submit that this *naïveté* is sometimes the consequence of repressing some utterly *non-naive* and expressive feature of the poem.

Let us have, then, a look at "Edward":[2]

(1)   Edward
          "Why dois your brand sae drap wi bluid,

---

[2]   From *The Oxford Book of Ballads*, ed. James Kinsley, 1969. London: Oxford UP.

Edward, Edward,
Why dois your brand sae drap wi bluid,
And why so sad gang yee O?"
"O I hae killed my hauke sae guid,
Mither, mither,
O I hae killed my hauke sae guid,
And I had nae mair bot hee O."

"Your Haukis bluid was nevir sae reid,
Edward, Edward,
"Your Haukis bluid was nevir sae reid,
My dear son I tell thee O."
"O I hae killed my reid-roan steid,
Mither, mither,
O I hae killed my reid-roan steid,
That erst was sae fair and frie O."

"Your steid was auld, and ye hae gat mair,
Edward, Edward,
Your steid was auld, and ye hae gat mair,
Sum other dule ye drie O."
"O I hae killed my fadir deir,
Mither, mither,
O I hae killed my fadir deir,
Alas and wae is mee O!"

"And whatten penance wul ye drie for that,
Edward, Edward,
And whatten penance wul ye drie for that,
My deir son, now tell mee O."
"Ile set my feit in yonder boat,
Mither, mither,
Ile set my feit in yonder boat,
And Ile fare ovir the sea O."

"And what wul ye doe wi your towirs and your ha,
Edward, Edward,
And what wul ye doe wi your towirs and your ha,
That were sae fair to see O?"
"Ile let thame stand tul they doun fa,
Mither, mither,
Ile let thame stand tul they doun fa,
For here nevir mair maun I bee O."

"And what wul ye leive to your bairns and your wife,
          Edward, Edward,
And what wul ye leive to your bairns and your wife,
          When ye gang ovir the sea O?"
"The warldis room, late them beg thrae life,
          Mither, mither,
The warldis room, late them beg thrae life,
          For thame nevir mair wul I see O."

"And what wul ye leive to your ain mither deir,
          Edward, Edward,
And what wul ye leive to your ain mither deir,
          My deir son, now tell mee O"
"The curse of hell frae me sall ye beir,
          Mither, mither,
The curse of hell frae me sall ye beir,
          Sic counsels ye gave to me O."

All the repetitive features of this poem, by themselves, may be considered markedly expressive. The mere repetition of a line may be very emphatic, and so may be a doubled apostrophe, as "Edward, Edward", or "Mither, mither", and so, of course, the addition of the interjection "O" (at the middle and last line of each stanza). All these features tend to lose their emphasis when they occur regularly, in their pre-assigned places. Then we tend to assign no thematic emphasis to them, but ballad-style features (since, however, we do not perceive the poem at once, like a picture, but in chronological sequence, we may attribute more emphatic value to them in the first stanza than in the subsequent ones).

The final line of the stanza may have two opposite effects: it may either 'round off' the stanza in a 'soft' ending, or it may 'cut it off' with a sharp, pointed, epigrammatic ending. If we compare the last lines of the first three stanzas, we may find that two of them ("And I had nae mair bot hee O" and "That erst was sae fair and frie O") have the 'rounding' effect, in harmony with the other, repeated lines, whereas the third one ("Alas and wae is mee O!") has a sharp contrasting quality. The same may be said of the last three stanzas.

There are a number of small differences in the undividual stanzas, which together make up the different impressions of 'rounding' and 'contrasting' effects:

- The shocking revelation at the end of stanza 3 and the brutal statement at the end of stanza 7 contribute to the quality of sharpness.

- All the last lines, except for stanza 3 and 7 are syndetic; all the syndeta are here of a connecting character *(that, for, and),* never contrasting.
- The abrupt, asyndetic lines at the end of the third and the seventh stanza are perceived as indicating some break. In fact, the last but one line of the stanza, too, becomes 'sharper' when it is end-stopped, in virtue of the asyndetic new start in the next line.
- The last line of the ballad reveals a hitherto concealed, highly essential piece of information. The repetitions in this stanza, anticipated as they are, are most functional.

> (2)   The curse of hell frae me sall ye beir

strikes the reader by its unexpected character. The apostrophe "Mither, mither" has a double function here: (a) in this unexpected context, it regains some of its original emotive quality; (b) it defers the solution of this striking riddle. The repetition, in spite of its expectedness, further stretches the reader's anticipation, till the last line brings, at last, the unexpected, long-awaited solution.

- The last line of the third stanza, too, revives, so-to-speak, the formulaic *O,* restoring high emphasis to it. This is due to over-determination: its presence is justified by the formula as well as by the local pattern of the exclamatory sentence, in which *O* is the third in a sequence of three interjections *(Alas... wae... O).*

The ballad has an action in the Aristotelian sense: it has a peripeteia (reversal) with an anagnorisis (revelation), or, to be precise, two revelations (one at the end of the third stanza, and one at the end of the seventh); i.e., there is a shift from one extreme situation to its opposite, in this case from ignorance to knowledge.

The ballad itself is seriously limited in its expressive resources. It consists, actually, of a series of questions and answers, expressed in a rigidly formulaic way and virtually leaving no room for dramatic manipulation. In spite of this, the peripeteia is brought about with pointed dramaticality. There is, as a matter of fact, no continuous action, but rather a series of fragmentary, abrupt, formulaic dialogues; it is left for the reader to complete the situation in his own mind and to offer some hypothesis in order to make a coherent whole out of the "fragments".

Stanza 1, besides advancing the action by dialogue, sets the "stage" for the action and provides the necessary information simultaneously serving as exposition. We learn that the dialogue occurs between mother and son. Metonymies bring to the foreground information that lingers in the background (in the past, or *within* the protagonist). From "your brand sae drap wi bluid", the reader should infer that Edward has just committed a murder. *Sad* in mediaeval usage frequently meant "heavy, firm, steadfast". Consequently, "so sad gang yee" is primarily a physical metonymy, indicating Edward's state of mind. Both together awaken the reader's curiosity and seem to be sufficient motivation for the mother's inquisitiveness.

As such, the rigid formula seriously impairs, as we have seen, the possibilities of expression. The expressive elements are turned into style. On the other hand, the very use of formula offers a most effective means of expression (if duly exploited), namely, *significant variation.*

> Significant variation is a type of structure in which the effect is secured by an alteration in a pattern of action which has become familiar by repetition. (Brooks and Heilman, 1966, Glossary: 51)

In "Edward", the pattern is set by the first two stanzas, by the mother's questions, Edward's answers and, again, the mother's rejecting the answers. The deviation from the pattern occurs in stanza 3, where the mother does not reject the answer (moving the reader to believe that this time the truth has been told). The same holds true, in a more sophisticated manner, of the last three stanzas. Here, it is more difficult "to alter the pattern"—the reader has two contradictory expectations (so it seems more difficult to disappoint *both*). Here, again, two stanzas set the dominant pattern. The mother asks Edward "And what wul ye doe wi your towirs and your ha", "And what wul ye leive to your bairns and your wife". The answer to both questions is, virtually, "I don't care". This pattern requires the same answer to the third question too: "And what wul ye leive to your ain mither deir". However, by now, a rival pattern has been established: the third stanza has to end in another fashion; one expects that his beloved mother would concern Edward more than his towers, wife, and children. The end of the ballad frustrates both expectations: this time, Edward does not answer "I don't care", but, disappointing all previous expectations, he shows a 'concern' for his mother which is unlike anything one might expect. Therefore, the revelation is both expected and unexpected at one and the same time, revealed to the reader as well as to the mother (although the 'information' the mother gets here is of quite a different quality and weight than that offered to the reader).

One can, therefore, give too different answers—one "stylistic", the other "expressive"—to the question "Why are there exactly *three* parallel questions and answers?" The first answer states that exactly *three* repetitions is what the popular formula requires; the other suggests that three repetitions are required, since this is the smallest unit in which significant variation may be effective, that is, in which a pattern can be established and altered.

The differences between a 'stylistic' and an 'expressive' solution to questions of text interpretation can be highlighted by a closer analysis of the ballad. Let us begin by asking, again, why is the mother so inquisitive? Obviously, from a stylistic point of view, this is her part in the formula. But there is more to it. Let us assume that the reader does not know yet the end of the ballad. He observes the mother's steady questioning. During the first stanza, he could conclude that these are the questions of a loving mother, troubled by her son's unusual looks. During the second and third stanza, he is brought to modify this appreciation somewhat: the mother is questioning—Edward is evading the questions, but his mother is cleverer than that; she presses him with his back to the wall. Revelation I throws new light on this hide-and-seek. Obviously, Edward's motives may be understood in his attempt to conceal the terrible truth from his mother. Revelation II changes the reader's point of view, and creates a new puzzle: why does Edward conceal the murder from his mother, when he knows that she is bound to welcome it?

There is an obvious Oedipus-situation in the ballad. The son kills his father, in order to please his mother. In the course of the dialogue, the reader gradually discovers its meaning, as it emerges little by little, through his more or less adequate assumptions and expectations, while the ballad keeps refuting and satisfying them. This *emerging* meaning is more complex and rich, and qualifies the basic Oedipal situation. So it cannot be summed up, but rather, must be followed step by step. We have seen the mother worriedly inquisitive on seeing her son so troubled. Although the reader's perception of the events is changed by the two revelations, he is expected not to abandon his conception, but rather, qualify it constantly. At the beginning we hear that the son looks sad, or rather *walks* sad. *Sad* may have a wide range of degrees, even when qualified by *so*. This vagueness renders the word ambiguous and, as we shall see, this ambiguity will prove crucial.

The reader may be puzzled by the mother's expertness in comparing blood of different hues: "Your Haukis bluid was nevir sae reid". One may even wonder whether there is any meaningful difference between the possible degrees of redness. Therefore, the reader is induced to find some metaphorical sense. Assuming that the mother does not know more at this stage than the reader, one might conjecture that there is some metonymic connection between this blood and Edward's sorrow and, red being an intense color, the mother's question might imply something like "Your sorrow is too intense to let me believe that it is only your hawk you have killed, so let me question you further". But since this is not explicitly stated, there is some mysterious flavor about the mother's illogical statement—by some, readily ascribed to the "balladic atmosphere". Since the reader does not see Edward, he may attribute to him *sad* looks in several meanings and of any degree, for having slain his hawk or having murdered his father. When he reveals the murder, *redness* acquires connotations of **guilt** (without lessening the connotations of graveness and sorrow); it is as if the mother had said "You look more guilty than that". One may even be reminded of the Biblical verse (*Isaiah*, 1: 8): "Though your sins are like scarlet, they shall be as white as snow; though they are red like crimson, they shall become like wool". The mother, in rejecting Edward's evasive answers (e.g., by "Your steid was auld, and ye hae gat mair") draws our attention to Edward's eagerness to conceal the truth from his mother (apparently inconsistent with his mother's share in his guilt, revealed at the end).

Why does Edward mention precisely the hawk and the steed? One may offer, again, a "stylistic" and an "expressive" answer. The hawk and the steed are nearest to the Mediaeval knight; should the formula have allowed for a third animal, no doubt the hound would have been mentioned. On the other hand, the knight and his hunting animals have the duty of mutual loyalty, according to the Mediaeval world picture. Killing one's hawk or steed, although a lesser crime than parricide, would be considered in a knightly society as far graver a guilt than in our days. So, there is a gradual cumulation of sense of guilt, before the real crime may be revealed. Furthermore, there is an ironical overtone in this preparation for the real guilt. While one might justly ask "If you loved your hawk and steed so much, why have you slain them?" without getting a reasonable answer, Edward's ambivalence toward his father is almost explicit in "O I hae *killed* my fadir *deir*", and seems to be quite adequate as motivation—to a post-Freudian mind, at least.

Revelation II compels the reader to change mental sets, to re-evaluate everything he has encountered so far in the ballad, including Revelation I. "And what wul ye leive to your ain mither deir" has to be interpreted, on first reading, as a rather conventional expectation that the son might perhaps prefer his mother to his wife and children. The final revelation puts quite a different emphasis upon "your *ain* mither *deir*"—there is a particularly close relationship between mother and son—a sharing of guilt, at least.

The reader may become aware of the ambiguous silence after stanza 3. Assuming that the mother was ignorant, one might well expect her to react in some violent way. Instead of this, she goes on, rather quietly, inquiring: "And whatten penance wul ye drie for that". The reader need not really be too troubled with the mother's silence: he may readily attribute it to the ballad's formulaic style (e.g., there was no place in the formula for the expression of the mother's shock). Only the final line reveals that presumably, she had no reason to feel thunder-stricken at all. We see how the balladic formula becomes, time and again, structurally and expressively significant in the course of "decoding" the poem.

The final revelation shows the reader a bit of Edward's ambivalence towards his mother. Now the reader may discover that Edward, in trying to hide what he had done, was not afraid that his mother would be too hard upon him. One might be even tempted to interpret now her "And why so sad gang yee O?" as an invitation "let us now make merry". Nevertheless, Edward tries to conceal what he has done, as if he were rather unwilling to let his mother feel satisfaction—let alone express her affection for him. This shameful confession of his *crime* becomes a shameful *confession* of his crime (that is, both mother and son know quite well every constituent of the situation, but Edward *now* shies away from her participation in his murder). This throws some new light upon the mother's stubborn inquisitiveness: not being satisfied with the mere effects of the murder, she wants to have her share in her son's affection (emphasized, again, by "your *ain* mither *deir*" in the last stanza). One might then *re*interpret their disguised discussion of the hawk's blood and its hue, as if each of the two had said: "I know exactly what you mean, but I want *you* to speak out first".

The foregoing reading of "Edward" throws into focus the hypothesis character of our interpretation. During the first three stanzas, the reader projects a consistent situation on the abrupt dialogue. He imagines an initial set of conditions, compatible with the questions-and-answers presented in the text, as well as with known human behavior and mental processing. We may take this "initial set of conditions" to be *highly plausible* in view of the available evidence, but not *strictly true.*

> The characteristic feature of critical interpretation that is philosophically most interesting is its tolerance of alternative and seemingly contrary hypotheses [...]. Given the goal of interpretation, we do not understand that an admissible account necessarily precludes all others incompatible with itself. (Margolis, 1962: 116)

> Where the statements "P is true" and "Q is true" are contraries, the statements "P is plausible" and "Q is plausible" are not. (ibid., 117)

Our set of hypotheses, conceived as highly plausible in the course of reading the first three stanzas, seems to be inconsistent with the final revelation. Since, however, hypotheses are to be held as plausible rather than strictly true, the reader may change his mental set and offer some different hypothesis, seemingly contrary to the initial one. As we have seen, even the mother's ambiguous silence after the third stanza, which is highly functional to the understanding of the poem, becomes only possible mediating two contrary hypotheses: she may or may not have been shocked by Edward's first revelation. Such an interpretation, however, requires the reader to assume an attitude toward the "merely possible", while continuing to be highly tolerant of the emotionally loaded, ambiguous situation.

A final word about the question: What exactly is the mother's reason to have her husband murdered by her son? Saying that she wanted to enact her part in the Oedipal situation would be a platitude. It seems to me that an illuminating, though disquieting answer is given in Aristotle's *Poetics,* Chapter 9. When dealing with the difference between history and poetry, he remarks that the latter is the more philosophical, because history deals with particulars like "What Alcibiades did or suffered", whereas poetry deals with universals like "How a person of a certain type will on occasion speak or act, according to the law of probability or necessity" (Aristotle, 1951: 37-38). Following this line of thought, the mother's immediate motives seem of no relevance to the ballad. The murder sets the occasion on which the persons of certain types are to act, while its lack of explicit motivation contributes to the mysterious balladic atmosphere—an atmosphere which is easily eliminated when we supply a motivation for her action—such as in the case of the Oedipus, enabling a rapid closure on the reader's part.

I have earlier mentioned "rigidity" or "intolerance of ambiguity", as similarly constituting a psychological syndrome. One of its most notorious symptoms is the incapability to be in uncertainties, mysteries, doubts, without any "irritable reaching after fact and reason"—in Keats's famous phrase. It will be readily noticed that the Aristotelian answer to the question "What exactly is the mother's reason to have her husband murdered by her son?" is bound to frustrate any attitude of "irritable reaching after fact and reason". Another possible symptom of this syndrome is a concern with concrete details and their functioning, that is, in the present case, a preference for dealing with such particulars as "What Alcibiades did or suffered", rather than with such universals as "How a person of a certain type will on occasion speak or act, according to the law of probability or necessity". Now, "the law of probability" in Aristotle's proposition poses another difficulty to rigid persons, as one of the symptoms of rigidity is an unwillingness to assume an attitude toward the "merely possible" (Goldstein and Scheerer, 1941: 1-10; see also Frenkel-Brunswick, 1968: 136).

I have begun the present chapter by making a distinction between "diagnosis" and "hypothesis". One could call these notions, less formally, *labeling* and *meaning-making*. The meta-critical distinction between *labeling* and *meaning-making* is by no means recent in critical theory. And it would appear, as well, that *labeling,* in literary criticism, satisfies some personal need rather than the requirements of any discipline or critical school. There is, probably, no critical art so readily associated with labeling as classical rhetoric. This notwithstanding, we find the following observation in one of the classical authorities on rhetoric:

> For it makes no difference by which name is either called, so long as its stylistic value is apparent, since the meaning of things is not altered by a change of name. For just as men remain the same, even though they adopt a new name, so these artifices will produce exactly the same effect, whether they are styled *tropes* or *figures,* since their values lie not in their names, but in their effect. (Quintilian, no date, Book IX: 7-8 H. E. Butler (trans.))

These pairs of terms contrast two different critical activities which, in turn, are frequently behavioral corollaries of different psychological attitudes. "Labeling" (or "diagnosis", as I have defined it above), instead of bringing out the complexity of a given experience, rather reduces experience to a single item which falls under acknowledged and well-classified categories (the Oedipus-complex, the ballad-genre). Classifying moods, feelings, or human situations is a means of taking the disquieting element out of them.

CHAPTER 14

Archetypal Patterns

Archetype as a Regulative Concept

Archetype is a Jungian, depth-psychological term. Jung postulates archetypes that are transmitted through a collective unconscious, by virtue of which some poetic patterns can be assumed to be more valuable than others. While I find much of Jung's discussion irrelevant to a Cognitive Poetics, certain aspects of *archetype* are, in my opinion, most illuminating. In the present chapter I propose to discuss this notion from two perspectives that may serve to emphasize its cognitive facets: *archetype* as a regulative concept, and *archetype* as an emotional pattern. The Jungian notion will be marginal to my argument, and I shall draw upon Maud Bodkin's Jungian notions rather than on Jung himself; sometimes I shall even consult non-Jungian sources. I shall focus these discussions on the CINDERELLA archetype in the Biblical story of David and Goliath and in Shakespeare's *As You Like It;* and on the DEATH-AND-REBIRTH archetype in *Faust I.*

Much archetypal criticism is reductionist and simplistic. It quite frequently forces on the work a schema that is alien to it (cf., e.g., my discussion of Eva Metman's interpretation of *Waiting for Godot,* below in Chapter 21). One of the aims of the present chapter is to explore the possibilities of increasing both the complexity and unity of the work, rather than reducing its complexity in favor of a unifying schema. This, however, will involve us in sometimes rather lengthy analyses of the works mentioned above.

As for the title of the present chapter, 'Archetypal Patterns', a slightly greater emphasis on the second word of this phrase than is usual in literary criticism seems to be in place. Archetypal *patterns* can be discussed in terms of literary structures, whereas *archetypal* patterns are, rather, discussed in psychological terms. One of the most illuminating passages in Maud Bodkin's analysis (1963) of Coleridge's "Ancient Mariner" is that in which she compares two contrasting descriptions of the ship, one of its being in a state of "death", stuck, with the "very deep" rotting underneath; the other, by contrast, indicating "rebirth", when the ship glides homewards with full speed. This contrast is indisputably there in the poem, and the reader may directly perceive it.

As I said, Jung and his followers postulate a collective unconscious, by virtue of which some literary structural patterns can be assumed to be more valuable, *a priori,* than others. The great Canadian critic Northrop Frye, on the other hand, "is not interested in causal explanation and rejects the collective unconscious as an unnecessary hypothesis. What concerns him is mostly a new theory of genres [...]" (Wellek, 1965: 337). In Frye's practice, archetypes have an *a posteriori* character, in spite of his terminology being drawn from mythology, and even though the archetypes themselves can be (and by some critics are) used in an *a priori* way. In the present section of this chapter I shall explore some possibilities of archetypes as **regulative concepts.**

"Archetypes are", says Frye (1968: 102) "associative clusters and differ from signs in being complex variables". In terms of our distinctions in the preceding chapters, this reminds us of style-as-hypothesis rather than style-as-diagnosis, especially since "associative clusters" and "complex variables" are emphasized. The impression is reinforced by Frye's following statement:

> [...] the *topoi* of rhetorical commonplaces [...] like other ideas in literature, are [...] dull when stated as propositions, and [...] rich and variegated when they are used as structural principles in literature. (ibid., 103)

That "associative cluster" which is so dull in isolation and so rich within its proper literary context has, indeed, a *regulative* function. It emphasizes certain elements of the pattern, and "backgrounds" the divergent, poorly articulated ones, thus creating a hierarchic system, and bestowing "depth-dimension" upon the whole complex.

Let me illustrate this point by a fairly simple example, after which I shall briefly compare the Jungian and the "regulative" approach to archetypes. In Orlando's wrestling with Charles in *As You Like It,* the underlying situation and pattern of events is rather reminiscent of the situation in the Biblical story of David and Goliath. Similarities and differences can be noticed on various levels and scales of the two stories. The central event, the inexperienced youth overthrowing the bragging "alazon", gains in its emotive appeal by virtue of the "dramatic irony" inherent in the situation (the wrestler is sure of himself, and there are indisputable facts that speak for him; this makes his downfall the more impressive). It is Celia who, before the event, draws attention to its "archetypal" nature:

(1) Le Beau: There comes an old man and his three sons,—
     Celia: I could match this beginning to an old tale [...]
     Le Beau: The eldest of the three wrestled with Charles, the duke's wrestler; which Charles in a moment threw him, and broke his ribs, that there is little hope of life in him; so he served the second, and so the third. Yonder they lie [...].

The three sons' function in the play is to 'speak for' Charles's invincibility. Celia's remark—which, by the way, is in keeping with her and Rosalind's jocular comments on all and sundry—prevents the three sons from becoming more than a parable, and "the old man, their father, making such pitiful dole over there" from attracting too much sympathy and so 'stealing the play'. At the same time, she reinforces the 'archetypal' character of the wider situation.

There are some slightly different facts to speak for Goliath: "All the men of Israel, when they saw the man, fled from him, and were sore afraid" (1 Samuel, 17: 24).

In both the Biblical story and in the play, nobody knows who the victorious youth may be, and this adds a flavor of mystery to his emergence from obscurity to brilliant success. In accordance with common sense, both King Saul and Duke Frederick attempt to dissuade the inexperienced youth from a hopeless endeavor. Both youths insist on having a try, but for different—in fact opposite—reasons. Orlando is so desperate that he doesn't mind risking his life; David, on the contrary, has faith and confidence in God's help. These motivations enhance certain central issues of the works in which they occur.

After the surprising victory, both King Saul and Duke Frederick ask for the name of the youth's father. This may be due to social, rather than literary conventions. It has not been reported what King Saul answered when he heard Jesse's name; he was presumably formal, or even formulaic. At any rate, we read in the next verse: "When he had finished speaking to Saul, the soul of Jonathan was knit to the soul of David, and Jonathan loved him as his own soul. And Saul took him that day and would let him go no more back to his father's house". Similarly, Rosalind's soul was knit to Orlando's soul; and Celia, in turn, loved Rosalind as her own soul. But Duke Frederick deviates from the by now expected pattern, setting the plot of the whole play into action. At the same time, this deviation gives us a glimpse into the Duke's character, and reinforces the underlying theme of "traditional moral virtues violated". And conversely, a comparison with *As You Like It* draws attention to a usually neglected passage in the Bible: "Now Eliab his eldest brother heard when he spoke to the men; and Eliab's anger was kindled against David, and he said 'Why have you come down? I know your presumption, and the evil of your heart; for you have come down to see the battle'" (1 Samuel, 17: 28). The more David is chided before the duel, the more impressive his victory. One cannot however, insist too much upon the difference. Oliver keeps Orlando, deliberately, in a Cinderella status, for no apparent reason, and seemingly, out of pure wickedness. There is nothing to suggest that David was deliberately *wronged* by his family. Still, the central episode of the Cinderella story is enacted in Bethlehem too. Jesse parades seven (!) of his sons, only three (!) of whom are named, before Samuel, so that he may find among them God's chosen one. Finally,

(2)   Samuel said to Jesse: "The LORD has not chosen these". And Samuel said to Jesse: "Are all your sons here?" And he said "There remains yet the youngest, but behold, he is keeping the sheep". And Samuel said to Jesse: "Send and fetch him; for we will not sit down till he comes here". And he sent and brought him in. Now he was ruddy, and had beautiful eyes, and was handsome. And the

> LORD said "Arise, and anoint him for this is he" (1 Samuel, 16: 10–12).

The story carefully makes a point of the fact that it is the smallest brother who becomes the greatest. This irony is emphasized by the Lord who chides Samuel "Do not look on his appearance or on the height of his stature [...]. For the Lord sees not as man sees; man looks on the outward appearance, but the Lord looks on the heart". This dramatic turning of the tables is repeated later, when the small David overthrows the giant Goliath. God probably takes pleasure in announcing His will in a way that most astounds His creatures; and the traditional Cinderella archetype serves this end exceedingly well. According to Muecke, "the pure or archetypal ironist is God—'He that sitteth in the heavens shall laugh: the Lord shall have them in derision'. He is the ironist *par excellence* because he is omniscient, omnipotent, transcendent, absolute, infinite, and free" (1970: 37–38).

We have, then, three levels of abstraction in these two plots. First, we have the actual chain of events, which is very dissimilar in the two. Some elements, however, become somewhat more distinctly perceptible, owing to their coincidence with a pre-established pattern of events viz., the astounding rise of the small and insignificant one by his overthrowing the one supposed to be invincible (the "David-and-Goliath" archetypal pattern). On the lower level, the two plots remain unlike; moreover, their similarities on the abstract level only emphasize the dissimilarities on the concrete level. Because we expect Duke Frederick to keep the young champion in his court, it is the more surprising that he rejects him, reinforcing the underlying theme of the play, involving the distortion of the traditional scale of values. Or, take the characterization of the "invincible" one. Goliath is a braggart, and gets what he deserves. His downfall is in the centre of our attention, and when David is summoned before Saul, he comes "with the head of the Philistine in his hand" (1 Samuel: 57). David, the small one, fought on behalf of a humiliated nation and its true God, derided. With the rise of the one, the others rose too. With Goliath's fall, his people as well as his gods were proved to be vain.

Charles shows a much more humane face when he warns Oliver so that he may prevent his younger brother from getting in trouble. The play is not interested in the moral downfall of Charles. Charles rather becomes an instrument to foreground, first, the moral deficiency of Oliver, and then the moral deficiency of the Duke; then he disappears from sight. Shakespeare—unlike the Biblical story-teller—makes no effort to render Orlando's victory technically credible. What he is interested in is the web of human relationships around it. So, the David-and-Goliath archetype becomes a regulative concept in both plots, ordering much material of various kinds. In the Biblical story, the diverse issues (religious, national, moral, familial) are subsumed in an overall antithesis and reversal. It arouses more *convergent* interests than the Orlando–Charles story. In neither of them does the archetype occur in its purity, in its isolated dullness.

The third level in the hierarchy consists of what may be called the Cinderella archetype. In *As You Like It,* it is rather incomplete, but serves as a plausible motivation for Orlando to challenge Charles, and to reinforce the atmosphere of wickedness in the new régime. In the Biblical story, on the contrary, the pattern of the Cinderella story is far more complete, but precisely the wickedness element is missing, or has only a remote echo in Eliab's chiding. It serves mainly to enhance the irony (or the miracle?) inherent in the extreme reversal of the situations, both the forgotten one preferred, and the small and insignificant one killing the boasting giant and becoming great himself.

To be sure, there is not the slightest indication in the Bible that David was kept with the sheep out of wickedness; we should not read anything of the sort into the story. Still, his success is all the more impressive since he was not the first of the brethren to be inspected: he was neither among the first three, nor among the first seven; in fact, he was with the sheep and hence almost forgotten. This is precisely the point I wish to make. The archetypal pattern lends significance to elements that occur in a story or poem; but the actual work must not be *reduced* to the archetype. On the contrary: the archetype must hover flexibly in the back of one's mind, almost non-existent. It is only "brought into existence" when it comes into contact with corresponding elements of the verbal context, like the invisible ink which appears in vivid colors when another liquid is applied to the sheet. The two elements realize each other.

An abstract archetypal pattern has, by its very nature, a "strong shape". The predictable elements of the "associative cluster" foreground certain aspects of a structurally weak verbal texture, while some others, the unpredictable ones, are backgrounded. In this sense, the archetypal pattern has an organizing, regulative effect. That is why they seem so dull to Northrop Frye: there is nothing to be organized.

The 'regulative-concept' approach would, then, focus attention on an abstract pattern that consists of two opposite states along with a dramatic reversal from a lowly to an elevated state, and insist that when it performs at its best, this approach organizes as much and as diverse material as possible, without going into the specific nature of the material. A Jungian analyst would handle the episode in 2 quite differently, for instance, where Jesse parades his sons before Samuel. A Jungian would embrace the other approach's abstract pattern, but would focus more attention on the specific contents of the action and imagery. Thus, he would suggest that the scene in 2 enacts the FOOL archetype. The fool, like David, who is with the sheep (and, we might add, like Cinderella, who is in the kitchen), has a degraded status, and is excluded from "decent" company. When, however, the issue at stake is the renewal of life, when Israel is in need of a new king, or the Prince of a bride to give him heirs, it is precisely the degraded and excluded one who is found to be worthy of rising; he is not merely reintegrated into society, but is raised above it, and becomes the source of its 'rejuvenation', the renewal of its vitality. The seeds of new life are frequently found to be represented by an imagery derived from the basic elements of the human condition: detritus, dirt, decay, all connoting somehow the primordial slime; the grimy figures of David tending the sheep (and certainly of Cinderella, the kitchen-maid) may be a remote indication of this.[1] In short, the Jungian analyst emphasizes the element of the *Rebirth* archetype in this cluster (the remainder of this chapter is devoted to a study of this archetype). The literary critic *qua* literary critic is interested in all the elements and their relative weight within the cluster. For him, the Jungian analyst over-stresses certain marginal issues, as the elements of fertility and rejuvenation; at worst, he *reduces* the whole cluster to these elements.

An Abstract Emotional Pattern as "Hub"

The "associative cluster" discussed above may become an "emotional pattern" when it organizes a structurally weak texture of emotional information. In the remainder of the present chapter, I shall explore this possibility through an analysis of the DEATH-AND-REBIRTH archetype in *Faust Part I*. In order to prevent the archetype from becoming "dull" in Frye's word, I shall follow up, in considerable detail, its intricate relationships, as a "structural principle" in the play, interacting with a variety of other elements (imagery, action, scene, etc.).

My discussion starts with the trite observation that *Faust* has no underlying **action** in the Aristotelian sense, but consists, rather, of a series of loosely connected episodes: in Stuart Atkins' phrase, *Faust* is an "enigmatic segment". It will be argued that, even though the play does not "imitate" an Aristotelian action, there are in it, nevertheless, some elements that are typical of the Ritual Drama as "Hub", as characterized by Kenneth Burke (1957: 87) and (in a somewhat different context) by Francis Fergusson. Also, there is in the play an overall rhythm that is akin, in a sense, to what Fergusson called *the tragic rhythm of life* in Greek tragedy. What is more, there is in it some indication of a "Great Chain of Being", not unlike the one underlying Greek and Shakespearean tragedy, with a hierarchic system of analogous planes, in which the analogous actions of DEATH AND REBIRTH take place in a way that is somehow related to the RESURRECTION of the dead God in Ritual Drama. Further, "examining first the relation between scene and act", we shall adopt from Kenneth Burke "the principle whereby the scene is a fit 'container' for the act, expressing in fixed properties the same quality that the action expresses in terms of development" (Burke, 1962: 3). It will be suggested that these scene-terms constitute, at the same time, the underlying death and rebirth imagery that is pervasive in *Faust Part I,* and is drawn out into *Part II*. In this way, the play's spiritual *space* will be worked out (in Wilson Knight's term). It will be further suggested that this imagery conforms, both in its contents and sequence, with the emotional pattern of what Maud Bodkin called THE DEATH AND REBIRTH ARCHETYPE. At the same time, the potential of this imagery to enter into an emotional sequence will be explored from a cognitive point of view.

---

[1]   I am indebted to Professor Henry Abramovitch for this analysis.

I have adopted, then, Kenneth Burke's characterization of "the Ritual Drama as 'Hub'". Burke proposes to take

> *ritual drama* as the Ur-form, the "hub", with all other aspects of *human* action treated as spokes radiating from this hub. [...] Ritual drama is considered as the culminating form, from this point of view, and any other form is to be considered as the "efficient" overstressing of one or another of the ingredients found in ritual drama. (Burke, 1957: 87)

I shall not go here into a discussion of whether really *all* other aspects of human action may be treated as spokes radiating from this hub; suffice it that in *some* types of literary works, this is indeed approriate; at any rate, this seems to be the case for a Romantic drama such as *Faust*. Nevertheless, such a choice, outside drama, at least, could appear quite arbitrary, even if it **happens** to work; and "the 'efficient' overstressing of one or another of the ingredients found in ritual drama" may seriously damage the "spokes radiating from this hub". So it might be quite useful to improve our metaphor by situating the "hub" at the core of human experience, from where the spokes are supposed to radiate outward, to ever-widening scopes of human activities. The "hub" then will become a certain 'abstract' emotional pattern. In this sense, *ritual drama* will be only one possible instantiation, or 'incarnation', of this abstract emotional pattern.

The most obvious candidate for such an "abstract emotional pattern" is Jung's DEATH AND REBIRTH ARCHETYPE; however, the pattern may be stated in Freudian terms as well.[2] I am going to draw upon both Jungian and Freudian formulations, but shall emphasize as much as possible the cognitive facet of the process.

First, let me refer to Ehrenzweig (1965), who combines gestalt-psychology with psychoanalysis to explore art; he demonstrates throughout his admirable book how in music and painting, artistic experience involves some low differentiated "depth-perceptions" *behind* the highly differentiated "surface-perceptions" of articulate *gestalts*. In Chapter 3, above, "Constructing a Stable World", I briefly quote from a later book by Ehrenzweig (1970: 135), where the author speaks of "a creative ego rhythm that swings between focussed gestalt and an oceanic undifferentiation". Let me quote Ehrenzweig at greater length:

> The London psychoanalysts D.W. Winnicott and Marion Milner, have stressed the importance for a creative ego to be able to suspend the boundaries between self and not-self in order to become more at home in the world of reality where the objects and self are clearly held apart. (Ehrenzweig, 1970: 135)

---

2   Maud Bodkin, on whose work I am heavily drawing, is committed to a Jungian view, but is careful to point out where the two approaches overlap and differ; furthermore, she also suggests some implications for a gestaltist conception of creativity.

> Seen in this way, the oceanic experience of fusion, of a "return to the womb", represents the minimum content of all art; Freud saw in it only the basic religious experience. But it seems now that it belongs to all creativity. (ibid.)

> As the ego sinks towards oceanic undifferentiation a new realm of the mind envelops us; we are not engulfed by death, but are released from our separate individual existence. We enter the manic womb of rebirth, an oceanic existence outside time and space. (ibid., 136)

Why should such a rhythm help man "become more at home in the world of reality"? A cognitive explanation—in accordance with our argument in Chapter 1—would point out that hard and fast categories (that eventually amount to *cognitive stability)* are indispensable for such elementary abilities as recognizing a person or a place as the same person or place, or identifying a series of vastly different sound-stimuli emitted by different speakers as the same word. But this cognitive stability is bought at the price of relinquishing subtle and minimal pre-categorial cues, perceivable only by intuition, which are equally indispensable for survival. What is crucial for our present inquiry into the abstract emotional pattern as "hub" is the opposition *focused gestalt ~ undifferentiation.* One of man's greatest achievements is his cognitive differentiation. This accomplishment, however, plays the tyrant to him: the less differentiated processes become less accessible to him, as well as less reliable. The passages quoted from Ehrenzweig imply, in fact, that religion, art, and creativity in general, are among the means that may yield some heightened consciousness of these less differentiated processes.

The suspension of the boundaries between self and not-self by the creative ego is thus said to lead to oceanic undifferentiation. In this state, we are said to be released from our separate individual existences; as such, it is similar to death. On the other hand, in this state, energy may be revived and released, which leads to the opposite extreme, the state of ecstasy. Ecstasy may be said to consist in a state of oceanic undifferentiation, loaded with enormous energy; which is why in ecstatic poetry we so frequently encounter death-imagery loaded with undifferentiated energy (cf. above, Chapter 11).

Imagery and Predisposing Factors

Thus, certain abstract emotional patterns may be 'individuated' in psychological processes. Some of these are more, others less conscious and mainly of an emotional nature; they exist in a wide variety of human activities, ranging from religious rituals, through drama, both ritual and romantic, and emotional behavior to creative thinking (in art or science) in general. Maud Bodkin (following Jung) called this pattern an ARCHETYPAL PATTERN. A characterization of an ARCHETYPAL PATTERN is suggested in the following statement:

> I shall use the term "archetypal pattern" to refer to that within us which, in Gilbert Murray's phrase, leaps in response to the effective presentation in poetry of an ancient theme. The hypothesis to be examined is that in poetry—and here we are to consider in particular tragic poetry—we may identify themes having a particular form or pattern which persists amid variation from age to age, and which corresponds to a pattern or configuration of emotional tendencies in the minds of those who are stirred by the theme. (Bodkin, 1963: 4)

Implicit in this definition is a distinction between *archetypal **pattern*** and *archetypal **contents*** (see below, footnote 5). Bodkin's insistence on *themes* suggests the latter; her insistence on *form* or *pattern* or *configuration* suggests the former. A slightly greater emphasis on the second word of this phrase seems to be in place in literary criticism. Archetypal *patterns* can be discussed in terms of literary structures, whereas *archetypal* patterns—rather in psychological terms.

Where do these archetypes come from?

> In Jung's formulation of the hypothesis, and in the more tentative metaphorical statement of Gilbert Murray, it is asserted that these patterns are "stamped upon the physical organism", "inherited in the structure of the brain". (Bodkin, 1963: 4)

Bodkin, however, warns us against an uncritical acceptance of such an assumption.

> Of more force in the present state of our knowledge is the general argument that where forms are assimilated from the environment upon slight contact only, predisposing factors must be present in mind and brain. (ibid., 4–5)

This caution with reference to "the present state of our knowledge" seems to be appropriate today no less than nearly sixty years ago, when Bodkin published her study (1934). Bodkin appears to have in mind, in this context, only such "predisposing factors" that, in Bartlett's phrase, "stir within us larger systems of feeling, of memory, of ideas, of aspirations" (ibid., 5), and that can be described as some large "pattern or configuration of emotional tendencies in the mind". But elsewhere in her book, she discusses other, more fine-grained elements that also might be described as "predisposing factors". She discusses these as related to a particular image; but I shall try to apply them to Bodkin's overall schema as well; at present, I shall concentrate on these latter factors.

The elements in question are mentioned in Bodkin's discussion of the emotional symbolism of caverns, in connection with Coleridge's "Kubla Khan". The very notion of *emotional symbolism* implies that she is not so much interested in what images mean as in what images *feel* like. Caverns and abysses often symbolize hell;

and by being opposed to high mountains, they may serve in the ARCHETYPE of Heaven and Hell. She begins her discussion of this issue, like so many "Kubla Khan" critics, with introducing a collection of myths and geographic (or pseudo-geographic) descriptions of caves and subterranean streams and seas. But from these myths and descriptions, she abstracts certain common qualities that are much subtler, and more elementary as experiences, than the usual symbolic meaning. At the same time, she indicates how the "gross" symbolic meanings may arise from those subtle, elementary sensations.

> Here is the "eternal essence" gathered from experiences of cavern and abyss —an essence of cold, darkness, and stagnant air, from which imagination may fashion a place of punishment, the home of the Evil One. (Bodkin, 1963: 101)

Conspicuous in this passage is that it does not merely state a simple equation: CAVERN = HELL. Rather, it abstracts from caverns such elementary sensations as "cold, darkness, and stagnant air"; these sensations are unpleasant, and in extreme cases unfavorable to life. Such an analysis has several advantages for the literary critic. For one thing, it explains how a certain visual image may generate (in the appropriate circumstances) a "thing-free" atmosphere with a marked emotional direction. Second, as a result it can fill with specific contents, applicable in changing circumstances, Kenneth Burke's above quoted "principle whereby the scene is a fit 'container' for the act, expressing in fixed properties the same quality that the action expresses in terms of development" (Burke, 1962: 3). This is, in fact, what may be meant by "a place *of* punishment": a place that expresses in fixed properties the same qualities that punishment expresses in action (and the *Evil* One in *potential* actions).

Now, consider such attributes of caverns as "cold, darkness, and stagnant air", with their antonyms "warmth, light, and fresh air". Such attributes arouse some of our most elementary sensations and are "assimilated from the environment upon slight contact only", hence "predisposing factors must be present in mind and brain". These are some of the most vital conditions for living beings, and hence may be imagined as most immediately experienced. In terms of the foregoing discussion, human beings are *predisposed* to respond to such qualities, or oppositions of qualities, even if the sensations are presented to the imagination only by means of words.

The Rebirth Archetype

I shall now point out three dimensions in the REBIRTH ARCHETYPE: a dialectical sequence, an emotional sequence, and a sequence of spatial imagery.

The following self-characterizations of Mephistopheles have become favorite slogans of later dialecticians:

(3)   MEPHISTOPHELES.   Part of that Power, not understood,
Which always wills the Bad, and always works the Good.
(1335–1336)[3]

or

(4)   I am the Spirit that Denies!
And justly so: for all things, from the Void
Called forth, deserve to be destroyed ...
(1338–1340)

and

(5)   Part of the Part am I, once All, in primal Night,—
Part of the Darkness which brought forth the Light ...
(1349–1350)

This conception suggests that everything in the world implies its opposite: birth implies death, darkness implies light. Death and destruction are followed by rebirth and life renewal. Mephistopheles knows that "Evil", the denial of life, his "proper element", entails "Good", creation, the renewal of life. Now, Mephistopheles expresses this as a more or less abstract paradox, involving two movements in opposite directions: from inexistence to existence, and *vice versa* (in this context, darkness is but the **absence** of light). This paradoxical state, or paradox of simultaneous processes, is sometimes "split" into two successive processes; but even then, the pivotal point is conceived of as containing the two opposite directions at one and the same time.

In Chapter 3, we have defined emotions as tendencies toward an object judged suitable, or away from an object judged unsuitable. These tendencies are frequently analyzed into a process of situation appraisal plus a state of undifferentiated energy. In the DEATH AND REBIRTH ARCHETYPE, the situation appraisal consists in taking cognizance of some such opposite processes as described above, individuated in a concrete situation; the undifferentiated energy is manifested in a fluctuation of energy between a higher than usual and lower than usual level of vital forces. The "pivotal point" is reached through "periods of inertia or brooding, normally occurring while latent energies gather strength for activity on a fresh plane" (Bodkin, 1963: 73). These, then, are at once "periods of inertia" and of "latent energies gathering strength", accounting for the "ambivalent feelings" in which opposite tendencies are individuated. This brings us back to the "creative ego rhythm that swings be-

---

[3]   All quotations from *Faust* are from the Bayard Taylor translation.

tween focussed gestalt and an oceanic undifferentiation".[4] Both oceanic undifferentiation and focused gestalt are of a double-edged nature (that is, give rise to opposite qualities in different, or ambiguous contexts). According to Ehrenzweig, "at an extreme limit, [oceanic dedifferentiation] may remove the boundaries of individual existence and so produce a mystic oceanic feeling" (Ehrenzweig, 1970: 304). Hence, oceanic undifferentiation, too, is of a double-edged nature, embodying one of two opposite modes of existence: being "engulfed by death", or "released from our separate individual existence" in an ecstatic rapture. Likewise, focused gestalts may be of a double-edged nature: they may represent structured reality and firm existence but, in certain circumstances, they may serve as the stringencies that restrain the expansion of the ego, or the outburst of vital forces. In the light of the foregoing discussion, the double-edged nature of oceanic dedifferentiation may account, in an interesting way, for such opposite states' (as death and ecstasy) implying each other: during the "period of inertia or brooding [...] latent energies gather strength for activity on a fresh plane", and so it becomes the "pivotal point" around which the state of ecstasy comes into being.

The sequence of spatial imagery associated with the rebirth archetype in poetry as well as in other kinds of human activity, serves to reinforce the other two dimensions, and to "externalize" the rebirth process to some extent. From the cognitive point of view, spatial imagery is a means for the effective coding of information. In the present case, spatial imagery is rich with those fine-grained elementary sensations that may be described as "predisposing factors", discussed at some length in the preceding section, a fine instance of which is pointed up by Bodkin's discussion of what caverns feel like, and of their emotional symbolism, as being full of "cold, darkness, and stagnant air, from which imagination may fashion a place of punishment, the home of the Evil One". In ARCHETYPAL *PATTERNS*, such images become part of a *sequence* of spatial imagery.

The sequence of images relevant to the REBIRTH ARCHETYPE has been described by Bodkin as follows:

> I have compared, also, myth and the metaphor of religious confession and of psychological exposition, selecting material in accordance with similarity of imagery, especially of form or pattern. Particular words and images, such as those of wind, of storm-cloud, of slime, of red colour, have been examined for their emotional symbolism, but mainly with reference to their capacity to enter into an emotional sequence. Within the image-sequences examined the pattern appears of a movement, downward, or inward toward the earth's centre, or a cessation of movement—a physical change which, as we urge a metaphor closer to the impalpable forces of life and soul, appears also a transition toward a severed relation with the outer

---

4   As I suggested in chapter 9, in some of his publications, Ehrenzweig uses the term *undifferentiation,* in some, *dedifferentiation.* The former term suggests a state, the latter a process.

world, and, it may be, toward disintegration and death. This element in the pattern is balanced by a movement upward and outward—an expansion or outburst of activity, a transition toward reintegration and life-renewal. (Bodkin, 1963: 54)[5]

The underlying emotional pattern is described as "a pattern of rising and sinking vitality, a forward urge and backward swing of life, reflected in an imagery deployed in time" (ibid., 114–115).

The Rebirth Archetype in *Faust*

Now I would like to draw together my discussions of Ritual Drama, hierarchy, and of the REBIRTH ARCHETYPE by focusing them on a crucial passage in the "Outside the City Gate" scene in *Faust*.

(6)   FAUST. Released from ice are brook and river
By the quickening glance of the gracious Spring,
The colors of hope to the valley cling,
Now weak old Winter himself must shiver,
Withdrawn to the mountains, a crownless king:
Whence, ever retreating, he sends again
Impotent showers of sleet that darkle
In belts across the green o' the plain.
But the sun will permit no white to sparkle;
Everywhere form in development moveth;
He will brighten the world with the tints he loveth,
And, lacking blossoms, blue, yellow, and red,
He takes these gaudy people instead.
Turn thee about, and from this height
Back on the town direct thy sight.
Out of the hollow, gloomy gate
The motley throngs come forth elate:
Each will the joy of the sunshine hoard,
To honor the Day of the Risen Lord!
They feel, themselves, their resurrection:
From the low, dark rooms, scarce habitable;
From the bonds of Work, from Trade's restriction:

---

5   It should be noted that one important distinction (already alluded to above) this passage makes is between *archetypal* **contents** and *archetypal* **patterns** ("emotional symbolism" on the one hand, and "capacity to enter into an emotional sequence" on the other). It is not explicitly stated, but it appears to be Bodkin's rule not to check images for their emotional symbolism, unless they possess a "capacity to enter into an emotional sequence."

> From the pressing weight of roof and gable;
> From the narrow, crushing streets and alleys;
> From the churches' solemn and reverend night,
> All come forth to the cheerful light.
> How lively, see! the multitude sallies,
> Scattering through gardens and fields remote,
> While over the river, that broadly dallies,
> Dances so many a festive boat;
> And overladen, nigh to sinking,
> The last full wherry takes the stream.
> Yonder afar, from the hill-paths blinking,
> Their clothes are colors that softly gleam.
> I hear the noise of the village, even;
> Here is the Peoples proper Heaven;
> Here high and low contented see!
> "Here I'm a Man,—dare man to be!".
>   (903–940)

I have already pointed out that *Faust* has no proper action in the Aristotelian sense. The present scene is one of those that are most conspicuously incompatible with a rigorous Aristotelian structure. The only element in the present scene that advances the dramatic action is the encounter between Faust and the poodle-Mephistopheles. The rest of the scene consists of a disproportionately large *background*. The mini-episodes involving short exchanges of words between groups of apprentices, servant girls, students, burghers, burghers' daughters, etc., serve one purpose: to create a background of realistic plenitude. Superficially, "the image is not a gratifying one. There is little elevation to be found in the materialistic types which Goethe depicts. [...] The people have little to say that is not concerned with sex, beer, brawling and political discontent" (Gillies, 1957: 34). However, according to the present conception, this is slightly to misread the situation. The same concern with "sex, beer, brawling and political discontent" has another facet, too: a general atmosphere of outburst of human activity. All these persons feel that their vital forces are released, and spend their time at their pleasure and leisure. This is the "meaning" even of the mini-episode of the burgher complaining of the new mayor. "The materialistic types which Goethe depicts" represent Life on an earthly plane.

None of these mini-episodes is continued in any way in the play; so the reader (or spectator) handles them by fusing them into a large "vista" of background texture. At the same time, surrounding nature (mostly expressed in terms of action) is perceived as a background to these mini-scenes.

On the other hand, the scene becomes a most important dramatic juncture, precisely by virtue of its background qualities. In Kenneth Burke's phrasing, "the scene is a fit 'container' for the act, expressing in fixed properties the same quality that the action expresses in terms of development": surrounding Nature, too, is "released from ice", and flourishing at leisure. With the appearance of Faust, the surrounding cheerful festive crowds too become a living background to the principal actor, who has discarded the gloomy mood in which he was left in the preceding scene, in his study. There is, then, a single underlying situation in this scene, that of **Resurrection**. The scene contains the entire scope of existence as a single "chord"—to use one of Kenneth Burke's favorite metaphors—spread out over time by Faust's interpretation into an "arpeggio": he spells out, one by one, the various links of "the Great Chain of Being", all of which appear to him as implicit in the situation. At the top he mentions the resurrection of the dead god ("of the Risen Lord"). To this corresponds the resurrection of Nature, after the withdrawal of "weak old Winter himself". The third level is that of the resurrection of the throngs, the fourth—the resurrection of the individual, who can say of himself "Here I'm a Man". All this is, as suggested above, thrown onto the stage as a single "sheaf of light", to be decomposed into parallel "beams" of resurrection, through the prism of Faust's interpretation.

When speaking of the throngs that are reborn today, Faust also mentions the previous conditions from which they have come out to the "cheerful light": it is a kind of "death-in-life". It is "out of the *hollow, gloomy* gate", "from *low, damp* rooms", "from the *pressing weight* of roof and gable", and "from *narrow, crushing* streets and alleys" that "the *motley* throngs come forth *elate*". In Bodkin's terms, this is "a movement upward and outward—an expansion or outburst of activity, a transition toward reintegration and life-renewal". The state of "death-in-life" is described in terms of a scene that is characterized by conditions that are not favorable to life: dampness and rot (as opposed to fresh, running water), darkness (as opposed to light), stagnant (as opposed to open, fresh) air, pressing weight and narrow space (as opposed to open space, huge mountains), etc. All these are elementary sensations, coded into two coherent, diametrically opposed spatial images, and thus entering into an "emotional sequence". It is these spatial images that determine both the scenery and the pervasive figurative language of the play, underlying its "emotional movement" as well as its symbolic contents. The *motley throngs* move from one type of scene to the other.

Such a background permeated with death, as described verbally by Faust, becomes an actual setting on the stage, anticipating real death, in the last scene of Part I. Faust and Mephistopheles, having galloped on their black horses over fields with gallows prepared for the executions next morning, enter the prison where Gretchen "dwells within the dark damp walls", waiting for the hangman. Here, again, "the scene is a fit 'container' for the act, expressing in fixed properties" the action that is going to take place next morning. Gretchen herself says:

> (7)   Under the steps beside us,
>   The threshold under,
>   Hell heaves in thunder!
>   The Evil One

> With terrible wrath
> Seeketh a path
> His prey to discover!
>   (4454–4460)

The paradoxical joining of opposite elements is most poignant at the very end of Part I., in the following words:

> (8)   MEPH. She is judged!
>   VOICE *(from above).*   She is saved!
>   (4611)

Here, the fall and destruction of Gretchen is, at the same time, her redemption, accompanied by a powerful epiphany. In Fergusson's formulation, we have here elements of "the mourning, the rejoicing, and the contemplation of the final stage-picture or epiphany—as imitating and celebrating the mystery of human nature and destiny" (Fergusson, 1949: 40). In scene-terms, the boundless world above intrudes into the confined, dark damp prison cell.

A less poignant, but more elaborate instance of opposite scene-terms we find in the Evening-scene, in Gretchen's "small, neatly kept chamber". Here, the same setting is perceived differently by Faust and Gretchen, since for the latter it implies corruption and destruction, whereas for the former—the beginning of a new life. Thus, for instance, Gretchen's room is praised by Mephistopheles as "Not every girl keeps thing so neat" and by the enamored Faust as "How all about a sense impresses/ of quiet, order and content!" But when Gretchen enters, she feels "It is so close, so sultry here! *(She opens a window)*". Faust, on entering, invokes the twilight "O welcome, twilight soft and sweet", whereas Gretchen enters, a few minutes later, "carrying a lamp". To be sure, there is a realistic motivation for this difference: some time has passed, and it has become darker. But for the sensitive Gretchen, her room is felt to be at once dark, sultry, and close: she has some elementary sensations adverse to life. On the moral-symbolic level, Mephistopheles' deadly treasure-box is already hidden in her room. In this way, Gretchen's elusive sense-impressions become a metaphor for her keen intuition (also manifested by her instinctive shrinking from Mephistopheles from the very first moment). The death-motive is reinforced when she sings her famous song about the King of Thule who, at the moment before his death, throws his goblet into the sea. Notice, however, this: the goblet "plunging and filling, and sinking deep in the sea" is only "released from its separate individual existence", in Ehrenzweig's words, "removing the boundaries of individual existence and so producing a mystic oceanic feeling"; furthermore, fresh water, too, is part of the life-principle within the play's imagery, dimly suggesting some "resurrection"-theme.

The Play's Structure and Setting

The play's structure consists, then, of a fluctuating rhythm of "life and death", or, more precisely, of the increase and the decrease of "life-forces", each of them implying (or containing the germs of) its opposite. A person striving to achieve a better, fuller, happier life, realizes the potentials implicit in his state, and so reaches a dead end, a point of stagnation. But precisely this point of stagnation contains the germs of growth, of the opposite state, of new life. With the renewal of life, new potentials arise; and after having exploited them, the protagonist finds himself again at the lowest point of stagnation, the state of "death", and so on.

Let us review the sequence of sceneries at the beginning of the play. First we find Faust in his study, in a state of depression and despair, having realized his intellectual potential, but failed to find happiness in all seventy wisdoms. His room is narrow, damp, and appears a prison to him. Next, in the morning he goes outside the city gate, where he experiences a kind of resurrection, and feels he is a Man again. Everything I have said above of light, resurrection, and the outburst of life, is relevant here. But when the light disappears from the fields and meadows, Faust returns to his home:

(9)   Behind me, field and meadow sleeping,
        I leave in deep, prophetic night ...
                    (1178–1179)

That night is Easter night, with a solemn atmosphere that arouses the love of our fellow creatures:

(10)   Within whose dread and holy keeping
            The better soul awakes to light.
                    (1180–1181)

This solemn state of mind is disturbed by its opposite: the poodle's unrest. In a more ordinary state of mind, Faust may have not noticed such an unrest at all. Faust sees yet nothing out of the way in this behaviour, and promises the poodle decent hospitality. His own promise induces him to sermonizing upon new friendships and new hopes:

(11)   Ah, when, within our *narrow* chamber,
        The lamp with friendly *luster glows,*
        Flames in the breast each faded ember,
        And in the heart, itself that knows.
        Then Hope again lends sweet assistance,
        And Reason then resumes her speech:
        One yearns, the *rivers* of existence,
        The very *founts* of Life, to reach.

(1194–1200; my italics)

The italicized words in this passage show that its figurative language uses, precisely, what I have described above as life-and-death imagery: light, water, flowering (in line 1199, the German original says "und Hoffnung wieder an zu blühen", that is, 'Hope then resumes her *blooming'*). What is more, the first line would suggest that within the death-scenery (narrow cell) the germs of new life imagery may be found. The poodle's snarling induces Faust to some self-ironic comments concerning man's despising "what he never comprehends", as well as concerning his own solemn mood. This leads him, eventually, to some opposite mood expressed, again, in terms of fountains and thirst:

> (12)   But ah! I feel, though will thereto be stronger,
> Contentment *flows* from out my breast no longer.
> Why must the *stream* so soon *run dry* and fail us,
> And burning *thirst* again assail us?

(1210–1213; my italics)

During Faust's attempts to translate a passage from the New Testament, the poodle begins to snarl, and then to expand, first as a hippopotamus, and then as an elephant, until "it fills the space entire" (1311). As a result, Faust finds himself in desperate straits, both physically and mentally. When, finally, Mephistopheles is "born" out of the poodle, as a Traveling Scholar, "the space entire" becomes available again, and Faust feels *relief:* "A traveling scholar, then? The *casus* is diverting"; narrow space and its opposite indicate at the same time Faust's successive mental states.

After having signed the pact, Mephistopheles does not lead Faust straight away to new life as he promised. First, Faust must extinguish his own previous self, so that he may be *restored to youthful vigor.* Mephistopheles leads Faust to narrow, confined, dark spaces which, according to the play's visual symbolism, suggest death. By the same token he leads him *away* from spirituality. First they go to Auerbach's *cellar,* where "jolly companions" are engaged in "foolishness" and "swinish ribaldry"—as one of them put it. From there they descend, further, to the Witch's kitchen. It is here that he is to undergo the rejuvenation rites; and it is here that he first gets a glimpse of Gretchen, who brings the prospects of new life to him.

I have suggested that in Faust's descent to the witch's kitchen, the scene expresses "in fixed properties the same death-quality that the action expresses in terms of development". This is not mere toying around with words. Faust, in agreeing to take part in the Witch's "hocus-pocus", in her ceremony of sense-deception, proves false to his previous self, betrays his own pure spiritual being. After all, Faust was characterized by Mephistopheles on their first encounter (though ironically) as "one whose mind the Word so much despises, / who, scorning all external gleams, / the depths of being only prizes" (1328–1330). The confined space narrows even further around Faust: "The Witch with fantastic gestures draws a circle" etc., and Mephistopheles forces Faust—who refuses to take part in such rites-of-bogus—into the circle. When, eventually, "the Witch breaks the circle and Faust steps forth", Mephistopheles widens the scope beyond all the immediate limits, saying "And now, away!" (in German, "Nun frisch, hinaus!"). If Faust's descent to the Witch's kitchen and entrance into her magic circle suggest, in 'scene-terms', a symbolic suicide, it is followed by a symbolic Resurrection, again in 'scene-terms'.

Earlier in the scene, when Faust expresses his annoyance with such witchcraft, and asks Mephistopheles whether there is no other way of rejuvenation, the latter admits that there *is* such a way, and in describing it, he again resorts to imagery that in scene-language expresses death and rebirth:

(13)   *Betake thyself to yonder field;*
        There hoe and dig, as thy condition;
        Restrain thyself, thy sense and will
        Within a narrow sphere to flourish ...
                    (2353–2356; my italics)

Again, Faust's rejuvenation (death and rebirth) becomes possible by *going out* and *restraining himself within a narrow sphere*. That is, one type of scene contains the germs of its opposite.

Gretchen's imminent death was already immanent in the scene-language of the preceding episodes, in which she took part. After the consummation of Faust's and Gretchen's love, there begins a slow process of dying. "By the ramparts", "in a niche of the wall a shrine, with an image of the *Mater Dolorosa*" we see Gretchen "placing fresh flowers in the jars": the narrow space of the scene expresses death; Gretchen's action expresses the renewal (perhaps, a request for the renewal) of life. In the next-but-one scene we see Gretchen in a Gothic cathedral, at a Mass, surrounded by people, tortured by an Evil Spirit standing behind her, the choir singing the *Dies Irae* (part of the Mass for the Dead). Gretchen expresses her distress in a scene-imagery of confined space and lack of fresh air for breathing, introduced in Faust's speech outside the city gate:

(14)   I cannot breathe!
        The massy pillars
        Imprison me!
        The vaulted arches
        Crush me!—Air!
                    (3816–3820)

Next we meet Gretchen in jail, with all the scenic implications we have mentioned earlier. This time, however, only her real death can grant her new life—eternal Life-in-Death. This time, *life* has a different meaning for Gretchen and for Faust: she finds it in her death (which may rescue her life after death); he finds it in physical existence. Apparently, it is her madness that is responsible for the following dialogue:

> (15)   FAUST.   If thou feel'st it is I, then come with me!
> MARG.   Out yonder?
> FAUST.   To freedom!
> MARG.   If the grave is there,
> Death lying in wait, then come!
>
> (4536–4540)

In the light of the foregoing analysis, however, the dialogue suggests in scenic terms the paradoxical joining of life and death (unlimited space within the very limited space of the *grave,* at the same time a metonymy for death).

The play begins in Heaven, in the most "elevated" spheres, and ends in the prison, beneath whose threshold "Hell heaves in thunder". The protagonist's progress is parallel to this, in an important sense: he repeatedly destroys his previous self, only to be reborn again, in a less spiritual, more earthly shape. Thus we see at the beginning of the play the philosopher who despises anything that is not purely spiritual; at the end we see the lustful lover who comes to the girl whom he made pregnant to rescue her from physical death (ready to sacrifice, by the same token, the salvation of her soul). Here, he is concerned only with the welfare of the body; this is emphasized, by contrast, by Gretchen's choice of physical death in preference of eternal life. Part I of *Faust* ends, then, at a point when Gretchen is granted Life-in-Death, while Faust chooses Death-in-Life, so to speak. At the beginning of Part II, he experiences a kind of purification and resurrection, in terms of the play's scenic symbolism: the first scene is placed in a "pleasant landscape"; Faust, "bedded on a flowery turf, fatigued, restless, endeavoring to sleep". Later, "a tremendous tumult announces the approach of the Sun". Ariel and the chorus sing of a rain of flowers, of spring, of dawn; and Faust himself, on awaking, speaks of "Life's pulses [which] with fresher force awaken". Unlike what happened throughout Part I, this time the renewal of life occurs in the higher spheres.

Faust's Study at Night: The Rhythm of Death & Rebirth

The above overview and analysis intends to show how the play's characteristic imagery embodies the REBIRTH archetypal pattern, described by Bodkin as follows:

> [According to Jung's view,] the regression, or backward flow of the libido, that takes place when conscious or habitual adaptation fails and frustration is experienced, may be regarded as a recurring phase in development. It may

be felt by the sufferer as a state of compulsion without hope or aim [...]—
and if the condition continues it means degeneration and death. But if the
contents which during the introverted state arise in fantasy are examined for
the hints, or "germs", they contain "of new possibilities of life", a new attitude may be attained by which the former attitude, and the frustrate condition which its inadequacy brought about, are "transcended". We may take, I
think, these two terms, "frustration" and "transcendence", as happily expressing the stages of the Rebirth process. (Bodkin, 1963: 72)

Now, the special effect of the play does not reside only in this significant overall
sequence of scenes, but also (or even first and foremost) in the rhythmic alternation
of imagery in the single scenes. The best illustration is provided, perhaps, in the
scene in "Faust's Study at Night". The setting is a "death"-setting, and at the outset
Faust soliloquizes on the dead end which he has reached in his search for truth and
happiness. Later, his reluctance to translate literally the Biblical verse "In the beginning was the Word" is interpreted by Mephistopheles as Faust's despising the Word,
because it yields only "outward forms", and does not reveal "the depths of being". In
his invocation to the moon, Faust draws attention to the narrow room where he is
staying and from where he is longing to *go out*. As we have seen in Chapter 10, his
invocation starts a series of short passages in which death and life imagery alternate
almost regularly. Faust sees from his desk the moon "climb the sky", whereas the
moon beholds him bending over books and papers in his room. It is from within
this room that Faust longs to the *out,* to unrestricted space in nature, in order to
bathe in nature's "dewy fountains". By reaching this climax, Faust almost forgets
his actual surroundings, almost achieving an ecstatic rapture—only to discover the
discrepancy between his wishful thinking and actual state, thereby amplifying his
depression ("Alas! my prison still I see!"). This suffocating world, in which he is
"Hemmed in by many a toppling heap of books ... ancestral lumber stuffed and
packed", is paralleled by the closed space of his own body:

(16)   And do I ask, wherefore my heart
         Falters, oppressed with unknown needs?
         Why some inexplicable smart
         All movement of my life impedes?
         Alas! in living Nature's stead,
         Where God His human creatures set—
         In smoke and mould the fleshless dead
         And bones of beasts surround me yet.
                                        (410–417)

We have seen that one of the elementary sensations unfavorable to life which Faust
associates in (6), above, with the enclosed spaces from which the "motley throng" is
pouring forth, is "pressing weight". In (16) this sensation is perceived in the en-

closed space of Faust's own body, suggesting again the hierarchic-analogic conception of the Universe revealed in (6). It is the heart oppressed within the *bosom* that is the scenery of "all movement of life impeded" within him; this state of emotional "death" is paralleled by the "high-vaulted *narrow* room" in which Faust himself is placed, further narrowed by such metonymies of death as *mould* or *the fleshless dead and bones of beasts*. It is from this point of "death" that Faust, again, longs to be reinvigorated in Mysticism, through Nostradamus' *Book of Mystery:* "Fly! Up, and seek the broad, free land!" *Broad, free land* is, again, the spatial expression of the kind of spiritual vigor sought. The experience of his first encounter with the book is described in terms of *starlight* and as the opposite of *dry mind* (that is, in terms of light and vital moisture); it leads to the ecstatic rapture discussed in connection with quotes nr. (6) in Chapter 10 and (2) in Chapter 17, culminating in the line

> (17)   How grand a show! but, ah! a show alone.
>
> (454)

This line aptly demonstrates how one state may contain the germs of its opposite, how the ambiguity of the word *show* (German *Schauspiel)* may constitute the pivotal point for ecstatic rapture turning into frustration and depression. One of the meanings of the word is "spectacle", that is, anything presented to sight or view, especially something of a striking kind; here, it is used in an exclamation expressing wonder and admiration. Another of its meanings suggests "theatrical appearance", as opposed to "reality". Thus, the *show* is both the source of Faust's ecstatic rapture and despair: it again emphasizes the discrepancy between his vision and actual state, as expressed in terms of *boundlessness* and *founts* on the one hand, and *draught* and *pining* on the other:

> (18)   Thee, boundless Nature, how make thee my own?
> Where you, ye breasts? Founts of all Being, shining,
> Whereon hang Heaven's and Earth's desire,
> Whereto our withered hearts aspire,—
> Ye flow, ye feed: and am I vainly pining?
>
> (455–459)

Next, the conjuring up of the Earth Spirit arouses in Faust feelings both of *glowing,* and of *mists* and *clouds* gathering over him. The paradoxical encounter between Faust and the Spirit is also expressed in scene-terms: "Thou, who around the wide world wendest, / thou busy Spirit, how near I feel to thee!" (Here *near* may suggest both "near in space" and "near in essence"). The Spirit's infinite perspectives are confined to Faust's narrow room and *nearness*. The Spirit rejects Faust's declaration of kinship: "Thou'rt like the Spirit which thou comprehendest, not me!" As an answer to Faust's question "Whom then?" "Enter *Wagner*, in dressing-gown and nightcap, a lamp in his hand". This recognition brings Faust to a "desperate state", from which it is precisely Wagner, "the dullest of mortal men", who relieves him. Wagner's lamp can be contrasted to the spirit's "life, all-glowing" on the one hand; but is still light, on the other hand, and as such containing "the germs" of the opposite state. It will be remembered that Faust sums up his ecstatic experience as paradoxically great and small at once. At the same time, he encapsulates the romantic conception of the paradox of imagination in terms of a paradox of space and time, of the infinite and the confined:

> (19)   If hopeful Fancy once, in daring flight,
> Her longings to the Infinite expanded,
> Yet now a narrow space contents her quite,
> Since Time's wild wave so many a fortune stranded.
>
>   (640–643)

Not only such metaphysical entities as Space and Time are paradoxical, but the tools inherited from our ancestors, too, possess an inherent paradox.

> (20)   What from your fathers' heritage is lent,
> Earn it anew to really possess it!
> What serves not, is a sore impediment,
> The Moment's need creates the thing to serve and bless it!
>
>   (682–685)

Consequently, the "hundred shelves", instead of widening his horizons, merely "constrain" Faust in his "mothy den".

We have followed in considerable detail the rhythm of alternating death and life imagery in Faust's long soliloquy in the night-scene in Faust's study. We have found here a significant configuration of elements. First, we have an imagery suggesting some *immediate* awareness of physical restriction (narrow rooms, caverns, confined circles, niches, etc.), associated with death; its opposite, boundless space is associated with life and resurrection. Concomitantly, we have such oppositions of immediate sensations as darkness opposed to light, or draught, thirst, rot, dampness opposed to dew, or fresh, running water. All this is closely associated with an opposition between a drastic reduction, as opposed to an unrestrained outburst of activity and of vital forces. It will be recalled that quite frequently, we have encountered a most significant paradoxical co-occurrence of the two extreme states. One such paradoxical combination of overwhelming life-forces and death-imagery is the state of ecstasy, quite frequently associated with glimpsing the *world beyond;* others are the great religious paradoxes traditionally called *Death-in-Life* and *Life-in-Death.* An exquisite instance of the latter, with a religious taint, we found in the last episode of Part I, when Gretchen prefers to die, rather than to be rescued by Faust; it was accompanied by an epiphany, a kind of Divine revelation of the world beyond. Still another, completely secular version of *Life-in-Death* we find in the scene under discussion.

Having reached total despair, Faust decides to commit suicide, and discovers Infinity *in* a small vial (of poison). I shall quote only the part of this long section that contains the embodiment of the above principle:

> (21)   Out on the open ocean speeds my dreaming;
> The glassy flood before my feet is gleaming,
> A new Day beckons to a newer shore!
> A fiery chariot borne on buoyant pinions,
> Sweeps near me now! I soon shall ready be
> To pierce the ether's high, unknown dominions,
> To reach new spheres of pure activity!
> This godlike rapture, this supreme existence,
> Do I, but now a worm, deserve to track?
> Yes, resolute to reach some brighter distance,
> On earth's fair sun I turn my back!
> Yes, let me dare those gates to fling asunder,
> Which every man would fain go slinking by!
> 'Tis time, through deeds the word of truth to thunder:
> That with the height of Gods Man's dignity may vie;
> Nor from that gloomy gulf to shrink affrighted,
> Where Fancy doth herself to self-born pangs compel ...
>
> (700–715)

The quintessence of this passage lies in such expressions as "to reach new spheres of pure activity!" or "This godlike rapture, this supreme existence", or "out on the open ocean", "the glassy flood before my feet", "some brighter distance" than "earth's fair sun", in opposition to "that gloomy gulf". It should be also noticed that Faust intends to overcome the "ultimate limit" by daring "those gates to fling asunder" that lead to the "world beyond". It seems as if the passage uses death-imagery to express ecstatic rapture; in fact, the exact opposite happens: the passage uses ecstatic imagery to convey the experience of *Life-in-Death*. Faust intends to commit suicide, and thus get freed of earthly limitations. Thus, if "death" and "seeing the other world" are to be understood metaphorically in relation to the ecstatic experience, they are to be understood literally in the present context.

If this last section contains the Death-and-Rebirth archetype in a rather un-Christian manner, it unexpectedly gives way to the prototypical Christian version of this archetype: the Angels' Chorus announces Easter Night with a chorale beginning "Christ is arisen!" ("Christ ist erstanden!"). This chorale transports Faust out of his desperate state ("What hollow humming, what a sharp, clear stroke, / Drives from my lip the goblet's, at their meeting?"), leading on to the play's next scene,

"Outside the City Gate", on Easter day (which we have discussed in relation to quote (6), above).

Thus, we have seen a sustained instantiation of a rhythmic emotional sequence deployed in time through imagery that is a perfect instantiation of the abstract pattern according to which "with the emotionally pre-determined fall of the hero goes a pre-determined resurrection. The life-force which, in one manifestation, perishes, renews itself in another. So the tragic lament passes into exultation" (Bodkin, 1963: 60).

The Nature of Recurrent Imagery in Drama

In the present chapter, I have devoted much attention to archetypal patterns with respect to recurrent imagery in *Faust*. It would appear that problems of archetypes and of recurrent imagery in drama are inextricably interwoven in *Faust*. In this section, I am going to summarize my argument concerning *Faust,* making some further generalizations towards a cognitive account of the nature of recurrent imagery in drama, with special emphasis on archetypal patterns.

I have discussed at considerable length the interaction of imagery, the DEATH-AND-REBIRTH ARCHETYPE, the setting of the scene, the structure of the action, and the underlying existential situation in *Faust Part One*. In doing this, I have carefully avoided any attempt to "reduce" the play to some external meaning. My assumption has been, rather, that the play draws its effectiveness from three kinds of "predisposing factors", owing to which various large-scale and small-scale forms "are assimilated from the [poetic] environment upon slight contact only" by the audience, as quoted above from Bodkin: elementary sensations, the *"immediate* awareness of restriction", as quoted in Chapter 10, above, from Kaufman, and the REBIRTH ARCHETYPE.

The smallest-scale factors concern relatively elementary sensations such as cold, darkness, dampness and stagnant air, or their opposites, which the organism swiftly recognizes as unfavorable or favorable to life. On this level, it should be noticed that it is not the absolute contents of imagery (which would require careful examination of the information received) that affects the audience immediately, but rather the *opposition of sensations* (which enables fast and crude judgments of a vast amount of information) that can be compared along such dimensions as the *evaluation* of the sensations (that is, whether they are favorable or unfavorable to life), their relative *intensity*, and their *direction,* that is, whether this relative intensity is increasing or decreasing. These fast judgments are based, mainly, on "opponent processes": oppositions are more salient, and hence more rapidly perceived, than any other relation. This process seems to serve as a fast-orientation device (cf. Chapter 1).

Actually, the process referred to here seems to be the *raison d'être* of recurrent imagery in dramatic works of art. When figures of language that have considerable common elements are perceived, they are compared, and from the similar images, similar sensations are abstracted. These elementary sensations may be perceived, in appropriate circumstances, as some "airy", diffuse mass that constitutes the play's emotional *atmosphere*. In this way, we may receive from clusters of images information that appears to be isomorphic with emotional processes.

As I have argued in Chapters 1 and 3, emotions are streams of information that is held in a highly active state, rather than being allowed to settle in hard and fast categories. Emotions serve, among other things, as mechanisms of fast orientation in rapidly changing (physical, or social, or intellectual) environments, in which much input, from many kinds of sources, must be rapidly and effectively processed, without pre-empting everything else in one's mental processing space. The human mental apparatus is conceived of as of a system with limited channel capacity, which may efficiently handle only a certain amount of mental processes. It may make numerous and careful distinctions concerning a relatively small amount of information, or many and crude judgments concerning a large amount of information. The former kind of processes are felt to be more intellectual, the latter of a more emotional nature. Recurring imagery in dramatic works of art as characterized above may generate diffuse information of opposing directions, which may be efficiently handled by a mechanism of fast orientation.

The foregoing discussion may elucidate an issue which has been rather summarily handled in the course of the present chapter. I have sometimes spoken of a state or process of death (and its converse—rebirth); and sometimes of some depressive state of mind (and its opposite—ecstasy). Now, there is a world of difference between death and depression—a thing which, oddly enough, literary critics tend to overlook. However, in a psychological atmosphere of fast and crude judgments comparing sensations not for their absolute contents but as to their evaluation, intensity, and direction, *death* and *depression* are perceived as approaching, to various degrees, the same pole of the spectrum.

In a concrete situation, elementary sensations may be presented as thing-free and gestalt-free qualities, thus closely resembling the structure of some *atmosphere*. Or they may be coded in some image that has a stable and characteristic visual shape. Such visual images are the most efficient way of encoding a large amount of sensory information as a coherent whole. This seems to be one (cognitive) reason that visual images are, typically, the language of dreams and myths. On the other hand, such stable visual images are all too much unlike the emotional way of handling information. Visual shapes are stable and require careful, differentiating processing; they easily usurp the focus of attention, pre-empting everything else in our mental processing space; by contrast, emotions tend to be diffuse, as we have seen above. In poetry, there appear to be two (not too sharply distinguished) techniques for overcoming this difficulty. Either the text may focus our attention on fluid information (similar in structure to that integrated in fast orientation), and on the process of *locating oneself* in one's environment with reference to time, space, and people (which is *The American College Dictionary*'s psychological definition of *orientation)*, rather than on the stable objects of the landscape (see below, Chapter 14). Or the poetic text may orient us towards visual images. Especially in the dramatic text, such visual images may be employed on two different levels: On one level, they may make their contribution to the immediate dramatic situation or developments, *in the focus of attention;* at the same time, on another level, they may be compared *off-focus* in the manner described above, for their emotional tendencies only (see above, Chapter 8).

Maud Bodkin abstracted the "essence of cold, darkness, and stagnant air" from "experiences of cavern and abyss", opposing these essences to qualities abstracted from huge mountains. This pair of images is prone to be conceived of as archetypal, owing to both their extreme opposition and their being "good examples" of sublime natural objects. In this respect, two comments seem to be required on *Faust's* imagery and scenery. First, in *Faust* the opposite scene-terms are somewhat "domesticated", mainly in the "Outside the City Gate" scene, both in their sublimity aspect and their extremity aspect: the caverns are domesticated into such man-made objects as a "hollow, gloomy gate" and "low, dark rooms, scarce habitable". Second, no automatic identifications may be made: while we have found *caverns* to be an archetypal coding of sensations *unfavorable* to life, nevertheless, we find in quote nr. (5) of Chapter 10 the following: "But would that I, on mountains grand, / amid thy blessèd light could stand, / with spirits through mountain caverns hover, / float in thy twilight the meadows over". Here, *mountain caverns* are part of a "life-scene": they are referred to as the "irrelevant texture" of the unrestricted, sublime space in which the imagined scene takes place, and attention is *not* directed to "cold, darkness, and stagnant air" as their "essence".

"Predisposing factors" on a larger scale are those parts of the imagery and of the visual setting of the play, arousing *"immediate* awareness of restriction", of being "hemmed in", that may be extended to metaphoricallly suggest the **ultimate limit.** This enhances the negative emotional value of the small, damp, dark enclosed spaces that abound both in the play's setting and figurative language. In moments when any one or any combination of the "four fundamental types of limiting experience" (mentioned by Kaufman, see above, Chapter 10) are felt to be overcome, there is an overwhelming feeling of outburst of energy culminating in some ecstatic experience, or act of resurrection. Finally, opposing emotional tendencies may enter into a wider emotional sequence, yielding the abstract emotional pattern of DEATH-AND-REBIRTH ARCHETYPE, each polar state containing "germs" of its opposite. This abstract emotional pattern is the "hub" of the play's action, as well as of many human activities—predisposing, again, the audience to respond to the play "on slight contact only", "with all other aspects of human action treated as spokes radiating from this hub". It has been pointed out that Romantic tragedy may, in this respect, have some intimate links with Classical tragedy, on the level of "imitating and celebrating the mystery of human nature and destiny. And this mystery was at once that of individual growth and development, and that of the precarious life of the human City" (Fergusson, 1949: 40–41). There is, however, a difference, too, in this same respect. Whereas in Sophocles' tragedy "Oedipus is shown seeking his own true being; [and] at the same time and by the same token, the welfare of the City" (ibid., 41), Faust too "is shown seeking his own true being"; but there are only occasional indications of this process overlapping with the rebirth of the Savior, and that of the vegetation as well as of the human society. Classical tragedy takes place against a background of a world picture organized in a hierarchy ("The Great Chain of Being"). In *Faust,* this "Great Chain of Being" is merely indicated by a few (albeit significant) hints. Nonetheless, in *Faust,* as in Classical tragedy, this hierarchy arouses a feeling that it is the *totality of life* that is experienced; it adds the "vertical" dimension to the emotional space in which the mechanisms of fast orientation are to be deployed.

Conclusions: The Nature of Archetypes in Literature

Much archetypal criticism attempts to reduce the literary works of art to some mythological or depth-psychological system outside the work. Many critics treat archetypes as meaning relationships: X in the text means a in the external system; Y in the text means b in the external system; Z in the text means c in the external system; and so forth. In this way, the (putative) archetype is forcibly turned into an allegory. In literary criticism, I have suggested, archetypal *patterns,* rather than archetypal *meanings,* are illuminating, as they allow the description of existing structures, rather than having to impute meanings from the outside. A slightly greater emphasis on the second word of the phrase "archetypal *patterns"* seems to be in place, however; this emphasis can be achieved by discussing the patterns in terms of literary structures. Archetypes (like *topoi* in Frye's sense) are associative clusters which are "so dull when stated as propositions, and so rich and variegated when they are used as structural principles in literature" (Frye, quoted above). According to Wellek, Frye's theory of archetypes is, in fact, a new theory of genres; and indeed, according to the present conception, archetype is similar to genre (or to period style, for that matter) in that it is a regulative concept that organizes a great variety of elements on a variety of strata of the work. By the same token, archetype, just like the other regulative concepts, can be applied as cognitive hypotheses (see chapters 3, 11 and 12, above).

In another important respect, archetypes are like symbols, as discussed in Chapter 8. There I suggested a constraint on symbolic interpretation: that some concrete features in the proposed symbol should be deleted, and only some of the most general meaning structure retained, so that no feature of the symbolic interpretation should conflict with the information more or less explicitly given in the text. The same would apply to archetypal interpretation. Consider for a moment the Cinderella archetype and the Biblical story of David. The wicked stepmother parades her favorite daughters one by one before the prince, but none of them fits the shoe; eventually, they have to bring in Cinderella from the kitchen. Likewise, Jesse parades seven of his sons before Samuel, but none of them turns out to be God's chosen one; eventually, they bring in David, who was with the sheep. Here we observe an abstract pattern with several common ingredients. There is one brother or sister who is kept in a lower status or esteem than his brothers or her stepsisters; initially they are doing the "dirty" jobs, but in the end, they rise enormously in status as compared to their brothers or stepsisters. The germs of new life (not only for the protagonist, but perhaps for the whole community) are found where the dirty jobs are done.

There is a drastic reversal between the low status of the protagonist at the beginning of the action and his or her high status at its end. There is also a most effective reversal scene *(peripeteia,* in Aristotle's terminology), in which the more favored candidates are paraded by the parent, before the Prince or Samuel—the person of authoritative status, empowered to make the choice, and having his own infallible criterion for choosing: the foot fitting the shoe, or God's approval. Now consider this: if we decide to let the story of David be an instantiation of the Cinderella archetype, then we have to delete from the "shoe" and the "fitting foot" all those concrete features which conflict with the explicitly stated corresponding element in the story of David: God's approval. These elements become an abstract category, such as "infallible touchstone for excellence" (or, perhaps, "for being the chosen one"). The same is true of "being in the kitchen" and "being with the sheep". Both stand for an abstract, "lowly status". Even God's chiding of Samuel "Do not look on his appearance" has its counterpart in the Cinderella story: the stepsisters are supposed to look attractive in their expensive dresses, whereas Cinderella, dressed as a kitchen wench, is supposed to look rather unattractive. "Dress" is a prototype of "outward appearance", as opposed to inner quality. Both stories make the point "[ordinary] man looks on the outward appearance, but the Lord [or the Prince] looks on the heart".

What appears to be rather trivial with reference to the Cinderella archetype, becomes less trivial in some other instances. Consider the following sentence by Ehrenzweig, quoted above: "We enter the manic womb of rebirth, an oceanic existence outside time and space". And consider the following description by Bodkin, also quoted above: "Within the image-sequences examined the pattern appears of a movement, downward, or inward toward the earth's centre, or a cessation of movement—a physical change which, as we urge a metaphor closer to the impalpable forces of life and soul, appears also a transition toward a severed relation with the outer world, and, it may be, toward disintegration and death. This element in the pattern is balanced by a movement upward and outward—an expansion or outburst of activity, a transition toward reintegration and life-renewal". Such an image-sequence of movement toward the earth's center is typically treated by some psychologists and literary critics as if it *meant* Ehrenzweig's "manic womb of rebirth". According to the present conception, if we wish to refer the archetypal womb-image to the image of the movement inward toward the earth's center, we have to delete from the *womb* those features that are incompatible with the other image, and retain such features as "confined space", "cessation of movement", "transition toward a severed relation with the outer world" and, at a later stage of the pattern, "a movement upward and outward—an expansion or outburst of activity, a transition toward reintegration and life-renewal". Where there is no such image as "Kubla Khan's" underground caverns, or *Faust's* "low, dark rooms", the "confined space" feature, too, must sometimes be deleted, making us retain only the more abstract elements. Thus, the womb-image is not conceived of as *the underlying image* for which all other enclosure-images stand, but as a spatial image that serves as the most efficient cognitive coding of features relevant to the emotional sequence (see above, Chapter 10). This is a very far cry from, e.g., Eva Metman's archetypal approach (see below, Chapter 20), who identified the various personae in Beckett's *Waiting for Godot* with certain specific archetypal categories derived from Jungian psychology.

The same must be said of my own treatment of the DEATH-AND-REBIRTH ARCHETYPE in *Faust*. In most instances when I am speaking of "death-scenery" or "rebirth-imagery", the words "death" and "rebirth" contain some concrete features that are incompatible with the play's action, and must be deleted, so that only such more general features are retained as "extreme decrease of vitality", or "an expansion or outburst of activity"—both mainly in the emotional sphere.

I have discussed above at some length the Cinderella archetype and the death-and-rebirth archetype. The former is a pattern of external events, the latter an emotional pattern. Now, these two patterns are not unlike each other. Both consist of an initial and a final state that are polar opposites, and a marked reversal that leads from the former to the latter. In both patterns, the transition is from a less favorable to a more favorable state. In the Cinderella archetype, however, the transition is from a lower to a higher social status, whereas in the death-and-rebirth archetype the transition is from one mental state to another, from distress, depression, inactivity, severed relation with the outer world, to an expansion or outburst of activity, acceptance by the outer world, joy or elation, and the like. It is quite plausible that the audience, upon following the sequence of events in the Cinderella plot, experiences a similar emotional sequence. Perhaps the best way to view this relationship is as follows. When an archetypal pattern (characterazed by Frye as an "associative cluster") organizes convergent actions, it is perceived as a sequence of external events; when in the course of such an organization, attention is focused on diffuse sense impressions (especially, if these sense impressions are perceived as favorable or unfavorable to life), the sequence is perceived as an emotional sequence, embodied in spatial imagery unfolding in time. Alternatively, this relationship can be viewed in terms of our initial conception of an abstract emotional pattern as *hub,* with all other aspects of *human* action treated as spokes radiating from this hub.

CHAPTER 15

Space Perception
and Poetry of Orientation

Space Perception

Poetry is essentially a "time" art. Nevertheless, an overwhelming majority of poetic images is related to space perception. One reason for this is that spatial organization is of central importance in human cognition. This and the next chapter will explore how mechanisms of space perception are turned to aesthetic ends.

Space perception is not a unitary phenomenon. The *perception of shapes* differs in important respects from *orientation.* Physiologically, there is convincing evidence that different brain centers are involved. From the cognitive viewpoint, the latter activity is *global,* whereas the former is *analytical.* Object-centered perception involves analysis, a separation of the object from oneself, and from other objects and organisms (cf. Ornstein's discussion of "ordinary consciousness" in Chapter 1). We may get an understanding of what this separation may imply when we consider Neisser's description of the opposite pole: the orienting schema "always includes the perceiver as well as the environment. Ego and world are perceptually inseparable" (Neisser, 1976: 117).[1]

> Since movement is a continuous process, it creates continuous changes— flow patterns—in the optical structure available to the eye. Not only do different faces of objects come into view as the perceiver moves, but the optically projected shapes of these faces undergo systematic changes. [...] The point is not that one momentary retinal projection is correct while the others are distorted, but that the optical transformations produced by movement specify the real layout of the environment. [...] The observer's movement does not provide information only about the environment. The pattern of change and invariance available to the eyes specifies his own movements as well. As he moves forward, for example, the retinal projection of every visible surface in the forward half of the environment becomes steadily larger. [...] Moreover, the manner in which the projections grow larger is

---

1 Some of the main issues discussed in the present chapter (deixis, orientation, the sublime, and their poetic effects) are now updated and amplified in Chapter 24).

not arbitrary: every projected point except one moves steadily outward. The single exception is the very point toward which the perceiver is moving. Thus, not only the fact that he is moving but the direction of his motion is fully specified. The availability of this kind of optical structure means that one can see one's own position as well as the layout of the environment. [...] J. J. Gibson coined the term *visual proprioception* for the pick-up of self-specifying information from the optic array. (Neisser, 1976: 115–116)

In Chapter 1, we have discussed *perceptual constancy* and *cognitive stability*. The above passage from Neisser gives a masterful description of the way in which a constant and stable scene is constructed from fluid visual information. On the other hand, it also indicates how this flux of continually changing information may become a versatile device of fast orientation. We are usually not aware of "flow patterns", but of stable objects of constant size, shape, and location, and of the fact that we are moving in a certain direction. For most people, most of the time, this perception is categorial. People who respond, intuitively, to this rich pre-categorial visual information, are said to have good (or even superb) sense of orientation. We see again that cognitive stability and intuition are expanding at each other's expense. (In Chapter 24 I quote findings of brain science that may account for such self-perception in relation to surrounding space; it may also be regarded, perhaps, as the cognitive mechanism underlying deixis).

As regards orientation, the above described locomotion need not actually take place. One may *imagine* the continuous changes of the optical structures available to the eye. They may be present to one's mind as "perceptual anticipation". Thus, orientation is more prepared to pick up the *arrangement* of objects in one's environment, whereas shape perception is centered on the properties of the *object itself*. Orientation is ready for taking in the environment in large lumps, the flux of information coming from the whole environment; shape perception concerns relatively small sections of the immediate environment, by constructing stable objects from the constant flux of information. Orientation depends on one's integration of the environment, and on locating oneself with relation to that environment; object perception depends on differentiation: that is, separating the objects from oneself. An orienting schema is a schema on a large scale, in relation to which ego constitutes a relatively small point; by contrast, the perception of an object involves a schema on a relatively small scale. The pick-up of self-specifying information from the optic array "can be simulated only by manipulating the entire optic array at once"; the act of orientation has, therefore, an integrating effect on the environment in awareness.

As to the *kinds of* schemata involved in shape perception and orientation, we notice a difference, too. Measurements of how quickly people can report on minor details of an imagined object have shown faster responses for objects imagined as large or close by, than for those imagined small or far away. According to Neisser (1976: 147), rather than ascribing the delay with small objects to a process of first "blowing up" and then describing, this delay may be explained as follows: "Plans for looking at distant and small objects are necessarily different from those for examining things that are large and near at hand. Searching for small details is compatible with the latter plans, but not the former. Subjects who are asked to imagine small details while they are visualizing a far-away object are essentially in an interference situation". This explanation may suggest some of the reasons behind different schemata for the perception of shapes and for orientation. In Chapter 17, it will be suggested that poetry may generate effects of disorientation by creating just such an "interference situation".

Neisser is preoccupied with the *process* of information pick-up and the *mechanism underlying* it, rather than with its appearance in consciousness. And indeed, in well-practiced situations in our everyday life, we are aware of the objects around us, their shapes and relative positions, as well as of our relation to those objects; by contrast, we do not *perceive* the orientation processes that are involved. When, however, the process of information pick-up is slowed down for some reason—in not so well practiced situations, or (as with Bartlett's subjects) for introspection or, more important for us, for aesthetic purposes—the process appears to consciousness as affect. In this respect, affect is a flux of unstable, shape-free information changing over time, *or a readiness to pick up* information which is prevented from settling into solid objects. Here, the visual mode is the dominant, but not the only, mode of perception of human beings; the stream of visual information is undifferentiably intermingled with information in other sensory modes, most notably the auditory and olfactory modes (hearing and smell).

A further problem should be noted here. Our business here is not merely with space perception, but with space perception in verbal art; that is, with space perception in a temporal medium. Making this distinction is not just toying around with words, but involves very real issues. Temporal and verbal information processing is sequential and is typically associated with the left cerebral hemisphere, whereas spatial information processing (orientation in particular) is global and is typically associated with the right cerebral hemisphere.

> The left hemisphere (connected to the right side of the body) is predominantly involved with analytic, logical thinking, especially in verbal and mathematical functions. Its mode of operation is primarily linear. This hemisphere seems to process information sequentially. This mode of operation of necessity must underlie logical thought, since logic depends on sequence and order. Language and mathematics, both left-hemisphere activities, also depend predominantly on linear time.
>
> If the left hemisphere is specialized for analysis, the right hemisphere (again, remember, connected to the left side of the body) seems specialized for holistic mentation. Its language ability is quite limited. This hemisphere is primarily responsible for our orientation in space, artistic endeavour, crafts, body image, recognition of faces. It processes information more diffusely than does the left hemisphere, and its responsibilities demand a ready integration of many inputs at once. If the left hemisphere can be termed analytic and sequential in its operation, then the right hemisphere is

> more holistic and relational, and more simultaneous in its mode of opera-
> tion. (Ornstein, 1975: 67–68)

The nature of orientation in particular is illustrated by the two hemispheres' different
ways of processing input:

> The right side of the cortex processes its input more as a "patterned whole",
> that is, in a more simultaneous manner than does the left. This simultane-
> ous processing is advantageous for the integration of diffuse inputs, such as
> for orienting oneself in space, when motor, kinesthetic and visual input
> must be quickly integrated. This mode of information-processing, too,
> would seem to underlie an "intuitive" rather than "intellectual" integration
> of complex entities. (ibid., 95)

This specialization of operation in different modes may explain much about the fundamental duality of our consciousness. "This duality has been reflected in classical as
well as modern literature as between reason and passion, or between mind and intuition. Perhaps the most famous of these dichotomies in psychology is that proposed by Sigmund Freud, of the split between the 'conscious' mind and the "unconscious'" (ibid., 74).

   The difference between the two cerebral hemispheres and the two types of information processing has, as we shall see later, important repercussions for poetic language. Since poetry is written with words, and language is typically a sequential, rational activity, the left-hemisphere functions will be taken for granted in the present
chapter; this will cause a certain asymmetry in our discussions: greater emphasis
will be laid in what follows on the outstanding global, less rational, right-hemi-
spheric functions.

On the Sublime

It is noteworthy in the framework of our present inquiry that the two kinds of predicates of aesthetic judgments in Kant's aesthetics, the "beautiful" and the "sublime"
appear to be akin to the above-mentioned mechanisms of space perception. I shall
resort to some of Beardsley's lucid summaries of Kant's thought:

> Beauty and sublimity are contrasted in two respects: that the former is con-
> nected with form, hence the boundedness, of an object, while the latter in-
> volves an experience of boundlessness; and that the former depends upon the
> purposiveness of an object, making it seem "as it were, pre-adapted to our
> judgment" (ß 23) while the latter is aroused by objects that seem "as it were
> to do violence to the imagination". (Beardsley, 1966: 218, quoting Kant,
> 1951)

Visual shape perception quite obviously is connected with the boundedness of an object; at the same time, it may be suggested that orientation is connected with relating the self to the great directions of the surrounding space, extending beyond the visible horizon, and thus involving an experience of boundlessness.

In the present section, we shall focus attention on the *sublime*. "We call that *sublime* which is *absolutely great*" (Kant, 1951: 86), *"what is great beyond all comparison"* (ibid.). We still need some definition that may attach a descriptive content to these critical terms. *Absolutely great* may be regarded as a positive description of the negative notion *boundlessness* or *infinity*. Kant suggests that the sublime be defined in psychological terms. "As this, however, is great beyond all standards of sense, it makes us judge as *sublime,* not so much the object, as our own state of mind in the estimation of it" (ibid., 94). The 18th-Century Hebrew poet in Hungary Shlomo Levisohn devotes about half of his treatise on poetics *Yə'urun's Poetry* to discussions of the sublime in Biblical and post-Biblical Hebrew poetry. He characterizes the sublime state of mind as follows: "The sublime is that which by the thunders of its activities seizes the mind, leaving no thoroughfare in it for any other thought". Thus, the sublime not only receives a psychological definition; it becomes part of a whole system of states of mind relevant in one way or other to the reading and writing of poetry. It becomes, in an important sense, the opposite of what, according to Walter Jackson Bates (1964: 56), is possibly an aspect of the quality denoted by Keats's phrase "negative capability": the ability "to make up one's mind about nothing—to let the mind be a thoroughfare for all thoughts" (this notion of Keats's will be discussed at some length in Chapter 21). In the "Conclusions" section of Chapter 17, I briefly compare and contrast the sublime with the grotesque. Both are qualities that suddenly seize and fill the human soul, leaving no thoroughfare for any other emotion; and both threaten to exceed the imagination's power to take it all in at once. One might say that both qualities are thrust upon the mind from the outside, unless one deliberately resorts to avoidance strategies. Negative capability, by contrast, "is an imaginative openness of mind, and heightened receptivity to reality in its full and diverse concreteness" (ibid., 56). This openness comes from within—sometimes as a natural disposition, sometimes through deliberate spiritual exercises. "To be dissatisfied with such insights as one may attain through this openness, to reject them unless they can be wrenched into a part of a systematic structure of one's own making, is an egoistic assertion of one's own identity" (ibid., 57). Now it is most significant that the sublime, the grotesque, and negative capability all alike are *total* experiences of the mind, consummated in a heightened exposure to reality (or poetic qualities), reached after the surrender of "an egoistic assertion of one's own identity"; but whereas in the former two, one is shaken out of it, as it were, by force, in the latter the surrender of this assertion comes from the inside.

But let us proceed now with some of Kant's conceptual distinctions, as discussed by Beardsley.

When we estimate magnitudes through numbers, that is, conceptually, the imagination selects a unit, which it can then repeat indefinitely. But there is a second kind of estimation of magnitudes, which Kant calls "aesthetic estimation", in which the imagination tries to comprehend or encompass the whole representation in one single intuition. There is an upper bound to its capacity. An object whose apparent or conceived size strains this capacity to the limit—threatens to exceed the imagination's power to take it all in at once—has, subjectively speaking, an absolute magnitude: it reaches the felt limit, and appears as if infinite. [...] imagination reaches its maximum capacity, shows its failure and inadequacy when compared to the demands of Reason, and makes us aware, by contrast, of the magnificence of Reason itself. The resulting feeling is the feeling of the sublime. (Beardsley, 1966: 218–219)

In my book on "Kubla Khan" (Tsur, 2006: 80–81, 88), I pointed out that in Coleridge's poem, both kinds of estimation are in evidence. We find them, among other places, together in the following stanza:

(1)   Five miles meandering with a mazy motion
        Through wood and dale the sacred river ran,
        Then reached the caverns measureless to man,
        And sank in tumult to a lifeless ocean:
        And 'mid this tumult Kubla heard from far
        Ancestral voices prophesying war!

Here (and elsewhere in "Kubla Khan") we have, then, both kinds of estimation, the indefinitely repeatable unit selected ("miles"), and the immense forces of the infinite and the sublime, as incarnated in the "caverns measureless to man" (twice), the "deep romantic chasm", "lifeless ocean", or "sunless sea", exceeding the imagination's capacity to comprehend or encompass the whole in one single intuition. Bodkin's characterization of "the imagination, seeking something enormous, ultimate" seems to be relevant here, "as when standing on some precipice edge, amongst peaks and chasms, one feels their lines overpowering and terrible through the suggested anguish of falling. That horror overcome adds a kind of emotional exultation to the sight of actual mountain chasms" (1963: 104).

In relation to the sublime, a further Kantian distinction is required, viz., that "between the mathematical sublime, which is evoked by objects that strike us as maximally huge, and the dynamic sublime, which is evoked by objects that seem to have absolute power over us" (Beardsley, 1966: 218). In a very important sense, "Kubla Khan" proceeds from the former to the latter kind of sublime. It is this feature that infuses the natural landscape with tremendous energy: beginning with the maximally huge "caverns measureless to man", through the dynamic sublime in the holy, enchanted, and haunted landscape, to the speaker's frenzy at the end of the poem by which the speaker seems to have absolute power over his audience.

It should be noted, however, that "infinite" space is only one among a variety of phenomena providing instances of the sublime; but it is, beyond question, its *best example*. What is more, in poetry the spatial aspect of the sublime prevails, usually reinforced by the other phenomena. Or, conversely, these other phenomena are frequently presented in spatial terms. Levisohn enumerates the following things that are perceived as sublime: enormous distances, enormous heights, enormous depths, the distant past, enormous sound, but also great silence and great darkness (cf., Milton's "darkness visible", commented on above, in chapter 4). Observe furthermore that in harmony with the localistic point of view,[2] I had to translate in the above summary from Levisohn, his term for "far-awayness" of the past by the adjective *distant,* referring to a spatial relationship. As the localists have pointed out, prepositions indicating temporal relationships are derived in many languages from prepositions indicating spatial relationships. In poetry, the metaphor that is most often used for infinite time is infinite space. It should be noticed, too, that some of the enormities mentioned above are negative entities experienced as positive presence. *Depth, silence, darkness* indicate "absence"—absence of substance, of sound, and of light, respectively. The passage quoted above from Bodkin may also indicate why, in certain circumstances, precisely these aspects of the sublime may be experienced as overpowering. In all these domains, "the imagination, seeking something enormous, ultimate", is left with nothing to rest on for support. Here, perhaps, again, the spatial relationship is the basic template for cognition. The fourth line in (1) above, "And sank in tumult to a lifeless ocean", suggests both the mathematical and the dynamic sublime; and "lifeless ocean" has something of the negative entity about it, frustrating "the imagination, seeking something enormous, ultimate". In lines 6–7, "And 'mid this tumult Kubla heard from far / Ancestral voices prophesying war!", the spatial aspects of the sublime (from far") are reinforced by enormous sound ("tumult"), and distant past ("ancestral voices"). What is more, the "solid" ancestors are absent, and are replaced here by a thing-free metonymy.

I have further discussed the sublime at considerable length in two pieces of Romantic poetry in which the landscape described "reaches [even transcends] the felt limit, and appears as if infinite": a poem by the Hebrew Romantic poet Saul Tchernikhovsky (v. supra, Chapter 11, excerpt 3), and Shelley's "Ozymandias" (v. infra, Chapter 24, passim). In the latter chapter I have also elaborated at greater length on orientation and the sublime. I have devoted a full chapter to "The Sublime and the Absolute Limit" in my book on religious and mystic poetry (Tsur, 2003: 141–165).

2 "The term localism is being used here to refer to the hypothesis that spatial expressions are more basic, grammatically and semantically, than various kinds of non-spatial expressions [...], they serve as structural templates, as it were, for other expressions; and the reason why this should be so, it is plausibly suggested by psychologists, is that spatial organization is of central importance in human cognition" (Lyons, 1977: 718).

Orientation and Shape Perception in Poetry

One of the central assumptions of the present study has been that in the response to poetry, ordinary cognitive processes are turned to aesthetic ends; some of the major effects of poetry being the result of disturbance of these processes. The immediate space extending beyond the visible horizon can be experienced only by responding to it as a whole, relating oneself to its great directions. The affective impact of the physical description in, e.g., "Ozymandias", is reinforced by an unfulfilled readiness to pick up self-specifying visual information in a vast surrounding space with fewer than usual cues for orientation. In Shape perception, by contrast, the key word is "distinction": distinction between objects, and between the objects and the perceiver.

In the last lines of Keats's "When I have Fears", perceptible space consists in the archetypal notion of absence: *nothingness,* which has been turned into infinite space by the verb *sink to.* The circumstances of unfulfilled readiness to pick up self-specifying information from the optic structure of the environment are amplified here: the scope of the orientation space is increased (beyond the shore of the wide world), whereas the possible self-specifying visual cues are reduced to zero:

(2)   then on the shore
       Of the wide world I stand alone, and think,
       Till love and fame to nothingness do sink.

Much romantic poetry, like this last passage, is aimed at a reintegration of the self with the environment, or at its total dissolution in it; in other words, it is an attempt to overcome, wholly or partially, the separation of the self from its environment, with the help of the orientation mechanism.

Above, in Chapter 4, I have compared two seventeenth-century applications of the compass-image, the one in Donne's "Valediction Forbidding Mourning",

(3)   If they be two, they are two so
          As stiffe twin compasses are two,
          Thy soule, the fixt foot, makes no show
          To move, but doth if th'other doe.

          And though it in the centre sit,
          Yet when the other far doth rome,
          It leans and hearkens after it,
          And growes erect as that comes home.

and the other from Milton's *Paradise Lost:*

(4)   Then stayed the fervid wheels, and in his hand
          He took the golden compasses, prepared

> In God's eternal store, to circumscribe
> The universe and all created things.
> One foot he centered, and the other turned
> Round through the vast profundity obscure.
> Thus God the heav'n created, thus the earth,
> Matter unformed and void. Darkness profound
> Cover'd th'abyss; but on the wat'ry calm
> His brooding wings the Spirit of God outspread,
> And vital virtue infused, and vital warmth
> Throughout the fluid mass ...   (VII. 224–237)

There, too, we contrasted the two passages to illustrate split and integrated focus, generating witty and emotional qualities. Here, we have to add that the two passages illustrate poetry of shape perception and of orientation, respectively. The respective witty and emotional effects of the two passages crucially depend upon these mechanisms of space perception. From the foregoing analysis, one may infer that orientation is closely associated with GLOBAL-EMOTIONAL, shape perception with ANALYTICAL-RATIONAL. As I have indicated in Chapter 5, according to gestalt theory (and confirmed by the Rorschach inkblot test), good form realization is correlated with a quality of strong intellectual control. Where, on the other hand, there is chaotic over-differentiation or primordial homogeneity, says Meyer (quoted in Chapter 5), "the lack of distinct, tangible shapes and of well-articulated modes of progression is capable of arousing desires for, and expectations of, clarification and improvement". As pointed out in Chapter 4, in order to extract the spiritual message from Donne's compass image, one must carefully visualize the compass in all its movements. The analytical-rational quality of this perception of shape reinforces the witty quality of the passage, as discussed in that chapter.

In Milton's passage, we encounter a different strategy. In line 228, attention is focused on the *exact* use of a compass (almost domesticating the Sublime Act of Creation): "One foot he centered, and the other turned". But, the design drawn by the golden compasses is not allowed to solidify into a "bounded" circle (as in Donne). The second foot is lost in the vague and infinite and shapeless, or even the matterless, so to speak. Space is presented here not only as sublime, lost beyond the visible horizon. Such information as "Matter unformed and void", and the subsequent thing-free and gestalt-free qualities are treated as information that has not settled into stable objects in the process of orientation; the information surrounds a fixed center that indicates, as it were, the location of the perceiving consciousness.

The Double-Edgedness of Abstract Nouns

The foregoing conception may illuminate an important stylistic property of abstract nouns, which otherwise would remain puzzling (to say the least): what may be called their **double-edgedness.**[3] 'Double-edgedness' denotes the phenomenon that a given element, device, or structure can give rise to incompatible or even opposite effects in different stylistic environments. In the present case, abstract nouns are perceived in certain circumstances as clear-cut concepts, intellectual abstractions; in others, as evoking undifferentiated, often emotionally loaded, qualities. The latter occasionally embrace qualities perceived as a vague, elusive, but intense atmosphere; on other occasions, as the presence of the ineffable, the possibility of getting a glimpse into some supersensory, spiritual reality; then again, as the source of some "oceanic" experience, of being totally immersed in some supersensory, but dense, substance. What those "certain circumstances" are, and what cognitive mechanisms underlie them, is the question explored here. I shall argue that the opposition between the varieties of experiences has to do with the mechanisms of space perception.

I propose to begin my discussion with a "minimal" pair of examples. The first example is from Wordsworth's famous "Observations Prefixed to 'Lyrical Ballads'" (1800), the second one from his "Solitary Reaper". In both examples, he uses the word *overflow* in a figurative sense, in relation to an abstract noun. This abstract noun, in both cases, is a highly generic term, the hyponyms of which refer to a wide range of immediately experienced qualities.

(5)   For all good poetry is the spontaneous overflow of powerful
       feelings [...].

(6)   Behold her, single in the field,
       Yon solitary highland lass!
       Reaping and singing by herself,
       Stop here or gently pass!
       Alone she cuts and binds the grain,
       And sings a melancholy strain;
          O listen! for the vale profound
          Is overflowing with the sound.

Wordsworth critics have drawn attention to the similar use of *overflow* in the two quotations and suggested that the two passages are closely related within the Wordsworthian conception of poetry. In what follows, I shall explore the perceptual *difference* between the two metaphors, in the light of the above-mentioned double-edgedness of abstract nouns.

Insofar as "feeling" is perceived as a 'regional quality' (see above, Chapter 4) of (5), this is due to the way the meaning of *overflow* is perceived in this phrase. *Overflow* denotes a movement of liquid in space, implying some vessel or riverbed that cannot contain all the liquid. Some of the meaning components relevant to the

3   The present discussion is an extract from a much more detailed treatment presented elsewhere (Tsur, 1987b: 145–190).

context are suddenness, superabundance, an outlet for excess, an uncontrollable discharge rising in a container with a necessity comparable to that of physical processes. Since *overflow* is associated here with *feeling* rather than with *water* (or some other substance), there is a conflict between the selection restriction features and the noun selected. As a result of this conflict, the features [+MATERIAL +LIQUID +SPATIAL MOVEMENT] tend to be canceled (or at least weakened) in *overflow*. As a result, one way of realizing this particular quality of meaning is to regard *overflow* as a bundle of conceptual predicates including "suddenness", "superabundance", "an outlet for excess", "an uncontrolled discharge rising inside a container" providing the information required for the definition of "all good poetry" and simultaneously canceling the visual-spatial image.

A psychologically-oriented approach might reveal the following. Most of my readers, I believe, when presented with the above excerpts, would probably report having some kind of single, unified sensory image, involving elements of *overflow:* a smooth but powerful movement from one's inside to the outside, involving visual, tactile, and kinaesthetic sensations. This "moving mass" will have its material components canceled; on the other hand, since it explains the existence of good poetry, many readers will perceive the metaphor as having a psychological atmosphere of specific direction and patent purpose. This psychological atmosphere seems to be just enough to tilt the balance of the material meaning components in the direction of "knowing", so as to have them assume the conceptual nature required to fulfill its role in conceptual discourse (i. e., in the definition of "all good poetry"). In this process, such meaning components of *overflow* as 'suddenness' and 'arising inside itself' tend to reinforce the meaning of *spontaneous*; 'superabundance' and 'excess' tend to reinforce the meaning *powerful*, whereas the tactile and kinesthetic sensations (if any) tend to reinforce the meaning *feelings*. This is why the first passage above is perceived as **almost** conceptual discourse, but still including a perceptual ingredient.

Now turning to the last two lines of (6), one notices an intense, "thing-free" quality that can be contemplated "without regard to thought or perceived object", so to speak. *Sound* itself denotes a thing-free quality. But notice that the verb *overflow*, which is associated with the visual and tactile senses, takes the object *sound*, which is associated with the aural sense. This conflict between the senses weakens (for some readers even cancels the auditory components in *sound,* and leaves the presence of a thing-free quality as a component. This thing-free quality becomes "infested" with undifferentiated sensations—the residuum of the tactile sensation of being immersed in water, after specific tactile properties have been canceled. Some readers report that they have a feeling as if the surface of their body became peculiarly important, accentuated somehow. From the visual sensation, only the spatial presence of 'superabundance' and 'movement' in space is left. Thus, in (6), but not in (5), there is an intense regional quality of "feeling", in the sense of "physical sensation not connected with sight, hearing, taste, or smell".

Thus, the overflow of sound is perceived as an intense, undifferentiated, supersensory presence, in which one might totally be immersed, so as "to suspend the boundaries between self and not-self". Here, then, *overflow* contributes to the presence of a "gestalt-free" and "thing-free" quality, that is, a quality that is intensely **felt**, but not interpreted (there is no awareness of inferences). This kind of feeling is not unlike a "process of immediate experience" that "links perception with sensation", at its most "refined".

It should be noted that semantic information is processed in different ways in the two metaphors. In (5), *feeling* is a solid frame of metaphor, in which no features (or components) are canceled; all the burden of feature-cancellation and transfer is "inflicted" upon *overflow*. In (6), feature-cancellation has been performed in both terms, so as to generate a "thing-free" and "gestalt-free" presence. The meaning-components activated by the metaphor in the first quotation are rapidly conceptualized, so as to serve the purposes of a conceptual discourse. The conceptualization of the meaning components activated by the metaphor in the second quote is relatively delayed, so as to serve for as long as possible as the object of pre-conceptual, "immediate" experiencing. As a corollary, the feature of spatial presence is more emphatically retained in (6) than in (5).

The two quotations (5) and (6) have been compared in four respects. First, they were shown to contain the same kind of metaphorical construction. Second, the felt differences between their perceived effects were characterized. Third, some of the supposed semantic mechanisms responsible for them were described. Fourth, certain apparently significant correlations between the semantic mechanisms and the perceived effects were suggested. It remains to be determined whether there is any indication in the texts themselves that could bias the reader in the perceptual direction in the one case, and in the conceptual direction in the other.

Sequential and Spatial Processing

The comparison of the two Wordsworth quotations might suggest such an indication, viz., the presence or absence of a particular physical setting as a background for the abstract nouns in question. One of the definitions of "abstraction" in *The American College Dictionary* is: "act of considering something as a general object apart from special circumstances". This definition matches exactly the process described in the first quote as "the spontaneous overflow of powerful feelings"; by contrast, the phrase "overflowing with the sound" in the second quotation is set in a particular physical setting, in carefully emphasized "special circumstances", thus confirming our hypothesis above. One of the necessary conditions for perceptual categorization is that "responses must occur at the time the sensory material is received"; therefore, a gestalt-free and thing-free perception arising from an abstract noun may occur only when the noun is set in an imagined situation defined *here and now*, as it were, from the point of view of the perceiving consciousness. And indeed, such exclamations as "Oh listen!", or the imperative in line 4, or *behold* and *yon* in the first two lines of "The Solitary Reaper" do serve as emphatic deictic devices, that is, serve emphatically to define the situation *here and now*.

This explanation may be approached from a different direction as well. Language is conceptual and linear by its very nature. Thus, it is best suited for logical discourse. Even such words as *feeling, emotion, intuition, orientation* refer to concepts, intellectual abstractions. It would appear impossible to evoke, only with their help, the non-linear experiences from which they have been abstracted. In other words, words appear to be particularly ill-suited to some of the most universally acknowledged aims of poetry. This problem, as well as its solution, may be better understood with reference to the results of the lateralization process in the human brain. Such experiences as feelings, emotions, intuitions, orientation are diffuse, global, non-linear processes, and are related to the right hemisphere, whereas the words that refer to them do so *via* concepts that are compact, analytic, linear, and are related to the left hemisphere. Hence, the problematic nature of the telling-and-showing dichotomy as illustrated in this particular case. **Telling** about diffuse, global, illogical **experiences** becomes necessarily compact, analytic, logical.

In the end, however, it is the problem itself that, by its very nature, suggests a solution to our poetic enigma; and our comparison of the two Wordsworth passages offers a typical example of such a solution. Considering that global activities such as emotions on the one hand, and spatial orientation on the other, are intimately associated with the right hemisphere, one might surmise that in "The Solitary Reaper", the definite spatial setting may be an instrument for transferring part of the processing of the verbal message to the right hemisphere. This conception could be further elaborated in the following way. At least two kinds of information about semantic categories are stored in memory: the **names** of the categories, and the representations of their **properties**. In the course of normal speech, we perceive the representations of these properties **categorially** (for this term, see Chapter 8, above); we do not perceive the semantic features (or meaning-components), but the single compact semantic entity which they constitute. Ornstein brings some convincing experimental evidence that when some memory image concerning spatial orientation is called up, the right hemisphere may be activated, even though one may be engaged in some verbal activity. "Which direction a person gazes is affected by the question asked. If the question is verbal analytical (such as 'Divide 144 by 6, and multiply the answer by 7' [or 'How do you spell *Mississippi?*]), more eye movements are made to the right than if the question involves spatial mentation (such as 'Which way does the Indian face on the nickel')" (1975: 77). When a landscape description (in the world stratum of the poem), and certain stylistic devices (such as repetitive schemata both on the semantic and phonetic level) transfer a significant part of the processing of the message to the right hemisphere, representations of some or even many properties of these categories escape the control of categorial perception, and constitute some global, diffuse atmosphere in a concrete landscape[4]. At the extreme of this technique, there may be no stable objects at all in the description, the concrete landscape being compellingly indicated by emphatic deictic

4 My discussion of the 'tip-of-the-tongue phenomenon' (Tsur, 1987b: 273–288) provides ample support for these speculations.

devices only. Moreover, in several cultures, emotionally loaded exclamations are intimately related with what is called the 'pathetic fallacy', that is, the bestowal of the speaker's feelings upon surrounding Nature. The reason, again, seems to be that the bestowal of emotions on the surrounding landscape transfers part of the information processing to the right hemisphere of the brain. As Ornstein indicates (see the quote above), the right hemisphere's simultaneous processing is advantageous for the integration of diffuse inputs, such as for orienting oneself in space, when motor, kinesthetic, and visual input must be quickly integrated. Our foregoing discussion might suggest that this mode is responsible not only for "the integration of diffuse inputs", but also for "the diffusion" of compact inputs, so as to create the impression of an "intuitive rather than intellectual integration of complex entities".[5]

To conclude this section, I would like briefly to consider, in the light of the foregoing distinctions, a verse line by the great Hebrew poet, Nathan Alterman:

זְמַן רָחָב, רָחָב. הַלֵּב צִלְצֵל אַלְפַּיִם.

zman raḥav, raḥav. hallev ṣilṣel ʾalpayim

(7)   Wide, wide time. The heart rang two thousand.

At first glance, the first phrase of this line may be perceived as a witty play, nothing more. If there is a "long, long time", there may be a "wide, wide time" as well. The Russian formalists and their disciples would perhaps regard this as a brilliant exercise in "making strange", in "de-automatization", in "reviving a dead metaphor". And as such, it is quite effective indeed. For some readers, however, the phrase has an intense emotional quality, which cannot be accounted for by the witty alienation device. Some readers feel as if they were wrapt in a low-differentiated texture of "time", or, as it were, "plunged" in it; as if the boundaries between self and not-self were suspended, while they (the readers) were "immersed" in "time". Some even report a faint tactile sensation all over the outer surface of their bodies.

The two parts of this verse line present an experience of a time period of very great magnitude. The second part estimates this magnitude conceptually: the imagination selects a unit, which it can then repeat indefinitely. Still, when it is the heart that strikes (as a clock) "two thousand", the description assumes some marked emotional quality. And the two thousand strokes (or beats of the heart) definitely exceed the imagination's power to take it in all at once, even though it can be expressed in numbers, that is, conceptually: the two thousand beats are collapsed into an undif-

---

5   The application of neurophysiology to poetics and other "higher" mental processes is controversial. I have defended my practice in an Appendix at the end of my book *On Metaphoring*) (Tsur, 1987b: 289–308). Also, see some recent developments below, Chapter 24.

ferentiated experience of time. The first phrase, by contrast, suggests the Kantian "aesthetic estimation", in which the imagination tries to comprehend or encompass the whole representation of a time period in one intuition. The apparent size of this period strains this capacity to the limit. "Long, long time" would suggest that its size threatens to exceed the imagination's power to take it all in at once. Now, as "long" refers to a spatial dimension, there would seem to be no reason why one should not refer to duration with equal naturalness by the name of another spatial dimension, e.g., "wide". However, as it has been noted, sequential time is a "linear" experience, typically associated with the left hemisphere of the brain. Whenever we refer to only one spatial dimension, we refer to *length*. As such, the adjective *long* is felt to be naturally appropriate to a linear use with reference to 'time', even though its original use is for spatial relationships. When *wide* is substituted for *long*, we are not dealing with just another spatial dimension, one that might refer equally well to duration. *Long* refers to that spatial dimension of which there is *more;* and we tend to associate directionality with it. *Wide* implies that the space referred to has another, more extensive (in fact, *longer)* dimension as well, which gives its intuitive direction. Space that extends in all directions into infinity, that is, beyond the horizon, has no length, only width. This is how Coleridge's Ancient Mariner describes infinite space leading nowhere, in which he was hopelessly stuck:

(8)   Alone, alone, all, all alone,
        Alone on a wide wide sea!   (232–233)

It is felt intuitively that one could not change the adjective into "a long long sea". *Wide* is precisely the spatial dimension that changes the "linear" character of duration into a "patterned whole", having a simultaneous existence or presence. It seems most likely that this involves the heightened activity of the right hemisphere of the brain which is responsible for the diffuse, low differentiated quality of the percept.

Allegory and Symbol

In this last section of the present chapter, I am going to discuss at some length the first five lines of Keats's sonnet "On Seeing the Elgin Marbles". From this discussion, I shall derive a distinction between allegory and symbol which reduces, I claim, the subjective impressionist element normally present in this distinction.

(9)   My spirit is too weak—mortality
        Weighs heavily on me like unwilling sleep,
        And each imagined pinnacle and steep
        Of godlike hardship, tells me I must die
        Like a sick eagle looking at the sky.

Keats's "Elgin-Marbles" sonnet contains a considerable number of abstractions and thing-free qualities (mainly in the parts not quoted here; see, e.g., Chapter 1, quote (8)), which are the source of emotionally loaded, undifferentiated qualities.[6] Here, I want to point out that *mortality* in this quotation makes an impression that may be described as a diffuse, though intense, essence or quality. The sonnet begins in a way that could be perceived as almost plain conceptual language. *My spirit is too weak* is a straightforward enough conceptual statement of an emotional state; *weighs heavily on me* is, in ordinary language, a dead metaphor, in the sense "troubles me". Nevertheless, the first two lines are rather perceived as undifferentiated and non-conceptual. Why? One reason could be the peculiar tension between the abstract and the concrete in the sentence "Mortality weighs heavily on me like unwilling sleep". Another reason may be the peculiar nature of the concrete element in this tension. Finally, the perceived quality generated in this way is reinforced by the relation of this phrase to the surrounding phrases.

To see this, let us first compare Keats's own words to a paraphrase such as "Death weighs heavily on me". This paraphrase appears to be somewhat less diffuse. While *mortality* is relatively rare in poetry, *death* is far more common. Though both are abstract nouns, *mortality* is more abstract than *death*, in the sense that the potential is more abstract than the actual. Besides, we are accustomed to personifications of *Death* in poetry, myth, and even our every-day thought, to the extent that we no longer associate such personifications with pure abstractions; by contrast, *mortality* is shape-free in our awareness. In this sense, *mortality* stretches the expression into the abstract direction. *Weighs*, on the other hand, attributes to *mortality* a property which is the exclusive property of physical objects. Now, when an abstraction is associated with a physical object that has a characteristic visual shape, the typical result is a figurative expression in which the abstraction has a compact, differentiated, conceptual character. When, however, the abstraction is associated with a physical quality that belongs to the domain of one of the least differentiated senses, such as the tactile or thermal sense, or the sense of weight (see above, Chapter 10) it tends to be registered as a diffuse, undifferentiated, though intense and saturated percept. By attributing weight to *mortality*, one endows it with potency, or power, while at the same time dramatizing a feeling of "di**stress**" or "de**press**ion". In this way, the present metaphor joins a highly abstract (differentiated) noun with a very low-differentiated predicate; there is a "hole" left at what Wimsatt (1954) calls **the substantive level** (that is to say, the expression suggests the kind of feeling for which our vocabulary has no name). In the present case, inasmuch as the metaphor is immediately preceded by a direct expression "My spirit is too weak" on the substantive level, it serves as a standard for deviation in either direction. Notice that the analysis depends on a certain mental performance: it takes for granted that the predicate *weighs* is not taken in the straightforward idiomatic sense of "troubles me". But the qualities that are suggested here as inherent in the predicate can be detected only if one understands *weighs* as a physical attribute proper, and conceives of the term as

6   I have elsewhere provided a more comprehensive reading of this sonnet (Tsur, 2002).

allowing, at one and the same time, for a more abstract and a more concrete interpretation of the expression on the substantive level than it, taken by itself, would suggest. Here, such a reading is encouraged by the sequel, "like unwilling sleep" (meaning either unwilling to come or to go), suggesting an altered state of consciousness of low differentiation. The expression metonymically transfers an undifferentiated sense of heaviness from the limbs to *mortality*, the abstraction being related to the speaker from the outside, as it were.

In the following, I shall propose a few comments on the poem's ensuing landscape description. According to our initial assumptions concerning the relationship between landscape descriptions and emotional qualities in poetry, one might expect that the "pinnacles and steeps" amplify the emotional quality of *mortality*, by increasing its diffuseness. This, however, is not necessarily the case. Alternative mental performances may be involved (see Chapter 2), and the reader may switch back and forth between them. Horizontally, "Each imagined pinnacle and steep" may be conceived of as of part of an actual, continuous landscape; vertically, as of strikingly representative examples of "godlike hardship", that is, of a circumstance in which excessive and painful effort of some kind is required. Qua *exemplary*, the landscape tends to bring the conceptual nature of *hardship* into sharp focus.

Now, the more emphasis is placed on the *actual* (rather than the exemplary) nature of the landscape, the softer (the more diffuse) becomes the focus of perception of the abstraction *hardship*. Alternatively, the more our awareness is focused on the *shapes* of the "pinnacles and steeps", the sharper the definition gets of the conceptual quality; and, conversely, the more one's awareness is focussed on **locating oneself in space and time** with reference to the pinnacles and steeps, the more diffuse (the more 'perceptual') the concept becomes. In other words, as I will argue in Chapter 24, the deictic element plays here a crucial role. All this is implied by our discussion of shape perception and orientation.

The line "Like a sick eagle looking at the sky" has a multiple relationship to the preceding utterance. First, the eagle reinforces connotations of loftiness in "pinnacles and steeps". Second, the eagle enacts the sense of desperate helplessness; it combines in one visual image impending death with what the eagle *might* be in the sky, and thus reinforces a tragic feeling. Third, the mere appearance of the eagle enhances the suggestion that the "pinnacles and steeps" may constitute an actual landscape. Fourth, the eagle represents a consciousness in the very act of locating itself with reference to space, that is, it emphasizes the aspect of spatial orientation, rather than the exemplary aspect in "each pinnacle and steep", and thus increases the diffuse, rather than the compact perception of *mortality* and also, possibly, of *hardship*.

Our discussion of the two aspects of "each imagined pinnacle and steep" upon which awareness may be focused, raises an additional issue of the utmost importance. The theoretical equipment introduced in the present chapter can help to discern some crucial respects in which allegory is distinguished from symbol. Traditionally, both suggest a kind of 'double-talk': talking of some concrete entities and implying some abstract ones. But whereas in allegory the concrete or material forms are considered as the "mere" guise of some well-defined abstract or spiritual meaning, the symbol is conceived to have an existence independent from the abstractions, and to suggest, "somehow", the ineffable, some reality, or quality, or feeling, that cannot be expressed in ordinary, conceptual language. The landscape in Keats's sonnet can be perceived as an allegorical landscape, strikingly representative of "godlike hardship", or as a symbolic landscape, suggesting certain feelings that tend to elude words.

Now, ineffable experiences are ineffable precisely because they are related to right-hemisphere brain activities, in which information is diffuse, undifferentiated, global, whereas the language which seeks to express those experiences is a typical left-hemisphere brain-activity, in which information is compact, well-differentiated, and linear. Traditional allegory bestows well-differentiated physical shapes and human actions upon clear-cut ideas, which can be represented in clear, conceptual language as well; by contrast, the symbol manipulates information in such a way that some (or most) of it is perceived as diffuse, undifferentiated, global. The symbol does this by associating information with the cognitive mechanism of spatial orientation, or by treating it in terms of the least differentiated senses, or by presenting its elements in multiple relationships; all these techniques can be reinforced by what I have called (in Chapter 4) "divergent structures" (cf. Tsur, 2006: 11–14).

In what follows, I shall use the term *symbol* in the very restricted sense used with reference to 19th century French symbolist poetry, in which the above principle appears at its extreme. Mallarmé "defined Symbolism as the art of evoking an object little by little so as to reveal a mood or, conversely, the art of choosing an object and extracting from it an 'état d'âme' " (Chadwick, 1971: 1). Mallarmé's disciple, Henri de Régnier, "defined the term 'symbol' as being a comparison between the abstract and the concrete with one of the terms of the comparison being merely suggested—'une comparaison de l'abstrait au concret dont un des termes reste sous-entendu'" (ibid., 2). Back in 1888 a critic hostile to the Symbolist movement, Jules Lemaître, offered a very similar description: "Un symbole est, en somme, une comparaison prolongée *dont on ne nous donne que le second terme*, un système de métaphores suivies. Bref, le symbole, c'est la vieille 'allégorie' de nos pères" (quoted by Brooke-Rose, 1958: 32; emphasis in the original).

Mallarmé's disciple and the hostile critic, despite their differences of opinions, do agree upon the description of the symbol as a linguistic device. Where they differ is in the implications for the term "merely suggested". This is brought out clearly if we read on in Chadwick's account:

> And, as Régnier further pointed out, because the symbol thus frequently stands alone, with the reader being given little or no indication as to what is being symbolized, Symbolist poetry inevitably has a certain built-in obscurity [...]. The sad and mournful landscapes of Mallarmé's contemporary, Paul Verlaine, are intended to convey to the reader the poet's profound melancholy though his poems rarely state explicitly that this is their purpose. (Chadwick, 1971: 2)

One might add that if according to Régnier, symbolist poetry has a built-in obscurity, the spiritual meaning that this poetry suggestively alludes to represents an undifferentiated transient mood for which language has no name, whereas "good old-fashioned allegory" could be said to have a certain built-in lucidity: the spiritual term suggested is a clear-cut, differentiated idea, regularly named by conceptual language. It is also noteworthy, and certainly in harmony with the basic ideas expressed in the present chapter, that, according to Chadwick, Verlaine chooses to convey his profound melancholy through the description of "sad and mournful landscapes". In other words, what Lemaître is doing in the above quotation, is to "level out" the difference between symbol and allegory (I shall return to this issue in Chapter 21). One feature that symbolism has in common with impressionism is that they both "desire [...] to capture the fleeting impression at the very moment in which sensations are transformed into feelings" (Weisstein, 1974). And this, I claim, symbolism accomplishes by activating the mechanisms of spatial orientation of the reader, through (as in the present case) manipulating certain ways of describing a space such as a landscape.[7]

---

7 I have elsewhere (Tsur, 1987b: 168–174) compared at considerable length Spenser's allegorical apparatus in a short passage from *The Fairie Qvene* (III. xii. 1), to a deceptively similar apparatus in Baudelaire's sonnet "Recueillement", and pointed at the subtle differences that render the former allegoric, the latter symbolic.

CHAPTER 16

Poetry of Disorientation

Throughout the present work, I have treated wit and emotion in association with metaphors, as human adaptation devices turned to aesthetic ends. **Emotion** is, in fact, the unique, conscious quality of information that is held in a fluid state, and that is capable of adjusting itself to rapidly changing physical or social circumstances. This is why emotion is so apt to serve as a device of fast orientation. **Wit** is the unique, conscious quality of a sudden shift of **mental sets,** that is, a sudden shift of readiness to respond in a certain way. Human beings appear to have a third kind of adaptation device relevant to poetic styles, whose unique, conscious quality may be characterized as **emotional disorientation.** In what follows, I shall discuss some typical mannerist poetic devices of disorientation as adaptation devices turned to aesthetic ends.

Sensuous Metaphors and the Grotesque

Romantic poetry is a poetry of integration and orientation that makes ample use of rich pre-categorial, or lowly-categorized information. In the instances discussed in the preceding chapter, an interference with the operation of the orientation-mechanism was exploited for poetic effects. This, however, is not necessarily the case in all poetry. To show what I mean, let me begin with an extensive discussion of two lines by the Hebrew poet Abraham Shlonsky:

יָרֵחַ מֵת תָּלוּי עַל בְּלִי־מָה,

כְּשָׁד לָבָן זוֹלֵף אֶת חֲלָבוֹ.

        yareaḥ met taluy ʿal bli-ma,
        kəˊad lavan zolef ʾɛt ḥalavo

(1)   A dead moon is hanging on nothingness
          Like a white breast shedding its milk.

Let me begin by reporting intuitions that some of my students had about these lines. In a seminar group, some of the students tended to interpret the "breast shedding its milk" as the embodiment of the principle of **giving**, of the life principle, having a contradictory relationship to the moon as "hung" and "dead" in the preceding line. The moon is associated here, paradoxically, with the principles of both life and death, with the principles both of passivity and of "giving". Running into difficulties, one of the students changed his interpretation and said that "shedding its milk" implies waste rather than of feeding. All these interpretations, however, were incompatible with the intuitions of other participants in the seminar, including myself. Before going into a possible other interpretation, it should be noted that the above kind of interpretation is far from illegitimate. It relies on one of the most important principles of **literary competence**, formulated thus: "The primary convention is what might be called the rule of significance: read the poem as expressing a significant attitude to some problem concerning man and/or his relation to the universe" (Culler, 1975: 115). The interpretation is further corroborated by one of the fundamental aesthetic principles, viz., that good poetry is paradoxical, that is, it consists in the fusion of incompatible or discordant qualities. The "rule of significance", peculiar as it may seem from a literary point of view, is an operating instruction realizing, in the literary domain, a principle that has much wider cultural applications. This principle is formulated by D'Andrade (1980) as follows: "In fusing fact and evaluational reactions, cultural schemata come to have a powerful directive impact as implicit values".

The above interpretation of Shlonsky's lines also relies on "the convention of metaphorical coherence—that one should attempt through semantic transformations to produce coherence on both levels of tenor and vehicle" (Culler, 1975: 115). There is an attempt to produce coherence on the level of the tenor, associating the moon with the principles of life and death, through the appropriate semantic transformations. The level of the vehicle, however, is "incoherent": there is a "mixed metaphor" here. The moon as hung and dead (like the head of a hanged man?) is conflicting with the moon as a white breast. This line of thought may lead us to an alternative way to handle such metaphors. The first step in this direction goes *via* Christine Brooke-Rose's work (1958). "Very broadly speaking, metaphors can be divided, from the point of view of idea-content, into functional metaphors (A is called B by virtue of what it does), and sensuous metaphors (A is called B by virtue of what it looks like, or more rarely, sounds like, smells like, feels like, tastes like)" (Brooke-Rose, 1958: 155).

Now, let us use Brooke-Rose's categories here to apply explicit structural descriptions to the conflicting intuitions. It is clear that the former interpretation of Shlonsky's image treated it as a functional metaphor, whereas in the latter, "the moon [...] like a white breast shedding its milk" is treated as a conspicuous sensuous metaphor. Hence the conflicting intuitions. The moon is called "a white breast shedding its milk", not by virtue of its life-giving activity, but by virtue of what it looks like: the moon is a round object, near which a white mass, "the Milky Way" is seen (pouring forth from it, as it were). Now, why should a poet bother to provide such rich imagery, if it were not to obtain some human significance? For the precision of description, some critics say. But the precision-explanation breaks down when one considers the incompatible details that the various images lump together. By contrast, one of the major assumptions of cognitive poetics is able to explain the conflict. Such sensuous metaphors as Shlonsky's interfere with the normal process of orientation; the conflict delays the appraisal of the human significance of the image.

I have elsewhere claimed that a psychoanalytic discussion of puns and caricatures may illuminate certain aspects of figurative language (Tsur, 1987b: 19–32).[1] On first approximation, it seems obvious that the image in (1) fuses two visual images into one, while preserving their warring identity. The visual conflict on the one hand, and the saving of mental energy resulting from the fusion on the other hand, generate the particular witty effect typically associated with caricature. On a closer look, however, such an explanation cannot account for the intuitive difference between a "functional" and a "sensuous" construal of the images involved. At most, we may say that the saving of mental energy intensifies the reader's involvement in

---

[1] Ernst Kris, in his contributions to the psychology of the comic (partly written in collaboration with Gombrich), assigns the source of comic pleasure to the following: "a part of the pleasure derives from a saving of mental energy, another from the relation to infantile life" (Kris, 1965: 174). Saving mental energy is the effect of puns and caricatures, too. They give two things in one. Kris and Gombrich mention caricatures in which politicians or types are presented as animals, or a series of four caricatures showing the "metamorphosis" of Louis Philippe into a pear. In addition, caricatures and puns can be considered as a regression to infantile life. They also resemble in some respects dreams, and thus can be suspected of having direct access to the preconscious mind. The authors explain these ideas as follows:

> Conscious logic is out of action, its rules have lost their forces. One of the mechanisms now in action can cause, in a dream, two words to become one, or merge two figures in one. This peculiarity of the psychic apparatus is sometimes exploited in jokes. If, for instance, we describe the Christmas vacations as "Alcoholidays", we understand that the new word, the pun word, is obviously composed of two parts: of "alcohol" and "holidays": they are united or—as we say—"condensed". An analogous condensation could also have arisen in a dream. But unlike the dream, the pun is thought out, created. We make use intentionally—which is not synonymous with consciously—of a primitive mechanism in order to achieve a particular aim".

> In fact—as Freud has shown us—in all play with words, in puns as well as nonsense talk, there is a renewal of the child's pleasure when it just learns to master language. [...] At bottom caricature, too, renews infantile pleasure. Its simplicity [...] makes it resemble the scribbling of the child. [...] Caricatures like those of Louis Philippe as a pear are at bottom nothing but visual puns, and the taste in puns may change but their mechanism remains the same (Kris and Gombrich, 1965: 196–197).

whatever quality is generated by the metaphor, whether construed as "functional" or "sensuous".

More generally speaking, the urgency to evaluate the significance of a stimulus appears to be a deeply rooted biological response.

> Most emotions involve an intuitive appraisal of a stimulus as good (beneficial) or bad (harmful). [...] It is very unlikely that organisms can unequivocally evaluate all stimuli with which they make contact. Some period, extended or brief, is necessary before tissue damage occurs, or internal injury develops, or pleasurable sensations occur. During this critical period of direct contact with an unevaluated object, a pattern of behavior apparently develops which, at the human level, is usually called surprise. (Plutchik, 1968: 72)

Sensuous metaphor may, then, be regarded as another literary device to delay the smooth cognitive process consisting in the contact with some unevaluated image; the device's function is thus to prolong a state of disorientation and so generate an aesthetic quality of surprise, startling, perplexity, astounding, or the like.[2]

Thus, Shlonsky's simile generates, under the pretense of precise description, a perceived effect of startling, or even emotional, disorientation. But the two lines contain additional devices of emotional disorientation, which will be discussed in the following.[3]

[2]   Such a prolongation may cause a feeling of unease that may be intolerable for some readers. Not all people are equally capable of enduring the contact with uncategorized or meaningless objects or stimuli; this depends, to a considerable extent, on personality style. "The leveler is more anxious to categorize sensations and less willing to give up a category once he has established it. [...] For him the unique, unclassifiable sensation is particularly offensive" (Ohmann, 1970: 231; cf. Tsur, 1975a; 2006: 11–77; and below, Chapter 21).

[3]   This usage of sensuous metaphors is highly sophisticated and rather exceptional. Gardner, Winner and their associates have produced ample evidence that preschool children are highly creative in producing metaphors; but all the metaphors they create are sensuous. Only at later stages of their development do children produce functional metaphors, or metaphors whose tenor is conceptual or pertaining to psychological dispositions. As understanders, young children tend to prefer sensuous metaphors, whose grounds are similar shapes or, later, similar colors. Only at later stages, after a so-called "literal period", they develop a taste for the other kinds of metaphors (cf. Gardner, 1982: 158–167; Gardner & Winner, 1979: 125–134; Silberstein et al., 1982). In the years preceding adolescence, when children have begun to allow a metaphoric renaming, their practice is characterized by "a greater awareness that tension has been overridden" (Gardner and Winner, 1979: 134); not so the preschool child whose practice is characterized by a "more carefree experimentation" (ibid.).

I have elsewhere (Tsur, 1987c: 154–158) attempted to show that Mediaeval Hebrew poets, especially in the genre of garden-descriptions, indulged in sensuous metaphors in a manner that is closer to a "more carefree experimentation" than to the arousal of surprise and or to the creation of perplexity, startling, astounding. To be sure, in this

The "sensuous" reader lingers at the visual images, without appraising their significance. These images, in spite of their common elements, are visually incompatible. The moon, the female breast, and the head of a dead person may be similar in their round shapes, but they are different in many details. The reader can join them visually only by the essentially comic technique of caricature, thereby demonstrating that the intolerable, inextricable mixture of incompatibles is a fact of life, perhaps the most crucial one. No wonder that such a reader perceives the image as grotesque, in an essentially divided response, which conveys the notion of something that is simultaneously laughable and horrifying or disgusting. Both laughter and horror or disgust are defense mechanisms in the presence of threat, the latter allowing the danger its authority, the former denying it (cf. Burke, 1957: 51–56). The grotesque is *the experiencing of emotional disorientation* when both defense mechanisms are suddenly suspended (cf. Thomson, 1972: 58). Shlonsky's image contains additional components of the grotesque. Some writers on the grotesque claim that "the grotesque is essentially physical, referring always to the body and bodily excesses and celebrating these in an uninhibited, outrageous but essentially joyous fashion" (Thomson, 1972: 56). "Our laughter at some kinds of the grotesque and the opposite response—disgust, horror, etc.—mixed with it, are both reactions to the physically cruel, abnormal or obscene" (ibid., 8). There is in the grotesque a kind of "delight in seeing taboos flouted". The white breast of cosmic dimension represents such an obscenity, or bodily excess (these issues will be discussed at greater length in the next chapter).

The quotation from Shlonsky presents us with yet another device of emotional disorientation, the 'realization of the idiom' "Milky Way" that is, the unexpected use of the idiomatic expression in its literal sense. Such sudden shifts of meaning may produce in the reader "a strange sensation—making one suddenly doubt one's comfortable relationship with language—not unlike the sense of disorientation and confusion associated with the grotesque" (Thomson, 1972: 65).

The grotesque, then, makes use of poetic devices that produce an emotional disorientation which is experienced as a shock, perplexity, surprise, or the like. It is, indeed, this quality that enables the various devices to combine and be integrated into a whole.

If one looks for an aesthetic justification of the above process, a sufficient answer will be: emotional disorientation is an intensive human quality perceived by the reader. One may justify one's positive evaluation of an aesthetic object with ref-

---

manner, too, they often achieved enormous complexity, but still in a relatively "more carefree experimentation". It is interesting to note that critics are reluctant to acknowledge sensuous metaphors in either the carefree, or the disorienting version, and that they presumably do this for different, or even opposite, reasons: while the disorienting use of sensuous metaphors may be painful to face, effects of the "carefree" use of sensuous metaphors may be experienced as too naïve, or even too childish, for their sophisticated taste. I am still collecting information in order to work out this distinction between the two uses of sensuous metaphors in greater detail.

erence to three general canons: unity, complexity, and some intensive human quality (cf. Beardsley, 1958: 465–469). It is obvious from the above analysis that Shlonsky's two lines are quite complex from the viewpoint of figurative language. Insofar as this complexity is achieved by means of what Neo-Classical critics would call "mixed metaphors", these lines appear to be deficient from the point of view of unity. Notice, however, this: the various kinds of poetic devices, each in its own way, are aimed at giving a shock and arousing a sense of emotional disorientation. This generates an intense human quality of perplexity and emotional disorientation. This quality, in turn, bestows perceptual unity upon the diverse images. In this respect, the role of cognitive poetics is to describe the mechanisms of defense and orientation, the disturbance of which has generated the intense human quality. It also helps to define the nature of this quality and to relate it, systematically, to the poetic structures (these issues will be further discussed in chapter 22).

What I have said so far is, in my opinion, sufficient to justify the foregoing analysis. There is, however, an additional set of significant correlations, which the cognitive approach may explain and, I submit, in a less trivial manner than some other approaches. We have observed two kinds of poetics, a poetics of integration and orientation, and a poetics of analytical expressions and disintegration. Now, these are not mere whimsical expressions of the poet's genius. There appear to be certain significant correlations between the general trends of poetic praxis and their socio-cultural background. Consider the following two passages.

> Where the previous ages had seen in it merely the principle of disharmony run wild or relegated it to the cruder species of the comic, the present tendency—one which must be welcomed as a considerable step forward—is to view the grotesque as a fundamentally ambivalent thing, as a violent clash of opposites, and hence, in some of its forms at least, as an appropriate expression of the problematic nature of existence. It is no accident that the grotesque mode in art and literature tends to be prevalent in societies and eras marked by strife, radical change or disorientation. (Thomson, 1972: 11)

> The style of James (and, for that matter, of Hopkins) shows then the characteristics recurring in certain periods of the history of art and poetry—in the periods when the ideals of serenity and formal balance are broken by a spirit of uncertainty and search; the search makes for the refinement both in themes and expression, for subtler and subtler penetration of meanings and attention to details rather than to the structure as a whole. So, that there is a loss of balance and at times of proportion: details are worked out with a goldsmith's care, and this makes for an enormous gain in insight and precision—but the total effect is frequently lost sight of, and is reached through accumulation rather than through a harmonious disposition of structural parts. Uncertainty too contributes to the lack of balance, or, with reference

to graphic representations, lack of symmetry; it induces a preference and taste for undulating, twining, whorling lines. (Melchiori, 1966: 138)

Both writers suggest, and I agree with them, that there tends to be some positive chronological correlation between the occurrence of the elements of "mannerist" poetry and a certain kind of socio-cultural background. However, neither author probes very deeply into this correlation. Thomson's phrase "appropriate expression" raises a host of questions, usually brought up in connection with the **expressive theory of art,** such as: 'What is an appropriate expression?', or: 'What is the relationship of poetry to questions of existence?', and so on. Apart from these, there is the central problem that art, on the one hand, is supposed to express the emotions of the poet while on the other, we also must surmise that the poet's emotions are somehow "expressive" of the socio-cultural environment in which he lives. While this seems to be a plausible assumption, it remains quite trivial as long as no "mediating structure" is offered to explain these expressive relationships. (Somewhat similar questions arise concerning the relationship between the "details worked out with a goldsmith's care" and the "enormous gain in insight" in the passage quoted from Melchiori).

The Metaphysical Conceit

Thomson (1972) is not alone in observing that mannerist devices such as the grotesque tend to be prevalent in the poetic styles of "societies and eras marked by strife, radical change or disorientation" that is, in societies dominated by more than one set of values; a similar relationship between such societies and other mannerist devices (as, e.g., the metaphysical conceit) has been observed by many literary critics and theorists. We have conceptualized the mechanisms underlying the response to poetry as adaptation mechanisms whose operation is disturbed and then exploited for aesthetic purposes. As suggested in the preceding chapter, an unfulfilled readiness to pick up self-specifying information, a mind-set which is so fundamental in the process of orientation, may be the mechanism underlying the affective impact of certain romantic descriptions. I have also suggested that the mechanism involved may have a strong integrating effect on the environment in which it functions (e.g., the landscape suggested by the poem). Now, it should be noticed that not only mannerist, but also romantic poetry was prevalent in an age and societies that were marked by strife, radical change, or even disorientation. In fact, the romantic era on the one hand and the seventeenth or twentieth centuries on the other, differ mostly in their relative degree of disintegration. The greater the disintegration, the more pointed the effect of the mechanism of integration and orientation—but only up to a certain point. Beyond that point, the disintegrating environment escapes from the orienting mechanism's control and a *different kind* of coping procedure must be instantiated. For want of a better term, we might call this procedure *meta-awareness.*

Let me try to illuminate the issue of the sudden disintegration of self-specifying information with a concrete example taken from our everyday physical reality. When you are sitting in a stationary train and the train nearby pulls out, you may feel it as if your own train were moving in the opposite direction, even though you don't experience the characteristic rocking movement of your body. Similarly, many drivers experience panick, when the parked car they are about to pass suddenly pulls out. The reason is that the self-specifying information in the optic array is being destroyed.[4]

The point of the example is that information "about oneself, like all other information, can only be picked up by an appropriately tuned schema" (Neisser, 1976: 116). When something suddenly seems to go wrong, one has to check the tuning of his own schemata. "Consciousness, according to Bartlett, enables an organism 'to turn around its own schemata'" (Miller and Johnson-Laird, 1976: 150). Interestingly enough, critical philosophy is characterized in similar terms: "thought turns around and examines itself instead of examining its own shadows in the void" (Pears, 1971: 30). In order to indicate that this analogy is not incidental, it ought to be pointed out that critical philosophy, not unlike the poetry of disorientation, tends to be prevalent in societies dominated by more than one set of values, and where there appear to be no unquestionable truths.

Modern poetry (and modern art in general) is just as much *about cognitive processes* as about its subject matter. Returning to the issue of *meta-awareness:* when the clashing emotional tendencies of the grotesque, of the metaphysical pun, or of the metaphysical conceit shock us out of tune with our environment, our own coping mechanisms (linguistic or otherwise) become perceptible to ourselves. The unique conscious quality of the moment of shock is experienced as confusion and emotional disorientation. One of the major functions of poetry is promoting heightened awareness, either awareness of the reality perceived, or of the cognitive mechanisms that enable us to perceive reality. The self-examination of cognitive mechanisms is still a matter of empirical investigation; an investigation moreover, which has lost its directness (cf. Pears, 1971: 31).

Whereas Romantic poetry tends to attend away from images (and language in general) to affect (which is a device of fast orientation), and thus may be called a **poetry of orientation,** there is another kind of poetry which may be called **poetry of disorientation** (mannerism, or metaphysical and modern poetry), and which focuses attention upon language and images. Furthermore, whereas in Romantic poetry

---

[4] "A one-year-old child standing on the floor of the room will fall down if the walls are silently and suddenly moved forward a few inches, although nothing touches him. This is, because the optical pattern produced by the moving walls would normally specify that the observer was plunging backward. The child compensates by shifting forward, overbalances and falls. Even an adult who knows about the experimental arrangement can be 'knocked down' in this way if he is balancing on a narrow beam" (Neisser, 1976: 116). Similarly, in a fluid society, where there are no stable points of orientation, and where the self-specifying information from the social and spiritual environment is contradictory, serious emotional or mental disorientation may result.

affect is an important integrating factor (in addition to the descriptive situation), in the poetry of disorientation one of the most important devices of integration is the sustained metaphor, the metaphysical conceit, or some of their equivalents.

> When human thought turns around and examines itself, where does the investigation start? [...] The short answer [...] is that there are two forms in which the data to be investigated may be presented. They may be presented in a psychological form, as ideas, thoughts and modes of thought: or they may be presented in a linguistic form, as words, sentences and types of discourse. Kant's critique starts from data of the first kind, and the second wave of critical philosophy, the logico-analytic movement of this century, starts from data of the second kind. (Pears, 1971: 27–28)

It is noteworthy that, correspondingly, mannerism too "has two modes, technical and psychological" (Sypher, 1955: 116). Sypher speaks of "Donne's false and verbal (perhaps false? perhaps verbal?) resolutions—his incapacity to commit himself wholly to any one world or view" (122). "The resolution is gained, if at all, only rhetorically, not [through] reason" (123). I suggest that this is one possible way in which poets in Thomson's words (1972: 65) "smash language, destroy man's naive trust in this most familiar and unquestioned part of his life [...] producing in the reader a strange sensation—making one suddenly doubt one's comfortable relationship with language—not unlike the sense of disorientation and confusion associated with the grotesque".

In the light of the foregoing discussion, let us now consider again Thomson's observation that "it is no accident that the grotesque mode in art and literature tends to be prevalent in societies and eras marked by strife, radical change or disorientation". Why should the authors and readers of mannerist poetry have recourse to the poetry of disorientation? Is it not enough for them to have to cope with disorientation in their social reality, so that they also seek out disorientation in poetry? As I have suggested above, following Neisser, "information about oneself, like all other information, can only be picked up by an appropriately tuned schema". When something suddenly seems to go wrong, one has to check the tuning of his own schemata. When the clashing emotional tendencies of the grotesque, of the metaphysical pun, or of the metaphysical conceit shock us out of tune with our environment, our own coping with the environment, and especially the linguistic mechanisms involved in this process become perceptible to ourselves. If a considerable number of members of a given society have acquired such coping mechanisms for adaptive purposes, they cannot be stopped from applying them for poetic purposes, and from putting them to work in a given poetic praxis, such as Mannerism. When the reader in a mannerist age contemplates such disorienting qualities as surprise, perplexity, startling, or astounding effects, or similar things associated with sensuous metaphors or metaphysical puns and conceits, far from having a painful experience, he may derive pleasure from the recognition that he is well equipped with the cognitive equipment required for coping with a reality in which the regular orientation devices are of little use. Poetry that utilizes only such adaptive devices that have been super-seded by more radical ones is usually experienced as affectedly delicate, or 'nice', or childish.

Thus, the metaphysical pun and conceit on the one hand, and the disorienting emotional shocks on the other (which eventually result in what Grierson, 1921, de-scribed as "strain of passionate paradoxical reasoning" in metaphysical poetry) seem to perform in one mode what critical philosophy is said to perform in another: they make thought turn around to examine itself. Intuitively, however, metaphysical (or manneristic, or modern) poetry and critical philosophy are rather unlike, and their differences seem to be no less significant than what they have in common. Shklov-sky's formulation aptly encapsulates these differences from the angle of art in gener-al: "The purpose of art is to impart the sensation of things as they are perceived and not as they are known" (Shklovsky, 1965: 12; cf. above, chapter 1). In metaphys-ical poetry in particular, one gets a sensation of perceptual and adaptive mechanisms as they are perceived and not as they are known, whereas in critical philosophy, one seeks an understanding rather than an immediate perception: "The understanding which is sought is understanding of our own conceptual system" (Pears, 1971: 31).

In this way, we may account for three kinds of human activities: the understand-ing of one's own conceptual system yields critical philosophy; the understanding of the perceptual system yields cognitive psychology; the immediate perception of one's own perceptual and/or conceptual system yields metaphysical poetry. Such a conception of the poetry of disorientation throws the metaphysical conceit into new perspectives (as we will see in the following).

The Metaphysical Conceit—Influence or Creation?

Let us begin our discussion with Abraham Cowley's 'ingenious' conceit of ex-change of hearts in "The Change":

> 2.   Oh take my Heart, and by that means you'll prove
>   Within, too stor'd enough of love:
>   Give me but yours, I'll by that change so thrive
>   That love in all my parts shall live.
>   So powerful is this change, it render can
>   My outside Woman, and your inside Man.

Ransom (1951: 784) quotes this stanza as containing a notorious example of the metaphysical conceit. "A conceit originates in a metaphor; and in fact the conceit is but a metaphor if the metaphor is meant; that is, if it is developed so baldly that no-thing else can be meant". And further on he says, "such is Metaphysical Poetry; the extension of a rhetorical device" (ibid., 786).

Admittedly, Cowley is not the first poet to substitute *heart* for *affection* (cf. Sidney's "My true love has my heart and I have his"). The startling quality of this image seems to be due to the fact that this metonymic device is developed so literally that this meaning must be intended. In this way, Cowley succeeds "in depositing with us the image of a very powerful affection" (Ransom, ibid.).

Yet, contrary to common belief, neither this way of handling imagery nor this particular image is the exclusive invention of seventeenth century metaphysical poets. Consider, for instance, two centuries earlier, Villon's Rondeau on the death of his mistress:

> 3.   Deux étions et n'avions qu'ung cuer;
>   S'il est mort, force est que devie,
>   Voire, ou que je vive sans vie
>   Comme les images, par cuer,
>   Mort!

The heart is traditionally considered as the seat of thought, feeling or emotion, and Villon, like Cowley, develops the "miraculous" element in his image in two steps: first, by a metonymic transfer from "affection" to *heart,* and then, by developing this device so literally that it must be *meant*. The idea that the two lovers were inseparably united by a single affection is expressed as "we were two, and had only one heart", which appears to be miraculous enough, if you conceive of the heart as of a hollow muscular organ, of which you know that there must be one and only one in every human body. That is, by a logical development of those aspects of "heart" that are irrelevant to "affection", Villon achieved a miraculous, or witty, effect. The image is, then, further developed, and "too" literally: since she died with the only heart we had, I have been left without a heart. The image thus developed may suggest further metaphoric or metonymic implications (based on the fact that the heart is traditionally considered as the seat of life or vital powers): since there is no life without a heart, my life is in fact no life; and since there is no body without a heart, my body is no body any more, but a mere lifeless image. Notice also that although the physiological aspects of the heart image have been developed according to a consistent logic, the various figurative implications of the image need not be logically consistent with one another.

Nor is Villon the first poet to have had recourse to this particular conceit. Rabbi Shlomo Ibn Gabirol, the eleventh-century Hebrew poet in Spain employed it more than once. Consider his verses on his physical separation from his friends:

וְאֵיכָה יִחְיוּ עוֹד אַחֲרֵי זֹאת   פְּגָרִים נוֹתְרוּ מֵאֵין לְבָבוֹת

wəʾexa yiḥəyu ʿod ʾaḥăre zot   pəgarim notəru meʾen ləvavot

(4)   How after all this the corpses can live
             having remained without hearts?

or

בְּנָסְעָם וְהֵם רוּחִי וְנִשְׁמָתִי   וְאֵיכָה אֶחִי אַחַר פְּנוֹתָם וְאֶשָּׁאֵר

הֲכִי נִשְׁאֲרָה מֵאֵין נְשָׁמָה גּוּיָתִי   הֲיִחְיֶה אֱנוֹשׁ מֵאֵין נְשָׁמָה וְיִשָּׁאֵר

wəʾexa ʾɛ̆ḥi ʾaḥar pənotam wəʾɛ˅˅aʾer
     bənosəʿam wəhem ruḥi wəniˇmati
hǎyihyɛ ʾɛ̆noˇ meʾen nəˇama wəyiˇˇaʾer
     hǎxi niʾˇǎra meʾen nəˇama gəwiyyati

(5)   How can I live after their departure
             they being my spirit and my soul?
         Can a human being live and stay here without a soul
             for my corpse has remained without a soul?

Ibn Gabirol worked in a literary tradition different from that of Villon or Cowley, in a tradition imported to Spain from the Orient by the Arab conquerors. One
should not be surprised very much if one found that he, too, had been preceded, may
be by some Arab poet, in the use of this conceit, though I have no evidence for this.

How can one account for the same, highly ingenious use of images in widely
different languages, in widely different poetic traditions? Two radically different explanations come to mind at once. Our choice between them depends, in the first
place, on whether we decide to establish literary organization on the level of the
immediately observable elements of the literary universe, or consider them as the
manifestation of an abstract structure (cf. Todorov, 1975: 20). This decision is influenced by our conception of the nature of literary creation and, ultimately, by our
conception of Man: whether we regard him as hopelessly conditioned by his past
experience, or are willing to grant him creative powers; in other words, whether we
adopt a behaviorist or a cognitive model of Man and his culture.

According to the first conception, embodied in what might be called the 'migratory' theory, someone at the dawn of the history of literature happily "hit" upon a
particular conceit, such as, in our case, the heart-conceit. From this point on, the
conceit migrated until it reached the Arab poets in Spain, who transmitted it to the
Hebrew poets of the eleventh century is Spain, as well as to the Provençal poets,
who are known to have influenced the poets of the *dolce stil nuovo* in Italy, who, in
their turn, have influenced English Metaphysical Poetry. The geographical proximity of Provence to Paris may then account for the appearance of the conceit in Villon's poetry. This explanation is not without geographical or chronological plausibility; but it appears to be too pedestrian, too circumstantial, too 'behavioristic',
and leaves too much to chance. Above all, it does not explain how poets and readers

of poetry handle *novel conceits*. It fails to explain why an earlier poet should be more likely to "hit" upon a certain conceit than a later one. In addition, the above explanation is counter-intuitive from the point of view of what we think we know about the inventiveness and ingenuity of the Metaphysical Poets.[5]

The rival explanation would rely on the possession of two cognitive devices, innate or acquired for adaptive purposes. These two devices (which we may loosely conceive of as principles or rules) are supposed to account for, not only the arise of the 'heart-conceit', but also for the generation of an indefinite number of additional conceits. Accordingly, one must assume that both the poets who had recourse to the heart-conceit and their reading public must know two generative rules: one may be called the principle of metonymy, and it concerns the figurative transfer from some activity or result to the tool or the organ that performs it (or from the faculty to its "seat"—depending on whether we conceive of affects or life as of something that is the *result* of the heart's activity, or something that is *seated* in the heart). The other one may be labeled, for want of a better term, the principle of "miraculism"; this rule is at work, according to Ransom, "when the poet discovers by analogy [or contiguity—R.T.] an identity between objects which is partial, though it should be considerable, and proceeds to an identification which is complete" (Ransom, 1951: 786). In other words, it is a metaphor [or metonymy—R.T.] that is "developed so literally that it must be *meant*" (ibid., 784).

This explanation has the obvious advantage that with the help of two relatively simple rules, it can account for a large number of conceits that have been and will be thought up in a wide range of languages, cultural traditions, and historical periods. It can also account for the fact that readers who have acquired the knowledge of these two rules have understood, and will understand, not only already established, but also novel conceits. This conception furthermore does justice to our intuitions concerning the inventiveness of the Metaphysical Poets: the "conditioning"-conception is, indeed, incapable of accounting for the invention, appreciation, and acceptance of a conceit *for the first time*. We may, then, assume that each one of the poets who have recourse to this conceit, has acquired these two rules, and may create (or generate) that same conceit every time anew, without having to be previously exposed to it in another poet's work. Moreover, even under the unlikely supposition that Villon knew Hebrew, and that he owned a collection of manuscripts of eleventh century Hebrew poetry; and even if we discovered the manuscripts of these two poems by Ibn Gabirol, with annotations in Villon's handwriting, we still might ask why Villon adopted, out of the treasure-house of Arabic-Hebrew conventions, precisely this one. Obviously, the answer would have to be that he accepted the influ-

---

5   As to the metaphysical poets' inventiveness, see, for instance, Dr. Johnson's essay on Abraham Cowley: "If Wit be well described by Pope, as being 'that which has been often thought, but was never before so well expressed', they [the metaphysical poets—R.T.] certainly never attained, or ever sought it; for they endeavoured to be singular in their thoughts, and were careless of their diction" (460); or, "the reader, far from wondering that he missed them, wonders more frequently by what perverseness of industry they were ever found" (461).

ence of precisely those specific poetic devices of which he had acquired the generative principles.

The term *miraculism* used by Ransom appears to be all the more significant, since eleventh century Hebrew poetry in Spain includes a set of rhetorical devices that are said to yield "pretended wonderment" in secular, and "genuine wonderment" in sacred poetry. Nonetheless, it is hard to evade the disturbing question: Is this miraculous quality sufficient account for the widespread use of metaphysical conceits by poets in widely different cultural traditions? After all, the principle of "miraculism", as defined by Ransom, is little more than an abstract rule. We also must find the answer to an additional question: Where do we get the principles of "metonymy" and "miraculism" from? Is this another story of migration—this time, of two abstract principles, rather than of a specific conceit, from Arabia to Spain, Provence, France, Italy, and England? Or are these rather abstract rules transmitted in the structure of the brain? If so, is this "structure of the brain" not a mere tautology, something that is coextensive with the poetic conventions involved and inferred from them? (As to the principle itself, I will argue below that it is based on a 'logical fallacy').

The Metaphysical Conceit—An Adaptive Device?

The following passage by D'Andrade (1980) may suggest a reasonable beginning for an answer to the above questions:

> An important assumption of cognitive anthropology is that in the process of repeated social transmission, cultural programs come to take forms which have a good fit to the natural capacities of the human brain. Thus, when similar cultural programs are found in most societies around the world, there is reason to search for psychological factors which could account for these similarities.[6]

While I do not pretend to know whether the conceit under discussion is found "in most societies around the world", or, in fact, in any cultural tradition other than the

---

[6] In a recent article, "Some Cognitive Foundations of 'Cultural Programs'" (Tsur, 2002), I coupled this quote with another observation, derived from the Introduction to the website "Literature and Cognition". In their light I explored, with reference to metric systems, the relative merits and deficiencies of the "culture begets culture" and the "cognitive constraints" conceptions of cultural processes:

> The past twenty years of cultural studies have focused on the ways in which culture begets culture, ignoring the cognitive capacities that are the conditions of possibility for cultural change. We would like to investigate the complex relations between the mind, the world that at once determines it and is determined by it, and the cultural forms that spring from this interaction and feed back into it.

ones mentioned here, I do believe that the facts discussed above warrant a search for psychological factors which could account for those similarities.

As for the principle of metonymy, it has been unequivocally established by Jakobson's classical study (1956) reflecting a major natural resource of the brain, and I shall not discuss it here.

The principle of "miraculism" can be further explored in three areas. First, let us consider the *metaphysical pun*. It is the most condensed expression of what Sypher (1955: 122) characterized as Donne's "false and verbal (perhaps false? perhaps verbal?) resolutions—his incapacity to commit himself wholly to any one world or view". The pun "resolves" two sufficiently different meanings in a single verbal sign. The resolution is achieved on the verbal level alone, in a manner that can be reasonably characterized as illogical, or as obeying a false logic. In the metaphysical pun, both meanings are so literally developed that both must be meant. This device has a remarkable ontological corollary: what is being said can exist only on the verbal level, the verbal sign being brought into the focus of consciousness. In such a pun, we cannot "attend away" from the verbal sign vehicle to any one of its meanings without suppressing the other meanings. Our examination of the metaphysical pun may thus conveniently start with, in Pears's words, "human thought turn[ing] around and examin[ing] itself", as a paramount technique in the service of the "poetics of disorientation" when, in order to check the tuning of our own schemata, our own coping or linguistic mechanisms become perceptible to ourselves.

Second, the *metaphysical conceit* has all the ingredients that we have considered for the metaphysical pun. But, in addition, it includes a visual mental image. The cognitive importance of mental imagery cannot be overestimated. From the vast literature on the subject, I shall pick three issues for a brief consideration:

According to Neisser (1976: 37), our image of an object as being in a particular place is simply a readiness to pick up information specifying the object when we get to the place. "Any delay between the anticipation and the pick-up creates a state of unfulfilled perceptual readiness, and the inner aspect of the active schema is a mental image" (138). "When two objects are in a close spatial relationship, the perceptual cycle takes a different course than it would if each were seen by itself" (139). Now, when two aspects of a spatial image are consistently developed so as to suggest conflicting or incompatible meanings, their coexistence is confined to the level of language or mental imagery; the chances are small that we will pick up all the information specified from the external world. This, again, forces the image into the focus of our attention, in order for us to examine the tuning of our active schemata.

According to Neisser (1968: 320), "the amount of information may require less capacity coded in terms of spatial relationships than in terms of temporal sequence. [...] This assumption would explain the predominance of visual imagery in dreams, and perhaps also our preference for visual models and metaphors for thinking, from 'insight' to 'point of view'".[7]

Finally, there is the "localistic" view of language, as summed up by Lyons (1977: 718): "Spatial expressions are linguistically more basic, according to the localists, in that they serve as structural templates, as it were, for other expressions; and the reason why this should be so, it is plausibly suggested by psychologists, is that spatial organization is of central importance in human cognition" (cf. Miller and Johnson-Laird, 1976: 475ff).[8]

Thus, spatio-visual imagery appears to have some fundamental function in cognitive processes. As it is manipulated in the metaphysical conceit, spatio-visual imagery as an active perceptual schema is submitted to the inspection of what we have called *meta-awareness.*

It should be noted that vital as imagery may be in cognitive processes, it is not just imagery that we become aware of. The metaphysical conceit draws attention to a **functional relation,** in which normally, "we know the first term only by relying on our awareness" of it "for attending to the second" (Polányi, 1967: 10). We are dealing here with Polányi's conception of *tacit knowledge;* as Polányi says, "all meaning tends to be displaced *away from ourselves"* (13). In an act of tacit knowing, we *attend away from* something in order to attend *to* something else; namely, *from* the first ("proximal") term *to* the second ("distal") term of the tacit relation. "In the case of a human physiognomy [...] we rely on our awareness for attending to the characteristic appearance of a face. We are attending *from* the features *to* the face, and thus are unable to specify the features. And [...] we are relying on our awareness of a combination of muscular acts to the performance of a skill. We are attending *from* these elementary movements *to* the achievement of their joint purpose, and hence are usually unable to specify these elementary acts" (10; cf. above, Chapter 1). We do not see retinal images, but outside objects. We usually do not perceive the acoustic cues for the muscular movements that produce speech sounds, but only the sounds themselves; and we are inclined to attend away from speech sounds to the meanings conveyed by them. In short, we tend to attend away from signs, to their joint meaning, appearance or function. And this is what typically happens in the poetry of orientation, as suggested here and in the preceding chapter. The metaphysical conceit, as described here, assigns two or more meanings or functions—that is, two "distal terms"—to a single image vehicle; thus it prevents us from attending away from the image, and at the same time, heightens our awareness of our mechanisms of knowing and perceiving. Repeated examination of one's cognitive apparatus—in this case, of the functional relation between the proximal and distal terms— proves to be a powerful means of improving one's being attuned to reality in a state of disorientation. Such an account can point up the adaptational *raison d'être* of the

---

[7] In Chapter 23 I point out that the "efficient coding" conception of spatial imagery is more useful for literary criticism than the "embodied mind" conception.

[8] Some additional research on the role of visual imagery in the psychological processes involved in the comprehension of metaphors is summarized by Pavio (1979).

metaphysical conceit, characterized by Dr. Johnson as "the most heterogeneous ideas yoked together by violence".

Third, a further word must be said about the *logical fallacy* that I said was involved in "miraculism", the poet discovering a partial identity between objects and proceeding to establish a complete identity. If it is true that poetry exploits adaptational mechanisms for aesthetic purposes, what is the adaptational value of the false logic encountered in the metaphysical conceit? Notice that we frequently encounter this particular kind of false logic in jokes, as in the joke about the person who had to go to a funeral but couldn't find a florist in the last minute; so he brought a box of candy. The hero of the joke clearly saw some functional equivalence between a bunch of flowers and a box of candy (i.e., you may bring either as a present when you are invited for dinner). This equivalence, however, is only partial: you may put a bunch of flowers on a grave, but it is conspicuously improper to put a box of candy there. So, when the hero of the joke develops the logic of this identification so consistently that the identification must be *meant,* the audience discovers the incompatibility of the results of this consistent but misguided logic with the objective circumstances. As a result, the reader must perform a shift of mental sets, followed by a process of rapid re-adjustment. Consistent thinking is a powerful means for handling reality; but if it is based on deceptive evidence, even the most consistent logic will lead to maladapted solutions. It is not enough to be logical; one's logic must be verified time and again against reality. From this point of view, "the partial though considerable identity" may serve to disguise, to some extent, the fallacious nature of the evidence upon which the reasoning is founded (letting the audience believe that the hero of the joke had, at least, *some* reason to identify flowers with candies: a fancy dress or a cork-screw would have been no less improper than candy, but then there would have been no joke, and the story would have been meaningless).[9] The process of rapid re-adjustment makes the working of the adaptation mechanisms involved perceptible to our consciousness, so that their attunement to reality is exposed to inspection and control.

A further aspect of the adaptational value of the conceit was already discussed in Chapter 3, in relation to Piaget's familiar conservation test: whether five-years old children judge a given amount of water to remain the same after it is poured into a container of different shape and size. Three kinds of arguments were set forth by the children to support their judgment, one perceptual, one having to do with action, and finally, a "transformational" argument. "Of the children who thought the water was not equal in amount after pouring, 15 per cent used nonperceptual arguments to justify their judgement. Of those who recognized the equality of water, two thirds used nonperceptual arguments" (Bruner, 1968: 393). The metaphysical conceit develops consistently, by using a false logic, a perceptual argument; at the same time, it

---

[9] This is most blatantly brought out by the "pointless" episodes of the Eskimo story "The War of the Ghosts" (used in Bartlett's classical experiments (1932)), in which the Western reader can discover no underlying schema that might render it intelligible.

develops consistently some genuine, nonperceptual argument. As a result, it plays up a maladaptive mechanism against an adequate, adaptive mechanism. In a developmental perspective, the conceit presents an opportunity to examine one's "outgrown", childish level of intellectual performance in the light of one's adult level of functioning, which results in a feeling of relative freedom, superiority and amusement; in short: Enter irony!

The foregoing considerations seem to furnish good reasons for assuming that the principles of "metonymy" and "miraculism" reflect some natural capacities and constraints of the human brain. They turn adaptive mechanisms to poetic purposes. Thus, we can not only explain the fact that people invent or understand novel conceits; we may account for the reappearance of the same conceit in fairly different cultural environments, in the works of poets noted for their originality and ingenuity, as well as for the significant association of the metaphysical conceit with precisely the poetics of disorientation.

CHAPTER 17

The Grotesque as an Aesthetic Mode

The present chapter attempts to establish a many-sided view of the grotesque as an aesthetic mode; it consists of four loosely connected sections. The first section discusses a reader-response approach to the problems of defining the grotesque—as an extreme example of the complex problems encountered with relation to aesthetic definitions in general. The second section focuses on the grotesque element in poems of the great Mediaeval Hebrew poet Shlomo Ibn Gabirol; it provides us with an instance of the difficulty involved in tackling aesthetic problems across some enormous cultural gap, both in time and in taste. The third section will put to work the distinctions we have introduced earlier concerning the grotesque, in order to account for the elusive "magical quality", reported by many readers of some poems by the great Hungarian poet, Endre Ady. As does the second section, the third makes the additional point that in grotesque poetry at its best, the grotesque is not just an isolated, so to speak casual, element: it joins forces with a great variety of devices to contribute to some overall quality of emotional disorientation (this point is reinforced by my discussion of Morgenstern's "Der Werwolf" in chapter 22 below, and of Shlonsky's two verse lines above, in Chapter 16). In such poems, the quality of emotional disorientation is typically characterized by what Kant called a "purposefulness without purpose". The final section of the present chapter attempts to characterize the aesthetic nature of the grotesque, within the basic assumptions of Cognitive Poetics, as presented in Chapter 1.

Aesthetic Definitions: The Grotesque
A Reader-Response Approach

The point of departure of the present section is an apparent "vicious circle". For the interpretation of a piece of literature, we have to make reference to the wider aesthetic categories to which it belongs; these wider aesthetic categories, in turn, are defined with reference to the particular works of literature that make up its membership. This is what Beryl Lake, in a wider perspective, called the *irrefutability* of certain aesthetic theories. The present section is to be seen in the perspective of the much wider enterprise of exploring "The Implied Critic's Decision Style" (cf. below, Chapter 21); I shall attempt to cut across this vicious circle, using as my hypothesis the implied critic's cognitive complexity. My test case will be the definition of the grotesque, and its application to a few paradigmatic works of literature.

I am not going to pass judgment on the correct interpretation of a certain work of literature, nor on the question which definition of the grotesque, or of a genre or style concept is the correct one; rather, I will ask what critical attitudes are reflected in these various notions. As for critical attitudes, I shall refer to a dichotomic spectrum, negative capability vs. quest for certitude (this is further elaborated below, in Chapter 21). Negative capability was described by Keats as the capability "of being in uncertainties, mysteries, doubts, without any irritable reaching after fact and reason". My main reason for choosing the grotesque among all aesthetic categories is that the grotesque makes the greatest demand on the reader's cognitive complexity, tolerance of ambiguity, and "negative capability".

Similar problems as those encountered here arise with regard to the definition of the genre or style category of Kafka's and Beckett's best-known works, or some of Agnon's "absurd" short stories. In Chapter 11, I suggested that the style of such works is based on the "efficient overstressing" of the conception of Man's condition in the world as "hemmed in". The author places his protagonist in an "extreme situation", in which Man's sense of limitedness is "heightened, to any degree heightened"—to use Hopkins' phrase outrageously out of context. In Chapter 21, I shall compare two readings of Beckett's *Waiting for Godot,* one that insists on interpretation in a conceptual system outside the play, and one that suggests that the play has no "meaning" in this sense: it merely presents a heightened sense of Man's limitedness. In the former case, we may speak of "allegoric" or "metarealistic" fiction; in the latter case—of a "literature of extreme situations" that demands an unusually high degree of negative capability.

Let us begin a thought-experiment. Suppose we have two "algebraic" definitions, call them *a* and *b*. Furthermore, without explicitly stating their contents, we assume that *a* and *b* are definitions of the grotesque. The problem now is the following: When comparing the two definitions in detail, how can we decide, which one is the "real" definition? We are confronted with *a priori* definitions, which cannot be refuted or supported with reference to examples. For any example I may offer to refute definition *a* or *b,* my opponent (who subscribes to the competing definition) may agree with my description of the putative counter-example, but still claim that it does not undermine his definition: he may, e.g., claim that this example is not 'really' grotesque. In fact, there even may be a partial overlap between the two definitions, but it still will be impossible to determine the boundaries of the grotesque. Suppose, for instance, that Kafka's "The Metamorphosis" will be found grotesque under both definitions, but Gogol's "The Nose" will be found grotesque only under one of them. Can this help us determine which one is the better definition? An exponent of definition *a* may claim: my definition is better, because it is applicable both to "The Metamorphosis" and "The Nose"; and both are grotesque. An exponent of definition *b* may claim: my definition is better, because it is applicable to "The Metamorphosis" only, and excludes "The Nose", which is not really grotesque. In this way, we are not very likely to make much progress in evaluating the two definitions. At most, we shall find, following Beryl Lake (1967), that both definitions are irrefutable, the contest will end in a tie. This however doesn't seem to be the proper way to handle the issue. Concluding an insightful paper on the role of theory in aesthetics, Morris Weitz writes:

> Thus, the role of theory is not to define anything but to use the definitional form, almost epigrammatically, to pin-point a crucial recommendation [...]. [Aesthetic theory] teaches us what to look for and how to look at it in art. [...] To understand the role of aesthetic theory is not to conceive it as definition, logically doomed to failure, but to read it as summaries of seriously made recommendations to attend in certain ways to certain features of art. (Weitz, 1962: 59)

This suggests that one must be careful when handling what appear to be definitions of aesthetic categories, such as "the Grotesque" (or, for that matter, "Metarealistic Fiction", or "Literature of Extreme Situations"—see Chapter 22). In most cases, it will be futile to try to discover which is the "correct" definition. And for our discussion, it will be better to regard definitions of the grotesque as 'serious recommendations' what to look for, and how to look at it in what are considered to be grotesque pieces of literature. When we are confronted with two incompatible definitions of a particular aesthetic category, or with attempts to apply different genre categories to the same corpus of fiction (such as "metarealistic fiction", or "literature of extreme situations"), we need not ask which is the "correct" definition or the "correct" genre, but rather, what we stand to gain or lose by adopting the one or the other; and, by the same token, what are the attitudes 'recommended' by these definitions or genres. The alternative attitudes, in turn, may be compared *in terms of the perspectives* adopted by the reader or critic (consciously or unconsciously). Thus, for instance, a reader or critic who views the pieces of fiction in the perspective of the nature of the aesthetic object may prefer a different set of attitudes from that preferred by a reader who views these pieces in a perspective of a system of extra-literary ideas. And again, the specific conception of the aesthetic object as "purposefulness without purpose", or "purposefulness without concept" may justify the preference of a set of attitudes that is different from that justified by a conception of the aesthetic object as one whose purpose is "to please and instruct".

The present section will elaborate on an additional perspective: that whereby the attitudes recommended by the aesthetic definitions and concepts are judged with reference to the reader's mental needs. Some of Agnon's or Kafka's fiction may induce distress, anxiety, or horror that are greater than what is tolerable for some readers. These readers may prefer a definition of the grotesque that minimizes the amount of anxiety or other irritating emotions; or they may want to apply to the corpus of fiction under consideration a genre category that minimizes the uncertainty involved. On the other hand, readers who are considerably tolerant of uncertainty may regard as the greatest achievement of these authors precisely their way of coping with "the irruption of the irrational" (cf. Warren, 1962: 131), and will prefer precisely the rival definition of the grotesque and of the relevant genre category. Furthermore, some of these perspectives are dependent upon each other. Thus, for instance, seeing a given whole as exceeding a certain limit in complexity may induce a feeling of uncertainty; consequently, readers with a limited tolerance of uncertainty will be inclined to adopt attitudes that are incompatible with a conception of the aesthetic object as "unity-in-variety", for instance. The same holds true for the aesthetic object as "purposefulness without concept": one conspicuous symptom of the "quest-for-certitude" syndrome is illustrated by what has been said above (Chapter 16, note 2) about the "leveler", who "is more anxious to categorize sensations and less willing to give up a category once he has established it. [...] For him the unique, unclassifiable sensation is particularly offensive" (Ohmann, 1970: 231). Such a reader will, therefore, tend to keep away from attitudes entailed by a "definition" of the aesthetic object as "purposefulness without concept".

One possible result of the present discussion, though not stated as its explicit purpose, is that the critics are forced to bring out into the open their implicit assumptions concerning the nature of the aesthetic object, that were hidden behind the interpretations; they will have a chance to consider whether these *implicit* assumptions are compatible with their *consciously* held aesthetic theories.

Let us now substitute some definite values for our algebraic symbols in our definitions of the grotesque. Most theoreticians would probably agree that the grotesque originates in a special mixture of conflicting qualities, such as the sublime and the ridiculous. The nature of this special mixture will become clear if we realize that both these qualities are *alternative* responses to threat. We are dealing with a defense mechanism against threat, as frequently mentioned in post-Freudian psychology. Thus, Kris (1964) discusses the sublime and the uncanny in the chapters described as contributions to the psychology of the comic. Similarly, Burke (1957: 52), in a chapter on "Beauty and the Sublime", explains the *sublime* and the *ridiculous* in their relationship to *threat:*

> Some vastness of magnitude, power, or distance, disproportionate to ourselves, is "sublime". We recognize it with awe. We find it dangerous in its fascination. And we equip ourselves to confront it by piety, by stylistic medicine, and by structural assertion (form, a public matter that symbolically enrols us with allies who will share the burdens with us). The ridiculous, on the contrary, equips us by impiety, as we refuse to allow the threat its authority.

Kris speaks of the "double-edgedness" of the comic. When the defense against the threat is dismantled, the ridiculous stops being ridiculous and becomes painful (a man who suspects, for instance, his wife of being unfaithful, will not find a comedy about a cuckold funny at all, but rather painful or distasteful). The comic originates in some threatening event, which is observed at a sufficient distance from the danger for the observer to feel safe. An observer who does not feel sufficiently safe will respond in an opposite manner. What characterizes the grotesque, according to some psychologists and literary theorists, is *a disruption of alternativeness*. Instead of deciding unambiguously in favor of one or another defense mechanism, the grotesque leaves the observer in an intermediate state, in uncertainty, in a state of indecision. He has a sense of "emotional disorientation". Many people find such an emotional state difficult to bear. Thomson (1972), at any rate, considers such an emotional state to be the distinctive feature of the grotesque, distinguishing it from other aesthetic qualities in which there is a co-presence of amusement and seriousness, as in irony and tragi-comedy.

> Irony depends on the resolvability, intellectually, of a relationship (appearance/reality, truth/untruth, etc.), while the grotesque presents essentially the unresolvability of incompatibles. (Thomson, 1972: 50)

> Tragi-comedy points only to the fact that life is alternately tragic and comic, the world is now a vale of tears, now a circus. The grotesque, in the form it takes in a play like King Lear, has a harder message. It is that the vale of tears and the circus are one. (ibid., 63)

Thomson introduces the quality of emotional disorientation that is associated with the grotesque by way of quoting a 41-line long passage from Beckett's *Watt* describing the many members of a certain Lynch family, all of whom are afflicted with all sorts of disgusting and improbable ailments. Then he goes on:

> Chances are that the reader's reaction will be somewhat confused, or at least divided. He will presumably respond to the tragic, disgusting or deformed nature of the unfortunate Lynches with a certain amount of horror, pity— perhaps even nausea. On the other hand the undoubtedly comic aspect of the description will rather induce him to respond with amusement or mirth. [...] Re-reading may only reinforce what is essentially a clash between incompatible reactions—laughter on the one hand and horror or disgust on the other. (ibid., 2)

> What will be generally agreed upon, in other words, is that "grotesque" will cover, perhaps among other things, the co-presence of the laughable and something that is incompatible with the laughable [...]. After the initial response to this passage, which as I have suggested will be essentially divided, the reader may well do one of two things as a further reaction. He may decide that the passage is more funny than horrifying, he may "laugh it off" or treat it as a joke; alternatively, he may be indignant and regard it as an outrage to his sensibilities that such things should be presented in a

humorous light. Both these secondary responses, if I may term them such, are highly interesting psychologically [...]. They both involve rationalization and defence-mechanisms, suggesting that the grotesque (assuming that this is in fact what we are confronted with) is hard to take, and that we tend to escape the discomfort it causes. (ibid., 3)

There is a famous anecdote about the astronomer Galle and his discovery of the planet Neptune. Supposedly, Galle was asked: "How do you know that the planet you have discovered is really Neptune?" The parenthesis toward the end of the preceding passage is directed against this kind of "skepticism". Thomson has given us a detailed description of the phenomenon in which the laughable is present together with the horrible, or the disgusting, or the pitiable, and called this phenomenon "the grotesque". But how can he know that the phenomenon described by him is really "the grotesque"? Galle's naïve interrogators assumed that the mythological names are inherent in the planets they designate, and not assigned by arbitrary decisions. So, if the name 'Neptune' is not written on the planet, how can the astronomer know that the planet he has discovered is indeed Neptune? He who intends to analyze the grotesque is even worse off. He may begin his analysis with an observation that many people use the term "grotesque" in relation to a wide range of undefined phenomena. When Thomson defines the grotesque, he is but offering his readers a "crucial recommendation" as for the attitude to be adopted toward these phenomena, termed "grotesque" by many. Most probably, the majority of critics would agree that his example of the Lynch family, at least, is an instance of the grotesque. If someone would not grant this much, Thomson will probably not try to give him more convincing "proofs".

The grotesque, then, as described by Thomson, is a quality that, in the first place, is "hard to take". In the grotesque, there is a clash between incompatible responses—the laughable on the one hand, and the horrible, the disgusting, and the pitiable on the other. The element that is so "hard to take" is the uncertainty, the emotional disorientation, the indecision in front of a threat. Making a decision in one or the other direction provides, according to some psychologists, a defense against the threat; whereas indecision causes discomfort, pain, distress, or anxiety. Consequently, the grotesque stays grotesque—according to Thomson—as long as the reader (or the observer) is capable of staying exposed to the incompatible emotions, without seeking relief in one of these "secondary responses" or "rationalizations" that resolve the conflict in favor of the laughable, the disgusting, or the pitiable. In a short excursus on the grotesque in his book on Kafka and Agnon, Barzel (1972: 72–74) refutes—and rightly—the view that the laughable in Kafka's work serves as relief from horror. "In this case, laughter is part of the horrible, and does not serve to relieve the reader's emotions" (ibid., 72). This does not imply, however, that the grotesque for Barzel consists in that state of clash or indecision, causing discomfort and distress. The difference between "The Nose" and "The Metamorphosis" is, he says, that "Gogol's story amuses us, whereas Kafka subdues all dimension of amusement" (ibid., 72).

Even if we refrain from deciding whose definition of the grotesque, Barzel's or Thomson's, is "correct", we can describe the attitudes presupposed by the two definitions relative to each other. Thomson regards the grotesque as requiring a response that consists in the willing exposure to threat, through the disruption of the defense mechanisms, that is, through indecision wavering between the "ridiculous" and the "disgusting". A person who is intolerant of "emotional disorientation", of the violent clash between conflicting emotional tendencies, is bound to seek relief by resolving the conflict in one of the opposite directions. Barzel recognizes the grotesque in the second stage of the process, in the stage of "rationalization". In Gogol's story, the amusing element is dominant, whereas Kafka's story "subdues all dimension of amusement". In each of the two stories, the conflict has been resolved, in one direction or the other.

We do not know whose definition is "right"; but we do know whose definition makes more complex psychological demands. He who views "The Metamorphosis" as a short story embodying the grotesque as defined by Thomson, is bound to be capable of "being in uncertainties, mysteries, doubts, without any irritable reaching for fact and reason", that is, capable of viewing both life and art through an attitude of negative capability. The contemplation of the grotesque, as this quality is defined by Barzel, presupposes a much lower degree of negative capability. A person whose quest for certitude exceeds a certain degree may be prevented from contemplating the grotesque in accordance with Thomson's crucial recommendation, even though he may be well capable of contemplating it as recommended by Barzel. It would appear, then, that the two definitions do not differ so much in the scope of their application as in the attitude which the observer is willing or able to assume.

Thus we are not dealing with a simple dichotomy, but with a dichotomic spectrum having fine shades between the two extremes. Thus, for instance, Barzel regards "The Metamorphosis" as a short story that "subdues all dimension of amusement"; he simplifies the story relative to Thomson's conception. At the same time, the quality which he considers to be dominant in the Kafkaesque situation may arouse an anxiety that is intolerable for a person being extremely given to the quest for certitude: "The emphasis in the succession [of Kafkaesque situations] is on the pangs of fear, the distressful musing of doubt" (ibid., 74).

I have no intention of diagnosing the critic Hillel Barzel's personality style here; rather, I will concentrate on what, following Booth, might be called "the implied critic's decision style" (see further on this, Chapter 21, below). In this respect, things are not simple at all. A critic's decisions may be determined, to a considerable extent, not only by the needs of his personality, but also by the intellectual and academic context in which he is acting. Thus, for instance, the definition of the grotesque adopted by a critic may be influenced by theoretical discussions to which he has been exposed. Suppose now, if we were witness to Barzel explicitly rejecting Thomson's position, we were witnessing a deliberate decision. However, in the case that Thomson's work was unknown to Barzel, or to any other critic who preceded Thomson, the mere fact that they did not act upon Thomson's "crucial recommendation" would tell us nothing about their personality styles. In fact, as we have seen, Barzel did reject the more simplistic position with regard to the elements of amusement in Kafka as "comic relief". Instead, he suggested that the laughable and distressful elements are not perceived one after another, but simultaneously; however, he does not regard them as preserving their warring identity, but rather as arranged in an unambiguous, relatively comfortable hierarchy.

Consequently, in order to learn about the decision style of Barzel's implied critic, we must have recourse to rather complicated procedures. His position concerning the grotesque may be the result of two completely different kinds of reasons (that do not exclude one another). On the one hand, it may be the result of casual reading of theoretical writings on the grotesque, or of critical writings on Gogol, Kafka, etc.; on the other hand, it may reflect his personal decision style and needs viz., to achieve a considerable degree of certitude, and of cognitive and emotional stability. In order to find out whether or not a certain critical position is merely casual, one must formulate a hypothesis based on the syndrome of the quest for certitude, and check whether the other decisions of the 'implied critic' would support such a hypothesis, or not. As I suggested above, the hypothesis must be formulated in the most careful manner. One must assume that the critic's decisions will not reflect the naïve position of an extreme quest for certitude; but, on the other hand, one should always expect to find (or at least, allow room for) the possibility of decisions that presuppose a higher degree of negative capability. And this is, indeed, what happens throughout Barzel's excursus on the grotesque. We have seen, for instance, that Thomson does not analyze the ailments of the Lynch family as laughable or distasteful, according to whether or not such 'reliably diagnostic' indications as the words *laughter, smile, comic,* or the like occur in the text; he treats the comic element as a *regional quality,* perceived as the cumulative effect of the ailments and deformations that are repulsive in themselves. This kind of analysis presupposes a considerable degree of tolerance of uncertainty. Barzel, by contrast, seeks the comic element, first and foremost, in explicit key-words in the text, rather than in 'regional' qualities. The recognition of the word *smile* is quicker, more certain, less complex, than the recognition of the comic effect in the cumulative impact of repulsive ailments and deformations. Moreover, the word *smile* is an obtrusive but unreliable sign of the comic. For the word *smile,* or its referent in extra-linguistic reality, do not necessarily arouse a "smiling" response in the reader. Consider the following passage by Barzel:

> The Land Surveyor's assistants are characterized (before their separation) by the smile on their faces. It is doubtful whether this laughter or smile may change the dog-like or animal-like image. "—and then K. pointed also to his assistants who stood linked together, cheek against cheek, and smiling, but whether submissively or mockingly could not be determined. All these

he pointed out as if presenting a train of followers forced upon him by circumstances—" *(The Castle,* p. 28). The element of horror consists in the deformation of the strange presence. [...] The smile enhances the effect of the strange, the dehumanized, and does not act toward the release of tension in the scene. (Barzel, 1972: 72–73)

Well, the smile does enhance the impression of the extraordinary, of the dehumanized, of the dreadful, but the scene in itself is not perceived as ridiculous at the height of dread. Furthermore, there are at least two details in the short passage quoted by Barzel that may be relevant to his purpose: the word "smiling", that refers to a well-defined category of behavior, and the phrase "smiling, but whether submissively or mockingly could not be determined", which suggests some point of indecision between conflicting emotional tendencies. Characteristically enough, Barzel makes use of the former, but not of the latter. Further on, he remarks:

Likewise in the typical Kafkaesque situation in Agnon's short stories. "When I raised somewhat my eyes, I saw a professor at the right of my acquaintance. His beard was yellowish and short, his-walking stick between his knees, and a smile hiding between his lips" ("The Document", p. 116). The laughter must not deceive us. [...] His smile is a grotesque, deformed mask, incapable of making one laugh. It would seem that the smiling appearances of the Satanic characters in the *Book of Acts* are part of the seduction pattern, rather than an instrument for the author to alleviate the reader's tension. (ibid., 73)

Does the perception of a smile typically make one laugh, or does it rather arouse a "warm feeling" or the like? By asking this question, I want to emphasize the futility of focusing on words like *smile* as indications of comic qualities. The phrase "grotesque, deformed mask" merely restates the grotesqueness of the smile, but does not indicate the cognitive complexity recommended for its contemplation. Barzel does not seem to distinguish between 'perceiving' and 'naming' a quality. Although he rejects the simplistic conception that laughter in the grotesque constitutes comic relief, he insists that the reader perceives the smiling characters in these short stories as part of a seduction pattern that is governed by horror, and does not perceive that the quality of amusement precisely is mixed with horror here. Under his analysis, the smile is not part of some unresolvable, violent clash of opposites; although it seemingly conflicts with *threat,* the two, smile and threat, are harmoniously integrated in the notion of *seduction.* When, however, Barzel does perceive the element of amusement as a *regional quality* of a piece of fiction, rather than as a merely *named* quality, he attempts to achieve certitude in another direction: contrary to what he has said above, he reverts to a conception of the grotesque-as-comic-relief:

The relieving laughter appears, in the grotesque-Kafkaesque situation, when the reader becomes an accomplice, is admitted into the knowledge of events, by the author's will, in front of the game of masks. "'Then who am I?' asked K. as blandly as before. And after a pause the same voice with the same defect answered him, yet with a deeper and more authoritative tone: 'You are the old assistant'" *(The Castle,* p. 27). The reader knows K.'s identity [does he? R.T.]. When the voice confuses his identity with that of the "old assistant", the narrative arouses a sense of relief and alleviation of tension. Dense horror becomes mirthful for a moment". (ibid.)

Here, at long last, Barzel speaks of the regional quality of a situation; but if the situation is meant to be grotesque—in Thomson's sense, at least—it does not relieve us from the painful, but is combined with it. K. has been hired to perform a certain task, but he is denied access to anybody with whom he could discuss this task. He does not know whether his assistants are the same as the persons who traveled with him to the place where he is now, and so forth. One possible way to handle the above dialogue is to view it as forming part of K's total loss of orientation, amplifying rather than alleviating the nightmarish atmosphere. The passage may be perceived either as painful or as amusing or as a blend of the two, inasmuch as it results from the utter purposelessness of K.'s telephone conversation and of his posing as the Land Surveyor's assistant. The possibly ludicrous quality of confused identities is added to the nightmarish confusion of the over-all situation.

A glance through Thomson's historical chapter reveals that in the course of history, conceptions of the nature of the grotesque range from "ludicrous exaggeration" to "a *co-presence* of the ludicrous with the monstrous, the disgusting or the horrifying", "producing a strange and often unpleasant and unsettling conflict of emotions" (Thomson, 1972: 14). From Romanticism on, there is an increasing awareness that the grotesque is "an appropriate expression of the problematical nature of existence" (ibid., 11). The present chapter has assumed that neither of these conceptions is simply right or wrong; I have accepted Morris Weitz's view, according to which aesthetic definitions are to be read as summaries of seriously made recommendations to attend in certain ways to certain features of art. The greater the critic's cognitive complexity, the more complex a conception of the grotesque he is capable of adopting, the more unpleasant and unsettling a conflict of emotions he is capable of tolerating and, perhaps, the more problematic in nature the existence he is capable of accepting. Psychologically, the grotesque is not the mere co-presence of the ludicrous with some quality that is incompatible with it: it is an exposure to threat, with the conflicting defense mechanisms neutralizing each other. It is precisely for this reason, as we have seen, that additional distinctions and concepts are appropriate and necessary. The critics cope with this necessity in various ways: some tend to name isolated entities that in some way are related to the clashing constituents of the grotesque; whereas others handle the grotesque as the perceived regional quality of some whole, a quality that is based on a more or less direct experience of the unpleasant and unsettling conflict of emotions.

Ibn Gabirol's Grotesque Disease

Shlomo Ibn Gabirol is one of the most important figures in Mediaeval Hebrew poetry in Spain, and surely one of the greatest representatives of the poetry of disorientation; this poetry reaches its peak in the poems where the poet describes his disease in great detail (see above, Chapter 12, note 5). Here, I wish to mention two of these poems, viz., "I shall be right indeed" and "The showers of your tears". The former poem has been summed up by Levin (1980: 243) as follows: "The sick person unites in his metaphors the scar with red roses, the sound of his wounds when squashed with kissing lips, the membrane of the abscess with the curtains of the Tabernacle, the shapes of the wounds with Bezalel's art-works, etc., [...] calls them by proper names; he takes strange pleasure in "raking" in them, describes them in their finest details, their shape, color, sound and movement". These clashing emotional tendencies constitute a blatant violation of the rules of poetic decorum, as formulated by Horace: "Painters and poets have always had the prerogative of daring anything. We know it, and both demand and grant the same licence. But not so far as to unite the mild with the savage or that snakes should be coupled with birds, lambs with tigers" (quoted by Gombrich, 1984: 255). But not only Horace would have been puzzled by such poems, but so indeed is the most outstanding scholar of Mediaeval Hebrew poetry, Schirmann:

> In his attitude toward his disease, as it is manifest in its description, there is an important psycho-literary problem which may not be ignored. [...] None of his other poems arouses in us such a strange feeling and confusion, as this one does when we realize his reaction to one of the disasters of his life. [...] It is not the impact of suffering on his soul, nor a mere hint, as in the rest of his work, at issues that are essentially unfit as subject matter for poetry, but precisely their lengthy and detailed description. And if this description is not realistic but resorts to apparently far-fetched images, this mode may only increase the nausea of some readers. This poem contains a worship of ugliness; moreover, there is much witticism in his similes, which may arouse today the reader's smile. It is, however, beyond doubt that the poet did not intend to amuse us. If this is bitter sarcasm, its spirit is strange to us today, and we find its subject distasteful. In this respect, a partition separates us from Mediaeval men in general. (Schirmann, 1979: 229)

In a similar vein, though less elaborately, Schirmann writes about the poem "The showers of your tears":

> One must admit that even within Ibn Gabirol's poetry, which sometimes *is*
> inclined towards witticism and casuistic subtlety, the poem makes a bizarre
> impression with its unnatural figures of speech. Some of his verse lines are
> problematic, as if they were produced through some special effort—the rea-
> son for this should be sought, perhaps, in the state of his health. (ibid.,
> 266)

It seems to me that in our age, having been exposed to both Baudelaire and Samuel
Beckett, there is little reason to talk of "partitions" in this respect. In fact, the
grotesque is one of the prevalent artistic modes today. It would appear, rather, that
Schirmann—like so many of our contemporaries—finds the grotesque quality "hard
to take". And conversely, we have no more reason to suppose that eleventh century
readers were homogeneous, as far as taste is concerned, than we have for such an
assumption about present age readers. Moreover, we do have some indication that at
least one Christian contemporary of Ibn Gabirol, St. Bernard de Clairvaux, the
French monk, preacher, and mystical writer, found the grotesque in architecture
distasteful.[1] Rather, it is the case that such poetry of disorientation turns the sense
of confusion and emotional disorientation associated with the grotesque to aesthetic
ends, as was suggested above.

Next, I will discus here at some length the other poem by Ibn Gabirol. I shall
focus on two passages only in this long work.[2] .

In Mediaeval Hebrew poetry, jewels, rare perfumes, embroideries were widespread
in stylized *"précieux"* landscape descriptions (as we have seen earlier, Chapter 12).
Artistic pleasure typically arises when some emotional or perceptual tension is replaced, or rather, resolved by some structure that induces a feeling of stability. Jewels, rare perfumes, rich embroideries, "gold to airy thinness beat" are paradigms of
direct pleasurable sensations: there is no need first to undergo the experience of perceptual or emotional tensions (cf. above, Chapter 12). When describing the impact
of the disease upon himself, Ibn Gabirol neglects very many details of reality; on
the other hand, he builds some hyperboles upon some typical details, characteristical
of the "luxuries of a refined culture". Pretending that every civilized man wears nose-

---

[1]   "But in the cloister, in the sight of the reading monks, what is the point of such
       ridiculous monstrosity, the strange kind of shapeless shapeliness, of shapely
       shapelessness? [...] You can see many bodies under one head, and then again one
       body with many heads, here you see a quadruped with a serpent's tail, here a fish whith
       the head of a quadruped. Here is a beast which is a horse in front but drags half a goat
       behind, here a horned animal has the hindquarters of a horse. In short, there is such a
       variety and such a diversity of strange shapes everywhere that we may prefer to read
       the marbles rather than the books" (quoted by Gombrich, 1984: 255).
[2]   I have given a detailed close-reading of the whole poem "The showers of your tears"
       in an earlier book (Tsur, 1987c: 176–194). As one may see there, the generalizations
       proffered above hold true of the entire poem. In a recent article (Tsur, 2006c) I
       discussed at length the poem "I shall be right indeed".

rings, finger-rings, coronets, and anklets, he describes his own leanness resulting from the disease in terms of a change of the relationship of his jewels to his body:

עֲדִי הָיוּ נְזָמֵינוּ עֲטָרֹות / וְהָיוּ טַבְּעֹותָנוּ עֲכָסִים

ʿădey hayu nəzamenu ʿătarot / wəhayu tabbəʿotenu ʿăxasim

(1)   Until our nose-rings became coronets
       and our rings became anklets

By this, Ibn Gabirol achieves an additional effect: he represented the disease and its agony with the help of a series of objects, whose conventional aesthetic function is precisely to avoid the need to experience (offensive) cognitive tension, while deriving aesthetic pleasure. In Dr. Johnson's words, he "yokes by violence together" the *most* heterogeneous ideas: his plagues and diseases with markedly pleasurable objects. Thus, he generates a sense of confusion and emotional disorientation characteristic of the grotesque. The speaker has recourse to the afore-mentioned jewels not by virtue of their most conspicuous property, their power to cause pleasure, only by virtue of their similar shapes, yet different sizes, which show the results of his disease. Thus, the most conspicuous property of the objects used in these figurative expressions (hyperboles) are irrelevant to the explicit purpose of the description. At the same time, by piling up these pleasurable objects, the poem generates an effect that is incongruent with the situation presented: the poet thus brings about a loss of proportion that is essentially comic, and incongruous with the desperate situation described. The words *rings, anklets* refer to different categories that are similar in substance (gold), shape (round, with a hole in the middle), and function (to adorn). One of the most important corollaries of this hyperbole is that it blurs what usually are considered hard and fast categories. This is still another way of generating the sense of confusion and emotional disorientation that is characteristic of the grotesque.

A similar technique we find in *Through the Looking-Glass*. In the Humpty-Dumpty episode, the blurring of the categories of 'man' and 'egg' is highlighted by another blurring of categories: Alice cannot tell, whether Humpty-Dumpty (Figure 17.1) is wearing a necktie or a belt, that is, whether the creature is wearing the object in question on his neck or his belly. Since, however, the grotesque, with the emotional disorientation involved, is a quality that is hard to take, Lewis Carroll's readers *may* tend to turn it into a comic, playful quality; by contrast, in Ibn Gabirol's poem, there are additional elements related to the grotesque that firmly anchor the reader's feelings in a sense of emotional disorientation.

Ibn Gabirol piles up a series of images on the theme of category-blurring. However, the image "and makes me take a myrtle for an oak tree" (verse 14) is not just one more instance of category-blurring, of confusing two trees of different thickness.

It goes as far as to make us doubt our comfortable relationship to our habitual modes of perception. Or take the images in verse 16:

וָאֶהְגֶּה בָּם כְּיוֹנִים וַאֲצַפְצֵף / בְּשִׂיחִי כַּעֲגוּרִים אוֹ כְסִיסִים

wəʾɛhgɛ bam kəyonim waʾaṣafṣef / bəsihi kaʿăgurim ʾo kəsisim

(2)   And I am cooing in them like doves, and twitter
            when I speak, like cranes or swallows

Figure 17.1   Humpty-Dumpty: Does he wear a necktie or a belt?

These images, too, are based on "stylized" birds that inhabit, conventionally, the garden which itself is a luxurious product of a refined culture. The inlay language (see above, chapter 3, note 9) is based on the Biblical verse "Like a swallow or a crane I twitter, I coo like a dove" (Isaiah, 38: 14). In the Biblical verse, the images emphasize the sorrow and helplessness of the speaker. In the present context of drastic changes in size and thickness, the physical aspect of "twitter", too, becomes relevant: "twittering" is 'using a thin voice'—an aspect which is irrelevant to the content feature "expressing sorrow". The cumulative effect of these piled up images around one single topic is to suggest a creature that is smaller than a human being to an unnatural degree, once adorned with rings on its fingers and in its nose, now with rings for anklets on its legs and a nose-ring for a coronet on its head, and which twitters in a thin voice instead of speaking. The impact is grotesque indeed.

The second passage to be discussed here includes verses 17–18:

וְלוּ אֶרְאֶה שְׁחָקִים יִשְׁלְחוּ שַׁי / וְיוֹבִילוּן לְעַפְעַפַּי שְׁבִיסִים

וְעַפְעַפַּי, בְּהַבִּיטִי אֲלֵיהֶם, / כְּלוּלָאוֹת, וְהֵמָּה כַּקְּרָסִים

wəlu ʾɛrʾɛ ˘əhaqim yiˇləhu ˇay / wəyovilun ləˤafˤappay ˇəvisim

wəˤafˤappay, bəhabbiti ʾălehɛm, / kəlulaʾot, wəhemma kaqqərasim

(3)   And would that I saw the skies send me a present
              and carry to my eyelids head-jewels
       And looking at them my eyelids are
              like loops, and they are like hooks

At the beginning, the metaphor in the first hemistich is construed as functional: "would that the skies do me a deed of kindness". Sending a present is one specific instance of such a deed, the abstract act being translated into a concrete physical transfer of objects in space. The word *present,* nonetheless, is still very general; the second hemistich creates a synonymous parallelism, where *present* is replaced by a much more specific object, *head-jewels*, thus adding one more item to the list of jewels in the preceding verses. At the same time, *head-jewels* become a (rather stylized) sensuous metaphor for *stars*, as this verse is usually understood by the commentators.

Accordingly, the poem exploits those sensuous elements of the image that are irrelevant to the request for an act of kindness; the request becomes, at the same time, a conventional description of the sky at night, sprinkled with stars that look like jewels. The next verse, however, causes the semantic set in the image of the second hemistich to shift, bestowing on it a meaning paraphrasable as "I see the stars". The figurative process is complex, even bold. It is founded on the realization of a metaphor. Now we have to understand *carry* literally as "physical transportation": transferring the stars from the sky to the eyes of the perceiver. Alternatively, if 'seeing' means having the image of an object on the retina, the next verse develops precisely those physical aspects of the stars (or jewels) by virtue of which they differ from their images. Ibn Gabirol's image brings, then, to consciousness not only the results of perception, but also its underlying mechanism. Verse 18 turns, next, the image into a metaphysical conceit by turning a partial identity between the stars (or jewels) and their retina-images into a complete identification: it is no longer a thing-free image that bears only a visual resemblance to the physical object out there. Instead, there are two full-blown physical objects, both the "distal" stimulus (the star) and the "proximal" stimulus (the image), so that now even the latter may show resistance, and can be 'looped' into the eyelid's loop. One side-effect of the looping of a miniature star (or jewel) into the eye by its image, like a hook, is an imaginary unpleasant sensation.

Schirmann paraphrases this verse as "My eyes gaze in wonder at the sky, as if they were fastened to the stars". The image "my eyelids are like loops and they are like hooks" is a specific instance of "fastened to". This specific instance, too, is the realization of a dead metaphor. At the same time, it introduces concrete elements that are irrelevant to the meaning "I gaze at the stars, and can't withdraw my gaze", thus intensifying the metaphoric contradiction. Levin's paraphrase of this verse is quite different: "The rays hurt him, as if they were hooks stuck in his eyes, that are like loops". As the foregoing account has suggested, we are confronted here with a single image manipulated in a mannerist way, so that it reconciles two (or more) incongruous, remote meanings. I believe I have shown that these puzzling verses are excellent instances of a "poetics of disorientation", rather than of a poetry that needs apology.

In the preceding chapter, I have distinguished two mechanisms of space-perception: orientation and shape-perception. I have suggested that the two processes involve two different kinds of perception-schemata. As I have claimed there, there is some experimental indication that in situations where there exists a conflict between different applications of the two kinds of schemata, the perceiver is experiencing difficulties and delays. A part of the sense of confusion in verse 18 is derived from precisely such conflicting applications. The substitution of a specific-concrete image for the speaker's perceiving and locating himself with reference to the stars substitutes two of the distinct characteristics of shape-perception schemata for two of the distinct characteristics of orientation schemata.

As to the first of these, whether we accept the modern explanation of seeing or we subscribe to that offered by Empedocles (as did Ibn Gabirol himself) that is, "A stream of light issues from the eye and unites with the stream of light that issues from the object seen" (Schirmann, 1961: 262), seeing involves streams of energy in which information is held in an active and fluid state; this enables relatively fast adaptation to rapidly changing situations. In our poem, a stable relationship involving solid objects with stable characteristic shapes (hooks and loops) is substituted for the relationship between the eye and the stars derived from the flexible stream of energy. With regard to the second characteristic, plans for looking at objects near at hand are here substituted for plans for looking at distant objects.

These two substitutions may have four conspicuous effects: first, the conflicting schemata generate a sense of disorientation not unlike the sense of disorientation associated with the grotesque. Second, when the "proximal term" of perception appears in consciousness, a de-automatization of perception occurs: instead of the mere re-sult of the perception, it is the perceptual mechanism that is presented to conscious-ness. When this mechanism is laid bare, its perceived quality is a sense of emotional disorientation: it arouses a strange sensation, making one suddenly doubt one's com-fortable relationship with this most habitual part of one's life. Third, the realization of idioms and metaphors involves a similar process: here, the reader suddenly doubts his comfortable relationship with language. Finally, the drastic semantic shifts pointed out above prevent the reader from achieving any kind of consistent orienta-tion in the poem's semantic universe.

I have discussed here only two short passages from Ibn Gabirol's "strange" poem. One aim of my analysis was to show that his elaborate dwelling on his dis-ease is not a casual whim, but constitutes a concerted effort to generate a pervasive quality of emotional disorientation in the poem.

The Swineheaded Lord

Next, I wish to demonstrate the explanatory power of the combination of a variety of principles considered hitherto in the present book, by having a closer look at the work of the great Hungarian poet Endre Ady. This poet is usually categorized as "Symbolist" or "Expressionist". Here, I want to point to another, hopelessly eva-sive, quality of his poetry, a quality that many of his readers have intuitively felt: Ady's poetry is said to have an irresistible, magical, spell-weaving quality about it. My contention is that this quality is the result of the interaction of a variety of prosodic, figurative, and thematic elements, among which the grotesque plays a prominent part.

I shall begin with a relatively mild instance of the afore-mentioned quality, as illustrated in the first two stanzas of his poem "A muszáj-Herkules" ("The must-Hercules"):

> (4)   D″ltömre Tökmag Jankók *lesnek*:[3]
>   Úgy szeretnék gyáván kihúnyni
>   S meg kell maradnom Herku*lesnek.*
>
>   Milyen híg fejüek a *törpék*:
>   Hagynának egy kicsit magamra,
>   Krisztusuccse, magam meg*törnék.*
>
>   (For my fall Pumpkin-Seed Jacks are lying in waiting:
>   I would like so much cowardly to expire,
>   Yet I must stay a Hercules.

---

[3]   The italics indicate the rhymes in the Hungarian text.

How dilute-headed are the dwarfs:
Had they let me on my own for a little while,
So help me Christ, I would break down on my own.)

On the thematic level, we have got here an opposition of the high-mimetic *Hercules,* as opposed to the low-mimetic *Pumpkin-Seed Jacks,*[4] *dwarfs,* and *cowardly to expire.* On the lexical level, the high-mimetic words are opposed to a popular dialecticism such as *Krisztusuccse* ("So help me Christ") and substandard words like "must", *muszáj.* On the figurative level, there is the irrational quality related to the oxymoron in the title, "A muszáj-Herkules" ("The must-Hercules"), as well as to the substitution of the modal particle *must* for an adjective. A similar, but less straightforward oxymoronic quality one may perceive in the line "I would like so much cowardly to expire". To this, another affective ingredient is added by the line "How dilute-headed are the dwarfs". Compare this verse-line to a possible paraphrase: "How idiotic are the dwarfs". What the predicate *dilute-headed* adds, is a vaguely grotesque quality, with a mild atmosphere of emotional disorientation. An intense affective ingredient is added by the phrase "I would like so much", and the interjection "So help me Christ". Now, all these more or less irrational oppositions and qualities are fused and intensified by two prosodic features of the poem, both related to rhyme and rhyme-pattern. The first is related to the asymmetrical shape of the stanza. Owing to an expectation for stable gestalts, as well as to past experience with stanza-forms, the reader is inclined to expect some symmetrical rhyme-pattern, presumably of the form *abab.* This odd-numbered structure with its asymmetrical rhyme pattern contributes to an unstable feeling or irrational quality, reinforcing the illogical qualities encountered on the other levels of the poem.[5]

Finally, there is the perceptual quality of the *virtuoso* anti-grammatical rhyme. Consider the rhyme-pair *lesnek~Herkulesnek.* The first "rhyme-fellow" (Hopkins), *lesnek* ("are lying in waiting"), is a verb, consisting of a stem *(les)* and the suffix for the third person plural *(nek).* This word is entirely included in the other rhyme-fellow. Here, however, the same speech-sounds refer to completely different semantic and syntactic entities. The string of sounds *les* is the last syllable of the proper noun *Herkules;* whereas the string of sounds *nek* is the dative-suffix. Thus, the two rhyme-fellows are homonyms on the phonetic level, but at the same time, are most emphatically contrasted on the semantic, syntactical, and morphological levels. A similar story may be told of the second rhyme. The two rhyme-fellows *törpék* and *megtörnék* are near homonyms; phonetically, they are contrasted only in one consonant. Grammatically, however, *törpe* ("dwarf") is a noun; the sound sequence *-ék* results from the plural-suffix. In the second rhyme-fellow, *tör* ("break") is a verb; *-nék* is a complex of suffixes, indicating the conditional mode, as well as the first person

---

4   *Pumpkin-Seed Jack* is, in Hungarian folklore, an unnaturally small creature.
5   Ady's three-line stanza, taken in isolation, looks very much like a Dantesque *terzina.* But whereas in Dante, the middle verse line rhymes with the first and third lines of the next stanza (and so on, indefinitely), Ady's middle line is left as a loose end.

singular. Here, too, the two rhyme-fellows are most emphatically contrasted on the semantic, syntactical, and morphological levels. As I have suggested in Chapter 9, such rhymes are apt to intensify, and increasingly fuse, whatever qualities there may emerge from the interaction of the other elements on the various levels of the poem. This is one of the reasons, I submit, of the impetuous, "irresistible" quality and the magical character of the present poem.

Next I will examine, at considerably greater length, a poem in which a haunting magical quality of a much more extreme degree has been perceived by generations of Ady-readers. The poem I mean is his "Battle with the Grand Lord", a literal translation of which is provided below:

(5)   The swineheaded Grand Lord is going to kill me,
       I felt, he's going to kill me, if I let him,
       He grinned at me and was sitting stiff,
       On the gold he was sitting, on the gold,
       I felt, he's going to kill me, if I let him.

       His swinish body, the loathsome one, I
       Caressed. He trembled.
       "Look here, who I am" (I whispered to him)
       And cut open my skull,
       He looked into my brain and laughed.

       (Should you think me the wild adventurer
       Of wild desires?) And I fell on my knees there.
       On the shore of tumultuous Life we were,
       There were the two of us, the sun was setting,
       "Give your gold, your gold".

       "A single second is enough to kill me,
       I may not wait anymore,
       I am called forth for voyage, for pleasure,
       By mysterious, luring words,
       I may not wait anymore."

       "*Your* heart is protected by bristles,
       My inside is ulcerous, guileful,
       Still, *my* heart is blessed,
       Corroded by Life, by Desire.
       I need gold. I must go on.

       The sea is awaiting *my* yacht,
       A thousand tents are waiting for me,

An alien sun, alien balsam,
Alien intoxication, a new girl,
All are waiting for me, for me".

The entire life within me is panting,
Everything that is new, toward me is galloping,
My many dreams are a holy hurly-burly,
All of *your* dreams are deaf,
So, cleave your thorax of gold.

The mournful, blind evening has already fallen upon us,
I was groaning. The waves
Continually brought word:
We are waiting. Have you got gold yet?
The tumult of the waves, the waves.

And we clashed. The shore was shaking,
I thrust my hand into his flesh,
I rent it, ripped it. All in vain.
His gold rattled. He laughed.
I cannot go, I cannot go.

A thousand evenings passed upon a thousand evenings,
My blood is shedding, shedding, continually shedding,
They call me, lure me from afar,
And we are still battling wildly:
I and the swineheaded Grand Lord.

There is a considerable number of uncertainties in this poem, stemming from many sources. These uncertainties are greatly enhanced by a variety of means: the already mentioned devices of the anti-grammatical rhyme, and the asymmetrical stanza form, and, last but not least, the enormous energy involved in clashes on a cosmic scale, such as indicated, e.g., by "And we clashed. The shore was shaking".

As for the interpretation of this poem, some Marxist critics take their "clue" from the social status of the Grand Lord and from the fact that what he denies the speaker is *gold,* and interpret the poem as an allegory of some kind of class struggle. A rival approach, which will be the one adopted here, attributes no absolute meaning either to the Grand Lord, or to gold, and relies rather on the *relations* obtaining between the Grand Lord, the speaker, and gold. This lack of "absolute meaning" is a possible source of the mysterious, magical quality of the poem. The Grand Lord does have social status, does have means in excess of what he seems to need; means which he does not even know how to put to fruitful use. He is stiff, senseless, insensitive, inhumane, even bestial, loathsome. There is also a suggestion of "something mechanical encrusted upon the living" (Bergson) in a line such as "He grinned at me and was sitting stiff". The speaker is his opposite in most respects: enormous forces are active inside him, he has most intense feelings, he has no economic means whatever, but is called forth for all sorts of goals, ambitions, purposes, aspirations, desires. His goals are mysterious, exotic, of an unspecified nature.

In one, all-important respect, however, the speaker is not the unqualified opposite of his antagonist: he is not the simple opposite of loathsome, he merely has a different kind of loathsomeness. Consider the following lines: *"Your* heart is protected by bristles, / *My* inside is ulcerous, guileful, / Still, *my* heart is blessed, / Corroded by Life, by Desire". The Grand Lord's loathsomeness is fast and stable, passively powerful, incapable of action, whereas the speaker has loathsome, powerful, and destructive forces acting inside him. This typically post-Romantic attitude, very well-known from Baudelaire, contrasts stagnation, and lifelessness with outbursting life-forces, which are nevertheless destructive, loathsome, full of evil. This may explain the oxymoronic quality of the three lines *"My* inside is ulcerous, guileful, / Still, *my* heart is blessed, / Corroded by Life, by Desire". Now consider this: these lines do not just imply some logical contradiction; they arouse conflicting, intense emotional tendencies in response to the speaker's personality. The same kind of complexities we find in the two lines "My many dreams are a holy hurly-burly, / All of *your* dreams are deaf". There is a straightforward opposition between *"my* dreams" and *"your* dreams"; at the same time, "holy" and "hurly burly" are characterized by conflicting emotional tendencies. If such conflicting tendencies are reinforced by additional elements, they may lead to a sense of confusion and a feeling of emotional disorientation.

The reinforcements in question are amply provided by the grotesque elements in the poem. I have quoted, in the preceding section of the present chapter, two passages on the grotesque due to, respectively, Horace and St. Bernard de Clairvaux. Gombrich (from whose *Sense of Order* these passages are taken) comments on them:

> What these texts have in common is the reaction of exasperated helplessness provoked by hybrid creatures, part plant, part human; part woman, part fish; part horse, part goat. There are no names in our language, no categories in our thought, to come to grips with this elusive, dream-like imagery in which "all things are mixed" (to quote Dürer again). It outrages both our "sense of order" and our sense of meaning. [...] The point is that there is no point. [...] Each of these "shapelessly shapely" motifs offers us surprise after surprise [...]; here we receive one shock after the other. Not only do the limbs of these composite creatures defy our classifications, often we cannot even tell where they begin or end. [...] Thus there is nothing to hold on to, nothing fixed, the *deformitas* is hard to "code" and harder still to remember, for everything is in flux. What is equally vital to our understanding of these effects is that the uncertainty of response carries over from the perceptual to the emotional sphere. (Gombrich, 1984: 256)

Figure 17. 2 Master of the Die: Grotesque. Early 16th century.

The antagonist of Ady's poem is precisely such a "hybrid creature" that "defies our classification", with "the uncertainty of response carried over from the perceptual to the emotional sphere". Now, consider the following. The grotesque visual element could be attenuated or eliminated altogether, if "swineheaded" were understood in some metaphorical sense (perhaps, "pigheaded"?). The beginning of the second stanza, however, insists that "swineheaded" should be understood literally: "His swinish body, the loathsome one, I / Caressed. He trembled". What is more, these very lines strongly intensify the conflicting emotional tendencies: the loathsome body trembling with pleasure, when caressed by the speaker.

Bakhtin (1968: 320) adduces an additional aspect of the grotesque that is relevant to our discussion of this poem. He presents the grotesque against "the new bodily canon, [that] presents an entirely finished, completed, strictly limited body, which is shown from the outside as something individual". "Next to the bowels and the genital organs is the mouth, through which enters the world to be swallowed up. And next is the anus. All these convexities and orifices have a common characteristic; it is within them that the confines between bodies and between the body and the world are overcome" (ibid., 317). In this perspective, such descriptions in Ady's poem as "And cut open my skull", or "I thrust my hand into his flesh, / I rent it, ripped it", too, are instances of the grotesque.

Kayser (quoted by Thomson, 1972: 18) suggests that "the grotesque is an attempt to control and exorcise ('zu bannen und zu beschwören') the demonic elements in the world". While this may be a correct observation, it should be kept in mind that in order to "control and exorcise", the grotesque must also *conjure up* "the demonic elements in the world". Gombrich's inspiring discussion of the grotesque would strongly support both claims. Still, I believe, Thomson's reservation is well-taken: "We may object also to the somewhat melodramatic over-emphasis on the 'demonic', which totally removes the fearsome aspect of the grotesque to the realm of the irrational—almost supernatural" (Thomson, 1972: 18–19). To this, I would like to add that the relegation of the grotesque to the supernatural is an all too easy way of handling it. The grotesque is so affective, precisely, because of its *immediate* ambiguity, even before questions may be raised concerning the possible existence of the creatures involved. My claim is, at any rate, that the strange, magical haunting quality of Ady's poem has its source, among other things, in the pervasive quality of emotional disorientation, generated by a variety of means, of which the grotesque is only one; this quality is further intensified by a variety of means (to be discussed below), residing in the prosodic organization as well as in certain over-all stylistic characteristics of the poem.

I am discussing here the grotesque as an aesthetic mode, as part of a poetics of disorientation. Now one of the most shocking aspects of this poem is that, while being powerfully disorienting, it is, at the same time, amply endowed with ingredients that are prominent in what I have called the "poetry of orientation" (Chapter 15). Such ingredients include extensions of the immediate perception beyond the immediately perceptible horizon, as in "I am called forth for voyage, for pleasure, / By mysterious, luring words", "They call me, lure me from afar", or "The waves / Continually brought word". The effect is reinforced by the all-pervasive, low-differentiated, thing-free quality in "The mournful, blind evening has already fallen upon us", and by the clause "I was groaning", enclosed between the two immediately preceding "high-mimetic" quotations. By contrast, the verb for *groan* "én nyöszörögtem", would be felt by most readers of Hungarian as "low-mimetic", thus further reinforcing the quality of emotional disorientation. These elements of the poetry of orientation, as in so many instances of romantic nature poetry, introduce another aspect that typically lies beyond the scope of our ordinary consciousness, namely, a perception of the invisible powers active in the world.

Finally, the overall quality resulting from the interaction of the various elements discussed above is strongly enhanced by several prosodic elements, of which I should point out only two, already touched upon earlier, in my discussion of the poem "The must-Hercules", viz., anti-grammatical rhyme, and irregular stanza form.

For a further elucidation of this point, I will quote the fourth and seventh stanzas of the poem in Hungarian (again italicizing the rhymes):

(6)   "Engem egy pillanat megölhet,
       Nekem már várni nem *szabad,*
       Engem szólítnak útra, kéjre,
       Titokzatos hívó *szavak,*
       Nekem már várni nem *szabad* " (stanza 4)

           ("A single second is enough to kill me,
           I may not wait anymore,
           I am called forth for voyage, for pleasure,
           By mysterious, luring words,
           I may not wait anymore.")

       "Az egész élet bennem zihál,
       Minden mi új felém *üget,*
       Szent zürzavar az én sok álmom,
       Neked minden álmod *süket,*
       Hasítsd ki hát arany*szügyed* " (stanza 7)

           (The entire life within me is panting,
           Everything that is new, toward me is galloping,
           My many dreams are a holy hurly-burly,
           All of *your* dreams are deaf,
           So, cleave your thorax of gold.)

The rhyme *üget~süket* is a virtuoso anti-grammatical rhyme; on the semantic level it contrasts the verb "gallop" with the adjective "deaf"; on the phonetic level, the last four speech sounds are contrasted only in one distinctive feature, [±VOICED], in the sounds [g~k]. The rhyme *süket~szügyed* is peculiar in that each of the consonants is akin to its counterpart in one feature, but contrasts with it in one or two others. Thus, the pair [˘~s] are akin as sibilants, but contrast as to their place of articulation (cerebral vs. dental) or, if one prefers, [±PALATAL]; the pair [t~d] have the same point of articulation, but contrast in the feature [±VOICE]; finally, [k~ď] agree as to their quality of [−ANTERIOR] consonants, while they differ both as to the features [±VOICE] and [±PALATAL].[6]

One of Gombrich's stimulating insights into the nature of the grotesque is that when its effect is too audacious, it can be mitigated by symmetry. "The symmetry swallows up the curious creatures" (Gombrich, 1984: 279). "Symmetry itself, as we remember from the Kaleidoscope, has a masking effect" (ibid.). I suggest that the converse of this observation may also be true, thus accounting for some of Ady's favorite stanza forms. I have already mentioned the three-line long asymmetrical stanza in "The must-Hercules". In "Struggle with the Grand Lord", we find a five-line stanza, equally asymmetrical. The first four lines constitute a four-line stanza, the symmetry of which is emphasized by the rhyme at the end of the second and fourth lines. It is this symmetry that is overthrown by the addition of a fifth line, also rhyming with the preceding rhyme-pair.

A comparison of the two stanzas quoted above highlights an additional device, used for arousing a feeling of unpredictability. In the seventh stanza, the first and second lines express parallel, whereas the third and fourth lines express contrasting attitudes; thus, these lines exhibit a meticulously symmetrical structure. The fifth line overthrows this symmetry and leads to a logical conclusion from the preceding argument; as such, it tends to be perceived as different from the preceding lines, and perceptually isolated from them. In the fourth stanza, by contrast, no new information is given at all in the fifth line: it simply repeats verbatim the second line (a favorite device of Ady's). This has an illogical, emotional affect, as the different contexts highlight slightly different aspects in "I may not wait anymore": the line "A single second is enough to kill me" foregrounds a sense of urgency and danger, whereas the lines "I am called forth for voyage, for pleasure, / By mysterious, luring words" suggest some irresistible attraction.

The asymmetrical stanza form, or the unpredictable repetition of a rhymed line, or an anti-grammatical rhyme alone would hardly generate this emotional atmosphere of verbal magic; it requires their combined effect, further enhanced by the semantic and thematic elements discussed in the present section. Thus, the magic spell of Ady's poetry can be said to be an *emergent regional quality*. It should be noted that all these elements—antigrammatical rhyme, asymmetrical stanza form, unpredictability, illogically repeated whole verse lines, and differences in barely noticeable semantic (and sometimes phonetic) nuances—are means typically deployed by hypnotic poetry as well, for quite similar effects (see below, Chapter 19).

---

[6]   For reasons which Cognitive Poetics cannot explain (but perhaps structuralist phonology could), various dissimilar plosives and other consonants in the final position (as in this rhyme [d] and [k]) are more readily accepted as perfect rhyme in Hungarian than in any other language I know.

Conclusions

The grotesque is, in an important respect, similar to the sublime. Both are *total* experiences: both are qualities that suddenly seize and fill the human soul, leaving no thoroughfare for any other emotion. That which is sublime, as that which is grotesque, threatens to exceed the imagination's power to take everything in at once. In another respect, however, the two kinds of experience are diametrically opposed. The sublime is an experience of positive character, related to orientation mechanisms in unlimited space. By contrast, the typical essence of the grotesque is emotional disorientation. The most typical source of emotional disorientation in the grotesque is the co-presence of the laughable and something that is incompatible with the laughable, such as the sublime, the pitiable, the horrible, or the disgusting. In psychoanalytic terminology, two incompatible defense mechanisms disrupt each other's activity in the grotesque; as a result, the soul is suddenly and immediately exposed to some unintelligible and frightful reality, measureless to man, something most people are poorly equipped to cope with.

There are other sources of emotional disorientation, besides the co-presence of the laughable and its incompatible counterpart: e.g., the blurring of hard and fast categories, the violation of "an entirely finished, completed, strictly limited body", the realization of idioms and metaphors, or certain extreme uses of the metaphysical conceit, all of which are more or less conventional resources. The present chapter, however, has drawn attention to an important, relatively unfamiliar phenomenon. Poets may creatively invent new ways of generating the disorienting effect; and since it is achieved by some drastic interference with the smooth working of existing cognitive mechanisms, readers may appropriately respond to it, without any previous 'training'. Thus, for instance, just as symmetrical structures may mitigate emotional disorientation, asymmetrical stanza structures are exploited by Ady for the purpose of intensifying this disorientation. An even more palpable instance may be found in Ibn Gabirol's poem, where we notice an interference with the basic perceptual mechanism of seeing: plans for looking at objects near at hand are substituted for plans for looking at distant objects; when this mechanism is laid bare, it arouses a strange sensation, making one suddenly doubt one's comfortable relationship with one of the most habit-dominated parts of life. Thus, a virtually infinite number of techniques can be invented for the generation of emotional disorientation. This is one of the basic messages of Cognitive Poetics.

Psychologically, then, the grotesque is not the mere co-presence of the ludicrous with some quality that is incompatible with it: it is an exposure to threat, with the conflicting defense mechanisms disrupting each other. "The point is that there is no point", says Gombrich. As I have noted before, this quality of emotional disorientation is typically characterized by what Kant called "purposefulness without purpose", and "purposefulness without concept". The strange, magical haunting quality of, e.g., Ady's poem has its source, among other things, in this pervasive quality of emotional disorientation, generated by a variety of means, of which the grotesque is only one; and "it is heightened, to any degree heightened", by anti-grammatical rhyme, asymmetrical stanza forms, and sublime elements. The very existence of such a great variety of means contributes to the psychological atmosphere of purposefulness. Thus, the disorienting effect of the grotesque is turned to aesthetic ends, yielding an heightened awareness of the state of being exposed to threat in an unshielded, defenseless manner. In some extreme instances, at least, this may result in a haunting quality that is not unlike the haunting quality of hypnotic or ecstatic poetry. [7]

---

[7]   I have elsewhere (Tsur, 2003: 263–285) extended the present conception of the grotesque to the infernal element in religious art, focussing on a painting by Hieronymus Bosch and two episodes from Dante's *Inferno*.

CHAPTER 18

Poetry and Altered States of Consciousness

We have seen in Chapter 1 the significance of individuals' constructing an ordinary, personal consciousness. We have also seen that people's response to poetry capitalizes on the disturbance or delay in the cognitive processes that constitute this consciousness. Ordinary consciousness is one of the greatest achievements of Man. However, this achievement is bought at the price of losing one's ability to rely on certain "lower" adaptive processes that are not controlled by "ordinary" conscious will. Our entire Western education teaches us to trust our reason and to distrust our emotions. I have already mentioned (in Chapter 14) the emotional pattern described by Ehrenzweig as "a creative ego rhythm that swings between focussed gestalt and an oceanic undifferentiation". According to both Freud and Jung, this rhythm is of essential importance when it comes to maintaining our mental health. One important function of art and religion in human psychic economy is to make this rhythm work. *Altered states of consciousness* are mental states in which adult persons relinquish to some extent the already acquired control of "ordinary consciousness". Such states help them achieve some relatively immediate exposure to reality, an immediateness which somewhat alleviates the rigid defenses built up by ordinary consciousness. (In this, *altered states of consciousness* are not unlike exposures to the grotesque, to which they otherwise appear to be diametrically opposed; cf. Chapters 16–17 & 22). Consequently, it will not be too much of a surprise that, traditionally, certain poetic genres have been closely associated with such *altered states of consciousness* as meditation, ecstasy, and hypnosis. It should be remarked, however, that while it is almost impossible to distinguish strictly *between* these three states of consciousness in their poetic guise, it may be quite profitable to distinguish between minor regressions from ordinary consciousness, as discussed in Chapter 1 (some psychologists speak of "changes in cognition and perception that do not represent a drastic break with normal experience but are different enough to be worthy of notice"—see Glicksohn, 1989: 17–18), and the attempt to capture some "peak experience" or some altered state of consciousness by means of poetry. Although the border-line is quite blurred, the extremes seem to be clear and illuminating.[1]

---

[1] For a more rigorous definition of Altered States of Consciousness, with criteria testable in the psychological laboratory, see Glicksohn 1989: 1–34.

A major claim of certain schools of conventional literary theory as well as of Cognitive Poetics is that poetry yields an heightened consciousness. Some poetry gives an heightened consciousness of the self's relationship to the surrounding space ("poetry of orientation"); other poetry concerns the heightened consciousness of an environment "run wild", which cannot be integrated any more by regular "orientation-devices". Chapters 16–17 above were devoted to the "poetry of disorientation", and discussed a variety of devices characteristic of disorientation, most notably, the grotesque, the metaphysical conceit, and the sensuous metaphor. The present chapter, as well as the following chapters (19 and 20 below) discuss "Poetry and Altered States of Consciousness", and explore some ways in which an heightened consciousness may be gained of mental states that in one way or another escape the control of ordinary consciousness, such as, most notably meditation, ecstatic and hypnotic poetry. Also, some of the material discussed in Chapter 10 on literary synaesthesia, can be said to belong here.

In Chapter 11, I discussed Ferenczi's (1925) classical paper on the development of the sense of reality. According to his Freudian view, the foetus' state in the womb is the prototype of a long series of recurring situations. In this state, the mother's body supplies all the foetus' needs. The foetus fills all the available space and makes no distinction between "subject" and "object". As the foetus grows, however, enclosure and protection become confinement and restriction. From this perspective, birth is a (traumatic) transition to a less protective but also less restrictive state of existence. Further growth results in a series of such transitions to states of ever-decreasing protection and restriction. By the same token, from stage to stage, there is a steadily growing "abyss" between "subject" and "object". One of the main objects of mystics of all ages and religions is to reach through the abyss between the human and the transcendental, the Divine, and to overcome it (cf. Scholem, 1955: 7–10). Mysticism, says Dr. Mobley, is religion in which God "ceases to be an object and becomes an experience" (cf. Tsur, 1974: 413).

There is also a secular version of this experience of overcoming the abyss between "subject" and "object". The Romantic poets sought to discover, with the help of their **imagination**, the transcendental order inaccessible to the senses, in nature, that *is* accessible to the senses. In English Romanticism, says Bowra (1961: 271), "five major poets, Blake, Coleridge, Wordsworth, Shelley, and Keats, despite many differences, agreed on one vital point: that the creative imagination is closely connected with a peculiar insight into an unseen order behind visible things". The Romantic poets call the unlimited reality with which they seek communion "Infinity", "Eternity" or "Nothingness", rather than "God";[2] sometimes they merely seek **integration** with surrounding Nature. Similarly, in chapter 15, we have discussed at some length **orientation** defined as "the ability to locate oneself in one's environment with reference to time and place". So, in this latter-mentioned case (as well as, perhaps, in the former), it would appear that awareness of a major adaptive device

2   This practice is most familiar with the religious mystics as well.

is "heightened, to any degree heightened"—to use an expression coined by Hopkins, in an admittedly rather different context.[3]

In Chapter 15, on space perception, I discussed the last two lines of the first stanza of Wordsworth's "The Solitary Reaper":

(1)   O listen! for the vale profound
       Is overflowing with the sound.

Among other things, I commented there on the fact that the verb *overflowing*, which is associated with the visual and tactile senses, takes the object *sound*, which is associated with the aural sense. This conflict between the senses cancels the auditory components in *sound*, and leaves the component of the presence of a thing-free quality, which quality then becomes 'infested', via the verb *overflow*, with undifferentiated sensations—the residuum of the tactile sensation of being immersed in water, after the cancellation of the specific tactile in *overflow*, due to the conflict between the senses. Some readers report that they feel as if the surface of their body became peculiarly important, accentuated somehow. From the visual sensation, only the spatial presence of superabundance and the movement in space has been left. Thus, the 'overflow of sound' is perceived as an intense, undifferentiated, supersensory presence, in which one may be totally immersed, so as "to suspend the boundaries between self and not self". In a paper on "Oceanic Dedifferentiation and Poetic Metaphor" (Tsur, 1988b) I discussed at considerable length such poetic metaphors as "But ye loveres, that bathen in gladnesse" (Chaucer, *Troilus & Cresseyde*, I.), and "Steep'd me in poverty to the very lips" (Shakespeare, *Othello*, IV. ii.); these metaphors are of the shape [IMMERSED in an ABSTRACTION], which tend to cause an heightened effect of precisely this kind. In many instances, metaphors of this structure are used in mystic or Romantic poetry to arouse an intense feeling of communion with "Infinity", "Eternity", or "Nothingness", as suggested above. In certain circumstances, especially when placed in a context of the expansion of vast space, such metaphors may be perceived as a direct intuition of the "oceanic undifferentiation"-pole of the "creative ego rhythm that swings between focussed gestalt and an oceanic undifferentiation", of which Ehrenzweig speaks. Bearing in mind Wayne Booth's (1961: 211–240) distinction between **telling** and **showing,** this technique may be as good as any for "showing", so to speak, an altered state of consciousness, or a "peak experience" by verbal means.

At this point, it is very important to make a very clear distinction between the *perception* of such a quality in a poetic text, and certain of its *interpretations* in the psychoanalytic tradition. Some critics, among them Ehrenzweig himself, are prone to take some image with a focused gestalt and construe it as an image of "oceanic undifferentiation" of some kind, as we will see in the following.

---

[3]   As to the brain mechanism invovlved in this process, see below, in Chapter 24, my discussion of Figure 24.1, derived from Newberg et al.

Oceanic Imagery in *Faust:* Ehrenzweig against Ehrenzweig

Ehrenzweig refers several times to the Homunkulus-episode in *Faust Part Two* as "oceanic" imagery. This episode seems to have an enormous grip on Ehrenzweig's imagination; as he says himself, "Nowhere in literature is there a more condensed image of the self-creating and self-scattering womb, or rather the divine parentless child identified with the womb from which he delivers himself in a threefold act of birth, love and death" (Ehrenzweig, 1970: 215). Since Homunkulus appears as a *dramatis persona,* rather than as a literary or linguistic figure in *Faust,* a *persona* furthermore who engages in dialogues and longer speeches over substantial stretches of time, I shall quote here only one of Ehrenzweig's several summaries of the episode:

> The chemical manikin, Homunkulus, achieves his own suicidal rebirth in love. I have already mentioned the extreme oceanic undifferentiation of the episode. Homunkulus is still unborn, enclosed in a glass phial which can become incandescent and lift itself into the air (this is an additional phallic symbolism). The manikin achieves rebirth by shattering his glass in a fiery explosion at the feet of the sea goddess, Galatea, amidst a general scene of orgiastic self-abandon. (Ehrenzweig, 1970: 215)

We must distinguish in this account between the **immediate presentation** of an undifferentiated state, and the **differentiated idea,** or the **differentiated image,** of that undifferentiated state. Had Ehrenzweig characterized only the events conveyed in the last sentence of this quotation as "oceanic undifferentiation", we might have accepted his account as a description of the achievement of such a state. But when he concerns himself with the image suggested in the last sentence but one (including the suggestion of "phallic symbolism"), or when he speaks of Homunkulus as of the man-made manikin "who is still unborn and encased in the glass womb he carries about" (ibid., 199), we may regard it at best as the differentiated idea of an undifferentiated existence in the womb, that is, an allegory of an oceanic state.

This conclusion is warranted by Ehrenzweig's own account of the oceanic experience as quoted in the chapter on Archetypal Patterns. My argument rests mainly on the opposition between "oceanic undifferentiation" and "focused gestalt". The stable glass case with a characteristic human shape in it may, perhaps, represent a "return to the womb", and thus *stand for* "oceanic undifferentiation"; but it also *presents* the audience or the reader with some focused, well-differentiated gestalt. Thus, far from being an "experience of fusion", of suspending "the boundaries between self and not-self", this image of Homunkulus represents a state in which "the objects and self are clearly held apart", the glass case serving to enhance this separation. From such a focused, stable shape one may perhaps abstract the idea of the "return to the womb"; but this shape cannot be perceived as the experience of fusion and undifferentiation. The image is basically allegoric in character.

Thus, there appear to be two alternative ways of introducing "oceanic" imagery into a poem. Either *via* some **differentiated stable visual shape**, as in the image of the encased Homunkulus, from which a visual resemblance to the unborn child in the womb may be inferred, or by some **dedifferentiation** process that "suspends many kinds of boundaries and distinctions; at an extreme limit it may remove the boundaries of individual existence and so produce a mystic oceanic feeling" (Ehrenzweig, 1970: 304). Earlier, I have mentioned one kind of metaphorical constructions as a technique of obtaining such a suspension of boundaries; and Goethe, in *Faust,* had recourse to this technique. Here, I only want to quote a single passage of this work, in which a crucial metaphor concerns immersion in an abstraction, seemingly leading to mystic insight.

> (2)   The spirit-world no closures fasten—
>   Thy sense is shut, thy heart is dead;
>   Disciple, up! untiring, hasten!
>   to bathe thy breast in morning-red!
>   (*Faust Part One,* 443–446, trans. Bayard Taylor)

In (2), the undifferentiated experience of being immersed in a "dense", thing-free and gestalt-free entity is reinforced by two aspects of the metaphorical abstraction. First, by canceling the material aspects of the colorless substance *water* (as in "bathe"), the abstraction process allows the experience to have a sensory attribute: color (as in "redness"). Hence, one of its effects here is to increase the "dense texture" of the thing-free entity into which one is to be plunged, and so intensify the resulting, undifferentiated sensation. Second, this abstraction itself is part of a large-scale spatial scene. Perhaps the most conspicuous condition in which abstract nouns may assume a low differentiated character is when they occur in the description of a concrete, specific landscape, in which the speaker (or the perceiving consciousness) is in an intensive relation to the environment. In (2), the redness of the morning both provides the abstraction and indicates the concrete landscape, without mentioning any object that may have some stable, characteristic visual shape.

Here, we may pause for a moment and reflect again on my use of psychoanalytical terms. Analytic philosophers distinguish between "description", "interpretation" (or "explanation"), and "evaluation" in critical statements. "Description" identifies elements *within* the text and the relationships between them, whereas "interpretation" points out the relationships between the text and something outside it. With relation to (2), "oceanic undifferentiation" is used as a descriptive term. It refers to the structure of imagery, or figurative language, and its perceived effects. With relation to Homunkulus encased in the glass phial, the term is used interpretively: it refers to a well-differentiated image in the text, and indicates its relationship to an undifferentiated experience outside the text, inside the womb, under reference to Freudian theory. In my paper on Oceanic Dedifferentiation (Tsur, 1988b), I have distinguished between "rapid" and "delayed categorization". The former leaves the perceiver with as short a period of indecision as possible, and thus spares him the discomfort of uncertainty. The latter requires a considerable period of uncertainty; by the same token, it allows the perception of low-structured sensory information, and a more reliable judgment. In the case of Ehrenzweig, an alternative way to handle his two kinds of interpretation would be to suggest that with reference to the Homunkulus episode, the interpretation concentrates on focused gestalts and enables rapid categorization; with reference to the immersion in "morning-red", the interpretation focuses on diffuse, unstructured gestalts, requiring delayed categorization; at the same time, it allows for the perception of a diffuse state that is not unlike oceanic undifferentiation.

Whitman's Catalog Technique and Cognitive Processes
"Illustrative" and "Meditative" Catalogs

The starting point of the present section of this chapter is a distinction made by Goodblatt (1990) between what she terms the "illustrative" and "meditative" functions of what is often called the Whitmanian 'catalog technique'. As an example of the former, Goodblatt quotes some lines from section 5 of "A Song for Occupations", in which the reader's response to a list of occupations is "to conceptualize the items as a particular statement or category. [...] As such, this catalog can be considered to fulfill an illustrative function" (Goodblatt, 1990):

(3)   The plum-orchard and apple-orchard....gardening....seedlings, cuttings, flowers and vines,
Grains and manures..marl, clay, loam..the subsoil plough..the shovel and pick and rake and hoe..irrigation and draining;
The currycomb..the horse-cloth..the halter and bridle and bits..the very wisps of straw,
The barn and the barn-yard..the bins and mangers..the mows and racks:
Manufacturers..commerce..engineering..the building of cities, and every trade carried on there.. and the implements of every trade,
The anvil and tongs and hammer..the axe and the wedge..the square and mitre and jointer and smoothing plane;
The plumbob and trowel and level..the wall-scaffold, and work of walls and ceilings..or any mason work:
The ship's compass..the sailor's tarpaulin..the stays and lanyards, and the ground-tackle for anchoring or mooring;

> The sloop's tiller..the pilot's wheel and bell..the yacht and
> fishsmack..the great gay-pennanted three-hundred-foot
> steamboat under full headway, with her proud fat breasts and
> her delicate swift-flashing paddles;
>
> > ("Song for Occupations")

In contrast to the illustrative function, Goodblatt distinguishes a meditative cata-log technique, whose function is to emphasize sensory experience (ibid). Goodblatt and Glicksohn (1986) give a good example of this from Whitman's "Song of My-self":

> (4)   The smoke of my own breath,
>   Echoes, ripples, and buzzed whispers....loveroot, silkthread, crotch
>   and vine,
>   My respiration and inspiration....the beating of my own
>   heart...the passing of blood and air through my own lungs,
>   The sniff of green leaves and dry leaves, and of the shore and dark-
>   colored sea-rocks, and of hay in the barn,
>   The sound of the belched words of my voice....words loosed to the
>   eddies of the wind,
>   A few light kisses....a few embraces....a reaching around of arms,
>   The play of shine and shade on the trees as supple boughs wag,
>   The delight alone or in the rush of the streets, or along the fields
>   and hillsides,
>   The feeling of health...the full noon trill....the song of me rising
>   from bed and meeting the sun. ("Song of Myself" II, 13–21)

These authors suggest that "this catalog is a poetic realization of the meditative technique of 'mindfulness'" (1986: 85).

For caution's sake, I shall use, instead of the technically precise term "realiz[ing] the meditative technique of 'mindfulness'", the vaguer description "indicating some altered state of consciousness". My phrase *indicating some altered state of con-sciousness* is meant to suggest that I do not wish to prejudice, at the present stage of my argument, two issues: first, whether we are confronted with a meditative or some other, likewise mystic, state of mind; and second, whether the poem "reflects" the poet's state of mind, "arouses" such a state of mind in the reader, or simply "may be perceived in the poem as one of its regional qualities", and thus is some-how "isomorphic" with such states of mind in human beings (in accordance with my argument in Chapter 4). Personally, I am inclined to adopt this third view. When critics speak of this meditative or mystic quality in some of Whitman's catalogs, they usually imply that it is a "meritorious" feature of the poem (that is, that some aesthetic worth may be attributed to the poem on these grounds).[4] It is not quite clear, whether Whitman's second kind of catalog is to be regarded as a mere failure to achieve this meditative or mystic quality, or as the realization of some other, hitherto unspecified aesthetic principle.[5]

Intuitively, then, the quote in (4) leans more toward the pole of a meditative, or some other altered state of consciousness; (3) appears to have a more conceptual character. In order to better understand the nature of the two kinds of catalog, let us consider Ehrenzweig's discussion of Bergson's "metaphysical intuition" as a gestalt-free vision:

> What Bergson calls metaphysical intuition is a gestalt-free vision, capable of superimposed perception. Let us hear his own masterful description of surface and depth vision:
>
> "When I direct my attention inward to contemplate my own self [...] I perceive at first, as a crust solidified at the surface, all the perceptions which come to it from the material world. These perceptions are clear, distinct, juxtaposed or juxtaposable one with another; they tend to group themselves into objects. [...] But if I draw myself in from the periphery towards the centre [...] I find an altogether different thing. There is beneath these sharply cut crystals and this frozen surface a continuous flux which is not comparable to any flux I have ever seen. There is a succession of states each of which announces that which follows and contains that which precedes it. In reality no one begins or ends, but all extend into each other". (Ehrenzweig, 1965: 34–35)

Bergson recognizes that juxtaposition is essential for surface perception, but not for depth perception. He gives a practical recipe to achieve intuition: he recommends one to visualize at the same time a diversity of objects in superimposition.

> "By choosing images as dissimilar as possible, we shall prevent any one of them from usurping the place of the intuition it is intended to call up, since it would then be driven away at once by its rivals. By providing that, in spite of their differences of aspects, they all require from the mind the same kind of attention [...] we shall gradually accustom consciousness to a particular and clearly defined disposition". (ibid.)

---

[4]   To justify such an evaluation, one might, for instance, appeal to the third (some Intensive Human Quality) of Beardsley's three **General Canons of Evaluation,** viz., the Canon of Unity, the Canon of Complexity, and the Canon of Intensity (Beardsley, 1958: 465–469).

[5]   The different handling of metaphors in the two kinds of catalogs tends to be systematic and thus suggests the second option. Since, however, I have failed to discover this particular aesthetic principle, I cannot rule out the first possibility.

It seems to be pretty clear that while it is possible "to visualize at the same time a diversity of objects in superimposition", it is impossible to imagine a diversity of *verbal expressions* in superimposition. All verbal expressions are received in succession, "in juxtaposition". One remedy to this state of affairs would be "to visualize at the same time the diversity of objects" denoted by the phrases of Whitman's catalogs "in superimposition". This, however, would hardly be consistent with the process of speech reception. Another possible remedy, more consistent with the conception of the poem as a verbal artefact, would be that the information conveyed by the succession of phrases of the catalog may, under certain conditions, result in a cognitive overload on the reader's processing space; in such a case, one might assume, the reader is compelled to handle this information by collapsing it into an undifferentiated mass (very much in the manner in which perceptual overload is handled by "dumping" the excess of perceptual information into an undifferentiated background mass). One possible way to handle a catalog such as that in (4) is to assume that the apparently declarative sentence

(5)   This catalog is part of a meditative poem

is to be understood as one that performs a different kind of speech act, describable as a **crucial recommendation.** In other words, the above (declarative) statement is to be construed as the crucial recommendation:

(6)   Perform the poem in such a way that it should be perceived as one that indicates some altered state of consciousness.

More specifically, (5) (and (6)) might be construed as

(7)   Perform the catalog in such a way that its itemization results in a cognitive overload on your processing space, thus compelling you to collapse the excess information into an undifferentiated mass.

Such a construal will most likely leave us in a state of utter confusion. If one needs the construal of (5) as (6) (or (7)) in order to realize (or experience) (4) as indicating some altered state of consciousness, the intuitive distinction between some meditative and conceptual quality in Whitman's catalogs becomes meaningless. The point, however, seems to be that some catalogs will lend themselves to a performance as recommended in (6) (or (7)) more readily than others. It will be observed, for instance, that in a sense, the items in (3), too, may cause a cognitive overload on the reader's processing space; on the other hand, they will hardly induce him to handle this information by collapsing it into an undifferentiated mass. Rather, the tendency on the part of the reader will be to "recode" the catalog by abstracting some general category from each line, and in this alleviate the burden placed on his memory.

When we first started to discuss these matters of the 'itemization' of catalogs such as exemplified by (3) and (4),[6] some people pointed out that a catalog like (3) does have a structure, since the items in each line belong to the same restricted field. We regarded this as a feature contributing to poetic structure. Later, by way of comparison to (4), we realized that on the contrary, it is precisely the arrangement of items in fairly homogeneous groups that induces consciousness into what may be termed "conceptual categorization". Hence it is this very kind of structure that accounts, to a considerable extent, for the conspicuous conceptual—and apparently non-poetic—nature of this kind of catalog.

Consider the contexts in which the word *vine* occurs in each of the two catalogs, (3) and (4). In (4), it occurs in the context of

> (8)   Echoes, ripples, and buzzed whispers....loveroot, silkthread, crotch and vine,

whereas in (3), it occurs in the context

> (9)   The plum-orchard and apple-orchard....gardening....seedlings, cuttings, flowers and vines,

While all the items in (9) clearly belong to the same semantic field (of plants or agriculture), the items in (8) (and, in fact, in the whole excerpt in (4)) belong to a diversity of fields, so that one may, perhaps, justly apply Bergson's formulation to these passages: "By choosing images as dissimilar as possible, we shall prevent any one of them from usurping the place of the intuition it is intended to call up".

There is another conspicuous difference between (4) and (3). Most items in (4) designate what in Ehrenzweig's terminology may be called **thing-free** and **gestalt-free** qualities, such as "The smoke of my own breath, echoes, ripples, and buzzed whispers, my respiration and inspiration ...", whereas most of the items in (3) designate objects that have stable, and sometimes even characteristic, visual shapes that seem to resist the kind of fusion that Ehrenzweig mentions. Consider, for instance, the verse

> (10)   The anvil and tongs and hammer..the axe and the wedge..the square and mitre and jointer and smoothing plane;

in which both qualities are present: the tools are taken from one semantic field (carpentery), and have well-defined boundaries that resist fusion.

---

[6]   In the Cognitive Poetics workshop at the Katz Research Institute for Hebrew Literature, Tel Aviv University.

Thus, the items in (3) indicate, in Bergson's words, perceptions that "are clear, distinct, juxtaposed or juxtaposable one with another", and that "tend to group themselves into objects"; by contrast, most items in (4) *can,* at least, be treated as "a succession of states each of which announces that which follows and contains that which precedes it. In reality no one begins or ends, but all extend into each other" — again, in Bergson's words. The impression of such a succession of states is further reinforced by a phrase like

> (11)   The sniff of green leaves and dry leaves, and of the shore and dark-colored sea-rocks, and of hay in the barn,

which is of the shape [SENSE-IMPRESSION of A and B and C and D and E], where A, B, C, D, and E designate a diversity of objects, fused in a single, momentary, low-differentiated sense-impression.

Thematized Predicate

"It is obvious", says Bierwisch, "that there is an essential mediation between the macrostructure and microstructure which results in the total effect, and that a rational literary theory must encompass both realms. Our present knowledge does not enable us to say anything meaningful about the type of relationship" (1970: 112–113). In my opinion, this is precisely one of the areas where Cognitive Poetics has more to offer than conventional poetics. In what follows, I shall discuss at some length the relationship between the overall structure of Whitman's "meditative" catalog, and a particular kind of phrase structure that happens to be very common in it.

The abundance of thing-free and gestalt-free qualities in (4) is foregrounded by phrases of the shape [the GERUND of the CONCRETE], as in "the beating of my own heart....the passing of blood and air through my own lungs" or "a few embraces....a reaching around of arms". Such phrases can be said to derive from clauses of the type "My own heart is beating" and "Blood and air are passing through my own lungs", or "Someone embraces" and "Arms reach around". We may want to call these derivations, respectively, processes of **nominalization** and **thematization,** by which, on the one hand, the abstract "action" is separated from the concrete "agent" who performs it, and, on the other hand, manipulated into the referring position of the phrase, i.e., into the focus of our attention (turning it into the "psychological subject" of the phrase). Likewise, such phrases as "The play of shine and shade on the trees" and "the rush of the streets", can be said to have been derived by similar processes. In the former of these two phrases, these processes are further enhanced by a pair of thing-free and gestalt-free qualities, viz., *shine and shade,* the *play of* which is perceived on the concrete things, *on the trees as supple boughs wag.*

Elsewhere (Tsur 1987 b: 128–143),[7] I have used the terms **Thematized Predicate,** or **Topicalized Attribute.** This terminology reflects the fact that we are

---

[7]   My present argument conveys here the gist of my argument there, with different examples, of course.

dealing both with verbal expressions and with the world of their referents. Thus, what on the syntactic level is usually called *subject* and *predicate,* on the level of referents is frequently called *topic* and *comment;* what on the level of referents is called an *attribute,* may be realized on the syntactic level as an adjective (pre-nominal or predicative), or as an abstract noun. Similarly, what in syntactic terms is called *nominalized* and *thematized predicate,* in referential terms may be called *topicalized attribute*[8] (see also below, in Chapter 24). In another (now somewhat antiquated but still useful)[9] terminology, one could say that what in the 'deep structure' is a predicate is, in the 'surface structure', nominalized and thematized in the figurative device under discussion. To put it more explicitly, what in the deep structure is a predicate, may be realized in the surface structure either as a predicate, or it may be adjectivalized and embedded as a prenominal adjective, or nominalized and thematized, that is, realized as a noun and manipulated into the referring position of the phrase. The surface structure of the phrases discussed here is, then, "the ABSTRACT of the CONCRETE", or "the GERUND of the CONCRETE", less frequently "the ABSTRACT (or GERUND) of the ABSTRACT".

Comparing the phrases *My beating heart* and *The beating of my heart,* we find that *beating* changes its grammatical form from the **present participle** (used as an adjective) to the **gerund** (in the sense of an abstract noun). In Strawson's (1967: 82n) terms, "The variation in form from 'pretty' to 'prettiness' [or, in our case, from the present participle to the gerund] supplies the substantive which is grammatically typical for referential position". Apart from this, there is little semantic difference between the two: both abstract nouns and adjectives serve to denote properties that may be said to have *grown together,* as the etymology indicates, in 'concrete' nouns. In psycholinguistic terms, there seem to be good reasons that, "if an element of the sentence receives focal emphasis as 'new information', it should occur towards the end rather than the beginning of the sentence" (Leech, 1974: 198): in this way, the sentence places a smaller burden on one's short-term memory. The obverse holds as well: if an element of the sentence receives emphasis as "old information", if the speaker wishes to bestow upon it a psychological atmosphere of familiarity, if he wishes to present it as that which denotes the thing what the sentence is "about", he should move such an element to the beginning, rather than having it at the end of the sentence or the phrase. This is the process of **thematization** or **topicalization**, as I have called it above. Nominalization and thematization turn the verb *beat* into an abstract noun, and transfer it to the beginning of a genitive phrase. Thus, an elliptic (i.e., predicate-less) sentence has been generated, conveying

---

[8] I am assuming that we know what *attribute* means, and will ignore the philosophical issues that are at stake here (see, e.g., the excellent paper by Moore, 1966, which I will quote on other issues below).

[9] As Richard Ohmann once put it, "the idea of alternative phrasings, which is crucial to the notion of style, has a clear analogue within the framework of a transformational grammar" (1970b: 267).

an abstract event. Whereas a declarative sentence as a predication serves to **affect** the beliefs of the addressee, a noun phrase without predication places some event (or state of affairs) at the disposal of the addressee's **perception**, without requiring him to believe that the event actually **has** taken place.

Hearking back to Ohmann's remark quoted in footnote 9, one could be tempted to ask how one is supposed to know, in terms of transformations, which 'deep' structures underlie the given 'surface' forms. For instance, how do we determine that the starting point for the 'transformation' described above ('beating heart' to 'the beating of the heart') is precisely the (prenominal or predicative) adjective *beating,* rather than the regular, referring noun in the NP *the beating?* One may answer this question, in Ohmann's spirit, that the above 'transformation' provides us, if not with *the underlying* string, at least with *some alternative* formulation, to which the stylistic effect of Whitman's phrases can fruitfully be compared.

A more systematic answer is to be found in Strawson's philosophical logic. The word *heart* denotes a spatio-temporally continuous particular, which typically occurs in a referring position, whereas *beating* is a more general term that organizes certain spatio-temporally continuous particulars into **groups** (together with, say, *drums* and *hammers);* such grouping terms occur typically in predicative position. Consequently, in our case, it is this general "grouping" term that is manipulated by the process described above into the referring position. This may also explain why, in an important sense, such phrases are perceived as relatively more marked, that is, why we have the impression that the less marked construction *"beating* heart" has been deliberately avoided.

Having considered the phrase from the point of view of the semantic effect of the 'transformations', let us now turn to another aspect of this process, viz., the absence of a special morpheme for predication. Regardless of how one envisions this absence from the point of view of theory, one thing is certain: one's attention is focused on *beating* rather than on *heart* (cf. also Weinreich, 1970: 122–124). In this fashion, attention is directed **away** from the solid physical object **to** some thing-free and gestalt-free quality. Syntactic constructions like the above (viz., the GERUND of the NOUN) may serve as a convenient tool for the separation between sense-data (or perceptual qualities) and physical objects. In everyday life and language, we do not usually distinguish the two. Perceiving (or speaking of) the one, we almost automatically identify it with the other. However, from the logical point of view, the two are far from identical:

> Now I cannot help thinking that in every case in which I point at an object which I am perceiving and say significantly "This is a tame tiger", "This is a book", my proposition is in fact a proposition about some sense-datum, or some set of sense-data, which I am perceiving; and that part of what I am saying is that this sense-datum (or these sense-data) is "of" a physical object in the sense in which it is true to say of an after-image which I see with my eyes shut that it is *not* "of" a physical object. [...] If "of" stood

here for a relation, we might say that "This is a book" was short for "The thing which this sense-datum is 'of' is a book". (Moore, 1966: 92–93)

We may hypothesize, therefore, using Moore's terminology, that one of the tasks of the "ABSTRACT-of-the-CONCRETE"-genitive-phrases is to generate a de-automatization of the relationship between the sense-data (or perceptual qualities) and the physical object. In terms of "old information", the emphasis is on the sense-data which I perceive *(beating),* rather than on the physical object *(heart).* One way to handle such nominal phrases is to consider them as if, in uttering them, the speaker were saying: I am expressing no facts, no propositions that may be "true" or "false"; I am merely conveying evasive, fragmentary sense impressions, the relationship of which to one another, or to some physical object, is not clear yet.

Such a way of expressing ourselves by way of **showing** (as opposed to **telling**) can be said to represent some low-level consciousness, the low level being due either to our functioning in a less distinct, "pre-conceptual" mental mode, or to certain less favorable perceptual conditions, such as speed, distance, darkness, or all of these together. Sense impressions, as well as "pre-conceptual" mental processes in general, are characterized by a kind of **immediacy:** they take place **here and now.** In order to realize these ends, the text resorts, as a rule, to some deictic device, that presents reality from the angle of the speaker, or the "perceiving consciousness".

Applying this to Whitman's text, this means that the deictic device will be realized, whenever the reader regards phrases such as the ones quoted above as **elliptic** expressions. Elliptic expressions have, typically, two kinds of meaning: deixis (e.g., "Here.", "After you."), and expressing some wish or exclamation (e.g., "Good night!", or "Just a minute!"). As to the former, these expressions suggest two semantic sets: a physical state of affairs on the one hand, and some mental process of immediate perception on the other.[10] To see this, consider expressions containing terms such as "smother…", "heat…", "silence…", "wind…", "rain…", "darkness…"; here, the latter four refer, as it were, to states of affairs, or processes in the physical world, whereas the former two refer to some impression or feeling. However, even a term such as "smother…" refers not only to some feeling, but also to the physical state of affairs that is perceived as causing suffocation; by contrast, the rest of the elliptic expressions refer explicitly to some state of affairs or physical process, as perceived at the time of speaking.

Now compare the following phrases from Whitman's catalog (both belonging to the long quote in (4) above):

(12)   The smoke of my own breath
(13)   The sound of the belched words of my voice

to the following set of phrases

---

[10] In this context, grammarians speak sometimes of feeling vs. state, but it is generally difficult to distinguish the two.

(11)   The sniff of green leaves and dry leaves, and of the shore and dark-
        colored sea-rocks, and of hay in the barn,

We will find significant differences among these phrases both as to their elements and their perceived qualities. First, unlike the phrases in (11), the spatio-temporally continuous particulars in (12) and (13) are thing-free and gestalt-free entities *(breath, words)*. Second, again in contrast to (11), in (12) and (13) both the specific particulars and their abstract properties are **simultaneously present** (I cannot perceive "The **smoke** of my own breath" without "my own breath").

In (12) and (13), *smoke* and *sound* must be regarded as attributes, or properties, or aspects of *my own breath* and of *the belched words of my voice* respectively. These aspects are "grown together" with other properties or attributes, from which they must be abstracted; consequently, their transmutation into the referring position serves, *inter alia*, to destroy the "con-crete" **thing** and to create sets of loosely connected qualities. That is, the process of transformation de-automatizes the relationship between the perceptual quality and the thing "of" which it is a perceptual quality.

We may make, then, the following interim summary of the foregoing discussion. Genitive phrases of the form "the ABSTRACT of the CONCRETE" or "the GERUND of the CONCRETE", which are the result of a nominalized and thematized predicate, that is, of a **topicalized attribute**, tend to de-automatize the relationship between sense data or perceptual qualities and the things "of" which they are the sense data or perceptual qualities. Sometimes, this transformational process is reinforced by additional figurative and syntactic processes; in such cases, the result may be the "destruction" of the physical object in which the various abstract qualities are "grown together", and a set of diffuse, loosely related, abstract qualities is generated. There is a series of conditions that tend to intensify this process: first, the second term of the genitive phrase, the spatio-temporally continuous particular in the CONCRETE position, may itself be a thing-free and gestalt-free entity; second, the attribute topicalized in the phrase may be perceived as not being able to stand apart from the particular term of which it is an attribute; third, the particular term in the second NP may exhibit unlimited spatial expansion, so that the topicalized attribute itself is perceived as diffused over considerable space, thereby enhancing the impression of some low-differentiated, diffuse, dense percept. These conditions seem to be ordered, each later one presupposing the earlier one. The more the linguistic expression obeys the conditions in this series, the more evasive and intense the impression appears to be.

"Shape may", says Meyer (1956: 161) "be regarded as a kind of stylistic 'mean' lying between the extremes of chaotic overdifferentiation and primordial homogeneity". The device of the topicalized attribute causes a dissociation between sense-data (or perceptual qualities) and physical objects; by the same token, it increases chaotic overdifferentiation. Thus, it does not merely increase the number of thing-free qualities in the text, but it may also increase the need for collapsing information into an undifferentiated mass.

In Chapters 1 and 14, I claimed that cognitive stability is bought at the price of relinquishing subtle and minimal pre-categorial cues, perceptible only by intuition: the less differentiated processes become less accessible and less reliable. In some of the amplest instances, the referents of metaphors generated by way of topicalized attributes are typically such information that escapes conceptual-verbal categorization. According to Ehrenzweig, religion and art are among the means that may yield some heightened consciousness of such less differentiated information; hence their great emotional impact. Now, whereas the visual arts and music may have easy recourse to subtle, low-articulated textures, the medium of poetry is language, which is conceptual and logical by its very nature. Cognitive Poetics explores a variety of poetic devices, the purpose of which is to emancipate poetry from the tyranny of concepts and logic, the **topicalized attribute**, as discussed in the present section, being one of them.

The Control of Attention

In (7) above, I reformulated the instruction for the mental performance of (4) in a manner that implied alternative ways of handling verbal and poetic information. But I gave no indication as to what these alternative ways might be in the case of the specific verbal material of the catalog. Our discussion of the **nominalized predicate** in the foregoing section supplies the description of the verbal units which can be handled in a variety of ways, so as to cause, respectively avoid, cognitive overload on one's processing space.

Let us now return to a simplified version of the quotation in (11).

> (14)   The sniff of the dark-colored sea-rocks

Two comments seem to be appropriate here: first, that **both** the noun *sniff* and the phrase *dark-colored sea-rocks* can easily occur in referring position, since they can be perceived independently from one another; and second, that the latter phrase denotes a solid object. In both these respects, (14) contrasts with such phrases as the ones in (12) and (13); (14) is, therefore, more in harmony with what I have called *cognitive stability*. This, however, does not imply that the phrase in (14) cannot receive, quite legitimately, **different kinds of attention.** When we contrast it with wordings in which some semantic equivalent of *sniff* is grammatically subordinated, as an adjective, to *sea-rocks* as, for instance, in

> (15)   The odorous dark-colored sea-rocks,

we still perceive that *sniff* in (14) is the main noun, gaining some independent existence by loosening, to some extent, its close association with the stable visual object. Thus, when we compare (14) to (12) or (13), it is the stable categories and objects that are foregrounded in it; when we compare it to a version in which the solid object with a prenominal adjective is in the referring position, it is the unstable, evasive perceptual quality that is foregrounded. This is not necessarily a mere academic exercise, but may have some psychological reality. The reader seems to have some control over his cognitive resources in performing such a line, so as to perceive it in one way rather than another.

Hence, we seem to have considerable freedom in allocating our cognitive resources. Under certain circumstances, we may quite freely shift our attention back and forth from the stable categories to the inarticulate, "unstable", pre-categorial information. In this connection, I wish to invoke Jerry Fodor, who, in trying to find some psychological evidence for "the structure of the internal code", came up against two competing models, the one put forward by Treisman, the other by Lackner and Garrett. Both models were developed through a kind of studies in which the subject listens to tape-recorded signals presented dichotically through headphones, with a different signal being transmitted through each phone. We are interested here in the way Fodor handles the inconsistencies between the competing models.

> [...] what the data uncontrovertibly show is that the all-or-none model (either a full representation of the input is available or nothing is) won't do. [...] In either case, the hearer apparently has a good deal of freedom in deciding how the internal representation of an impinging stimulus is to be handled. Remember that, in both the Treisman and the Garrett and Lackner studies [...] the processing differences are determined, at least in part, by [the subject]'s decision to attend to the material in one channel and to ignore the material in the other. (Fodor, 1975: 163)

In our case, we might paraphrase Fodor to the effect that the reader has a great deal of freedom in deciding whether to attend to the stable categories, or to the inarticulate precategorial information. In other words, we may imagine two readings of (11) (and of (14)), one in which *cognitive stability* is reinforced, and one in which it is undermined. In still other words, (11) (and (14)) are, in spite of their topicalized attribute, capable of a performance that does *not* generate a thing-free atmosphere, but rather evokes a solid world of physical objects. As Fodor puts it,

> On either model, the psychological states of the organism are implicated in determining which of the potentially available representations of the stimulus is the one that in fact mediates the production of behavior. To put the point more generally, the organism's exploitation of its representational capacities is, in some systematic way, responsive to its utilities. (Fodor, ibid.)

Applied to our case, this is to say that the psychological states of the reader "are implicated in determining which of the potentially available representations of the stimulus" will generate the perceived quality of the verse-passage. The reader's attitude, in turn, is determined to a considerable extent by the psychological atmosphere of the specific text: whether it contains solid objects or thing-free qualities. This determination, however, is not total: *some* voluntary control over the direction of his attention the reader still does have.

This last issue regarding control of attention throws some new light on the recommendations formulated in (6) and (7):

> (6)   Perform the poem in such a way that it should be perceived as one that indicates some altered state of consciousness.

> (7)   Perform the catalog in such a way that its itemization results in a cognitive overload on your processing space, thus compelling you to collapse the excess information into an undifferentiated mass.

Suppose we offer some such recommendation to a reader of (4), what are the specific cognitive attitudes that we might expect him to assume? Or what specific cognitive operations could we expect him to perform? We might expect him, for instance, to focus attention upon the topicalized attributes in the referring position, so as to destroy the **things** and to create sets of loosely connected qualities; that is, to focus upon the de-automatized relationship between the perceptual quality and the thing "of" which it is a perceptual quality. This would both increase the cognitive load on his processing space, and facilitate the "collapsing" of this information into an "undifferentiated mass". This might indicate, by way of **showing**, (rather than explicitly telling about), some low-level consciousness resulting from a low-level cognitive functioning, from some "pre-conceptual" mental process underlying the altered state of consciousness associated above with (4).

Poetry of Meditation

The poetry of meditation is one of the most conspicuous kinds of poetry related to altered states of consciousness. As Louis Martz has rightly insisted, it is quite difficult to distinguish instances of poetry of meditation from instances of ecstatic poetry, as poetry of meditation frequently has recourse to ecstatic imagery; and conversely, as the foregoing discussion has suggested, the different varieties of mystic poetry *may* have clear-cut secular versions.

The poetry of meditation may be approached from a variety of directions. The foregoing discussion of Whitman's meditative catalog does not presume to exhaust the poetic significance of meditation. At least two more approaches ought to be considered as relevant to the subject of the present book. In what follows, I propose briefly to indicate the place of the present approach in relation to these.

When Louis Martz (1962) defined "The Poetry of Meditation", he did so with special reference to the meditative tradition of Jesuit writings and practices. In the concluding chapter of the first edition of his book, Martz extended his referential framework, and spoke of a "meditative style" in general; by the time he was preparing the second edition, he had come to the conclusion that it is more accurate to speak of the "meditative poem", as a genre that can be composed in a variety of styles. In the concluding chapter, Martz points to a number of romantic and modern poets who wrote poems in this genre in a variety of styles, obeying its intuitive rules, without being necessarily aware of them. Here, I shall adopt his definition:

> A meditative poem is a work that creates an interior drama of the mind; this dramatic action is usually (though not always) created by some form of self-address, in which the mind grasps firmly a problem or situation deliberately evoked by the memory, brings it forward toward the full light of consciousness, and concludes with a moment of illumination, where the speaker's self has, for a time, found an answer to its conflicts. (Martz, 1962: 330)

Martz believes that the emotional force of methodical meditation (and of the meditative poem)

> may be attributed to the fact that it satisfied and developed a natural, fundamental tendency of the human mind—a tendency to work from a particular situation, through analysis of that situation, and finally to some sort of resolution of the problems which the situation has presented. (Martz, 1962: 39)

Of the three stages which Martz (following St. Ignatius in the introductory instructions to his *Spiritual Exercises*) distinguishes in formal meditation and in meditative poetry, composition (memory), analysis (understanding), and colloquy (affection, will), the first one, more precisely called "composition of place" (*compositio loci*), deserves special attention here. Saint Ignatius was very particular about it: "the composition will be to see with the eyes of the imagination the corporeal place where the thing I wish to contemplate is found" (ibid., 27). "Even more important for the poet, St. Ignatius directs that one also use the image-forming faculty to provide a concrete and vivid setting for a meditation on invisible things" (ibid., 28). This, on the one hand, should be seen in connection with what was said above, in Chapter 11, viz., that we do not experience abstractions but particular situations: "the awareness of finitude is not purely conceptual or hypothetical; it is an awareness of *my actual being* as being here (in this time and place) rather than there, as restricted in this particular concrete way". On the other hand, the notion of composition of place must be connected with my conception of the relationship between space perception and emotional qualities in poetry. As I have remarked in Chapter 15, both Romantic and Metaphysical poetry are typically set in a concrete situation sharply defined *here and now*. This is why the typical Romantic version of the medi-

tative poem so often begins with a meticulous description of the surrounding nature—the "composition of place", if you like. It should be further examined to what
extent this notion of meditative genre can be fruitfully applied as a "regulative concept"; at any rate, the immediate eperience of a particular situation and the emotional
qualities associated with space perception may certainly account for the great emotional impact of these romantic "meditative poems".

Another, quite different approach, was propounded by the present author in a previous work (Tsur, 1974): I tried to show there how the same "Holy Sonnet" by
Donne can be read as a poem, a prayer, and a meditation at different times. I distinguished between these categories in terms of Jakobson's language functions, but extended these so as to entail further semantic and pragmatic distinctions. In the present theoretical framework, this explains how the same Holy Sonnet by Donne can
be read as a poem, a prayer, and a meditation, in different mental performances.

The section on Whitman of the present chapter is an attempt to characterize
"meditative" in terms of the reader's mental activities as well as of the various texts'
verbal structures. By doing this, it contributes in two important aspects to an understanding of mental performance: as a pair of mental devices for handling cognitive
overload in poetry reading: *conceptual categorization,* and *dumping into an undifferentiated "ground"-mass;* and as a conception according to which significant stylistic
distinctions between similar poetic structures can be made, depending on the kind of
mental performances they require or afford. Finally, the "essential mediation between
the macrostructure and microstructure which results in the total effect" of the
Whitman catalog has been detailed as the relationship between the overall meditative
structure and one particular kind of genitive phrase, the "topicalized attribute", which
is relatively rare in language in general, but is quite conspicuous in this specific
passage.[11]

To sum up: The present chapter has illustrated the relationship between poetry and
altered states of consciousness, explaining the latter in their relationship to Cognitive Poetics' conception of poetry, from a variety of angles. We have considered
these altered states of consciousness in poetry in the light of the *telling ~ showing*
dichotomy, and have distinguished between a low-differentiated image of a low-differentiated state of mind, and a high-differentiated image of such a state. Finally, we
have considered the different mental activities involved in a conceptual and a meditative performance of Whitman's catalogs.

---

[11] The argument of this chapter, especially of the last section, has been considerably
expanded in a recent book (Tsur, 2003).

CHAPTER 19

Obtrusive Rhythms
and Emotive Crescendo

This chapter is devoted to two important principles of poetic organization which are of relevance in connection with the altered states of consciousness discussed in the previous chapter. The first principle is one of prosodic organization, which I call "Obtrusive Rhythms"; it underlies what Snyder (1930) has called "hypnotic" or "spell-weaving" or "trance-inductive" poetry. The second consists in a pattern of gradually intensified emotion; I call it "emotive crescendo". In Chapter 4, above, I distinguished between convergent and divergent poetry. The former is typically witty or rational, the latter typically emotional. In the present chapter, I shall claim that regular, convergent rhythms are "double-edged": in certain circumstances, they may underlie some altered states of consciousness, most notably "hypnotic poetry". In such instances I speak of "Obtrusive Rhythms".

Obtrusive Rhythms & Hypnotic Poetry

In this section of the present chapter, I shall consider a rather puzzling phenomenon of poetry. In a number of poems by Poe, Coleridge, and certain other poets, readers are inclined to "attend away" from the meaning of the words, and to become "spell-bound" by their sound. The reader feels as if he were entangled by the sounds of these poems, and tends to perceive their meaning relatively dimly. Among the most conspicuous features of these poems are their "obtrusive rhythms", rhythms that impose themselves upon the reader, as it were. Such rhythms are derived from a meter that is more than usually regular. I have elsewhere (Tsur, 1977: 83–96) discussed at great length a widely noted phenomenon in poetry: the trochaic and the ternary meters in many languages "exert their will" more vigorously than the iambic meter, and therefore tend to be, by their very nature, perceived as more obtrusive. In English poetry, where the most widespread meter is the iambic, these "obtrusive rhythms" are sometimes trochaic, and sometimes ternary (even though, sometimes, iambic meters do appear as "obtrusive"). In addition, obtrusive rhythms draw upon repetitions at "higher" ranks of organization, such as verse lines repeated with no sufficient justification by the contents, or significantly repeated phrases (which are not infrequently formulaic). Sometimes, too, anaphoric or epiphoric repetitions (the ending of a series of units of discourse with the same word or words) are in evidence. In several of the poems containing obtrusive rhythms, the regular stanzaic organization is "disrupted" in one way or other, either by (regular or irregular) alternation of various stanza forms, or due to the occurrence of a longer than usual sequence of lines ending with the same rhyme, or of a casual order of verse lines, that is, where the order of rhymes or the number and length of lines is unpredictable. At other times, on the contrary, everything is all too predictable: not only the number of lines and order of rhymes is fixed in every stanza but, what is more, certain formulaic key terms recur in the rhymes at pre-determined points.[1]

It has been observed time and again that poems of the kind discussed here tend to puzzle the critics: "Critics tend to praise the kind of poetry they understand", as Snyder succinctly has put it. By contrast, one of the prevalent critical responses to such poetry is disapproval or disparagement. Some critics argue that the poet must have got carried away by the rhythms of his own poem, forgetting, as it were, the dimension of meaning; they treat the poem as if it were no more than a "glorified nursery rhyme"—in Elizabeth Schneider's phrase. Other critics follow an opposite strategy: they decide to "attend away" from the sound dimension, back to the dimension of meaning. These critics dwell in great detail on the meaning context of the poem, on the immediate situation and the plot of which it forms a part—whether they speak of the literal meaning of the poem, or indulge in allegoresis. On such a reading, the sound dimension of the poem is relegated to a marginal position. Only very rarely one may encounter an interpretation which has as its point of departure the assumption that we are confronted with a peculiar interplay of sound and meaning, that the particular effect of the poem derives precisely from an increase of the relative weight of the sound texture and a decrease of the relative weight of the meaning—and this as a special achievement, not as a failure to achieve some aesthetically more respectable accomplishment.

Above, I quoted Snyder who, in his remarkable little book (1930), calls such poems "hypnotic", or "spell-weaving", or "trance-inducing". He argues that such

> poems have a peculiar trance-inducing technique; that they owe their mysterious "spell" to a magic no more incomprehensible than that of hypnotism; that by intensifying the listeners' suggestibility they permit experiences where—for better or for worse—the poet holds sway over the listeners' conscious and subconscious mind. (Snyder, 1930: 38)

Second, in my various writings on prosody, I have assumed that the effect of verse with a tendency to metric regularity is "double-edged", in fact "triple-edged" (cf. Tsur, 1983: 30–33; 1985; 2006). (a) Regular meter implies a clear contrast be-

---

[1]   In my book on Hebrew hypnotic poetry (Tsur, 1988a), I have shown that the same poetic devices underlie the same kind of poetic effects in certain poems by Nathan Alterman and Jonathan Ratosh.

tween prominent and non-prominent syllables. In this sense, regular meter has a strong rational quality (as in, e.g., Pope's poetry); it has good shape (strong gestalt), "it creates a psychological atmosphere of certainty, security, and patent purpose"; it exhibits definite directions and organizes percepts into predictable orders (see above, Chapter 5). (b) Regular meter may indicate a simplified mastery of reality, as in nursery rhymes. (c) The vigorous impact of regular meter may have the effect of heightening the emotional responsiveness that underlies hypnotic or ecstatic experiences; this is the business of the present chapter. In other words, regular meter shares some important properties with conscious control and the exercise of will; at the same time, it is akin to some basic involuntary physiological processes, many of which consist of regularly recurring events. Intense physical and emotional activities in humans and animals increasingly tend to establish a regular rhythm and to transcend voluntary control. Consequently, one factor that differentiates between the regular meter underlying a witty poem and that underlying an ecstatic poem is the energy level inherent in other layers of the poem. Thus, whereas the first two effects are the unmarked potentials of regular meter, the third is the marked effect; it obtains in special circumstances only. To point out these "special circumstances" requires lengthy analyses at a great variety of strata of the poem (as a "stratified system of norms").

The concept at the root of this double- (or triple-) edged effect is *security*. It is intimately related to the dichotomy propounded in Chapter 21, between *negative capability* and the *quest for certitude*. As research by Frenkel-Brunswick (1968) has shown, the intolerance of ambiguity may interfere with one's free emotional responses. Another author, J. C. Ransom, has suggested that a fairly predictable meter may dispel anxiety in the presence of ambiguity—give "false security to the Platonic censor in us" (quoted by Chatman 1965: 212)—so that the reader may feel free to attend to ambiguities in the other layers of the poem. The crucial question seems to be whether the psychological atmosphere generated by "good metric shape" is of genuine or false "certainty, security, patent purpose", etc. That is to say, if other layers of the poem, too, have a rational quality, then the psychological atmosphere is one of genuine certainty, etc. If, however, some other layers of the poem induce some intense psychological atmosphere of uncertainty—as, for example, the "unreal" visions of "Kubla Khan" or "The Ancient Mariner"—regular meter will impart "false security", it will lull the vigilant "Platonic censor in us" and make it accept the emotional quality of the poem. By the same token, and at the same time, vigorous rhythms have a strong bodily appeal, amplifying whatever irrational qualities there may be.

The third and fourth aspects to be discussed are related, within the foregoing framework, to rhyme: grammatical and anti-grammatical rhyme (discussed above in chapter 9), and the grouping of verse lines by rhyme within the stanza (as discussed in Chapter 5). The fifth aspect concerns the perceived emotional qualities of speech sounds (as discussed in Chapter 8).

My book on Coleridge's "Kubla Khan" (Tsur, 2006) devotes its second chapter to a lengthy demonstration of how an enormous variety of elements, some of which are discussed throughout Chapters14 and 18–20 of the present work, are integrated in that poem, so as to contribute to its unusually intense hypnotic and ecstatic quality. Here, I shall only occasionally refer to that earlier work; instead, I shall attempt to present some of the essentials of hypnotic poetry with reference to brief passages from three poems by Edgar Allan Poe.

Poe's poems are notorious for their "obtrusive", regular meter. Excerpts (1)–(4) meet, to a considerable extent, the requirements of the metric rule "Stressed syllables occur in strong positions only". Such compounds as *woodland* and *ghoul-haunted* in (2), and *lamp-light* in (4) have their first main stress (as is the case in Pope's poetry) in strong positions (not as in Milton's, in weak positions). Even the stressed syllables in weak positions *(bright* in (1) and *mid, dim,* and *dark* in (2)) are perceptually overridden by the strenuous ternary meter.

Let us approach our subject through a consideration of the contribution of the rhymes in these excerpts to the "hypnotic" effect in question.

In Chapter 9, I distinguished between grammatical and anti-grammatical rhyme, and have suggested that the former is perceived as "tame", the latter as "vigorous". One way to increase the vigor involved in anti-grammatical rhyme is to increase the number of phonemes shared by the rhyme-fellows, while contrasting in them as many meaning components, as high on the list of features as possible (see above, Chapter 9, for details on the 'list'). A "monotonous" sound points up the diversity of meaning components, and vice versa. A further means of increasing vigor would be to contrast more than one morpheme in the rhyming words. Let us consider the rhyme structure in three of Poe's most famous poems.

(1)   For the moon never beams without bringing me dreams
              Of the beautiful Annabel Lee.
        And the stars never rise but I see the bright eyes
              Of the beautiful Annabel Lee.

                                    ("Annabel Lee")

(2)   The skies they were ashen and sober   *Adj.*
        The leaves they were crisped and sere—
        The leaves they were withering and sere: *Adj.*
        It was night in the lonesome October   *Noun*
        Of my most immemorial year.   *Noun*
        It was hard by the dim lake of Auber,   *Noun*
        In the misty mid region of Weir—   *Noun*
        It was down by the dank tarn of Auber,
        In the ghoul-haunted woodland of Weir.

                                    ("Ulalume")

(3)   Ah, distinctly I remember: it was in the bleak December,
       And each separate dying ember wrought its ghost upon the floor...

                                                      ("The Raven")

(4)   And the Raven, never flitting, still is sitting, still is sitting
       On the pallid bust of Pallas just above my chamber door;
       And his eyes have all the seeming of a demon's that is dreaming,
       And the lamp-light o'er him streaming throws his shadows on the

                                                              floor;

       And my soul from out the shadow that lies floating on the floor
       Shall be lifted — nevermore.

                                                      ("The Raven")

There is a double semantic opposition in (1), between *beams* and *dreams:* here the
verb *beams* is contrasted to the noun *dreams,* while the phoneme /s/ contrasts two
morphemes of opposite nature, [–PLURAL +3d PERSON] and [+PLURAL]. Likewise,
eyes forms an echo rhyme with *rise* (is wholly included in it), contrasting a verb
with a noun, as well as an /s/ that forms a suffix with an /s/ that is part of the root.
By contrast, line 4 in (1) is a verbatim repetition of line 2, with no contrast in
meaning (though the second line in itself may be ambiguous: here, the preposition
of has two different meanings, expressing an 'object' vs. a 'subject' relation, respectively). As to (4), I only wish to point out that in the rhyme *seeming ~ dreaming ~
streaming* we have, under the identical surface structures, three different 'deep' parts
of speech: the first one is a noun (gerund), the second one a verb (present progressive), the third one an adjective (present participle). Lines 2, 4 and 5 rhyme with
more in the last line; and this is the case in all the stanzas of this poem ("The
Raven"). Moreover, lines 4 and 5 both end with the same phrase, in the same literal
meaning, *on the floor.* Poe offers here an additional opposition: an extreme case of
unity-in-variety (the anti-grammatical rhymes) vs. extreme cases of unity-without-
variety (verbatim repetition posing as rhyme). What may be the intended effect of
such a construction? In order to clarify this, let us have a look at the excerpts in (1),
(2), and (3), inasmuch as they represent the respective poems from which they are
culled. From the point of view of theme, as well as of atmosphere, these poems
range from communication with the other world, through the presence of the uncanny, to the intrusion of the preternatural into our world.
    In Poe's poetry, the face-to-face encounter with the irruption of the uncanny is
closely related with a notorious musical quality, that has its source in the more than
usually regular meter and a combination of anti-grammatical rhyme with *epiphora*
replacing rhyme. This peculiar combination is directed toward a peculiar effect which
goes beyond the opposition of the extremely monotonous with the extremely diver-
sified. My claim is that the repetition of identical (or nearly identical) lines and
rhyme words (or even of anti-grammatical rhyme pairs as in *floor ~ more* at pre-assigned places) enhances the regular effect of metrical convergence which, under cer-

tain circumstances, may have an incantatory effect and contribute to an uncanny atmosphere in the poem. One of those "certain circumstances" is that the atmosphere is felt to be loaded with high energy; the anti-grammatical rhyme then increases this level of energy. In a paper on emotional qualities in poetry, I concluded the discussion of the emotional quality in Blake's "The Tyger" as follows:

> Convergent rhythmic patterns typically count for non-emotional qualities. In this poem, the tremendous energy and emotional qualities implied by syntactic structure and figurative language override, so to speak, the witty or playful (or, for that matter, simplifying) potential of the rhythm. ... (Tsur, 1978: 177)

The value of Poe's poetry is highly controversial. Mallarmé and his circle regarded Poe as the grand master of poetry, who penetrated into the core of Mystery, and had an insight into the weird forces at work behind the visible world. Today, Poe's poetry enjoys a considerably lower esteem. I would like to suggest that the present conception can account for these contradictory evaluations. It is not only that some readers are unwilling to grant that it is worth having an insight into Poe's version of the uncanny. The issue at stake is whether "the tremendous energy and emotional qualities" in the poem are strong enough to override the simplifying quality of the regular rhythm, and confer an incantatory quality upon it or, on the contrary, whether the (more than usually) regular meter has a simplifying effect on what pretends to be an emotional quality.

A few more observations seem to be pertinent here. Feminine rhymes are particularly effective in English, because they seem difficult to achieve (they draw upon a very limited reservoir of words). This effectiveness is heightened in excerpt (2) by the adjective ~ noun rhyme *sober ~ October (Auber),* and in excerpt (3) by the verb ~ noun rhyme *remember ~ December,* followed by the echo rhyme *ember.* Poe seems to have been fond of month names in rhymes. In excerpt (2), he rhymes *October* with the adjective *sober,* and with the proper name *Auber,* in excerpt (3)—*remember* with *December,* thus producing unfamiliar feminine rhymes. Representing abstract conceptions of time and being proper names, they may be conveniently contrasted not only with other parts of speech, but even with most nouns (as *ember)* by features fairly high on our list (see above, Chapter 9), such as [±CONCRETE] and/or [±PROPER]. In addition, *December* and *October* are metonymies for seasons; they denote an abstraction and connote a winter or autumn atmosphere, respectively, an atmosphere that is reinforced by the epithets *lonesome* and *bleak.* In the present context, I wish to make an additional point. The three members of the rhyme *sober ~ October ~ Auber* appear to have an increasing impact of musicality, in this order. As we recalled in Chapter 3, proper names have no descriptive contents; however, such month names as *December, October* still carry some connotations of an emotional atmosphere. Thus, the members of this rhyme appear to occur in a decreasing order of descriptive content. This may perhaps provide a specific illustration of the inverse relationship that has been observed between the weight of meaning and perceived musicality in this kind of poetry.

As to *October,* it fulfills a very peculiar poetic function in excerpt (2). From the prosodic point of view, it is highlighted by being part of a sophisticated, feminine, anti-grammatical rhyme. From the semantic point of view, it must be considered in the context of the cognitive mechanisms discussed in the chapter on space perception (above, Chapter 15). In the present case, we have a scene quite strictly defined in time and space; but no objects have been mentioned in it that have stable, characteristic visual shapes. This is typically a scene in which the perceiving consciousness can only relate itself to the great directions of the dimly-perceptible surrounding space. *October* contributes here to the definition of the scene in time and, by the same token, it provides an abstraction that is heavily loaded with an emotional atmosphere, to be perceived *diffusely* in a concrete landscape. The immediate landscape is indicated merely by the description of the skies in the first line, and of the leaves in the second and third lines. But this seems sufficient to prevent the "misty mid region of Weir" and the "dim lake of Auber" from remaining an abstraction on an imaginary atlas: they become part of an immediate concrete landscape, contributing specific perceptual qualities to its atmosphere.

The stanza in question has nine verse lines, and consists of two rhymes only; one of them is masculine, and its vowel is a long, front, high vowel: *sere* (twice), *year,* and *Weir* (twice). The other rhyme is feminine, and its stressed syllable contains a long, back, mid vowel. The two rhymes appear to be inextricably interwoven, on the one hand; on the other, they are contrasted in almost every respect, as I have suggested. In addition, the [FRONT ~ BACK] opposition entails a perceptual opposition as well: that of bright ~ dark. From this point of view, the rhymes introduce a considerable sense of movement into the stanza. Contrasting with this, within each rhyme we find a peculiar combination of movement and static reiteration which is, as indicated above, quite characteristic of this kind of "spell-weaving", "hypnotic" poetry. *Sere ~ year* and *sober ~ October* constitute, as suggested above, vigorous anti-grammatical rhymes, that are further spun out by the (imaginary) geographic names which *(qua* proper nouns) have no descriptive contents. At the same time, we have got the monotonous reduplication of *sere, Weir* and *Auber* instead of rhymes.

At the present point of my argument, I wish to consider excerpt (2) from the point of view of a principle pointed out by Snyder in his discussion of Gray's "Elegy Written in a Country Churchyard" as a specimen of hypnotic poetry. Let us follow his description of the first quatrain, which he considers to be "one of the most harmonious stanzas". "The meter is iambic with only two such slight departures from regularity as serve to keep it from being painfully mechanical" (Snyder, 1930: 51).

> The vowel effects are singularly interesting; but as the present state of knowledge on the psychological effectiveness of "dark" and "light" vowels is rather dubious, I will not risk giving evidence on this point, however

tantalizing the temptation may be. But the consonantal effects—to consider only the most obvious ones—are, I think, unique. Even Poe with his
adroit choice of the name "Lenore" and his rather artificial coinage of the
name "Ulalume", never quite equaled the skill with which liquids and
nasals are repeated in the *Elegy*. […] Thus, a careful inspection shows that
in these four lines every accented syllable save one—and it is the accented
syllables that really count—either ends in a vowel sound or involves a liquid or a nasal! […] Liquids and nasals are capitalized.

> the cuRfew toLLs the kNeLL of paRtiNG day,
> the LowiNG heRd wiNd sLowLy o'eR the Lea,
> the pLowMaN hoMewaRd pLods his weaRy way.
> aNd Leaves the woRLd to daRkNess aNd to Me.

The second and third stanzas, like the first, continue, so far as versification
is concerned, to employ the very highest artistry to satisfy and soothe the
ear; and, with only slight modification, the same thing may be said of the
whole poem. (Snyder, 1930: 51–52)

I have discussed this observation at some length in another context, that of the
emotional symbolism of speech sounds (Tsur, 1992: 45–47; cf. also above, Chapter
8); I shall reproduce part of that discussion (of course, with the necessary changes)
here. One of my main arguments is that in the "speech mode", all of the acoustic
impulses that carry the phonetic information are excluded from consciousness. In the
"poetic mode", some of these acoustic impulses subliminally *do* reach awareness,
and—when interacting with some other aspects of the text—may have a crucial influence on its perceived emotional quality. It is in this framework that one must
consider Snyder's observation that "every accented syllable save one […] either ends
in a vowel sound or involves a liquid or a nasal". What vowels, nasals, and liquids
have in common is that all are acoustically periodical. And in periodical sounds, the
acoustic sensory information reaches awareness more easily than in aperiodical
sounds. Snyder only vaguely indicates what the significance of this observation may
be (such as when he says that even Poe "never quite equaled this skill", and that it
had to do with "soothing the ear"). Now, the significance of Snyder's observation on
the vowels, liquids and nasals in Gray's "Elegy" will become apparent when we realize that Snyder pointed out some of the characteristics of hypnotic poetry in terms
that are very similar to my description of periodic and aperiodic sounds. Two such
aspects of hypnotic poetry mentioned by Snyder are the "skillful avoid[ance of]
whatever is 'startling'", and the "preserv[ation of] a marked regularity of rhythm"
(Snyder, 1930: 41). In other words, "practically all of these poems show an interesting parallel to hypnotism [in] their freedom from any abrupt changes which would
be likely to break the spell, and especially freedom from such ideas as compel mental alertness" (ibid.). In my own book on the poetic mode of speech perception, pe-

riodic sounds were characterized as "the recurrence of signal portions with similar structure" (see above, Chapter 8); this, on a miniature scale is akin to "regularity of rhythm" on a larger scale. Likewise, aperiodic sounds were said to have "randomly changing wave form", with "more idiosyncratic features to be remembered". This seems to be akin, on the detailed acoustic level, to what has been characterized on the level of ideas as abrupt changes that compel mental alertness, "skillfully" to be avoided by hypnotic poetry. As to the effects of periodic compared to those of aperiodic sounds, these have been characterized as follows: "The recurring signal portions with similar structures may arouse in the perceiver a relatively relaxed kind of attentiveness (there will be no surprises, one may expect the same wave form to recur). Thus, periodic sounds are experienced as smoothly flowing. The randomly changing wave forms of aperiodic sounds, with their 'idiosyncratic features', are experienced as disorder, as a disruption of the relaxed kind of attentiveness" (Tsur, 1992: 45). Thus, it seems quite plausible (as Snyder may have felt intuitively) that vowels, liquids, and nasals in prominent positions in a hypnotic poem reinforce, on the sub-phonemic acoustic level, a quality that is typically experienced in such poems on other, more easily discernible levels. The prominence of such periodic sounds in stressed syllables is **not** an indispensable characteristic of "hypnotic" poetry; but once it is there, it may greatly enhance the effects noted on the more palpable levels, at the same time rendering these effects somehow more evasive. In particular, for our discussion of "Ulalume" one should also note that the rhyme words *day ~ way* in Gray's "Elegy" (that do not end with a vowel or a liquid or a nasal) end with the glide [j]; as we know, glides are acoustically quite similar to the afore-mentioned phonetic categories of vowels, liquids and nasals.[2] This observation is also relevant for our discussion of Poe's poem "Ulalume" (a portion of which was reproduced above as (2)). About this poem, Bowra writes, among other things:

> [Poe] sometimes tries to make words appeal entirely or almost entirely through their sound [...]. On the whole, he limits this process to proper names which create an unearthly atmosphere and suggest that we are no longer in the familiar world. A striking example of this is in "Ulalume". Poe sets the scene in a landscape of his own invention to which he gives names appropriate simply because of their sound. It would be useless to ask more about them, and we accept at their sound-value the *dim tarn of Auber,* the *misty mid region of Weir,* and the volcano **M**ou**n**t Yaa**n**ek. (Bowra, 1961: 191)

It will be noticed that I have printed in bold letters the liquids, nasals, and glides in the quoted phrases. The consonants in the name *Ulalume* itself are liquids; its initial sound is the glide /j/. But this technique is not confined to proper names, even though it may be more palpable there. On the next page, Bowra writes:

---

[2]   By this criterion, the consonantal occurrences of *w* in Grey's stanza would increase the total number of periodic sounds by five.

> The meaning of *immemorial* is "old beyond memory", and since this is
> purely negative, it does not admit degrees of comparison. Of course, it is
> possible that, in defiance of linguistic usage, Poe is trying to suggest an
> infinitely remote past. But is it not plausible that he is trying to do some-
> thing else, to give *immemorial* a new meaning, which, according to his
> precepts, is indefinite and amounts to some such significance as "deep in
> memory"? (ibid., 192)

Notice again that all the consonants in this long word are liquids and nasals; furthermore, its stressed vowel is a "dark", back vowel (something to which I shall return in a moment). In addition to the words and phrases already mentioned, we find
in this stanza such expressions as "The leaves they were withering and sere", and
"In the ghoul-haunted woodland of Weir". Special attention is deserved by the word
lonesome in line four. Three out of its four consonants are liquids or nasals, and
both its vowels are "dark", back vowels. Its stressed vowel recurs in the stressed syllables of *October, most,* and *immemorial.* The first three sounds of *most* are included in *lonesome,* albeit in a different order. Such a phonetic crisscross reinforces,
in the memory of the reader, the traces of the speech sounds involved, by generating
an intense sound texture that impresses itself on the reader's perception.

The intrusion of the mysterious, low-differentiated otherworldly quality into this
world is indicated by "the ghoul-haunted woodland of Weir" (incidentally, does the
word *Weir* sound, its etymology notwithstanding, like a variant of *weird?).* This
quality is enhanced through reference to entities that indicate, in one way or another,
impeded sensory or general cognitive functioning: *ashen, night, immemorial, hard,
dim, misty, dank,* and perhaps also *woodland.* In other words, the perception of the
scene is very low-differentiated. It is in this context that we should consider the relative abundance and prominence of "dark", back vowels in Poe's "Ulalume".

In Chapter 8 above, I summarize some of my arguments in my book on the poetic mode of speech perception (Tsur, 1992) drawing, among others, upon Fónagy
(1961: 194). Fónagy mentions Macdermott who, through a statistical analysis of
English poems, found that "dark vowels are more frequent in lines referring to dark
colours, mystic obscurity, or slow and heavy movement, or depicting hatred and
struggle". To account for such findings, I have provided some empirical evidence
that pre-categorial sensory information is perceived in back vowels as considerably
undifferentiated. Relatively low differentiation in vowel perception is, then, naturally matched with darkness when the FRONT ~ BACK and dark ~ bright continua are
perceived as analogous. Furthermore, frequent back vowels in verse lines that refer
to dark colors realize their dark potential by combination with the dark elements of
the meaning. Readers may have an intuition that the sound is somehow "an echo of
the sense", or that the sounds are somehow "expressive" of the sense. Somehow (as
implied by Macdermott), the conventionally established metaphorical relationship
between darkness and mystic "obscurity", or between darkness and such emotions as

hatred, seems to mediate between vowel color and such meaning components. Following my analysis, I suggest in Chapter 8 that the relatively undifferentiated perceptions associated with the back vowels may be *directly related to* the low-differentiated perception associated with mystic "obscurity"; there is no need for a mediating metaphorical concept.

There is one more crucial issue which we ought to consider in connection with excerpt (2): the structure of the stanza and the grouping effect of rhymes. As I have indicated in the introductory paragraph to this section, hypnotic poetry, quite characteristically, tends to have peculiar stanza structures. In three instances we find repetition of the same word instead of rhyme, in the examples quoted above. The various instances of the phenomenon in question are not of one kind: they represent two different patterns. The last four lines of this stanza show the *abab* pattern, with a strong, symmetrical shape. This pattern is, however, defective, as instead of *rhyming* words, the same words are repeated. This has a particularly "tame", or even "stale" effect, especially when contrasted to the vigorous, anti-grammatical rhymes in the same stanza. Looking at the first five lines of the stanza, we find an entirely different picture. Here, the repetition disturbs, rather than confirms, the *abab* pattern. Suppose we omit line 3, then we obtain a quatrain with an unusually vigorous effect, owing to its symmetry and virtuoso anti-grammatical rhymes. Here, one of the conspicuous effects of the near-iteration of the second line is the weakening of the strong shape of the symmetrical stanza. Now, suppose we remove all the identical endings, obtaining a six-line stanza as in excerpt (5):

(5)   The skies they were ashen and sober
       The leaves they were crisped and sere:
       It was night in the lonesome October
       Of my most immemorial year.
       It was down by the dank tarn of Auber,
       In the ghoul-haunted woodland of Weir.

In Chapter 5, I have discussed at length the principles which may account for the various perceptual groupings of a stanza such as the one discussed here. Its rhyme structure, *ababab,* can be grouped in two different ways. According to one grouping, the first two units are divided into two identical parts, *ab.* While the first two lines "disturb" the perceptual field, the next two lines "close" its shape and balance it, by matching each line with a similar ending. This yields a symmetrical, closed *abab* quatrain, that has a strong, balanced, stable shape. But this can be done only at the price of isolating the last two lines, leaving a loose end in the shape of an additional unit *ab,* anew disturbing the perceptual field, without providing the matching, "balancing" lines. These two lines tend to "re-open" the closed and balanced structure, and dispel the feeling of focal stability already achieved. Thus they may lead to the other grouping, according to which the stanza is divided into three identical groups of *ab* lines. In this case, no closed, symmetrical, stable shape arises, but rather a fluid set of similar, but unstable units, a running sequence of *ab*–groups which could be continued indefinitely. The syntactic, thematic, or rhetorical structure of the text may induce the reader to group lines in each stanza either in one way or the other.

Let us have a look at a stanza originally written in that form, taken from Byron's "Hebrew Melodies".

> (6)   While sadly we gazed on the river
> Which roll'd on in freedom below,
> They demanded the song; but, oh never
> That triumph the stranger shall know!
> May this right hand be withered for ever,
> Ere it string our high harp for the foe.

Now, how does Byron handle the perceptual problem in this particular stanza? First of all, he does not leave it to the reader's discretion to decide whether the shape is closed at the end of the fourth line. The sentence run-on from the third to the fourth line considerably weakens the third line, making it dependent on the whole, and requiring a strong closure at the end of the fourth line. The conclusive tone of the exclamatory sentence, and of the all-exclusive *never,* does indeed indicate such a closure, where the rhyme pattern, too, becomes completed, at the end of the fourth line. Second, what happens to the "loose end" left by the last two lines? They are perceived, on the one hand, as deviating from the closed quatrain; on the other hand, by virtue of the *ab* rhyme, they *refer back* to it. In certain circumstances this may be perceived as a reinforcement of the closure. In the present case, for instance, the resolute vow expressed in lines 5 and 6 is perceived as an amplification of the exclamation in lines 3 and 4. Such a strong-shaped, closed unit has the psychological atmosphere of patent purpose and definite direction, leading to the closure. As for the contents of the stanza, it contains both a narrative element and an argumentative element, the latter expressing an emphatic, active attitude. The narrative and the argumentative element, too, express a psychological atmosphere of patent purpose and definite direction; thus, the similar psychological atmospheres of the content and of the perceptual shape tend to reinforce each other.

A comparison of excerpt (5), and possibly of (2), with the organization depicted here can be most illuminating. In the first place, (5) has no narrative or argumentative, but rather a descriptive content, the psychological atmosphere of which is not one of patent purpose and definite direction. While both narrative and argument refer to a sequence deployed in time, a landscape has no "beginning, middle, and end" (cf. Chapter 4, "Excursus"). The landscape described in excerpt (5) is vague, contains no stable characteristic visual shapes; it *leads* nowhere, it merely *is.* The fifth and sixth lines of (5) do not reiterate or amplify previously conveyed information. Still, by virtue of the anaphora "It was" at the beginning of lines 3 and 5, the last two lines are perceived as referring back to the quatrain. Here, however, in contrast to Byron's stanza, there is no mutual reinforcement between the psychological atmosphere of patent purpose and definite direction of the content and the perceptual shape of the stanza. A strong gestalt is the product of the actively organizing mind. Intense textures arising from the dissolution of focused gestalts can be perceived only when the actively organizing mind is held in abeyance (this is what Keats called *negative capability*). The vigorous strong shape of the stanza in (5) inhibits the vague interaction of elements on the semantic, phonetic, and world stratum of the poem, and represses the diffuse atmosphere. Thus, the effect of the rhymes tends to be perceived as rather flat.

Now, it should be remembered that (5) has been obtained by re-writing (2), Poe's authentic version. I have already pointed out that one of the main effects of the near-iteration of the second line as the third line in (2) is to upset the symmetry of the stanza and to weaken its perceptual shape. The reiteration of *Auber* and *Weir* at the end of the last two lines of (2) further increases the uncertainty in grouping the lines. On the one hand, as I have already suggested, the similar endings organize the last four lines into a symmetrical, closed quatrain. At the same time, these similar endings are repetitions of the same words, not genuine rhymes. Thus, the last four lines may also be perceived as a rather unstructured pile-up of reiterated units, involving a certain degree of saturation. Thus, one of the main effects of these repetitions is to leave the reader with a feeling of uncertainty as for the grouping of the verse lines in this stanza. As a result, the diffuse elements are not controlled, their interaction is not inhibited; and a vague atmosphere, involving rich pre-categorial information, may be perceived.

Let us have now a closer look at the two "tokens" of the repeated verse "types". In the second and third line of (2), there are three near-synonyms: *crisped, sere,* and *withering.* Lines 2 and 3 are literally identical, except for the substitution of the adjective *withering* for its near-synonym *crisped.* This generates a near-minimal semantic pair, based on the opposition *crisped ~ withering,* the latter emphasizing the process of losing moisture and vitality, the former emphasizing the resulting texture. These synonyms emphasize, by way of analogy, different features in *sere.* Thus, the two tokens of *sere* both have, and do not have, identical meanings, at one and the same time. Now, a world description based on such semantic subtleties may easily lead to "chaotic overdifferentiation", something which—as we have seen in the preceding chapter—may be an essential element in the verbal representation of an altered state of consciousness. This structure generates, in fact, an additional *uncertainty:* is the aim of the repetition to achieve semantic subtlety by contrasting three near-synonyms, or is repetition merely to be regarded as an emphatic device, icluding some "elegant variation", so as to avoid boredom?

Now, if we compare the sixth to the eighth line and the seventh to the ninth, it becomes apparent that not only the ending words are identical in these pairs, but also, that the lines constituting the pairs have very similar phrase structures. "It was hard" changes into "It was down"; and "by the dim lake of Auber" changes into "by the dank tarn of Auber". *Lake* and *tarn* are near-synonyms; and *dank* may be per-

ceived as uniting the meanings of *dim* and *misty,* adding some unpleasant components. Likewise, "In the misty mid region of Weir" changes into "In the ghoul-
haunted woodland of Weir". *Misty* may be related with the uncanny, and it is this
element that is intensified in *ghoul-haunted.* Further, it should be noticed that in all
cases, the change is from the "brighter", front vowels to the "darker", back vowels.
This change seems to have two consequences: the reader is forced to notice—subliminally perhaps—certain subtle and evasive perceptual features in the sound texture of
these lines, features which, again, "threaten" with chaotic overdifferentiation; and he
may also notice, perhaps, that the change is from the "brighter" to the "darker",
from the more to the less differentiated (as to the relationship between "bright"
sounds and differentiation, see above, Table 8.1 in Chapter 8). Again, should we
regard these repetitions as intended to point up certain semantic and phonetic
relationships, or as mere emphatic reiterations with "elegant variation"?

Bowra noted about Poe's poetry:

> Poe's belief that vagueness is essential to poetry gave to his work its most
> characteristic quality. No doubt through it he hoped to hypnotize his readers
> into a trance, and for this reason he uses words as incantation. (Bowra,
> 1961: 192–193)

I have discussed the first stanza of "Ulalume", at perhaps unprecedented length, in
order to show how such "trance-inducing" works in "hypnotic" poetry. My central
claim is that vagueness on a variety of levels is a necessary condition for the generation of what I have called "obtrusive rhythms". If the function of more than usually
regular rhythm is to give *false* (rather than *genuine)* certainty to the 'Platonic Censor' in us, there must be a more than usually pervasive quality of vagueness and
uncertainty in a hypnotic poem. On the other hand, regular repetition, too, must be
more than usually pervasive. Poe's poems are notorious for their regularity of meter. At the subphonemic level, we find the periodic acoustic information characterized by a more than usual frequency and prominence of liquids, nasals, and glide. On
the higher levels, we find reiterated words and phrases instead of rhymes, sometimes
at pre-assigned places of the stanza, and verbatim (or near-verbatim) repetition of
whole lines, or at least of similar phrase structures. Likewise, vagueness and uncertainty occur at a variety of strata and levels. On the world stratum, we find in (2) an
immediate situation defined in space and time, in which no concrete objects with
stable characteristic visual shapes are mentioned, so that the perceiving consciousness can only relate itself to the great directions of the environment. A great variety
of expressions indicate darkness and impeded vision, resulting in low-differentiated
perceptions. On the sound stratum, at the subphonemic level, we find an abundance
and prominence of "dark" vowels, with low-differentiated pre-categorial acoustic information. At the higher levels, we find an ambiguous and unpredictable grouping
of verse lines by rhyme and epiphora, yielding weak, ambiguous perceptual shapes.
The reiterations and near-iterations of phrases and verse lines contribute to the total

effect in a variety of ways. First, they enhance the sense of repetition; second, they weaken the perceptual organization of the stanza; and third, they tend to generate a richness of subtle and evasive semantic and sensory-phonetic information. The second and third aspects tend to contribute to cognitive overload which, in turn, tends to be handled by our 'dumping' information into an undifferentiated mass. The 'Platonic Censor' in us is incapable of facing the uncertainties inherent in such pervasive vagueness, undifferentiation, ambiguity, and mystic obscurity. At the same time, regular rhythm is predictable, and arouses a sense of control and security. By the same token, regular (and especially, more than usually regular) rhythm tends to enhance the poem's irrational qualities by compensating for the uncertainties inherent in the poem's vagueness and undifferentiation, thus fooling the 'Platonic Censor' in us.

Emotive Crescendo

In Chapter 14, we examined the spatial imagery of archetypes with reference to their capacity of entering into an emotional sequence. One such emotional sequence was the death-and-rebirth archetype. The present section examines an emotional pattern that consists of the second stage of this archetype, an expansion or outburst of vital forces. This archetypal pattern is prevalent in all sorts of mystic and ecstatic poetry, including much of romantic and post-romantic poetry.

At first glance, there appear to be two insurmountable problems with ecstatic poetry. First, language is conceptual and logical by its very nature, whereas ecstasy is most conspicuously not: it involves a different kind of consciousness. Accordingly, while "ecstatic poetry" ought to be a contradiction in terms, we know it is not. Still, a poet who announces that he is having an ecstatic experience loses his credibility; thus, we are clearly up against the **telling ~ showing** dichotomy. Second, ecstasy is a state of mind with great emotional intensity. If the poet attempts to express (or "show") it by using words of great emotional intensity, his effort will be regarded as reflecting an empty pose rather than a credible ecstatic experience. In poetry, something can be perceived as intense only when it is *compared to something else*. Indeed, one of the poetic techniques for overcoming these difficulties is to use an emotional pattern, in which two emotional states are compared to one another, the later being far more intense than the earlier one. When the two states occur at the beginning and the end of a relatively independent section of a poem, and when the 'high' end of the pattern is perceived as an extremely intense peak, I call the pattern an *emotive crescendo*—emotive, as the pattern frequently consists in two contrasting ends of an emotive scale. The poem begins with a regular, everyday tone or, at any rate, in a low emotive pitch; at the other end, there is an intense emotive tone or state of mind; between the two ends, we find elements that have an heightening effect. One more observation is necessary here. The "emotive crescendo" is not an "objective fact" of the poem: it crucially depends on a certain kind of mental performance. When the critic states "This is an "Emotive Crescendo", one should understand such a statement as a crucial recommendation to *perform* the poem as an "emotive crescendo" (cf. the preceding chapter); other mental performances, too, may be conceivable. At most, the critic is describing the poem as *affording* or *encouraging* a performance that imposes an "emotive crescendo" on it.

Frequently enough, the two ends of the "emotive crescendo" are marked by some similar or even identical element. Thus we find that Keats's sonnet "When I have fears" begins with "ceasing-to-be" and ends with "nothingness"; Wordsworth's poem, whose first line is "I wandered *lonely* as a cloud", ends with a state of *solitude*. Such "recapitulations" call for a comparison of the two ends, emphasizing the extreme change in tone that has taken place and—as Barbara Herrnstein-Smith (1968) has shown—it may induce a tone of *finality*. As I have pointed out above, in Chapter 12, there is in romantic poetry a "preferred" theme at the *fortissimo* end of the pattern: Death (or Nothingness). This theme, coupled with the emotive *fortissimo,* yields an oxymoron, whether explicitly stated or implied. The "alchemy" of this figure is remarkable; it serves to evoke a quality that seems to be inaccessible to our rational faculties: that of ecstasy. In one respect, Death and ecstasy are irreconcilable opposites. Death is a state in which vital force is totally absent, whereas ecstasy is a state in which all the forces of the soul are mobilized to an extreme degree; hence the apparent contradiction. In another respect, however, the two states are similar: in both, the everyday rational faculties disappear: in death, through the disappearance of all functions; in ecstasy, when our rational faculties are absorbed in the overwhelming experience of the *whole* self. The use of the actual word *ecstasy* or any of its synonyms may tend to classify this state conceptually under one fixed category, whereas the use of this most irrational of figures tends to keep categories fluid. The energy built up in the course of the poem, ending in the *fortissimo,* fulfills a double function in this scheme. On the one hand, it constitutes one of the incompatible terms of the figure. On the other hand, incompatible terms may generate a witty quality. As we have seen in Chapter 4 with reference to emotional qualities, one of the features that differentiate emotional from nonemotional experiences is an extreme change in the level of psychic energy. Furthermore, since the contradiction between the death-imagery and the level of high energy usually remains implicit, the element of sharp contradiction is "mitigated", as "Longinus" would have put it—even where both incompatible terms come explicitly to the fore, as in the emotive *fortissimo* of Keats's "Bright Star":

(7)   And so live ever—or else swoon to death!

The disjunction *or* mitigates the contradiction, smoothing over the opposition on the surface. Even though the opposition "live" ~ "death" is reinforced by the opposition "ever" ~ "swoon", with its element of **sudden change** of mental state, the rational mind is appeased so as to accept these incompatible terms; however, in the domain of poetry, whenever one says "this *or* that", the depth-mind perceives "this *and* that".

With the foregoing distinctions in mind, let us have a look at Wordsworth's "Daffodils":

(8)   I wandered lonely as a cloud
        That floats on high o'er vales and hills,
        When all at once I saw a crowd,
        A host of golden daffodils;
        Beside the lake, beneath the trees,
        Fluttering and dancing in the breeze.

        Continuous as the stars that shine
        And twinkle on the milky way,
        They stretched in never-ending line
        Along the margin of a bay:
        Ten thousand saw I at a glance,
        Tossing their heads in sprightly dance.

        The waves beside them danced; but they
        Outdid the sparkling waves in glee:
        A poet could not be but gay
        In such a jocund company:
        I gazed—and gazed—but little thought
        What wealth the show to me had brought:

        For oft, when on my couch I lie
        In vacant or in pensive mood,
        They flesh upon that inward eye
        Which is the bliss of solitude;
        And then my heart with pleasure fills,
        And dances with the daffodils.

This poem begins with a notion of "loneliness", and ends on a note of "solitude", developing as it were from "floating on high" to some "vacant or pensive mood", through a constant process of **intensification.** Consider the group of synonyms and closely related words

        sprightly→ glee→ gay→ jocund→ bliss.

First of all, these words have a cumulative impact, as far as the impression created by the poem goes. Second, when comparing the first and the last member of the group, there appears to be a considerable difference in intensity between them. The intervening members occur in a casual order; and conform with the crescendo pattern only in a certain mental performance: when the pattern is "retro-related"[3] from the last member. Thus, for instance, the word *pleasure* may indicate a lower degree of pleasure than *bliss;* but it would still indicate the peak of the experience, by virtue of its place in the pattern. Harold Bloom has pointed out that there are here pairs of successive words in which the second member tends to be more "ample" (perhaps, only by virtue of the crescendo pattern): *crowd→ host*; *fluttering→ dancing*; *shine→ twinkle* (add to this *sparkling*). Now, consider the contribution of the following two lines to this pattern: "The waves beside them danced; but they / Outdid the sparkling waves in glee". Here, *danced, sparkling* and *glee* are made *somehow* to participate in the same scale. This "somehow" becomes less mysterious if we recall from Chapter 4 that emotional qualities involve a sudden deviation from normal energy level, and that emotions related to joy and ecstasy involve *increase* of energy to varying degrees. Consequently, the verb *outdid* acquires a crucial function in suggesting or generating the crescendo pattern. The expressions of movement and joy (reinforced by the expressions of shining) are drawn together in the metaphor of the last two lines:

(9)   And then my heart with pleasure fills,
       And dances with the daffodils.

Paradoxically enough, the height of intense movement occurs in a relaxed, "pensive mood", when the speaker is lying on his couch. "I gazed—and gazed—but little thought" connotes a kind of self-oblivion, while denoting 'I had no idea' (the speaker could not, at the moment of gazing, estimate how significant the 'show' was). Although there is here a break in the continuity of the experience, indicating, as it were, "emotions *recollected* in tranquillity", the last stanza takes up this connotation, and heightens it to "vacant" (denoting 'unoccupied with thought or reflection') and "pensive" (which suggests 'dreaminess or wistfulness', and may involve 'little or no thought to any purpose').

As I have suggested, regular meter can be related to altered states of consciousness, when it gives, in Ransom's words, "false security to the Platonic Censor in us". Security in regular meter may be rendered *false* when, among other things, there is asymmetry or irregularity at higher prosodic ranks. In "Daffodils", however, there is a control of strong gestalts on all prosodic levels, at the foot rank, at the line rank, and at the stanza rank. The iambic meter in this poem is one of the most regular occurrences in most of the major English poets. As I have argued elsewhere, the organization of the tetrameter line tends to be more symmetrical than that of the ubiquitous pentameter line, and thus exhibits a more conclusive tone. The first four lines of each stanza constitute a symmetrical closed quatrain, followed by a couplet with an even stronger gestalt (cf. above, Chapter 5). What is more, the narrative structure of the contents, too, induces in this poem a psychological atmosphere of "definite direction and patent purpose", as L. B. Meyer has it. There seems, never-

---

[3]   That is, when a pattern is elaborated from its end point backward (see next chapter).

theless, to be an ecstatic quality in this poem (as reported by a great number of readers), something which possibly is explained by two aspects of the poem. First, as I have suggested, the rational effects of convergent rhythms and witty structures can be overridden by tremendous poetic energy; in this way, an intense emotional quality may be generated. In "Daffodils", the effect of the regular rhythms is channelled into the dancing movement of the flowers which, in its turn, contributes the energy level required. Second, the psychological atmosphere of patent purpose and definite direction indicated above is most palpably counteracted by the emphatic **purposelessness** of the speaker's "wandering lonely as a cloud" in the first two lines, and by his "vacant or pensive mood" in the last stanza. The second line of the last stanza "In vacant or in pensive mood" suggests, then, a state of mind devoid of certainty, security, and patent purpose, that is, a state in which the experiencer relinquishes all sense of control and power. In the mental performance of some readers, this state of mind is weighed against the sense of control and power aroused by predictable, symmetrical stanza structures. In the final resource, the overall effect of the poem depends on which of the two states of mind eventually subdues the other. A reader in whose performance the sense of control aroused by the predictable, symmetrical stanza structures is dominant, may experience the poem as a "glorified nursery rhyme"; a reader in whose performance the loss of control involved in the vacant or pensive mood prevails, will experience it as an ecstatic poem. And we do, indeed, receive from readers both kinds of report.

Critics are far from unanimous as for the character of this poem. A few weeks after dispatching the manuscript of this book to the publisher, I attended a conference on psychology and literature, where David Ellis presented a paper on Wordsworth in which he focused on this poem. His view of it is not unlike the one presented here. He summarizes some of the conflicting views on this poem in two passages.

> The British critic A. C. Bradley, in the Oxford Lectures, called it "entirely happy"; the American critic Geoffrey Hartman in his important study of Wordsworth, recalling Bradley's comments, referred to it as "a pretty thing"; and another American, Carl Woodring, in his book *Wordsworth* described it as a poem of "unclouded majesty and joy". ... (Ellis, 1991)

> Coleridge categorized this poem as an example of Wordsworth's "defects". He objected to the disparity between the beauty and poignancy of the penultimate couplet and the final couplet. There is a falling off, he argued, a sinking effect. While that may be true, I would argue that these two couplets, coming at the conclusion of the poem, are the respective climaxes of the two plains, inner and outer, that they are equally essential, and that they do connect meaningfully in Wordsworth's mind, although the connection is not always understood by the reader—a situation that gives rise to the common criticisms of Wordsworth. (ibid.)

I claim that my conception of obtrusive rhythm, according to which varying relative weights may be attributed to the elements of certainty and uncertainty, may account for both the "pretty thing" and the "unclouded majesty and joy" views on this poem. If no awe-inspiring element is perceived in this poem, its energetic rhythms will give rise to *genuine* security, and the resulting quality will be judged as "a pretty thing"; if, however, at some point in the poem the reader has to relinquish his conscious control over his experiences, the same energetic rhythms will cause *false* security, and the resulting quality will be a perception on the part of the reader of his soul being held in sway. My notion of the double-edgedness of death and nothingness imagery, and the ensuing conception of the emotive crescendo may account for both Coleridge's and Ellis' judgments of the end couplets of the last two stanzas. The "vacant or pensive mood" of the last stanza can be perceived either as an anticlimax, or an ecstatic hyper-climax, after the climax has been reached at the end of the penultimate stanza.

By comparison, in Coleridge's "Kubla Khan", too, we find a more than usually regular meter and a dancing movement contributing most effectively to the overpowering obtrusive rhythms of an "emotive crescendo". In the following lines of the poem, the metric superordinate has a very strong shape—the symmetrical couplet.

(10)   And from this chasm, with ceaseless turmoil seething,
        As if this earth in fast thick pants were breathing,
        A mighty fountain momently was forced:
        Amid whose swift, half-intermitted burst
        Huge fragments vaulted like rebounding hail,
        Or chaffy grain beneath the thresher's flail:
        And 'mid these dancing rocks at once and ever
        It flung up momently the sacred river.

These lines, however, are grouped according to two diverging grouping principles, of which either blurs the other. In one respect, these lines are simple couplets, and accordingly, grouped by rhyme. Syntactically, however, a second pattern is superimposed. The line "A mighty fountain momently was forced" is grouped, rhymewise, with the next line. Syntactically, however, it is grouped with the preceding line. From the preposition *from* in the first line, a verb is predicted; this prediction is fulfilled as late as the end of the third line, running on to the next couplet. Thus, the interpolated simile "As if this earth in fast thick pants were breathing" not only adds the mythological dimension, but also weakens the perceptual shape of the whole passage, by delaying the fulfillment of syntactic predictions and by upsetting, for a considerable stretch of lines, the convergence of sentences and couplets. The next clause, two lines long, is again "straddled" across two couplets. When it ends, in mid-couplet, another line is needed to complete it; consequently, an "extra" simile ("Or chaffy grain beneath the thresher's flail") is introduced after the fulfillment of the syntactic predictions. Only the last two lines of the passage—the "summary" of the description—entirely converge with the couplet. Therefore, perceptually, too, it has a "rounding-off" effect. In addition, such phrases as *ceaseless turmoil seething, mighty fountain, Huge fragments vaulted* indicate tremendous energy, much beyond what we encounter in "Daffodils". Thus, the dancing movement of "huge fragments" realizes here the most energetic potential of regular rhythm, which gives great security to the Platonic Censor in us. This security becomes *false* because of the blurred shapes of the metric superordinates, owing to the two rival, symmetrical patterns blurring each other. Wordsworth and Coleridge resort to the same principle in creating the ecstatic effect of their poems; but Coleridge takes it many steps further.

In discussing the ecstatic qualities of poetry, we have arrived, then, at a configuration of elements which (or a substantial subset of which) we may expect to recur in ecstatic poetry of this kind. First, we have some gradual increase of energy, the "emotive crescendo". This energy may be expressed by physical motion, as in "Daffodils", or by a mental tension of some sort (as e.g. in Keats's sonnet "When I have fears"; cf. Chapter 5, example 14). Second, there is an element that can best be described as a state of "self-abandonment" or "self-oblivion". This element may occur, as in "Daffodils", in the guise of some "vacant or pensive mood", reinforced by "I gazed—and gazed—but little thought", or of death, or nothingness; in fact, there seems to be no limit on the poets' inventiveness in this respect. Third, there is an element of "sharing" ("And dances *with* the daffodils"), or of union with some unlimited thing-free entity (God, infinity, eternity, nothingness, night), or of "integration" with one's environment. Fourth, such an experience often triggers, at its peak, some overwhelming insight, such as the immediate perception of some highly significant reality, inaccessible to ordinary senses, either because it belongs to the past, or to a transcendental world ("They flesh upon that inward eye"); alternatively, it may result in the cognition of some truth, a cognition which is independent of any reasoning process. Fifth, the experience is often accompanied by an extreme degree of bliss; sometimes there is a feeling of "purification", or "transsubstantiation", or "improvement" of the self. Sixth, there is what Kenneth Burke calls "the mystic oxymoron". "Identification in itself is a kind of transcendence. [...] So identification attains its ultimate expression in mysticism, the identification of the infinitesimally frail with the infinitely powerful. Modes of identification with the 'sublime' in nature would then be analyzable as large 'fragments' of the mystical motive" (Burke, 1962: 850). Thus, the individual becomes "infinitely powerful" and *"lost* in the infinitely powerful" at one and the same time.

Finally, a word about the phrase "That floats on high o'er vales and hills". Occasionally, "floating" imagery occurs in hypnotic–ecstatic poetry (cf. "floated midway on the waves" and "his floating hair!" in "Kubla Khan"). In a recent book I reproduced the gist of my discussion of "Daffodils", and added a few "neuro-theological" observations (Tsur, 2003: 24–28), of which I will reproduce here one. The nature of the phrase "floats on high" in this poem will be illuminated by a comment by Maud Bodkin, speaking of "flight as it is known in dreams", with reference to a very different image in Dante's "Paradiso", characterising its effect as "the absence of any sensation of effort, the wonder at effortless attainment of a new sphere". To this we may add Michael A. Persinger's comment in his neuro-psychological study (1987), speaking of "God Experience involving temporal lobe instability" (26). "Few people appear to acknowledge the role of vestibular sensations in the God Experience. However, in light of the temporal lobe's role in the sensation of balance and movement, these experiences are expected. [...] Literature concerned with the God Experiences are full of metaphors describing essential vestibular inputs. Sensations of 'being lifted', 'feeling light', or even 'spinning, like being intoxicated', are common" (Persinger, 1987: 26). After quoting an account of such an experience, he observes: "Note the repeated references to vestibular sensations: 'floating,' 'lifted,' 'moving,' 'spinning'" (27). The phrase "as a cloud floating high" is introduced, as it were, merely as a simile for loneliness; by the same token, it suggests effortlessness as well as elements of the spiritual experience toward which it leads (cf. Tsur, 2006: 91–92; I appealed to the same mechanism in my discussion of the phrase "a most dizzy pain" in Keats's "On Seeing the Elgin Marbles" [Tsur, 2002: 305] as well).

On the basis of the above, it seems possible to identify the following typical features of ecstasy: emotional intensity, the experiencing of union, and insight. It is hard to tell which of the three is to be regarded as the causal antecedent of the other two. Perhaps the process varies from case to case; maybe the ecstatic experience occurs only when the three are present simultaneously.

In Chapter 11, we have distinguished between a "personal" and a "teleological" conception of the "ultimate reality"; consequently, we have two ways of transcendentally identifying with that reality. In *Faust,* identification is usually of the latter kind. One of the most conspicuous instances of a revelation of the former kind is Faust's encounter with the Earth Spirit. Faust sums up this experience as follows:

> (11)   When that ecstatic moment held me,
>   I felt myself so small, so great ...
> (626–627)

The scene consists in the direct perception of some ultimate reality, usually inaccessible to ordinary senses; it involves tremendous energy, as well as "the mystic oxymoron". One of the fullest and most interesting instances of the configuration suggested above occurs in the episode in which the protagonist contemplates committing suicide. But there is an interesting twist in the configuration: instead of using death imagery in relation to ecstasy, Faust uses ecstatic imagery in relation to *real* death (see above, Chapter 14, example (21)).

In other romantic poems we find a more complex pattern: the crescendo pattern culminates in supreme bliss, to be followed by a further stage, disillusionment and depression. Let us consider Blake's "The Crystal Cabinet":

(12)   The Maiden caught me in the wild,
         Where I was dancing merrily;
         She put me into her Cabinet
         And Lock'd me up with a golden Key.

         This Cabinet was formed of Gold
         And Pearl and Crystal shining bright,
         And within it opens into a World
         And a little lovely moony Night.

         Another England there I saw,
         Another London with its Tower,
         Another Thames and other Hills,
         And another pleasant Surrey Bower,

         Another maiden like herself,
         Translucent, lovely, shining clear,
         Threefold each in the other clos'd—
         O, what a pleasant trembling fear!

         O, what a smile! a threefold Smile
         Fill'd me that like a flame I burn'd;
         I bent to kiss the lovely Maid,
         And found a threefold kiss return'd.

         I strove to seize the inmost Form
         With ardor fierce and hands of flame,
         But burst the Crystal Cabinet,
         And like a weeping Babe became—

         A weeping Babe upon the wild,
         And weeping Woman pale reclin'd,
         And in the outward air again
         Fill'd with the woes the passing Wind.

In this poem, there is a certain analogy between the first and the last stanzas, an analogy which is stressed by their positions in the pattern. Both stanzas are at a *low point* as compared with the first half of the penultimate stanza. In addition, the last stanza is depressing, because, first, it comes right after the utmost bliss of ecstasy, accompanied by a striving "to seize the inmost form"; and second, it represents an anti-climax not only in comparison with the preceding stanza, but also when compared with the "original" state, as depicted in the first stanza. It should be noted that the sudden "fall" is a direct consequence of the *fortissimo* at the end of the crescendo.[4]

In résumé, the present chapter explored the obtrusive rhythms underlying hypnotic poetry by way of a detailed analysis of one stanza from Poe's "Ulalume". More briefly, I have discussed another pattern relevant to altered states of consciousness in poetry: the "emotive crescendo". When the emotive crescendo is superimposed upon a piece of poetry with obtrusive rhythms, it may contribute to the generation of an ecstatic quality. But the emotive crescendo may also be superimposed upon a passage of a different character; then it yields a rather different kind of ecstatic poetry, involving the dissolution of focused gestalts. This possibility will be explored in the next chapter.

---

[4]   The two subsequent stages of intense passion and depression may become condensed in an ambiguity such as, for instance, the one found in Keats's "Ode on a Grecian Urn":

> All breathing human passion far above
> And leaves a heart high-sorrowful and cloy'd,
> A burning forehead and a parching tongue.

At the core of the ambiguity is the verb *leaves,* which may suggest a growing distance in time or space, simultaneously contrasting "human passion *far above*", with the "heart high-sorrowful and cloy'd" left below, and the subsequent stages of "human passion" with the "heart high-sorrowful and cloy'd" remaining behind (that is to say, remainders of the great passion). A similar pattern of a gradually intensifying experience, all the way up to ecstasy, to be followed by a sudden hit of soberness, we find also in some of the best romantic Hebrew poetry by Bialik and Tchernikhovsky.

CHAPTER 20

The Divergent Passage
and Ecstatic Poetry

Baudelaire's "Correspondances" as an Ecstatic Poem

The main purpose of the following reading of Baudelaire's "Correspondances" is to demonstrate in it a very complex poetic structure from which typically ecstatic qualities may arise. At the same time, additional distinctions made in the foregoing chapters will be considered in relation to this poem; thus it becomes a node in which a wide variety of issues discussed in the present book are drawn together.

At the beginning of Chapter 1, I located Cognitive Poetics between analytic and impressionistic criticism. Here, I shall offer an (analytic) close reading of Baudelaire's poem in the tradition of "New Criticism". At the same time, I shall briefly allude to Henri Peyre's impressionistic comments, illustrating critical impressionism and its deficiencies. At the end of the chapter, I shall discuss two cognitive mechanisms that may help to account for the emerging ecstatic quality of the poem.

To help us attain this goal, let us briefly review the signposts that were set up along our path so far. In Chapter 4, I distinguished between convergent and divergent style, the latter having great emotional potential. In Chapter 14, I suggested that archetypes are emotional patterns, emerging when some abstract associative cluster organizes a texture of rich, divergent elements. One such abstract pattern was the death-and-rebirth archetype; its second stage, an expansion or outburst of vital forces, is the emotional pattern that organizes the texture of divergent elements in ecstatic experience. In Chapter 12, I proposed a model of defining poetic styles, as well as a model that will account for the Versatile Reader's acquisition of his versatility. Both models are based on a gradual process of differentiation, from the more general to the more specific category, by contrasting style types within poetry, styles within types, poems within styles and, eventually, the various parts of one and the same poem. Exactly such a contrast, with highly significant stylistic implications, will be found between the two quatrains of Baudelaire's sonnet.

Correspondances

La Nature est un temple où de vivants piliers
Laissent parfois sortir de confuses paroles;

L'homme y passe à travers des forêts de symboles
Qui l'observent avec des regards familiers.

Comme de longs échos qui de loin se confondent
Dans une ténébreuse et profonde unité,
Vaste comme la nuit et comme la clarté,
Les parfums, les couleurs et les sons se répondent.

Il est des parfums frais comme des chairs d'enfants,
Doux comme les hautbois, verts comme les prairies,
— Et d'autres, corrompus, riches et triomphants,

Ayant l'expansion des choses infinies,
Comme l'ambre, le musc, le benjoin et l'encens,
Qui chantent les transports de l'esprit et des sens.

>   Nature is a temple, where living pillars
>   Emit sometimes indistinct words;
>   Man passes there through forests of symbols
>   That observe him with familiar gazes.
>
>   Like long echoes that mingle in the distance
>   In a dark and profound unity,
>   Vast as the night and as the light,
>   The perfumes, the colors, and the sounds respond to one another.
>
>   There are perfumes, fresh as the flesh of children,
>   Sweet as oboes, green as meadows,
>   And others, corrupt, rich, and triumphant,
>
>   Having the expansion of infinite things,
>   Like amber, musk, benzoin, and incense,
>   Which sing the raptures of the spirit and the senses.

In Chapter 4, I suggested that repeated sound clusters stand out more clearly in poetry of witty than of emotional quality. I also suggested that when the discordance of elements in a poem is palpable, it tends to induce a witty quality. Intense emotional qualities, on the other hand, typically arise when repeated sound clusters as well as discordant semantic features tend to fuse, imperceptibly, into one another. I shall begin my discussion of this poem with an observation that in itself can hardly be regarded as compelling evidence, viz., the fact that at least one very experienced reader of Baudelaire (Henri Peyre) did not notice in this poem any such readily perceptible features.

> There is no virtuoso musical effect in the quatrains, no attempt at surprising the reader, no metaphor that fuses discordant elements. (Peyre, 1964: 9)

As I shall try to show in a moment, the informative value of this apparently descriptive statement is doubtful. It seems to have, rather, an impressionistic function, viz., that of tuning the reader's mind to respond to the poem in a certain way. It is not very common in genuine descriptive critical statements to enumerate what is absent in a piece of poetry, without suggesting why one should expect it to be present.[1] The rhetorical effect of this passage is clear enough: Look at the poem's noble simplicity; how rich, nevertheless, is its atmosphere! Isn't that mysterious?

With regard to the other features named by Peyre, I find that at least the elements of line 7 are somewhat discordant: "Vaste comme la nuit et comme la clarté". As I suggested in Chapter 9 (where I referred to this poem), this line contains a "marked" simile (that is, *light* is not a very "good example" of "vast things"). Not only is it somewhat unusual that *clarté* is offered as a simile for 'vastness', even more unusual is the fact that in the course of this simile, *nuit* and *clarté* have been made somehow to equal one another. To use the terminology introduced above, what may have constituted a sharp split focus, turns out to be an instance of soft integrated focus, by virtue of the smooth fusion of its rather discordant elements. What actually happens here is that while the reader's attention is given to the aspect of vastness (which he will readily attribute to *night*), he has been "cheated", without realizing it, into accepting the implied equation of night and light. Moreover, incompatible elements that are gestalt-free are more smoothly, less perceptibly fused than when they have some stable, characteristic visual shape. About a similar effect, although less sophisticated in nature, "Longinus" (p. 97) states: "In the same spirit, Aristotle and Theophrastus point out that the following phrases serve to soften bold metaphors— 'as if', and 'as it were', and 'if one may so say', and 'if one may venture such an expression'; for the qualifying words mitigate, they say, the audacity of expression". In this line by Baudelaire, mitigation is brought about by the fact that night and light have been compared, *as it were,* for vastness' sake *only*. But is this not precisely that of which, according to H. Peyre, there is no trace in the quatrain ("no metaphor that fuses discordant elements")? Or does he only mean that no formal metaphor is involved here? I wonder.

The same holds true of the phrase "no virtuoso musical effect". I take "musical effect" to mean a pattern of perceptible repetition of sound, or a deviation from such a pattern. I would consider such a repetition as "virtuoso" if it is, first, more frequent than usual; second, more intensive than usual (that is, comprises many speech sounds); third, more 'elegant' than usual (that is, it does not violate the naturalness

---

[1]   Neither are there any iambic pentameters, or acrostichs, or many other such things in this poem; but there is no need to mention them.

of other prosodic, syntactic, or semantic features, such as metric scheme, rhyme-scheme, diction, word order, etc.).

One might, however, notice that the musical effects in this stanza—virtuoso or not—are extremely rich and intricate. In line 5, the *l* and the nasality feature of *longs* are repeated in *loin,* while it "rhymes" with *sons* in line 4; it also has the nasal vowel *-on* in common with *confondent ... profonde ... répondent.* The first and third of these three words make a formal rhyme as expected, while the second appears unexpectedly. The first three consonants of *profonde* reappear in *parfums;* the first two are found (in a reversed order) in *répondent,* the third in *confondent.* To this, one might add *Dans une ténébreuse et profonde unité;* remember that /b/ and /p/ differ only in voicedness. The sounds of *unité* are anticipated by *une* and echoed by *ténébreuse,* while most of its sounds are resounded in *nuit* in the next line. *Clarté,* while rhyming with *unité,* contains all the consonants of *couleurs,* in the same order.

If a scholar like Henri Peyre, who devoted a considerable part of his professional life to Baudelaire's poetry, says about this quatrain that there is no virtuoso musical effect in it, one possible interpretation of this saying is—and a very plausible one—that he did not notice the effect, owing to the fusion of the sound clusters in the un-differentiated musical background texture. It should be pointed out that most of these repetitions are **sound clusters,** involving two, three, or more elements. The clusters are perceived and compared to each other; the reader, however, cannot focus his awareness on any particular string, because his attentive perception has been dis-tracted from one string to another, so that a network of highly significant sounds has been generated, rich in effects, but only semi-consciously perceived. This dif-fuseness of perception is further reinforced on other strata of the poem. The imagery suggests vague, gestalt-free and thing-free qualities, some of them being discordant, lumped together in a more or less irrational manner, and thus generating a thick tis-sue of diffuse perceptions on the stratum of imagery, too (cf. our discussion above of the simile in line 7). The adjective *profonde* means "profound", that is, "deep" on the one hand, and "going far beyond what is superficial, external, or obvious; ex-tremely intense" on the other. While the former meaning suggests some thing-free and gestalt-free visual image, as a qualifier of *unité,* it is the latter meaning which becomes foregrounded. Notice also the interesting ambiguity of the rhyme-words at the end of lines 5 and 8. *Se confondent* means both "are mingled" and "are thrown in disorder or disconcerted"; *se répondent* means "are in harmony", but also, "exhibit mutual understanding". Thus, the meanings "are mingled" and "are in harmony" characterize the sensory texture of the percepts; whereas the meanings "are thrown in disorder or disconcerted" and "exhibit mutual understanding" superimpose an organiz-ing pattern on this texture. Thus, there is a process of gradual organization in this quatrain, from chaotic confusion to harmonious responsiveness, indicated by mere "overtones" and ambiguities. Thus, the semantic and prosodic structure of the second quatrain join forces to generate a very sophisticated artistic effect (which, as I shall argue, is characteristic of the poem as a whole, on a larger scale too). Both the sound patterns and the semantic structure of the stanza yield a thick, but diffuse and blurred gestalt-free texture which, at the same time, is rather clearly articulated as a unit, by the rhyme pattern on the one hand, and by the superimposed semantic pattern on the other. On the syntactic stratum, much like the imagery, the sentence has a form-blurring effect.

Such a thick tissue of diffuse perceptions is necessarily the substratum of an intense atmosphere in a poem. Diffuse perceptions of this kind may be the source of the almost mysterious intuition that some people say they experience in reading this sonnet.[2]

I have tried to account for the unique mystic flavor of this stanza by structural analysis. By contrast, Peyre wishes to account for it by resorting to a metaphor grounded in Platonic philosophy, thereby intending to attune the reader's mind to the poem itself, rather than pointing out the poetic structures that give rise to it:

> He tore off the veil that covers the true nature of objects thus to reveal the identity behind the illusory appearances, the one behind the many, as Plato and Shelley had put it. (*loc. cit.*)

If Peyre's earlier-quoted impressionistic remark missed the point (in that the textual facts do not conform with it), the present statement misses it by being applicable to too many poetic works (that, besides, are very unlike each other). James Smith in his discriminating article on "Metaphysical Poetry", for instance, argues that treating the problem of the one behind the many is one of the main characteristic features of Metaphysical Poetry (cf. above, Chapter 12). In this context, the first part of the above quotation is indeed misleading, as it has *the air* of bearing on this particular poem more than on any other. Consider, however, the following statement on the role of poetry *in general*: "This is the role of poetry. It unveils, in the full meaning of the term" (Cocteau, 1955: 121). Erlich (1965) quotes the same passage from Cocteau (actually translating "takes off the veil"), and comments in a footnote:

> One wonders whether the above phrase is a direct echo from a passage in *Anna Karenina,* in which the painter Mixajlov describes the creative art as "taking the veil off" the actual, i.e. reaching beyond the surface of things into their very essence. (Erlich, 1965: 180)

Peyre's suggestion is, then, inadequate to a considerable extent. What *might* make such a general statement meaningful, would be if one were to specify in what sense it bears upon this particular poem. On closer inspection, it becomes fairly clear that the same generalization holds true of the two quatrains of this sonnet in two different ways. The first quatrain conveys an atmosphere of perceiving more

---

[2] Bergson's and Ehrenzweig's discussion of metaphysical intuition, quoted and discussed at length in Chapter 18, is most relevant here too.

than a physical reality in a way that might well be termed "animistic". The second quatrain presents such an atmosphere with the help of thing-free qualities.

Let us examine this distinction between the two quatrains through the prism of Hedvig Konrad's theory of metaphor (1958). Its relevant part is aptly summarized by Christine Brooke-Rose (1958) in the following words (already quoted earlier, Chapter 4):

> When we use a noun metaphorically, we make abstraction of certain attributes which it possesses, leaving out others which would not fit; for instance in "the roses of her cheeks", we think only of fragrance, pinkness and softness, not of thorns, leaves, yellowness or dark red.

We might continue by quoting further Hedvig Konrad's own words: "Ce ne sont que les traits dominants de ces métaphores qui ressortent, ces attributs ont ainsi obtenu un caractère *général et abstrait*" (Konrad, 1958: 87; italics in original). From this description, Konrad derives a criterion for "defective metaphors": "La majeure partie des métaphores défectueuses est du à ce fait que les attributs secondaires ne peuvent être éliminés dans notre esprit" (ibid., 86).[3] A further development in such a conception of metaphors would allow those "secondary attributes that cannot be eliminated" to be exploited for the benefit of the poem.

With these distinctions in mind, we may now attempt to pinpoint the difference between the sonnet's two quatrains. There is, in fact, an intense "thing-destruction" in the metaphorical use of words in both quatrains, by which "thing-free", "general and abstract" qualities are abstracted from the things referred to by the nouns. But, while in the second stanza the perceptions remain "thing-free", in the first stanza they are subjugated to a dominant image: *a forest*. Some of the secondary qualities of the images, irrelevant to the "invisible part of the world", have been connected (exploited) here, so that they render a rather coherent, visible and audible world. This double exploitation of the metaphor's potential stimulates an *impression* of a world perceptible by the senses, through which one may *intuit* another, suprasensuous world.[4]

"La Nature est un temple"—the metaphor may be paraphrased as "Nature is a place of worship, a place of communion with a supernatural (perhaps invisible) being". *Temple* also has certain pagan connotations, apt to suggest some animistic view of nature (one should bear in mind that "worship", "Being" etc. have not been explicitly mentioned; which is why they *are there* in a suprasensuous way). *Vivants*

---

3   I am not very happy with such a conception of "defective metaphors". Such a description may fit excellently some of the best mannerist metaphors (as I suggested in Chapter 4, what is bad Classicism may be excellent Mannerism). The wit of the following text depends, precisely, on such a "defect": "Mary has roses in her cheeks—they are yellow and have thorns".

4   Wimsatt, in his "Structure of Romantic Nature Imagery" (1964a) arrives at similar conclusions concerning romantic nature imagery, albeit using a very different reasoning.

piliers ('living pillars') is a not too bold paraphrase for "tree", based on a hierarchic conception of {lifeless, growing, and living} things; the Noun Phrase uses the epithet *living* to qualify a headword taken from the lifeless domain, skipping the proper term on the "substantive level" (cf. Wimsatt, 1964b). This paraphrase is most functionally exploited. "Trees" reinforces "La Nature", "pillars" reinforces "temple", while the joining of a lifeless thing with the adjective "living" reinforces the animistic view of nature.

Line 2, "Laissent parfois sortir de confuses paroles", has a certain *indefinite* quality, reinforcing the "intuitive" perception of line 1. This indefiniteness is kindled, first of all, by *"confuses* paroles", and further enhanced by the indefinite article "de" and the adverb "parfois". *"Laissent* ... sortir" may suggest (1) deliberate action (causation), (2) deliberate allowance, or (3) merely being the source of something. In the latter case, *paroles* should be understood figuratively, referring to Nature's inarticulate noises, such as rustling leaves, etc. The two former senses would suggest "other-worldly", or animistic perceptions of variously intense degrees. The naturalist sense serves as motivation for the reader to open up his other senses too *en passant,* so to speak.

The famous phrase "forêts de symboles" links up with "trees", 'forêts' being their collective noun, and with nature, the 'forêts' being one of its concrete "incarnations", one of its "best examples". Since in this sonnet, Nature may or may not be identical with "forêts", one gets the impression that there is a concrete forest existing quite independently, while abstract Nature, too, may somehow linger behind it all. There is also some uncertainty and indecision as to which of the two incompatible terms in "forêts de symboles" is to be taken figuratively. It may mean real forests which serve as symbols, that is, point to the other, suprasensuous world; alternatively, from "forests" one may extract such semantic features as *plenty, disorderliness,* or *confused orientations and directions*; in the latter case, the main term would be "symboles", i.e., objects serving as symbols (the plural "forêts" may then either indicate a great number, or act as a "contour-blurring plural abstraction", in Leo Spitzer's phrase—cf. Chapter 22, below).

The phrase *l'observent* denotes a mental process and, as opposed to "seeing", it implies a directed mental activity, an action that is more perceiving than perceptible. Similarly, *familiers* denotes an attitude, that is, in Richards' (1925) phrase, "an incipient action", one that is implicitly present; it denotes some *intimate, inner* relationship with *l'homme.*

If the first quatrain consists of a rather coherent nature image, intimating, very much in the romantic manner, some suprasensuous presence, the second quatrain presents us with sensations of thing-free qualities, rather in the manner of impressionist poetry. Although the situational constraints are considerably relaxed in this stanza, as compared to the preceding one, even so a perceiving consciousness is indicated that relates itself to the immediate situation with deictic indications of "near" and "remote", especially through the phrase "de loin". There is here a boundless situation in which, according to the Kantian conception of the sublime, "the imagination tries to comprehend or encompass the whole representation in one single intuition"; at the same time, the representation exceeds the upper limit of the imagination's capacity (cf. above, Chapter 15). Thus, some of the gestalt-free information is perceived as if intruding or irrupting from "beyond the limits" (cf. Chapter 11). In this way, the second quatrain, too, conveys an atmosphere of perceiving more than physical reality, but in a way that is very different from that of the first quatrain. Earlier in this chapter, we have seen how the sound stratum and its ambiguities give rise to a sort of "intense vagueness" of diffuse perception. Incapable as they are of articulation, these ambiguities lend intensity to the other, more explicit, albeit thing-free images. The sense of thing-free *qualities* is aroused in this quatrain, first of all, by an unusually large number of abstract and collective (plural) nouns, denoting thing-free entities: "unité ... la nuit ... la clarté ... les parfums, les couleurs et les sons". The sense of *vagueness* (and of intensity) is enhanced by words suggesting immense expansion, like "longs ... de loin ... profonde ... vaste", or by words suggesting *indistinctness,* such as "echo" (two steps away from the *thing:* it is but the reflection of a sound, while the sound itself only indicates its [possibly] hidden source); or by words suggesting impediments to perception, like "ténébreuse et profonde ... la nuit".

These diffuse sense perceptions exhibit, nevertheless, some remarkable *coherence,* by virtue of several cohesive factors:

- coherent syntactic structure (even though less coherent than in the preceding quatrain);
- highly repetitive sound elements;
- highly repetitive semantic features;
- the conventional stanza form;
- words denoting **unity** and **fusion** of various kinds: "se confondent ... unité", reinforced by the organizing process in the second quatrain, noted above, proceeding from "se confondent" to "se répondent".

Many readers of the poem have experienced the uneasy feeling that at the point of transition from the octet to the sestet, something important has been lost: as if an element of offensive arbitrariness had stolen into the poem. While in the first two stanzas, there is a situational constraint on the represented world (even if it seems to be gradually loosening up), in the sestet all such constraints seem to be removed. The sestet begins with an all too indefinite "Il est des", merely asserting the existence of certain sophisticated odors, anywhere, at any time; it appears to be a "feast" of synaesthetic metaphors based on intense olfactory sensations grouped together here merely for their own sake. As will be seen, this loose semantic structure is amply corroborated by a similarly loose syntactic structure. In addition, the rhyme pattern of the sestet constitutes a much weaker gestalt than that of the octet. On the other hand, however, this state of affairs may be conceived of as of a further stage in a continuous process of gradual removal of situational and formal constraints.

In Chapter 10, we have discussed literary synaesthesia at some length. Here I want to recall that synaesthesia, in general, is deemed to be a regression to a less differentiated mode of perception (i.e., to a stage when the mind does not differentiate between the stimuli registered by the various senses). This is of special significance in a sonnet such as the present one, the "essence" of which is said to lie in indistinct, "mystical" intuitions. Further, it should be recalled that when a higher, more differentiated sensory domain is treated in terms of a lower, less differentiated one, intense emotional effects may be achieved. These effects are considerably enhanced when they occur in a context of thing-free and gestalt-free qualities, where no stable, characteristic visual shapes are involved. By contrast, when a lower, less differentiated sensory domain is treated in terms of a higher, more differentiated one, some witty effect is typically achieved. This effect, however, may be overridden in a context that can be described as "chaotic overdifferentiation": in this case, there arises some kind of "perceptual overload", which the cognitive system handles by fusing the "overwhelming" amount of information into some continuous, low-differentiated mass, very much in the way that in painting and music, all the information that exceeds the system's capacity is "dumped" into the background (cf. also Chapter 18). Impressionist and Symbolist poetry occasionally resort to such 'downward' transfers (transfers that treat a lower, less differentiated sensory domain in terms of a higher, more differentiated one) in a context that generates precisely this chaos and overdifferentiation. In line 8, "Les parfums, les couleurs et les sons se répondent", we are faced with a "chaotic" state of fusion, in which it is quite insignificant whether the less differentiated senses draw upon the more differentiated ones, or *vice versa*. The immense "intuitive" effect of this description is reinforced by the fact that the sensations or percepts are mentioned here apart from the objects or events of which they are attributes.

In lines 9–10, we have a series of mainly downward transfers, "Il est des parfums frais [...], Doux comme les hautbois, verts comme les prairies": *sweet perfumes* involves an insignificant downward transfer, between two related senses; *sweet sounds of oboe* involves an upward transfer, whereas the perfumes described in terms of the sounds of the oboe and in terms of the greenness of the prairies are downward transfers of the most prominent kind. Nevertheless, owing to the thing-free and gestalt-free vision in the vast dimensions of an infinite setting, and owing to the intense fusion of the senses, we have here an overdifferentiated, chaotic universe that cannot be disturbed, only corroborated, by these downward transfers, so that the mystic-ecstatic effect also is reinforced, rather than disturbed.

The first tercet gives an "overview" of odors: some are "fresh" and "sweet", some—foul. The oboe's sound is explicitly said to be "sweet"; but it also has a "thick", sensuous quality, readily transferred to the perfumes. "Green" may suggest here "refreshed, invigorated"; while the prairies, introduced, as it were, merely as a simile for greenness, may also serve as a disguised **realistic motivation** for both greenness and natural fragrances. *Corrompus* (corrupted) suggests rot or overripeness, connoting excess. This "negative" excess is amplified by two prominently positive adjectives: "rich and triumphant". The beneficial and harmful abundance connoted by this line suggests, further, indulgence in the excess of odors and corruption, that is so characteristic of *Les Fleur du Mal*. By the same token, it suggests high energy level which, in turn, eventually contributes to an emerging pattern of emotive *crescendo* (cf. Chapter 19). On the sound patterns of this tercet I shall remark only that *parfums* and *frais* have the consonant cluster *fr* in common, while *triomphants* shares the sounds r, f, and the nasalisation with *parfums*.

In the next phrase (run on to the second tercet), these ample immediate sensations are thrown into a much wider perspective. *L'expansion, infinies* (and *prairies* of the first tercet) join forces with the vague, vast qualities of the octet. *Choses* emphasizes here some *"indefinite* object", which cannot be named more closely. In its local context, line 12 acts, I would say, in a "diffusing" function, preventing the phrase *riches et triomphants* of the preceding tercet from focusing its intenseness too vigorously.

Perfumes are the prototypical instances of thing-free and gestalt-free percepts. Here, too, this is one of their conspicuous functions. The perfumes *l'ambre, le musc, le benjoin et l'encens,* act by cumulation of thing-free, sensory stimuli, as a preparation for the final metaphor. Only when we arrive at the last line, it becomes clear that this feast of diffuse sensations throughout the sonnet did have a well-conceived end: a rapture of ecstasy. This is what *les transports de l'esprit et des sens* suggests, quite clearly; also, perhaps, emphasizing some exalted features of *chantent.* The latter verb, however, continuing *se répondent,* has some harmonizing effects as well. Add to this the verb "singing", with its combination of spiritual and sensuous aspects from which, in a context of excessive olfactory sensations, some sense like "bring forth" or "express" may be abstracted.

The last line seems to have, then, retroactively, some organizing effect. While reading the sonnet, we have gradually passed from "thing-like" to "thing-free" perceptions, finding these perceptions constantly increasing in strength. The disorder that was apparent before we became aware of the underlying pattern has its own intensifying and "thing-destroying" effect. Retroactively, all of these factors take on a new significance (i.e., order): they become part of the "transport of spirit and senses".

It seems, therefore, unjustified to say with Henri Peyre that "our senses [...] perceive the central mystery of nature differently and render it into parallel languages, which are convertible into one another". According to Erhardt-Sieboldt's distinction (1932), synaesthesia may enable the poet either to combine the power of several sense impressions into one collective impression, or to translate one sense impression into the terms of another sense. As I have argued in Chapter 10, literary synaesthesia joins *terms* derived from the *vocabularies* of the various sensory domains, exploiting the resulting effect for specific literary purposes. Here, clearly, Erhardt-Sieboldt's first option is at work: the incompatible terms of the intersensory transfer act upon one another, and from this illogical interaction arises the metaphorical power of the sonnet, which, in turn, stimulates in the reader the *impression* that he has intuited some "central mystery of nature".

The changes in the syntactic structure of the sonnet reinforce the effects of its imagery. In the first quatrain, as contrasted to the second, the sentence acts, conspicuously, as an organizing principle, emphasizing the symmetry of the quatrain: it divides the quatrain into two equal parts, in each of which there is a main clause and a subordinate one; in each clause the order of words is: subject phrase—predicate—complements. In the second quatrain, the sentence structure—much like the imagery—has a blurring effect on the form of the stanza. The main clause of the only sentence in the stanza runs from the first line to the end of the last, where its multiple subject and the predicate finally occur: "Comme de longs échos [...] Les parfums, les couleurs et les sons se répondent". What is in between is elaboration, obstructing the sense of integrity in this quatrain, "emancipating", to a large extent, the individual clauses and phrases from their subordination. At the end of lines 5 and 6, an evenly continuing, rather long sentence is articulated (jointed) by the end parts of the prosodic units (the rhymes). "Vaste comme la nuit et comme la clarté", as we have seen, comprises largely discordant elements; the phrase formally modifies *unité,* but because of its rather weak semantic links to it, acquires a large degree of autonomy, and makes the image contribute its connotations to the general atmosphere of the quatrain, rather than to the noun which it modifies.

The sestet's syntactic structure is even looser, and enhances the sense of diffusion: its first five lines consist of a long series of juxtaposed noun phrases containing images largely inconsistent with one another. Their only pretext to syntactical coherence relies upon a rather weak formal subject and predicate *(il est).* Compared to lines 5–13, in which the syntactic integrity of the sonnet is gradually lost out of sight, the relative clause with its finite transitive verb in the last line presents a marked contrast indeed. After a prolonged process of gradual syntactic weakening, it imputes to the sonnet a vigorous closure, enhancing the already by itself emphatic *transport,* the ecstatic rapture that constitutes the peak of the sonnet.

We may, therefore, sum up the process of perceiving this sonnet as follows. In the first quatrain, there is a fairly consistent central image, through which one can "intuit" some suprasensuous presence, by perceiving some less articulate secondary meanings. In the following stanzas, the process of thing-destruction becomes increasingly dominant, thing-free perceptions are gradually intensified, culminating in a rapture of the senses, an overwhelming ecstasy. As I have suggested, the second stage of the death-and-rebirth archetype consists in an expansion or outburst of vital forces; it is also this emotional pattern that organizes the texture of divergent elements in ecstatic experience. As we have seen in the preceding chapter, the pattern may also occur in instances of more than usually convergent poems. In other Romantic and Impressionistic poems, e.g. by Blake, Wordsworth, and Keats, a similar process is found, which I have called "emotive crescendo". On reaching the culminating point of ecstasy, the reader "retro-relates" it (William James's term, quoted by Ehrenzweig, 1965) with the preceding scattered sense perceptions, so that he may perform what Ehrenzweig would call a "secondary elaboration", or a "superimposition", of an all-pervasive pattern.

The Divergent Passage and Two Cognitive Mechanisms

In the sonnet by Baudelaire, then, the "emotive crescendo" is superimposed upon what I have elsewhere (Tsur, 1977: 199–214; 1998: 256–264) called a "divergent passage"; the following discussion is adapted from there. In the quoted works, I discuss this kind of structure in a variety of rhymed and unrhymed passages (including sonnets) by Milton, Wordsworth, Shelley, and Keats. The 'divergent passage' brings to an extreme the principle expounded by Coleridge in Chapter 14 of his *Biographia Literaria,* according to which the poem "diffuses a tone and spirit of unity that blends, and (as it were) fuses" each of its elements into the others. The shapes of metric and syntactic units, when considerably weakened, tend to "blend" quite inseparably, in the presence of appropriate integrating forces at higher ranks. When such integrating forces are present, the poem tends to balance and reconcile "discordant qualities [;..] a more than usual state of emotion with more than usual order". The process has the unpredictability of life and nature, of a "feeling profound and vehement" which, at the same time, is brought "under the irremissive, though gentle and unnoticed, control of will and understanding".

In some of the more distinguished divergent passages, the flickering, fluid, diffuse perceptual quality assumes overwhelming dimensions, very much like a "landslide", threatening to get out of control. The "secondary elaboration", or "superimposition" of an all-pervasive pattern imposes an "irremissive, though gentle and unnoticed, control". The main agent of this control is a powerful closure (see Herrnstein-Smith, 1968). *Prospectively,* following the sequence of lines and phrases, closure prevents the poem from becoming "like a river followed up from the mouth, each of [whose] tributaries ends in a moorland bog". The sequence becomes organized and disorganized at one and the same time. It proceeds, apparently, in an indefinite direction, waywardly, leaving syntactical and metrical loose ends; at the same time, all this *leads up,* "purposefully", to a specific point, where all the loose ends meet, where linguistic units converge with the prosodic ones. This is sometimes reinforced by further "closural devices". In the present case, the reaching of a "peak experience", the ultimate point of emotional excitement, is such a closural device.

In retrospect, closure does even more for the psychological organization of a divergent passage. Direct experimentation with readers' perception of such complex material seems hardly possible. We may, however, attempt to take some fruitful cues from Ornstein's sophisticated experiments, showing how perceived time, depending on the coding of stimuli, is different from clock time. In spite of the dissimilarity of experiences (the experience of time and of perceiving a divergent passage), the analogy is not as far-fetched as it would seem. It is not the duration of a divergent passage that matters, but the dynamism involved in the processes of coding and recoding. Both in the experience of duration and in perceiving the perceptual qualities of a divergent passage, a nonconceptual experience is determined by the amount of processed information which reaches the awareness of the observer, and the efficiency with which the information is structured. Ornstein found that "when a stimulus situation is efficiently coded (chunked into few elements) the experience of duration shortens" (Ornstein, 1969: 106). The more an interval constitutes a "unit" in the observer's experience, the shorter the experience of duration. The most impressive experiments in Ornstein's study were the ones that proved beyond a shade of doubt that "by recoding a 'random' or complex stimulus into a simpler one *after the interval was completed,* the experience of duration was shortened relative to those who did not recode the stimulus" (ibid., 108; my italics).[5]

One of the fundamental assumptions of the present study is the Gestalt Law of *Prägnanz,* according to which psychological organization will always be as good as the prevailing conditions permit. Our foregoing analysis deals, first and foremost, with the "prevailing conditions" in divergent passages, examining our findings in the light of the laws of "psychological organization". Ornstein's last-but-one experiment (described in footnote 5) disclosed an important principle of psychological organization. Observers tend to improve the psychological organization of a nonconceptual experience, and modify their awareness of it, even after the event, when a

---

[5]   For his experiment Ornstein used one of Koffka's Gestalt figures, which can be coded in either a simple or a complex manner, depending on the instruction received. Stimuli were presented to observers in four stages: I. "An example of the kind of stimulus you will be looking at" (20 sec.); II. a 1-min. segment of a tape with "random" noises; III. test stimulus (1 minute); IV. next page (20 sec.). Observers were assigned to three conditions, which varied in Stages I and IV. For the first condition, in Stage I the "complex set" figure was shown, in Stage IV, an empty page. For the second condition, in Stage I the "coded set" figure was shown, in Stage IV, an empty page. For the third condition, in stage I the "complex set" figure was shown, while in Stage IV the page consisted of the "coded set" stimulus with these words written on it: "What you have just seen was the word "man" written on its mirror image". After 20 seconds, Observers were instructed to turn to the next page and answer the duration question. This question asked them to compare the length of the tape with that of the interval following the tape (it will be remembered that, measured in clock time, they were of equal length). "The over-all differences of groups are significant [...] coding either before or after the interval, makes a significant reduction in duration length [...] wether the interval was coded before or after seems to make little difference" (Ornstein, 1969: 93–94).

| Test figure | Complex Set figure | Coded Set figure |

previously unknown "meaning" is revealed. "Meaning", in this context, is not restricted to referential meaning, but includes any systematic organizational principle. This throws some light on the nature of the divergent passage. Strong closure "marks it off" as a "unit" by a clear-cut limit. As a result, the integrating factors of the passage are emphasized, turning it into a whole that determines the character of its parts. The unit is "coded" on two different levels. On reading the passage, it appears to be "random" or, at any rate, highly complex. When the closure gives the "erratic sequence" a "structural meaning", the "random or complex stimulus" is recoded into a simpler one, imposing upon the passage "the irremissive, though gentle and unnoticed, control" of good shape, of simplicity-in-complexity, of unity-in-variety, of-order-in-disorder.

At the beginning of the present chapter, I suggested that repeated sound clusters stand out more clearly in poetry of witty than of emotional quality. In divergent textures, they tend rather to fuse into some vague, harmonious musicality. I have also noted that at least one very experienced reader of Baudelaire failed to notice the unusually intense clusters of repeated speech sounds of the quatrains. Elsewhere, I discuss another cognitive mechanism which appears to offer an explanation for this and similar perceptual phenomena in poetry (see Tsur, 1977: 186–189). In what follows, I shall adapt some of my discussion there to the present issue.

In Chapter 5, above, I made an attempt at explicating what the metaphor "shading" and "shape" may mean in the context of poetic structure. The divergence of stress pattern and meter, "a-metrical" alliterations, run-on lines and stanzas tend to "blur the lines", generating "shadings". On the semantic level, this is reinforced by the mentioning of entities that do not have stable characteristic visual shapes. It will be noticed that the same prosodic elements constitute both "shadings" and "lines", each of them increasing at the expense of the other. In drawing, many divergent lines yield shading; similarly, as Ehrenzweig has suggested, in polyphonic music, "the ear constantly oscillates between the harmonic fusion and polyphonic separation of the melodic lines" (1970: 173). "To the extent to which a musical tone is fitted into a clear melodic 'line' it is prevented from fusing into harmonic 'colour'; conversely, a strong chord will temporarily fuse the loose strands of polyphony into solid tone colour so that the separate melodic lines disappear altogether" (ibid.).

It has been observed time and again that various prosodic elements behave in vastly different manners in differing environments. Alliteration may be felt to "click" into place in a convergent poem, and blend in the general harmonies of the "miraculous organ music" of Milton's divergent verse, or in French Symbolist poetry. One striking fact may be observed in a great variety of verses. The "interblending" of deviant stresses is somehow contained in end-stopped lines and couplets, their power to affect their environment is kept down. Divergent passages are more spacious, less tightly kept in restraint. Their elements are felt to be at large, rather loosely fixed into their places. They are more apt to "melt", be fused into weakly differentiated masses; their heightened interaction is felt to generate fluid structures, with notable emotional qualities.

It seems impossible to test objectively, in the psychological laboratory, this intuitively felt tendency of "gestalt-free" elements in poetry to heighten their interaction whenever the shape of metric superordinates (lines, stanzas) is weakened. The reader who followed our comparison of alliteration in Milton and Spenser in Chapter 4 will readily concede that too many variables are involved here to allow for meaningful experiments. Again, we can do little more than establish (whatever their worth) analogies with visual perception, where this phenomenon was most dramatically demonstrated.

> When Chevreuil, in the early nineteenth century, made artists familiar with colour induction, he did not touch directly on the problem of form and colour. The experiment which demonstrated interaction most clearly was to place a small grey square on a large ground of colour. On a green ground the grey square would turn a distinct pink. Obviously the more saturated the surrounding green, the stronger was the induced pink in the square. A few years later a most paradoxical phenomenon was observed; when a sheet of semi-transparent tissue paper was placed over the whole area the saturation of the green ground was of course severely diminished. One would have expected that the colour induction in the grey square would also become much paler. But the opposite happened: the pinkness of the grey square became more pronounced. Many years passed until no less a man than the great Helmholtz gave the trite explanation of the paradox. The tissue paper made the outline of the grey square fuzzier and this weakening of its form increased colour interaction. A more impressive documentation of the overriding importance of line and form could scarcely be imagined. A comparatively crude weakening of the line was sufficient to compensate—indeed more than compensate—for the enormous loss in the saturation of colours. (Ehrenzweig, 1970: 170–171)

> We can summarize therefore that colour-interaction between figure and ground stands in inverse proportion to the good gestalt of the figure [...] the ambiguity of a weak figure on a strong ground immensely increases colour interaction. Gestalt psychology, without the help of Helmholtz's discovery, stated independently that colour interaction increases within the boundaries of a good gestalt while it is inhibited across its boundaries. (ibid., 172)

Following the description of Helmholtz's discovery, Ehrenzweig makes the following observation:

> As in all relationship between form and colour the reverse effect can also happen. Strong colour interaction tends to make sharp outlines seem much softer than they are; it levels down differences in tone. (ibid., 171)

To sum up In this chapter, we have described, at great length, the structural elements that generate in Baudelaire's "Correspondances" a 'divergent passage', as well as a superimposed pattern of "emotive crescendo". In this, we have to a large extent followed the techniques developed by such traditional critical schools as "New Criticism". But even at this level of critical activity, such terms as "gestalt-free qualities" could not be developed without some cognitive framework. Furthermore, the intense ecstatic quality perceived by many readers of this poem can be accounted for only with the help of the two cognitive mechanisms discussed in the present section. The phonetic analog of the visual mechanism of color interaction discovered by Helmholtz explains why gestalt-free elements are perceived under certain, special conditions, as more fused and more diffuse than in other, more regular circumstances. And the cognitive mechanism discovered by Ornstein can explain why the same text can be experienced "at one and the same time" as disintegrating, trembling on the brink of chaos, and as highly organized in an "emotive crescendo"; in my view, the "mysterious" ecstatic quality perceived in this type of poetry crucially depends on these mechanisms. In the fourth chapter of my book *What makes Sound Patterns Expressive?* (Tsur, 1992) I have offered a close reading of Rimbaud's sonnet "Voyelles"; here, I point out the same structural principle, of a "disintegrating" divergent passage, superimposing on the poem an emotive crescendo, 'retro-related' from its last, "ecstatic" line.

Finally, we should recall Hepburne's distinction between "detecting and experiencing an emotion" (see above, Chapter 4). One should not expect anybody to *experience* ecstasy, but rather to *recognize* an ecstatic experience on reading this or similar poems. Furthermore, the foregoing analysis should be regarded as a "crucial recommendation" for one possible performance of Baudelaire's poem: the ecstatic quality may be perceived in this poem only if it is performed in a way that is similar to the one recommended here.

CHAPTER 21

The Implied Critic's Decision Style

Two Critical Attitudes

When in a piece of criticism, or in the output of a critic, certain cognitive devices are consistently deployed in a way that is characteristic of a certain cognitive style, I call this "the implied critic's decision style". Paraphrasing Booth (1961: 71–76) on "the implied author", *the implied critic* can be defined as the person whose decisions are reflected in a given piece of criticism. "We infer him as an ideal, literary, created version of the real man; he is the sum of his choices" (74–75). The present chapter will look into the critic's possible decision styles; it will do this by elaborating on two critical attitudes. They can be defined relative to each other as ranking higher or lower on a scale, one extreme of which may be marked as what Keats called *negative capability;* the other—as *positivism* or *factualism.*

One extreme of the spectrum may be characterized, then, by Keats's description of the quality

> which Shakespeare possessed so enormously—I mean *Negative Capability,* that is when man is capable of being in uncertainties, Mysteries, doubts, without any irritable reaching after fact & reason—Coleridge, for instance, would let go by a fine isolated verisimilitude caught from the Penetralium of mystery, from being incapable of remaining content with half knowledge. (Keats, 1956: 103–104)[1]

In general, various works of literature may be ranked as demanding various degrees of negative capability (ecstatic and mystic poetry, for instance, or Kafka's *The Castle* require a conspicuously higher degree of negative capability than does Pope's *An Essay on Man*). Moreover, various readings of one and the same work may rank higher or lower in negative capability.

---

[1] Keats (1956: 103) did not have in mind, necessarily, the achievement of writing poetry; indeed, it was during a "disquisition" with his friend Dilke that "at once struck [Keats] what quality went to form a Man of Achievement, especially in Literature, and which Shakespeare possessed so enormously [...]". Both Walter Jackson Bates (1964: 56–57) and Lionel Trilling (1956: 26) claim Keats meant that Dilke lacked negative capability when he said he "was a Man who cannot feel he has a personal identity unless he has made up his Mind about every thing".

Returning to the Keats quotation above, I hope to show that around the mid-area of this spectrum of attitudes, within the boundaries of more or less legitimate literary criticism, there are pieces of criticism that exhibit the capability of "being in uncertainties, Mysteries, doubts", an "ability to make up one's mind about nothing— to let the mind be a thoroughfare for all thoughts" (Keats, 1956: 26) while other pieces of criticism suffer from "irritable reaching after fact and reason [...] from being incapable of remaining content with half knowledge". To be sure, works of criticism are often meant to dispel ignorance and uncertainties in one way or other, but one can't help feeling that in some cases "reaching after fact & reason" is "irritable" indeed; the most conspicuous cases occur in polemics or in the interpretation of works of literature that demand an unusually high degree of negative capability. If we accept Peter Berek's (1978: 121) characterization of *symbol* as "a yearning after allegory in the *absence of positive ideas* to allegorize", the symbol too will require a considerable degree of negative capability, something which will lead certain critics craving for certitude to "irritably reach after" some "positive ideas to allegorize", to paraphrase Keats and Berek.

At the pole opposite to negative capability we find Mr. Gradgrind's slogan "facts, facts, facts" (in Dickens' *Hard Times):*

> "Bitzer," said Thomas Gradgrind. "Your definition of a horse".
>
> "Quadruped, Graminivorous. Forty teeth, namely twenty four grinders, four eye-teeth, and twelve incisive. Sheds coat in the spring; in marshy countries sheds hoofs too. Hoofs hard, but requiring to be shod with iron. Age known by marks in mouth." Thus (and much more) Bitzer.
>
> "Now girl number twenty," said Mr. Gradgrind. "You know what a horse is".

There is, of course, a wide range of possible attitudes from negative capability to lifeless Victorian factualism. Few readers approximate Keats's sensitivity in reading poetry, and the majority of readers are not ruthless factualists of the Gradgrind type. In dealing with factualism, it will be most profitable, therefore, to stick to the more moderate "factual" approaches, staying well within the boundaries of legitimate and discriminating criticism.

Factualism is not defined (as many seem to think) by the exclusion of conjectures, interpretations, and integrating hypotheses. On the contrary, it is sometimes marked by an inability to discriminate between what is known for certain and what is merely possible: thus, when it comes to conjectures, interpretations, or integrating hypotheses, factualism is inclined to treat them as though they were facts. As an epitome of this attitude, in its extreme form, consider the Policeman in Pushkin's *Boris Godunov*. He hands (by chance) the warrant of arrest to Gregory, who is himself the wanted suspect (my translation—R.T.):

Policeman: Read it then aloud.

Gregory: (reading): "[…] It has been found that this accursed Grishka has
    fled in the direction of the Lithuanian border. […]"

Policeman (to Missail): *Can it be anybody but you?* [Italics mine].

Gregory: "And the King has ordained to arrest him. […]"

Policeman: And hang him.

Gregory: The warrant doesn't state *hang him.*

Policeman: Nonsense! Some things are stated, some things implied. Read
    then: To arrest and hang him.

Gregory: "… and hang him …"

In literary criticism, too, we find such instances of 'concrete' thinking, as when critics confronted with the uncertainty of whether Ophelia committed suicide or was accidentally drowned, infer from the sexual overtones of her mad songs that she was pregnant and therefore, realizing that she was now barred from marrying Hamlet, the father of her child, went mad and committed suicide (cf. above, Chapter 3). It is perhaps worth noting in parentheses that *Hamlet* as a whole ranks very high in its demands on one's negative capability.

As Margolis (1962) has suggested, the proper logic of literary interpretation is to answer questions in terms of what is more or less plausible, rather than with an un-qualified yes or no (which would be proper in answering factual questions). "The characteristic feature of critical interpretation that is philosophically most interesting is its tolerance of alternative and seemingly contrary hypotheses" (1962: 116). Like-wise, Weitz (1972: 258) suggests: "These explanations can only be adjudicated in vague terms as for their adequacy but not in precise terms as to their truth or fal-sity". This, in turn, makes a considerable psychological demand on the audience's tolerance of uncertainty. Some critics, realizing this disquieting need for "tolerance of alternative and seemingly contrary hypotheses," seek certitude—paradoxically—in multiplicity: if seemingly contrary hypotheses are tolerated, it means that anything goes; consequently, one may cling with absolute confidence to one's own interpreta-tion).[2]

---

2   Donne rightly realized, in stanza IV of his "Litanie", a fundamental kinship between
    "being in anxiety" and being overconfident, in persons that have an inclination
    toward unambiguous attitudes, that is, toward making up one's mind and coming to
    all-inclusive or all-exclusive conclusions:

> From being anxious or secure,
> Dead clods of sadnesse, or light squibs of mirth,
>   From thinking that great courts immure
> All, or no happinesse, or that this earth
>   Is only for our prison fram'd,
>   Or that thou art covetous
>   To them thou lovest, or that they are maim'd
> From reaching this worlds sweet, who seek thee thus,
> With all their might, Good Lord deliver us.

The value of scientific treatises can often be judged by the amount of ignorance they dispel. In literary criticism, there seems to be an inherent antinomy: on the one hand, such criticism reaches after knowledge; on the other hand, this knowledge is illuminating only if the critic (and his reader) are capable of being, to some extent or other, "in uncertainties, mysteries, doubts," and of making up their minds about nothing. What Keats gives us in these words is a masterful description of what psychologists of 'perception and personality' call *delayed closure.* Closure happens, for instance, when the scientist reaches his conclusion, thus dispelling ignorance regarding a particular matter of study. Now one major difference between scientific and literary thinking concerns *rapidity of closure.* While science, in general, is characterized by *rapid* closure, as opposed to the exercise of literary criticism, it remains nevertheless true that any fruitful inquiry presupposes some degree or other of delayed closure; in particular, "being in uncertainties, mysteries, doubts," making up one's mind about nothing, is an essential part of the process of understanding, even on a second, third, or hundredth reading.

This dichotomy, between *negative capability* and *quest for certitude,* based as it is on "literary" formulations in Keats's letters, is astonishingly similar to dichotomies familiar among psychologists some 80–100 years later. Here we find, e.g., liberal vs. authoritarian personality; open vs. closed mind; flexibility vs. rigidity; tolerance vs. intolerance of ambiguity; abstract vs. concrete personality; "sharpeners" vs. "levelers" (see above, Chapter 2, for this distinction); rapid vs. delayed closure, and so forth. In the present chapter, I have preferred not to resort to any of these familiar pairs of terms—in spite of my frequent recourse to the psychologists' findings—for two reasons. First, these dichotomies are similar to one another, but are not synonymous; thus, for instance, the attitude of the quest for certitude (supposed to be akin to that of the "leveler"), has sometimes to rely on "sharpening" tactics, especially in cases where "leveling" would cause coarse distortions, or when "sharpening" is an effective means of dispelling uncertainty. Second, the present work is concerned with *the implied critic's* attitudes as they are manifest in his choices in critical works; it does not pretend to know anything about the flesh-and-blood critic's psychology, in extra-literary reality. The above mentioned dichotomies, as they are used by the psychologists, reveal a series of specific tactics that can be detected in critical writings, too. These tactics seem to be in the service of the dichotomy offered here (*negative capability* and *quest for certitude*), which may be regarded as "general strategies".

"For art comes to you proposing frankly to give nothing but the highest quality to your moments as they pass, and simply for those moments' sake" says Walter Pater (1951[1873]: 897). The poets, says the great Hebrew poet Bialik, are chasing all the time those aspects that make things unique, the fleeting moment that will never again return ("Veiling and Revealing in Language"). These are precisely the aspects that the quest for certitude tolerates least.

The leveler is more anxious to categorize sensations and less willing to give up a category once he has established it. Red is red, and there's an end on't. He levels (suppresses) differences and emphasizes similarities in the interest of perceptual stability. For him the unique, unclassifiable sensation is particularly offensive, while the sharpener at least tolerates such anomalies, and may actually seek out ambiguity and variability of classification. (Ohmann, 1970b: 231)

Above, I introduced the notion of "the implied critic's decision style". I refer by this term to cases when in a piece of criticism, or in the output of a critic, certain cognitive devices are consistently deployed in a way that is characteristic of a certain cognitive style. Let us consider briefly a short instance in which several such devices are engaged in the service of one possible cognitive style. In Chapter 15, I quoted the following adverse comment by Jules Lemaître (1888) on 19th century French Symbolism:

Un symbole est, en somme, une comparaison prolongée *dont on ne nous donne que le second terme,* un système de métaphores suivies. Bref, le symbole, c'est la vieille 'allégorie' de nos pères.[3] (Quoted by Brooke-Rose, 1958: 32)

I do not pretend to know anything about Lemaître's cognitive style or, in fact, anything about him beyond what is said in the above quotation. But what he is doing here, first of all, is to *level* the differences between symbol and allegory. Furthermore, he not only levels the differences and emphasizes the similarities between allegory and symbol, but he does this for an obvious purpose: viz., to deny the existence of the unique, unclassifiable sensation. One feature that impressionism has in common with nineteenth century French Symbolism is that both desired, in Weisstein's (1974) phrase, "to capture the fleeting impression at the very moment in which sensations are transformed into feelings". When Lemaître resorts to the strategy of debunking, stating that the poetic symbol is *nothing but* the good old allegory of our fathers, he denies in fact that "the fleeting impression at the very moment in which sensations are transformed into feelings" can be captured by poetry, or that such an experience does exist at all. Toward the end of Chapter 15, I suggested that the difference between symbol and allegory does not necessarily reside in the *kind* of information, but in that information in the former is more diffusely *organized* than in the latter. It is precisely this diffuse quality that is intolerable for rigid persons, that are characterized by an "intolerance of ambiguity".

As for rapid and delayed closure, they may be described by reference to two types of *parable*. A parable treats some moral or truth in terms of a story. The parable

---

[3]   "A symbol, in sum, is a prolonged comparison *in which only the second term is given,* a system of sustained metaphors. Briefly, the symbol is nothing but the old 'allegory' of our fathers".

may be (1) an allegory, in which case *X* stands for *a*, *Y* for *b*, *Z* for *c*, and so forth. Each character is interpreted in a framework outside the story. But a parable need not be an allegory, in which case, (2) the "lesson" is drawn from the internal structure of the story, from the more or less complex relationships between its elements. Here, the story situation is analogous to certain life situations, since *X, Y,* and *Z* are related in the story in a way not unlike *a, b,* and *c* in life.

In La Fontaine's parable of the Grasshopper and the Ant, it is customarily assumed that the former stands for the idle, the latter for the industrious person. This knowledge defines the reader's attitudes throughout the narrative. However, if one allows oneself freely to follow the internal relationships of this parable, one may arrive at an interpretation that is less favorable to the ant, but no less plausible. I shall return to this possibility later.

By contrast, consider the parable of the father and the son on their way to the marketplace to sell their donkey. Regardless of which of the two rides on the donkey or walks beside it, they were severely criticed by the passers-by. As a consequence, the father and the son decide to drown the donkey in a nearby lake. Now, clearly, neither the father nor the son nor the donkey stand for anything here. The lesson, viz., that one cannot possibly satisfy all one's critics, depends on the whole of the story; one cannot make up one's mind about its meaning at an early stage. In the first-mentioned parable, *rapid closure* can be achieved by drawing on the available information concerning the received 'meaning' of the ant and the grasshopper. In the latter parable *closure* must be *delayed* until one understands what the *whole* means. In other words, in the former kind of parable, the meaning of the agents can be established in a one-to-one relationship to some entities outside the story; in the latter, it is determined by a part-whole relationship inside the story.

Two important observations must be made about the distinction between the two kinds of parables. First, in type 2 motivation is conspicuously internal. The moral, or the general truth of the parable cannot be inferred unless the parable's structure, the relationship between its elements, is sufficiently realized by the reader. Type 1 allows more easily of external motivation. The key to what stands for what, lies in a conceptual system prior to, or "outside", the parable. In type 2 one need not know that *X* stands precisely for *a*, *Y* for *b*, and so on. On the contrary, such a secondary elaboration of a type 2 parable makes one feel that the parable has been narrowed down or oversimplified in an arbitrary manner. Second (and perhaps as one possible source of this feeling), type 1 allows of more rapid closure, whereas type 2 requires a considerable delay. One's ignorance concerning the meaning of the parable cannot be dispelled before one has read (or heard) enough to realize the complex relationships between the various parts. In type 1, the interpreter may (though need not) authoritatively state at the very beginning what stands for what; thus, closure may be rapidly achieved. Readers who are intolerant of "being in uncertainties, mysteries, doubts" (that is, of delayed closure), are inclined to look for authoritative, external explanations, rather than making delicate distinctions and grasping complex part-whole relationships. Only readers who are able "to make up their minds about nothing", that is, who are capable of remaining in uncertainty, have sufficient leisure to perceive subtle and minimal cues, and so may appreciate complex or ambiguous *emergent meanings* in the course of their reading.

Waiting for Godot: Two Readings

Only a very few literary masterpieces require a degree of negative capability comparable to that demanded by Beckett's *Waiting for Godot.* Everything done or said in this play seems utterly pointless. Nevertheless, the play has an unusually strong appeal. This state of affairs has induced critics, time and again, to try and find the *real* meaning of the play, and thus dispel or mitigate ignorance. I propose to consider at some length the different degrees of negative capability manifested rather consistently in the two interpretations of the play by Eva Metman and by Günther Anders, printed in a collection of critical essays on Beckett (Esslin, ed., 1965: 117–132 and 140–151). In his introduction, the editor notes that

> [...] there can be no doubt that these critics are, above all, responding to an overwhelming emotional, almost a mystical experience. [...] Whether they analyze the language and structure of the texts or track down the philosophical allusions, or even use them as the starting point for sociological analysis (like Günther Anders) or psychological interpretation (like Eva Metman), they are all clearly impelled by a profound experience of insight which has obviously had an exhilarating effect on them. (14)

The paradoxical fact seems to be this: the powerful, almost mystical impact of the play, the "profound experience of insight", has its source in the uncertainties, mysteries, doubts that the play arouses; on the other hand, the "mysterious meanings" assigned to it *dispel* this mysterious impact. The present study assumes that sociological analysis and psychological interpretation illuminate the "overwhelming emotional, almost mystical" quality of the play in proportion to the critics' capability of elucidating it without irritably reaching after facts and reason, without unduly dispelling the "uncertainties, mysteries, doubts" inherent in the play.

The interesting thing to notice is that although both essays are rich in important observations about the play, there is a consistent difference of attitude between them. Metman's essay more frequently reaches after more clearly identifiable ideas, facts, and reasons, which are (frequently more external to the play) than Anders' does. To be sure, Metman also acknowledges the uncertainties of the play: "in so far as the onlooker [...] is captivated by the strangeness of what he witnesses, he begins to hope for a turn or solution which never comes" (120); or "[Godot] seems to be a kind of distant mirage" (124).

Let us now consider the question "Who is Godot?". To this question, several answers may be given, of which I shall present three possible types, in an order of increasing demand on one's tolerance of "being in uncertainties". Some of the most concrete and unambiguous answers are summarized in an unsympathetic account by Alain Robbe-Grillet in his essay in the same volume quoted above:

> Explanations flow in from all quarters, each more pointless than the last. Godot is God. Has not the author borrowed the root "God" from his native language? After all, why not? Godot—again, why not?—is the earthly ideal of a better social order. Don't the tramps long for food and shelter and the possibility of not being beaten? And doesn't Pozzo, who is specially said not to be Godot, hold thought in bondage? Or else, Godot is death, and they will hang themselves tomorrow if death doesn't claim them first. Godot is silence: you have to wait for it in order to have the right to be still at last. Godot is the inaccessible self that Beckett pursues through all his work, always with the ultimate hope that "This time, perhaps, at last, it will be I". (Robbe-Grillet, 1965: 110)

The kind of interpretation caricatured here is, all too obviously, an "irritable reaching after fact and reason". First, it reduces the explanation of an extremely complex situation to a single quality of the awaited person. Second, it turns a *negative* entity (the person who does not come) into a positive trait. Third, it shifts attention from the play's main theme *Waiting* for Godot, to Waiting for *Godot,* from pointless waiting to the abstractions for which Godot is alleged to stand, thus mitigating the pointlessness of waiting. If we know *who* Godot is, it is easier to understand *why* he doesn't come; thereby, we may attain closure regarding a series of unexplained matters.

   Next, consider Eva Metman's answer to the question "Who is Godot?". From her observation "He seems to be a kind of distant mirage" we might infer that he is mere illusion, the reflected image of some distant object, probably non-existent. However, what she does instead, is to bring the distant image nearer in an attempt to reveal what he "really" is, or may be.

> In the first act we hear that he does not beat the boy-messenger, who is a goatherd, but beats his brother who is a shepherd. [...] At the end of the second act we hear two more items: Godot does nothing and his beard is—probably—white.
>
>   From all this we may gather that Godot has several traits in common with the image of God as we know it from the Old and New Testaments. His white beard reminds one of God's old-father aspect. His irrational preference for one brother recalls Jehovah's treatment of Cain and Abel; so does his power to punish those who would dare drop him. The discrimination between goatherd and shepherd is reminiscent of the Son of God as the ultimate judge; as a savior for whom men wait and wait, he might well be meant as a cynical comment on the second coming of Christ; while his

doing nothing might be an equally cynical reflection concerning men's forlorn state. [...]

Whereas Matthew (25.33) says: "And he shall seat the sheep on his right hand, but goats on the left", in the play it is the shepherd who is beaten and the goatherd who is favored. What Vladimir and Estragon expect from Godot is food and shelter, and goats are motherly, milk-providing animals. In antiquity even male goats among the deities, like Pan and Dionysos, have their origin in the cult of the great mother and the matriarchal mysteries, later to become devils. (Metman, 1965: 125)

Now this is hardly reductive; on the contrary, it is rather elaborative. Metman takes up certain cues or pseudo-cues from the play and elaborates them to suit the Jehovah-image as closely as possible. Since the text itself offers very few such cues, Metman relies on external authorities rather than on internal evidence. She selects certain features of God-the-Father, or Jehovah, to which she adjusts the little information she has, torn out of its context. What she says of goats and the cult of the great mother reflects her Jungian preoccupation rather than anything verifiable in the text. Her metonymic transfer from goats to goatherd, from sheep to shepherd, and her reversal of the placement of the boys (to the left and the right) are somewhat puzzling, to say the least. It is significant, perhaps, that not only, in Metman's interpretation, Godot's composite picture relies on external authorities (Scripture, classical mythology, Jung), but she makes a barely warranted, positive picture out of sequences in which ignorance, half-knowledge, and uncertainties seem to be the central issues.

As a matter of fact, nothing has been said about Godot (except perhaps his name) that would suit an angry Jehovah better than a stereotyped, arbitrary feudal landlord. Why should Godot's white beard remind one of God's old-father image rather than of an old arbitrary landlord, or of any old man, for that matter? The only reason that comes to mind is some *a priori* assumption on Metman's part that he *ought* to stand for something, which is precisely the Policeman's logic in *Boris Godunov.*

Such critical activities originating in the quest for certitude illustrate the misapplication of cognitive tools, that were discussed in earlier chapters. In Chapter 3, we looked at Wason's experiment on the application of hypotheses and the failure to eliminate them; as Wason clearly demonstrated, when subjects look for supporting, rather than disconfirming, evidence—this mental strategy necessarily leads to the wrong conclusions. Only in literary criticism, where there is no feedback from the experimenter, is it the case that "anything goes". In chapter 9, I discussed the derivation of figurative meanings from literal ones by feature deletion. I suggested there that symbolic interpretations are frequently generated by introducing themes from outside the poetic work. In these instances, the ostensible theme of the work and the imported theme have a wide range of shared features at the higher levels. The lower-level features must be deleted from the "imported" theme, so as to avoid a conflict of features—something which Metman obviously has neglected to do.

It is worth noting that all the information given by the messenger boy seems to enhance, rather than dispel the ignorance and uncertainties about Godot. There are two brothers, one who keeps the sheep, one who keeps the goats. Is this a meaningful distinction, or are they each other's doubles? On the surface, the distinction seems stereotypical. It makes little difference which boy keeps which herd. It is the lack of certain knowledge that is emphasized in the dialogue between Vladimir and the boy. Vladimir wants to find out whether Godot is a kindly person. The boy is quite unlikely to give any sophisticated information. As a messenger, he has been admirably chosen to keep the tramps (and the audience) in perfect ignorance. He knows that Godot doesn't beat him, but beats his brother; he has no idea why. We see that this boy is simple-minded and possibly incapable of any purposeful wrongdoing. But his brother might be the devil himself. Information is simply lacking as to why one brother is beaten. The same holds true of Godot's beard. The boy can testify that Godot has a beard, but he is rather uncertain about its color; he believes it's white. One does not get sufficient information to make up one's mind as to whether Godot is a real person, a stereotype, or some allegorical figure. If Vladimir could find out what Godot does, it might give him a better idea what he is like. But the boy's answer ("Nothing") leaves us again in a state of negative knowledge. The introduction of the archetype of the Son who "shall seat the sheep on the right, but the goats on the left" seems a bit far-fetched, considering that the only cue we have is that the shepherd is beaten, but the goatherd isn't. Equally far-fetched is all that is said about goats, milk-giving animals, and matriarchal mysteries.

Three observations can be made about Metman's interpretation of Godot: it relies on external rather than internal evidence; it utilizes cues which in the play are meant to indicate ignorance, uncertainties, doubts, in order to create a positive, Jehovah-like image of Godot; it seems to assume, *a priori,* that Godot stands for something rather than nothing.

Let us now consider Anders' answer to the same question, "Who is Godot?":

> But exposed as they are to the daily continuation of their existence they can't help concluding that *they must be waiting* and exposed to their continual waiting, they can't help assuming that they are waiting for *something.* Just as we, seeing people at night waiting at a bus stop, are forced to assume that they are waiting, and that what they are waiting for will not be long in coming. Thus, to ask who or what the expected Godot is, is meaningless. *Godot is nothing but the name for the fact that life which goes on pointlessly misinterprets itself as "waiting", as "waiting for something".* The positive attitude of the two tramps thus amounts to a double negation: their inability to recognize the senselessness of their position. (Anders, 1965: 143–144)

I will not argue that this is the "correct" or "wrong" interpretation. I will, instead, consider the stategies underlying this analysis. First of all, this passage does not reach after facts and reasons; on the contrary, it points to a de-automatized relationship between actions (or rather non-actions) and reasons. It inverts logical priorities in the cause-and-effect relationship, and discriminates two loosely related processes, where we are used to seeing a single, firmly organized process (thereby enhancing rather than dispelling uncertainty). It suggests that human actions go on pointlessly, that it is merely a habit of mind to postulate *some* reason for *any* action or even for such non-actions as remaining and waiting. *"I remain, therefore I am waiting for something"*, instead of the more logical—or, at least, less sophisticated—"I am waiting, therefore I remain".

Second, in this passage Anders decomposes the positive attitude of the tramps into a double negation, indicating that it would be a mistake to assume that because Godot is a name, it must refer to someone. The effect is to keep the mind from the comfort of contemplating positive and concrete objects.

Third, this passage relies mainly on the complex and fluid interrelationships between the elements of the play; that is, it looks for internal motivation. When it goes outside the play, it does not search out well-established authorities in order to complete what is missing; rather, one's thought turns around, so to speak, and critically examines itself and, to a considerable extent, abandons its own authority. The comparison to people waiting at the bus stop provides neither facts nor reasons which might have some direct bearing on the identification of Godot with this or that abstraction. It rather illustrates a (mostly) unnamed principle which may help us to interpret the behavior of the tramps.

The point is not that Metman's interpretation is less accurate than Anders' (even though I believe it is). Rather, the point I wish to make is that, whereas the former is persistently striving for certitude, the latter, equally persistently, is relinquishing it. It is only a methodological coincidence that this difference shows up more readily in the interpretations of a work to which Anders' approach is more adequate.

A theoretical formula can dispel uncertainty as efficiently as any fact and reason, but only if it does not raise doubt as to its applicability to the case in hand. A formula may be more comforting than immediate experience, which is far more fluid and complex and offers far more evasive cues. On the other hand, the appeal to such a formula easily becomes maladaptive, in that it may bar the perception of immediate experience and, at the same time, lead us to read some irrelevant interpretation into it. Metman quotes Jung: "Why have we not long since discovered the unconscious and raised up its treasure-house of eternal images? Simply because we had a religious formula for everything psychic—and one that is more beautiful and comprehensive than immediate experience" (Metman, 1965: 131). Ironically enough, this may be true, *mutatis mutandis,* of Metman's own essay. She, too, has a comprehensive formula (and a Jungian one to boot), which comes time and again between herself and the immediate experience of the play. Consider the following quotation from the play:

> Astride of a grave and a difficult birth. Down in the hole, lingeringly, the gravedigger puts on the forceps. We have time to grow old. The air is full of our cries. But habit is a great deadener. (From *Waiting for Godot,* quoted by Metman, 1965: 127).

In discussing this passage, Metman uses the seemingly harmless simile "our existence in which the womb and the tomb seem to fit together like two hemispheres" (ibid.). One page later, however, the hemispheres are taken as a fact of the play and turn out to be the missing image required to adjust Beckett's play to a mythologically oriented interpretation:

> This episode may well explain why there are no women in this play, that is to say women on the human level: the mother goddess, who is both the womb and the tomb, envelops all and everything with her power. In ancient Egypt this goddess was known as an upper and lower hemisphere, not only feared but worshipped in her two aspects as Nut and Naunet. Beckett, however, refrains both from differentiation and from valuation. (Ibid., 128)

Here, Metman's reaching after facts and reasons becomes "irritable" indeed. She implies that every fact (positive as well as negative) about the play must have some reason, and a weighty one at that. For example, although there is no female character in the play, she takes the dubious "Great Mother" archetype as a *fact* of the play and offers it as a *reason;* a way of reasoning which, by the way, is characteristic of concrete thought (cf. the Policeman in *Boris Godunov).* When such thinking resorts to abstractions (e.g., Femininity), it is not always careful about distinguishing between them and the things from which they are abstracted; in this case, as if the mother-goddess, symbolized by two hemispheres that are not mentioned in the play, could be treated just as concretely as a Iocasta, as an Ophelia, as a Phèdre. It might perhaps be more readily granted that an unconventional play like Beckett's is unconventional in this respect too, in not having a female character. As it is now, it appears that Metman has found a problem to suit her solution.

Spheres and circles have frequently served as mythical symbols by virtue of their geometrical perfection or their strong unitary shape. When Plato speaks of men and women as hemispheres, he has in mind some potential harmony between them. Do Vladimir's words about the gravedigger with his forceps indicate such a harmonious view of life? Or do they have merely some grotesque quality? We may grant that giving birth is customarily related to femininity and that in many cultures (ours included), earth is metaphorically related to motherhood. But are Vladimir's words focused on this feminine principle, or on the absurdity of our *condition humaine?*

Let us work out the internal logic of this image, in terms of mental habits and their manipulation by literary means. *Life,* marked at its extremes by birth and death, is the center of the universe in the consciousness of the ordinary men and women. By contrast, in Christian religious traditions it is only a transient episode for the soul which "seeketh heaven, and comes of heavenly breath". Religious poetry may attempt to bring man to an insight into this truth, by a sudden shift of attention from the habitual *figure* to its *ground,* the markers of its extremes, as in Sir Philip Sidney's sonnet "Leave me, O love which reachest but to dust":

> let that light be thy guide
> In this small course which birth draws out to death ...

Vladimir sharpens this inverted image to absurdity: Man passes straight from the womb to the tomb, assisted by the gravedigger's forceps. In a world in which "God is dead", there is nothing beyond, and what is in between is meaningless and negligible. The emotional disorientation aroused by this state of affairs is reinforced by the grotesque image.

Let me quote an additional passage in which Metman achieves certainty by similar means:

> Neuman describes the emergence of self-consciousness in adolescence as one in which "feelings of transitoriness and mortality, impotence and isolation" prevail, "in absolute contrast to the [child's] situation of contentment and containment". *Obviously,* the figures of the play are *exactly* on the border between the two phases. (ibid., 129; italics mine)

For our present purposes, the question of the general validity of theoretical assumptions carries little weight in this and similar passages. Of far greater importance is (1) whether one's theoretical formula is validated by the play as a whole, or whether isolated details of the play are made to comply with that formula; and (2) whether or not the critic discriminates between what is known for sure and what is only more or less probable.

Here, I wish to mention briefly two additional ways of achieving certainty which lead Metman toward concreteness and positivistic interpretations. One is to take out the disquieting element from complex feelings, relationships, and personalities by labeling them, preferably with some psychological term. Thus we are told that "in Lucky [...] we can see the destroyed contact with the creative sources of the psyche"; there is "a mutual sado-masochistic relationship between himself and Pozzo", which is "a mutual fixation" (Metman, 1965: 123). "The wish to control (Pozzo) and the wish to be protected (Lucky) remain inseparable. So do the impotence of consciousness (Vladimir) and the power of unconsciousness (Estragon)" (ibid., 132). This last quotation in particular, with its insistence on rapid or immediate closure in experiencing the play, seems to turn the parable into allegory.

By contrast to Metman, who removes the disquieting element from experience by boiling down the complex phenomena to a single label established in a psychological system outside the play, Anders goes the other way 'round. He foregoes the certitude inherent in such well-worn terms as *time,* "making them strange", so to speak, by proffering operational definitions with a highly descriptive content. After claiming that life in the play is life without time, he explains:

> By this I mean that what we call "time" springs from man's needs and his attempts to satisfy them, that life is temporal only because needs are either *not yet* satisfied, or goals have *already* been reached, or objectives reached are *still* at one's disposal. Now we have seen that in Estragon's and Vladimir's lives objectives no longer exist. For this reason in the play time does not exist either. (Anders, 1965: 146)

The other way to dispel uncertainty is to quote an external authority preferably of a certain status, such as Beckett himself. Metman quotes from other works by Beckett, mainly from his *Proust,* assuming that what he says of Proust applies to *Waiting for Godot* as well. These quotations are beautifully framed and doubtless may have a point, and some bearing on Beckett's preoccupations; however, their applicability to *Godot* should not be taken for granted. And although such a use of quotations is not necessarily illegitimate in literary criticism, however, in this general atmosphere of quest for certitude they definitely create a bias against negative capability.

As I have already suggested, it would be foolish *not* to expect a theoretical discourse or literary interpretation to dispel ignorance. However, one also may expect a literary discourse to communicate some observations which do not cling so desperately to facts and reasons, observations that involve what in psychology is called a "shift of mental sets" ("set" understood as the readiness to respond in a certain way, cf. above, Chapter 1). An increased readiness to change one's mental sets, to relinquish the psychological atmosphere of security offered by facts, reasons, labels, and theories, is tantamount to what Keats called an ability "to make up one's mind about nothing—to let the mind be a thoroughfare for all thoughts".

The main difference between Metman and Anders has to do with their readiness to change sets. Metman seems reluctant to revise and modify her external authorities in the light of internal evidence of the play. As we have seen in Anders' bus-stop comparison, he relinquishes the psychological atmosphere of security inherent in the cause-and-effect chain by decomposing it into an objective set of observed facts and a psychological set of thinking habits. Thought is directed toward some external object; at the same time, it examines itself. Notice also how Anders' comparison is more flexible than Metman's hemisphere simile. In the latter, the image is supposed to "complete" the image mentioned in the play; then it is shown that the "complete" image occurs in Egyptian mythology (hence it is an archetype; hence it has a beneficial effect on works of literature), and then it is accepted as a fact in the play. In the bus-stop comparison, by contrast, a (nameless) principle is extracted, which in turn is to be applied to the structure of the play. Anders also explains, from a different angle, the negative entity denoted by the positive name "Godot" as a *double negation.*

Anders' essay is characterized by a virtually total absence of technical terms. Instead, we find a sequence of threefold set-shifts: comparison→ abstraction→ application. To see this, compare the places where his explanations come close to those of Metman's. Both authors say that there is, in the group of works to which *Godot* belongs, an *alienation effect.* In discussing this issue, Metman is inclined to shift the focus of attention away from the process of changing sets, either to the facts observed or to psychological terms that label the factors involved in the process. Thus, we read that Beckett "strips his figures so thoroughly of all those qualities in which the audience might recognize itself that, to start with, an *alienation effect* is created that leaves the audience mystified" (Metman, 1965: 120); or that Beckett's new form of drama "creates a vacuum between the play and the audience so that the latter is compelled to experience something itself, be it a reawakening of the *awareness of the archetypal powers* or a *reorientation of the ego* or both (Brecht has given this the name of alienation effect)" (ibid.; italics mine).

At the outset of his essay, Anders states that *Waiting for Godot* is a parable. Characteristically, he does not use this generic term merely for the classification or labeling of the play. Nor does he use it as an excuse for indulging in a what-stands-for-what type of interpretation. Instead, he focuses attention on the mechanism of parables, implying a concern with internal motivation and delayed closure. Parables work, he says, through "inversion", a principle typically conducive to changing sets. His next step is to demonstrate how the principle of inversion works in classical parables. Finally, he shows how this principle can be applied to *Waiting for Godot,* with the added twist, or change of sets, that *Godot* is a *negative* parable.

> When Aesop or Lafontaine wanted to say: men are like animals, did they show men like animals? No. Instead they reversed—and this is the peculiarly amusing alienation effect of all fables—the two elements of the equation, its subject and its predicate; that is, they stated that animals behave as men. A quarter of a century ago Brecht followed the same principle, when, in the *Three-penny Opera,* he wanted to show that bourgeois are thieves; he too turned the subject into the predicate and presented thieves behaving as bourgeois. It is this process of substitution which one must have grasped before starting to interpret Beckett's fable. For Beckett too uses it in an extremely subtle way. (Anders, 1965: 140)

The drastic shift of view from the obvious to the incredible-yet-true is conspicuous in the following passage (the parenthetical italics are mine):

> In those situations in which we, the more fortunate ones, play football and, once we have finished, can start all over again, Estragon plays the *da capo* game "shoe off, shoe on"; and not in order to exhibit himself as a fool, but to exhibit *us* as fools; in order to demonstrate through the device of inversion that our playing of games *(the pointlessness of which is already made*

> *invisible by its public recognition)* has no more meaning than this. (Ibid.,
> 148–149)

The real meaning of the scene is not stated here in terms of "Estragon stands for
...", but in terms of "Unlike anything in life as this scene may seem, it still has an
important ingredient in common with life", which implies that closure may not be
achieved before the intricate life situation is grasped, the scene is grasped, and the
two compared:

> The inverted meaning of the scene in which Estragon plays "shoe off, shoe
> on" reads: "Our playing of games is a shoe off, shoe on, too, a ghostly
> activity meant only to produce the false appearance of activity". And, in the
> last analysis: "Our real shoe on, shoe off—that is, our everyday existence—
> is nothing but a playing of games, clownlike without real consequences
> ...". (Ibid., 149)

Anders' shifts of attitudes do not stop here. He keeps a further shocking change in
store, one highly illuminating of the tragic quality so many readers have felt in the
two clowns: "'We are their brothers—only that the two clowns *know* that they are
playing, which we don't'. Thus it is not they but we who are actors in the farce.
And this is the triumph of Beckett's inversion" (ibid., 149). One very important implication of this kind of analysis is the loosening of the rigid categories that are so
vital for "factualist" thinking: "Is there really a recognizable boundary line between
our 'real life' and our 'playing'?" (ibid., 148).

   Whereas Metman makes her point through "disambiguation" and excessive reliance on psychological labels, Anders' analysis of Estragon's "shoe off, shoe on"
game is counter-reductive, so to speak. Its subtlety consists in presenting this game
from several angles, from a shifting point of view. Estragon is shown to be an ironic if unwitting comment on generally accepted views and ideas. Anders' essay focuses upon changing angles, fluid experience, so as to arrive at structural principles
behind the contents. Metman's essay focuses upon Jungian psychology as "corroborated" by the play. It arrives at those contents of the play which are comparable to
the archetypal contents of the collective unconscious.[4]

   Anders' and Metman's readings of *Waiting for Godot* raise, in all its rigor, the
question: how can we know whether the personae of a play or a story do or do not
stand for certain abstractions; whether a given piece of literature achieves its effect
through its meaning or through its lack of meaning? Or, in terms of our earlier ty-

---

[4]   I wish to emphasize again that my critique of Metman's interpretation concerns the
    implied critic's lack of negative capability, and *not* Jung's theory of archetypes. As
    will be clear from chapter 14, above, and from my book on "Kubla Khan" (Tsur,
    2006), I consider Maud Bodkin's Jungian interpretation of this poem as one of the
    most successful efforts for appreciating this poem; in addition, it is an outstanding
    example of exercising negative capability in literary criticism.

pology of parables: whether *Waiting for Godot* is a parable of type 1 or type 2? In Chapter 11, I suggested that the style of this and similar works is based on the "efficient overstressing" of the conception of Man's condition in the world as "hemmed in". The author places his protagonist in an "extreme situation", in which Man's sense of limitedness is "heightened, to any degree heightened". I propose to call this kind of literature "literature of extreme situations". Of the two conceptions of the play considered here, one (Metman's) links its interpretation to a conceptual system outside the play, while the other (Anders') insists that the structure of the *whole* play must be grasped, if one is to perceive the hopelessness of the tramps' situation and the pointlessness of their waiting. Only in the very final episode, when the messenger boy announces for the second time that Mr. Godot cannot come this time, can we decide that the waiting is pointless indeed—whatever external idea Godot may or may not stand for. My claim is that one cannot infer from the details of the play itself which path should be followed. In general, this decision depends on the work's genre or style; the critic must make a deliberate, *a priori* decision as for which genre or style concept he wants to attribute the play to. As I have argued in Chapter 17, such an attribution (or even the definition of the concepts involved) crucially depends on the critic's tolerance, respectively intolerance of uncertainty and, in the final analysis, on his cognitive complexity.

Two Attitudes: A Recapitulation

We have compared at some length two readings of *Waiting for Godot* for the sake of what might be called their psychological settings. As we have seen, the readings differ in their strategies of "reaching after fact and reason", and the corresponding psychological settings can be described in terms of greater or lesser tolerance of uncertainty and ignorance; the respective strategies in terms of the easier vs. the more difficult route toward the achievement of certainty and knowledge. We have been interested in the contents of the two interpretations only insofar as the former strategy tends to be maladaptive. Our major interest has been directed toward such structural considerations as isolation vs. integration of observations; rigid vs. fluid categories; external vs. internal motivation; simple vs. multiple relationships; labeling vs. discrimination; inert vs. changing sets; etc.

The persistent quest for stability inherent in positivism and factualism, as well as their excessive reliance upon external evidence, may remind us of those ancient drawings which represent the earth firmly fixed on the back of a giant turtle or elephant. The "cosmology" of negative capability, on the other hand, prefers to conceive of the earth in terms of *Job* 26:7:

> He stretches out the north over the void,
> And hangs the earth upon nothing.

Or, in more modern terms, the earth "hangs" upon the sun through the invisible forces of gravitation, just as the innumerable suns of the universe "hang" upon one another, with no Archimedean point outside them.

As I have suggested above, the critical tendencies ascribed to negative capability and the quest for certitude, respectively, bear a remarkable resemblance to such psychological tendencies as flexibility vs. rigidity, abstract vs. concrete personality, tolerance vs. intolerance of ambiguity. The attitude of the flexible person, the one who is tolerant of ambiguity, has been characterized as follows:

> The categorical or conceptual attitude is characterized by ability or readiness to assume a mental set voluntarily, to shift from one aspect of the situation to another, to keep in mind, simultaneously, various aspects, to grasp the essentials of a given whole, to break up a given whole into parts and to isolate them voluntarily, to abstract common properties, to plan ideationally, to assume an attitude toward "the merely possible", to think and perform symbolically, and finally to detach our ego from the outer world. (Frenkel-Brunswick, 1968: 136)

Conversely, the attitude of a rigid person, one who is intolerant of ambiguity, has been characterized as follows:

> Too much existing emotional ambiguity and ambivalence are counteracted by denial and intolerance of cognitive ambiguity. It is as if everything would go to pieces once the existing discrepancies were faced. To avoid this catastrophe everything that might abet the uncertainty and opaqueness of life is desperately avoided by a selection of undisturbing, clear-cut, and therefore too general or else too concrete aspects of reality. (ibid., 134)

Although what Keats called negative capability presupposes a flexible personality, the quest for certitude is not necessarily correlated with a rigid personality. Frequently, the two show some correlation, in which "situational interferences" such as academic climate and conventions, limitations of communication, and so on may be involved. Consequently, when I claim to have discerned the correlatives of the quest for certitude in a certain piece of criticism, I do not pretend to have "diagnosed" the critic's empirical personality. I am interested in those generalizations that are "capable of unfolding their meaning in particular application, and [in] those which suggest how the mind works in certain classes of experience"—to quote Knights (1964: 229); my aim is to establish the relevance of such classes of experience to the response to literature and, mediately, to literary criticism, scholarship, and the teaching of literature.

I have treated the implied critic's decisions in the perspective of a "decision style". Two characteristics of these decisions are of importance here: that they exhibit some consistency with respect to the tolerance of incertitude, over considerable periods of time and a wide range of critical tasks; and that at a lower level of generalization, a wide range of cognitive devices or strategies are deployed that deeply imply one another (or, are significantly correlated). The present discussion is only meant to give a general orientation in this problematic domain. I have elsewhere discussed the variety of specific issues encountered in critical discussions of two kinds of literature that exact greater than usual degrees of negative capability.[5]

In fact, the psychological dichotomies mentioned above are treated as personality *styles,* or cognitive *styles.* According to Else Frenkel-Brunswick, the signs of such syndromes as the intolerance of ambiguity can be detected at a number of personality levels. The same author also indicates some significant psychoanalytical correlates of this syndrome. Such findings are in complete harmony with the basic hypotheses of the present book. In the following, I am going to investigate the roots of the tolerance or intolerance of incertitude; I will do this in psychological terms, using the concept of 'cognitive complexity'. In Chapter 1, I have discussed ordinary consciousness as a personal construct. In Chapter 3, I have followed in greater detail the acquisition of cognitive tools for constructing a stable world from the constant flux of information. Doing that, I dwelt at some length on the problem of achieving "cognitive stability" on the one hand and, on the other, of adequately handling the constant flux of information in one's physical, social, and spiritual environment. I suggested there that one must be assured that the world remains essentially the same, if one is to shift mental sets without apprehension, in accordance with the demands of a reality changing in its concrete details. And conversely, only whoever is capable of shifting his mental sets according to the demands of changing reality, whoever is capable of relinquishing cognitive categories created on the evidence of a small section of reality, is capable of constructing a cognitive model that is stable over a considerable period of time, without having to ignore details of this constant flux on the more concrete levels. In what follows, I shall suggest that this psychological "mission impossible" is accomplished through the construction of a hierarchic system of information-processing.

Levels of Information Processing in Reading Poetry

In the present chapter I have based my psychological hypotheses on studies in perception and personality. Originally, these were two independent areas of research; but by the late forties, the two supposedly unconnected problem clusters came to be seen as different aspects of one and the same process. For instance, a low tolerance

---

5   In my paper "Kubla Khan and the Implied Critic's Decision Style" (Tsur, 2006: 11–77), I discussed at great length the cognitive devices and strategies deployed in dealing with this ecstatic poem. In a Hebrew paper, "Solving Riddles and the Quest for Certitude: Hebrew Critics Confronting Literature of Extreme Situations", I have identified similar devices and strategies in the handling of a very different genre: "literature of extreme situations", including fiction by Kafka, Agnon, and A. B. Yehoshua (Tsur, 1996: 119–206).

for perceptual ambiguity and cognitive dissonance was found to be significantly correlated with lacking emotional responsiveness, dogmatism, and authoritarianism; conversely, a high tolerance for perceptual ambiguity and cognitive dissonance was found to be significantly correlated with emotional ambivalence, openness to new experience, and a liberal world view.[6] Later studies, primarily those conducted in the sixties, then established strong correlations between these findings and the different styles of information-processing.

Information processing involves the selection of stimuli from the environment, and their arrangement into "dimensions" (in our case, the "environment" will be that of the poem); the resulting dimensions are then compared and/or combined according to certain rules. H. M. Schroder and his colleagues (upon whose work I have drawn liberally) have established correlations between personality styles and styles of information processing. For example, a personality characterized by intolerance of ambiguity—that is, one with a low integration index, as we will call it below, following Schroder—"identifies and organizes stimuli in a fixed way, and the rules derived from existing schemata are explicit in defining this one way" (Schroder et al., 1970: 177). What psychologists identify as an "abstract personality" is defined in terms of "flexibility" or "tolerance of ambiguity", corresponding to what we, in the present and earlier chapters, have termed "negative capability". Such a personality is not necessarily characterized as lacking rules, but rather as possessing a greater number of conflicting rules on a lower level which may be accommodated by rules on a higher level.

It should be emphasized that the mere number of dimensions used does not necessarily determine a person's level of information processing:

> A person using two dimensions may be able to use them conjointly, combine them in different ways and compare outcomes, while a person using three dimensions may use them independently in a compartmentalized way. The number of dimensions taken alone, then, has no necessary relationship to the level of information processing; but given complex combinatory rules, the potential for generating new attributes of information is higher, and the degree to which one stimulus can be discriminated from another is increased as the number of perceived dimensions increases. (ibid., 176)

Moreover, the very nature of systematic inquiry may confine a given piece of literary criticism to the exploration of a single dimension. It would be absurd, therefore, to assume an inflexible personality whenever a critic explores only one dimension

---

6   See the two symposia on these matters, held in 1948 and 1949 (Bruner and Kretch eds., 1968[2], and Blake and Ramsey eds., 1951). Although, as Else Frenkel-Brunswick says, "rigidity in one respect may go with flexibility in another", she also adds: "There is some indication that in the case of distinct intolerance of emotional ambivalence one may as a rule be able to locate at least some aspect of intolerance of cognitive ambiguity although these may often be apparent on a higher level than that of perception proper" (Frenkel-Brunswick, 1968: 139–140).

of a work. One may, rather, distinguish various degrees of integration (versus compartmentalization), various degrees of tolerance for uncertainties, alternatives, ambiguities, cognitive dissonance, and the like. As Schroder and his colleagues point out,

> [The] shift from absoluteness to the generation of alternatives increases the amount of functional information available at a given time. Uncertainty increases with the presence of more abstract properties, not in the sense that the world is more chaotic, but rather in the sense that alternatives exist. Much more information is sought before resolutions are made; when they have been made, these resolutions are less fixed and the system remains open to the perception and effects of alternatives. (Ibid., 182)

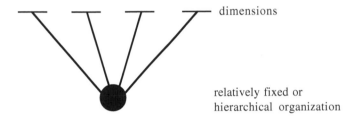

dimensions

relatively fixed or
hierarchical organization

Figure 21.1   Low Integration Index (from Schroder et al., 1970: 177).

Let us now return to La Fontaine's fable "The Grasshopper and the Ant", which is a rather simple poem. The stimuli provided by the actants (grasshopper and ant) can be arranged into a singing vs. working dichotomy, which in turn can be interpreted as either idle vs. industrious or artistic vs. materialistic.

A person with a low integration index will read the stimuli at any time unidimensionally, and never consider the possibility of ambiguity or conflict. For example, the ant's final dictum, "Well then go now and dance", will be taken as a witty answer, which teaches the grasshopper a good lesson. Dancing will be categorized as another form of idleness; singing and dancing will not be thought of as creative artistic activities. We could, however, interpret the ant's closing comment less favorably, as selfish, self-righteous, or insensitive to art.[7] If we accepted that interpretation categorically, we would again be exhibiting a low integration index. But if we perceive *both* interpretations *as alternatives,* our integration index will be somewhat higher, of "moderately low", in Schroder's terms:

---

[7]   Only recently, when writing Chapter 25, I ran into the same interpretation of La Fontaine's parable in Edmond Rostand's *Cyrano de Bergerac*. The poet–baker Ragueneau tells his wife (who has just slurred his poet–friends, "your wretched scribblers"): "Fourmi !... n'insulte pas ces divines cigales!" (Ant!... don't insult these divine grasshoppers!). Here, obviously, Rostand seeks a witty effect, and does not presume to offer a "plausible" interpretation.

The generation of alternatives or of uncertainty is an important step in increasing abstractness, but at this level the system is characterized by ambivalence. Unlike low-level structure, for which the problem of choice is minimal, moderately low structure generates alternate interpretations without fixed basis for choice or organization. For example, there is no fixed rule for what is right or wrong (ibid., 180).

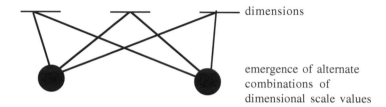

dimensions

emergence of alternate
combinations of
dimensional scale values

Figure 21.2   Moderately Low Integration Index (from Schroder et al., 1970: 179).

Now, if we attempt critically to *choose* between alternatives, we will exhibit a moderately high integrative capacity; for that, we must develop a rather sophisticated mechanism for comparing and relating alternatives. In Schroder's terms, "the significance of moderately high structure may be described as the initial emergence of rules for identifying more complex relations than alternation" (ibid., 182). To return to our example, in order to judge whether the ant's behavior is right or wrong, we must relate its answer to the possible interpretations of the singing vs. working dichotomy: we must decide whether the grasshopper's singing is mere "fiddling time away", or an artistic activity and whether the ant is industrious or concerned solely with its material needs. What is required from us here is quite complex; we must assume an attitude toward what may or may not be the case: if p then q; but if r then s.

La Fontaine's fable is not sufficiently complex to allow an integration of both readings. We are required to choose one of the alternatives basing ourselves on internal evidence. For instance, the grasshopper's expressed assurance that he is going to repay the loan with interest before the autumn seems strongly to suggest that he is a deceiver; we have little reason to suppose that he will be better off next year. Thus, the idle vs. industrious reading is reinforced. Genre considerations, too, would support a similar conclusion: neo-classical parable was more interested in universal moral traits than in social class distinctions. But notice: an automatic acceptance of the traditional interpretation may be right in its results, but maladaptive in its procedure. If alternative possibilities are automatically excluded, the reading will be "projective".

As long as we are dealing with a relatively unsophisticated piece like "The Grasshopper and the Ant", a rigid, low-integrated, authoritative reading may "work". However, the same sort of reading will become projective in a more sophisticated text. "When a person continues to perceive the world completely in terms of his own schemata, ignoring subtle situational changes and the alternate interpretations of others around him, he is 'projecting'. Thus, projection may be considered to be a defense mechanism commonly used by individuals low in integrative complexity" (Schroder et al., 1970: 178–179).

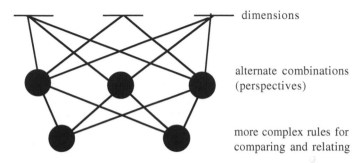

Figure 21.3 Moderately High Integration Index (from Schroder et al., 1970: 182).

Conversely, those who possess a high tolerance of ambiguity frequently react against projective readings. New Criticism, for instance, which was part of what René Wellek called "the revolt against Positivism", furiously opposed interpretations that minimized conflict by excluding from consideration traits of characters that did not fit into the preconceived black-and-white categories. Thus, the *Scrutiny* group not only objected to such projective questions as "How many children had Lady Macbeth?" or "Where was Hamlet at the time of his father's death?", but also emphasized those traits of Hamlet that did not exactly fit the image of the "sweet prince" and those characteristics of Othello that were dissonant with the image of the "noble hero". In this way, they arrived at more complex characters, that were less consonant with the reader's initial sympathetic attitude. For the same reasons, they stressed again and again that characters could not be isolated from the dramatic structures which embodied them. Characteristically, the New Critics often engaged in "ambiguity hunting" at the text's verbal level.

Goethe's "Erlkönig"
Let us turn now to a more sophisticated example, Goethe's ballad "Erlkönig".

> Wer reitet so spät durch Nacht und Wind?
> Es ist der Vater mit seinem Kind;
> Er hat den Knaben wohl in dem Arm,
> Er faßt ihn sicher, er hält ihn warm.
>
> "Mein Sohn, was birgst du so bang dein Gesicht?"—
> Siehst, Vater, du den Erlkönig nicht?

Den Erlenkönig mit Kron' und Schweif?—
"Mein Sohn, es ist ein Nebelstreif."

"Du liebes Kind, komm, geh mit mir!
Gar schöne Spiele spiel' ich mit dir;
Manch' bunte Blumen sind an dem Strand,
Meine Mutter hat manch gülden Gewand."

Mein Vater, mein Vater, und hörest du nicht,
Was Erlenkönig mir leise verspricht?—
"Sei ruhig, bleibe ruhig, mein Kind;
In dürren Blättern säuselt der Wind."

"Willst, feiner Knabe, du mit mir gehn?
Meine Töchter sollen dich warten schön;
Meine Töchter führen den nächtlichen Reihn,
Und wiegen und tanzen und singen dich ein."

Mein Vater, mein Vater, und siehst du nicht dort
Erlkönigs Töchter am düstern Ort?—
"Mein Sohn, mein Sohn, ich seh' es genau:
Es scheinen die alten Weiden so grau."

"Ich liebe dich, mich reizt deine schöne Gestalt;
Und bist du nicht willig, so brauch ich Gewalt."—
Mein Vater, mein Vater, jetzt faßt er mich an!
Erlkönig hat mir ein Leids getan!—

Dem Vater grauset's, er reitet geschwind,
Er hält in den Armen das ächzende Kind,
Erreicht den Hof mit Müh' und Not;
In seinen Armen das Kind war Tot.

Who is that riding so late through the night and the wind?
It is the father with his child.
He holds the boy well in his arms,
Retains him safely, keeps him warm.

"My son, why are you hiding your face, so frightened?"—
"Father, don't you see the Erlking,
The Erlking with crown and robe?"—
"My son, it is a stripe of haze."

"You, darling child, come, go with me!
I will play such nice games with you;
There are lots of bright flowers on the shore;
My mother has many golden robes."

"My father, my father, don't you hear
What the Erlking promises me whispering?"—
"Be calm, stay calm, my child,
The wind is rustling in the dry leaves."

"Will you, fine boy, go with me?
My daughters will look after you nicely,
My daughters will dance the nocturnal ring
And will rock and dance and sing you to sleep."

"My father, my father, don't you see over there
The Erlking's daughters at that darkish place?"—
"My son, my son, I can see it quite well:
It is the old willows that gleam so grey."

"I love you, your beautiful shape attracts me;
If you won't come of your own will, I will use force."—
"My father, my father, now he's taking hold of me!
He has hurt me, the Erlking!"

The father shudders, he rides fast,
He holds the groaning child in his arms,
He reaches the manor with troble and strain;
In his arms the child was dead.

In this poem, the environment can be tracked in at least two ways: the sense stimuli can be interpreted from the son's point of view as "the Erlking with crown and robe", "what the Erlking promises in a whisper", "the Erlking's daughters" or, from the father's point of view, as "a stripe of cloud", "the wind rustling in dry leaves", "the willows that gleam so grey". Any interpretation will have to decide, eventually, whether the son's or the father's vision, or a combination of the two, reflects the ballad's reality. A supporter of the father's vision may rely, for instance, upon facts observable in our everyday, extra-literary environment; by contrast, an advocate of the son's vision may appeal to the conventions of the ballad genre. Even the son's death at the end of the poem does not confirm either vision; each uni-dimensional interpretation will account for the event equally well, neither disproving, nor proving incontrovertibly the existence of the Erlking. The boy may have been critically ill, and the Erlking the figment of his feverish imagination. As the history of philosophy shows, the world can thoroughly be interpreted in either materialistic, or in idealistic (or transcendentalistic) terms. This seems true of the poem too.

In Chapter 3, I quoted Bruner on perception: "Perceiving takes place in a 'tuned organism'" (1951: 124). A hypothesis "may be regarded as a highly generalized state of readiness to respond selectively to classes of events in the environment" (Bruner, 1951: 125). As a rule, we order structurally weak percepts with the help of hypotheses (ibid., 126–130). Figure 3.1 in Chapter 3 demonstrates this on a very elementary level; the present case, that of "Erlkönig", provides an infinitely more sophisticated example. Low-differentiated noises in the forest are perceived by the son as "what the Erlking whispers", by the father as "the wind rustling in dry leaves"; the same happens with the low-differentiated visual information in the stormy midnight forest.

Many years ago, at a faculty seminar, I used this poem to support a theory of interpretation according to which conflicting data in a poem could be reconciled by a hypothesis; moreover, conflicting hypotheses could, in certain cases, be reconciled by means of a "superhypothesis". In the present instance, the father and the son give conflicting accounts of the same environment. As suggested above, many readers tend to achieve certainty by denying the existence of the Erlking, attributing his appearance in the poem to the boy's imagination; these readers support their conclusion by arguments taken from our every-day experience; others try to achieve certainty by accepting the Erlking's existence, justifying their decision by reference to the conventions of the ballad genre. By contrast, the present view would prefer to accommodate these two incompatible hypotheses in a wider conception, arguing from our fundamental uncertainty as to the "correct" view of the universe, viz., idealistic or materialistic. Alternatively, we might accommodate the conflicting visions in a "romantic" view of the universe, according to which there is a physical reality accessible to the senses, beyond which a "more real" reality may be intuited (the father and the son, respectively, representing the two kinds of perception).

Two of the people attending the seminar failed to see the point of my argument. They maintained that there was only one correct construal of the reality represented in the poem; one person argued for the father's vision, the other for the son's. Curiously enough, while both were quarreling with my theory, which admitted both points of view, were barely taking notice of each other's arguments.

In terms of the present chapter, we may make some modest claims about the levels of information processing apparent in these particular persons' responses to this particular poem at that particular time. Even the presence of a steadfast advocate of an opposing interpretation could not make any of them admit the need (or at least the possibility) of alternate schemata or of some more complex structure which could accommodate the conflicting visions. My interpretation, which attempted to integrate the conflicting views, was perhaps experienced as threatening, and dismissed as overly sophisticated or overly ingenious (a defense strategy favored by people with a low-complexity attitude); by contrast, each of the conflicting hypotheses representing the single-minded non-integrative attitude, ignored the opposite view (as to acknowledge it would have required fixed criteria for preferring one view to the other). There seems to be little doubt that both these persons strove to achieve stability and to eliminate cognitive dissonance through organizing stimuli in a fixed hierarchy. Their levels of information processing, in responding to this poem, appear to be of low or moderately low integration. In Schroder's words, "the more undifferentiated the schemata, the lower the potential for generating [or tolerating—RT] conflict or ambiguity or for resolving ambiguity by means other than exclusion" (ibid., 177). The two systems, though contradictory in the hierarchic organization of their contents, appeared to be of a similar level of integration and structures.

An integration system having fairly complex rules for comparing and relating schemata might handle Goethe's ballad in a different way. The ballad presents a pathetic situation. The child, irrespective of whether the Erlking is objectively or merely subjectively real, is terrorized by his advances; the father, anxious to comfort his child, does not particularly care whether or not there is an Erlking. The highly emotional content of the poem is reinforced by the fact that the two perceptions of the environment are not only *incompatible* but, in the dramatic sense, also *conflicting*. The reader, in order to respond with due awe, apprehension, and anxiety, must perceive that the same elements in the poem contribute to two different readings, and he must assume an attitude toward the text which does not rule out either possibility.

Now, if we characterize the father's and the son's visions as equally valid, can we reconcile the conflict and posit some form of unity at a higher level? I would argue that the Romantic view of the world embraces both realities—the sensuous and the supersensuous, the materialistic and the idealistic—in one harmonious vision: neither reality is rejected; each becomes a complement to the other. As I argued in Chapter 11, Romantic poetry at its best aspires to overcome the limitations of the physical world, in order to experience the "other" world that is inaccessible to the senses; sometimes, this is achieved by "the use of imagery to express the otherworldly in terms of this world and the divine in terms of human life, the other side in terms of this side". Romantic poetry aspires to perceive the supersensuous reality *through* the perception of the sensuous reality. Goethe's ballad puts these two visions side by side. Nevertheless, it must be stressed that while the two views, the father's and the son's, achieve unity at a high level, they are still perceived as conflicting at a low level; furthermore, as we have seen, the poem exploits the emotional potential of this dissonance to a considerable extent.

A superhypothesis entertained by seventeenth or twentieth century readers would attempt to accommodate such alternative models of reality by relying on *uncertainty* rather than on *integration*. The two visions of reality in Goethe's ballad may thus be treated as symptoms of a fundamental uncertainty. Likewise, e.g., in Book VIII of *Paradise Lost,* Raphael gives Adam lengthy accounts of both the Ptolemean and the Copernican models of the world, and concludes:

> whether heav'n move or earth,
> Imports not, if thou reckon right; the rest
> From man or angel the great Architect
> Did wisely to conceal ...   (ibid., 70–73)

In the twentieth century, when "God is dead", such uncertainties are "heightened, to any degree heightened", and treated as signs of the meaningless nature of existence.

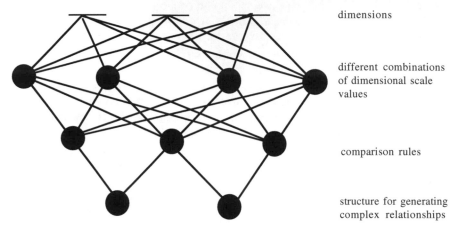

dimensions

different combinations
of dimensional scale
values

comparison rules

structure for generating
complex relationships

Figure 21.4   High Integration Index (from Schroder et al., 1970: 18).

The value of the parsimonious working hypothesis offered here is that it provides a structure for generating complex relationships. In Schroder's terms, it would be an example of fourth-level integration.

> Unlike the low level, which consists of a hierarchical set of established rules and procedures, high-level functioning (which again reaches a form of unity in the system) is characterized by the ability to generate the rules of the theory, the complex relations and alternate schemata, as well as the relationships between the various structures. It has the potential to generate alternate patterns of complex interactions (ibid., 184).

Literary History, Value, and Information Processing

The model of cognitive structure proposed here by way of analyzing La Fontaine's and Goethe's poems may also illuminate various approaches to literary history. When disagreements arise, one need not necessarily assume that all theoretical approaches are equally valid and respectable. One should ask, instead, to what extent a given approach conforms with the complexity of the subject matter, or with the needs of a person possessing a certain level of cognitive complexity. Consider, for instance, the following passage by Wellek and Warren:

In practice, such clear-cut choices between the historical and the present-day point of view are scarcely feasible. [...] The answer to historical relativism is not a doctrinaire absolutism which appeals to "unchanging human nature" or the "universality of art".We must rather adopt a view for which the term "Perspectivism" seems suitable. We must be able to refer a work of art to the values of its own time and of all the periods subsequent to its own. [...] Relativism reduces the history of literature to a series of discrete and hence discontinuous fragments, while most absolutisms serve either only a passing present-day situation or are based (like standards of the New Humanists, the Marxists, and the Neo-Thomists) on some abstract non-literary ideal unjust to the historical variety of literature. "Perspectivism" means that we recognize that there is one poetry, one literature, comparable in all ages, developing, changing, full of possibilities. [...] Both relativism and absolutism are false; but the more insidious danger today [that is, in the nineteen-forties—RT], at least in the United States, is a relativism equivalent to an anarchy of values, a surrender of the task of criticism (Wellek and Warren. (1956: 31–32)

Perspectivism as described by Wellek and Warren may serve as a paradigm of abstract or "high-level functioning". It conceives of a particular work of literature both as unique and as part of larger categories such as period style, genre, and, ultimately, literature and art. In Schroder's terms, "the more integratively complex the structure, [...] the more perspectives [...] a person can generate and integrate about each stimulus (stimuli are finely discriminated)" (op. cit. 187).

Relativism and absolutism, on the other hand, are typical of concrete or low-level functioning. Both are not only "false" but false in a similar way: both try to avoid complexity in an extremely complex situation. Both relativism and absolutism exhibit "poor capacity to act 'as if', to assume the role of the other or to think and act in terms of a hypothetical situation" (Harvey, 1970: 316).[8] We can also apply our model in a somewhat different fashion. New Humanism, Marxism, and Neo-Thomism, for instance, may be regarded as very different, or even contradictory, at a low level of integration. At a higher level, they may be regarded (without obscuring differences between them) as varieties of an absolutist approach. And at a yet higher level of integration, absolutism and relativism can be reconciled, since both seem to

---

[8]   Occasional confusion of terminology should not obscure the issue. What Wellek and Warren call "relativism" is included by most psychologists in "absolutism"; and what the same psychologists call 'relativism", Wellek and Warren would call "perspectivism". In the following passage, accordingly, we might read "perspectivism" for "relativism": "More abstract functioning, [...] because of a more complex and enriched mediational system and a greater ability to transcend and depart from the immediate and perceptual characteristics of the impingements, results in less absolutism, that is, greater relativism in thought and action" (Harvey, 1970: 315).

pursue the same quest for certitude and exhibit the same intolerance for ambiguities, complexities, and uncertainties.

I would like to end this chapter with a note on values. Wellek and Warren's phrase, "a relativism equivalent to an anarchy of values, a surrender of the task of criticism", raises the question whether artistic values and moral values are related. If we take, for example, such criteria as the three dramatic unities as the basis for literary value, and such commandments as "Thou shalt not kill" and "Thou shalt not commit adultery" as the basis for moral values, artistic taste and moral integrity will seem pretty irrelevant to each other. In the psychological sense, however, both are concrete and absolutistic, when they establish such explicit rules to be followed. Today, it seems to be generally accepted that both life and art are apt to present complex and unforeseeable situations that cannot be handled by a finite system of explicit rules. However, the alternative to a "hierarchical set of established rules and procedures" in both life and art need not be total anarchy (as it might appear to some inflexible, concrete personalities). The more viable alternative seems to be a high-level functioning characterized by the ability to generate its own rules, by sensitivity to subtle and minimal cues and hence less susceptibility to false but obtrusive ones, and by a tendency not to form and generalize impressions of people (or of poems) from incomplete information (Hrvey, 1970: 316–317). This process is a highly internal one "in the sense that it is not anchored in established rules, in the sense that it represents a projection into the future, and in the sense that many different interactions can be generated in the same external situation" (Schroder et al., 1970: 184).

In short, as I have suggested, what we might term either negative capability, or perspectivism, or moral integrity is characterized neither by rigidly fixed rules nor by the absence of rules, but by a greater number of conflicting rules on the lower levels which may be accommodated by rules on higher levels. Although artistic taste and moral integrity are not one and the same thing, both seem to presuppose similar psychological structures. Thus, it would appear (as I would argue) that studies in personality psychology and cognitive structure have much to offer in bridging the gulf between stylistic studies and studies of literature's relevance to human values.

CHAPTER 22

The Critic's Mental Dictionary

The Critical Code

The philosopher of science and the unsympathetic layman alike are rightly suspicious of attempts to introduce novel terminologies. It happens all too frequently that the new terminology is nothing but a one-to-one translation of old terminology. In such instances the usual question is asked: What can one do with the new terminology, and in the new theoretical frame of reference from which it is derived that one could not with, or in, the old ones? This question and its possible answers are an important touchstone of new theories.

In the case of Cognitive Poetics, there are many illuminating answers to the above question. But the most significant and the most general answer, I believe, is this: Cognitive Poetics, by its new terminology and its new framework, reclaims the reader's aesthetic impression from the domain of arbitrary impressionism, and relates perceived effects, or "aesthetic qualities" (in Sibley's sense), to objectively describable structures in a consistent manner. By the same token, it provides tools to bestow human significance upon linguistic and poetic devices that were so meticulously unearthed by analytic criticism, and upon the structures they constitute. As Bartlett (1932) insisted, structural relationships are experienced as affect. If one is to attribute affects to structural relationships in a non-arbitrary manner, one must have some understanding of the cognitive processes by which this is done. The present work has provided numerous such examples.

The problem of justifying novel terminologies becomes apparent when one considers specific terms. In some of my discussions, I have adopted from contemporary semantics and psycholinguistics the terms *hyponym* and *superordinate,* and the hierarchical organization which they constitute. Now, is this no mere one-to-one substitution of *hyponym* for Aristotelian *species,* and *superordinate* for Aristotelian *genus?* One way—and not a very inspiring one—to answer this question may be that the Aristotelian terms refer to extra-linguistic categories, whereas *hyponym* and *superordinate* refer to word meanings (such an explanation may be analogous to the distinction between *topic* and *comment* on the one hand, and *subject* and *predicate* on the other).[1] But there is a less trivial answer, too. We have been dealing here with two different systems with analogous organizations. It may be found eventually that

---

[1]   Note that Cohen (1979) uses the first pair of terms to make essentially the same kind of points as Strawson (1967) does, using the second pair.

these organizations reflect the basic organization of the human mind. But what concerns us here is that this semantic organization enables us to perform certain operations, as a result of which we may account for such semantic phenomena as synonymy, antonymy, language acquisition and—more important for our present concern—for the relative naturalness of figurative expressions. By the latter, in turn, we may account for a whole series of aesthetic qualities regularly attributed to poetic and colloquial metaphors. Last but not least, the theory of marked and unmarked metaphors based on hyponymy may explain how linguistic intuition constrains literary interpretation (see, e.g., Tsur, 1987b: 105–116).

Let us try and compare a semantic definition of literature to a possible cognitive definition, such as the one proposed above, in Chapter 1: "A literary work is a discourse in which an important part of the meaning is implicit" (Beardsley, 1958: 126). Our characterization of a literary work, from the cognitive point of view, can correspondingly be re-formulated as a discourse in response to which an important part of the cognitive correlates is categorized at a relatively low level. If we ask now how we can recognize relatively low categorization in the cognitive correlates of a poetic discourse, a conspicuous candidate is "implicit meaning".

Thus, the two definitions may appear to be synonymous. However, "implicit meaning" is not coextensive with "relatively low categorization" of cognitive correlates. The latter category also includes, on the semantic level, thing-free qualities, gestalt-free qualities, weak gestalts, certain instances of "making things unfamiliar", and so forth. On the prosodic level, it may include diffuse patterns of alliteration, weak metric shapes, etc. Thus, we have here two levels of description, which appear to be somehow related, but with two important modifications. In the first place, there is no straightforward correspondence between the elements belonging to the two levels. In the second place, the terms that belong to one level of description are better suited for one kind of operations, while the terms that belong to the other level of description are better suited for others. If we want to connect our metalanguage to the object language level of a poem, we will probably choose terms that have a relatively high descriptive content. Let us call this *the descriptive level of metalanguage.* If we want to connect our metalanguage to perceived effects or aesthetic qualities, we will have to make conversion from one set of terms to another set: terms that are related, by theory, to emotional or aesthetic qualities. Let us call this *the combinational level of metalanguage.* At the former level, we may describe our text as abounding in implicit meanings, gestalt-free qualities, diffuse patterns of alliteration and weak metric shapes; at the latter level, we will probably describe these phenomena as a regression to relatively low categorizations which, in turn, have been related to affective qualities.

This last-mentioned issue suggests a possibility that promises to be extremely fruitful: that which appears to be a mere translation of terms from one set to another may in fact, in some significant instances at least, be a complex recoding. Just as *language* is best transmitted in one form and stored in another (see above, Chapter 1), *metalanguage* is best used for the description of a text in one form, and for relating it to aesthetic principles or emotional qualities, in other forms. Just as we use the speech code to convert the stream of information from acoustic to phonetic representations, or the various linguistic codes to convert from surface levels of representation to deeper, eventually semantic ones, thus there may be a *critical code* which may govern the conversions from one set of metalanguage to another. As in the speech code and the language code, in this critical code, too, none of these conversions is straightforward and trivial, requiring only the substitution of one segment or representation or critical term for another. Thus far, it is not clear to what extent we find "grammatical rules" embodying the critical code, or only general principles. At the present stage of my investigation, I tend to opt for the second option. Here, I only want to elaborate a model of the critical code, with conversions from one level to another, each level being shaped and constrained by the requirements of the task to be accomplished, their joint designation being to yield critical insight.

Let us have a closer look at the statement that there is no straightforward correspondence between the terms on two different metalinguistic levels. Suppose that we have, on the descriptive level, the terms *a, b, c,* and on the combinational level the terms *x, y, z.* There will be a complex coding if in certain conditions *a* may be converted into *x,* in other conditions *a* into *y.* Conversely, *x* sometimes may be converted into *a,* sometimes into *b,* and sometimes into *c,* and so forth. Let us begin with a fairly simple, but quite interesting example. The term "plural" is well-designed to mark certain grammatical forms, whereas its stylistic implication is virtually nil. Nevertheless, the plural form can be used for certain stylistic effects, for which another set of terms could be expected to be more serviceable. Thus, for instance, the plural may be used for *intensification,* as in

(1)   Was this the face that launched a thousand ships?[2]
(Marlowe: *Dr. Faustus*, XIII)

Leo Spitzer (1969), on the other hand, suggests that the plural is one of a long series of "muting devices" used by Racine:

We have already discovered that in *soupirs, désirs,* there is one of those contour-blurring plurals of abstractions, which inhibit too sharp a definition of the emotions of the characters. Such genuinely Racinian plurals as *amours, fureurs, flammes* are well known. [...] Where a metaphor or figurative usage is employed, the plural is weakening of the sensuous content: the indefinite plural blurs the sensuous outline of the image. The eighteenth century objected to the plural in

Il n'a plus aspiré qu'à s'ouvrir *des chemins*

---

[2] Although not a plural in itself, *a thousand* emphasizes precisely the *multitude* of the ships.

Pour éviter l'affront pour tomber dans leurs mains.
(*Mithridate,* V, 1569–1570)

(*"Un* seul chemin tout overt suffisait pour éviter l'affront"). But *un chemin*
would have been taken literally: the reader would imagine a road, whereas
"way" is intended to be equivalent to "means". (Spitzer, 1969: 127)

Notice such phrases of Spitzer as "contour-blurring", "weakening of the sensuous
content", "blurs the sensuous outline", or, on the next page, "He could do so, because by the plural the physical aspect is somewhat concealed". As we shall see in
example (2), the "blurring of the sensuous outlines" of the image by the plural may
be crucial not only where figurative expressions are concerned, but also in literal
language. It follows from our discussion of ordinary consciousness in Chapter 1 and
in other chapters that "sharp definitions" of things, clear-cut shapes, clear-cut concepts, or even clear-cut emotions, are a result of our focusing our attention on them,
of our relegating all other information to a low-differentiated ground. The use of the
plural prevents, then, our attention from being focused on any single item *with all
its characteristics;* the many similar items prevent each other from "usurping our attention" (to use a Bergsonian phrase; cf. Chapter 18).

"Plural" is, then, a double-edged category. It may either have an intensifying or a
muting potential. The intensifying potential depends on the cumulative effect of,
e.g., "a thousand ships". The muting potential depends on more sophisticated relationships: the cognitive differentiation of information into a unique, stable item, and
a "regression" to a less differentiated mode of cognition, effected by a multiplicity of
items preventing each other from usurping our attention. Thus, the muting use of
the plural may be regarded as a moderate version of "thing destruction", in which no
"thing-free" or even gestalt-free qualities are generated, only what might be called
"blurred gestalts". A notorious instance of the plural as a muting device in this
sense we find in Wordsworth's Westminster-Bridge Sonnet:

(2)   Earth has not anything to show more fair:
        Dull would he be of mind who could pass by
        A sight so touching in its majesty:
        This City now does, like a garment wear
        The beauty of the morning; silent, bare,
        Ships, towers, domes, theatres, and temples lie
        Open unto the fields and to the sky;
        All bright and glittering in the smokeless air.

My main point in quoting this example is to show how the "contour-blurring plural" is one contour-blurring device among many, on several strata of the poem. The
many and diverse items in the sixth and seventh lines blur each other's sensuous
outlines, by preventing each other from "usurping" attention. This contour-blurring

effect of the plural combines, on the semantic level, with "the beauty of the morn-ing", and "the smokeless air"—both thing-free qualities that infuse the city. The former expression, a genitive phrase, contains a "thematized predicate" (see above, Chapter 18) in the referring position, derived in several steps from "This morning, the city is beautiful". Thus, attention is directed away from *things* that are beautiful, to an all-pervasive, but indistinct *quality*. On the prosodic level, the effect combines with other processes of category-blurring. The tense enjamebment *"lie/open"* blurs the prosodic shape of the line and, at the same time and by the same token, the se-mantic and syntactic category of *lie*. This verb is at first perceived as a full lexical word, with full lexical stress; in *lie open* it is downgraded into a complex predicate comprising a verb with an adjectival complement, its stress being reduced, too. A similar downgrading occurs in *pass by,* where *by* is the stressed member of the collocation, whereas in *pass by a sight* it becomes an unstressed preposition (I have discussed some of the prosodic aspects of this sonnet at greater length in Tsur, 1972; see above, Chapter 5, example (18)).

The straightforward correspondence between the metalanguage levels is even more conspicuously absent when we look at it from the semantic end. The process that Ehrenzweig calls "thing destruction" may operate in other, less moderate forms, too, compared to the use of the plural. In fact, the "nominalized predicate" mentioned in the preceding paragraph serves precisely such a purpose in Wordsworth's poem. Tak-ing a bird's eye's view of thing-free qualities, Josephine Miles (1965) in her valu-able study of what she calls "The Pathetic Fallacy" (not to be confused with Rus-kin's earlier use of the term), traces, among other things, the shift from bestowing emotions on solid natural objects (as generally practiced by Wordsworth), to at-tributions that are more familiar with Shelley, Keats, and (later) Tennyson. Her find-ings, as usual in her studies, are supported by ample statistical evidence. Thus she sums up some essentials of the process of changes:

> Shape, hue, odor and sweet sound are the new agents of feeling, as the senses have acquired new powers, they spread away from *scene* into the air. (Miles, 1965: 29)

> [...] the change was [...] from the solids of the scene and the liquids of lark and stream to the vapours of cloud and airy fragrances. (ibid.)

> The vision is one of the sensed qualities, not objects, as the associates of human emotions. Immediately felt color and atmosphere takes the place of representative objects and arrangements. The adjective rather than the noun is clue to the emotion. (ibid., 33)

No explanation is offered for the perceived effect of this shift. What difference does it make that human emotions became associated with hue, odor, sound, vapours of cloud and airy fragrances, rather than with solid objects? Miles tries to make up for the lack of systematic theoretical explanation by having recourse to such terms as "immediately felt", or "spread away". To be sure, she does this in an exceptionally perceptive and intelligent way, and her description is anything but counterintuitive. According to my understanding, however, Miles is enumerating thing-free and gestalt-free entities; in the same understanding, the relationship of these to low-categorized information and, in turn, to affects, may account for the shift, not only in the themes, but also in the emotional qualities of 19th-century poetry, and thus fill such phrases as "the senses have acquired new powers" with more precise meaning.

Miles's work, as exemplified in the quoted passages, constitutes a piece of most illuminating descriptive poetics. The terms she uses are well suited for the description of poetic texts, but they are relatively inefficient in accounting for these texts' perceived effects or "aesthetic qualities". When we convert our categories from the descriptive to the combinational level, we are, indeed, converting between categories that are not coextensive. "Plural" may correspond to "intensification" or to "muting" ("contour-blurring") on the combinational level; "muting", in turn, can be converted so as to become a specific instance of "low categorization", "thing destruction", or the like. "Low categorization" or "thing destruction", in turn, may correspond, on the descriptive level, to a whole series of other categories, such as hues, sounds, etc. The *principles* of such conversions are supplied by cognitive poetics.

Notice that "low categorization", "thing destruction", "thing-free qualities", "gestalt-free qualities", etc., are synonymous from a combinational point of view; still, they differ, albeit to a low degree, in descriptive content. It is through these descriptive contents that they combine with the other, more descriptive terms.

One more observation is required at this point. Spitzer, Miles, and Ehrenzweig were each working within a largely different frame of reference. Spitzer was doing very small-scale stylistic-philological analysis; Miles conducted large-scale statistical investigations; whereas Ehrenzweig propounded a psychology of music and the visual arts. Ehrenzweig's categories have almost no descriptive content that can be directly applied to poetry; Spitzer and Miles had some brilliant insights into the perceptual (and combinational) potentials of their categories, but the categories themselves were mainly ad hoc and pre-theoretical. The present model establishes equivalences and combinational potentials via *perceived effects,* in a creative (one might even say 'generative') manner, thus enabling us to handle novel instances and terms. These terms can be conceived of as of parts of a modular set of units, "designed", as it were, to be joined in a variety of ways, on different levels of description.

In Chapter 4, the problematic relationship between aesthetic and non-aesthetic concepts was discussed. The present chapter takes up the issue from a different aspect. In order to be used in a verifiable statement about a text, a metalinguistic term must have considerable descriptive content. Even so, a metalinguistic statement may be *true,* and still *trivial,* not worth making. For a "true" metalinguistic statement to have aesthetic significance, it must be related to some general model or theory. And conversely, a general model or theory can be related to some text only *via* terms that have considerable descriptive content. Let me illustrate this through a shamefully simple example. The statement "This poem contains 83 lines" may be perfectly true, but trivial from the aesthetic point of view. By contrast, the statement "This poem contains 14 lines" may be more significant from the aesthetic point of view, through reference to the SONNET MODEL. The SONNET MODEL, in turn, may be related to some text only *via* such descriptive terms as "14 lines", *"abba* rhyme pattern", etc. Significant distinctions in a poem can be made only with the help of terms that have precise descriptive contents; conversely, these distinctions may become significant only when they can be related to some widely accepted theoretical model. The theoretical models, in turn, can fruitfully be applied to a poem only *via* some term with a precise descriptive content. We cannot know whether a poem is a sonnet, without being aware of the *number* of lines and their *grouping* by rhyme-scheme. A good critical term is, then, one that has a well-articulated, precise descriptive content on the one hand, and can be related to some general model or commonplace (in the rhetorical sense of the term) on the other. A good model, in turn, is one that combines with terms on more specific levels, giving them precise descriptive meanings, improving their articulation, or rendering the distinctions made with them significant.

The preceding paragraph is crucial in understanding one of the main conceptions of the present book: the relationship between traditional poetics and cognitive science. In Chapter 1, I have discussed this relationship at some length, and have mentioned the problem of "reductionism": I have warned against any attempt to reduce poetics to some other, cognitive, discipline, and have presented Polányi's "principle of marginal control" as a safeguard against it. This, however, is a general principle; how can it be applied in specific instances? There appears to be a converse problem, too. Many analyses in the present book can be said to be derived from good old traditional poetics. Why should we, then, bother about this thing called Cognitive Poetics? The solution offered by the present chapter to both problems is this: the theories and models of Cognitive Poetics are related to specific texts *via* extensive analyses in terms of more traditional poetics.

This conception can also explain why critics must sometimes have recourse to those eternal masterpieces called "commonplaces". What gives commonplaces their peculiar character is that they are so indisputably true; and as such, there is little doubt that they satisfy Grice's Maxim of Quality, that is, "try to make your contribution one that is true". The issue at stake seems to be, then, whether they satisfy Grice's Maxim of Quantity, that is, "make your contribution as informative as required". Now, the great virtue of commonplaces is that one may appeal to them in order to justify certain arguments on a lower level of generality. For a piece of literary criticism to be informative, it must suggest some distinction or conclusion on a less general level of argument.

In Chapter 20, in discussing Baudelaire's "Correspondances", I have quoted Henri Peyre's attempt to account for the almost mysterious intuition that some people say they experience in reading this sonnet: "He [Baudelaire—R.T.] tore off the veil that covers the true nature of objects thus to reveal the identity behind the illusory appearances, the one behind the many, as Plato and Shelley had put it". There, too, I made an effort to show that this description fits, in some sense, almost all poetry or, for that matter, almost all art. At this point, the description becomes a commonplace. The critical terms I offered in that chapter have relatively great descriptive contents; using those, I have shown that the same commonplace may apply to various poetic styles in different ways: thus I have been able to make significant distinctions even between the two quatrains of the same sonnet. In terms of the present discussion, Peyre did provide relevant commonplaces; but these do require additional critical terms that have sufficient descriptive content, so that significant distinctions can be made.

Perspectivism & Canons of Evaluation

My first test case for the above distinctions will be a brief consideration of a venerable issue in aesthetics and literary theory: the possible approaches to literatures of the past, as propounded by Wellek and Warren (1956; see above, Chapter 21, last section). These authors describe three possible approaches to such literatures: relativism, absolutism, and perspectivism. With respect to this distinction, they point out, among other things:

> In practice, such clear-cut choices between the historical and the present-day point of view are scarcely feasible. [...] The answer to historical relativism is not a doctrinaire absolutism which appeals to "unchanging human nature" or the "universality of art".We must rather adopt a view for which the term "Perspectivism" seems suitable. We must be able to refer a work of art to the values of its own time and of all the periods subsequent to its own. [...] Relativism reduces the history of literature to a series of discrete and hence discontinuous fragments, while most absolutisms serve either only a passing present-day situation or are based (like the standards of the New Humanists, the Marxists, and the Neo-Thomists) on some abstract non-literary ideal unjust to the historical variety of literature. "Perspectivism" means that we recognize that there is one poetry, one literature, comparable in all ages, developing, changing, full of possibilities. [...] Both relativism and absolutism are false; but the more insidious danger today [that is, in the nineteen-forties—RT], at least in the United States, is a relativism equivalent to an anarchy of values, a surrender of the task of criticism. (op. cit., 31–32)

In Chapter 12, I quoted Wimsatt's conception of the Coleridgean critic who says, as it were: "We will defend the essential concept of a poem, a work of verbal art, and insist that it applies always differently to an indefinite number of individual instances". In order to account for the acquisition and applicability of this Occamian principle, I proposed there a hierarchic model of conventions, realized by way of contrasting stylistic categories to other, neighboring categories. My example was Coleridge's conception of the poem as "the balance or reconcilement of opposite or discordant qualities", and I insisted "that it applies always differently to an indefinite number of individual instances". My extensive treatment of the issue there can be summed up in terms of the present discussion. Coleridge's essential concept of a poem, "the balance or reconcilement of opposite or discordant qualities", became one of the great commonplaces of our critical heritage; many critics appeal to it when attempting to justify their close reading or favorable evaluation of poems. This slogan, however, cannot directly be applied to specific texts; the critic must use a wide range of more specific terms, having precise descriptive contents. The range of these terms is almost infinite, depending on the critical school to which the individual critic may adhere, as well as on the specific texture and structure of the individual poem discussed. Some of these terms are invented *ad hoc,* justified with reference to their adequate descriptive contents suited to the specific text on the one hand, and with reference to Coleridge's slogan on the other. Above, in Chapter 12, I have supplied relatively specific terms with sufficient descriptive content to distinguish between three "style-types". At a still lower level of specificity, one might create terms with sufficient descriptive content to distinguish between individual styles. Yet, no matter how divergated the distinctions at the lower end of the hierarchy, at the higher end the unity of such general notions as *art, literature, Mannerism, Seventeenth-Century Metaphysical poetry* is preserved.

Let us consider now a closely related issue. From Wellek and Warren's isolated quotation, one might receive the mistaken impression that the following formula is active here: **relativism + absolutism = perspectivism.** As has been suggested in the preceding chapter, relativism and absolutism are equivalent, in an important respect, from the psychological point of view. We may, therefore, expect both attitudes to occur in the same piece of criticism, without necessarily rendering it "perspectivist". In order for an approach to become truly perspectivist, there must be some essential relationship between the two attitudes present in the piece of criticism. The example discussed in the preceding paragraph, for instance, might suggest a hierarchical relationship, as, e.g., that between *genus* and *species.* One excellent example for such a relationship we may find in the relationship between "general canons" and "specific canons" of aesthetic evaluation, as presented by Beardsley:

> I think when we take a wide survey of critical reasons, we can find room for most of them, with very little trouble, in three main groups. First, there are reasons that seem to bear upon the degree of *unity* or disunity of the work [...]. Second, there are those reasons that seem to bear upon the degree of *complexity* or simplicity of the work [...]. Third, there are those reasons that seem to bear upon the *intensity* or lack of intensity of human regional qualities in the work. (Beardsley, 1958: 462)

Upon this distinction, Beardsley founds the three General Canons of Criticism, the Canon of Unity, the Canon of Complexity, and the Canon of Intensity (ibid., 466). These three Canons are relevant to all the arts, while the principles dealing with defects and merits in one particular art may be called *Specific Canons* (ibid., 465). I should add here that also the principles about defects and merits in one stylistic period (that may or may not cut across the various arts) may be called *Specific Canons*. One of the questions which concern Beardsley is whether the specific canons can be subsumed under the general canons. His solution is very similar to the conception propounded here, provided one construes the verb *appeal to* in the following quotation with reference to the relationship between critical "commonplaces" and terms with considerable descriptive contents. "The three general standards unity, complexity, and intensity can be meaningfully appealed to in the judgment of aesthetic objects, whether auditory, visual or verbal. Moreover, they are appealed to constantly by reputable critics" (ibid., 469). Here I wish to point out only one possibility. Neo-Classical criticism judged drama according to the principle of the three unities: unity of time, place, and action. In Shakespeare's plays, all three unities are drastically violated. In many of them there are several actions between which the causal connection is rather loose; some plays are spread over long periods of time, sometimes many years, and over several countries and continents. Romantic critics defended Shakespeare's aesthetic reputation by claiming that in spite of the violation of these "external" standards, his plays do have great "organic" unity. Now, while the Neo-Classical terms *unity of time, place,* and *action* have considerable descriptive content, and are directly applicable to individual works, *organic unity* has no descriptive content at all: thus, it might be impossible to answer the question "How can I know that a certain play does have organic unity?". Some modern critics have pointed out significant analogies (e.g., Fergusson, 1955) between the parallel actions; thus, the various actions are unified at a higher level. Some other critics (e.g., Wilson Knight) have pointed at the recurrent imagery that generates the plays' particular spiritual space. Thus, the specific standards for unity are different in these three ages, but all can be related to the general canon of unity. What is more, Fergusson's and Wilson Knight's notions can directly be related to the general canon; but is it not possible that these are the descriptive terms with which the romantic slogan "organic unity" can be related to specific plays?

To conclude the present section, consider the following: The specific canons are precisely those specific conventions with which the relativist is concerned, and which cannot be compared to specific conventions in some other age, unless *via* some general canon. The absolutist, on the other hand, may find the general canons most convenient for presenting the literature of all periods as a uniform mass. It is only when the critic justifies his use of specific canons by appealing to the general canons that he takes a perspectivist view of literature.

Morgenstern's "Der Werwolf"

In the following, I propose to elaborate the foregoing seminal presentation into a more comprehensive conception of the critical code. This will be no more than a tentative first approximation of the subject: a coding of critical terms which may indicate the structure of the critic's mental dictionary. I shall also attempt to explore what kind of coding of critical terms may lead to significant insights into the aesthetic structure and quality of a poem. I shall do this by comparing the model of critical terms introduced here, to the term "folk etymology", introduced by Keyser and Prince (1979), with reference to one of their most interesting literary examples, Christian Morgenstern's "Der Werwolf". The following are the crucial points of the definition of the term:

> [Folk etymology] is the process whereby unfamiliar terms are made into familiar ones often with accompanying mythologies. […] What is the logic of the examples considered thus far? First, there is a word which in itself has a single referent in the world. […] The word is for all intents and purposes, made up of no subparts. […] The word, however, then is divided into parts […] and a fable is attached to the reanalyzed word. At this point the word has been made to enact the world, as it were, through the medium of a fable. (Keyser and Prince, 1979: 66–67)

Let us have now a close look at Morgenstern's "Der Werwolf":

3.　Ein Werwolf eines Nachts entwich
　　von Weib und Kind, und sich begab
　　an eines Dorfschullehrers Grab
　　und bat ihn: "Bitte, beuge mich!"

　　Der Dorfschulmeister stieg hinauf
　　auf seines Blechschilds Messingknauf
　　und sprach zum Wolf, der seine Pfoten
　　geduldig kreuzte vor dem Toten:

　　"Der Werwolf", sprach der gute Mann,
　　"des Weswolfs, Genitiv sodann,
　　dem Wemwolf, Dativ, wie mans nennt,
　　den Wenwolf, — damit hats ein end".

　　Dem Werwolf schmeichelten die Fälle,
　　er rollte seine Augenbälle.
　　"Indessen", bat er, "füge doch
　　zur Einzahl auch die Mehrzahl noch!"

Der Dorfschulmeister aber musste
gestehn, dass er von ihr nichts wusste.
Zwar Wölfe gäbs in grosser Schar,
doch "Wer" gäbs nur im Singular.

Der Wolf erhob sich tränenblind —
er hatte ja doch Weib und Kind!
Doch da er kein Gelehrter eben,
So schied er dankend und ergeben.

One night a Werwolf escaped
from his wife and child and went
to the grave of a village schoolmaster
and said to him, "Please decline me".

The village schoolmaster climbed up
on the brass pommel of his tin nameplate
and said to the Wolf, who patiently
crossed his paws before the dead man:

"The Werwolf", said the good man,
"the Werwolf's, genitive then,
to the Werwolf, dative, as it is called,
the Werwolf, — there is an end to it".

The cases flattered the Werwolf,
who rolled his eyeballs.
"Meanwhile", he said, "add
the plural to the singular!"

The village schoolmaster however had
to confess that he did not know it.
While wolves may occur in large troops,
 still "Wer" occurs only in the singular.

The wolf got up blind with tears —
he had after all a wife and child!
However, since he was no scholar,
he departed thankful and submissively.[3]

Does the above definition of "folk etymology" help the authors to a better insight into Morgenstern's poem? The authors explain what is a Werwolf; and then

---

[3]   Keyser and Prince's plain prose translation.

they show at some length the discrepancy between the genuine and the "folk" ety-mology of the word, as "folk-etymologized" by the schoolmaster. So far, so good. Then, however, they further list the grammatical cases as enumerated in the poem (and in their prose translation). From an informative point of view, this is com-pletely redundant. Psychologically, it may be the sign of an uneasy feeling that something important still remains to be said; that some elusive intuition has not yet been captured by the conceptual apparatus. Furthermore, how many readers do really feel that, in this case, "an unfamiliar term has been made into a familiar one" through folk etymology? Would it not be more correct to say that an unusual yet meaningful word has been "made stranger" through strange manipulation in a strange story?

Keyser and Prince conclude: "The entire point of Morgenstern's poem is based upon a joke which is itself based upon folk etymology, that is, the idea that lan-guage enacts life. It is the disparity between language and life that is the cause of the werwolf's unhappiness" (ibid., 72). I submit that the point of Morgenstern's poem is more than "a resonant joke". For instance, why should the werwolf go to pre-cisely a dead schoolmaster? What should we make of the end of the poem ("How-ever, since he was no scholar, he departed thankful and submissively")? This seems quite irrelevant to the "folk-etymological" joke. It would appear that the poem is more complex: it may have several layers of meaning which—as I shall argue—constitute one solid whole. Let us start our inquiry with the observation that one literary theorist, at least, has held a radically different conception of Morgenstern's games with words.

> Morgenstern's playfulness [...] has a serious side to it. He is on record as claiming that man's basically unsatisfactory relationship to his fellows, his society and the world in general stems from his being imprisoned by lan-guage, which is a most unreliable, false and dangerous thing, and that one must "smash" language, destroy man's naive trust in this most familiar and unquestioned part of his life, before he can learn to think properly. Morgen-stern's brilliantly witty games with words are thus, seen from this point of view, devious devices of alienation, and at their most radical succeed in pro-ducing in the reader a strange sensation—making one suddenly doubt one's comfortable relationship with language—not unlike the sense of disorienta-tion and confusion associated with the grotesque. (Thomson, 1972: 165)[4]

I would like to point out four elements in this passage. First, it credits Morgen-stern's word plays with something that is much more than a poetic joke. Second, and more important, it attributes to them an effect that is the opposite of the one at-tributed to folk etymology by Keyser and Prince. Not a "process whereby unfamiliar terms are made into familiar ones", but rather a "devious device of alienation" de-

---

4   See my discussion of Thomson's conception of the grotesque (above, Chapters 15–16).

stroying "man's naive trust in this most familiar and unquestioned part of his life". This process, rather than "enacting" the world in the service of a "mythological impulse", compels man to readjust to society, and to the world in general, as it really is. One may, of course, include this, too, in Keyser and Prince's phrase (for this purpose, "enact" is an admirably chosen verb), but then, "language enacts the world" will come to mean "language has something to do with the world". Third, this effect can be the source, in certain circumstances ("at their most radical"), of an emotional quality. Fourth, this emotional quality is "not unlike the sense of disorientation and confusion associated with the grotesque".

I must concede that Morgenstern's witty word-game in this poem is hardly at the poet's most brilliant. Still, its effect is marked enough to contribute to the poem's "regional quality", provided the effect is reinforced by some other element in the poem. And this, precisely, provides one possible explanation for the occurrence of the dead schoolmaster. Morgenstern not only prefers him dead, but also makes him "climb up on the brass pommel of his tin nameplate"; in short, the word-play and the grotesque are presumably meant to contribute to a common effect: a quality of emotional disorientation. Whether the dead schoolmaster climbing up the brass pommel is perceived as grotesque, depends of course on the reader's ability or willingness to expose himself to the scene, stripped of the security of the available defense mechanisms, that is, neither "laugh off" the bizarre scene, nor become indignant "that such things should be presented in a humorous light". Whoever refuses to experience the hard-to-take quality of the grotesque will necessarily regard the poem as a joke. On this level of observation, the more elements contribute to that "grotesque" quality, the more they increase the unity, complexity, and intensity of the poem (thus providing more possible reasons to support a favorable aesthetic judgment).

There is an unmistakable satirical dimension in the poem. It presents the village schoolmaster as an automaton, who is so well drilled and so indiscriminating in the exercise of his profession that, irrespective of the circumstances, he is always eager to cooperate in anything that may give an opportunity for rote declension. At the other end of the satire, we see the werwolf who, we are told, is unlearned; and therefore would accept anything from "learned" people, thankfully and submissively, no matter how insensible it may be. This satirical dimension exploits material that has been introduced into the poem on other grounds, such as the "smashing" of the phonemic and morphemic sequence /wer + wolf/, with the grotesque ingredient contributing to the overdetermination of its elements; this dimension is not without interest in its own right. It is, however, integrated into the overall effect of the poem, since its wit reinforces the ridiculous component of the grotesque (while the dead schoolmaster rising from his grave takes care of the horrifying component).

The relationship between presenting the village schoolmaster as a senseless automaton and the selection of the grave as the scene of events may be put in a slightly different perspective, and one that may have far-reaching consequences. There is a proverbial idiom in many Central European countries about someone who, e.g., is very familiar with a poem: "He could recite it even when awakened from his deepest sleep". The basic situation of the poem can be derived from this saying in two steps. First, it is hyperbolized by the substitution of "from the grave" for "from his deepest sleep"; second, the hyperbolic expression is literally understood in the poem: the werwolf awakens the schoolmaster from his grave to recite what he has learnt by rote.

The above derivation is of some interest for the issue we have been discussing. On the one hand, it clearly hooks up with Morgenstern's conception of language as something that must be 'smashed', i.e., decomposed in certain ways in order to create the central affect in this poem: disorientation and readjustment. On the other hand, my interpretation clearly relates Morgenstern's technique to the Metaphysical conceit, as I have discussed it in Chapter 16. A conceit originates in a metaphor (or some other trope); indeed, the conceit *is* but a metaphor, if its tenor and vehicle are equally intended; that is, if they are developed so literally that they both must be meant (cf. Ransom, 1951: 784).

Thus, Morgenstern's "smashing" of language turns out to be a specific (though extreme) instance of a more general literary device which, in turn, is at play within a wide range of more general aesthetic principles. Let us mention, briefly just one of them:

> "The function of poetry", wrote Jakobson in 1933, "is to point out that sign is not identical with its referent": why do we need this reminder? "Because", continued Jakobson, "along with the awareness of the identity of the sign and the referent (A is A_1), we need the consciousness of the inadequacy of this identity (A is not A_1)".
>
> This antinomy is essential since without it the connection between the sign and the object becomes automatical and perception of reality withers away. (Erlich, 1965: 181)

What we have in a conceit, then, is one single sign function, in which each the tenor and the vehicle are so consistently developed that one is compelled to be aware of both their identity and incongruity. Jakobson's formulation, even in its details, is not unlike Thomson's formulation of Morgenstern's attitude toward language. It emphasizes the disorienting effect of "language-smashing" and of the grotesque, and the witty affect of the metaphysical conceit in the semiotic-aesthetic perspective of a heightened awareness of reality, a perspective which might apply to very different kinds of poetry (such as Romantic poetry) as well. Notice, too, that Jakobson's conception is a semiotic formulation of the principle put forward by Shklovsky in cognitive terms, and quoted in Chapter 1 as one of the basic assumptions of Cognitive Poetics.

We may attempt now to draw together several threads from the foregoing generalizations. The phonological-morphological sequence /wer + wolf/ can be regarded as consisting of two different signs (the two separate etymological derivations of Key-ser and Prince). Both are so literally developed that both must be meant. From the semiotic point of view, the sequence serves as two sign vehicles which, in turn, may or may not refer to two different sets of objects: these must be kept separate (since both are too literally developed). It is here that the following remark of Key-ser and Prince becomes relevant: "It is this disparity between language and life that is the cause of the werwolf's unhappiness"; that is, somehow the disparity between the signifier and the thing signified is of importance in the poem. They locate this disparity in the contents of the poem, whereas what is of aesthetic significance is the disparity as perceived by the reader (of which the disparity in content is only one possible aspect).

Psychologically speaking, through this forceful separation of tenor and vehicle, the reader faces a situation that produces a strange sensation of emotional disorienta-tion, which is the intense human quality of the poem. This emotional quality is re-inforced by the poem's grotesque character and by its satirical elements. A similar story can be told about the conceit in the poem. In the hyperbole "he knows it so well that he can recite it even if awakened from the grave", both the tenor ("he knows it so well") and the vehicle ("awakened from the grave") are developed so lit-erally that both must be meant. However, the grave-situation includes elements that are irrelevant to the grotesque component (thus, the awakening from the grave is overdetermined). On the other hand, the learning-by-rote aspect of the image hooks up with that sign vehicle of the sequence /wer + wolf/ which is evoked by the de-clension of the interrogative pronoun *wer*. Thus, all the loose ends of the poem are tied up in a complex network of sign-functions, and what at first looks like a joke (the arbitrary switching from one aspect of the *signifiant* to another), becomes an overdetermined network of signs, in which the switching is no longer arbitrary (the "loose end" is motivated by other elements in the poem) and, by the same token, the *signifiant* and the *signifié* are the same and not the same, at one and the same time.

As we see, the passage from Thomson in which he discusses Morgenstern's view of language with reference to his word plays, is most helpful in obtaining an insight into the aesthetic qualities of Morgenstern's poem. Let us now carefully examine the way Thomson characterizes the critical tool he is offering here. One unusual thing about the quoted passage is that Thomson offers no term as the definiendum (such as, e.g., "language-smashing")[5] of his definition; usually, we expect to find a term, and then its definition. But let us consider the merits of Thomson's definition of his (missing) term. First, he places Morgenstern's word plays in the wider con-text of language, and the experience of language in human reality. Second, he indi-cates the possibility of another, radically different alignment of language, reality, and experiencer; the word play may be instrumental in bringing about the drastic

5   I am emphasizing this fact, because it happens all too frequently that critics *label* literary phenomena, ignoring their *significance* (for example see above, Chapter 13). Thomson, on the contrary, provides a description of the phenomenon and its significance, but provides no *label*.

shift from one alignment to the other. Third, he indicates the phenomenological quality that may accompany such a drastic shift (that is, he describes the observed features of the mental experience of the shift). Fourth, but not least, he points out that the unique conscious experience of "language-smashing" is not unlike the unique conscious experiencing of the grotesque.

Such a coding of critical terms is a metalinguistic, or metapoetic, equivalent of Eco's semiotic conception of the coding of lexical items, that is, a conception concerned both with establishing the meaning of the term and its combinational possibilities. "In this way the notion of independent combinational rules can be avoided, for they are a part of the coded representation of the sign-function" (Eco, 1979: 91). The proper coding of a critical term opens up, then, the possibility of a wide range of connections. From now on, Morgenstern's "playfulness" can be related to grotesque elements in the poem; it can be used to account for its complex emotional quality. Furthermore, this playfulness may be related to Jakobson's semiotic conception of poetry as a way of inducung a heightened awareness of reality; alternatively, it can be viewed as a radical instance of a wider literary principle, represented by John Crowe Ransom's conception of the metaphysical conceit, which, again, can be related to Jakobson's principle. Thus, my conception of the coding of critical terms in the mental dictionary may lay the foundation for the study of "critical competence", another item to be added to the list of "competences", comprising, so far, linguistic, poetic, and communicative competence.

Critical Terms and Insight

I have implied that one requirement of a serviceable critical code is that its proper use yield insight into the aesthetic nature of literary texts. In the present section, I shall attempt to explore the nature of insights in general, and in critical activity in particular. Let us begin with a standard definition of "insight" as "the ability to see and understand clearly the inner nature of things" *(Webster's New Twentieth Century Dictionary)*. It seems to me that such a definition of "insight", in itself, brings rather little insight. There are two reasons for this: first, the definition overlooks the element of sudden flash; second, and more important, "the inner nature of things" is a very fuzzy notion. This is best brought out if we revisit Peer Gynt peeling his onion, in an attempt to discover its core, as we saw him do it above, in Chapter 12. There exists no "inner nature of things", or "inner spirit", or "essence" *per se*. What appears to be the "inner nature of things" is a "regional quality" of wholes. There are only layers and layers combined into a whole; elements and structure. This is true not only of onions; I have proposed, following Wellek and Warren, to consider poems, literary periods, and genres as stratified systems of norms. The analytic mind can take such a whole into pieces; this may (but need not) be an important step toward insight: the better the articulation of the elements in one's awareness (other things being equal) the more likely it is to lead to insight. Insight occurs when one becomes aware, in a sudden flash, of many, clear relations between the well-articulated units that constitute the whole.

In our discussion of "Der Werwolf", insight was gained into the poem's putative aesthetic "essence" by realizing that a variety of well-defined elements belonging to the various strata of sound, units-of-meaning, and of the world all contribute to the same overall quality of emotional disorientation. Thus, the perception of a single, all-pervasive quality is substituted for the awareness of a variety of elements. Sometimes, insight is gained through building a bridge between different disciplines, or between different levels of generalization within one discipline, using aspects that are usually thought of as unrelated. At other times, insight is gained by contemplating literary works that are generally thought of as very dissimilar in nature, and discovering that they belong to the same (established or ad hoc construed) category. In all these cases, two stages seem to be indispensable (although they may be inseparable in the consciousness of the experiencer): first, becoming aware of a large number of well-articulated elements in the various works; second, realizing that a considerable number of these well-articulated elements are shared by all these works. When this process results in the cognition of a single perceptual quality or category, the number of entities to be handled by the mental processes is reduced, and a complicated feeling "is replaced by a single feeling of greater intensity" (Peirce, as quoted by Eco, 1979: 132). This cognitive result, according to the view presented here, is an essential part of the peculiar conscious quality of insight.

This, furthermore, seems to be one of the main purposes of introducing new critical terms. If properly defined, such terms may help us divide up familiar works in new ways, by naming previously not discussed elements; also, the new terminology may point up some of the shared elements in familiar works. Sometimes the shared elements, being quite central to these works, may "amalgamate", establishing some new conceptual category.

This is precisely why the term *folk etymology,* as a descriptive label of the process described above, fails. The term is fuzzy at the lower levels, it fails to make the essential distinction that might meaningfully contrast and relate the various texts; at the most, they are united by one common label. This is the case with Keyser and Prince: their conclusions remain on the trivially general (though true) level of commonplaces. The term "folk etymology" does not lead to insights, that is, to a series of combinations as might furnish a connection between this level of generalization and the description of a specific work.[6] Conversely, Thomson's (missing) term is

---

6   The insights yielded by Keyser and Prince's paper are summarized in its "Conclusion" section. This passage, in particular, abounds in those eternal masterpieces called "commonplaces". One of them is the "observation that language is often held to enact the world"; another, the assumption that "words are literally saturated with meaning". In their paper, the authors discuss in detail the episode, masterfully recounted by Freud in his *Psychopathology of Everyday Life,* of the young man who forgot the word *aliquis* in a verse line by Virgil. In this example, the authors say, folk etymology "is hypothesized to be a psychological phenomenon of some depth", which is said to lie "behind some sophisticated creative thinking". In the

well-articulated at the lower level. The description of its meaning not only makes unfamiliar yet acute distinctions; it opens up, by the same token, the possibilities of further combinations, on a variety of theoretical and descriptive levels. Innovative and original critical terms may provide insights also then when, as in the case of Thomson's description of "language-smashing" and the grotesque, they establish possible combinations between the structure of the aesthetic object and the reader's response.[7]

In the light of the foregoing discussion, let us now consider the coding of the term "insight" itself. Webster's definition of this term, while useful in helping to establish my *preference* of Thomson's "language-smashing" to Keyser and Prince's "folk etymology", it could not *account* for the preference. According to *The American College Dictionary,* "insight" may be defined as "penetrating mental vision or discernment; faculty of seeing into inner character or underlying truth". As a psychological technical term, it defines "insight" as "the sudden grasping of a solution; configurational learning". Add to these Peirce's observation about replacing a complicated feeling by a single feeling of greater intensity, and suppose that these different phrases describe various aspects of the same kind of event. We will have, then, a term that describes an event in terms of its **results** (seeing inner nature or underlying truth), its **structure** (sudden grasping, configurational learning), and its **unique conscious quality** (single feeling of greater intensity). The structural description establishes correspondences between the term and a certain kind of mental event, whereas the "functional" and "phenomenological" descriptions open certain combinational possibilities. It is, in fact, such an intuitive coding of "insight" that helped us to explain how Thomson's, rather than Keyser and Prince's term led to an insight into Morgenstern's poem.

As an additional example of what makes a critical term yield insight, I wish to discuss briefly another set of terms, in metrical theory this time, that earned S. J.

---

same vein, their claim that Morgenstern's word-play "forms the basis of a resonant joke" is a commonplace. Finally, the principle implied by the quotation from Wallace Stevens' poem "The Man with the Blue Guitar", namely, that in the modern world, poetry takes the place of myth and religion, is little more than a commonplace. As I have suggested, the great virtue of commonplaces is that one may appeal to them, in order to justify certain arguments on a lower level of generality. In order for the contribution of a piece of literary criticism to be informative, it must suggest some conclusion on a less general level of argument; and that is, precisely, what seems to be lacking in Keyser and Prince's paper. The term "folk etymology" does not seem to be too well qualified to bridge the gap between these high level generalizations and the description of the various individual texts, for which I submit that the "modular" conception of critical terms propounded in the present chapter is tailor-made—at any rate, it yields a much more significant insight into the aesthetic character of Morgenstern's poem than do the scattered commonplaces provided by Keyser and Plince.

7   An additional factor's presence is crucially required for significant insights to happen, as I have discussed in the preceding chapter: the processes discussed above may lead to insights only if the critic has the necessary mental flexibility, and a tolerance for shifting mental sets.

Keyser and Morris Halle a world-wide reputation. This theory has been criticized for being circular. If we define a "metrical line" as one in which no stress maximum occurs in a weak position (see above, Chapter 6), and a stress maximum as a syllable that bears lexical stress between two unstressed syllables with no intervening syntactic or prosodic junctures, then we may not, in addition, claim that our theory is able to explain the fact that a stressed syllable may occur in the first (weak) position of an iambic line, or in a weak position after a major syntactic juncture, and thus credit it with special explanatory powers.[8] All that the stress-maximum theory says—thus goes the argument—is that stressed syllables may occur in weak position either after a line onset, or after a major syntactic juncture, or when preceded or followed by another stressed syllable; all this was well known to prosodists long before Halle and Keyser came along.

Justified as this criticism may be in its essentials, one is hard put to explain the fact that in spite of all, the Halle-Keyser theory has been one of the most influential metrical theories in the twentieth century, and the source of innumerable exciting insights for prosodists all over the world. The "secret" of the stress-maxima theory seems to corroborate my present argument. The notion of metrical ictus (and all its synonyms) was a very fuzzy notion, even in the minds of experienced prosodists; it consisted of an indiscriminate mixture of metrical and linguistic stress. The first achievement of the Halle-Keyser theory was to separate out and clearly define the notions of stress pattern and metric pattern, with clearly articulated correspondence rules. Its second great achievement was the theoretical construct "stress maximum", which coded all those conditions for the acceptance of stressed syllables in weak positions (which had been well known to prosodists for centuries) into one well-articulated, easily manipulable concept.[9] The third great achievement of the theory concerns the "modularity" of the notion. One can make up one's mind whether a given syllable is a stress maximum or not, by checking the various relevant criteria; it takes a *separate* step to decide whether the line is metrical or not. In this way, fuzziness is dispelled, and the critic may make decisions in clear-cut steps. Given a well-established practice, the critic performs these steps with the speed of intuitive processes.

[8]   "If we define the fish course as that which comes after the soup, then if a hostess serves fish first, it cannot be the fish course" (Wimsatt, 1971: 208).

[9]   The mental economy involved in such a process has been described by George Miller as follows:

> The input is given in a code that contains many chunks with few bits per chunk. The operator recodes the input into another code that contains fewer chunks with more bits per chunk. There are many ways to do this recoding, but probably the simplest is to group the input events, apply a new name to the group, and then remember the new name rather than the original input events. (Miller, 1970: 44)

This is exactly what is obtained by using the term "stress maximum". For another way of recoding see above, Chapter 2, Figure 2.2.

One great virtue of the term "stress maximum" is that it bestows articulation and structural organization upon the whole field of stress in poetic rhythm. As the name indicates, its core concept is the notion of a maximal contrast to unstressed sylla-bles. By the same token, the term constitutes a partial contrast of varying degrees to stress that is "neutralized", partially or wholly, by adjacent junctures or stresses. And consequently, as an extra bonus, the term "stress maximum" suggests the no-tion of a contrast that can be sharpened or leveled, opening up the possibility of connecting the term with gestalt theory.

That the Halle-Keyser theory became the source of so many insights was due to the clear-cut articulation of its concepts and the efficient coding of its notion of "stress maximum"; in terms of information processing, this saved mental process-ing space, allowing for a flexible manipulation of metrical entities and for the cre-ation of unexpected connections, both within the domain of metrics and between the domain of metrics and other domains of literary studies.[10] i).Keyser;

The Keyser-Prince paper has the psychological atmosphere of exciting insights. One feels all along that the authors had the keen intuition that something important was hiding behind their examples. Unfortunately, however, the authors failed to put this intuition into words. For one thing, there is the "So what?" objection: "So what if all your examples derive from folk etymology? You still haven't made your point: that this term bestows on them some kind of deeper significance". Further-more, it is a fact that there is little "family resemblance" between the authors' vari-ous examples; most of them are based on different subsets of elements in their char-acterization of "folk etymology". By the same token, their characterization intro-duces certain noisy elements. A central notion in their definition is the phenomenon usually called "paronomasia" in traditional rhetoric (in plain English, "pun"), by which one single verbal sign is realized (consecutively, or simultaneously) in two alternative sign-functions. To this characterization, the term "folk etymology" adds two components, first, that these two sign functions have to do, somehow, with the origin and development of the words concerned; and second, that one of the two functions is somehow less acceptable than the other. In fact, however, these two components are relevant only to some of the marginal examples, and are utterly ir-relevant to the most interesting ones. Still another reason for the poor persuasive ef-fect of Keyser and Prince's terminology is that it refers to certain elements in the examples, but fails to refer to the pervasive quality of a poem like "Der Werwolf". And finally, there is the theory's failure to fill in the "space" between the descrip-tions of the texts and the highly generalized commonplaces of the conclusion sec-tion, with a properly articulated network of terms. My claim is that a considerable part of the blame for this goes to the term "folk etymology" and the authors' use of the verb "enact".

---

[10] As far as I know, none of the adherents—let alone critics—of the "stress-maximum" theory has shown signs of awareness of this aspect of the term. I have discussed at great length several related issues in my books Tsur, 1977 and 1998; see also above, Chapter 6).

I have speculated at some length on the ways critical terms must be coded in one's mental dictionary in order to be conducive to critical insight. But the mere use of a term coded in a particular way is no guarantee for insights. Other terms, too, must be coded in one's mental dictionary in similar ways; and so must the great commonplaces of our critical heritage. In this way, one's critical dictionary may serve as the groundwork for a kind of metalinguistic or metapoetic creativity, by generating "well-formed" critical utterances which may be used for "successful", or even "insightful", reference to poetic qualities and structures. The coding in question must give information about both the descriptive content of a term and its combinational possibilities. As to the other side of the coin, **combinational restrictions**, I have had nothing to say, at least explicitly: a proper articulation of the terms should take care of these.

Sound Patterns in Wallace Stevens

Let us proceed to show that the tools proposed above, in discussing "Der Werwolf", are not *ad hoc* categories, but are equally well suited (in fact, better than are categories such as "folk etymology" or "enact") to deal with the issues raised by Keyser and Prince in connection with the Wallace Stevens poems. The way Keyser and Prince treat repeated sound clusters in these poems raises a fundamental question: are we to attribute additional referential meaning to the superimposed sound clusters, and thus turn them into puns, or are we to regard them as a euphonic sound texture in its own right, with no extra meaning assigned? In other words, are we to regard, e.g., the repetition of the sound sequence /yu/ in

(4)   **You** are that white **Eu**lalia of the name

as a musical effect or as a pun? Does the sound sequence /yu/ confer the referent "you" to "**Eu**lalia"? In pun, each of the two sign functions is "striving" to reassert itself in the reader's perception, to preserve, as it were, the two functions' "warring identity"; the result being a perceptual quality of wit. In alliteration, the alternative sound patterns do not vie in rivalry for the reader's attention; they are peacefully arranged in a hierarchic order, the arbitrary referential sign being in the foreground, with the non-referential expressive sound clusters constituting a more or less "thick" musical background texture. Psychologically, then, the two conceptions of sound repetition are incompatible. This incompatibility is curiously similar to that obtaining between the elements which constitute the grotesque. That is to say, if the strict separation of the respective arrangements could somehow be interfered with, one might expect a resulting "high tension" effect, not unlike the strange sensation of confusion and disorientation associated with the grotesque.

Let us consider Keyser and Prince's quotations from Stevens' "Ordinary Evening in New Haven":

(5)   When the mariners came to the land of the lemon trees,
       At last, in the blond atmosphere, bronzed hard,
       They said, "We are back once more in the land of the elm trees,

       But folded over, turned around". It was the same,
       Except for the adjectives, an alteration
       Of words that was a change of nature, more

       Than the difference that clouds make over a town.
       The countrymen were changed and each constant thing.
       Their dark-colored words had redescribed the citrons.

Keyser and Prince (op. cit., 76) comment: "The shift of letters in the first syllable of *lemon, lem,* produces *elm,* and, as Stevens says, this change of language, in
itself, produces a change of nature". Here, the term "folk etymology" has picked out
those elements to which it was tuned, and molded Stevens' poetic technique in its
own image, with little regard for the possibility that the phoneme sequence /lem/
repeated as /elm/ may or may not be a case of plain alliteration. But notice that this
repeated sound cluster is actually embedded here in a rich texture of alliteration,
about which Keyser and Prince say nothing. Thus, the phonological sequence
/blond/ is repeated in the same order (with the liquid replaced by another liquid and
with the addition of a voiced sibilant) in /bronzd/. Both phoneme sequences, /l-n-d/
and /r-n-d/ are repeated, in the same order, in *land* (twice), and in *turned around.*
These sound clusters have further ramifications in the quoted passage, on which I
shall not dwell here.

It is interesting to observe the two consecutive phrases "in that blond atmosphere, bronzed hard". The two phrases are related on three levels: First, they constitute a syntagmatic sequence; second, their sound clusters are related by a paradigmatic pattern; and third, they are contrasted by such semantic components as [±DARK]
and [±HARD]. These contrasting components form semantic patterns that are redundant from the syntagmatic point of view, and it would appear that they are absorbed
in the background texture, together with the phonological clusters. *Prima facie,* the
repeated cluster /lem/ — /elm/ is just one more thread in this network of sound texture, which appears to be non-referential, superimposed upon the syntagmatic sequence of arbitrary linguistic signs.

In the second tercet of the excerpt, however, the tables are turned on the reader. "It
was the same, / Except for the adjectives, an alteration / Of words that was a change
of nature". One wonders what could be substituted for "was", in the last clause, of
more specific verbs, such as "produced" or "reflected". Keyser and Prince paraphrase
"was" as "produced", without any reservation. From the context of the poem, I
gather that "reflected" might be no less appropriate. What the poem says is quite
sophisticated, and could be, I think, paraphrased as follows: "When they came to the
land, they found there was a change of nature: elm trees were replaced by lemon

trees; in the language of the poem that describes this change of nature, the shift is rather slight: only the word *lemon* has been replaced by *elm* (the letters of which are already contained in the replaced word). The reader who has access to this real-world state of affairs only through the language of the poem (description first, landscape last), may think that it is the slight change of language that produced the change of nature". That is why the copula *was* is so much more appropriate here than either of the content verbs "reflected" or "produced"; it fits into both orders of representation.

The reader is shocked out of his complacent indulgence in poetic language in three different ways at one and the same time. First, there is a shift of the chain of causation: the thing experienced first (language) produces, as it were, the thing experienced later (landscape), irrespective of the logical sequence of events. Second, there is a shift from language to metalanguage ("adjectives"). Third, if Keyser and Prince are right, a referential sign function is assigned to a non-referential pattern of potential sign vehicles (the "shift of letters" signifies a "change of nature"). Thus, the alliteration is turned into a pun *after the event.* The non-referential sound pattern becomes the sign vehicle of a sign function, emerges from the background texture, and "strives" to establish its "warring identity", to establish itself in the reader's perception. In other words, both the sign vehicle and the signified are so literally developed that they both assume independent existences of their own.

This way of "smashing" language would appear, then, to be infinitely more sophisticated and more effective than that observed in "Der Werwolf". The identity and discrepancy of signifier and signified has been forced into the foreground by three simultaneous shifts. The emotional disorientation is all the more baffling here, since the same sound clusters that have already been accepted as euphonic sound texture, are now smashed, and remolded in the shape of a pun. The examples quoted by Keyser and Prince in the same paper from Stevens' "Infanta Marina" appear to provide a still more sophisticated instance of the same technique.

Once more we see, then, that (as demonstrated here by our analysis of some poems by Wallace Stevens) our choice of critical terms may pre-judge the outcome of the analysis. The descriptive content of the notion "folk etymology" is not sufficiently articulated to distinguish "pun" from "alliteration", nor does the descriptive content of "enact the world" enable us to make such sophisticated distinctions as are required to handle "an alteration of words that *was* a change of nature".

Keyser and Prince's discussion of Stevens' technique amounts to saying that the poet developed his sign vehicles so literally that they assumed an existence of their own. As I have tried to show, this technique is not very new; and if that were all, it would not even be very original. The fact that Stevens' preferred sign vehicles for operating this device are exotic proper names, may point to an interesting idiosyncrasy, but it leaves the core of his originality untouched. I submit, as a hypothesis to be yet confirmed, that Stevens' peculiarity in handling this particular technique consists in the great sophistication of his "smashing" of language; a smashing that occurs at several levels at one and the same time, and in the unique role he assigns to this process in the phonological component.

Some Further Perspectives

There remain to sum up and further explore some general questions: (1) The intuitive use of critical terms by critics who display (respectively, enhance) insight; (2) the characteristics of fruitful critical terms; (3) the nature of critical competence, with insights resulting from the application of critical terms. The critic may be assumed to have intuitively used terms whose coding is similar to that of words in natural language. Such intuitive use is witnessed, e.g., by the fact that Thomson does not even bother to create a proper technical term for his "language smashing".

In general, in order for a critical term to be fertile, its meaning should be well articulated, and its coding should include several kinds of information. Only thus will it facilitate a structural, a functional and a phenomenological description of literary phenomena (that is, it will enable the critic to describe a literary phenomenon in terms of its structure, its results, and its unique conscious quality). The structural description may establish correspondences between the term's meaning and a certain kind of literary phenomenon, whereas the functional and phenomenological descriptions open certain combinational possibilities. In order for a critical term to lead to insights, it is of the utmost importance that its coding include information not only about its meaning, but also about its combinational potentials. Some "flexible" (as I have called it above, Chapter 21) and experienced critics will be able to abstract the relevant features even when encountering the term (or the literary phenomenon) for the first time.

There is some indication that the meaning structure of critical terms is similar to that of words in natural languages. One important resource of creativity in natural languages is the hierarchical (hyponymical) organization of its mental dictionary. The hierarchical organization of the lexicon of natural languages is a major asset for the creative processes, both of language learning and of establishing meaning relationships between words that are removed from each other to varying degrees. "A single concrete object can be referred to as a *dinner table, table, furniture, artifact, object* and *thing,* but each of these terms is shared with a different range of other *things"* (Miller, 1978: 79).

Hyponymy is an obvious way of saving mental storage space, and sometimes mental processing space as well; thus, hyponymy also becomes a device that facilitates language acquisition. "In order to account for a child's speed in learning new words once he has learned a few related words, it suffices merely to suppose that there is a common part being learned over and over, and that learning that part gets faster with practice" (Miller, loc. cit., 81).

The heterogeneous elements jumbled together in the notion of "folk etymology" have no internal structure, and that is why they fail to generate significant insights. "Assigning two sign functions to a single phoneme sequence", "inventing a myth", "enacting the world", and "having to do with the derivation of words" have a rather fuzzy relation to each other. At any rate, none can be counted as a direct superordinate of the others, in the sense in which *furniture* is a superordinate of *table, chair,* and *bed.* Most of them do have a remote common superordinate, such as "having to do with language"; but combinations at this level of abstraction will be quite trivial. Triviality in this sense is a function of the empty slots in those parts of the hierarchy where the respective hyponyms and their superordinate term occur.

Here, Keyser and Prince might argue that certain elements in "folk etymology" are regularly associated with each other, nonetheless. Couldn't that be regarded as the basis of some meaningful relationship? It seems to me that such a possibility has little psycholinguistic validity. One of George Miller's examples serves to illuminate this:

> An urban child might have some verbal understanding of what farmers are and do, and might know the difference between friends and strangers, but he would not necessarily conclude that *farmer* is a hyponym of *stranger*, just because all farmers are strangers to him. His evidence about *table* and *furniture* might be very similar. If it seems reasonable that this child would not believe that farmers must be strangers, why should it seem unreasonable if he did not believe that tables must be furniture? (Miller, 1978: 81)

The answer seems to be that, as Miller has suggested, when a child learns the words *chair, table, bed,* etc., he learns over and over again whatever these words have in common with furniture; and this facilitates the process of learning.

> Presumably the meaning of *stranger* is not a part of what he learns when he learns *farmer;* therefore a similar facilitation of subsequent learning would not occur in that case. In this way a knowledge structure can be built up with an organization that conforms to what are called redundancy rules, but without any rule learning (in the usual sense) on the part of the child. (Ibid.)

To put it somewhat crudely, the term "folk etymology", as defined by Keyser and Prince, does not lead to significant insights because the generalization levels of its elements are not sufficiently differentiated (in the sense that they are not on different levels of the same scale). Since none of the elements imply the others, the gerneralizing term has no meaning structure that might facilitate any cognitive processes. Integrating some of the notion's elements in a piece of literature does not call up other parts of the definition, except by a kind of conditioned reflex nor does it generate intuitions about significant relationships with other pieces of literature, in which different parts of the same definition are incarnated.

Now let us take Thomson's definition of the grotesque. Suppose we have the object language sentence "The dead village schoolmaster climbed up the brass pommel of his tin nameplate". Suppose we describe it in a metalanguage as "grotesque". According to Thomson's analysis, this term would suggest the co-presence of the ridiculous with the horrible in the scene described. At a higher level of abstraction, one could speak of the co-presence of the ridiculous with some quality that is incompatible with it, widening the range of phenomena to which the term "incompatible with the ridiculous" is applicable (including e.g., the sublime, the pitiable, the disgusting, besides the horrible). The next stage, though outside the usual scale of hyponymy, involves a systematically different language stratum: it describes the phenomenological quality of the grotesque ("a sense of confusion and emotional disorientation"). The range of phenomena to which this term is applicable is wider than the range of "grotesque": it includes, as we have seen, at least one other hierarchy, that of "language smashing". We have thus established a relationship between a class of psychological contexts and several hierarchies of linguistic and non-linguistic contexts. Items belonging to various hierarchies may be perceived as equivalent to each other, and may reinforce the same aesthetic quality of a poetic text, by virtue of their relationship to the same psychological context.

Traditionally, the relationship between a hyponym and its superordinate is defined in terms of logical entailment ("This is a chair" entails "This is a piece of furniture", or "an artifact", or "a physical object", and so on). "This definition is not sufficient", says Miller.

> It is necessary to add, at the very least, that the direct hyponyms of a superordinate term form a contrastive set of terms whose extensions are mutually exclusive and whose combined extensions exhaust the extension of the superordinate term. (op. cit., 79)

Miller's addition to the definition of hyponymy supplies a more exact description of what I have called "articulation". "The horrible", "the pitiable", "the disgusting", and "the sublime" constitute such a set of contrastive terms, the direct hyponyms of "a quality incompatible with the ridiculous". That is one reason for the clear-cut articulation of the term "grotesque". On the other hand, I have claimed there is no relation of hyponymy between "assigning two sign functions to one phoneme sequence", "inventing a myth", "enacting the world" and "having to do with the derivation of words", etc. From *this* point of view, they may be regarded as being "on the same level of generalization". However, they do not form a set of contrastive terms either (or part of such a set), whose combined extensions would exhaust the extension of some direct superordinate. That is why the term "folk etymology" is poorly articulated.

Generative linguistics has coined and promoted the term "linguistic competence"; this refers to the native speaker's underlying knowledge, that enables him to produce and understand an indefinite number of utterances to which he may not have been exposed before. By analogy, in order to account for the ability of human beings to produce and understand literary works of art to which they have not been exposed before, the notion of "poetic competence" or "literary competence" has been proposed (Bierwisch, 1970; Culler, 1975: 113–130; see also above, Chapters 2 and 3). Both forms of competence imply some kind of *creativity,* linguistic or artistic. By analogy, I have proposed here the notion of "critical competence", to account for the ability of human beings to use and understand critical terms in a creative manner.

It is noteworthy that these analogic types of competence form an entailment hierarchy: each later one presupposes the preceding one. One cannot have poetic competence without having first acquired linguistic competence; and, in turn, one cannot have critical competence, without having first acquired poetic competence

As I have suggested in Chapter 1, such a hierarchy is not a mere chain of subordinations; it is governed by what Polányi (1967: 40) calls "the principle of marginal control", that is, the control exercised by the organizational principle of the higher level on the particular elements forming its lower level; the successive working principles control the boundary that is left indeterminate on the next lower level. "Moreover, each lower level imposes restrictions on the one above it, even as the laws of inanimate nature restrict the practicability of conceivable machines; and again, we may observe that a higher operation may fail when the next lower operation escapes from its control (Polányi, op. cit., 41).

I have elsewhere discussed how linguistic intuition constrains literary interpretation (Tsur, 1987 b: 105–116). Here, I shall only point out that this hierarchic conception of critical competence can explain the frequently observed phenomenon that a critic who has applied to a poem the legitimate tools of his discipline, according to its proper logic, may reach conclusions that are conspicuously counter-intuitive. In Polányi's terms, we might say that his critical competence has failed to operate, because some of the operations of his poetic or linguistic competence have escaped from control.

Such a failure must be distinguished from another, functional kind of "operational failure" which, too, is relevant to our present business. Poetic competence exploits, at a lower level, a variety of linguistic, as well as cognitive mechanisms. As suggested in Chapter 1, not infrequently, it is precisely the failure of those mechanisms that is exploited by poetic competence for certain specific effects; Chapter 17 identified the grotesque as a case in point.

Some emotional as well as aesthetic qualities, such as the sublime, the pitiable, the horrible, or the ridiculous, are the result of the operation of various defense mechanisms designed to cope emotionally with threat. There is, furthermore, a marked difference as to the individual emotional or aesthetic qualities: the ridiculous is basically incompatible with the others, and the defense mechanisms involved are mutually exclusive. The ridiculous, in Kenneth Burke's words, "equips us by impiety as we refuse to allow the threat its authority" (Burke, 1957: 52), whereas the sublime, the pitiable, or the horrible do "allow the threat its authority". In other words, in the presence of the ridiculous, the perceiver has a feeling of superiority and relative freedom, whereas in the presence of the sublime, the pitiable, and the horrible, he has a feeling of smallness, helplessness, or even of being trapped. The grotesque, the sense of confusion and emotional disorientation associated with this feeling, results from an interference with the smooth operation of these defense mechanisms, preventing the system from settling in any one of these mutually exclusive emotional states. The grotesque occurs, we might suggest now, when poetic competence exploits the failure of these lower-level mechanisms to function "properly".[11]

One obvious advantage of the above conception is its conspicuous cognitive economy. At the lower-level forms of competence one need not learn lists of conventions (see above, Chapter 12) for, e.g., the grotesque and its related qualities, nor acquire specific mechanisms to deal with them. The reader may exploit, in the service of his poetic competence, the proper functioning of his linguistic and cognitive mechanisms, *and* the obstruction of their proper functioning as well. By the same token, this conception may account for the emotional impact literary works of art may have. It may also account for the fact that *some* readers (those, I have called above, Chapter 12, "the versatile reader,") can respond, in a fairly adequate manner, to a variety of poetic styles with which they may have had only superficial acquaintance.

At the higher end of the hierarchy, critical competence presupposes these lower-level operations. It consists, however, not only in an ability to *use* the term "grotesque", but also in an ability to *see* and *state* the actual or potential combinations of this quality with other qualities in a poem. Thus, there is a two-way traffic between the various levels of competence. Critical competence presupposes, and draws upon, poetic competence. On the other hand, it aids, *via* the "properly-coded terms", the creative functioning of poetic competence, and in some instances determines the character of its parts.

Metalanguage, Metaeffusion & Infinite Regress

> Achilles had overtaken the Tortoise, and had seated himself comfortably on its back.
>
> "So you've got to the end of our race-course?" said the Tortoise. "Even though it DOES consist of an infinite series of distances? I thought some wisacre or other had proved that the thing couldn't be done?"
>
> "It CAN be done," said Achilles. "It HAS been done! *Solvitur ambulando.* You see the distances were constantly DIMINISHING; and so—"
>
> "But if they had been constantly INCREASING?" the Tortoise interrupted. How then?"
>
> "Then I shouldn't be here," Achilles modestly replied; "and YOU would have got several times round the world, by this time!"
>
> (Lewis Carroll: *What the Tortoise Said to Achilles*)

The Tortoise proposes to Achilles to explore "a race course, that most people fancy they can get to the end of in two or three steps, while REALLY consists of an infi-

---

[11]   We have encountered a similar effect, arising from a similar interference with the separation of two mutually exclusive organizations of sound clusters, in the Wallace Stevens poems.

nite number of distances", by taking "a little argument" in that "beautiful" First Proposition of Euclid:

(A) Things that are equal to the same are equal to each other.
(B) The two sides of this Triangle are things that are equal to the same.
(Z) The two sides of this Triangle are equal to each other.

The Tortoise proposes to consider what happens if a reader accepts Z but not A and B, or does accept A and B but not Z. Both kinds of readers, says Achilles, "would do wisely in abandoning Euclid, and taking to football".

> Well, now, I want you to consider ME as a reader of the SECOND kind, and force me, logically, to accept Z as true".
> "A tortoise playing football would be—" Achilles was beginning.
> "—an anomaly, of course," the Tortoise hastily interrupted. Don't wander from the point. Let's have Z first, and football afterwards!"

In an attempt to force the Tortoise to accept Z as true, Achilles successively formulates the following propositions, entering them into his notebook, one after the other:

(C) If A and B are true, Z must be true.
(D) If A and B and C are true, Z must be true.
(E) If A and B and C and D are true, Z must be true.

And so on infinitely. Now the literary critic's work appears to be, in an important sense, similar to Achilles' attempt to force the Tortoise to accept Z as true. Would it not be better if we all took to football? I propose to consider this question first with reference to impressionist criticism, and then with reference to analytic criticism that uses a critical metalanguage.

Take the case of the impressionist critic. He has a poetic text, which expresses certain emotions. He feels that his reader is in need of some guidance in order to appreciate these emotions. So, he expresses his own emotions *à propos* the poem, in order to tune the reader's mind to the emotions of the poem. Let us call this *meta-effusion*. In fact, he has produced now a rival text, one which is not an equivalent of the original one. Chances are that it is less complex than the original. Likewise, chances are that in this meta-effusion there are certain noisy elements, irrelevant to the original text of the poem. Insofar as the meta-effusion is more easily accessible to the reader than the poet's own effusion, it is only because it is less complex and artistically inferior to the original poem. So, rather than directing the reader's attention *to* the poet's text, it tends to direct attention *away* from it. Now, the reader may turn for further help to a meta-critic, who would tune the reader's mind to the critic's meta-effusion with a meta-meta-effusion. And so it goes on without end, with the meta-meta-meta-effusion of the meta-meta-critic, and the meta-meta-meta-meta-effu-sion of the meta-meta-meta-critic. There is only one constraint on this endless series: if the number of METAs before *critic* is n, their number before the corre-sponding *effusion* must be n+1. And the distance between the text and the reader's mind will gradually increase.

Apparently, the same is true if we substitute *metalanguage* for *meta-effusion.* But this similarity is only *apparent.* Why? The answer is indicated by Lewis Carroll's parable (or Zenon's, if you wish), when considered against our foregoing discussion. Achilles, in one giant step, overtakes the Tortoise and gets to the end of the race-course. In the same way, the critic needs only two levels of metalanguage, the descriptive level and the combinational level; then, with a giant step, he may leap from the foothold of the combinational level of his term into his reader's mind.

The analytic critic, using a metalanguage, does not produce a rival text to the poet's first order text; on the contrary: his text is viable *only* in the poetic text's presence. The descriptive contents of the metalanguage can be used as a rather pre-cise instrument to direct the reader's attention to certain aesthetically significant aspects of the poem's object language. It is this use that is typically absent from meta-effusion. As I have argued earlier, in order to assign aesthetic significance to a "true" metalinguistic description, it must be related to some general model or the-ory. Furthermore, both must be coded in a way that their combinational potentials may be activated and interlocked. A metalinguistic description of a poetic text will assume aesthetic significance for a reader, only if he already is familiar with the rel-evant general models and theories, and if these are *actively present* in his mind at the time of reading the piece of analytic criticism. Further, the process will be success-fully accomplished, if similar combinational potentials are activated with reference to the metalanguage describing the poetic text on the one hand, and with reference to relevant general models and theories on the other.

I have indicated several times that there appear to be certain similarities between the structure of the mental lexicon of natural languages and that of the vocabulary of critical terms. In the respect under discussion, too, there may be a significant simi-larity. Without subscribing to Fodor's "innateness" hypothesis, I find that his de-fense of a mental language against the charge of infinite regress makes a point that is rather similar to my point above. Fodor illustrates his conception of the relation-ship between external language and internal representation by an analogy with com-puters.

> Real computers characteristically use at least two different languages: an in-put/output language in which they communicate with their environment and a machine language in which they talk to themselves (i.e., in which they run their computations). "Compilers" mediate between the two lan-guages in effect by specifying biconditionals whose left-hand side is a for-mula in the input/output code and whose right-hand side is a formula in the machine code. [...] What avoids an infinite regression of compilers is the

fact that the machine is *built* to use the machine language. (Fodor, 1979:
65–66)

How can the critic ensure that the relevant general models and theories are *actively present* in the reader's mind at the time of reading the piece of analytic criticism? One way to do this is meticulously to enumerate all the relevant emotional and aesthetic models required (assuming that the reader *already* knows them). This is, indeed, what is done in the introductory sections of many critical writings. Sometimes this is performed in a more sophisticated manner, by way of polemics: the critic is responding to the work of some other critic. In many cases, however, all this may be time-consuming and tedious. In "practical criticism", the critic is forced to strike an acceptable compromise between the rigorous exposition required by his discipline, and the time and patience he may exact from his reader. Many excellent critics do indeed compromise in such a way. And this is where critical impressionism may come in usefully. With a brief impressionistic remark, or a well-chosen metaphor or joke, the critic may tune his reader's mind, that is, he may arouse the relevant cognitive, emotional and theoretical models in his reader's mind, and then proceed with his rigorous analytic criticism, use critical terms to describe poetic structures in the text, point at combinational potentials both in the critical vocabulary and the mental models, so that they may hook up and interlock with each other. That is, precisely, how a metalinguistic description of a poetic text may become meaningful to a reader.

Language Strata: The Liar's Paradox

> Take the case of the Liar, that is, of a man who says "I am lying"; if he is lying he is speaking the truth, and if he is speaking the truth he is lying. We might interpret this statement as saying "All the propositions which I assert are false". Is this proposition itself true or false? [...] The decisive point to realize is that the phrase "all propositions" is an illegitimate totality. [...] We may put it like this: if somebody were to tell us he is a liar, we could ask him, "Well, a liar of what order?" If he says he is a liar of the first order he is making a statement of the second order, and this statement may be perfectly true. When he says "I am a liar of the second order (including the totality of first-order statements) this would be a statement of the third order; and so on. [...] Once we reach this stage, there is no contradiction. (Waisman, 1966: 17–18)

Philosophy did not stay for long in this euphoric state of freedom from paradox. One of the central theses of Douglas Hofstadter's (1981) *Gödel, Escher, Bach* is that the elimination of this and similar paradoxes is neither possible, nor desirable; they are conditioned by the structure of the human mind as reflected in the works of Gödel, Escher, and Bach.

> There seems to be one common culprit in these paradoxes, namely, self-reference, or "Strange Loopiness". So if the goal is to ban all paradoxes, why not try banning self-reference and anything that allows it to arise? This is not so easy as it might seem, because it can be hard to figure out just where self-reference is occurring. It may be spread out over a whole strange loop with several steps, as in this "expanded" version of Epimenides, reminiscent of [Escher's] *Drawing Hands:*
>
> > The following sentence is false.
> > The preceding sentence is true.
>
> Taken together, these sentences have the same effects as the original Epimenides paradox; yet separately, they are harmless and even potentially useful sentences. The "blame" for this Strange Loop can't be pinned on either sentence—only on the way they "point" at each other. In the same way, each local region of [Escher's] *Ascending and Descending* is quite legitimate; it is only the way they are globally put together that creates an impossibility. (Hofstadter, 1981: 21)

For Waisman, language, metalanguage, meta-metalanguage and so forth, are only one—though a very interesting—kind of instances of a wide variety of language strata. Other kinds of strata include "object language", "sense-datum language", "mental-process language", and so forth, with interestingly different kinds of logic.

> A thing is, so to speak, a hard core that resists at any attempt at breaking it up and reducing it to the level of other data, whatever they may be. All this talk about material objects and sense-data is a talk about two language strata, about their relation, about the logic of this relationship. The problem arises along the plane where the two strata make contact, so to speak. The difficulty is to understand in precisely which way a material object statement is related to a sense-datum statement; that is, what sort of relations hold between members of different strata; and that is a problem of logic. (Waisman, op. cit.: 29)

As the readers will have noticed, throughout the present chapter—indeed, throughout the present book—I have been discussing a variety of language strata and the relationships between them. The discussion has focused not only on the relationship between an indefinitely long series of "meta"-languages, but also on that between language strata, such as "object language", "sense-datum language", "mental-process language", and so forth. Thus, for instance, when in Chapter 18 I discussed the concept of **topicalized attribute (thematized predicate)**, I was in fact discussing the cognitive relationships between these three language strata. And this is, indeed, a crucial difference between Waisman's and Hofstadter's work on the one hand and the present work on the other: while they are focusing attention on logical relationships, my work is focused on cognitive relationships (with the logical ones hovering only in the background). The quotations from Waisman and Hofstadter, however brief, may help us to pinpoint the elements which I have discussed from the cognitive point of view.

Take, for instance, the issue of self-reference. Waisman and Hofstadter are interested in such questions as whether paradoxes can be eliminated or not, and whether their elimination is desirable or not; according to Hofstadter, the common culprit in these paradoxes is self-reference. I have been concerned in the present chapter with an entirely different question: unexpected self-reference in poetic language, either as it occurs in "Der Werwolf", or in the way it appears in the Wallace Stevens poems, tends to generate a quality of "emotional disorientation". In both instances, we also find a sudden leap from object language to metalanguage. Self-reference in Escher's *Drawing Hands,* too, tends to arouse "emotional disorientation". In Bach's *Art of the Fugue,* however, it does not—here I disagree with Hofstadter. "In what he planned as the next-to-last fugue, [Bach] inserted his own name coded into notes as the third theme" (Hofstadter, 1981: 86). Hofstadter insinuates that this act had an overwhelming effect on Bach's health and his leaving eventually the *Art of the Fugue* incomplete. I have nothing to contribute to an understanding of this kind of events. Since we are engaged here in "audience response" rather than in "author response", we may note that self-reference in this case is no perceptual part of the music, since the names of the sounds that constitute the musical scale constitute no part of the music. Furthermore, for a person who enjoys Bach's music, but does not know the names of the notes B-A-C-H in German, but only, e.g., "si bemolle-la-do-si", self-reference in this sense does not exist. The best way, perhaps, to show that self-reference is no perceptual part of this music is to point out that while in transposition the music remains the same, the "self-reference" is lost. In genuine self-reference, the reader or beholder is shocked out of his mental set, that is tuned to one consistent sign system, his own cognitive mechanisms thereby becoming perceptible to him. Bach's self-reference remains for the listener a witty or playful meta-idea *referring to* the music; it does not affect the listener's perceptual process.

I have claimed that I was more interested in the cognitive than in the logical issues involved in, e.g., self-reference—even though there were considerable overlappings between them. The same holds true of the interface between language strata. I have mainly been concerned with problems of coding and conversions from one stratum to the other, less with the logical relationship between them. My basic conception of the issues involved is hierarchical. I conceive of linguistic, poetic, and critical competence as arranged in a hierarchy, governed by Polányi's principle of marginal control. The structure of the critical terms is envisaged as hyponymical, by analogy with the lexicon of natural languages. Likewise, I have relied on a hierarchic series of first, second, third (and so forth) order languages. Now, one crucial point must be noted in all these ways of organizing the conceptual universe. Although they display a tendency towards hierarchy, this hierarchy is not rigidly fixed in all instances: sometimes, there appear to be alternative routes, which the reader or critic may exploit creatively. Wherever there are gaps in the hierarchy, modularity is substituted for hierarchy; gaps are filled in by interlocking modules from different language strata. A further suggestion has been that both lexical items and critical terms may be encoded together with their combinational potentials; thus the need for specific combinational rules can be obviated. These combinational potentials are sometimes on a fairly specific level; but we also seem to have a highly general mechanism for the generation of combinational potentials in unforeseen instances, such as we have been exposed to for the first time. These combinational potentials "point at each other" from the various language strata, and with their help, crucial gaps may be bridged. The most crucial of these gaps is the one between the descriptive level of metalanguage and the reader's mental models. In this connection, I have shown a way in which the problem of infinite regress in the use of metalanguages can be avoided. I have discussed all of these issues with reference to two fundamental poetic modes, that of orientation and that of disorientation. With reference to the former, I have discussed critical terms propounded by Leo Spitzer, Josephine Miles and Anton Ehrenzweig; this was done in the first section of the present chapter. As for the latter, this has been the focal point of the rest of this chapter.

CHAPTER 23

Lakoff's Roads Not Taken

This chapter is a critique of George Lakoff's theory and practice as presented in his "Contemporary Theory of Metaphor" (Lakoff, 1993).[1] It addresses the issue on several planes, on each plane comparing Lakoff's approach to some alternative. The highest plane, affording the widest perspective, concerns two approaches to interpretation and scientific thinking: one that relies on a pre-established set of meanings, and one that assumes that "all the work remains to be done in each particular case". The two approaches involve different cognitive strategies, rapid and delayed conceptualization. Another plane concerns the cognitive explanation for using spatial images in metaphoric and symbolic processes. Here the "embodied-mind hypothesis" is confronted with the "efficient-coding hypothesis". It is argued that the latter is more adequate, and can better account for the mental flexibility required for "delayed conceptualization". On the third plane, Lakoff's "Contemporary Theory of Metaphor" is compared to Beardsley's "Controversion Theory of Metaphor". I will assert that precisely in those respects in which Lakoff claims superiority for his theory it is inferior to Beardsley's. On the most concrete plane, Lakoff's handling of three texts is considered, two literary and one nonliterary. It is argued that in two cases Lakoff's conceptual apparatus is less than adequate to handle the arising problems; in the third case it allows him to say about the text exactly what every critic would have said about it for the past seven hundred years.

Rapid and delayed conceptualization

The point of departure for the following exercise is the observation that the history of the interpretation of symbolic processes and of figurative language is dominated by two polar attitudes: one pole relies on more or less pre-determined meanings, the

[1] This chapter does not presume to offer a wholesale criticism of "cognitive linguistics". It is focussed on *one* of its forcible statements. Lakoff (1993) modestly claims to speak on behalf of the Contemporary Theory of Metaphor, challenging much that appears in the other papers in Ortony's (1977, 1993[2]) collection, "many of which make certain assumptions that were widely taken for granted in 1977" (204). Thus, I am not going to consider all the examples ever discussed by cognitive linguistics, only three of them which, Lakoff claims, illustrate the explanatory power of his theory. The business of this chapter is to show that the challenge is less of a challenge than it purports to be.

other one insists on certain "meaning potentials" of the sign unit, the final meaning(s) being determined by its unforeseeable interaction with the signs that constitute the context. These are two alternative cognitive strategies. The former yields rather quick results and arouses in the interpreter a feeling of certainty, but tends to be rigid and maladaptive: it may miss some of the most legitimate possibilites. The latter is slower, and requires considerable tolerance of uncertainty; but it is much more flexible in its application. I have called these strategies "rapid" and "delayed conceptualization". In what follows, I will briefly explore these cognitive strategies.

In the psychoanalytic interpretation of dreams, Wilhelm Stekel compiled a dictionary of dream symbols. Freud regarded this as inadequate: "after warning that such a gift as Stekel's is often evidence of paranoia, he decides that normal persons may also occasionally be capable of it" (Burke, 1957: 228). As it is frequently said, sometimes a cigar is just a cigar. Freud and some other practitioners and theoreticians believe that one cannot know what a dream symbol means until it is viewed in the context of the dream and the free associations of the dreamer; and the cigar, for instance, will change its meanings according to the unique stream of associations provided. In literary theory, in the first third of twentieth century, Richards (1929) led an assault on contemporary academic education and critical practice, because they encouraged "stock responses", that is, some undifferentiated responses to images and symbols whenever they occur, irrespective of context. He vigorously insisted that symbols change their meanings and require subtle changes of response when they enter into different contexts.[2]

At the crossroads

I have a problem with Lakoff's application of the "conceptual metaphor" to literary texts. To indicate its nature, consider his discussion of three lines by Robert Frost:

> Two roads diverged in a wood, and I—
> I took the one less traveled by,
> And that has made all difference.

Since Frost's language often does not overtly signal that the poem is to be taken metaphorically, incompetent English teachers occasionally teach Frost as if he were a nature poet, simply describing scenes. (I have actually had students whose high school teachers taught them that!) Thus, this passage could be read nonmetaphorically as being just about a trip on which one encounters a crossroads. There is nothing in the sentence itself that forces one to metaphorical interpretation. But, since it is about travel and

---

[2]   I have elsewhere discussed at considerable length "rapid" and "delayed conceptualization" with reference to interpretation in psychotherapy and to the interpretation of poetic metaphor. See Tsur (1988).

encountering crossroads, it evokes a knowledge of journeys. (Lakoff, 1993: 238)

There is a much larger number of equally incompetent English teachers who teach their students that whenever you encounter travel and crossroads, you have to activate, automatically, the LIFE IS A JOURNEY conceptual metaphor. (I have actually had students whose high school teachers taught them that!) Now what is so powerful about Frost is his irony: he pretends to know nothing, not that he is metaphorical, not even ironical. His "language often does not overtly signal that the poem is to be taken metaphorically". The proper response to Frost's poem involves the uncertainty whether the image is metaphorical or not. Now what I would expect a competent English teacher to do is to teach his students, first, that in some contexts crossroads are metaphorical, and in some not; second, that crossroads may have a wide range of metaphorical meanings; third, that they should look for principled arguments that may support the claim that in a certain instance "crossroads" should or should not be understood metaphorically, and in what sense(s); and fourth, that there is a stylistic difference between poems that do and those that do not overtly signal that they are to be taken metaphorically, and they require different kinds of response. The suggestion that "crossroads" can be metaphorical is trivial; it is the proper handling of these four issues that would make a competent English teacher. It is the third of these four points that poses the greatest difficulty to Lakoff. In order to find such principled arguments one must admit that something is wrong with the literal meaning of the poem; for instance, that "And that has made all difference" violates some of Grice's conversational maxims. But this would contradict one of Lakoff's pet assumptions, namely, that metaphors do not violate communication maxims.

Ray Gibbs's discussion of conversational maxims may account for the source of Lakoff's problem; by the same token it may throw some light on the nature of rapid and delayed conceptualization.

> One reason many scholars believe figurative language violates communication maxims is that they confuse the *process* and *product* of linguistic understanding. All language interpretation takes place in real time ranging from the first milliseconds of processing to long-term reflective analysis. This temporal continuum may be roughly divided into moments corresponding to linguistic comprehension, recognition, interpretation, and appreciation. Comprehension refers to the immediate moment-by-moment process of creating meanings for utterances. Recognition refers to the products of comprehension as types (i.e., determining whether an utterance conveys a particular type of meaning such as literal, metaphorical, ironic and so forth). Interpretation refers to the products of comprehension as tokens (i.e., determining the specific content of the meaning type). Apprecia-

tion refers to some aesthetic judgment given to a product either as a type or token. (Gibbs 1993: 255–256)

My point is that Gibbs's distinction between *process* and *product* works both ways: it may suggest that in some instances metaphor need not violate communication maxims; but it may also explain why insistence on this distinction may lead Lakoff to the mishandling of Frost's metaphor. When Lakoff and myself disagree as for what is a competent or incompetent English teacher, we do, in fact, disagree about the proper uses of Gibbs's sequence "linguistic comprehension, recognition, interpretation, and appreciation". Judging from the above example, for Lakoff, literary response concerns only comprehension; for me, it concerns much of the whole sequence. What is more, at each step, decision involves uncertainties—not only in the *process* of decision, but also in its *product*. That is what my foregoing description of a competent English teacher implies. The moment-by-moment account of the process by Gibbs may illuminate the nature of rapid and delayed conceptualization, but with a twist. Confining the process to its first step allows relatively rapid conceptualization. As much is evident. But the ability to give a thorough account of the whole process is not necessarily evidence of delayed conceptualization. Delayed conceptualization implies that one is capable of perceiving much of the process "in a flash". (I cannot tell, however, how the phenomenological quality "in a flash" should show through Gibbs's experimental procedures). One may, of course, produce experimental evidence that readers or listeners are able "to create *some* interpretation for a trope during the earliest moments of comprehension" (Gibbs 1993: 255). My point is that creating "*some* interpretation for a trope" is not necessarily a competent response to a piece of literature.

Or, let me introduce another example: *Oedipus the King*. "Laius was slain where three highroads meet". One could plausibly argue that the overwhelming importance of the location is, first, its uniqueness: that the place is almost uniquely identifiable, and for Oedipus it leaves little doubt as for the identity of the murderer; and second, that it "sounds" somehow very significant, partly because of the meeting of *three* highroads (not two and not four). This meeting of the roads, in turn, may indicate metaphorically some "strange coincidence" (which is not the same as the implications of the LIFE AS A JOURNEY metaphor). Indeed, the play is governed by some strange coincidences. Iocasta had a child, killed long before, who was said to be destined to kill his father when he grows up; and Oedipus received a similar prophecy. Laius was killed where three highroads meet; and Oedipus killed an old man at exactly such a place. But the strangest coincidence is when everything "ties in": the analogies are revealed as identities. The existence of the LIFE AS A JOURNEY conceptual metaphor too *may* have to do with this "air" of significance; but its specific aspects are of low salience at best. One could argue, of course, that the play is concerned with Oedipus' life, and his life is a journey to discover its hidden meaning; and that this crossroads has significantly changed it. But then, any person travelling on a road also has a life, and this road could be symbolic of this life. With some good will any crossroads and journey can be forced to become symbolic. Let me put it differently: Is there for Lakoff any way for a crossroads to escape being symbolic? Or to put it differently, one may claim that the meeting of three high-roads too can be derived from the LIFE AS A JOURNEY metaphor. But then anything can be derived from anything, and the whole system becomes utterly trivial. Briefly, it is not at all clear what are Lakoff's constraints.

The "Embodied Mind" and the "Efficient Coding" hypotheses

My present suggestion is that we use visual spatial imagery for a variety of reasons, one of them being that it is a very efficient coding of many kinds of information. According to Neisser (1968: 320),

> the amount of information may require less capacity coded in terms of spatial relationships than in terms of temporal sequence. [...] This assumption would explain the predominance of visual imagery in dreams, and perhaps also our preference for visual models and metaphors for thinking, from 'insight' to 'point of view'.

In the chapter "The Concrete and the Abstract in Poetry" of my book *On Metaphoring* I have discussed at great length this aspect of the use of concrete images, also quoting Brooks and Warren:

> The word *peach* implies certain qualities: a certain shape, a certain colour, a certain kind of sweetness. But *peach* implies these qualities as "grown together" as we should actually find them embodied in a peach. (The Latin word from which *concrete* comes means literally "grown together"). We can, of course, *abstract* (this word literally means "to take away") these qualities from the actual peach and refer to them in isolation: *sweetness, fuzziness, softness*. Isolating these qualities in such fashion, we get a set of ABSTRACT words. *Sweetness* is a quality common to peaches, of course, and to many other things; the quality is thought of as an idea in its own right. (Brooks and Warren 1958: 298)

In a concrete noun or verb a wide range of features are "grown together", which constitute its "meaning potential". One or several of them may be actualized in a specific context. In this way, several meanings may be encoded in one expression. "Where three highroads meet" provides, first, a precise, identifiable description of the location of the murder; and second, it indicates some outstanding significance. In addition, one may evoke, of course, some implications of the LIFE AS A JOURNEY metaphor. But one must be aware that only a small subset of these implications, if at all, is relevant to the text, and at a very low salience. Such a conception of concrete images in literature allows the reader or critic to move from one aspect to another, yielding great flexibility and considerable accuracy in interpretation. Such an attitude requires strongly delayed conceptualization, to allow a differential response to the image, moving from one aspect to another, choosing the relevant ones, and to respond differentially to the relative salience of the various aspects. To sum up this discussion of roads, I would like to quote L. C. Knights's (1948: 229) comment in a very different context: "But to say this is to admit that all the work remains to be done in each particular case". Lakoff, by contrast, smuggled in through the back door the stock responses so forcefully exorcised by Richards.

What kinds of insight can we get into poetic language, according to these examples, with the two kinds of conceptual apparatus based on the "Embodied Mind" and the "Efficient Coding" hypotheses, respectively? Lakoff's apparatus can help us to reduce a wide variety of expressions to one underlying image. It can point out that the opening lines of Dante's *Divine Comedy*

> In the middle of life's road
> I found myself in a dark wood...,

as well as Bunyan's *The Pilgrim's Progress*, along with Frost's poem, the three highroads meeting in *Oedipus Tyrannos*, and such colloquial expressions as "Look *how far we've come*. It's been *a long, bumpy road*. We can't *turn back now*. We are at a *crossroads*. We may have to *go our separate ways*. The relationship isn't *going anywhere*. We're *spinning our wheels*. Our relationship is *off the track*. The marriage is *on the rocks*. We may have to *bail out* of this relationship" (Lakoff, 1993: 206) are all derived from the same underlying conceptual metaphor. The apparatus I have proposed may show, by contrast, how several potential meanings are condensed in one expression; by this, in turn, it may account for its expressive force and uniqueness among the other terms derived from the same conceptual metaphor. Finally, it can indicate an image's potential to combine with a wide variety of additional images at the same time; that is what I call its *combinational potential*.[3]

The reader may ask whether I can produce some experimental evidence for my conception of concrete images in figurative language. Ray Gibbs, I believe, has provided some very convincing experimental evidence—unintentionally, though. In a paper presented on 31 Deember 1997 at the Porter Institute, Tel Aviv University,[4] Gibbs spoke of elementary bodily experiences as the basis of metaphors, such as "balance", or "the body as a container". "The idea is that balance is something that we learned with our bodies and not by grasping a set of rules [...] And the point here is that it's not just an arbitrary thing, that we happen to use balance and talking about these other kinds of things", such as "people's personalities are balanced or out of balance", or that "certain views are balanced". "It's motivated because it makes sense in terms of talking about these things, given the nature of our valued

---

3   My "alternative" proposal was elsewhere worked out at great lentgth. See Tsur 1998; Tsur 2002 and, in an earlier version, Tsur 1987.
4   I am quoting the transcript of a tape-recording of the session.

experience of balance". Likewise, "we have a very strong sense of ourselves as bottles and containers". Such conventional metaphors as "he spilled the beans" or "he blew his stack" can be produced and understood by our interlocutors, because "we have a very strong sense of ourselves as bottles and containers"; hence we all share the underlying conceptual metaphor "the body as a container".

In order to test the psychological reality of this hypothesis, Gibbs conducted the following experiment. He gave three paraphrases of the expression "he blew his stack", that pointed out one, or two, or three ingredients it shared with "anger". He asked observers to make preference judgments. He found, not surprisingly, that preference increased with the number of shared ingredients. "So this suggests that our understanding of what "blew his stack", for instance, means is not just that John got very angry. It means more specifically that John got very angry because he has felt a great deal of internal pressure; perhaps he unintentionally expressed his anger, and he did so very quickly and forcefully". Gibbs interpreted these results as evidence for the "mind–body" hypothesis. It seems to me, however, that this experiment provides little evidence for that hypothesis. To be sure, this specific idiom does have one ingredient of "internal pressure", because we are speaking of a mental state that *is* internal, and does involve a sense of pressure; and we are using the image of "blowing up", that does entail the building up of internal pressure. In this sense, "internal pressure" is predetermined by the specific image and the specific referent of this specific idiom, and is accidental to the use of metaphors in general. But as for metaphors and idioms in general, the experiment provides, rather, evidence for the cognitive hypothesis proposed here, namely, that people use spatial imagery in thinking or in figurative language, because spatial imagery is an efficient coding of information. Preference of spatial imagery increases with the amount of information coded in it. Subjects prefer that interpretation of "he blew his stack" which contains the meaning components "perhaps he *unintentionally* expressed his anger, and he did so *very quickly and forcefully*" not because it corroborates the BODY AS A CONTAINER conceptual metaphor (it does not); but because it increases the number of meanings encoded in one spatial image. If the metaphor concerns basic bodily experiences, its effectiveness may receive additional reinforcement.

Such a conception of figurative language, in turn, entails different modes of practical criticism, that yield much subtler insights into poetic language. Thus, for instance, there is also a practical consideration for preferring my hypothesis to the "mind–body" hypothesis. Subtler and more flexible intertextual or intratextual distinctions can be made, and of greater aesthetic significance, by pointing out the amount of information coded in the various spatial images than by pointing out that such expressions as "he spilled the beans" or "balance sheets" can be traced back to some basic body experience.

Stock Responses

My argument has two facets. On the one hand, I point out some general problems with Lakoff's theory of metaphor from the logical and cognitive point of view, as compared to other theories of metaphor; on the other hand, I claim that its literary application may be harmful. One of the issues relevant in the latter respect is Richards' discussion of stock responses. I have suggested that Lakoff smuggled back through the back door the stock responses exorcised by Richards.

> A stock response, like a stock line in shoes or hats, may be a convenience. Being ready-made, it is available with less trouble than if it had to be specially made out of raw or partially prepared materials. And unless an awkward misfit is going to occur, we may agree that stock responses are much better than no responses at all. Indeed, an extensive repertory of stock responses is a necessity. Few minds could prosper if they had to work out an original, "made to measure" response to meet every situation that arose [...]. But equally clearly there are in most lives fields of activity in which stock responses, if they intervene, are disandvantageous and even dangerous, because they may get in the way of, and prevent, a response more appropriate to the situation. These unnecessary misfits may be remarked at almost every stage of the reading of poetry, but they are especially noticeable when emotional responses are in question. (Richards 1929: 228)

Stock responses have a semantic and a pragmatic aspect. Words enter into verbal contexts, and assume different meanings in different contexts. These verbal structures may convey emotionally and ideologically significant situations. One of the significant differences between the poetic and the non-poetic uses of language is that in the poetic use the semantic changes of words are somehow more significant, and require subtler and more frequent shifts of "mental sets" on the understander's part. These semantic changes need not be figurative, they may well be literal. Consider the case of the panda who orders a steak sandwich; after eating it he shoots the bartender and walks out without paying. The manager stops him at the entrance: "What do you think you are doing?" The panda answers: "As you may have noticed, I am a panda; look me up in the dictionary; it says "bearlike animal; eats shoots and leaves". In this instance, the words "shoots and leaves" change their literal meanings, including their word class and syntactic function. Even "eats" undergoes an admittedly more evasive change of meaning—from a transitive to a middle verb. The phenomenological quality of this shift is "wit". Emotional qualities are generated by streams of subtler and more frequent shifts. One aspect of stock responses involves a refusal to shift mental sets as required by the stream of shifting meanings. Another aspect concerns a refusal to shift one's mental attitudes towards certain emotionally or ideologically loaded situations when the wider context is changing. Richards' attack is directed against both kinds of refusal; but he applies the term "stock responses" only to the latter. One source of the enormous appeal of conceptual metaphors is that whenever one encounters a certain spatial image in a text, say, "journey", or "crossroads", one need not shift one's mental sets neither *across* contexts, nor *within* some evolving context. This is, in fact, the main point of my foregoing criticism of Lakoff's handling of Frost's crossroads and of what he considers an "incompetent teacher".

There is an inherent paradox in Lakoff's work. He and his associates invested almost unprecedented subtlety and intellectual rigour into working out the "meaning potential" of such conceptual metaphors as LIFE IS A JOURNEY, SEEING IS KNOWING, or the BODY IS A CONTAINER. By the same token they have prepared "an extensive repertory of stock responses". By this they made an enormous service and disservice at one and the same time to literary studies. On the one hand, "we may agree that stock responses are much better than no responses at all"; and Lakoff's system allows critics intolerant of "delayed conceptualization" to do reasonable practical criticism. On the other hand, "stock responses, if they intervene, are disadvantageous and even dangerous, because they may get in the way of, and prevent, a response more appropriate to the situation". As the foregoing discussion may suggest, the enormous lure of stock responses may prove irresistible not only to some of Lakoff's less sensitive disciples, but to Lakoff himself too. What is at stake here is cognitive strategy: rapid or delayed conceptualization. The road not taken would have required exposure to uncertainty for too long; and that might be particularly offensive to some persons.

The "Contemporary" and the "Controversion" Theory of Metaphor

Lakoff claims in his paper under discussion that he and his followers have radically changed the state of the art in the study of metaphor. He claims that three of their most outstanding achievements are: (1) the discovery that a wide range of metaphors in colloquial language, literature, dreams etc., can be reduced to a relatively small number of underlying "generative metaphors"; (2) that the main bulk of these generative metaphors rely on spatial imagery: abstract, mental and social processes are typically expressed in spatial images; and (3) that their theory is more adequate than the traditional Controversion Theory of metaphor. I have no quarrel with the first claim, though I have my doubts as for its usefulness regarding the analysis of literature. I have no quarrel with the second claim either (which was quite widespread before Lakoff as well), except that, as I have already argued, their spatial model is not as adequate as it could be. In what follows, I will devote some attention to the third claim.

Consider Lakoff's following statement:

> A major difference between the contemporary theory [i.e., Lakoff's theory] and the classical one is based on the old literal–figurative distinction. Given that distinction, one might think that one "arrives at" a metaphorical interpretation of a sentence by "starting" with the literal meaning and employ-

ing some algorithmic process to it (see Searle, this volume). Though there do exist cases where something like this happens, this is not in general how metaphor works, as we shall see shortly. (Lakoff 1993: 205)

Lakoff argues, then, against "the old literal–figurative distinction". In figurative language, just as in literal language, he says, we need not assume contradictions and meaning-cancelations. Research in pragmatics and artificial intelligence during the past twenty years or so suggests, rather, a reverse possibility the processing of literal language too is riddled with inferences, implied expectations confirmed or refuted, contradictions and conditions in which meanings are or are not cancelled. In his "Conceptual Dependency Theory", Schank (1975: 68–70) uses the "BUT-test" to distinguish between straightforward assertions and inferences. From "John went yesterday to the movies", an AI program will assume that John saw a movie; however, "John went yesterday to the movies but all the tickets were sold" involves no logical contradiction, whereas "John went yesterday to the movies but he stayed at home" does. Notice that the "BUT-test" cancels in the first instance an *inference* and not a *feature*. Dascal distinguishes "sentence-based and context-based 'excesses'", and points out that cancelation is a matter of degree.[5]

It is difficult to argue against Lakoff by counter-examples, since he admits in advance that "there do exist cases where something like this happens"; so, apparently, the only way to refute him would be to analyse all metaphors in the world, and show that the majority of metaphors don't behave as he claims they do. Since I am not prepared to do that, I propose to try an alternative way, which has its logical shortcomings, but considering the alternative, this would be a viable way to take. I am going to take some of Lakoff's own examples, see what he does to them, and see what one could do to them with some other, pre-Lakoffean theory. This method

---

5   Consider the following paragraph:

> One characteristic property of the excesses or modifications of the sense [in cases in which the utterance has meaning in excess of (or distinct from) the sense of the sentence uttered] is that they can be usually canceled without generating a contradiction. Thus one can say *The dog is on the carpet, but it will not piss because it just came back from the garden*, thus canceling the possible warning and request aspects of the first part of the assertion. It is hard to imagine, however, how one could say, without contradiction, *The dog is on the carpet, but it is not touching the carpet's surface.* It is important to notice that sentence-based 'excesses', though cancelable, are more difficult to cancel than context-based ones. The 'hint' that there was an expectation that John would not come, conveyed by an utterance of *Even John came*, is very hard to eliminate. In order to eliminate it, one has to imagine a very special context of utterance which is able to retain the assertion (*John came*) and to filter out the hint. Similarly, the suggestion that the captain is usually drunk, conveyed by *The captain was sober today*, is not easy to cancel, in spite of the fact that its denial is not logically nconsistent with the 'sense' of the assertion. Cancelability, therefore, seems to be a matter of degree (Dascal, 1983: 26).

does not rule out the possibility that Lakoff has ill-chosen his examples, and that they are among those few "cases where something like this happens". But, again, considering the alternative, this is the best I can do. In fact, the issue at stake is not factual at all, as this paragraph might suggest. Paraphrasing Morris Weitz (1962), theories of metaphors are no factual statements, but crucial recommendations as for what to look for in metaphors, and how to look at it. When we have two or more such theories, we need not verify them against the facts, but rather carry out the various recommendations and compare outcomes.

I am going to compare Lakoff's approach to Beardsley's Controversion Theory of metaphor. According to this theory, "a metaphor is a significant attribution that is either indirectly self-contradictory or obviously false in its context, and in which the modifier connotes characteristics that can be attributed, truly or falsely, to the subject" (Beardsley 1958: 142). The opposition between the two approaches is obvious. One of the advantages Beardsley claims for his theory is this:

> The Controversion Theory explains one of the most puzzling and important features of metaphor, its capacity to create new contextual meaning. [...] Sometimes we invent, or hit upon, a metaphor and find that it gives us a new idea. The reason is that the connotations of words are never fully known, or knowable, beforehand, and very often we discover new connotations of the words when we see how they behave as modifiers in metaphorical attributions. The metaphor does not create the connotations, but it brings them to life. (Beardsley 1958: 143)

I would like to make two comments on this statement: that, as we have seen, Lakoff's system has been devised, by contrast, to create meanings that show little sensitivity to changing context; and that Beardsley's statement is highly compatible with the conception of spatial imagery I have suggested above. Unforeseen contexts create unforeseen contextual meanings by "bringing to life" unrealised "features" (in my terminology) or "connotations" (in Beardsley's) terminology. There appears to be only one (rather trivial) difference between Beardsley's and my formulation, namely, that "connotations" are better suited to "words", whereas "features" are better suited to "spatial images".

Notice that the sentence "John went yesterday to the movies but he stayed at home" serves above as an example of logical contradiction. But, in certain circumstances, it can be used figuratively to make one of several perfectly meaningful statements as, e.g., "John went yesterday to the movies but he couldn't enjoy it, because he was thinking of his sick child left at home with the baby sitter"; or, "John has a rich imagination: he imagined seeing a full movie without leaving his home". This is what the Controversion Theory is about. The understander applies the Principle of Congruence to an incongruent text, generating unforeseeable meanings in unforeseeable circumstamces. Now suppose we supply some relevant conceptual metaphors (such as GOING TO AS IMAGINING, or STAYING AT A PLACE AS EMO-

TIONALLY LOADED THINKING OF IT), we also have to supply some rules or principles to account for the understanders' amazing ease to switch from one underlying metaphor to another. We must assume perhaps that when the situation changes, the understander perceives some incongruence between the metaphor and its context which, in turn, requires him to substitute one underlying metaphor for another. But then we are back at the Controversion Theory, complicated by the Conceptual Metaphor Theory.

Now consider Disraeli's remark, quoted by Lakoff from Searle:

> I have climbed to the top of the greasy pole.

I will fully reproduce here Lakoff's discussion, to make sure I am not making some unfair selection—assuming that Lakoff executes the crucial recommendations of his theory. Then I will do my best to carry out the crucial recommendations suggested by Beardsley's conceptual apparatus as for what to look for in this sentence, and how to look at it; then I will compare the two in light of the two theories. Let us begin with the question how can we know that this sentence must be understood metaphorically?

> This could be taken nonmetaphorically, but its most likely metaphorical interpretation is via the CAREER IS A JOURNEY metaphor. This metaphor is evoked jointly by source domain knowledge about pole climbing, which is effortful, self-propelled, destination-oriented motion upward, and knowledge that the metaphor involves effortful, self-propelled, destination-oriented motion upward. (Lakoff 1993: 238)

Lakoff admits that "this could be taken nonmetaphorically", but tacitly assumes that it is metaphorical, then proceeds to the assertion that "its most likely metaphorical interpretation is via the CAREER IS A JOURNEY metaphor", skipping the question why we should think of it as metaphorical at all. Beardsley would have a very straightforward and principled answer to that, namely, that it is "obviously false in its context". Why did Lakoff not come to a similar conclusion? Not because such a conclusion is beyond his logical capacities; rather, I think, because he explicitly set out in the first place to show that "this is not in general how metaphor works" (Lakoff 1993: 205). So, as far as this specific instance is concerned, Lakoff is forced tacitly to assume that which Beardsley can support by principled arguments. As far as Beardsley is concerned, there are here two incongruous domains. One of them is a long-term social process, requiring great mental and social effort; the other one is a relatively short-term physical movement in space, involving great physical effort. That is why they are incongruent. Now the Principle of Congruence requires us to render the incongruent domains congruent. In this case, the modifier (climbing to the top of the greasy pole) connotes such characteristics as "effortful, self-propelled, destination-oriented motion upward" that can be attributed, truly or falsely, to the subject (career).

I have already argued that the existence of a conceptual metaphor does not guarantee that it is applicable in a certain instance. By claiming that the CAREER IS A JOURNEY metaphor is evoked jointly by source domain knowledge and by target domain knowledge, Lakoff is assuming that which he has set out to prove in the beginning. If CAREER IS A JOURNEY, it does not guarantee that A JOURNEY IS CAREER; and even if THE JOURNEY *IS* CAREER, it does not guarantee that GREASY POLE CLIMBING IS CAREER. As we have seen, one of the most important achievements Lakoff claims for his theory is that it has superseded the incongruence conception of metaphor. This forces him to play down two crucial stages of the process. First, he must tacitly assume that an expression is metaphorical though it could be nonmetaphorical as well. And second, he must tacitly skip a rather illuminating stage of his argument: that mapping must take place between two incongruent domains, so as to render them congruent.

The Controversion Theory can be complemented by the "feature-cancellation theory of metaphor" (see above, Chapter 9). Those features of the source that conflict with features of the target are cancelled. The cancellation of the conflicting predicates abstracted from the source foregrounds the relevant ones; at the same time it may facilitate the fusion of the two domains. In the present instance, such abstract predicates as difficulty, effort, insecurity etc. are foregrounded, whereas such features as the material of the pole, the colour of the grease, the climbing movements of the climber are cancelled.

But let us follow the rest of Lakoff's argument:

> Part of the knowledge evoked is that the speaker is as high as he can get on that particular pole, that the pole was difficult to climb, that the climb probably involved backward motion, that it is difficult for someone to stay at the top of a greasy pole, and that he will most likely slide down again. The CAREER IS A JOURNEY maps this knowledge onto corresponding knowledge about the speaker's career: he has as much status as he can get in that particular career, it was difficult to get that point in that career, it probably involved some temporary loss of status along the way, it will be difficult to maintain this position, and he will probably loose status before long. (Lakoff 1993: 238–239)

Thus Lakoff. Now what would Beardsley say about the same issues? He would probably say word by word the same, except one sentence. Instead of "The CAREER IS A JOURNEY maps this knowledge onto corresponding knowledge about the speaker's career" he would have said: "the modifier connotes characteristics that can be attributed, truly or falsely, to the subject". And Beardsley's modifier does, indeed, connote all those things enumerated by Lakoff. If so, Lakoff and his followers' claims for great innovativeness is less than warranted. Thus far, then, Lakoff's conceptual system added nothing to Beardsley's, except substituting the predicate "maps this knowledge onto" for "connotes characteristics that can be attributed, truly or falsely, to". On the other hand, it had tacitly to skip a range of issues which Beardsley's system can handle in a principled way. Then Lakoff concludes:

> All this follows with nothing more than the conventional CAREER-AS-JOURNEY mapping, which we all share as part of our metaphorical systems, plus knowledge about climbing greasy poles. (Lakoff 1993: 239)

Now suppose we ask a panel of judges to list the properties of CAREER and of JOURNEY, and then rate them for relevance and salience. Of all the features enumerated above by Lakoff, perhaps "self-propelled, destination-oriented" would turn up in JOURNEY, and not as the most salient ones. All the burden of understanding this metaphor is laid on the *ad-hoc*, pre-theoretical notion of "plus knowledge about climbing greasy poles". Apart from this, Lakoff can merely enumerate a list of specific "connotations". Beardsley's conceptual system, by contrast, is tailor-made for this situation: "The Controversion Theory explains one of the most puzzling and important features of metaphor, its capacity to create new contextual meaning. [...] The connotations of words are never fully known, or knowable, beforehand, and very often we discover new connotations of the words when we see how they behave as modifiers in metaphorical attributions. The metaphor does not create the connotations, but it brings them to life". The CAREER-AS-JOURNEY mapping can explain very little about Disraeli's sentence; it rather adds the noisy element of a journey. Whereas Beardsley's crucial recommendations provide everything one needs for understanding it, from identifying it as a nonliteral statement, through bringing to life dormant connotations, to attributing them, truly or falsely, to the subject. What is more, when the conceptual metaphor system breaks down, Lakoff himself resorts to those instructions.

As Odette de Mourgues (1953) remarked, pigeonholing gives certainty but no insight. Pigeonholing the sentence "I have climbed to the top of the greasy pole" as an instance of the CAREER-AS-JOURNEY metaphor gives, indeed, little insight. Insight is gained not because of it, but in spite of it. In the present instance, the best we can say about it is that it didn't prevent Lakoff from acting, intuitively, upon the instructions implied by Beardsley's theory.

Whose Theory and Principles Become Unnecessary?

The business of this chapter has been to point out two opposite approaches to the handling of meaning in figurative language and symbolic systems, that dominate the history of interpretations both in psychotherapy and literary criticism. One of them works with pre-established meanings; the other one with an indefinite range of potential meanings, changing subsets of which may be realized in changing contexts. These are two alternative interpretative strategies. The respective cognitive attitudes are rapid and delayed conceptualization. They have different advantages and disadvantages. The former is advantageous when speed of response is required, while accuracy and subtlety are less important; the latter is advantageous when the obverse is the case. In light of this summary, let us consider Lakoff's following paragraph (with reference to another example: "the hours crept by as we waited for the plane"):

> Searle accounts for such cases by his Principle 4, which says that "we just do perceive a connection" which is the basis of the interpretation. This is vague and doesn't say what the perceived connection is or why we "just do" perceive it. When we spell out the details of all such perceived connections, they turn out to be the system of conceptual metaphors I have been describing. But given that system, Searle's theory and his principles become unnecessary. (Lakoff 1993: 239)

Going back to our discussion of Disraeli's "I have climbed to the top of the greasy pole", we should remember this: when we spell out the details of all such perceived connections, they *don't* turn out to be the system of conceptual metaphors. On the contrary, we are forced "to admit that all the work remains to be done in each particular case". To put it more explicitly: if we ask whether *some* connection between journeys and climbing greasy poles (e.g., movement in space) can be pointed out, the answer is yes (they turn out to be the system of conceptual metaphors); if we ask whether this exempts us to do all the work in this particular case, the answer is no.

We might re-write, then, Lakoff as follows: "given Beardsley's theory and principles, Lakoff's system of conceptual metaphors becomes unnecessary". The rule appears to be this: when one set of principles can account for a metaphor, the other set becomes unnecessary. Now, how can we decide whose principles or system become unnecessary? It depends on the circumstances and the purpose of our inquiry. In well-practiced circumstances, relying on the system of conceptual metaphors may be quite sufficient, and Searle's or Beardsley's principles may become unnecessary. When, however, unforeseen circumstances arise, Lakoff's system may become unnecessary, while Beardsley's theory and principles may become all-important. It is illuminating to observe Lakoff's own performance in the two test cases we have considered above. When facing Frost's verse lines, he displays excessive self-confidence, but little literary subtlety. When confronted with Disraeli's sentence, he cannot tell why he thinks it is to be understood metaphorically, but takes it for granted. In his principles of interpretation he is forced to fall back on the *ad hoc*, pre-theoretical notion of "plus knowledge about climbing greasy poles"; whereas in practice, he acts upon the recommendations of Beardsley's (supposedly false) theory. Obviously, in these test cases, the rival models are better suited.

It is not an easy task to catch Lakoff doing this: the reader accepts his analysis, without noticing that the theory does not cater for it. We have just seen how Lakoff does this. He suggests some abstract logical connection between journeys and climbing greasy poles, indicating that his theory *is* relevant to this instance; that is just enough to induce the reader to a willing suspension of disbelief. By mentioning "plus knowledge about climbing greasy poles", he appeals to the trained reader's willingness to bracket certain issues to preserve the lucidity of the argument: the reader has the knowledge; is shown how Lakoff uses it; and does not notice that he has not been told the principles according to which he is to use it. Finally, suppose Lakoff is right in his claim that "when we spell out the details of all such perceived connections, they turn out to be the system of conceptual metaphors I have been describing". In such a case he ends up with the barren pigeonholing of the metaphor. The productive stage is that of "spelling out the details" which, as we have seen, is not necessarily taken care of by the system. Now suppose Lakoff adds CAREER IS CLIMBING GREASY POLES to the system of conceptual metaphors. There will always be unforeseen cases that can be related to the existing system in the final act of pigeonholing—after working out the unpredicted details with the help of some model as the ones suggested by Beardsley or Searle. Indeed, I have just been told that Lakoff and his colleagues have recently assimilated the "feature-cancellation theory of metaphor". Turner's work on blended spaces using Lakoff's "invariance hypothesis" attempts to formulate exactly how and why such feature cancelletion happens. If you can't beat them, join them.

Metaphor Processing and the Stopwatch

Speed of response becomes relevant to our business in two different respects. One of them has to do with accuracy of response; the other with establishing the route of information processing in understanding metaphors. In the former, delay is qualitatively estimated; in the latter—measured on the stopwatch. The time that elapses between reading a metaphor and responding to it has two crucial aspects. First, it allows rapid or delayed closure, depending on its duration, involving a period of uncertainty to which some language-users are more tolerant, some less. Such New Critics as Richards and L. C. Knights elaborated on the speed element in literary response, anticipating, in the first quarter of the twentieth century, the notion of rapid and delayed closure elaborated by psychologists of perception and personality in the late forties. My own contribution in this respect lies merely in pointing out a close relationship between the two. Stock responses require less time than more subtle responses; so, speed may come at the expense of the subtlety of response.

Secondly, since the second half of the twentieth century speed of response has been used to indicate the mechanism of information processing in understanding metaphors; it became an index of the intervening stages of processing. Response times are measured by the stopwatch in the psychological laboratory. An enormous number of empirical studies was produced, proving that the understanding of a figurative expression takes the same time as the understanding of literal expressions. This, of course, was more consistent with Lakoff's "Contemporary Theory", that assumed direct understanding, than with the stages postulated by the "Controversion Theory". Then, however, an enormous amount of empirical research emerged that demonstrated the opposite: the understanding of figurative expressions takes longer than that of literal expressions. Rachel Giora reviewed all this experimental evidence, and came exactly to the same conclusion as I arrived above speculatively. "Both approaches account for only a limited number of findings". Her concluding paragraph is most illuminating (Giora, 1997: 201):

> At this stage it seems possible to formulate the conditions under which various processing models apply. Thus, direct process assumed by contemporary cognitive psychologists, seems to apply when highly salient meanings are intended. For example, the salient figurative meaning of highly conventional idioms is processed directly (Gibbs, 1980). Parallel processing applies when alternative meanings are equally salient, as in the case of conventional metaphors (Blasko & Connine, 1993), or when less conventional referring expressions are used innovatively (Gerrig, 1989). Sequential processing, assumed by the traditional pragmatic model, applies when language is used innovatively, as in the case of novel metaphors (Blasko & Connine, 1993), novel uses of highly conventional language (Gerrig, 1989), novel referring expressions (Gibbs, 1990), or literal uses of highly conventional idioms (Gibbs, 1980).

The above speculative conclusions, supported by stopwatch experiments in the psychological laboratory have been reinforced by an fMRI study in the neurological laboratory, suggesting that different brain centers are involved in understanding novel and conventional metaphors: "a unique network, consisting of the right homologue of Wernicke's area, right and left premotor areas, right and left insula and Broca's area, is recruited for the processing of novel metaphors but not for the processing of conventional metaphors".

Conclusions

One of the most impressive parts of Lakoff's theory (for me at least) was its hierarchic organization. "Metaphorical mappings do not occur in isolation from one another. They are sometimes organized in hierarchical structures, in which 'lower' mappings in the hierarchy inherit the structures of the 'higher' mappings" (Lakoff 1993: 222). Consider the following three levels:

> Level 1: The event structure metaphor
> Level 2: A PURPOSEFUL LIFE IS A JOURNEY
> Level 3: LOVE IS A JOURNEY; A CAREER IS A JOURNEY

Now, after having written the foregoing discussion, I am somewhat less enthusiastic about it. Judging from Lakoff's handling of Disraeli's metaphor, it didn't help him to get an insight into its meaning. But after having received an insight by other means, it helped him to pigeonhole it as another instance of the conceptual metaphor system. This may throw some light on the inherent merits of Lakoff's performance regarding some literary metaphors. Consider the opening lines from Dante's *Divine Comedy:*

> In the middle of life's road
> I found myself in a dark wood...,

What does Lakoff have to say on these lines? That light affords seeing, and seeing is knowing, while darkness suggests the opposite of knowing, confusion. The phrase "In the middle of life's road", in turn, suggests that life is a journey. I don't think there was a single critic since Dante's time to our own times, of any critical school, or pre-theoretical, who thought otherwise. Doesn't Dante himself say, after all, that it was "life's road"? The only new information Lakoff contributes is that this is an instance of the conceptual metaphor system. Now, I agree that it is difficult to say something different on this example. But then, I didn't choose the examples to illustrate the explanatory power of Lakoff's theory. Lakoff chose them.

CHAPTER 24

Deixis in Literature

What *Isn't* Cognitive Poetics?

Exposition

As I said in the Preface, it has been suggested to me that I add to the present edition a few case studies comparing my analysis to some cognitive linguist's analysis of one issue each, so as to highlight the difference between our approaches. This last section of chapters contains three such studies.[1]

The present chapter contains a case study of Peter Stockwell's chapter on deixis (Stockwell, 2002: 41–57). My response to Stockwell has a personal history too. There is a companion volume to Stockwell's book, Joanna Gavins and Gerard Steen (eds.) *Cognitive Poetics in Practice*. This volume is by various hands, and contains parallel chapters to Stockwell's chapters. I contributed the chapter on deixis. When Stockwell sent me his chapter on deixis, I sent him two long e-mails criticizing it, from which parts of the present chapter have been extracted. He has accepted some of my suggestions on "Ozymandias" as, for instance, that an inconclusive tone prevails in the last six lines, and a weak sense of closure in the last line, and that the two reinforce each other. But, as to the rest of the issues, our disagreement largely persists.

So, let me state at the outset what I mean by the term "cognitive". During the past sixty-five years or so the word "cognitive" has changed its meaning. Originally, it distinguished the rational from the emotional and impulsive aspect of mental life. Now it is used to refer to the psychological processes involved in the acquisition, organization, and use of information; in fact, in all information processing activities of the brain, ranging from the analysis of immediate stimuli to the organization of subjective experience. In this later sense, "cognitive" includes such processes and phenomena as perception, feeling, emotion, memory, attention, problem-solving, language, thinking, and imagery, most of which are excluded from the earlier sense, or even opposed to it. In the phrases "Cognitive Science", "Cognitive Psychology" and "Cognitive Poetics" as I understand it, the term is used in the latter sense. In what sense is it used in the phrase "Cognitive Linguistics"?

---

[1]   Some of the issues discussed in the present chapter (deixis, orientation, the sublime, and their poetic effects) update and amplify ideas presented in Chapter 15, above).

In what follows, I will ask two kinds of questions about critical statements: whether they do illuminate an aesthetic object or some aesthetic problem; and whether they may be regarded as Cognitive Poetics. At the outset I will bring a series of brief extracts from one of Stockwell's central sections and a comparable paragraph from E. M. Forster, with a few comments on them. Then I will present my arguments in a more orderly manner. They will include not merely a criticism of Stockwell's practice. I will also attempt to indicate, quite extensively, how deixis could be better utilized from the cognitive point of view, and in a way that would better illuminate works of literature.

Let us start, then, with the culmination of Stockwell's chapter. He offers what he calls a **Cognitive poetic analysis** of Emily Brontë's *Wuthering Heights* in order to demonstrate the explanatory power of his terms. Since I cannot quote here the whole section, I will confine myself to a selection of key sentences from it, to indicate its outline.[2] The rest of Stockwell's section is an elaboration of these key sentences, or "more of the same". The essence of this section is to enumerate the various kinds of "deictic centres", to exemplify them, and show their shifting sequence in the novel. I could find no trace of cognitive discussion (in the second sense of the term *cognitive*) in this section, and very little that can illuminate the sources of the novel's greatness, or unique character, or aesthetic quality; it rests, mainly, on the aesthetically (and cognitively) indifferent level. It is a sort of *Introduction to Point of View in Fiction*.

> [The novel] is narrated primarily by Mr. Lockwood. Though he is a character in the novel as well, he occupies only the framing level, and takes no real part in the central story.
> The first part of the story proper begins when Lockwood reads Catherine Earnshaw's diary-like comments in the margins of an old Bible he finds when spending a night at Wuthering Heights.
>
> *
>
> However, at this point we perhaps need more detail in terms of embedded narration.
>
> *
>
> The deictic shift is preceded by Lockwood inviting Nelly to tell him all about Heathcliff. The first part is clearly deictically centred on Lockwood.
>
> *
>
> The shift in deixis is perceptual (to Nelly), temporal (back twenty years), relational (Nelly's values are encoded hereafter), and textual (she becomes a new teller after the paragraph space, and her perceptions then apparently structure the narrative, though in fact the implied author 'Emily Brontë' continues to insert chapter headings across Nelly's narrative—'Brontë' retains the compositional deixis). The spatial deixis remains constant:

---

2   Such key sentences are usully the first sentences in their paragraph. Where this didn't suffice, I reproduced additional sentences.

'here' is Thrushcross Grange; though Nelly immediately shifts this to Wuthering Heights within a locative expression.

*

There is something of a blend in the edgework here, as 'I', 'she' and 'her' in the final sentence excerpted above all point deictically to Nelly Dean. ["Before I came to live here, she commenced—waiting no further invitations to her story—I was almost always at Wuthering Heights"].

*

Here we have the deictic shift initiated with textual deixis, referring back to the previous text. The 'I' narration suddenly shifts to a third person participant,

*

The narrative reverts to Lockwood on the last page,

All this leads to the following conclusion:

> The deictic shifts between different embedded narrators allow readers to track consistent threads through the novel. However, in the edgework, there are many examples where textual deixis and the compositional deixis of the implied author cut across chapter headings throughout.

That's it.

In *Aspects of the Novel* (first published in 1927), E. M. Forster gives a comparable (though much shorter) survey of shifting point of view in Dickens' *Bleak House,* which I will quote without omissions.

> This is a ramshackly survey and for me the whole intricate question of method resolves itself not into formulae but into the power of the writer to bounce the reader into accepting what he says—a power which Mr Lubbock admits and admires, but locates at the edge of the problem instead of at the centre. I should put it plumb in the centre. Look how Dickens bounces us in *Bleak House.* Chapter I of *Bleak House* is omniscient. Dickens takes us into the Court of Chancery and rapidly explains all the people there. In Chapter 2 he is partially omniscient. We still use his eyes, but for some unexplained reason they begin to grow weak: he can explain Sir Leicester Dedlock to us, part of Lady Dedlock but not all, and nothing of Mr Tulkinghorn. In Chapter 3 he is even more reprehensible: he goes straight across into the dramatic method and inhabits a young lady; Esther Summerson. 'I have a great deal of difficulty in beginning to write my portion of these pages, for I know I am not clever,' pipes Esther, and continues in this strain with consistency and competence, so long as she is allowed to hold the pen. At any moment the author of her being may snatch it from her, and run about taking notes himself, leaving her seated goodness knows where and employed we do not care how. Logically, *Bleak*

House is all to pieces, but Dickens bounces us, so that we do not mind the shifting of the view point. (Forster, 1962: 86–87)

For Forster, the whole intricate question of method resolves itself not into formulae but into the power of the writer to bounce the reader into accepting what he says. Stockwell develops, for the same purpose, the "Deictic Shift Theory" (DST). "Deictic shift theory models the common perception of a reader 'getting inside' a literary text as the reader taking a *cognitive stance* within the mentally-constructed world of the text. This imaginative capacity is a *deictic shift* which allows the reader to understand projected deictic expressions relative to the shifted deictic centre" (Stockwell, 2002: 46–47). My criticism, briefly, of this approach is that in his analyses Stockwell does not speak of the *cognitive stance,* only of the *shifted deictic centres.* Both writers assert that such shifts of point of view or of deictic centres do occur in novels and demonstrate the succession of points of view or of deictic centres. But neither of them tells us, beyond that, what kinds of arguments can be given to support the claim that a writer did succeed "to bounce the reader into accepting what he says", or what cognitive processes are involved. When it comes to analysing a work, both enumerate the succession of points of view or of deictic centres.

In Forster's case, we know at least what is the problem that his enumeration is meant to solve for him. It does not presume to be "cognitive analysis" (neither cognitive, nor analysis), merely one of several counterexamples (along with Gide's *Faux Monnayeurs,* and Tolstoy's *War and Peace*) to Percy Lubbock, who expects the author to adopt one consistent point of view in his novel. Even when Forster makes distinctions between various kinds of point of view, he does not do it in terms of subcategories such as perceptual, temporal, relational, textual and compositional deixis, but of functioning, such as "We still use his [the omniscient author's] eyes, but for some unexplained reason they begin to grow weak: he can explain Sir Leicester Dedlock to us, part of Lady Dedlock but not all, and nothing of Mr Tulkinghorn". By the way, while Stockwell regards shifting point of view as an outright virtue of a text, Forster carefully keeps descriptive and evaluative statements apart; he merely asserts that shifting points of view do exist in works generally accepted as masterpieces, *pace* Percy Lubbock's verdict.

The upshot of the comparison is the question: In what respects is Stockwell's analysis more cognitive than Forster's?

Labelling and Meaning-Making

Kinds of deictic centres (or, for that matter, of anything) can be endlessly multiplied and labeled by names through subclassification, such as *Perceptual deixis, Spatial deixis, Temporal deixis, Relational deixis, Textual deixis,* and *Compositional deixis.* "Perceptual deixis", in turn, may be further subcategorized into participant roles, as in

For example, the US President gives a speech (as speaker) written by a scriptwriter (source) in front of a crowd of schoolchildren (hearers) but the speech is addressed to the school principal who invited him (addressee), and the speech is recorded by TV camera crews (recipients) though the actual aim of the event is to communicate with the national electorate (target). (Stockwell, 2002: 49)

This is not necessarily an exhaustive list of subcategories. Stockwell encourages students to extend it: "Can you discern any other roles that might be evident in the communicative situation? How might these categories be adapted for written literary situations?" What constrains, then, the number of such sub-subclasses? I suggest that it is the usefulness of the classification. When Wayne Booth (1961) distinguishes "real authors, real readers, implied author, implied reader, narrator, narratee, etc.", he does it for a very good reason: to dispel confusion which used to riddle much critical discourse. But what confusion do these categories of Stockwell's dispel? Alternatively, what insight into an aesthetic object or some aesthetic problem, or critical discourse would they afford? It appears to be pigeonholing for pigeonholing's sake.

When I was interviewed by Beth Bradburn about cognitive poetics for the **Literature, Cognition, and the Brain** website, I suddenly realized about my work something that until then I was not fully aware of. In most of my work I use traditional critical tools, and I appeal to cognitive theory only when I encounter some issue that cannot be handled in more traditional terms. I am shamelessly using the methods and terminology of "New Criticism", of Structuralism, of Analytic Philosophy, and other, and don't feel obliged to naturalize them in the cognitive community. My impression is that Stockwell was working quite differently.[3]

---

[3]   In criticizing my claim that I appeal to cognitive theory only when I encounter some issue that cannot be handled in more traditional terms, one reviewer observed: "If we were truly to practice cognitive poetics, then it seems to be of paramount importance to show how these cognitive processes work, both in the production and the interpretation of literary texts"; and "If it can be shown that different literary terms are related through a more basic process of language use (here the linguistic notion of deixis), then this takes us a ways toward greater understanding of how we as human beings conceptualize our experience and express it through language, whether in response to real life situations or imaginative creativity". This, of course, could be true if we knew what are the cognitive processes or mechanisms underlying deixis. To the best of my knowledge, cognitive linguists do not usually discuss the cognitive processes underlying deixis, that is, the cognitive mechanism underlying the perception of self in relation to, e.g., surrounding space. My discussion below of the left and right orientation areas in the brain (based on Newberg et al.) may be a first step in that direction. Cognitive linguists simply acknowledge that deixis exists and indicates certain relationships. One may certainly "show how these cognitive processes work, both in the production and the interpretation of literary texts" with reference to traditional critical concepts as well (and that's what I usually do). My point was that one should not present the reinvention of the wheel as an epochal innovation.

What is more, Stockwell and I seem to be in disagreement as to what constitutes a cognitive explanation. My philosophy in this respect goes roughly as follows. When we use a word, any word, say "table, go, mysticism, I", extremely complex cognitive processes are involved. Recent cognitive research has devoted much effort to unearth these processes. The same is true of "deixis, metaphor" etc. Now, when we point out that a given poem contains the word "table" or "mysticism", or some deictic device or some instance of conceptual metaphor, this will not automatically render our discussion cognitive, in spite of the enormous research devoted in the past to the cognitive processes underlying them. A discussion becomes cognitive when certain problems are addressed which cannot be properly handled without appealing to some cognitive process or mechanism *in the specific discussion.* A critical discussion does not become cognitive by virtue of the amount of past research invested in the elements it handles, but by virtue of the cognitive research applied to the solution of problems that arise in the text under discussion. Being able to push an electric switch doesn't mean that we are doing physics, even though much physical research went in the past into its invention.[4]

I felt uneasy about three aspects of Stockwell's chapter. First, I have found very little in it that would justify the name "cognitive poetics". Even when he rechristens as deixis such well-worn terms as point of view, free indirect speech, suzhet, and so forth, it doesn't render them more cognitive than they were before. Besides, though I am trying to show in my contribution to *Cognitive Poetics in Practice* that deixis *may* have uses in poetry that can best be explained by assuming certain cognitive processes (see below), deixis in itself is no more cognitive than any other linguistic phenomenon. It is, of course, possible that deixis is underlain by illuminating cognitive processes that may account for important literary effects. But this remains to be shown.[5] According to my conception, cognitive poetics explores how cognitive processes shape and constrain literary response and poetic structure. I have found no

---

[4]   This is in harmony with Dascal's following observation: "Behind every technology created by humankind—be it the wheel, agriculture, or the cellular telephone—there is, of course, a lot of cognitive effort. But this does not make it, as such, a cognitive technology in the sense in which I propose to use this expression. What I have in mind are the main uses of a technology, rather than the process of its creation or its effects". The difference between Dascal's and my observation is, of course, that nobody claims that the wheel or even the cellular phone is a cognitive device.

[5]   David Miall quotes empirical evidence for some such underlying cognitive process, precisely as something that Stockwell's work fails to refer to. "Do readers interpret a text in terms of figure/ground relationships? Does cognitive deixis position a reader in relation to the points of view on offer in a narrative? In this context, we might consider the finding of Seilman and Larsen (1989) that during reading of a literary text compared with an expository text, the memories prompted by the literary text contained twice as many actor-perspective memories as the expository text, which mainly prompted observer memories. This suggests that the deictic indicators function differently in a literary text, inviting the reader to cast herself as an agent, as (in their words) 'a responsible subject interacting with one's environment'" (p. 174). "Deictic indicators, in other words, may be taken up differently according to the genre of the text being read" (Miall, 2006: 42–43).

trace of such cognitive processes in the chapter, unless one means such vague generalizations as "readers can project their minds into the other world, find their way
around there, and fill out the rich detail between the words of the text on the basis of
real life experience and knowledge". But if this is cognitive poetics then anything is
cognitive poetics. Nor would I regard a statement like "Reading is creative in this
sense of using the text to construct a cognitively-negotiable world, and the process
is dynamic and constantly shifting" as sufficient justification for calling my work
cognitive. I make this comment not because Stockwell's work doesn't endorse my
conception of cognitive poetics, but because if one accepts this as cognitive poetics,
then nothing remains in linguistics and literary theory that is not cognitive poetics.
Certainly, everything that is language or literature goes through the cognitive system of authors, readers, and critics.

Second, I am less than happy with Stockwell's attempt at classifying deixis into
six categories, and pigeonholing his examples in them. I must confess that I am not
a great fan of pigeonholing. Even where one might expect more labelling and
pigeonholing than anywhere else, in rhetoric, it is not universally welcome. As I
suggested before, changing the names of the pigeonholes doesn't solve the problem.
This is for instance what Quintilianus has to say on this issue: "For it makes no
difference by which name is either called, so long as its stylistic value is apparent,
since the meaning of things is not altered by a change of name. For just as men
remain the same, even though they adopt a new name, so these artifices will produce
exactly the same effect, whether they are styled tropes or figures, since their values
lie not in their names, but in their effect" (p. 353). Likewise, these artifices will
produce exactly the same effect, whether they are styled point of view in fiction, or
deictic centre. The section on *Wuthering Heights*, despite its heading **Cognitive
poetic analysis**, contains no cognitive analysis whatever, it is sheer pigeonholing
of successive, shifting points of view in the novel. Briefly, as Odette de Mourgues
said back in 1953, pigeonholing gives certainty but no insight. (This is a brilliant
cognitive observation by a non-cognitive critic).

Third, the distinction between "real authors, real readers, implied author, implied
reader, narrator, narratee, etc." is very useful for avoiding confusion; but has nothing
particularly cognitive about it, at any rate, no more than any other critical concept.
It doesn't even belong specifically to a chapter on deixis, unless one means to say
that when the real author says "I" it means something different from when the narrator says "I". But this is only trivially a statement about deixis; it is, more significantly, a statement about real authors and narrators, and not a very illuminating one.
Stockwell's discussion of Mary Shelley, for instance, could occur in almost any
non-cognitive introduction to fiction. But, to my taste, there is too much labelling,
and too little discussion of effects in it.

Meaning-Making in "Ozymandias"

To illustrate my three points above, I propose to make a few comments on "Ozymandias".

> (1)   I met a traveller from an antique land
>   Who said, Two vast and trunkless legs of stone
>   Stand in the desert. Near them, on the sand,
>   Half sunk, a shattered visage lies, whose frown,
>   And wrinkled lip, and sneer of cold command,
>   Tell that its sculptor well those passions read
>   Which yet survive, stamped on these lifeless things,
>   The hand that mocked them and the heart that fed;
>   And on the pedestal these words appear:
>   "My name is Ozymandias, king of kings:
>   Look on my works, ye Mighty, and despair!"
>   Nothing besides remains. Round the decay
>   Of that colossal wreck, boundless and bare,
>   The lone and level sands stretch far away.

How does Stockwell handle this poem? He points out three different persons in it, two different places (the implicit 'here' and 'the antique land'), and three different times, as well as a wide range of "deictic centres". Stockwell classifies deixis into six subcategories: *Perceptual deixis, Spatial deixis, Temporal deixis, Relational deixis, Textual deixis,* and *Compositional deixis.* He identifies instances of these subcategories in "Ozymandias", and labels them appropriately. In addition he enumerates "deictic centres" without calling them names. Thus we get "the deictic centre that says 'I' in the first line", "embedded deictic centre to understand the 'my' and 'ye' of the pedestal inscription", or "a time implicit in the present tense of 'met' and 'said'; the time in which the traveller was in the desert, chronologically in the past but deictically projected as a present tense 'stand' and 'these words appear'; and a deictic projection to the ancient time of the inscription when 'is', 'look' and 'despair' were written while Ozymandias was alive". We receive little indication what is the "stylistic value" of these deictic centres.

I have no doubt that "Ozymandias" is one of the most sophisticated poems in English literature, or in all the other literatures I know. This is due to the sophisticated use of point of view. As far as "deictic centre" is synonymous with "point of view", it is also due to deictic centre. But, as Quintilianus pointed out, it makes little difference by what name you call it, what matters is what the device does in the text. Here the manipulations of point of view (of deictic centres, if you like) are used to achieve various kinds of unprecedented ironic effects. The ironic narrator typically uses a detached, dispassionate tone; he pretends to know nothing, not even that he is ironic. In the present instance he is merely repeating what he has heard from a traveller from an antique land. He doesn't know what are the implications of the description, he doesn't even know whether it has any implications, and if you attribute to it any meaning, it is at your own responsibility. (The implied author, of course, knows a lot more, but this is besides the point). We do not know what was the traveller's sophistication or whether *he* understood the implications of what he reported. For all we know, he may have been impressed by the sublimity of the scenery, or by the emotions expressed by the shattered face, or by the sculptor's skill in mocking (imitating) them, and still be unaware of the other possible implications. The shift from the point of view of the narrator to that of the traveller is, then, trivial in itself; what is significant is that it is used in the service of an ironic attitude. But the same "deictic" device can be used to contribute to other very different qualities as well, as, for instance, in Verlaine's poem "Langueur" (Languor), in the line

(2) Là-bas on dit il est de longs combats sanglants.
 Far away they say there are long, sanguinary battles

Deixis or not, both poets use "farawayness" and reported evidence as a "muting device". Shelley resorts to it to mute any emotional overtone of the narrator, generating an ironic, detached tone, while foregrounding the powerful sublime effect of the scene described. Verlaine, by contrast, uses an attenuated emotional tone suggesting some emasculate, enfeebled attitude. Thus, the same verbal device is exploited for very different effects: to generate an ironic, unemotional tone, and to convey a feebled emotional mood.

Now the really great feast of point of view (or deictic centres, if you like) in Shelley's poem concerns the inscription. Its words change their meanings in different contexts, determined by different points of view. These changing meanings are ironical to each other. For Cleanth Brooks, "irony is not the opposite of an overt statement, but 'a general term for the kind of qualification which the various elements in a context receive from the context'" (Wellek, 1963: 329; Brooks, 1968: 171).

In my various writings I have insisted that critical terms must have considerable descriptive contents; but the description has little significance in itself unless it is understood in relation to a wider theoretical framework or model. A critical statement can be true, and still trivial and devoid of interest, unless a theoretical framework or model imputes significance to it (cf. Chapter 22, above; Tsur, 2003: 212). Brooks's conception could serve as an epitome of this. On the descriptive level, the critic may point out the meaning of an expression in one context, and then the change of its meaning in another. "Irony" bestows aesthetic significance on this trivial description. "Irony", in turn, is assumed to be a structural principle in literature expounded at great length in Brooks's work. As to perceived effect, this change of meaning also allows the ironic narrator to pretend to know nothing: he merely quotes the exact words.

It is the different contexts that prompt language-users to make different inferences from the same words. Ozymandias placed his statue, presumably, where the "store cities" or pyramids built for him by the children of Israel could be seen. The nineteenth-century traveller sees the wreck of the statue in the middle of the desert, where nothing but sand can be seen. Given these two different contexts (deictic centres if you like), Ozymandias meant one thing, the nineteenth-century reader understands another. Ozymandias means "Look on my Works, ye Mighty, and despair", you will never achieve my greatness. The nineteenth-century reader may understand "Look on my Works, ye Mighty, and despair", because your greatness too will come to dust. There is an additional point of view, context, or deictic centre (if you like), from which the situation can be viewed: what is the message of the scene to, say, Napoleon in his Egyptian expedition? Even the phrase "King of Kings" may be seen in a changing perspective. Ozymandias presumably meant, literally, that he was a ruler over many kings. In the nineteenth century, the phrase "King of Kings" would have meant "God". It suggests another irony: the victory of the spiritual power of the former slaves over the physical power of Pharao. There is very little chance that an undergraduate (or full professor) will remember all the kinds of deixis Stockwell enumerates, and even less that these categories will help him to realize these effects of these changing perspectives, whether you call them deixis or not. But the changing inferences prompted by changing contexts will be applied intuitively. One need not burden memory with subcategories; the rules are available in one's linguistic or communicative competence.[6]

A suggestion by Winner and Gardner (1993) may explain why the ironist's detached, impersonal tone is perceived as so powerful. A literal remark is rarely if ever equivalent to an ironic one, because the choice of irony carries with it particular social effects. The ironist (here the implied author, perhaps) is perceived as being a certain kind of person—wittier, less confrontational, and more in control, than the utterer of a literal expression of displeasure. We may even consider different degrees of irony if we compare Ozymandias' message to two more outspoken versions of it, in a "twin brother" of Shelley's poem by Horace Smith, and in the verse drama *The Tragedy of Man* by the great Hungarian poet, Imre Madách (1823–1864).

After having finished this chapter, I ran into the following poem by Horace Smith, a friend of Shelley's, composed on December 27, 1817 during a sonnet-writing competition with Percy Bysshe Shelley (who wrote "Ozymandias" as a result): **On a Stupendous Leg of Granite, Discovered Standing by Itself in the Deserts of Egypt, with the Inscription Inserted Below**.

> (3)   In Egypt's sandy silence, all alone,
>   Stands a gigantic Leg, which far off throws
>   The only shadow that the Desert knows.

6   Even the computer, in the artificial intelligence mode, can make inferences that change with the changing context. Consider a story like "John was sitting in a hotel room in Paris. He was exhausted and hungry. From his bag he took out X". If you substitute "a sandwich" for X, the computer will infer that John was going to eat it. If you substitute "the Michelin Guide", the computer will not infer that John was going to eat it, but that John is planning to go to a restaurant (cf. Schank and Abelson, 1977).

"I am great Ozymandias," saith the stone,
"The King of kings: this mighty city shows
The wonders of my hand." The city's gone!
Naught but the leg remaining to disclose
The sight of that forgotten Babylon.
We wonder, and some hunter may express
Wonder like ours, when through the wilderness
Where London stood, holding the wolf in chase,
He meets some fragment huge, and stops to guess
What wonderful, but unrecorded, race
Once dwelt in that annihilated place.
Available online: http://www.rc.umd.edu/rchs/reader/smith.html.

Were it not so conspicuously comparable precisely to Shelley's masterpiece, it would count as not a bad poem at all. It is based on exactly the same archeological findings, and the octet presents them in the same perspectives. At the same time it foregrounds, by way of contrast, Shelley's pretended ignorance I am talking about. It says explicitly what Shelley is so carefully tacit about. Consider the following two lines:

(4)   "… this mighty city shows
The wonders of my hand." The city's gone!

Shelley's irony is so subtle that I myself was sometimes wondering whether I was not reading certain things into his poem. In Horace Smith's sonnet it's all there, explicitly.

Now consider Madách's Tragedy. After the expulsion from Eden, "Adam and Lucifer travel through time to visit different turning-points in human history and the devil tries to convince Adam that life is (will be) meaningless and mankind is doomed. Adam and Lucifer are introduced at the beginning of each scene, with Adam assuming various important historical roles and Lucifer usually acting as a servant or confidante. Eve enters only later in each scene". In "Scene IV Adam is a Pharaoh, Lucifer his Vizier, Eve the wife of a slave" (Wikipedia Summary). In this scene we witness the following dialogue:

(5) ADAM *to Lucifer*
For one thing only long I in my heart,
Madly it may be, but yet grant it me,
I would upon the future boldly gaze
To know, when some few thousand years have passed,
Shall my renown endure?

LUCIFER
While thou didst kiss,

Didst thou not feel a gentle, cooling breeze
That swept across thy face and then flew on?
A little wave of dust doth mark its flight,
That mounts a few short inches in a year,
And some few cubits in a thousand years;
Yet a few thousand years shall overwhelm
Thy pyramids, and thy great name shall be
Buried beneath a barrier of sand.
Jackals shall in thy pleasure gardens howl,
And, in the desert, dwell a servile race.
    While Lucifer speaks all this becomes visible.
All this no raging storm shall bring to pass,
No shuddering upheaval of the earth,
Only a little breeze that gently plays!

             translation by J. C. W. Horne
    http://mek.oszk.hu/00900/00915/html/madach4.htm

This passage, like "Ozymandias", presents an ironic discrepancy between Pharao's presumption and a vision of destruction and oblivion. And here too there is an ironic discrepancy between the barely-noticeable breeze and layers of dust on the one hand, and their overwhelming destructive force on the other. But while the speaker (the narrator or, for that matter, the implied author) in "Ozymandias" pretends to know nothing and understand nothing, Lucifer's ironic vision is deliberate, explicit and inspires a psychological atmosphere of patent purpose. In keeping with the dramatic character, it even suggests a sense of superiority and malicious joy. The speaker in "Ozymandias" is subtler, less confrontational and more in control. By the same token, the victim of irony feels in Shelley's poem more vulnerable, more defenseless against some unsaid assault on his self-confidence. The manipulation of point of view has a decisive contribution to this effect.

But who is the victim of irony in Shelley's poem? The most evident answer seems to be: Ozymandias; this can be extended to other despots too, who want to immortalize their fame, e.g., Napoleon in his Egyptian expedition. This can be further extended: the victim of irony is the implied reader, who may entertain certain notions of power and greatness. In a deeper sense, however, one should consider two alternative possibilities: the implied reader may join the ironist as an ironic observer of Ozymandias; or may join the victim of irony. Ozymandias may become a striking representative of the *condition humaine*. If the grandiose building enterprises of the great and mighty come to such an end, then Everyman's petty exploits are doomed to failure from the very beginning. The question is whether Ozymndias is perceived as a representative of the category "despots", or the category "humankind". In harmony with his ironic tone, Shelley is tacit on this. Interestingly enough, in Horace Smith's sonnet, the sestet slightly tilts the balance in favor of the latter. "The archetypal victim of irony is man", says Muecke (1970: 38), seen "as trapped and submerged in time and matter, blind, contingent, limited, and unfree—and confidently unaware that this is his predicament". The fate of Ozymandias' pyramids may force this predicament upon awareness. The issue is, then, whether the line "The lone and level sands stretch far away" is supposed to arouse in the implied reader a feeling of superiority, freedom, amusement *vis-à-vis* Osymandias, as an ironic observer; or a sense of frustration for being contingent, limited, and unfree. The latter possibility may be corroborated by the absence of closure generated by this line. Closure, says Barbara Herrnstein-Smith (1968: 36), "gives ultimate unity and coherence to the reader's experience of the poem by providing a point from which all the preceding elements may be viewed comprehensively and their relations grasped as part of a significant design". In her chapter on anti-closure she quotes, per contra, Leonard B. Meyer on the lack of closure in modern music. "Underlying this new aesthetic is a conception of man and the universe": "The denial of the reality of relationships and the relevance of purpose".

I have tried to make aesthetic meaning out of the devices labelled as "deixis" or "point of view". Barbara Herrnstein-Smith's discussion of poetic closure is explicitly gestaltistic, that is, cognitive; much of the rest, however, could be said about the poem by any "New Critic". You need no Cognitive Poetics for it.

Now a few minor comments on this poem. There is room for distinguishing between the Shakespearean and the Italian sonnet from the cognitive point of view, but not necessarily in a chapter on deixis. Now, this poem, though containing 14 lines, approximates something like a sonnet, but is not exactly a sonnet, owing to deviations from the rhyme pattern. At any rate, neither this poem, nor the Italian sonnet, can be said to be a deviation from the Shakespearean sonnet. If at all, one could regard the Shakespearean sonnet with its closing couplet as a deviation from the Italian sonnet, and not the other way around. Stockwell writes: "We might even recognize that a prototypical sonnet form often has its most dramatic final flourish in the last two lines (sometimes rhymed, as in Shakespeare's sonnets). However, Shelley places his most dramatic pair of lines ('My name is Ozymandias ... and despair') five lines before the end, in order further to emphasize their multi-centred and polyvalent nature. The inconclusiveness of the form is matched, of course, by the very weak sense of closure in the final line ('The lone and level sands stretch far away'), which also takes the scene spatially away from the deictic centre of the ruin".

Stockwell founds the "inconclusiveness" of the last six lines on thematic grounds: the occurrence of the dramatic peak in lines 10–11, and the absence of a "dramatic final flourish in the last two lines (sometimes rhymed, as in Shakepeare's sonnets)". But while he is aware of the potential contribution of the final couplet to a "dramatic final flourish", he doesn't know what to do with the emotional quality generated by the absence of such a couplet in, e.g., the prototypical Italian sonnet, or in the present poem. I submit that cognitive theory is exceptionally well-suited to handle such an issue. Thus, for instance, Leonard B. Meyer, who applies gestalt theory to music, discusses strong and weak shapes and their respective perceived effects as follows: "Because good shape is intelligible in this sense, it creates a psychological atmosphere of certainty, security, and patent purpose, in which the listener feels a sense of control and power as well as a sense of specific tendency and definite direction" (Meyer, 1956: 160). This would suggest that a relatively unpredictable rhyme pattern would generate a psychological atmosphere of uncertainty and lack of purpose. Notice that the rhyme pattern here is not merely less predictable than the couplet; "kings" in the "sestet" rhymes with "things" in the "octet", which is not only unpredictable in its own right, but also leaves the rhyme patterns of the two parts in a state of confusion. So, this uncertainty too may reinforce the inconclusive tone derived from the lack of "dramatic final flourish" and the weak sense of closure.

Here I would also like to mention a minor matter of interpretation. Even in this shattered condition of the statue, its "frown, / And wrinkled lip, and sneer of cold command, / Tell that its sculptor well those passions read / Which yet survive, stamped on these lifeless things, / The hand that mocked them, and the heart that fed".[7] This visual image suggests the supremacy of the permanence of art over the transience of power. This is perhaps what the ambiguity of *mocked* (imitated / derided) too suggests. Here Stockwell inserts a curious assertion: "Even the printing process is echoed in the use of 'stamped'". It is difficult to understand how the printing process enters into the poem, except to satisfy Stockwell's need to adduce an example for what he calls *textual deixis*. The plain meaning of Shelley's phrase is that the passions were imprinted, or impressed upon the stone. Shelley's phrasing also involves an oxymoron: survive in a lifeless medium. I believe that, rather, "yet survive, stamped on these lifeless things" may have to do with the "paradox of imagination", what Coleridge called "the balance and reconciliation of opposite or discordant qualities" (Biographia Literaria, Chapter IV). Thus, the shattered face becomes a striking embodiment of this paradox. This draws attention to an interesting issue in the process of interpretation, which we have already encountered: are we looking for as many deictic centres as conceivable whatever their contribution to the poem as a whole, or are we looking for details that support the emerging overall meanings or effects? What are the constraints on adducing deictic centres?[8]

While the absence of a closing couplet doesn't undermine the sonnet form, Shelley does blur it in a variety of other means. Such sequences of stressed syllables as "sands stretch far" in the last line blur the metric shape of the poem. Syntax is exceptionally meandering in this poem: a series of relative clauses are linked in a

---

7   Not as Stockwell, who glosses the "hand" and the "heart" as both belonging to the sculptor, I read the line as referring to the sculptor's hand and Ozymandias's heart: Ozymandias's heart fed those passions, and the sculptor's hand "mocked" them.

8   The etymological relationship between *print* and *imprint*, or *press* and *impress* is insufficient excuse for dragging in the printing process. However, the actual verb used by Shelley is "stamped", which would rather point in the direction of the postal services. Paraphrasing George Miller (1993: 392), our task is not to search for a unique paraphrase of the text, nor to find out how many meanings can be attributed to it, but to search for grounds that will constrain the basis of interpretations to a plausible set of alternatives. The printing process and the postal services are obviously no part of such a plausible set.

long chain overburdening short-term memory, and run-on sentences background rhyme patterns, so that stanza shapes (as far as they exist) cannot easily be recognized; but they are also blurred by the deviation from the sonnet's rhyme pattern. Thus, Cognitive Poetics is exceptionally well suited to handle the perceived effects of prosodic structures, and one of the fascinating things about it is that it relieves us of the need to fall back on impressionistic statements about them (see, e.g., my discussion of the perceived effects of possible rhyme patterns in the sonnet form, in Chapter 5 above). Consider, for instance, the gestaltist distinction between strong and poor gestalts. Strong gestalts have, in certain conditions, a noted rational quality, poor gestalts display frequently some intense emotional quality. It is this correlation which Meyer's above analysis was meant to account for.

What can we learn from this about Shelley's poems in general, and this poem in particular? First of all, there is in romanticism a general tendency for weakened prosodic structures, mainly in Shelley and Keats. In most romantic poetry, the blurring of prosodic structures contributes to an emotional quality. In this poem prosodic structures are exceptionally blurred. Now the tone of this poem is anything but emotional. In irony at its best (and this is irony at its best) the speaker's attitude can be characterized as detachment, distance, disengagement, objectivity, dispassion. The manipulations of point of view in this poem, as I pointed out above, lead to imply grave things by saying apparently insignificant things in a detached tone. The fluid structures, the poor gestalts in this poem, have a potential to contribute to precisely such a tone: a psychological atmosphere *deprived* of patent purpose, of a sense of specific tendency and definite direction may reinforce a tone of irony that pretends to intend nothing. Thus, an emotional and an ironical context may actualize different potentials of divergent prosodic structures (cf. my discussion of the effect of strong and weak prosodic gestalts on an ironic quality [Tsur, 1998: 245]).[9] Both what Barbara Herrnstein-Smith (1968) calls "anti-closure" and the unpredictable rhyme pattern strongly reinforce this psychological atmosphere of the absence of patent purpose.

I don't mean to imply that this is what Stockwell should have written. I have discussed this poem at such outrageous length in order to make two crucial points. First, as Quintilianus said, it makes no difference by what name you call some literary device; what matters is its poetic effect. I wanted to show the effects of some poetic devices, and also how the effects of a wide range of devices combine to make some overall effect—in this case irony. I have even tried to suggest that irony has a social effect too which, in turn, may contribute to a detached but forceful tone. Second, through my prosodic discussion I also wanted to demonstrate how cognitive

---

9   There I compare a passage from Milton with a different alignment of verse and syntax conveyed by the same words, resulting in pentameter lines that have stronger gestalts than the original. So, other things are literally identical. When I asked students whether irony is equally subtle in both passages, they had no doubt that the original passage (with the weaker gestalts) "somehow" suggested subtler irony.

generalizations can be used for handling issues one cannot handle by earlier terminology (I will return to this poem below).

Deixis and Orientation

What is, then, the typical effect of deixis on a poetic passage? In this and the next section I will trace just two such typical effects. Consider David Miall's question "Does cognitive deixis position a reader in relation to the points of view on offer in a narrative [or poem]?" The ensuing analysis suggests: "probably yes". In several of my works I explored poetic passages in which a peculiar combination of deixis and abstract nouns is conspicuous.

Consider the poem "Shepherd", by the Hebrew poet Abraham Shlonsky:

(6)   This width, that is spreading its nostrils.
      This height that is yearning for you.
      The light flowing with the whiteness of milk.
      And the smell of wool,
      And the smell of bread.

A more sophisticated version I found in a poem by another great Hebrew poet (of the same school), Nathan Alterman:

(7)   This night.
      The estrangement of these walls.
      A war of silences, breast to breast.
      The cautious life
      Of the tallow candle.

Consider the phrases involving a concrete and an abstract noun.[10] In Chapter 9 I discussed at considerable length Strawson's logical distinction between *singular terms* and *general terms* in predicative position. According to Strawson, the normal, "unmarked", syntactic structure of such constructions would be that concrete, "spatio-temporally continuous particulars" as "bread", "wool", "walls", "candle" occur in the referring position (Strawson, 1967). (By "spatio-temporally continuous particulars" Strawson means objects that are continuous in space, and if you go away and come back after ten minutes, an hour, a week, or a year they still have the same shape). Such more abstract or more general qualities as "whiteness", "smell", "estrangement", should occur as attributes or predicates, e.g., "the white milk", or "the milk is white"; "the smelling wool", or "the wool has smell", or "the wool smells"; "the estranged walls", or "the walls are estranged". In these two excerpts, the adjectives are systematically turned into abstract nouns, and the abstract nouns

10   The enormous effect of versification is, of course, lost in these literal translations.

are manipulated into the referring position instead the spatio-temporally continuous particulars. (I have called such transformations *thematized predicates* or *topicalized attributes*). "We may think of this as governed by a 'good reason' principle: many linguistic systems are based on this principle, wherein one option (the 'unmarked' option) will always be selected unless there are good reasons for selecting otherwise" (Halliday, 1970: 159). Here the "good reason" for selecting the "marked" option is to turn the attribute into what Halliday calls the "psychological subject", "the peg on which the message is hung, the theme being the body of the message". Thus, in these two excerpts, not the concrete objects are manipulated into the psychological centre of the message, but their attributes that have no stable characteristic visual shapes.

When I read such poetic texts, I have an intense sensation, involving an intense emotional atmosphere in both stanzas. The phrase "The estrangement of these walls", for instance, shifts attention from the walls to the estranged atmosphere in the room. In this verse line attention is directed away from the persons to the atmosphere. The deictic devices 'this' and 'these' have to do with the generation of a coherent scene; at the same time, they suggest that there is some perceiving 'I' in the middle of the situation. The line 'This height that is yearning for you' reinforces the presence of such a perceiving self; the verb *yearning* charges the abstraction with energy, and turns it into some active, invisible presence. All the sentences of this stanza are elliptic, which have here a deictic function: they point to the percepts of the immediate situation. *Width* and *height* are pure geometrical dimensions; but here they are somehow emotionally charged. Some readers report a feeling "as if the emotional atmosphere were thick". Other readers report a feeling as if they were plunged in this thick atmosphere. Some of those who report the latter feeling say that they feel some faint tactile sensation all over their skin; and others, on the contrary, that the boundary between their body and this thick texture was suspended (see Tsur, 2003b; cf. Tsur 1988; Werner, 1978: 426).

Two unusual grammatic structures are conspicuous in these two excerpts. The first is what I have called *topicalized attribute,* the manipulation of an attribute into the referring position. Such transformations are quite characteristical of poetry that displays some intense, dense emotionally charged atmosphere. In everyday life and language we do not usually distinguish between physical objects and their attributes (or perceptual qualities). When we perceive (or speak of) the one, we are inclined automatically to identify it with the other. But the two are far from identical. One of the tasks of the "ABSTRACT of the CONCRETE" genitive phrases ("estrangement of these walls") may be to de-automatize the relationship between the attributes (or perceptual qualities) and the physical object. The other conspicuous grammatic structure concerns elliptic sentences. Elliptic sentences frequently contain a deictic element. This deictic element may have far-reaching poetic consequences. The function of an indicative predication is to *affect the beliefs* of the addressee, and to connect the utterance to extralinguistic reality (by suggesting "it occurred"). A noun phrase without predication places some event (or state of affairs) at the disposal of one's *awareness,* in abstraction from any claims concerning existence. If the phrase contains deixis it *may,* as we have seen, connect the utterance to extralinguistic reality, without affecting our beliefs (that is, as a percept, not as a statement).

About forty years ago I approached poetry from the point of view of "New Criticism" (it was "new" in the first half of the twentieth century). At that time I tended to explain the perceived quality of such poems as follows: we are confronted here with a *concrete* situation, but this concreteness is conferred on it only by the deictic devices; what we perceive in this situation are abstract nouns and qualities that have no stable characteristic visual shapes. Thus, our perceptions have a thicker texture than mere abstractions, but still lack some stable characteristic visual shape. Hence the intense, dense, but elusive feeling.

When in the late nineteen-sixties I began to develop my theory of cognitive poetics, I had come to realize that processes of knowing and feeling involve streams of information of the same kinds. The difference between conceptual thinking and percepts or emotions is not in the kind of information, but, among other things, their organization: the former is more compact and sequential, whereas the latter is more diffuse and simultaneous. This could explain how the loosening of the relationship between objects and their attributes rendered them less compact, more diffuse and emotional. While a logical argument has a beginning, middle and end (is sequential), a landscape is simultaneous. This may change the perception of even such abstractions as *width* and *height* into diffuse qualities (see also excerpts (5)–(6) in Chapter 15).

In the nineteen-seventies I came across cognitive psychologist Robert Ornstein's study of consciousness, in which he put forward the conception (which became the "received view") that while logical and rational consciousness is typically related to the left hemisphere of the brain, meditative consciousness is related to the right hemisphere. The left hemisphere processes information sequentially, and its output is experienced as compact and logical; the right hemisphere processes information simultaneously and its output is experienced as diffuse, integrating input from many senses. Orientation, emotions, and mystic experiences are all typically right-hemisphere activities (cf. supra, Chapter 15). Regarding the poetic structure discussed in the present section, I claimed, the emphatic deixis evokes a coherent scene arousing imagined orientation which, in turn, transfers a significant part of language processing from the left to the right hemisphere, rendering the related percepts more diffuse. Orientation involves not only a perception of the surrounding space, but also a sense of one's own body's position.

I was trying to stay, for as long as possible, within literary theory, linguistics, philosophy and cognitive science. But really compelling evidence began to turn up from the emerging brain science. During the past fifty years or so linguists have propounded a semantic-feature conception of meaning. Cognitive psychologists and brain scientists too speak of cognitive "features". The brain scientist Marcel Kinsbourne refutes the naïve belief that the right hemisphere's output is featureless: "A holistic approach, leaving features and their relations unspecified, is as alien to right-hemisphere function as it is inimical to rationality in general" (Kinsbourne, 1982: 417). I claim that the right hemisphere's output is "ineffable" not because no semantic features are involved, but because those features are *diffuse* and *simultaneous*. It is not the information that is unparaphrasable, but its integration and diffuseness. Diffuseness and integration are not semantic information *added,* but the *structure* of information *as it appears in consciousness*. Whereas semantic information can be paraphrased, the impression that arises from its structure can only be *described.*

In 2001–2002 I extended the above conception to seventeenth century-poetry of meditation as well. This poetry is said to have evolved from Jesuit meditation. The first stage of this meditation was "composition of place". The seventeenth-century Jesuits as well as twentieth century scholars claimed that the entire success of the meditation depended on a proper execution of the composition of place; but they never explained why. In a paper published in *Pragmatics and Cognition* (later included in my book: Tsur, 2003) Motti Benari and I argued that the composition of place requires the meditator to imagine himself in a specific situation of an episode from the life of Jesus or one of the saints and induce the meditative process through activating the right hemisphere by the orientation mechanism.

As I have suggested in various places (Tsur, 1987b: 4; Chapter 15 above; 1998), since language is compact and linear by nature, the phrases "emotional poetry" or "mystic poetry" ought to be, but are not, contradictions in terms. Now the phrases are not contradictions in terms, precisely because poets found exactly the same solution as Ignatius and the Jesuits found. In romantic nature poetry, for instance, the insights into supersensuous reality are intimately associated with detailed nature descriptions, a "composition of place", as it were. The orientation mechanism involved imposes diffuseness on the percepts conveyed by language.

There is no evidence in Orenstein's discussion for our conjecture concerning this effect of the orientation mechanism on meditation and poetic language. But after the article had already been accepted for publication by *Pragmatics and Cognition* we encountered brain research that may support this conception. Andrew Newberg, Eugene D'Aquili and Vince Rause (2001) conducted a SPECT camera brain-imaging study (the acronym stands for Single Photon Emission Computed Tomography) of Tibetan meditators and Franciscan nuns at prayer. To our pleasant surprise, these researchers claim that what they call the "orientation association area" (OAA) is "extremely important in the brain's sense of mystical and religious experiences, which often involve altered perceptions of space and time, self and ego" (29). This would massively support our speculations above based on the structure of literary texts, introspection, and earlier brain research. Their study attempted to obtain experimental evidence for their claim. They point out that there are two orientation areas, situated at the posterior section of the parietal lobe, one in each hemisphere of the brain:

> The left orientation area is responsible for creating the mental sensation of a limited, physically defined body, while the right orientation area is associated with generating the sense of spatial coordinates that provides the matrix in which the body can be oriented. In simpler terms, the left

orientation area creates the brain's spatial sense of self, while the right side creates the physical space in which that self can exist. (Newberg et al., 2001: 28)

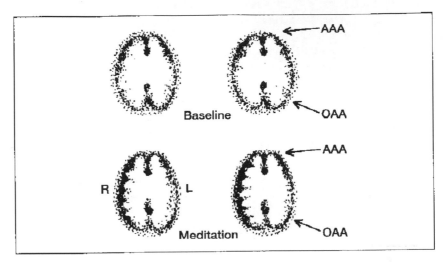

Figure 24.1 The top row of images shows the meditator's brain at rest and indicates an even distribution of activity throughout the brain. (The top of the image is the front of the brain and part of the attention association area, or AAA, while the bottom of the image is part of the orientation association area, or OAA.) The bottom row of images shows the brain during meditation, in which the left orientation area (on your right) is markedly decreased compared to the right side (from Newberg et al.).

These researchers found a sharp reduction in the activity levels of the left orientation association area during meditation. A SPECT image of the brain's activity during meditation indicates that the activity of "the left orientation area [...] is markedly decreased compared to the right side" (ibid., 4). They assume that both orientation areas were working as hard as ever, but in the left area the incoming flow of sensory information had somehow been blocked (6).

In a later chapter they highlight the right hemisphere orientation activity during what they call "the active approach" to meditation:

> Active types of meditation begin not with the intention to clear the mind of thoughts, but instead, to focus it intensely upon some thought or object of attention. A Buddhist might chant a mantra, or focus upon a glowing candle or a small bowl of water, for example, while a Christian might pray with the mind trained upon God, or a saint, or the symbol of a cross. For the sake of discussion, let's imagine that the focus of attention is the mental image of Christ. [...] In this case, since the intention is to focus more intensely upon some specific object or thought, the attention

facilitates rather than inhibits, neural flow. In our model, this increased neural flow causes the right orientation area, in conjunction with the visual association area, to fix the object of focus, real or imagined, in the mind. (ibid., p. 120)

We consider these findings extremely valuable for interpreting the meditative experience. If the boundaries between self and not self are to be suspended in meditation, that is, if the self is to dissolve in infinite space, the boundaries of the self must be de-emphasized, and the perception of the surrounding space overemphasized. The process must begin, therefore, with activities having opposing effects in the two orientation areas: in the right area "the sense of spatial coordinates that provides the matrix in which the body can be oriented" must be reinforced; in the left area "the mental sensation of a limited, physically defined body" must be reduced. What is more, the diffuse information-processing mode originating in the right hemisphere may help to blur, as an initial step, the mental sensation of a well-defined physical boundary of the body—whatever the later stages of the cognitive and neurological processes. In imaginative processes, objects that have stable characteristic visual shapes enhance the feeling of their separateness and our separateness from them; abstractions as well as gestalt-free and thing-free qualities enhance a feeling of the suspended boundaries.

This might account for certain verbal structures that are quite common in our corpus: these structures draw attention to the surrounding space, but focus on thing-free and gestalt-free entities (such as abstractions) rather than on stable characteristic visual shapes. Consider, for instance, the following phrase from a passage by the Jesuit writer, Dawson: "to have noted well the distance from one place to another, the height of the hills, and the situation of the townes and villages", or Ignatius' "the length, breadth and depth of Hell". (Indeed, it was claimed in Chapter 15 above that "orientation is more prepared to pick up the *arrangement* of objects in one's environment, whereas shape perception is centered on the properties of the *object itself*"). Here the focus of attention is shifted from spatio-temporally continuous objects to certain abstract relations: *distance ... height ... situation,* or *length, breadth* and *depth,* manipulated into the referring position. According to our interpretation, such abstractions and gestalt-free qualities are perceived differently by the two orientation association areas. In the left area they enhance a feeling of the blurring of boundaries; in the right area they are perceived as unstable, fluid information, comparable to the fast-integrated output of right-hemisphere orientation processes, that cannot settle as solid objects.

These findings suggest that the switch from "ordinary consciousness" to "meditative consciousness" involves the substitution of a holistic mode of operation for the analytic and sequential information-processing mode. Structurally, there is a drastic increase in the diffuseness of the brain's output. Hence, the "composition of place" is intended to evoke a right-hemisphere orientation process. The right-hemisphere process is responsible for the "diffusion" of compact inputs. The activation of the orientation mechanism arouses an information-processing mode that is diffuse, holistic, and simultaneous. This mode of functioning characterizes the meditative process, and typically involves diffuse and intuitive impressions.

I have extensively dwelt on the activity of the left and right brain orientation areas which in some extreme conditions may lead to some altered state of consciousness. But in normal conditions this activity may be responsible for the cognitive processes underlying deixis: the perception of self in relation to the surrounding space. This is the point where a discussion of deixis may become cognitive (as, for instance, in experiencing the sublime, discussed in the next section).

My position *vis-à-vis* Stockwell's work receives support in a wider perspective from David Miall. With reference to Stockwell's and his circle's work he comments: Cognitive poetics "has adopted a model of cognition that, surprisingly in the present stage of psychological research, is restricted almost entirely to information processing issues: in other words, the role of *feeling* has been neglected" (Miall, 2006: 41). Ironically enough, though I am usually credited with having coined the phrase "Cognitive Poetics", it came to designate, when not qualified, an approach to which I largely object. Two pages later, however, Miall adds: "Given that literary reading is so often imbued with feeling, it is surprising that feeling has still received so little attention from cognitive poetics. Of the major scholars in this field, only Reuven Tsur and Keith Oatley have made significant contributions" (Miall, 2006: 43).

As I have shown in Chapter 18 above and in my book *On the Shore of Nothingness*, such verbal constructions as the combination of emphatic deictic devices with abastract nouns in the referring position are very much in evidence in seventeenth-century poetry of meditation, in Romantic meditative poems (as Wordsworth's Calais-beach sonnet) as well as in Whitman's meditative catalogue. Thanks to such constructions, poetry is well-suited not only to *tell of*, but also to *show* altered states of consiousness; to evoke not only the concept of these states of mind, but also their feel. Regarding deictic devices, I have argued and attempted to demonstrate that the task of cognitive poetics is to shift attention from labelling and classifying them to accounting for their effect.

Deixis and the Sublime;

Finally, let us examine the relationship between deixis and the sublime as they occur in "Ozymandias". I have mentioned above how Stockwell classifies, labels and illustrates his deictic categories in "Ozymandias". Now that we know that when "the deictic centre that says 'I' in the first line" looks back on ancient times, it is temporal deixis, and when he looks at a faraway land it is spatial deixis—we are also entitled to know what is their "stylistic value", "their effect". The same could be said of the following: "All of the locating expressions follow the deictic centre in each case: 'near them' is spatially related to the traveller standing in the desert; 'those passions' and 'these lifeless things' are centred on the traveller looking at the shattered face; 'far away' is understood relative to the site". To be precise, however, "near them" is not spatially related to the traveller standing in the desert; the objects are spatially related *to each other*. Their proximity does not depend on where the traveller stands (cf. Langacker's examples in note[11]). Likewise, "those passions" and "these lifeless things" can be construed, with some good will, as deictic; more likely, however, those demonstrative pronouns indicate here co-reference with earlier expressions rather than spatial relationships focused on the speaker as reference point.

I have already suggested that in some instances the shifting deictic centres serve to establish a pervasive ironic tone in the poem. In what follows I will argue that, at the same time, deixis serves to evoke a sublime quality. Let me recapitulate a few aspects of the Kantian notion of the *sublime,* discussed at greater length in Chapter 15. "We call that *sublime* which is *absolutely great"* (Kant, 1951: 86), *"what is great beyond all comparison"* (ibid.). We still need some definition that may attach a descriptive content to these critical terms. *Absolutely great* may be regarded as a positive description of the negative notion *boundlessness* or *infinity.* Kant suggests that the sublime be defined in psychological terms. "As this, however, is great beyond all standards of sense, it makes us judge as *sublime,* not so much the object, as our own state of mind in the estimation of it" (ibid., 94).[12] From the poetic point of view, this poses an enormous problem: How can words convey that which "is great beyond all standards of sense", without falling back on empty superlatives? I submit that this requires a verbal technique in which deixis plays a crucial part. In the following passage Beardsley briefly summarizes those parts of the Kantian notion of the sublime from which the essentials of this technique can be inferred:

> When we estimate magnitudes through numbers, that is, conceptually, the imagination selects a unit, which it can then repeat indefinitely. But there is a second kind of estimation of magnitudes, which Kant calls "aesthetic estimation", in which the imagination tries to comprehend or encompass the whole representation in one single intuition. There is an upper bound to its capacity. An object whose apparent or conceived size strains this capacity to the limit—threatens to exceed the imagination's power to take it all in at once—has, subjectively speaking, an absolute magnitude: it reaches the felt limit, and appears as if infinite. [...] imagination reaches its maximum capacity, shows its failure and inadequacy when compared to the demands of Reason, and makes us aware, by contrast, of the magni-

---

[11]   In the following examples, *"Over* and *across* are", says Langacker (1987: 127–128), "deictic in (c) and (d), [...] but not in the other sentences":
     (a)   *There is a picture over the fireplace.*
     (b)   *An elderly man walked across the field.*
     (c)   *An old church lies just over that hill.*
     (d)   *There is a mailbox across the street.*
     (e)   *There is a mailbox across the street from the drugstore.*
[12]   Eighteenth-century theorists analyse in detail this state of mind (see my book *On the Shore of Nothingness*, pp. 141–145).

ficence of Reason itself. The resulting feeling is the feeling of the sublime.
(Beardsley, 1966: 218–219)

Eighteenth-century theorists discussed at considerable length what kinds of things
are sublime: among them, immensely large things, or things immensely remote in
space (both horizontally and vertically) or in time (such as pre-history, ancient history, or the mythological past). Visually, then, the sublime is that which exceeds
our ability to encompass it, that which transcends the limits of the visible horizon.
The Kantian "aesthetic estimation" presupposes, then, self-perception, or imaginary
self-perception, here and now, in the middle of the visual space encompassed by the
horizon. As we have seen in excerpt (6), deixis is *the* means to evoke such a
situation in a verbal context. In my various writings I have insisted that critical
terms, with their descriptive contents, have little significance unless they are understood in relation to a theoretical framework or model. Consider Stockwell's assertion: "The line 'The lone and level sands stretch far away' takes the scene spatially
away from the deictic centre of the ruin". What Stockwell's theoretical framework
imputes on the line is almost synonymous with its explicit contents: "The lone and
level sands stretch far away" = "takes the scene spatially away from the [...] ruin".
This is perfectly true, but trivial. The only thing it adds is that it specifies the point
of origin as the ruin. This addition may be accurate, but shifts attention away from
the deixis and its potential to evoke a sublime quality in the poem. First, as Langacker (1987: 127) put it, not all spatial relationships are deictic, "the position of
the speaker serves as a default-case reference point".[13] The line does not explicitly
indicate the deictic centre; from the cognitive point of view, the perceiving
consciousness (not the ruin) is the deictic centre, though the speaker (the traveller)
may stand near the ruins. Secondly, the Kantian perspective emphasizes here not the
"taking away from the centre" aspect of the description, but its "faraway" aspect, that
is, its "transcending the limits of perception" aspect, presenting the scene as
absolutely great, as sublime. This is reinforced by the adjective "boundless". Thus,
subcategorizing the domain as *perceptual, spatial,* and *temporal deixis* does the poem
a conspicuous disservice. As footnotes 11 and 13 suggest, for Langacker, for
instance, "the ruin" as a reference point or a phrase like "'far away' is understood
relative to the site" would be insufficient to warrant a deictic construal.

When we say "XIIIth Century B.C.", or "thirty three-centuries ago", the imagination selects a unit (century), which it can then repeat indefinitely. This indefinitely
repeatable unit allows us to ignore all the intervening perceptual information.
Likewise, when we say "Giza is so and so many miles away from London" the imagination selects, again, a unit, which it can then repeat indefinitely. However, when
we speak of a "faraway" or "antique land", the (spatial or temporal) distance becomes

---

[13] In a discourse like *Sharon asked the repairman to come immediately* there are two
speakers: the speaker of the whole utterance, and the speaker of a reported utterance.
Here the latter is construed as the "deictic centre" of *to come* (cf. Langacker, 1987:
127), sanctioned by established convention.

somehow vaguely perceptual, and "threatens to exceed the imagination's power to take it all in at once", it "has, subjectively speaking, an absolute magnitude: it reaches the felt limit, and appears as if infinite". This may illuminate the problematic usefulness of subcategorization when speaking of poetic effects: it makes little difference whether the distance is spatial or temporal. The overwhelmingly important thing is what this distance *does:* that it "threatens to exceed the imagination's power to take it all in at once".[14]

This effect interacts with the versification structure. I have already mentioned one effect of blurred prosodic gestalts in this poem: they reinforce the elusiveness of the ironic quality. Another effect concerns the sublime quality. There is precedent for the supposition that qualities generated by the blurring of boundaries on one level of a poem may be obstructed by sharp outlines on another level (in synaesthesia, for instance, as I argued in Chapter 10, the absence of stable visual outlines may be conducive to the smooth fusion of information from several senses, that is, to the obscuring of boundaries between the senses). So, the blurring of prosodic shapes may enhance the sublime effect generated by transcending the boundaries imposed by space and time.

Here a knotty problem arises. As Stockwell rightly observed, in "Ozymandias" there are three different points of view of three different persons, and two different places. Infinite space observed from the middle of the desert, infinite time observed from the present, and infinite space between the narrator and the desert are part of different deictic situations. Can the three be integrated into one cognitive experience "in which the imagination tries to comprehend or encompass the whole representation in one single intuition?" Let us consider such a possibility. First, the phrase "traveller from an antique land" integrates the latter two situations by suggesting both spatial and temporal distance in one. Secondly, Stockwell makes a rather sophisticated observation about "a time implicit in the present tense of 'met' and 'said'; the time in which the traveller was in the desert, chronologically in the past but deictically projected as a present tense 'stand' and 'these words appear'; and a deictic projection to the ancient time of the inscription when 'is', 'look' and 'despair' were written while Ozymandias was alive". But he does nothing with it. It would appear that the chronologically removed events "deictically projected as a present tense" may serve just such an integration.

Here, however, another knotty question arises, posed by David Miall, concerning the psychological reality of such integration of 'deictic centers': "Does cognitive deixis position a reader in relation to the points of view on offer in a narrative [or poem]?" In the present case the problem is even more difficult: Does such a cognitive device "bounce" a reader into a position in which he can integrate infinite space observed from the middle of the desert, and infinite time observed from the

---

14 To be sure, space and time are of central importance in cognitive organisation. Cognitive poetics may flexibly and creatively apply these notions in a wide variety of contexts, whereas freezing them into rigid taxonomies impedes rather than facilitates such creative application.

present into a single intuition? I don't know the answer, and doubt whether anybody knows it. I suppose that some readers are capable of this, some are not. I strongly hope that David Miall will find a way experimentally to test how many readers are, and how many are not capable of this. For the time being I am handling such problems in a different way. I would put my answer in a hypothetical form. If the reader is able to perceive or experience the sublime quality of Ozymandias' desert, it strongly suggests that he is able to position himself in relation to the spatial point of view on offer in the poem, or—more rarely—even integrate the spatial and temporal points of view. Likewise, if in excerpt (6) a reader can perceive the "thick" emotional quality in "this width" and "this height", it strongly suggests that he can place himself in the centre of the situation and experience the (imagined) orientation process. As long as there is no controlled empirical data, this is the best we can do. And it's not so bad, after all.

Finally, there is a significant mutual dependence between the ironic and the sublime in this poem. The detached, impersonal ironic tone amplifies the effect of the sublime; and the sublime effect of the boundless desert reinforces the sense of futility and meaninglessness of petty human aspirations.

Summary

David Miall criticized Peter Stockwell for being too much preoccupied with meaning, too little with feeling. I have argued against the way he handles his conceptual apparatus. More specifically, I argued that he had a predilection for labelling rather than meaning-making; and that I disagreed with him as to what counts as a proper cognitive explanation. I pointed out that in Stockwell's practice "cognitive analysis" sometimes consists in rechristening well-worn old terminology into new, "cognitive" terms. Everything that is language or literature goes through the cognitive system of authors, readers, and critics. However, a discussion becomes cognitive not when it resorts to a certain terminology, but when certain problems are addressed which cannot be properly addressed without appealing to some cognitive process or mechanism. On this issue, I invoked Quintilianus who had claimed that the value of stylistic devices lies not in their names, but in their effects, in their actions.

In the last three sections I tried to demonstrate how stylistic devices may interact with other devices and perspectives to generate (sometimes conflicting) poetic effects. Following Langacker I argued that not all spatial reference points are deictic, only where the position of the speaker serves as a reference point. At the beginning of his chapter Stockwell too makes a statement to this effect; but in his critical practice he does not always observe this restriction. Deixis proper is an essential ingredient in the verbal evocation of the sublime and of the emotional qualities and altered states of consciousness related to orientation. These arise in situations in which the perceiving consciousness is the reference point.

I am fully aware that one cannot expect Stockwell to go in a textbook into such lengths as I have gone here. Enough has been said, however, to support my claim that he devotes the available space to discussions that have little to do with Cognitive Poetics; and that he devotes too much space to labelling and pigeonholing, and too little to poetic analysis.

All three reviewers for *Pragmatics & Cognition* pointed out a crucial problem with the present submission: that a mere textbook chapter does not justify this kind of reaction, "unless the chapter from the textbook would be extremely controversial as well as important to the field". This is precisely my reason for writing and publishing the present chapter. Stockwell's book was published, from the beginning, as something that is not just a textbook. It has a companion volume by various hands, which contains parallel chapters to Stockwell's chapters. Besides, Stockwell is not an isolated, marginal case. Much of what I have to say on his work would apply to some degree to the work of many other Lakoffian critics.[15] At present, the book is well on its way to become *the* canonical book on Cognitive Poetics (see, e.g., "Stockwell has successfully re-defined the field"—Hamilton, 2005: 744); I therefore feel an obligation to point out that something in it *is* controversial. One of the reviewers accuses me of using Stockwell's argument in a different context for a different purpose: "Where Stockwell is presumably presenting the notion of deixis in a way that he feels students might learn some mastery over its identification and definition, Tsur criticizes his chapter for not showing how deictic application can illuminate a literary text". Even in this formulation Stockwell's discussion emerges as something that is not Cognitive Poetics, but rather "presenting the notion of deixis in a way that he feels students might learn some mastery over its identification and definition". As this referee rightly observes, I would expect a book on Cognitive Poetics to show "how deictic application can illuminate a literary text". Stockwell didn't purport to write a grammar book in which the texts for practicing happen to be literary texts, but an Introduction to Cognitive Poetics. But I also claim that learning some mastery over the identification and definition of deixis is not sufficient for calling one's critical activity "cognitive". Moreover, writing a textbook in poetics cannot be an excuse for ignoring the literary effects of stylistic devices. Finally, let me add a word to justify my focusing on a single chapter. I find the critical practice of wholesale evaluation without going into details particularly irksome. I believe that an unfavorable assessment of a piece of literary theory should be supported by detailed reasons and examples, followed by suggestions how it could be

---

[15] Indeed, in our correspondence Stockwell himself tried to refute my criticism by the following comment (17 Oct. 2001): "There are many people doing work in the interface between language, linguistics, literature, psychology and the study of mind in general who see themselves as being engaged in cognitive poetics". This may suggest that my criticism would apply to many other people as well. As a matter of fact, I regard myself too as "doing work in the interface between language, linguistics, literature, psychology and the study of mind in general"; in fact, my point of criticism is that in Stockwell's chapter there is too little psychology and the study of mind in general that would warrant the name "Cognitive Poetics".

done in a more satisfactory manner. Furthermore, as I said above in the first paragraph, my object in this chapter is not just to criticize Stockwell's work, but to highlight the difference between our approaches. Such a response requires to concentrate on a relatively short text.

CHAPTER 25

Comparing Approaches to Versification Style

in *Cyrano de Bergerac*

Preliminary

As I said in the preceding chapter, it has been suggested to me that I add to the present edition of this book a few case studies comparing my analysis to some cognitive linguist's analysis of one issue each, so as to highlight the difference between our approaches and provoke discussion.

This chapter contains one of those case studies: it focuses on Eve Sweetser's investigation, in the Lakoff tradition, of the contribution of rhyme and meter to a comprehensive interpretation of Edmond Rostand's *Cyrano de Bergerac*. I will extrapolate to Rostand's play the theoretical machinery I have elaborated during the years for the investigation of rhyme and meter. Sweetser says she is working within "blending theory"—somewhat stretching the concept, so as to apply to versification. At any rate, her approach is strongly meaning-oriented. My approach, by contrast, has gestaltist and phonetic orientation (as expounded in Chapters 5–8); when I have recourse to meaning, it is a semantic-oppositions approach (as expounded in Chapter 9). Thus, in the final resort, it is the suitability of two theoretical approaches to handle versification that stands to trial—a meaning-oriented and a gestalt-oriented approach. The purpose here is not to take Sweetser to task for not pursuing a certain kind of criticism, but rather to provide a case study comparing my approach to some other cognitive approach—in this instance, a case study of versification.

Let me state at once the bottom line of this comparison: Cognitive Poetics is not a homogeneous enterprise. Sweetser and I isolate the same text units for attention, but have different methodologies, ask different kinds of questions, and give different answers. Briefly, she concentrates more on meanings; I—on perceptual qualities (as expounded in Chapter 4). It would appear that quite frequently we have similar underlying intuitions; but our different methodologies lead us to ask different questions. I fully agree with the admirable interpretation of the play that emerges from Sweetser's handling of versification; but here I will concern myself only with versification and the perceptual qualities it generates.

The Lakoff school pays curiously little attention to the prosodic dimension of poetry. It is mainly interested in semantics. Two notable exceptions are Masako

Hiraga's work, and Eve Sweetser's paper "Whose rhyme is whose reason? Sound and sense in *Cyrano de Bergerac*".

As a preliminary, I will note that I disagree with Sweetser on one side issue. "Rostand's *Cyrano de Bergerac* is a particularly complex example of dramatic verse", she writes. "Its form is instantly salient, since its traditional hexameter [sic] (12-syllable lines) rhymed couplets metonymically evoke the frame of mid-17th-century France: the play's setting; and the time when 'classical' French drama was in flower and verse tragedy was considered its highest-prestige form" (p. 32). I claim that this metonymic evocation of the frame of mid- 17th-century France, the play's historical setting, is less significant than it would appear. The play's versification is a variable independent from its historical setting. Thus, for instance, Rostand's other verse drama, *L'Aiglon* (The Eaglet) is placed in the 19th century (1830–1832), in the Austrian Emperor's court, the "eaglet" being Napoleon's and Marie-Louise's son, with such historical personages for dramatis personae as Marie-Louise and Prince Metternich. The play is "l'histoire d'un pauvre enfant" within that historical setting. The two plays have recourse to exactly the same versification patterns of the alaxandrine couplet. Furthermore, I will argue that Rostand's alexandrine couplets, in both plays, are as different from Racine's as possible within the same versification tradition. In fact, with their occasional enjambments and "effaced" caesurae (see below) they are more similar to the couplets of Romantic than of Classical drama.[1]

I intend to compare my approach to Sweetser's consistently excellent work. We isolate the same kinds of text units for attention; so, on the descriptive level we would most probably provide quite similar descriptions of the text. The difference would be in the different theoretical frameworks within which we make those descriptive statements. Sweetser adopts the venerable Form–Content dichotomy; I adopt Wellek and Warren's more recent notion (1942) of "Materials" and "Structure". And, we are working within a meaning-oriented and a gestalt-oriented theory, respectively. The different theoretical perspectives generate considerable differences of focus or emphasis on the very same perceptions.

As a point of departure, let me quote Boileau's aphorism: "La rime est une esclave: et ne doit qu' obéir" [Rhyme is a slave, and must do nothing but obey]

---

[1]   My student Roi Tartakovsky commented on this paragraph: "Could one not argue, simply, that writing a play in verse in the late 19th century is highly conspicuous, and can potentially 'mean' different things. It has 'signifying potentiality' (my term). In the case of *Cyrano*, this potentiality is harnessed to evoking the 17th century, and in the other play—it simply is not." His notions "meaning different things" and "signifying potentiality" are well-taken; they have precedent in the theory of metaphor I embrace. The activation of "dormant features" or meaning potentials is the ground for understanding novel metaphors. I had, however, a second point too on this matter: *Cyrano's* versification is more similar to Romantic than to Classical tragedy. I don't think that putting all alexandrine couplets in one bin is very useful. More subtle distinctions are required. My main objection is to jumping to conclusions on the basis of obtrusive but doubtful cues, while ignoring subtle and minimal cues.

(*L'Art Poétique*, I. 30). But who is the master? According to Sweetser's conception it must serve meaning; according to the present conception—it must serve a perceptual whole of which it is a part; and meaning is just another part.

Articulateness and Requiredness

Sweetser introduces her section "The Hôtel de Bourgogne: rhyme, meter, and polyphonic voice" with the following example.

The pickpocket: La dentelle surtout des canons, coup**ez-la**!
       *(Particularly the canons' lace, **cut it off** !)*
A spectator:Tenez, à la première du *Cid* , j'étais **là**!
    (You know, at the first performance of le Cid, *I **was there**!)*
The pickpocket: Les montres ...*(the watches)*
The bourgeois: Vous verrez des acteurs très il**lustres** ...
    *(You'll see really **illustrious** actors...)*
The pickpocket:
Les mouchoirs ...*(the handkerchiefs)*
The bourgeois:
                Montfleury ....
Someone shouting from above:
                    Allumez donc les **lustres**!
    *(So light the **chandeliers**!)*
The bourgeois:...Bellerose, l'Epy, la Beaupré, Jod**elet** !
A page:Ah! Voici la distributrice!...
    (Oh, here's the food vendor!)
The vendor (female):   Oranges, **lait**,...
    *(Oranges, **milk**,...)*

She introduces this excerpt with the following comment:

> In the following example (I. i. 25–30), characters complete not only each other's couplets (25–6, *coupez-la* and *j'étais là*), but each other's lines: two speakers' words make up line 27 (*illustres*), and three speakers (including the preceding two) contribute to the other half of the same couplet, line 28 (*lustres*). More interestingly, and less typically of verse drama, these characters are not engaged in a single conversation, but in multiple parallel conversations between characters who might not interact directly (given social divisions), and in fact do not even all hear each other. The pickpocket is covertly advizing his trainees, the theater buff bragging to his friends, the bourgeois informing his son, the vendor advertizing refreshments, and the theater employee calling to colleagues for the lights to be lit.

This paragraph is a *description* of the excerpt. This, or a similar, description could occur in my discussion as well. What would be most important for me in her description concerns the segmentation of lines and distribution of speech between different speakers and even different conversations. I would focus, on the experiential level, on the perceptual qualities bestowed by them on the couplets. Sweetser, by contrast, says with so many words that she concentrates on meaning: "when multiple characters contribute to a line, or when 'enjambment' gives us salient differences between the two kinds of boundaries, the meaning affordances of metrical line units stand out more clearly" (34). I have nothing against such preoccupation with meaning; except that it misses the perceived qualities contributed by versification. She continues:

> By letting these multiple characters' voices 'collaborate' to make hexameter [sic] lines, and rhymed couplets—a structured and unified formal whole—Rostand's blend conveys the broader message that at the content level these parallel interactions between diverse individuals form a unified social whole. Perhaps the message is that Parisian society is somehow an organic whole, despite class and other social divisions; or perhaps a more interesting interpretation is that dramatic artistic performance brings together disparate segments of society into a community. This could well be Rostand's bourgeois late-19th-century message; and if so, it cannot reasonably be put in the mouth of any character within the play's 17th-century setting under the French monarchy. It is appropriately expressed not by those characters' words, but by their interleaving relationship to the metrical structure of the whole (37–38). [and so forth].

This paragraph concerns the *interpretation* or *significance*, not the *perceived qualities*, of the said segmentation and distribution. Sweetser offers, à propos versification, a brilliant interpretation of the play. As I said, I embrace most of her interpretation, some of it with great enthusiasm. But herein I will concern myself only with versification. This paragraph, however, contributes very little to this interpretation. It rather relates the segmentation and distribution to wider issues that are no organic part of the play's action (such as "Rostand's bourgeois late-19th-century message", or "the message that Parisian society is somehow an organic whole"). One thing, however, appears to be quite probable: this discussion is an indication of the author's strong intuition (which I share) that this versification structure is somehow very effective. Sweetser is looking for the key to this effectiveness under the streetlamp of the contents; I claim that versification does something to poetry that cannot be reduced to meaning.

I devoted no professional attention to this play before reading Sweetser's paper. But I have written quite a lot on English versification that, I believe, might fruitfully be extended to Rostand's versification as well. My first English publication (1972) was "Articulateness and Requiredness in Iambic Verse"; part of it was later included in Chapter 5 above. When we speak of articulateness, we imply that a whole has been broken into parts, and that this facilitates perception of the whole. When we speak of requiredness, we imply that each part is essential to the whole: when a part is omitted, there is an acute feeling of incompleteness, of imbalance. Articulateness and requiredness depend on the relative strength of the whole. Requiredness is possible only where the whole is highly organized. If the integrity of the whole is not felt, deficiency cannot be felt either. According to the gestalt assumption, a perceptual unit tends "to preserve its integrity by resisting interruptions": each of two conflicting units will tend to reassert itself in the reader's perception (As we have seen in Chapter 5, Fodor and his colleagues have empirically substantiated this assumption in a linguistic context; Fodor and Bever, 1965; Garrett et al., 1966).

As gestalt psychologists have insisted time and again, segmentation may facilitate the perception of a complex whole. Caesura is such a segmentation device in the middle of a verse line, rendering it symmetrical, stable, balanced (cf. Chapter 6 above). A word- or phrase-ending may confirm caesura; in its absence, syntax overrides caesura, generating tension or, alternatively, blurring the line's shape. There may be additional, syntacic breaks in a line. The nearer the break to the caesura, the less it threatens the balance and symmetry, and the less one is likely to mistake the segment for a full but defective line. When it occurs nearer to the end, one is more likely to mistake the segment for a completed unit manqué, and to regard it as a threat on the integrity of the line. Consequently, our relief will be greater when the missing part is supplied. This may generate, in certain cisrcumstances, a sharp, witty effect, turning the last string of syllables into a "punch-phrase", so to speak. As I tried to show in Chapter 5 (through quite a few examples), segmentation that generates articulateness and requiredness is a characteristic feature of Pope's wit. And it appears to be one of the characteristics of Rostand's wit as well.

Now, consider Sweetser's observation: "characters complete not only each other's couplets (25–26, *coupez-la* and *j'étais là*), but each other's lines: two speakers' words make up line 27 (*illustres*), and three speakers contribute to the other half of the same couplet, line 28 (*lustres*). More interestingly, and less typically of verse drama, these characters are not engaged in a single conversation". This observation points at something that is intuitively very significant, but Sweetser's theoretical framework cannot account for it. The present theoretical framework, by contrast, is tailor-made for it. The speaker has completed his part, but the verse line remains incomplete. This taking turns enhances the sense of segmentation and, by the same token, the sense of incompleteness, increasing the requiredness of the missing part. The greater the number of interruptions, the more vigorous the verse line's "effort" to reassert itself in the audience's perception (I will return to these two pairs of rhymes). This is, perhaps, the epitome of the argument of the present chapter. We both feel that the distribution of one line between several speakers and even several conversations is very significant from the poetic point of view. Blending theory is incapable of accounting for this, whereas gestalt theory is tailor-made for it.

This construal, that "the message is that Parisian society is somehow an organic whole, despite class and other social divisions" is very plausible. But I wish to make four further comments on it. First, in the "OUTSIDE THE CITY GATE" scene in Goethe's *Faust* there is a similar polyphony of brief conversations of several social groups, and we receive a similar "message" from it. Here, however, the versification strategy is quite different. There is a more complex, less regular rhyme pattern; on the other hand, in the whole 95-line section only one line is distributed between two speakers, with the segmentation not near the end but near the middle of the line. Furthermore, in Goethe's scene rhyme patterns do not "spill over" from one conversation to another. This might suggest, in Rostand, a sharpening of the paradoxical view of creating an organic whole despite class and other social divisions. Second, this structure dominates Rostand's both plays. *Cyrano* takes place in Parisian society which is said to be "somehow an organic whole, despite class and other social divisions". But we have the same versification structure in *L'Aiglon* too, which takes place in the Austrian Emperor's court and royal family, whose social structure is quite homogeneous. In fact, in *Cyrano* too we find the "social polyphony" only at the beginning of Act I, whereas the versification style prevails throughout the play. Third, whatever the social implications, Rostand's versification strategy has considerable "added value": it bestows a witty quality on the dialogues. Finally, a piece of philosophical hairsplitting: to the outright predications "the message is that" and "Parisian society *is* a" I would prefer a Wittgensteinian conception of "seeing as": "presenting Parisian society *as* an organic whole, despite class and other social divisions". In other words, this is not the meaning of the scene; merely, Parisian society is concretized in a certain way.

The versification pattern pointed out in Cyrano is no less conspicuous in Rostand's other play. Consider the opening lines of *L'Aiglon:*

LES DAMES, *au clavecin. [...]*
Elle manque tous les bémols. — C'est un scandale!
— Je prends la basse. — Un, deux! — Harpe! — La... la!... — Pédale!

BOMBELLES, *à Thérèse* .
C'est vous?

THERESE
        Bonjour, Monsieur de Bombelles.

UNE DAME, *au clavecin.*
                        Mi... sol...

THERESE
J'entre comme lectrice aujourd'hui.

UNE AUTRE DAME, *au clavecin.*
                Le bémol!

THERESE
Et grâce à vous. Merci.

BOMBELLES
                    C'est tout simple, Thérèse
Vous êtes ma parente et vous êtes Française.

(THE LADIES, *at the harpsichord*. She misses all the flats. — This is a scandal!
— I play the bass. — One, two! — Harp! La... la!... — Pedal!
BOMBELLES, *to Therese* It's you?
THERESE Good day, Mr. de Bombelles.
LADY, *at the harpsichord* Mi... sol...
THERESE I am starting today as a reader.
ANOTHER LADY, *at the harpsichord* Flat!
THERESE It's thanks to you. Many thanks.
BOMBELLES It's elementary, Thérèse
You are my kin, and you are French)

Consider the following sequence from the second line of this excerpt: "Un, deux! —
Harpe! — La... la!... — Pédale!". All are one- or two-syllable-long chunks, none of
them constitutes a clause. The first two chunks are *required* to complete the first
versification segment (that is, up to the caesura); the rest to complete the line. Here,
too, the "characters are not engaged in a single conversation, but in multiple parallel
conversations". Or consider the following sequence in the same scene: "C'est vous? /
Bonjour, Monsieur de Bombelles./ Mi... sol...". All this makes up a single line.
The first two chunks are spoken by two different persons, and the conversational
turns are completed (if not ended). But, alas, two more syllables are required. These
come, eventually, from the harpsichord string of conversation. What is more, these
two syllables constitute two semantically related, but syntactically disjunct words.

In the last couplet of the sequence, the first line is divided between two speakers
precisely at the caesura. Its second hemistich is further articulated by the vocative
"Thérèse" (by the same speaker!), that interrupts the syntactic flow and is highly
required. Finally, the sequence achieves stable closure by ending with a complete
line displaying perfect parallelism with a distinct caesura.

This effect of threatening the line's integrity may be further enhanced by a "false"
rhyme in mid-line, as in the following excerpt from the same scene:

MARIE-LOUISE, *se retournant, à Bombelles.*
Je viens d'écrire pour qu'on garde son cheval!

A Thérèse.

Depuis la mort du général...

THERESE, *étonnée.*
                                Du général?

(MARIE-LOUISE, *turning to Bombelles.*
I've just written that they should take care of his horse!
To Thérèse. Since the death of the general...
THERESE, *astonished.* Of the general?)

The audience is fooled into mistaking the first "général" for the expected rhyme word, yielding a grievously deficient verse line. Therese's astonished question "Du général?" provides the genuine rhyme and the missing part of the perceptual field. There are quite a few such instances of false alarm in Rostand's both plays. The next excerpt is from *Cyrano:*

UN BOURGEOIS, *conduisant son fils*
Plaçons-nous là, mon fils.
UN JOUEUR   Brelan d'as!
UN HOMME, *tirant une bouteille de sous son manteau et s'asseyant aussi*
                                Un ivrogne
Doit boire son bourgogne...
Il boit.
                                ... à l'hôtel de Bourgogne!

(BOURGEOIS, *leading his son*
Let us sit down here, my son.
CARD PLAYER   Triple ace!
A MAN, *taking out a bottle from under his coat, sitting down too*
                                A druncard
Must drink his Burgundi ...
Drinks.
                                ... in the hôtel de Bourgogne!)

The unity-in-variety aspect of the Parisian society may be an *additional* dimension of Rostand's dialogue in Act I of *Cyrano*; but cannot account for the witty effect of the lines; this can be traced to the unity-in-variety aspect of the dialogue, in perspective of gestalt theory.

Interruptions will increase the tendency of verse lines to reassert their integrity, up to a point. When this (theoretically undefined) point is passed, the verse line will begin to disintegrate. This effect crucially depends on performance. The actors may take advantage of such segmentation of the dialogue to suppress meter all in all, so as to render their speech as near as possible to realistic prose discourse. In this case, no requiredness will arise. But if the actors preserve the integrity of the verse to some degree, requiredness and the resulting witty effect will be most conspicuous. Paradoxically, the string of segments imitating the cadences of colloquial speech, too, will emphatically reassert itself. In this respect, segmentation is "double-edged".

To compare Rostand's alexandrine couplets to 17th-century verse drama, I have checked the first two acts of Racine's *Phèdre* (a total of 736 verse lines). There are notably few instances of verse lines distributed between two or more speakers. But the really striking thing is that none of these segmentations occurs in the second hemistich. Consider:

THÉRAMENE
Seigneur, la reine vient, et je l'ai devancée,
Elle vous cherche.

HYPPOLYTE
　　　　　Moi!

THÉRAMENE
　　　　　　　　J'ignore sa pensée ...

(THERAMENES Sir, the queen is coming, and I've arrived before her,
She is looking for you.
HYPPOLYTUS　　　　　For me!
THERAMENES　　　　　　　　I don't know what is her intention)

Even such a complex distribution of a line between two speakers as this divides the line into two exceptionally distinct hemistichs with a clear-cut caesura. "Moi!" completes the first hemistich, emphatically articulating the caesura; the second hemistich remains intact. It would appear that in the alexandrine couplet Racine cherishes balance and classical symmetry, whereas Rostand exploits, in the same versification pattern, the requiredness phenomenon, to generate a witty effect.

Caesura

Not as the iambic pentameter, the twelve-syllable line (English iambic hexameter and French alexandrine) demands, for good perceptual reasons, a rigidly fixed caesura precisely after the sixth position. The implied author of *Cyrano* is well aware of this. As Sweetser observes, "Even baking is poetic composition, as we see in Ragueneau's instructions to an apprentice baker" (II.i):

Vous avez mal placé la fente de ces miches:
Au milieu la césure, entre les hemistiches!

You misplaced the cut on these loaves;
the cesura should be in the center, between the half-lines!

Notwithstanding this, Rostand the empirical author is sometimes quite "careless" about it. In his plays caesura occurs sometimes in the middle of a word, as in

Depuis la mort du gé/néral... Du général?
or
Ah! Voici la distri/butrice!.. Oranges, lait,...

It is not enough, however, that caesura should be marked by a word boundary; classical poetics demands that it should be the boundary of a lexical word or even a phrase. In the following example from *L'Aiglon,* by contrast, it occurs after a preposition, in mid-phrase:

Je viens d'écrire pour / qu'on garde son cheval!

In the first line of the following excerpt from *Cyrano* we have a caesura right after a conjunction+preposition. The line ends with another stylistic device prohibited in classicist drama: a tense enjambment, introducing an incomplete line, which demands three syllables to complete it. This is eventually provided by another speaker:

On ne commence qu'à / deux heures. Le parterre
Est vide. Exerçons-nous / au fleuret.
                                    Pst... Flanquin...

As explained above, the versification style of Rostand's plays conspicuously differs from, for instance, Racine's classical style in several respects: a predilection for "requiredness" at the line ending; occasional "effaced" caesurae and tense enjambments. Consequently, the style of Rostand's alexandrine couplets is nearer to that of French Romantic Tragedy than that of 17th-century Classicist Tragedy.
    Caesura

Tame and Vigorous Rhyme

Let us turn now to the problem of rhyme. Sweetser comments on the first excerpt quoted above: "Individual rhymes here are meaningful in the usual ways: rhyming *lustres* ('chandeliers') with *illustres* ('illustrious') is an amusing change of register from the high-flown to the everyday concrete, as well as a play on the etymological relation between the two words". I would make three comments on this observation. First, we should make clear what it is that we have explained by "the etymological relation between the two words". That there *is* such an "etymological relation between the two words" is perfectly true; but that this enhances the rhyme's effect is rather doubtful. On the contrary, it appears to *tame* it. Rhyme is a conspicuous instance of unity-in-variety. The sound structure of its members should be as similar as possible; the meaning structure as different as possible. Its effect—both witty and emotional—crucially depends on this. (I am not speaking of modernist off-rhymes and incomplete rhymes). The etymological relation enhances the similarity of the meaning of the two members. Secondly, the change of register, by contrast, though not very salient, would enhance the opposition of meaning, if perceived at all. Actually, *lustres* ('chandeliers') need not be of a low register; after all, it is a decorative appliance, typically hung from the ceiling of some large, imposing building. Thirdly, the words *lustres* and *illustres* are opposed as parts of speech (noun vs. adjective), reinforcing the dissimilarity of meaning, *in spite of* the etymological relation.

I have taken the distinction between verse that rhymes similar and different parts of speech from W. K. Wimsatt. In his paper "One Relationship between Rhyme and Reason" (1964) he points out the difference between Chaucer's rhymes and Pope's. Chaucer's are "tame" rhymes, in which the same parts of speech are used in closely parallel functions. Not so Pope's, who achieves his witty effects, among other means, by rhyming, e.g., nouns with verbs, verbs with adverbs, in different syntactic positions. Such rhymes are perceived as *vigorous*. "We may say that the greater the difference in meaning between rhyme and words the more marked and more appropriate will the binding effect be" (Wimsatt, 1964: 168), or, as Wordsworth would put it, rhyme involves the pleasure of the discovery of similitude in dissimiltude. Roman Jakobson (1956: 82)[2] mentions Wimsatt's distinction between "tame" and "vigorous" rhymes and calls them "grammatical" and "anti-grammatical" rhymes. I have discussed this distinction at some length in Chapter 9, pointing up, in particular, the contrast between meaning components.

Verlaine's notorious attack on rhyme may illuminate certain aspects of the issue:

Prends l'éloquence et tords-lui son cou!
Tu feras bien, en train d'énergie,
De rendre un peu la Rime assagie.
Si l'on n'y veille, elle ira jusqu'où?

Take eloquence and wring its neck! / You will do well while you are about it / to render rhyme a little calmer. If one does not watch, till where will it go?

The phrase "elle ira jusqu'où?" suggests excessive length. If you do not watch, the parallel strings of sound will extend to monstrous lengths. However, the words "cou" and "jusqu'où" share no more than two speech sounds. Still, annotators usually make comments to the effect that this is an example of an acrobatic and funny rhyme. This effect is achieved by opposing the noun *cou* with *jusqu'où*. composed

---

2   "Anti-grammatical rhymes" are rhymes that oppose words belonging to different parts of speech, as *sober~October* in Poe's "Ulalume", or even sets of morphemes that belong to different parts of speech, such as Pope's in *endless error* **hurl'd~and** *riddle of the* **world**.

of a preposition and an adverb of place. The former is a unitary word, the latter derives its two speech sounds from two different words. So, the noun *cou* is opposed to two different words, that belong to different parts of speech.

Now let us take a similar but more elaborate case discussed by Sweetser:

> In the following passage from *Cyrano* IV. iii, Cyrano's Gascon regiment is at war, and starving because they are surrounded and their supplies cut off. Cyrano has a musician play a traditional Gascon folk tune on his fife, to distract them from their hunger; they become dreamily homesick instead, for a moment. The Captain fears that Cyrano is making the cadets 'soft' with this sentimental reverie.

> *Carbon*: Tu vas les affaiblir en les attendrissant!
> *(You'll weaken them by softening them too much!)*
> *Cyrano*:Laisse donc, les héros qu'ils portent dans le sang
> Sont vite réveillés! Il suffit ...
> *(Don't worry, the heroism in their blood*
> *is speedily awakened! All it takes...)*
> *[He gestures, a drum rolls, and the cadets leap to their feet,*
> *arms in hand.]*
> *Les cadets*:   Hein!...Quoi?...**Qu'est-ce**?
> *(Huh...What?...**What is it** ?)*
> *Cyrano*: Tu vois, il a suffi d'un roulement de **caisse**!
> Adieu, rêves, regrets, vieille province, am**our** ...
> Ce qui du fifre vient s'en va par le tamb**our**!
> *(You see, all it took was one **drum** roll!*
> *Farewell, dreams, regrets, old home province, and **love** ...*
> *The effects of the fife are chased off by the **drum**!)*

The pair of lines rhyming in *qu'est-ce / caisse* are of course parts of a single statement about the ease of bringing the cadets to attention—and the two rhyming words are closely linked in the meaning frame as well as in sound, since the drum (*caisse*) is what makes the sound which instantly brings a homonymous watch response ('What is it?') from the cadets. Similarly, the *amour / tambour* couplet is all about the contrast between sentiment (evoked by the fife) and soldierly courage (evoked by *tambour*, another word for drum); not only does the couplet encapsulate a complete aphorism on this subject, but the rhyme words come from the two contrasting models—the emotional state involved in one frame, and the musical instrument evoking the other. [...]. The presence of Cyrano's *is speedily awakened! All it takes* in the same line with the cadets' *What is it?* is a particularly graphic demonstration of Cyrano's point—indeed, a better completion of his meaning than he could have made by speaking himself.[3]

Rhyme and alliteration and meter all also make specific formal connections between smaller units: the rhyming or alliterating words, or the metrical half-lines, for example.

I've added Carbon's line to Sweetser's excerpt. In this passage we can, again, see most consistently Sweetser's and my contrasting approaches. We both feel that rhyme is particularly significant in this passage. Here, again, Sweetser looks for the key to this significance in the content. I claim, by contrast, that one of the advantages of Cognitive Poetics is that it provides tools to describe rhyme in a way that may account systematically for its perceptual qualities as directly experienced rather than as an appendage to contents.

Consider Sweetser's following observation: "The pair of lines rhyming in *qu'est-ce / caisse* are, of course, parts of a single statement about the ease of bringing the cadets to attention—and the two rhyming words are closely linked in the meaning frame as well as in sound, since the drum (*caisse*) is what makes the sound which instantly brings a homonymous watch response ('What is it?') from the cadets".[4] Whatever the topic of the utterance, such a virtuoso rhyme will always draw attention to it. Consequently, claiming that "the two rhyming words are closely linked in the meaning frame" is somewhat of a tautology. It merely translates a statement about contents into rhyme-language

Actually, a poet like John Donne must make special manipulations to prevent alliteration, for instance, from connecting meanings (see Chatman, 1956; Tsur, 1998: 49–53). This holds true, with the necessary changes, of the *amour / tambour* couplet as well. The antithesis between a "dreamily homesick" mood and a heroic, soldierly attitude rests in the contents of the couplet, and any pair of rhyme words taken from the description of the respective moods will be "all about the contrast between sentiment and soldierly courage". This would, in fact, be the default arrangement. A remarkable achievement would be if the contrast of moods and the contrast of rhyme words were arranged in counterpoint.

The phrase "homonymous watch response" is, again, an accurate description. But what is its significance? Sweetser drops in the word "homonymous", but does not elucidate its relevance. Her theoretical framework is focused on contents, not on verbal structure. The present theoretical framework is, again, tailor-made for it. Homonymity increases the phonetic similarity of the rhyme words; whereas the first member of the rhyme contrasts not one, but three words to the noun in the second

---

[3] Sweetser makes here an excellent point: the abrupt interruption of the verse line and of Cyrano's fluent speech by the cadets' disjunct interjections is directly experienced as an immediate iconic representation of the disruption of the cadets' "dreamily homesick" mood.

[4] The assertion that "the pair of lines are of course parts of a single statement" must be understood in a very special sense, since formally they are parts of different statements.

member. At the same time, the sequence "Hein!...Quoi?...**Qu'est-ce**?" forces the line to reassert itself by resisting segmentation—achieving considerable articulateness near the line ending, and generating effective requiredness. We have seen Verlaine's rhyme "cou ~ jusqu'où". Its first member is wholly included in the second; and the two rhyming sounds are derived in the second member from two different words. This was said to be "acrobatic" and "funny". In the present instance, the homonymous rhyme consists of four shared speech sounds, which in the first member of the rhyme are derived from three (!) different words, sharpening its witty effect. The rhyme "attendrissant ~ sang" is vigorous, but far from the vigour of the "qu'est-ce ~ caisse" rhyme pair. It rhymes different parts of speech, a present participle verb with a noun. The rhyming syllables are homonymous; but neither of them contain speech sounds derived from more than one word.

We have already encountered (but not discussed) a similar instance: "Jodelet ~ lait". Here, too, the second member of the rhyme is wholly included in the first one; and the two nouns are contrasted at lower levels: [±COMMON NOUN, ±ANIMATE, ±HUMAN]. In the "amour ~ tambour" rhyme both members are nouns, but are contrasted at a lower level: [±CONCRETE]. Or take another instance which we have already encountered:

> *The pickpocket*: La dentelle surtout des canons, coup**ez-la**!
> *A spectato*r:Tenez, à la première du *Cid* , j'ét**ais là**!

We have discussed Sweetser's observations on its versification. As to the rhyme itself, Sweetser merely foregrounds it by typography, without comments. Again, it neatly falls into our model. Both members of this rhyme are composite. The second word in them is the pair of homonyms "la" and "là" respectively, contrasting a pronoun with an adverb of place. The first word in each member is a verb; but the vowel that is part of the rhyme is contributed by different morphemes. Thus, the method proposed here can account not only for the perceptual effect—vigorous or tame—of rhymes, but also for its *relative* force.

Organizing Effect and Immediate Appeal

Sweetser points out in the last act of the play, when Cyrano is about to die, instances of what she calls "intertextuality". Here again she treats rhyme as an index to contents. I do not deny that in certain cases repeated rhyme pairs may juxtapose, so to speak, two passages far apart in the play, generating some ironic view, as in

> ROXANE L'âme, c'était la vôtre!
> CYRANO   Je ne vous aimais pas.
> ROXANE Vous m'aimiez!
> CYRANO, se débattant   C'était l'autre!
> ROXANE Vous m'aimiez!

CYRANO, d'une voix qui faiblit Non !
ROXANE Déjà vous le dites plus bas!

> This *bas-pas* rhyme echoes the final couplet of II. viii, where Le Bret is
> responding to Cyrano's *non, merci!*tirade against the world. The audience
> knows, though Le Bret does not, that Cyrano's intended love declaration to
> Roxane has just been thwarted by her revelation that she is in love with
> Christian. Eventually realizing that Cyrano's sudden extreme bitterness is
> really personal, despite his philosophical justifications, Le Bret says:

> Fais tout haut l'orgueilleux et l'amer, mais, tout **bas**,
> Dis-moi tout simplement qu'elle ne t'aime **pas**!
> *(Out loud [publicly], act the proud cynic – but **quietly** [in confidence],*
> *Just tell me she does **not** love you.)* (II.viii)

> In Act V it is Cyrano and Roxane, using the same rhyming forms, who
> renegotiate the relationship between low-voiced privacy and denial of love.

I am not suggesting that something is wrong with the investigation of the
organizing effect of rhyme, but that if you start straightaway with this effect, you
miss very much, most notably the immediate appeal of the rhymes. There are some
indications in Sweetser's paper that she did have strong intuitions regarding this
immediate appeal. But "blending theory" fails to account for the rhymes' verbal
structure or perceived effect, and directs attention away from the verbal structures to
the contents. This led Sweetser to a brilliant comprehensive interpretation of the
play, relating versification patterns to relatively large chunks of contents. In some of
my recent publications I introduced the notion of "relative fine-grainedness" in
critical discourse. Sweetser's discussion makes important observations on the play's
structure. The critical tools introduced here allow the critic to fill it in with reference
to more fine-grained texture. This is one of the great achievements of Cognitive
Poetics as I conceive of it.

   In her comment on the special issue of *Language and Literature* (on blending) in
which Sweetser's article was published, Margaret Freeman makes a point that may
illuminate my foregoing argument in a wider perspective:

> As Reuven Tsur (1992, 2003) has cogently argued, blending as defined by
> Fauconnier and Turner is not the whole story in literary production. In fact,
> he makes a case for the disruption of the forces that blending purportedly
> exists to achieve. Cognitive stability and economy, clear-cut categorization,
> and human-scale reasoning are, he claims, precisely those aspects that
> poetic devices are designed to unsettle, blur or delay. (Freeman, 2006: 111)

Theoretical Conclusion

Sweetser is working within a dichotomic conception based on form and content: "as Hiraga (2005) shows so clearly, blending theory lets us unpack the form–meaning relationships built up by rhyme and meter, giving us a language in which to start talking about poetic units and how they build meaning. This in turn opens the door for unpacking Rostand's particular uses of interaction between dialogue and poetic form". The present chapter points out different "particular uses of interaction between dialogue and poetic form".

I am working within a theoretical framework that proposes to do away with the form–content distinction:

> Things become even more disastrous for the traditional concepts when we realize that even in the language, commonly considered part of the form, it is necessary to distinguish between words in themselves, aesthetically indifferent, and the manner in which individual words make up units of sound and meaning, aestbetically effective. It would be better to rechristen all the aesthetically indifferent elements "materials," while the manner in which they acquire aesthetic efficacy may be called structure. This distinction is by no means a simple renaming of the old pair, content and form. It cuts right across the old boundary lines. "Materials" include elements formerly considered part of the content, and parts formerly considered formal. "Structure" is a concept including both content and form so far as they are organized for aesthetic purposes. The work of art is, then, considered as a whole system of signs, or structure of signs, serving a specific aesthetic purpose. (Wellek and Warren, 1956: 129)

Sweetser, or Hiraga for that matter, need the form–content dichotomy, because it enables them to talk about "iconicity", that is, to point out that one dimension of the text is similar in some respect to another. I prefer the Wellek and Warren distinction, because it allows for greater flexibility, and makes it possible to account for the emergence of a wide variety of perceptual qualities in a poetic text.

Contents, "projected world", word meanings, phonetic structure, metaphor, meter, rhyme, alliteration, are all materials (Wellek and Warren call them "norms"). Structures are the various combinations of these norms. Poetic effects arise from the subtle interaction of a great variety of norms. Configurations involving stressed syllables in weak positions, alliterative patterns occurring in consecutive syllables, run-on lines, the grouping of lines into asymmetrical or unpredictable structures, e.g. by rhyme, and abstract nouns in a landscape defined here and now, yield an exceptionally weak gestalt with an exceptionally strong emotional quality (such configurations are typical of Milton and Shelley, said to be the most musical poets in the English language). Configurations involving stressed syllables that occur only in strong positions and in all strong positions, alliterative patterns involving strong positions only (with one or more intervening positions), end-stopped lines, the grouping of lines into symmetrical, predictable structures, and objects with stable characteristic visual shapes in the world stratum of the poem yield an exceptionally strong gestalt, sometimes with an exceptionally strong witty quality. "Hypnotic" poetry typically involves exceptionally regular meter–stress mappings, alliterations of both kinds mentioned above, end-stopped lines, but unpredictable groupings of lines; and so forth. I usually treat these configurations under the heading of convergent and divergent poetry (cf. Chapter 4, and Chapters 19–20). Anti-grammatical rhymes typically generate a vigorous witty quality in a convergent context, and a vigorous emotional quality in a divergent or hypnotic context (in other words, they typically reinforce, even amplify, the gestalt qualities of the **whole**). Futhermore, the various configurations need not necessarily comprise homogeneous elements: in some poems, convergent elements serve to prevent a highly divergent poem from disintegrating. This may account for the observation that Milton's and Shelley's highly divergent poetry is typically perceived as musical and emotional, whereas Donne's more divergent poetry is typically perceived as harsh and witty.

This is not "iconicity", but "emergent gestalt qualities". "Iconicity" allows the critic to handle only those instances in which the similarity between form and content exists, or else compels him to read the similarity into them. According to the Wellek and Warren model a wide range of elements (which are independent variables) may occur in any combination, and thus it may serve to describe any unforeseen combination of elements in a poem. Any combination will display *some* gestalt quality which a poem may utilize or fail to utilize for aesthetic purposes; and gestalt theory may systematically account for the relationship between poetic structure and perceived qualities regularly attributed to them.

Finally, a sympathetic reader of the manuscript of this chapter asked a provocative question that gives me the opportunity to end on a more general note.

> What is your ultimate goal? Based on results, Sweetser's goal seems to be to produce a "good" interpretation or understanding of the play. Yours remains implicit, and maybe should be made explicit. I have always secretly thought of your work (of, for example, highlighting subtle prosodic effects) as ultimately providing better tools that can be applied, at the end of the day, to interpreting texts in a richer, more comprehensive way. Am I completely wrong?

In my answer I pointed out two ultimate goals. Sweetser and I share, I suppose, both these goals. First, much human research is directed to a better understanding of the world we live in, for its own sake. Just as we want to know how did our universe evolve from the Big Bang, for instance, or how did life emerge from inorganic matter, we also want to know how aesthetic qualities emerge from an aesthetically indifferent string of words. Secondly, a major goal of all aesthetic theory and criticism is to make a crucial recommendation as to what to look for in an aesthetic object, and how to look at it (cf. Weitz, 1962). Interpretation is one kind of activity toward this goal; my research on versification is another.

References

Ackerman, J. K. (1957) "A Theory of Style", in M. C. Beardsley and N. M. Schueller (eds.), *Aesthetic Inquiry.* Belmont, Ca. 54–66.

Addison, Joseph (1951 [1711–12[1]] from "Spectator Papers", in James Harry Smith & Edd Winfield Parks (eds.), *The Great Critics.* New York: Norton. 819–825.

Alcock, Theodora (1963) *The Rorschach in Practice.* London: Tavistock Publications.

Anders, Günther (1965) "Being without Time: On Beckett's Play *Waiting for Godot"*, in Martin Esslin (ed.), *Samuel Beckett.* Englewood Cliffs, N.J.: Prentice Hall (Twentieth Century Views). 140–151.

Aristotle (1951) *Poetics.* S.H. Butcher (trans.), in James Harry Smith & Edd Winfield Parks (eds.), *The Great Critics.* New York: Norton. 28–61.

Arnheim, Rudolf (1957) *Art and Visual Perception.* London: Faber & Faber.

Arnheim, Rudolf (1967) *Toward a Psychology of Art.* London: Faber & Faber.

Arnold, Magda B. (1968) *The Nature of Emotion.* Harmondsworth: Penguin.

Arnold, Magda B. and J. A. Gasson (1968 [1954[1]]) "Feelings and Emotions as Dynamic Factors in Personality Integration", in M. B. Arnold (ed.), *The Nature of Emotion.* Harmondsworth: Penguin. 203–221.

Bakhtin, M. M. (1968) *Rabelais and his World* (trans. Helene Iswolsky). Cambridge, Mass.: MIT Press.

Barzel, Hillel (1972) *Agnon and Kafka—A Comparative Study.* Ramat Gan: Bar-Uryan (in Hebrew).

Bartlett, Frederick C. (1932) *Remembering.* Cambridge: Cambridge UP.

Bate, Walter Jackson (1964) "Negative Capability", in Walter Jackson Bate (ed.), *Keats.* Englewood Cliffs N.J.: Prentice-Hall. 51–68.

Beardsley, Monroe C. (1958) *Aesthetics: Problems in the Philosophy of Criticism.* New York & Burlingame: Harcourt, Brace & World.

Beardsley, Monroe C. (1966) *Aesthetics from Classical Greece to the Present.* New York and London: MacMillan.

Ben-Porat, Ziva (1976) "The Poetics of Literary Allusion". *PTL 1:* 103–128.

Berek, Peter (1978) "Interpretation, Allegory and Allegoresis". *College English, 40:* 117–132.

Bialik, Hayim Nahman (1954) "Veiling and Revealing in Language", in *Essays in Criticism.* Tel Aviv: Dvir. 24–31 (in Hebrew).

Bierwisch, Manfred (1970) "Poetics and Linguistics", in Donald C. Freeman (ed.), *Linguistics and Literary Style.* New York: Holt, Rinehart & Winston. 97–115.

Blake, Robert R. and Glenn V. Ramsey (eds.) (1951) *Perception—An Approach to Personality.* New York: Ronald Press.

Bodkin, Maud (1963 [1934[1]]) *Archetypal Patterns in Poetry.* London: Oxford UP.

Booth, Wayne C. (1961) *The Rhetoric of Fiction.* Chicago: Chicago UP.

Bowra, Sir Maurice (1961) *The Romantic Imagination.* London: Oxford UP.

Bradburn, Beth "Interview with Reuven Tsur". *Literature, Cognition & the Brain.* Online: http://www2.bc.edu/~richarad/lcb/fea/tsurin/tsurmain.html

Brooke-Rose, Christine (1958) *A Grammar of Metaphor.* London: Secker & Warburg.

Brooks, Cleanth (1968) *The Well-Wrought Urn.* London: Methuen.

Brooks, Cleanth and Robert B. Heilman (1966) *Understanding Drama.* New York: Holt, Rinehart & Winston.

Brooks, C. and Warren, R.P. (1958) *Modern Rhetoric.* New York.

Brown, Roger (1968) *Words and Things.* New York: The Free Press.

Brown, Roger (1970) "The 'Tip of the Tongue' Phenomenon", in *Psycholinguistics: Selected Papers.* New York: The Free Press. 274–303.

Bruner, Jerome S. (1951) "Personality Dynamics and Perceiving", in Blake, Robert R. and Glenn V. Ramsey (eds.), *Perception—An Approach to Personality.* New York: Ronald Press. 121–147.

Bruner, Jerome S. (1968 [1964[1]]) "The Course of Cognitive Growth", in P. C. Wason and P. Johnson-Laird (eds.), *Thinking and Reasoning.* Harmondsworth: Penguin. 380–409.

Bruner, Jerome S. (1973) *Beyond the Information Given—Studies in the Psychology of Knowing.* New York and London: W. W. Norton.

Bruner, Jerome S. and David Kretch (eds.) (1968[2]) *Perception and Personality.* New York: Greenwood Press.

Burke, Kenneth (1957) *The Philosophy of Literary Form*, New York: Vintage.

Burke, K. 1957. "Freud—and the Analysis of Poetry", in *The Philosophy of Literary Form.* New York: Vintage. 221–250.

Burke, Kenneth (1962) *A Grammar of Motives* and *A Rhetoric of Motives* (in one volume). Cleveland & New York: Meridian Books.

Burnshaw, Stanley (ed.), *The Poem Itself.* Harmondsworth: Pelican.

Chadwick, Charles (1971) *Symbolism.* London: Methuen.

Chatman, Seymour (1960) "Comparing Metrical Styles", in Thomas Sebeok (ed.), *Style in Language.* Cambridge, Mass.: MIT. 149–172.

Chatman, Seymour (1965) *A Theory of Meter.* The Hague: Mouton.

Chatman, Seymour (ed.), (1971) *Literary Style: A Symposium.* London: Oxford UP.

Clark, Herbert H. & Eve V. Clark (1977) *Psychology and Language: An Introduction to Psycholinguistics.* New York: Harcourt, Brace & Jovanovich.

Clark, Herbert H. (1970) "Word Associations and Linguistic Theory", in John Lyons (ed.), *New Horizons in Linguistics.* Harmondsworth: Pelican. 271–286.

Cocteau, Jean (1955 [1922[1]]) from "Le Secret Professionnel", in Wallace Fowlie (ed. and trans.), *Mid-Century French Poets.* New York: Grove Press. 121.

Cohen, Jonathan L. (1979) "The Semantics of Metaphor", in Andrew Ortony (ed.), *Metaphor and Thought.* Cambridge: Cambridge UP. 64–78.

Coleridge, Samuel Taylor (1951) Biographia Literaria. In Donald A. Stauffer (ed.) *Selected Poetry and Prose.* New York: The Modern Library, 109–428.

Collins, A. M. and Quillian, M. R. (1969) "Retrieval Time from Semantic Memory". *Journal of Verbal Learning and Verbal Behavior.* 8: 240–247.

Conrad, R. (1964) "Acoustic Confusions in Immediate Memory". *BJPsych 55:* 75–84.

Cooper, C. W. and L. B. Meyer (1960) *The Rhythmic Structure of Music.* Chicago: Chicago UP.

Cooper, William E. and John Robert Ross (1975) "Word Order", in Grossman, Robin E., L. James San and Timothy J. Vance (eds.), *Papers from the Parasession on Functionalism.* Chicago: Chicago Linguistic Society. 63–111.

Culler, Jonathan (1975) *Structuralist Poetics.* London: Routledge & Kegan Paul.

Cumming, Robert (1961) "Literature of Extreme Situations", in M. Philipson (ed.), *Aesthetics Today.* Cleveland: Meridian. 377–412.

Curtius, Ernst Robert (1973) *European Literature and the Latin Middle Ages,* Willard R. Trask (trans.), Princeton: Princeton UP.

Cytowic, Richard E. (2003) *The Man Who Tasted Shapes.* Cambridge, Mass.: The MIT Press.

D'Andrade, Roy Godwin (1980) "The Cultural Part of Cognition", Address Given to the 2nd Annual Cognitive Science Conference, New Haven.

Daiches, David (1968) *A Critical History of English Literature.* London: Secker and Warburg.

Darwin, C. I. and A. Donovan (1979) "Perceptual Studies of Speech: Isochrony and Intonation". Paper presented at the Conference on Language Generation and Understanding, Bonas (Gers).

Darwin, C. I. and A. Donovan "Perceptual Isochrony" (demo tape).

Dascal, M. (1983) *Pragmatics and the Philosophy of Mind I: Thought in Language.* Amsterdam/Philadelphia: John Benjamin.

Dascal, M. (2004) "Language as a cognitive technology". In B. Gorayska and J.L. Mey (eds), *Cognition and Technology.* Amsterdam: John Benjamins, 37–62.

Donovan A. and C. I. Darwin (1979) "The Perceived Rhythm of Speech". Paper presented at the IXth International Congress of Phonetic Sciences, Copenhagen.

Davie, Donald (1960) "Syntax and Music in *Paradise Lost*", in Frank Kermode (ed.), *The Living Milton: Essays by various Hands*. London: Routledge and Kegan Paul. 70–84.

Dombi, Erzsébet (1974) "Synaesthesia and Poetry". *Poetics 11:* 23–44.

Duffy, Elizabeth (1968 [1941[1]]) "An Explanation of Emotional Phenomena without the Use of the Concept Emotion", in M. B. Arnold (ed.), *The Nature of Emotion*. Harmondsworth: Penguin. 129–140.

Eco, Umberto (1976) *A Theory of Semiotics*. Bloomington: Indiana UP.

Ehrenzweig, Anton (1965) *The Psychoanalysis of Artistic Vision and Hearing*. New York: Braziller.

Ehrenzweig, Anton (1970) *The Hidden Order of Art*. London: Paladin.

Empson, William (1968) "Rhythm and Imagery in English Poetry", in Harold Osborne (ed.) *Aesthetics in the Modern World*. London: Thames and Hudson. 340–361.

Erhardt-Siebolt, Erica von (1932) "Harmony of the Senses in English, German and French Romanticism". *PMLA 47:* 577–592.

Erlich, Victor (1965) *Russian Formalism* (2nd., revised ed.). Hague: Mouton.

Esslin, Martin (1965) (ed.), *Samuel Beckett*. Englewood Cliffs, N.J.: Prentice-Hall (Twentieth Century Views).

Ferenczi, Sándor (1925) "Stages in the Development of the Sense of Reality", in I. S. van Teslaar (ed.), *An Outline of Psychoanalysis*. New York: Modern Library.

Fergusson, Francis (1955) *The Idea of a Theater*. Garden City, N.Y.: Doubleday.

Fillmore, Charles J. (1971) "Types of Lexical Information", in Danny D. Steinberg and Leon A. Jakobovits (eds.), *Semantics*. Cambridge: Cambridge UP. 370–392.

Fodor, J., A. and T. Bever (1965) "The Psychologicl Reality of Linguistic Segments". *Journal of Verbal Learning and Verbal Behavioor 4:* 414–420.

Fodor, Janet Dean (1980) *Semantics: Theories of Meaning in Generative Grammar*. Cambridge, Mass.: Harvard UP.

Fodor, Jerry A. (1979) *The Language of Thought*. Cambridge, Mass.: Harvard UP.

Fogle, Richard H. (1964). "Synaesthetic Imagery in Keats", in Walter Jackson Bate (ed.), *Keats*. Englewood Cliffs, N.J.: Prentice-Hall. 41–50.

Fónagy, Iván (1961) "Communication in Poetry". *Word 17:* 194–218.

Fónagy, Iván (1971) "The Functions of Vocal Style", in Seymour Chatman (ed.), *Literary Style: A Symposium*. London: Oxford UP. 159–176.

Fontana Dictionary of Modern Thought, The

Forster, E. M. (1962) *Aspects of the Novel*. Penguin: Harmondsworth.

Fowler, Roger (1966) "'Prose Rhythm' and Metre", in Roger Fowler (ed.), *Essays on Style and Language*. London: Routledge and Kegan Paul. 82–99.

Fowler, Roger (1971) *The Languages of Literature*. London: Routledge and Kegan Paul.

Fraisse (1969) "Why is Naming Longer than Reading?". *Acta Philologica 30:* 96–103.

Freeman, Donald C. 1969. "Metrical Position Constituency and Generative Metrics". *Language and Style:*2: 195–206.

Freeman, Margaret H, (2006) "Blending: A Response" *Language and Literature* **15**(1): 107–117.
  Available Online: http://lal.sagepub.com/cgi/reprint/15/1/107.pdf

Frenkel-Brunswick, Else (1968 [1948[1]]) "Intolerance of Ambiguity as an Emotional and Perceptual Variable" in J. S. Bruner and D. Kretch (eds.), *Perception and Personality.* New York: Greenwood Press.

Fromkin, Victoria A. (1973). "Slips of the Tongue". In: *Scientific American* 229, No 6. 110–17.

Fry, D. B. (1958) "Experiments in the Perception of Speech". *Language and Speech 1:* 126–151.

Fry, D. B. (1970) "Speech Reception and Perception", in Lyons, John (ed.), *New Horizons in Linguistics.* Harmondsworth: Pelican. 29–52.

Frye, Northrop (1968) *Anatomy of Criticism.* New York: Atheneum.

Gardner, Helen (1972) "Introduction", in *The Metaphysical Poets.* Harmondsworth: Penguin. 15–28.

Gardner, Howard (1982) *Art, Mind, & Brain.* New York: Basic Books.

Gardner, Howard and Ellen Winner (1979) "The Development of Metaphoric Competence: Implications for Humanistic Disciplines", in Sheldon Sachs (ed.), *On Metaphor.* Chicago: Chicago UP. 121–139.

Garrett, M., T. Bever and J. A. Fodor (1966) "The Active Use of Grammar in Speech Perception". *Perception and Psychophysics 1:* 30–32.

Gavins, Joanna and Gerard Steen (eds.) (2003) *Cognitive Poetics in Practice.* London: Routledge.

Gibbs, R.W. 1993. "Process and Products in Making Sense of Tropes". In A. Ortony (ed) *Thought and Metaphor,* 2nd ed. Cambridge: Cambridge UP. 252–276.

Gibbs, R. 1997. "Conceptual Metaphors Underlying Conventional and Poetic Language", paper presented at the "Cognitive Theories of Intertextuality" research workshop at the Porter Institute for Poetics and Semiotics, Tel Aviv University: December 30, 1997 – January 1, 1998.

Gillies, Alexander (1957) *Goethe's Faust: An Interpretation.* Oxford: Blackwell.

Giora, R. (1997). Understanding figurative and literal language: The graded salience hypothesis. *Cognitive Linguistics*, 7, 183–206.

Glicksohn, J., R. Tsur and Ch. Goodblatt (1991) "Absorption and Trance-Inducing Poetry". *Empirical Studies of the Arts 9/2:* 115–122.

Goldstein, K. and M. Scheerer (1941) "Abstract and Concrete Behavior". *Psychological Monographs 53, 2:* 1–10.

Gombrich, E. H. (1963) "Visual Metaphors of Value in Art", in *Meditations on a Hobby Horse—And Other Essays on the Theory of Art.* London: Phaidon.

Gombrich, E. H. (1966) *Norm and Form*. London: Phaidon.

Gombrich, E. H. (1969 [1965¹]) "The Use of Art for the Study of Symbols", in James Hogg (ed.), *Psychology and the Visual Arts*. Harmondsworth: Penguin. 149–170.

Gombrich, E. H. (l984). *The Sense of Order: A Study in the Psychology of Decorative Art*. Oxford: Phaidon.

Goodblatt, C. & J. Glicksohn (1986) "Cognitive Psychology and Whitman's 'Song of Myself'". *Mosaic 14:* 83–90.

Goodblatt, C. (1990) "Whitman's Catalogs as Literary Gestalts: Illustrative and Meditative Functions". *Style 24:* 45–58.

Grierson, Herbert J. C. (1965 [1921¹]) "Introduction" to *Metaphysical Lyrics & Poems of the Seventeenth Century*. Oxford: The Clarendon Press. xiii–lviii.

Guilford, J. P. (1970 [1959¹]) "Traits of Creativity", in P. E. Vernon (ed.), *Creativity*. Harmondsworth: Penguin. 167–188.

Halkin, Simon (1984) *Trends and Forms in Modern Hebrew Literature*. Jerusalem: Bialik Institute (in Hebrew).

Halle, Morris and Samuel Jay Keyser 1966. "Chaucer and the Study of Prosody". *College English* 28: 187–219.

Halle, Morris and Samuel Jay Keyser (1971) *English Stress: Its Growth and Its Role in Verse*. New York: Harper and Row.

Halliday, M. A. K. (1970) "Language structure and language function". In John Lyons (ed,), *New Horizons in Linguistics*. Harmondsworth: Penguin Books. 140–165.

Hamilton, Craig A. (2005) Review of Peter Stockwell: *Cognitive Poetics: An Introduction*. *Cognitive Linguistics* 16–4: 743–747.

Harvey, O. J. (1970). "Conceptual Systems and Attitude Change", in Peter B. Warr (ed.), *Thought and Personality*. Harmondsworth: Penguin. 315–333.

Hasenfus, Nancy, Colin Martindale, and Dana Birnbaum (1983) "Psychological Reality of Cross-Media Artistic Styles". *Journal of Experimental Psychology: Human Perception and Performance 9:* 841–863.

Hepburn, R.W. (1968) "Emotions and Emotional Qualities: Some Attempts at Analysis", in Harold Osborne (ed.), *Aesthetics in the Modern World*. London: Thames and Hudson. 81–93.

Herrnstein-Smith, Barbara (1968) *Poetic Closure*. Chicago: Chicago UP.

Hirsch, E. D. (1972) "Three Dimensions of Hermeneutics", in *New Literary History, III. 2:* 245–263.

Hofstadter, Douglas R. (1981) *Gödel, Escher. Bach: An Eternal Golden Braid—A Metaphorical Fugue on Minds and Machines in the Spirit of Lewis Carrol*. Harmondsworth: Penguin.

House, Humphrey (1973 [1953¹]) "'Kubla Khan' and 'Christabel'", in Alun R. Jones and William Tydeman (eds.), *Coleridge: **The Ancient Mariner** and Other Poems—A Casebook*. London: Macmillan. 200–216.

Hrushovski, Benjamin (1968) "Do Sounds Have Meaning? The Problem of Expressiveness of Sound-Patterns in Poetry". *HaSifrut 1:* 410–420 (in Hebrew). English Summary: 444.

Hrushovski, Benjamin (1980) "The Meaning of Sound Patterns in Poetry: An Interaction View". *Poetics Today 2:* 39–56.

Hyman, Stanley Edgar (1955) *The Armed Vision.* New York: Vintage Books.

Jakobson, Roman (1956) "Two Aspects of Language and Two Types of Aphasic Disturbances", in Roman Jakobson & Morris Halle, *Fundamentals of Language.* The Hague: Mouton. 55–82.

Jakobson, Roman (1960) "Closing Statement: Linguistics and Poetics", in Thomas A. Sebeok (ed.), *Style in Language.* Cambridge, Mass.: MIT. 350–377.

Jakobson, Roman (1968) *Child Language, Aphasia, and Phonological Universals.* The Hague: Mouton.

Jakobson, Roman and Linda R. Waugh (1979) *The Sound Shape of Language.* Bloomington: Indiana UP.

Jensen, A. R. and W. D. Rohwer (1966) "The Stroop Color–Word Test: A Review". *Acta Philologica 25:* 36–93.

Johnson, Samuel (1951 [1779[1]] from "Abraham Cowley", in James Harry Smith & Edd Winfield Parks (eds.), *The Great Critics.* New York: Norton. 460–462.

Johnson-Laird, P. N. (1970) "The Perception and Memory for Sentences", in John Lyons (ed.), *New Horizons in Linguistics.* Harmondsworth: Pelican. 261–270.

Jones, John A. (1969) *Pope's Couplet Art.* Athens: Ohio UP.

Kafka, Franz (1957 [1930[1]]) *The Castle.* (trans.), Willa and Edwin Muir. Harmondsworth: Penguin.

Kant, Immanuel (1969) *Critique of Judgement* (trans.), G. H. Bernard. London: Hafner Press.

Kaufman, Gordon G. (1972) *God the Problem.* Cambridge, Mass.: Harvard UP.

Keats, John (1956) *The Selected Letters of John Keats,* Lionel Trilling (ed.). Garden City, N.Y.: Doubleday Anchor.

Keyser, Samuel J. and Alan Prince (1979) "Folk Etymology in Sigmund Freud, Christian Morgenstern, and Wallace Stevens". *Critical Inquiry:* 65–78.

Kinsbourne, M. (1982) "Hemispheric Specialization and the Growth of Human Understanding". *American Psychologist 37,* 411–420.

Klein, George S. (1951) "The Personal World through Perception", in R. R. Blake and G.V. Ramsey (eds.), *Perception—An Approach to Personality.* New York: Ronald Press. 328–355.

Knight, Wilson G. (1965) *The Imperial Theme.* London: Methuen.

Knights, L. C. (1964 [1928[1]]) "Notes on Comedy", in E. Bentley (ed.), *The Importance of Scrutiny.* New York: New York UP. 227–237.

Knowles, Gerry 1991. "Prosodic Labelling: The Problem of Tone Group Boundaries", in Stig Johannson and Anna-Brita Stenström (eds.), *English*

Computer Corpora. Selected Papers and Research Guide. Topics in English Linguistics vol. 3. Berlin: Mouton de Gruyter. 149–163.

Knowles, Gerry 1992. "Pitch Contours and Tones in the Lancaster/IBM Spoken English Corpus", in Gerhard Leitner (ed.), *New Directions in English Language Corpora—Methodology, Results, Software Developments.* Berlin: Mouton de Gruyter. 289–299.

Konrad, Hedvig (1958) *Étude sur la Métaphore.* Paris: Vrin.

Köhler, Wolfgang (1972) *The Task of Gestalt Psychology.* Princeton: Princeton UP.

Kreitler, Hans & Shulamit Kreitler (1972) *Psychology of the Arts.* Durham N.C.: Duke UP.

Kris, Ernst (1965) *Psychoanalytic Explorations in Art.* New York: Schocken.

Kris, Ernst, and E. H. Gombrich (1965) "The Principles of Caricature", in Ernst Kris, *Psychoanalytic Explorations in Art.* New York: Schocken.

Kris, Ernst and Abraham Kaplan, (1965) "Aesthetic Ambiguity", in Ernst Kris, *Psychoanalytic Explorations in Art.* New York: Schocken.

Krueger, F. (1968 [1928[1]]) "The Essence of Feeling", in Magda B. Arnold (ed.), *The Nature of Emotion.* Harmondsworth: Penguin. 97–108.

Lake, Beryl (1967) "A Study of the Irrefutability of Two Aesthetic Theories", in William Elton (ed.), *Aesthetics and Language.* London: Oxford UP. 100–113.

Lakoff, George (1987) *Women, Fire and Dangerous Things.* Chicago: Chicago UP.

Lakoff, G. (1993) "The Contemporary Theory of Metaphor". In A. Ortony (ed) *Thought and Metaphor,* 2nd ed. Cambridge: Cambridge UP. 202–251.

Langacker Ronald W. (1987) *Foundations of Cognitive Grammar* Volume I. Stanford, Ca.: Stanford University Press

Lazarus, R. S. (1968 [1966[1]]) "Emotion as Coping Process", in M. B. Arnold (ed.), *The Nature of Emotion.* Harmondsworth: Penguin. 249–260.

Leech, Geoffrey (1974) *Semantics.* Harmondsworth: Penguin.

Legouis, Émile and Louis Cazamian (1935) *A History of English Literature.* New York: Macmillan.

Levin, Samuel R. (1971) "The Conventions of Poetry", in Seymour Chatman (ed.), *Literary Style: A Symposium.* London: Oxford UP. 177–196.

Levin, Israel (1980) *The Embroidered Coat.* Tel Aviv: The Katz Research Institute for Hebrew Literature and Hakibbutz Hameuchad Publishing House (in Hebrew).

Liberman, A. M. (1970) "The Grammars of Speech and Language". *Cognitive Psychology 1:* 301–323.

Liberman, A. M., F. S. Cooper, D. P. Shankweiler, and M. Studdert-Kennedy (1967) "Perception of the Speech Code", *Psychological Review 74:* 431–461.

Liberman, Alvin M., Ignatius G. Mattingly, and Michael T. Turvey (1972) "Language Codes and Memory Codes", in A. W. Melton and E. Martin (eds.), *Coding Processes in Human Memory.* New York: Winston.

"Longinus" (1951) *On the Sublime.* W. Rhys Roberts (trans.), in James Harry Smith & Edd Winfield Parks (eds.) *The Great Critics.* New York: Norton. 65–111.

Losciuto, Leonard A., and Eugene L. Hartley (1970 [1963[1]]) "Religious Affiliation and Open-Mindedness in Binocular Resolution", in Peter B. Warr (ed.) *Thought and Personality.* Harmondsworth: Penguin. 373–377.

Lovejoy, Arthur O. (1961) "On the Discrimination of Romanticisms". in *Essays in the History of Ideas.* Baltimore, Johns Hopkins UP. 228-53.

Lyons, John (1977) *Semantics.* Cambridge: Cambridge UP.

Mack, Dorothy (1975) "Metaphoring as Speech-act: Some Happiness Conditions for Implicit Similes and Simple Metaphors". *Poetics 4:* 221–256.

Madách, Imre *The Tragedy of Man,* trans. J. C. W. Horne. Available online: http://mek.oszk.hu/00900/00915/html/madach4.htm

Maier, N. R. F. (1968 [1931[1]]) "Reasoning in Humans II. The Solution of a Problem and its Appearance in Consciousness", in P. C. Wason and P. N. Johnson Laird (eds.), *Thinking and Reasoning.* Harmondsworth: Penguin. 17–27.

Margolis, Joseph (1962) "The Logic of Interpretation", in Joseph Margolis (ed.), *Philosophy Looks at the Arts: Contemporary Readings in Aesthetics.* New York: Charles Scribner's Sons. 108–118.

Martz, Louis (1962) *The Poetry of Meditation.* New Haven: Yale UP.

May, Janet and Bruno H. Repp (1982) "Periodicity and Auditory Memory", in *Status Report on Speech Research SR–69.* New Haven, Conn.: Haskins Laboratories. 145–149.

Melchiori, Giorgio (1966) "Two Mannerists: James and Hopkins", in Geoffrey Hartman (ed.), *Hopkins.* Englewood Cliffs, N.J.: Prentice Hall (Twentieth Century Views).

Mervis, Carolyn B. (1980) "Category Structure and the Development of Categorization", in R. J. Spiro, B.C. Bruce & W. F. Brewer (eds.), *Theoretical Issues in Reading Comprehension.* Hillsdale NJ: Erlbaum.

Metman, Eva (1965) "Reflections on Samuel Beckett's Plays", in M. Esslin (ed.), *Samuel Beckett.* Englewood Cliffs, N.J.: Prentice Hall (Twentieth Century Views). 117–139.

Meyer, Leonard B. (1956) *Emotion and Meaning in Music.* Chicago: Chicago UP.

Miall, David S. (2006) *Literary Reading—Empirical & Theoretical Studies.* New York and Bern: Peter Lang.

Miles, Josephine (1965) *Pathetic Fallacy in the 19th Century.* New York: Hippocrene Books.

Miles, Josephine (1964) *Modes and Eras in English Poetry.* Berkeley: California UP.

Miller, George A. (1970) *The Psychology of Communication.* Harmondsworth: Pelican.

Miller, George A. (1978) "Semantic Relations among Words", in Morris Halle et al. (eds.), *Linguistic Theory and Psychological Reality.* Cambridge, Mass.: MIT. 60–118.

Miller, George A. (1979) "Images and Models, Similes and Metaphors", in Andrew Ortony (ed.), *Metaphor and Thought.* Cambridge: Cambridge UP. 202–250.

Miller, George A. and Philip N. Johnson-Laird (1976) *Language and Perception.* Cambridge, Mass.: Harvard UP.

Miller, J.G. (1950) "Unconscious Processes and Perception", in Blake & Ramsey (eds.), *Perception—An Approach to Personality.* New York: Ronald Press. 258–282.

Moore, G. E. (1966) "Is Existence a Predicate?", in A. G. N. Flew (ed.), *Logic and Language* (Second Series). Oxford: Blackwell. 82–94.

Mourgues, Odette de (1953) *Metaphysical, Baroque, and Précieux Poetry.* London: Oxford UP.

Muecke, D. C. (1970) *Irony.* London: Methuen.

Neisser, Ulric (1968 [1963¹]) "The Multiplicity of Thought", in P. C. Wason and P. Johnson-Laird (eds.), *Thinking and Reasoning.* Harmondsworth: Penguin. 307–323.

Neisser, Ulric (1976) *Cognition and Reality.* San Francisco: Freeman.

Newberg, Andrew, Eugene D'Aquili and Vince Rause (2001) *Why God Won't Go Away: Brain Science and the Biology of Belief.* New York: Ballantine Books.

Ohmann, Richard (1970a) "Generative Grammars and the Concept of Literary Style", in Donald C. Freeman (ed.), *Linguistics and Literary Style.* New York: Holt, Rinehart & Winston. 258–278.

Ohmann, Richard (1970b) "Modes of Order", in Freeman, Donald C. (ed.), *Linguistics and Literary Style.* New York: Holt, Rinehart & Winston. 209–242.

Oras, Ants (1957) "Spenser and Milton: Some Parallels and Contrasts in the Handling of Sound", in Northrop Frye (ed.), *Sound and Poetry.* New York: English Institute Essays. 109–133.

Ornstein, Robert (1969) *On the Experience of Time.* Harmondsworth: Penguin.

Ornstein, Robert E. (1975) *The Psychology of Consciousness.* Harmondsworth: Penguin.

Ortony, Andrew (ed.). *Metaphor and Thought.* Cambridge: Cambridge UP.

Ortony, Andrew (ed). 1977, [1993²] *Thought and Metaphor.* Cambridge: Cambridge UP.

Pagis, Dan (1970) *Secular Poetry and Poetic Theory: Moses Ibn Ezra and his Contemporaries.* Jerusalem: Bialik Institute (in Hebrew).

Pater, Walter (1951[1873¹]) "Conclusion", from *The Renaissance,* in James Harry Smith and Edd Winfield Parks (eds.), *The Great Critics.* New York: Norton. 894–897.

Pavio, Allen (1979) "Psychological Processes in the Comprehension of Metaphor", in Andrew Ortony (ed.), *Metaphor and Thought*. Cambridge: Cambridge UP. 150–171.

Pears, D. F. (1966) "Universals", in A. G. N. Flew (ed.), *Logic and Language* (Second Series). Oxford: Blackwell. 51–64.

Pears, David (1971) *Wittgenstein*. London: Fontana.

Persinger, Michael A. (1987) *Neuropsychological Bases of God Beliefs*. New York, Westport, Connecticut, London: Praeger.

Peyre, Henri (1964) Commentary on Baudelaire's "Correspondances", in Stanley Burnshaw (ed.), *The Poem Itself*. Harmondsworth: Pelican. 8–9.

Plutchik, R. (1968 [1962[1]]) "The Evolutionary Basis of Emotional Behaviour", in Magda B. Arnold (ed.), *The Nature of Emotion*. Harmondsworth: Penguin. 67–80.

Polányi, Michael (1967) *The Tacit Dimension*. Garden City, N.Y.: Anchor.

Preminger, Alex (1974) *The Princeton Encyclopedia of Poetry and Poetics*. Princeton: Princeton UP.

Preminger, Alex and T. V. F. Brogan 1993. *The New Princeton Encyclopedia of Poetry and Poetics*. Princeton: Princeton UP.

Posner, Michael I. (1973) *Cognition: An Introduction*. Glenview Ill. & Brighton, England: Scott, Foreman & Co.

Quintilian (n.d.) *Institutio Oratoria*, H. E. Butler (trans.). London and Boston: Loeb Classical Library. IX.i.8 Now available online: http://penelope.uchicago.edu/Thayer/E/Roman/Texts/Quintilian/Institutio_at oria/home.html

Rakerd, Brad (1984) "Vowels in Consonantal Context Are More Linguistically Perceived than Isolated Vowels: Evidence from an Individual Differences Scaling Study". *Perception & Psychophysics 35:* 123–136.

Ransom, John Crowe (1951) "Poetry: A note in Ontology", in James Harry Smith & Edd Winfield Parks (eds.) *The Great Critics*. New York: Norton. 769–787.

Repp, Bruno H. (1984) "Categorical Perception: Issues, Methods, Findings", in N. J. Lass (ed.), *Speech and Language: Advances in Basic Research and Practice, vol. 10*. New York: Academic Press. 243–335.

Richards, I. A. (1929) *Practical Criticism*. New York: Harcourt, Brace and Company.

Richards, I. A. (1961 [1925[1]]) *Principles of Literary Criticism*. London: Routledge and Kegan Paul.

Robe-Grillet, Alain (1965) "Samuel Beckett, or 'Presence' in the Theatre", in M. Esslin (ed.), *Samuel Beckett*. Englewood Cliffs, N.J.: Prentice Hall (Twentieth Century Views). 108–116.

Rorschach, Hermann (1951) *Psychodiagnostics*. Bern: Huber.

Rostand, Edmond. *L'Aiglon* and *Cyrano de Bergerac* Available online: http://abu.cnam.fr/BIB/auteurs/rostande.html

Rumelhart, David E. (1979) "Some Problems with the Notion of Literal Meaning", in Andrew Ortony (ed.), *Metaphor and Thought*. Cambridge: Cambridge UP. 78–90.

Schank, Roger C. (1973) "Identification of Conceptualizations Underlying Natural Language", in Roger C. Schank & Kenneth Mark Colby (eds.), *Computer Models of Thought and Language*. San Francisco: Freeman. 187–247.

Schank, R.C. 1975. *Conceptual Information Processing*. Amsterdam & New York: North Holland/American Elsevier.

Schank, Roger and Abelson, Robert (1977) *Scripts, Plans, Goals and Understanding: An Inquiry into Human Knowledge Structures*. Hillsdale, N.J.: Lawrence Earlbaum Associates.

Schirmann, Jefim (1979) *Studies in the History of Hebrew Poetry and Drama*. Jerusalem: The Bialik Institute (in Hebrew).

Schirmann, Jefim (1961) *Hebrew Poetry in Spain and in Provence*, 4 vols. Jerusalem and Tel Aviv: The Bialik Institute and Dvir (in Hebrew).

Schneider, Elisabeth (1975 [1953^1]) *Coleridge, Opium and Kubla Khan*. New York: Octagon Books.

Scholem, Gershom G. (1955) *Major Trends in Jewish Mysticism*. New York: Schocken Books.

Schramm, Wilbur L. (1935) *Approaches to the Science of English Verse*. Iowa City: Iowa University.

Schroder, H. M., M. J. Driver, and S. Streufert (1970) "Levels of Information Processing", in Peter B. Warr (ed.), *Thought and Personality*. Harmondsworth: Penguin. 174–191.

Searle, John R. (1971 [1969^1]) "The Problem of Proper Names", in Danny D. Steinberg and Leon A. Jakobovits (eds.), *Semantics*. Cambridge: Cambridge UP. 134–141.

Shankweiler, Donald, Winifred Strange, and Robert Verbrugge (1975) "Speech and the Problem of Perceptual Constancy". *Status Report on Speech Research, SR 42–43*. New Haven, Conn.: Haskins Laboratories.

Shen, Yeshayahu & Michal Cohen. (1998) "How come silence is sweet but sweetness is not silent: a cognitive account of directionality in poetic synaesthesia". In: *Language and Literature. Vol. 7(2). 123-140.*

Shen, Y. & David Gil. (forthcoming, 2007). "Sweet Fragrances from Indonesia: A Universal Principle Governing Directionality in Synaesthetic Metaphors". In: Willie van Peer & Jan Auracher (eds). *New Beginning for the Study of Literature*. Cambridge: Cambridge Scholars Publishing, 2007.

Shen Y. & Ravid Eisenamn (forthcoming, 2008). "'Heard melodies are sweet, but those unheard are sweeter': Synaesthesia and cognition". To appear in: *Language and Literature (17:2).*

Shklovsky, Victor (1965) "Art as Technique", in L. T. Lemon and M. J. Reis (eds.), *Russian Formalist Criticism*. Lincoln: Nebraska UP. 3–24.

Sibley, Frank (1962) "Aesthetic Qualities", In Joseph Margolis (ed.), *Philosophy Looks at the Arts: Contemporary Readings in Aesthetics*. New York: Scribner. 63–88.

Silberschlag, Eisig (1974) "Hebrew Poetry", in Alex Preminger (ed.), *Princeton Encyclopedia of Poetry and Poetics*. Princeton: Princeton UP. 336–343.

Silberstein, Lisa, Howard Gardner, Erin Phelps & Ellen Winner (1982) "Autumn Leaves and Old Photographs: The Developments of Metaphor Preferences". *Journal of Experimental Child Psychology 34:* 135–150.

Slobin, Dan I. (1971) *Psycholinguistics*. Glenview Ill. and Brighton, England: Scott, Foreman & Co.

Smart, J. J. C. (1966) "Theory Construction", in A. G. N. Flew (ed.), *Logic and Language*. Oxford: Blackwell. 222–242.

Smith, James (1934) "Metaphysical Poetry", *Scrutiny 2:* 222–239.

Snyder, E. D. (1930) *Hypnotic Poetry: A Study of Trance-Inducing Techniques in Certain Poems and its Literary Significance*. Philadelphia: University of Pennsylvania Press.

Snyder, E. D., & R. E. Shor (1983) "Trance-Inductive Poetry: A Brief Communication". *International Journal of Clinical and Experimental Hypnosis, 31:* 1–7.

Spitzer, Leo (1969) "The Muting Effect of Classical Style in Racine", in R. C. Knight (ed.), *Racine*. London: Macmillan. 117–131.

Stanford, W. B. (1942) "Synaesthetic Metaphor". *Comparative Literature Studies 6–7:* 26–30.

Stockwell, Peter (2002) *Cognitive Poetics—An Introduction*. London and New York: Routledge.

Strawson, P. F. (1967) "Singular terms and Predication", in P. F. Strawson (ed.), *Philosophical Logic*. Oxford: Oxford UP. 69–88.

Sweetser, Eve (2006) Whose Rhyme is whose Reason?: Sound and Sense in *Cyrano de Bergerac. Language and Literature.* 29–54.

Sypher, Wylie (1955) *Four Stages of Renaissance Style*. Garden City, N.Y.: Anchor.

Thomson, Philip (1972) *The Grotesque*. London: Methuen.

Todorov, Tzvetan (1975). *The Fantastique*. Ithaca, N.Y.: Cornell UP.

Trilling, Lionel (ed.) (1956) *The Selected Letters of John Keats*. Garden City: Doubleday.

Tsur, Reuven (1971) *A Rhetoric of Poetic Qualities*. Unpublished Sussex University Dissertation.

Tsur, Reuven (1972) "Articulateness and Requiredness in Iambic Verse". *Style 6:* 123–148.

Tsur, Reuven (1974) "Poem, Prayer and Meditation: An Exercise in Literary Semantics". *Style 8:* 405–425.

Tsur, Reuven (1975a) "Two Critical Attitudes: Quest for Certitude and Negative Capability". *College English 36:* 776–778.

Tsur, Reuven (1975b) *Convention and Rhetoric in Mediaeval Hebrew Poetry.* Tel Aviv: Daga (in Hebrew).

Tsur, Reuven (1976) "Anti-grammatical Rhyme and Linguistic Competence", *HaSifrut* 22 (in Hebrew, with English summary).

Tsur, Reuven (1977) *A Perception-Oriented Theory of Metre.* Tel Aviv: The Porter Israeli Institute for Poetics and Semiotics.

Tsur, Reuven (1978) "Emotion, Emotional Qualities, and Poetry". *Psychocultural Review 2:* 165–180.

Tsur, Reuven (1979) "Levels of Information Processing in Reading Poetry". *Critical Inquiry 5:* 751–759.

Tsur, Reuven (1983a) *What is Cognitive Poetics?* Tel Aviv: The Katz Research Institute for Hebrew Literature.

Tsur, Reuven (1983b) *Poetic Structure, Information-Processing and Perceived Effects.* Tel Aviv: The Katz Research Institute for Hebrew Literature.

Tsur, Reuven (l983c) *Critical Terms and Insight: The Mental Dictionary of "Critical Competence".* Tel Aviv: The Katz Research Institute for Hebrew Literature.

Tsur, Reuven (1985) "Poetic Language and Semantic Information-Processing". *Theoretical Linguistics 12:* 205–212.

Tsur, Reuven (1985) "Contrast, Ambiguity, Double-Edgedness". *Poetics Today, 6:* 417–445.

Tsur, Reuven (1986) "Decoding Secret Messages, and the Quest for Certitude: Hebrew Critics Confronting Literature of Extreme Situations" (in Hebrew). *HaSifrut 34:* 142–160.

Tsur, Reuven (1987a). *The Road to "Kubla Khan".* Jerusalem: Israel Science Publishers.

Tsur, Reuven (1987b). *On Metaphoring.* Jerusalem: Israel Science Publishers.

Tsur, Reuven (1987c) *Mediaeval Hebrew Poetry in a Double Perspective—The Versatile Reader and Hebrew Poetry in Spain..* Tel Aviv: University Publishing Projects (In Hebrew).

Tsur, Reuven (1988a). *Hebrew Hypnotic Poetry.* Tel Aviv: The Katz Research Institute for Hebrew Literature (in Hebrew).

Tsur, Reuven (1988b) "'Oceanic' Dedifferentiation and Poetic Metaphor". *Journal of Pragmatics 12:* 711–724.

Tsur, Reuven (1992) *What Makes Sound Patterns Expressive?—The Poetic Mode of Speech Perception.* Durham, N.C.: Duke UP.

Tsur, Reuven (1996) *Text, Reader, World—The Implied Critic's and the Real Reader's Decision Style* (in Hebrew). Tel Aviv: Hakibuts Hameukhad Publishing House.

Tsur, Reuven (1997) "Poetic Rhythm: Performance Patterns and their Acoustic Correlates". *Versification:* An Electronic Journal Devoted to Literary Prosody. (http://staff.washington.edu/versif/backissues/vol1/essays/tsur.html)

Tsur, R. 1998. "Light, Fire, Prison: A Cognitive Analysis of Religious Imagery in Poetry." *PSYART: A Hyperlink Journal for the Psychological Study of the Arts,* article 980715. Available HTTP: http//www.clas.ufl.edu/ipsa/journal/articles/tsur02.htm

Tsur, Reuven (1998) *Poetic Rhythm: Structure and Performance—An Empirical Study in Cognitive Poetics.* Bern: Peter Lang.

Tsur, Reuven (2000b) "Picture Poetry, Mannerism, and Sign Relationships". *Poetics Today* 24: 751–781

Tsur, Reuven (2000) "Phonetic Cues and Dramatic Function—Artistic Recitation of Metered Speech". *Assaph—Studies in the Theatre:* 173–196.

Tsur, Reuven (2000) "The Performance of Enjambments, Perceived Effects, and Experimental Manipulations" *PSYART: A Hyperlink Journal for the Psychological Study of the Arts.* http://www.clas.ufl.edu/ipsa/journal/articles/psyart2000/tsur04.htm

Tsur, Reuven (2001c) "Onomatopoeia: Cuckoo-Language and Tick-Tocking—The Constraints of Semiotic Systems". *Iconicity In Language.* Available Online: http://www.trismegistos.com/IconicityInLanguage/Articles/Tsur/default.html

Tsur, Reuven (2002) "Phonetic Cues and Dramatic Function—Artistic Recitation of Metered Speech". (Expanded version). *PSYART: A Hyperlink Journal for the Psychological Study of the Arts.* http://www.clas.ufl.edu/ipsa/journal/2002/tsur05.htm

Tsur, Reuven (2002) "Some Cognitive Foundations of 'Cultural Programs'". *Poetics Today* 23.1: 63–89.

Tsur, Reuven (2002) "Aspects of Cognitive Poetics", in Elena Semino and Jonathan Culpeper (eds.), *Cognitive Stylistics—Language and Cognition in Text Analysis.* John Benjamins Publishing Company: Amsterdam/Philadelphia.

Reuven Tsur (2002) "Some Comments on the Lakoffean Conception of Spatial Metaphor". In Thomasz Komendzinski (ed.), *Metaphor: A Multidisciplinary Approach.* Special issue of *Theoria et Historia Scientiarum* VI. No. 1. 245–267.

Tsur, Reuven (2003) *On The Shore of Nothingness: Space, Rhythm, and Semantic Structure in Religious Poetry and its Mystic–Secular Counterpart—A Study in Cognitive Poetics.* Exeter: Imprint Academic.

Tsur, Reuven (2003b) "Deixis and abstractions: adventures in space and time". In Joanna Gavins and Gerard Steen (eds.), *Cognitive Poetics in Practice.* London: Routledge. 41–54.

Tsur, Reuven (2006b) "Constraints of the Semiotic System—Onomatopoeia, Expressive Sound Patterns and Poetry Translation", in Uta Klein, Katja Mellmann, Steffanie Metzger (Hrsg.) *Heuristiken der Literaturwissenschaft— Disziplinexterne Perspektiven auf Literatur.* Paderborn: mentis. 246–270.

Tsur, Reuven (2006a) *"Kubla Khan"—Poetic Structure, Hypnotic Quality and Cognitive Style: A Study in Mental, Vocal, and Critical Performance.* Amsterdam: John Benjamins.

Tsur, Reuven (2006c) "'I Shall be Right Indeed' by Shlomo Ibn Gabirol: Rhythmic and Grotesque Effects—Is the Past Homogeneous?" *Criticism and Interpretation. Journal for Interdisciplinary Studies in Literature and Culture.* 39: 43–72 (in Hebrew).

Tsur, R., Glicksohn, J., & Goodblatt, C. (1990) "Perceptual Organization, Absorption and Aesthetic Qualities of Poetry". László Halász (ed.), *Proceedings of the 11th International Congress on Empirical Aesthetics.* Budapest: Institute for Psychology of the Hungarian Academy of Sciences. 301–304.

Tsur, R., Glicksohn, J., & Goodblatt, C. (1991) "Gestalt Qualities in Poetry and the Reader's Absorption Style". *Journal of Pragmatics 16 (5):* 487–504.

Tsur, Reuven and Motti Benari (2002) "'Composition of Place', experiential set, and the meditative poem (a cognitive–pragmatic approach)". *Pragmatics and Cognition,* 203–237.

Ullmann, Stephen (1945) "Romanticism and Synaesthesia". *PMLA* 60: 811–827.

Ullmann, Stephen (1957) "Panchronistic Tendencies in Synaesthesia", in *The Principles of Semantics.* Oxford: Blackwell. 266–289.

Waisman, F. (1966) "Language Strata", in A. G. N. Flew (ed.), *Logic and Language* (Second Series). Oxford: Blackwell. 11–31.

Warren, Austin (1962) "Franz Kafka", in Ronald Gray (ed.), *Kafka.* Englewood Cliffs: Prentice Hall. 123–132.

Wason, P. C. (1968) "'On the Failure to Eliminate Hypotheses …' A Second Look", in P. C. Wason and P. N. Johnson Laird (eds.), *Thinking and Reasoning.* Harmondsworth: Penguin. 165–174.

Watson, George (1973 [1966[1]]) "'Kubla Khan'", in Alun R. Jones and William Tydeman (eds.), *Coleridge: **The Ancient Mariner** and Other Poems—A Casebook.* London: Macmillan. 221–234.

Weinreich, Uriel (1966) "Explorations in Semantic Theory", in Sebeok, T. A. (ed.), *Current Trends in Linguistics* III. The Hague: Mouton. 395–477.

Weisstein, Ulrich (1974) "Impressionism", in Alex Preminger (ed.), *Princeton Encyclopedia of Poetry and Poetics.* Princeton: Princeton UP.

Weitz, Morris (1962) "The Role of Theory in Aesthetics", in J. Margolis (ed.), *Philosophy Looks at the Arts.* New York: Scribner. 48–59.

Weitz, Morris (1972 [1964[1]]) *Hamlet and the Philosophy of Literary Criticism.* London: Faber & Faber.

Wellek, René (1963) *Concepts of Criticism.* New Haven & London: Yale UP.

Wellek, René & Austin Warren (1956) *Theory of Literature.* New York: Harcourt, Brace & Co.

Wells, Rulon (1968) "Nominal and Verbal Style", in Thomas A. Sebeok (ed.), *Style in Language.* Cambridge Mass.: MIT. 213–220

Wimsatt, W. K. (1954) *The Verbal Icon.* New York: Noonday.

Wimsatt, W. K. (1971) "The Rule and the Norm: Halle and Keyser on Chaucer's Meter", in Seymour Chatman (ed.), *Literary Style: A Symposium.* London: Oxford UP. 197–220.

Wittgenstein, Ludwig (1976) *Philosophical Investigations*, G. E. M. Anscombe (trans.). Oxford: Blackwell.

Zemach, Eddy (1962) *Like the Tree's Root.* Jerusalem: Akhshav (in Hebrew).

Index

abduction, 280
Abelson, 11, 264, 604
Abramovitch, 360
abrupt, 226, 228, 229 see also
    continuity
absolute magnitude, 303
absolutism, 539–540, 548–550 see
    also *perspectivism*; *relativism*
abstract nouns, 21, 41,90, 96, 252,
    394–396, 453–456, 610–616, 638
ABSTRACT of the CONCRETE, 462–
    466, 610–616 see also *GERUND of
    the CONCRETE*; *thematized
    predicate*; *topicalized attribute*
abstract personality, 530
abstract thinking, 55, 59
abstract vs. concrete personality, 514
abstraction, 43, 44, 55, 69, 70, 72,
    105, 272–276, 332, 394, 396,
    397, 400, 401, 453–456, 476,
    477, 522, 526, 566, 615
absurd, 73, 296, 297–302, 424
Ackerman, 64
acoustic coding, 216–234
acoustic cues, 6–10, 21, 175, 239 see
    also *conflicting vocal cues*;
    convergent and divergent cues;
    phonetic cues
acoustic representation, 7
acrostich, 497
Adam, 605–606
adaptation, 43, 44, 48, 49, 52
Addison, 93
adequacy, 245
Ady, 423, 439–447, 448

aesthetic concepts, 80, 83–84, 206,
    546
aesthetic definitions, 423–433
aesthetic estimation, 303, 390, 399,
    617
aesthetic quality, 12, 40, 80, 83,
    206, 207 541, 542, 546, 567, 568
    aesthetic effect, 10, 11, 12
Aestheticism, 46
aesthetics, 2, 5, 6
affect, 15, 17, 18, 19, 21, 387, 412
affricates, 239, 240
Agnon, 55, 424, 425, 428–431, 529
alazon, 356
Alcock, 113, 114
alexandrine, 623–640
alienation, 266, 525, 553
allegoresis, 472
allegoric, 55, 424
allegory, 75, 382, 399–403, 442,
    454, 512, 515, 516, 523
alliteration, 5, 21, 73, 85–89, 90,
    101–103, 112, 508, 542, 563,
    564, 638
allowable deviations, 156
allusion, 71, 73, 103, 272–276
altered states of consciousness, 25–
    26, 37, 47, 320, 451–470, 471,
    613, 616
Alterman, 258, 271, 302–305, 398,
    472, 610–611
ambiguity, 108, 130, 165, 166, 185,
    305, 310, 344, 351, 353, 376,
    445, 473, 485, 498, 502, 509,
    515, 528, 530, 531, 533, 537

ambivalence, 36, 309, 311, 352, 528, 530, 532
amplitude, 205
anagnorisis, 349
analytic criticism, 1, 77, 112, 541, 570, 571–572
analytic philosophy, 206, 599
anaphora, 127, 278, 471
Anders, 517–527
angry vs. tender poems, 212–216, 221–223
animism, 500–501
anti-closure, 609
antithesis, 117, 120, 121, 145
antonymy, 13, 246, 364, 542
aphasia, 235–240
aphorism, 108
archetype, 32, 63, 343, 355–384, 485, 495, 518–526
    archetypal pattern, 297, 308, 355–384, 454, 485
    archetype of Heaven and Hell, 364
    cinderella archetype, 355, 356–360, 382, 383, 384
    death-and-rebirth archetype, 64, 307, 355, 360–382, 384, 485, 495, 505
    fool archetype, 359
    see also collective unconscious; Jung
Aristotle, 2, 349, 353, 354, 360, 368, 383, 497, 541
Arnheim, 30, 33, 34, 57, 61, 85, 112–119, 132, 141, 150, 161, 290, 314
Arnold, 56, 58
arpeggio, 369
articulateness, 127, 135, 140–154, 634
articulateness and requiredness, 623–629
articulation, 173–180, 191, 558, 561, 565, 567

artificial intelligence, 1, 15, 245, 264–266, 586, 604
aspect switching, 194, 229
    aspect-blindness, 64
    aspect-seeing, 64
Aspects of the Novel, 597–598
associative cluster, 356, 359, 360, 382
asyndeton, 349 see also syndeton
Atkins, 360
atomization, 55
authoritarianism, 530

babbling, 235, 236, 237, 242
Babits, 241
Bach, 572–574
back vowels, 229–235, 242, 480, 484 see also front vowels
Bakhtin, 445
ballad, 343–354, 533–537
Barney, 181
Baroque, 64, 97, 326
    Baroque drama, 325
Bartlett, 17, 18, 24, 387, 412, 421, 541
Barzel, 75, 428–433
Bates, 389, 511
Baudelaire, 37, 140, 149, 209, 238, 239–241, 259, 293, 434, 443, 495–506, 508, 510, 547
Beardsley, 79–80, 103, 175, 182, 206, 303, 391, 410, 458, 542, 549–550, 577, 587–592, 617–618
Beckett, 55, 302, 309, 327, 355, 384, 424, 427–428, 434, 517–527
behaviorism, 416
Ben-Porat, 273
Benari, 613
Benson, 195
Bentov, 232
Berek, 512
Bergson, 16, 37, 443, 458–461, 499, 544

Berko, 62, 63
Bever, 133–134, 627
beyond the information given, 43–76
Bialik, 46, 47, 294, 309–311, 494, 514
Bierwisch, 1, 68, 78, 80, 82, 238, 461, 567
Birnbaum, 326
bisyllabic occupancy of metrical position, 187–193
Blake, William 318–319, 452, 476, 492–494, 505
Blake, Robert R., 344, 530
blank verse, 98, 144, 174
Blasko & Connine, 593
Bleak House, 597–598
blend, 626
    blending, 637
    blending theory, 623, 627, 637, 638
Bloom, 488
Bodkin, 31, 32, 355, 360, 362–379, 381, 384, 390, 391, 491
BODY IS CONTAINER, 583, 585 see also *conceptual metaphor*
Boileau, 239–241, 624
Booth, Wayne, 429, 453, 511, 599
Boris Godunov, 512, 519, 522
Bowra, 331, 452, 479–480, 484
Bradburn, Beth, 599
Bradley, 489
breath-group, 172
Bridges, 156
Broca's area, 593
Brontë, Emily, 596
Brooke-Rose, 105–106, 248, 402, 406, 500, 515
Brooks, Cleanth, 21, 328, 329, 330, 350, 581, 603
Brown, Roger 14, 36, 37, 62–63, 165
Browning, 144–145, 146

Bruner, 44–56, 61, 313, 421, 530, 536
Bultmann, 308
Bunyan, 582
Burke, Kenneth 24, 31, 296–297, 314, 360–361, 364, 368, 369, 409, 426, 491, 568, 578
Burnshaw, 209
Bush, 103
but-test, 586
Butler, 354
Byron, 482–483

caesura, 100, 117, 135–140, 153, 163, 172, 190, 192, 193, 195, 205, 624, 627, 629, 631, 632
Callow, 187–204
cancellation, 586 see also *feature deletion*
    cancellation vs. multiplication, 247–251
canons of evaluation, 206, 452, 455, 458, 548–550 see also *complexity*; *intense human quality*; *unity*
cardinal vowels, 224–225
CAREER IS A JOURNEY, 588–593 see also *conceptual metaphor*
caricature, 407, 409
Carroll, 435, 569–570, 571
catalog, 456–468, 470
categorial, 386, 397
    categorial perception, 218, 398
categorization, 23
Cazamian, 318
Chadwick, 47, 402, 403
channel capacity, 185
chaotic overdifferentiation, 465, 483, 503
Chatman, 185, 186, 473
Chaucer, 155, 156, 158, 277, 453, 633
Chevreuil, 509

Chicago School, 328–330
child phonology, 235–240
Chomsky, 14, 29, 30, 328, 329
Christabel, 31
chronographia, 92
Citowic, 288
Clark, E. V., 278
Clark, Herbert H., 14, 245, 278, 279
Classic
Classicism, 23, 93, 240–241, 318,
    319, 320, 326, 500
    Classical tragedy, 381, 382, 624
    Classicist Tragedy, 632see also
    Neo-Classicism
closure, 89, 115–130, 147, 151, 153,
    167, 169, 278, 505, 506, 607,
    608, 629
    closural allusion, 124
Cocteau, 499
coding, 6, 9–12, 14, 15, 173, 366,
    369, 381, 384, 506, 508, 543,
    551, 557, 559, 565, 574
cognitive complexity, 529
cognitive dissonance, 530, 531, 537
cognitive growth, 44–56
Cognitive Linguists, 41
cognitive overload, 36–37, 89, 459–
    461, 466, 468, 470, 485
Cognitive Poetics, 2, 3, 4, 5, 19, 20,
    26, 27, 29, 30, 40, 43, 44, 46,
    61, 67, 77, 82, 86, 101, 103,
    112, 234, 238, 248, 289, 294,
    295, 298, 320, 336, 338, 355,
    407, 410, 423, 447, 448, 452,
    461, 466, 470, 495, 541, 546,
    547, 555; defined, 1
cognitive psychology, 1
cognitive science, 1, 2, 3, 6, 8, 547;
    defined, 1
cognitive stability, 17, 284, 362,
    386, 466, 529, 637
cognitive style, 511, 515
Cohen, 247, 253, 541

coinciding downbeats, 166
Coleridge, 31–33, 273–276, 328,
    330, 355, 363, 390, 399, 452,
    471, 473, 474, 489, 490–491,
    506, 511, 548, 549, 608
    Coleridgean criticism, 328–330
collective unconscious, 64, 355, 526
    see also *archetype*; *Jung*
Collins, 258, 259–263
color induction, 509–510
combinational potential, 9, 15, 165–
    171, 210–216, 542–548, 557–
    562, 565, 569, 571, 572, 575,
    582
combinational restriction, 562
comic, 262, 328, 426, 430, 431, 435
    comic pleasure, 407
    comic relief, 430, 431–432
comment, 541
commonplace, 356, 547–548, 558,
    561, 562
comparison, 524
compasses image, 49, 94–97, 114,
    334–335, 392–393
competence, 29–30
    communicative competence, 67–
    75, 557, 604
    communication maxims, 579–580
    see also *conversational maxims*;
    cooperative principle
    critical competence, 68, 557, 565,
    568–569, 574
    linguistic competence, 68–75,
    157, 279, 557, 567–568, 574,
    604
    literary competence, 43, 67–75,
    406, 567 see also *rule of*
    significance; *principle of*
    congruence
    metaphoric competence, 245–281
    phonetic competence, 182
    poetic competence, 30, 67–75,
    327, 557, 567–569, 574

rhythmic competence, 68
complex variable, 356
complexity, 206, 355 see also *canons of evaluation*
componential analysis, 13, 245–281, 395–396, 453, 455, 563
composition of place (compositio loci), 469, 613, 615
conceptual categorization, 460, 466, 470
conceptual dependency theory, 586
conceptual language, 20, 400, 402, 403
conceptual metaphor, 594, 600 see also *BODY IS CONTAINER*; *CAREER IS A JOURNEY*; *LIFE IS A JOURNEY*; *LOVE IS A JOURNEY*; *SEEING IS KNOWING*
conclusive tone, 482, 488 see also *inconclusive tone*
  conclusive vs. suspensive tone, 22, 102–103, 104, 109, 123, 124, 146–154
conflicting vocal cues, 181, 192 see also *acoustic cues*; *convergent and divergent cues*
connotation, 401, 476, 488
Conrad, 172, 173
conservation test, 45–46, 49–50, 52, 56
consistency, 54–55
constraint-seeking, 50–55, 65, 68, 69
constraints of semiotic systems, 223–230
Contemporary Theory of Metaphor, 577–594
  "Contemporary" and the "Controversion" Theory of Metaphor, 585 see also *Controversion Theory*
continuity, 181–208, 214, 240 see also *discontinuity*

continuous vs. abrupt, 215–216
  see also *abrupt*
contour-blurring plural, 543–545, 546
contrast set, 249, 258, 319, 320, 324, 330 see also *family resemblance*
control of attention, 466–468
Controversion Theory, 577, 587, 593
  see also *Contemporary Theory of Metaphor*
convergent vs. divergent, 41, 59–61, 82, 83–91, 100–104, 112, 113, 142, 146–154, 236–240, 278, 280, 471, 491, 508
  convergent, 201, 207, 490, 505
  see also *divergent*
  convergent and divergent cues, 193
  convergent and divergent delivery styles, 184–185
  convergent and divergent poetry, 639
  convergent rhythm, 489
conversational maxims, 579
  maxim of quality, 547
  maxim of quantity, 547
  see also *competence*; *cooperative principle*
Cooper, 139, 163, 179
cooperative principle, 68, 75 see also *competence*; *cooperative principle*
correspondence rules, 157
couplet, 88, 91, 116–122, 124, 125, 126, 127, 128, 129, 130, 141, 146, 147, 148, 278, 488, 489, 490, 607, 508, 608, 626, 629
Cowley, 93, 414–418
Crane, 328
Crashaw, 289
creativity, 362
  creative thinking, 59–60, 81–82, 362
criticism, 21

critical attitudes, 511–529
critical code, 15, 27, 541–575
critical philosophy, 412, 413, 414
critical terms, 541–575 see also
   competence, critical
cross-media styles, 326–327
crossroads, 578–582, 585 see also
   LIFE IS A JOURNEY
crucial recommendation, 207, 425,
   428–430, 459–461, 486, 510, 587
Culler, 43, 69, 73, 175, 250, 345,
   406, 567
Curtius, 337
Cyrano de Bergerac, 531, 623–640
Cytowic, 288

D'Andrade, 18, 20, 21, 297, 406,
   418
D'Aquili, 613–615
Daiches, 318–319
Danks, 218
Dante, 31, 32, 325, 440, 491, 582,
   594
dark vs. bright vowels, 223–234, 484
   dark vowels, 212, 213, 219, 480–
   481
Darwin, 175
Dascal, 586, 600
David and Goliath, 356–360 see also
   archetype
Davie, 149–151, 152
Dawson, 615
de-automatization, 398, 464, 465,
   468, 611
decision style, 27, 28, 511–540 see
   also *negative capability*; *quest for
   certitude*
decoding, 257, 352
deep structure, 6, 10, 11, 462 see
   also *surface structure*
defense mechanism, 336, 343
deixis, 397, 398, 464, 501, 595–622
   deictic centres, 596–622

deictic shift, 596, 597
Deictic Shift Theory, 598
Delattre, 230–231
delayed closure, 525
delayed conceptualization, 577, 585
delivery style, 171, 181–208
description, 455
descriptive content, 207, 476, 482,
   524, 542–548, 562, 564, 571
Deutsch, Diana, 63
Dickens, 512, 597
dictionary of dream symbols, 578
didactic, 328
differentiation, 329, 340, 386
   differentiated vs. undifferentiated,
   283, 294
Dilke, 511
dimeter, 123
disambiguation, 174
discontinuity, 181–208 see also
   continuity
disorientation, 24–25, 26, 55, 75,
   387, 405–422, 573 see also
   orientation
Disraeli, 588–591, 594
distal stimulus, 438 see also
   proximal stimulus
distinctive feature, 6
distinguishers, 250
divergent, 184, 201, 207, 356 see
   also *convergent*
   divergent passage, 495–510
   divergent prosodic structures, 609
   divergent style, 92, 402
Divine Comedy, 582, 594
dogmatism, 54, 530
Dolman, 145–146
Dombi, 285, 291, 293
domestication, 92, 95, 96, 98, 99,
   100, 291, 381, 393
Donne, 49, 94–97, 104, 114, 128,
   165–168, 289, 291, 314, 329,

333–335, 392–393, 413, 419,
    470, 639
Donovan, 175
Dos Passos, 317
double articulation, 278–281
double trochee, 162
double-edgedness, 21, 44, 91, 165,
    171, 212, 214–215, 222, 294,
    306, 366, 394–396, 426, 471,
    472, 473, 490, 544, 631
drama, 2, 171, 379
dramatic irony, 356
Drayton, 126–127
Driver, 530–538
duck-rabbit, 193, 194 see also
    Jastrow
Duffy, 57–58, 61
duration, 173–180
Dürer, 443

early peak, 196 see also *late peaking*
Eco, 14, 118, 278, 279–281, 557,
    558
ecstasy, 25, 275, 321, 322, 362,
    366, 375, 376, 377, 378, 380,
    451, 485, 486, 488, 493, 504,
    505, 510
    ecstatic poetry, 32, 61, 308, 316,
    320, 362, 449, 450, 466, 483–
    492, 493–504, 509
"Edward", 122–123, 337, 343–354
efficient coding, 185, 577, 581–583
ego rhythm, 46, 284, 361–362, 451,
    453
Ehrenzweig, 20, 21, 36, 37, 46, 114,
    236, 284, 336–337, 343, 346,
    361–362, 366, 370, 383, 451,
    453, 454–456, 458–461, 466,
    499, 505, 508, 509–510, 545,
    546, 575
El Greco, 150
elegant solution, 185
elementary sensations, 364, 379, 380

ellipsis, 346, 464
    elliptic sentences, 611
Ellis, 489–490
embodied mind, 577, 581–583
emergent gestalt qualities, 639
    emergent meaning, 517
    emergent regional quality, 449
    emerging meaning, 353
emotion, 18, 19, 25, 44, 56–61, 62,
    82, 92, 94, 100–103, 107, 297,
    301, 365, 380, 397, 398, 405,
    408, 415, 425, 428, 447, 448,
    451, 471, 510, 544, 545
    emotional, 84, 85, 94, 96, 148,
    299, 304, 471, 495, 503 see also
    feeling
    emotional disorientation, 48, 112,
    340, 405–422, 423–449, 553–
    557, 562, 564, 567–569, 574
    emotional effect, 242, 251, 283,
    393
    emotional pattern, 355, 360–362,
    364–379, 384, 485–494, 495
    emotional quality, 19, 41, 44,
    100–103, 106, 112, 117, 122,
    166, 206, 207, 221, 236, 278,
    283, 284, 399, 469, 470, 473,
    476, 478, 486, 488, 489, 496,
    508, 542, 543, 546, 554, 557,
    568, 584, 607, 609, 638, 639
    emotional symbolism, 363, 366,
    478
    emotive crescendo, 471, 485–494,
    504, 505, 506, 510
empathy-theory, 150
Empedocles, 438
emphatic stress, 162
Empson, 327
encoded, 227
    encoded vs. unencoded, 6–10, 21
    encoded vs.unencoded, 215–234
    encoding, 245, 309, 311, 380
energy level, 473

enjambment, 87, 88, 89, 91, 127, 132, 141–142, 143, 144, 147–154, 185–187, 482, 490, 505, 609, 624, 626, 632
Enlightenment, 324, 325
Epimenides, 573
epiphany, 370, 377
epiphora, 471, 475, 484
epithet, 96, 120, 290, 291, 476
equal or proportional time intervals, 180, 182
Erhardt-Sieboldt, 291, 504
Erlich, 281, 499, 555
Escher, 572–574
essence, 319, 320, 322, 323, 381, 557, 558
    essences and layers, 313–315, 322–326, 557–559
essentializing, 296, 313–315 see also *proportionalizing*
Esslin, 517
Euclid, 570
evaluation, 455
evaluative contents, 207
Eve, 605–606
exemplary vs. actual, 401–402
existentialism, 298
explanation, 455
explanatory adequacy, 82
Expressionist, 439
expressive sound patterns, 9, 15, 216
expressive theory of art, 411
extreme situation, 424, 425, 527, 529

factualism, 511, 512, 526, 527
Fairie Qvene, 88
fallacy of homogeneous past, 340
family resemblance, 258, 317, 319, 561 see also *contrast set*
farce, 526
Fauconnier, 637
Faurisson, 65

Faust, 276–277, 305–308, 355, 360–382, 384, 454, 492, 628
Faustus, 22
Faux Monnayeurs, 598
feature deletion, 247–257, 270–276, 395–396, 453, 455, 589, 592 see also *cancellation*
feeling, 395–396, 397, 403, 415, 515, 595, 607, 611, 612, 616, 620 see also *emotion*
Ferenczi, 309, 452
Fergusson, 360, 370, 381, 550
fermata, 184
figurative language, 245–263, 286, 325, 326, 327, 369, 372, 381, 407, 410, 455, 577, 586, 590
figure/ground, 16, 17, 20, 37, 523
Fillmore, 245
fine-grainedness, 637
FitzGerald, 34, 123
FK score, 114
flexibility, 344
    flexibility vs. rigidity, 514
fMRI, 593
focal stability, 481
focus
    integrated focus, 300, 304, 332, 497
    sharp focus, 92, 135, 305, 401, 497
    soft focus, 92, 106, 135, 147, 287, 304, 401, 497
    split focus, 147, 287, 291, 301, 305, 332, 497
    split vs. integrated focus, 84, 91–100, 103–104, 112, 145, 146
focusing sound patterns, 210
Fodor, 3, 7, 8, 15, 133–134, 467, 571–572, 627
Fodor, Janet Dean, 250
Fogle, 292
folk etymology, 551–564
Fónagy, 212–216, 221, 241, 480

form vs. contents, 324, 344
formant, 216–231, 242
    formant transition, 216, 217, 219,
    220
formula, 349, 350, 352, 471, 472,
    521, 523, 571
form–content dichotomy, 624, 638
    form–meaning, 638
Forster, E. M., 596–598
Fowler, 89, 168, 170–171
Fraisse, 111
Frank, 45
free indirect speech, 600
Freeman, Donld C. 189–190
Freeman, Margaret, 637
Frenkel-Brunswick, 354, 473, 528,
    529, 530
Freud, 5, 11, 36, 46, 47, 48, 49,
    307, 309, 312, 314, 339, 340,
    352, 361, 362, 388, 407, 426,
    451, 452, 456, 559, 578
fricatives, 220
front vowels, 229–235, 484 see also
    back vowels
Frost, Robert, 578–581, 582, 585
Fry, 214
Frye, 102, 172, 175–356, 359, 360,
    382, 384
    new theory of genre, 355
functional metaphor, 248–249, 406
fundamental frequency, 175

Gardner, 97, 408, 604
Garrett, 133–134, 467, 627
Gasson, 56, 58
Gaver, 227
Gavins, Joanna, 595
generative
    grammar, 7
    metrics, 162
    metrists, 182
    rules, 158

genre, 11, 25, 27–28, 63, 69, 72, 75,
    296, 297, 313, 314, 317, 319,
    320, 324, 326, 327, 328, 335,
    337, 339, 343–354, 356, 382,
    424–426, 451, 469–470, 527,
    529, 532, 535, 536, 539, 557
Gerrig, 593
GERUND of the CONCRETE, 461–466
    see also *ABSTRACT of the
    CONCRETE*; *thematized predicate*;
    topicalized attribute
gestalt, 7, 21, 34, 38, 46, 47, 85,
    87, 88, 89, 160, 166, 173, 236,
    237, 241, 279, 284, 361, 366,
    440, 451, 453, 454, 456, 473,
    488, 494, 502, 509, 542, 544,
    609, 619, 623, 624, 627, 638,
    639
    Gestalt Law of Prägnanz, 507
    gestalt principle of Proximity, 63
    gestalt qualities, 639
    gestalt theory, 111–154, 163,
    165, 184, 561, 607, 627, 630,
    639
    gestalt-free, 21, 22, 99, 103, 114,
    135, 240, 241, 284, 288, 291,
    292, 380, 393, 396, 397, 453,
    455, 466, 497, 498, 499, 502,
    503, 504, 509, 510, 542, 544,
    546, 615 see also *thing-free*
    gestaltistic, 607
Gibbs, Ray, 579–580, 582–583, 593
Gibson, 18, 386
Gide, 598
Gielgud, 187–207
Gillies, 368
Giora, Rachel, 593
Glicksohn, 28, 34, 126, 451, 457
glide, 479, 484
glissando, 337
glottal stop, 183, 184, 186
Glucksberg, 218
Gödel, 572

Goethe, 66, 276–277, 305–308, 355, 360–382, 492, 533–538, 628
Gogol, 424, 429
Goldberg, 140
Goldstein, 354
Gombrich, 64, 219, 229, 236, 314, 320, 336, 338, 407, 433, 434, 443, 445, 447, 448
good continuation, 116–119, 123–129
good example, 258–259, 319–322, 330, 334, 381, 391, 497
good reason principle, 610
Goodblatt, 28, 34, 126, 456–457
grand style, 171
Gray, 318, 329, 477–479
Great Chain of Being, 360, 369, 382
Greek Tragedy, 327, 360
Grice, 267, 547
Grierson, 97, 299, 331, 414
grotesque, 10, 11, 24, 25, 26, 318, 340, 389, 405–411, 412, 413, 423–449, 452, 522, 523, 553–557, 562, 566–569
grouping, 38, 39, 47, 48, 49, 107, 113, 115–132, 141, 166, 169, 252, 463, 473, 484, 490, 547
  grouping effect of rhymes, 481–484 see also *rhyme*
  grouping potential, 163–164
Guilford, 59

Ḥagiga, 266
Halkin, 140, 322–323
Halle, 38–39, 94, 157–180, 189–190, 204, 560–561
Halliday, 611
Halwes, 180, 219
Hamilton, 621
Hamlet, 32, 51–52, 115, 513, 533
Harley, 62
Hartman, 489
Harvey, 539

Hasenfus, 326
Haskins Laboratories, 229
Hayes, 135
Heidegger, 339
Heilman, 350
Helmholtz, 509–510
Hepburne, 100–101, 510
Herbert, 289
Herrick, 329
Herrnstein-Smith, 112–119, 153, 486, 506, 607, 609
high vs. low vowels, 229
Hiraga, 624, 638
Hirsch, 339, 340
historical perspective, 327–341
historicism, 339
Hodge, Douglas, 186
Hofstadter, 572–574
holistic mentation, 387, 615
Homer, 107, 288–289, 327
homonym, 73, 440
Hopkins, 289, 340, 410, 424, 453
Horace, 95, 433, 443
Horne, 606
horror joke, 10–12, 24, 26, 27–28, 48
House, 275–276
Hrushovski, 210–212
hub, 297, 307, 310, 360–362, 381, 384
Hubbard, 287–288
Hugo, 212–216, 273
human contingency, 295–312
Husserl, 39
Hyman, 296
hyperbole, 49, 345, 435, 555, 556
hypnosis, 451
hypnotic poetry, 61, 447, 449, 452, 471, 639 see also *spell-weaving*; *trance-inductive*
hyponymy, 13, 246, 255, 259–263, 394, 541, 542, 565–567, 574

hypothesis, 27, 32, 36, 50–55, 61–67, 76, 82, 173, 264, 274, 280, 313, 329, 343, 344, 349, 353, 363, 382, 396, 423, 430, 512, 513, 519, 529, 536, 538, 564, 571
hypotheses (perception of music), 63

iambic, 117, 123, 136, 137, 138, 140, 141, 142, 144, 151, 156–180, 182, 241, 471, 477, 488, 497
Ibn Ezra, 333, 338
Ibn Gabirol, 301, 314, 332, 339, 340, 415–418, 423, 433–439, 448
icon, 100
    iconicity, 638, 639
ictus, 157, 558
idyll, 302
illustrative and meditative catalog, 334–335
imagery, 85, 90, 97, 104, 147, 241, 296, 299, 302, 305–311, 359, 360–382, 537
Immanuel of Rome, 325
immediate memory, 136, 156, 172, 173
implied author, 511, 596, 597, 599, 601, 602, 604, 606
implied critic, 511–540
    implied critic's decision style, 341, 343, 423, 429
Impressionism, 64, 403
    impressionist poetry, 240, 285, 291, 293, 503, 505
    impressionistic criticism, 1, 76, 77, 82, 87, 209, 238, 239, 240, 399, 495–500, 539, 568–569, 570
inconclusiveness, 607
    inconclusive tone, 608see also *conclusive tone*
individual consciousness, 339–341
ineffable, 402, 612

infantile pleasure, 407
inference, 255, 604
infinite regress, 569–572
influence, 414–417, 418
information processing, 1, 2, 27, 44, 56, 245–281, 290, 330, 387, 388, 396, 398, 507, 529, 561
information theory, 113
information-confirming cycle, 66, 83
Ingarden, 39
Inhelder, 45
inkblot test, 112–114, 393
inlay language, 71, 72, 436
insight, 290, 308, 325, 420, 452, 455, 476, 491, 556, 557–562, 565–566, 581
instrumental phonetics, 175–180, 181–208
integration, 40, 41, 44, 50, 55, 85, 100, 112, 119, 286, 290, 304, 332, 386, 388, 398, 405, 409, 410, 411, 413, 452, 491, 502, 506–508, 512, 527, 530–538, 554, 561
intense human quality, 206 see also *canons of evaluation*
interference situation, 387
interlingua, 7
interpersonal transcendence, 300–301, 305
interpretation, 10, 11, 31–33, 50–52, 53, 64–66, 255, 263–276, 343, 344–354, 369, 382, 406–409, 423, 426, 455, 456, 472, 511, 512, 542, 568, 577, 579, 580, 585, 588, 590, 591, 599, 608, 623, 626, 639, 640
intertextuality, 636
intolerance of ambiguity, 340, 344, 353, 473, 515, 527, 529, 530, 540 see also *tolerance of ambiguity*
intonation, 141, 145, 173, 180, 195

intonation contour, 185, 192, 193,
194, 196, 198, 205, 225, 226
intuition, 13, 20, 60, 137, 157, 210,
219, 229, 231, 232, 233, 246,
253, 255, 264, 265, 266, 267,
269, 275, 278, 283, 284, 285,
289, 290, 294, 303, 314, 315,
324, 326, 362, 370, 386, 388,
390, 397, 399, 406, 417, 466,
480, 499, 503, 561, 566, 568
irony, 21, 50, 92, 145, 270, 273,
345, 358–392, 427, 579, 602,
603–607, 617–620
irrefutability, 423–425
irrelevant texture, 335
Isaiah, 351, 436
Italian sonnet, 607
Izmailov, 223

Jakobson, 5, 112, 219, 229, 235–
240, 277, 279, 281, 419, 470,
555, 557, 631, 633
James, Henry 410
James, William, 505
Jastrow, 194 see also duck–rabbit
Jensen, 111
Johnson, Dr. Samuel, 91, 174, 417,
421, 435
Johnson, Richard, 160
Johnson-Laird, 24, 89, 412, 420
Jones, 120–121
Joyce, 317
József, 140
Jung, 63, 355, 359, 361, 362, 363,
374, 384, 451, 519, 521, 526 see
also *collective unconscious*;
archetype
just noticeable differences, 315, 322

Kafka, 55, 74, 75, 297, 298, 327,
424, 425, 428–433, 511, 529

Kant, 41, 303, 339, 341, 388–391,
399, 413, 423, 448, 501, 617–
620
Katona, 36
Katz, 15
Kaufman, 297–301, 306, 308, 379,
381
Kayser, 445
Keats, 104, 108, 127–129, 130, 137,
158, 164, 176, 186–187, 240,
286–287, 292, 321–322, 329,
330, 354, 389, 392, 399–402,
424, 452, 483, 486, 491, 492,
494, 505, 506, 511–512, 514,
524, 528, 545, 609
Keats vs. Marlowe, 21–23
Keyser, 38–39, 157–180, 189–190,
204, 551, 560–566
Kinsbourne, 612
Kiparsky, 187, 198
Klauzner, 323–326
Klein, 35, 346
Knight, Wilson, 31, 276–277, 336,
343, 360, 550
Knights, L. C., 77, 82, 528, 582,
592
Knowles, 179, 181, 183, 191, 193
Koffka, 507
Köhler, 59, 60, 81–82, 115
Konrad, 105–106, 500
Kreitler, 272
Kretch, 530
Kris, 11, 236, 407, 426
Krueger, 315, 322, 324, 327
"Kubla Khan", 31–33

L'Aiglon, 624, 628–632
La Fontaine, 239, 516, 531–533,
538
labeling vs. meaning-making, 354,
556–557, 598–601, 620
Lachover, 322–326
Lackner, 467

Lake, 318, 423, 425
Lakoff, 577–594, 621, 623
Langacker, 617–620
language acquisition, 235–240, 242, 565
language functions, 470
language smashing, 553–557, 564, 565, 567
language strata, 572–574
late peaking, 134, 179, 184 see also *early peak*
lateralization, 387–388, 397–399, 402, 612–615
Lavy, 232
Lazarus, 57, 58
Leech, 139, 462
Legouis, 318
Leibnitz, 175
Lemaître, 402, 403, 515
Lessing, 107
leveler, 426
leveling and sharpening, 31, 33–36, 143, 162, 346, 514–515, 561
Levin, 192, 433, 438
Levin, Samuel R., 135
Levisohn, 389–392
Lewis, C. S., 183, 206, 207
liar's paradox, 572
liberal vs. authoritarian, 514
Liberman, Alvin M., 6–10, 14, 180, 216–235
libido, 374
Lieberman, 173
LIFE IS A JOURNEY, 579–594 see also *conceptual metaphor*
limited channel capacity, 36, 160, 171–173, 185, 380
Lindsay, 258
linguistics, 1, 2, 21
liquid, 563
liquids, 9, 10, 215, 222, 478–480, 484
listener response, 181, 200–206, 208

litany, 338
literal–figurative distinction, 585–586
literary criticism, 2
literary history, 2, 538–540, 548
literary synaesthesia, 452, 502–505
literature of extreme situations, 298
litotes, 345
LNR group, 258, 265
localism, 391, 420
Lock, 232
logical fallacy, 418, 421
long-term memory, 6, 7, 8, 19, 261, 262
Longinus, 93, 94, 96, 97, 486, 497
LoSciuto, 62
loudness, 175
LOVE IS A JOURNEY, 593 see also *conceptual metaphor*
Lovejoy, 315–322
Lubbock, 597, 598
Lucifer, 605–606
Lukács, 107
Luzzatto, 322–326
Lyons, 68, 391, 420
lyric, 328

Macdermott, 212, 480
Mack, 261–262
Madách, 604–606
Maier, 60
making strange, 266, 524
Mallarmé, 209, 402, 403, 476
man as prisoner, 297–302
mannerism, 73, 93, 195, 320, 335, 410, 412, 413, 500, 549
mannerist, 326, 335–339, 405, 438
mannerist poetry, 283, 413
marginal control, 3, 4, 5, 8, 547, 568, 574
Margolis, 64–66, 82, 206, 343, 353, 513

markedness, 139–140, 235, 246–247,
    248, 257–263, 269, 271, 276,
    286, 290, 463, 473, 497, 542
markers, 250
Marlowe, 21–23, 170–171
Marlowe Society, 187–198, 204
Martindale, 326
Martinet, 279
Martz, 468–470
Marxism, 537, 546
    Marxist critics, 442
materials–structure dichotomy, 324,
    344, 624, 638
mathematical sublime, 390
Mattingly, 218
May, 222
meaning
    meaning component, 107, 245–
    281
    meaning potentials, 578
    meaning units stratum, 41
    meaning-cancelations, 586
    meaning-component, 168
meditation, 25, 451, 452, 456–470,
    613–615
    meditative poetry, 320
Melchiori, 337, 411
memory, 2, 19
Mendelssohn, 323
mental dictionary, 15, 245–281,
    541–575
mental image, 419
mental performance, 29–41, 83, 137,
    341, 401, 466, 470, 485, 488,
    489
mental processing space, 37, 185,
    380
mental set, 11, 26, 43
mental space, 167, 172, 173, 185
mental storage space, 8
mentalism, 133
merkava mysticism, 338
Mervis, 258–259, 319, 330

meta–awareness, 24, 411–414
meta–language, 206
metaeffusion, 569–571
metalanguage, 541–575
metaphor, 14, 22, 23, 26, 51, 77,
    105–106, 107, 168, 172, 182,
    245–263, 283–294, 310, 319,
    331, 351, 363, 366, 369, 370,
    378, 381, 395, 396, 398, 400,
    402, 405, 406, 408, 413, 415,
    417, 437, 439, 448, 453, 455,
    466, 480, 488, 492, 497, 499,
    500–501, 504, 508, 515, 542,
    543, 555, 572, 577–594, 638
    metaphorical coherence, 406
    mixed metaphor, 406, 410
metaphysical, 24, 92, 93, 97, 98,
    296, 330–339
    metaphysical conceit, 24, 49, 273,
    331, 336, 411–414, 438, 448,
    452, 555, 557
    metaphysical intuition, 458–461
    metaphysical poetry, 21, 49, 93,
    283, 297–305, 314, 412–414,
    416, 469, 499, 549
    metaphysical pun, 336, 411–414
    metaphysical wit, 47, 91, 92, 301
metarealistic, 424, 425
meter, 5, 38–39, 41, 112, 132, 149,
    151–154, 155–180, 181–208,
    325, 623, 638–640
    metric, 21
    metric pattern, 156–180, 558
    metric scheme, 496
    metric shape, 278, 540, 606
    metric system, 314, 324
    metrical position, 155–180, 181–
    208
    metrical set, 38, 159, 166, 172,
    173
    metricalness, 158, 173
Metman, 355, 384, 517–527

metonymy, 305, 332, 349, 350, 351, 374, 376, 401, 415, 417, 418, 419, 422, 476, 519, 624

Meyer, 85, 112–119, 123, 155, 163, 166, 179, 293, 393, 465, 488, 607, 609

Miall, 610, 616, 619, 620

migration, 418
migratory theory, 416–417

Miles, 104–107, 545–546, 575

Mill, 74

Miller, 13, 14, 24, 51, 118, 135, 172, 412, 420, 560, 565–567

Miller, George, 608

Miller, J.G., 344

Milner, 361

Milton, 38, 84, 85–91, 94–97, 100–103, 104, 132, 137, 139, 149–154, 156, 158, 162, 164, 167–169, 171, 207, 209, 329, 391, 393, 474, 506, 508, 509, 638, 639
Milton vs. Donne, 94–97
Milton vs. Poe, 100–103
Milton vs. Spenser, 85–91

miraculism, 417–422

Mobley, 452

modernism, 73, 93
modern poetry, 21, 412
modern poets, 469
modernistic literature, 297, 298

modularity of the mind, 7

Molière, 1, 314

monism, 328

Moore, 108, 462, 464

More, 146

Morgenstern, 423, 551–559, 561, 562, 564, 574

Mosher, 50

Mourgues, 331, 599

Muecke, 358, 606

multiple relationship, 402

Murray, 363

musicality, 148, 476

mysticism, 452, 491
mystic experiences, 612
mystic oxymoron, 491
mystic poetry, 47, 286, 301, 453, 468, 485, 511, 613

myth, 65, 272, 316, 320, 364, 366, 380, 400, 559, 565, 567

mythology, 308, 356, 490, 524

Nair, 49

naming, 316

Napoleon, 604, 606, 624

nasals, 9, 10, 215, 222, 478–480, 484
nasal vowels, 236, 239

Nahman of Braslaw, 314

necessary and sufficient condition, 80, 83–84, 103, 317, 340

negative capability, 20, 276, 330, 389, 424, 429–433, 473, 483, 511–529, 530, 540 see also *decision style*; *quest for certitude*

Neisser, 16, 18, 19, 24, 36, 60, 171, 385–387, 412, 413, 419, 581

Neo–Classicism, 92, 124
Neo–Classic, 147, 326, 410, 550see also *Classicism*

Neo-Thomism, 539, 548

Neuman, 523

neutral sound patterns, 210

New Criticism, 495, 510, 533, 599, 612
New Critics, 329, 592, 607

New Humanism, 539, 548

new information, 462 see also *old information*

Newberg, 599, 613–615

nominal vs. verbal style, 104–109

nominalization, 459–466, 543
nominalized predicate, 23

nonspeech mode, 9, 10, 176, 216–234 see also *speech mode*

Norman, 258
norms, 29, 30, 32, 38, 39, 638
Nostradamus, 376
novel, 2, 317, 327
nursery rhymes, 473

obtrusive rhythm, 471–494
Occam, 247, 328, 548
oceanic dedifferentiation, 307
    oceanic imagery, 454–456
    oceanic undifferentiation, 46, 284,
        361–362, 366, 394, 451, 453–456
octet, 126–130, 131, 502, 504
Oedipus complex, 343–354
Oedipus the King (Oedipus
    Tyrannos), 580–581, 582
Oedipus-situation, 351
Ohmann, 408, 426, 462, 463, 515
old information, 462, 464 see also
    new information
Olver, 47
Omar Khayyám, 34–35, 123–126
On Seeing the Elgin Marbles, 22
onomatopoeia, 162, 210, 223–229,
    235, 239, 241, 242
ontological problem of the one and
    the many, 334–335
open concept, 313, 326–341, 343
open vs. closed mind, 514
opponent processes, 379
optic array, 386, 412
optical transformations, 385
oral stop, 236
Oras, 77, 85–91
ordinary consciousness, 15, 16, 20,
    25, 43, 67, 75, 320, 321, 385,
    451, 529, 544
organized violence, 4, 5, 8, 21
orientation, 17, 18, 19, 20, 21, 24–
    25, 284, 290, 292, 293, 304, 380,
    385–403, 405, 410, 411, 438,
    439, 448, 453, 575, 610–616 see
    also *disorientation*

fast orientation, 380, 382, 386,
    405, 412
    orientation schema, 386–387, 438
ornament, 313, 325, 336–338, 343
Ornstein, 15, 16, 385, 387–388,
    397, 398, 504–506, 610–611
Ortony, 577
Othello, 533
overarticulation, 179, 192–193, 205
overdifferentiation, 130, 284, 293
oxymoron, 89, 90, 151, 290, 294,
    321, 345, 440, 443, 486, 608
Ozymandias, 595, 602, 616–620

Pace non trovo, 35
Pagis, 69, 337
panchronistic tendencies, 289, 291,
    292
parable, 5515–517, 523–527, 532,
    571
paradigm of Enlightenment poetry,
    322–326
paradigm of Mediaeval Hebrew
    poetry, 322–326
paradigma, 424
paradigmatic, 563
Paradise Lost, 182
paradox, 117, 328–335, 338, 345,
    365, 370, 374, 377, 406, 414,
    509, 572–574, 608
    paradox of imagination, 608
parallel transmission, 218, 234
parallelism, 629
paraphrase, 400, 440, 608, 613
paronomasia, 73, 561
part–whole relationship, 2, 7, 118,
    136, 155, 160, 162, 313–315,
    322–326, 410, 516, 558, 625
past experience, 327, 416
Pater, 3, 47, 295, 514
pathetic fallacy, 398, 545
pattern of performance, 157–180
Pavio, 420

Pears, 25, 316, 341, 412–414, 419
Peer Gynt, 314, 322, 557
Peirce, 118, 280, 558, 559
Penrose, 53
pentameter, 156–180, 182
perceived effect, 1, 23, 29, 30, 77–
    104, 124, 165, 245, 277, 278,
    284, 304, 324, 327, 396, 541,
    542, 546, 609
perceived quality, 9, 29, 77–104,
    112, 222, 246, 278, 283, 286,
    289, 612, 626, 639
perceiving as, 206
perception and personality, 344, 514,
    529, 592
perceptual anticipation, 386
perceptual constancy, 17, 386
perceptual cycle, 419
perceptual forces, 132–154, 159,
    162, 184
perceptual isochrony, 176
perceptual overload, 459, 503
perceptual quality, 112, 149, 165,
    234, 280, 283, 289, 295, 463,
    464, 465, 467, 468, 477, 506,
    562, 623, 626, 638
perceptual readiness, 19, 419
perceptual stability, 515
perceptual vs. conceptual
    categorization, 394–403
performance, 29, 30–41, 185, 630
    see also *rhythmical performance of
    poetry*
    vocal performance, 29, 30, 38–39,
    137, 158–180, 181–208, 213
period and style
period style, 23, 64, 313–341, 343,
    382, 539, 550, 558
periodicity, 214, 242, 484
periodic vs. aperiodic, 215–216, 222–
    223, 240, 478–480
periodization, 322–326
peripeteia, 349, 383

Persinger, 492
personality style, 30, 35, 408
personification, 400
perspectivism, 539–540, 548–550
    see also *absolutism; relativism*
Petrarcan, 273
Petrarch, 35, 69
Pet˝fi, 212–213, 214
Peyre, 77, 209, 212, 495–500, 504,
    547, 548
phallic symbolism, 454
Phèdre, 631
philosophical logic, 463
philosophy of science, 1
phoneme, 5, 217, 239, 279
    phonemic opposition, 174
phonetics, 6
    phonetic cues, 206 see also
    acoustic cues
    phonetic representation, 6, 7, 21
phonology, 8
    phonological feature, 7
    phonological level, 279
    phonological universals, 235–240
phrasal vs. clausal style, 104–109 see
    also *verbal vs. nominal style*
Piaget, 45, 49, 421
Picasso, 64
pigeonholing, 345
pitch extract, 177–179, 188, 205
Plato, 274–275, 499, 548
pleasure, 47, 48, 49
    pleasure principle, 309
pluralism, 329
Plutchik, 408
Poe, 100–103, 210, 471, 474–485,
    494
poetics, 1, 2, 5, 6, 9, 15, 20; defined,
    1
    poetic mode, 10, 16, 216–234,
    478–479
    poetic qualities, 112–114

poetry of disorientation, 405–422, 423–449, 452
poetry of meditation, 468–470, 610, 613–616
poetry of orientation, 385–403, 412, 420, 445, 452
point of view, 304, 324, 420, 581, 595, 596, 598, 600, 601, 602, 603–622
Polányi, 3, 4, 6, 8, 112, 304, 324, 325, 420, 547, 568, 574
polyphony, 508
Pope, 38, 92, 116–122, 124, 126, 139, 141–144, 147, 148, 149, 158, 164, 169, 277, 278, 329, 417, 473, 474, 511, 627, 633
position, 278
positivism, 511, 523, 527, 533
Posner, 111–112
post-romantic poetry, 485
potential, 111, 158, 210–216, 309, 326, 476, 495, 500, 544
potential meanings, 590
Potter, 54
Prägnanz, 113, 123
pre-categorial information, 4, 9, 10, 17, 18, 20, 21, 25, 216–234, 242, 284, 286, 362, 405, 466, 467, 480, 483, 484
pre-categorial visual information, 386
pre-conceptual mental processes, 464, 468
pre-conscious, 407
Précieux, 330, 339
predication, 245, 252
predicative position, 252–257, 610
predisposing factors, 362–364, 381
preromanticism, 318–319
presupposition, 109, 245
Prince, 551–566
principle of congruence, 587, 588 see also *literary competence*

problem solving, 44, 45, 182, 207, 595
projected world, 638
proper names, 73–75, 476, 479, 564
proportionalizing, 296, 297, 313–315 see also *essentializing*
prose rhythm, 157–180, 183, 196, 206, 207
Prose vs. Verse, 173–180
prosodic, 21, 609, 619, 623, 639
protagonist, 344, 345, 349, 374, 383, 424
Proust, 524
proverb, 69
proximal stimulus, 438 see also *distal stimulus*
proximity, 113, 116, 117, 166
psychoanalysis, 284, 361, 407
   psychoanalytic interpretation of dreams, 578
   psychoanalytic literature, 309
   psychoanalytic theory, 236
   psychoanalytical terms, 455
psycholinguistics, 1
psychological reality, 619
psychological subject, 611
psychological syndrome, 343–354
pun, 93, 103, 236, 407, 562, 564
purposefulness without concept, 425, 426, 448
purposefulness without purpose, 423, 425, 448
Pushkin, 512–513

quantitative meter, 155, 174
quatrain, 117–119, 123–126, 127, 128, 129, 132, 278, 482, 488, 495, 498, 500, 501, 502, 505, 548
quest for certitude, 112, 424, 429–433, 473, 511–529 see also *decision style; negative capability*
Quillian, 258, 259–263

Quintilianus, 354, 601, 602, 609, 620

Racine, 117, 327, 543–544, 624, 631, 632
Rakerd, 234
Ramachandran, 287–288
Ramsey, 344, 530
Rand, 220
Ransom, 414–418, 473, 488, 555, 557
rapid and delayed closure, 592
rapid and delayed conceptualization, 577–578, 580, 585, 591
rapid vs. delayed categorization, 456
rapid vs. delayed closure, 343–354, 514–517
rationalism, 320
Ratosh, 472
Rause, 613, 615
reader-response approach, 423–433
reality principle, 309
realization of the idiom, 409
recoding, 6, 8, 9–12, 14, 21, 36–37, 160, 172, 173, 334, 459, 506, 542, 560
reductionism, 2, 382, 547
reductionist, 296
referential vs. nonreferential use of speech sounds, 235–240, 242
referring position, 252–257, 610, 615–616
regional quality, 78–80, 103, 395, 396, 430–432, 457, 554, 557
Régnier, 402, 403
regression, 47, 48, 50, 236–240, 272
regulative concept, 295, 313–341, 343–354, 355–384, 470
reintegration, 311
relativism, 539–540, 548–550 see also *absolutism*; *perspectivism*
Renaissance, 35, 207, 274, 337
    Renaissance poem, 314

repetition, 346, 481–484, 485, 497, 498
Repp, 220, 222
representative anecdote, 295–312
represented world, 325
requiredness, 115–116, 121, 127, 128, 135, 140–154, 636
retrieval, 8, 19
retro-relating, 488, 505, 510
return, law of, 123–130
rhetoric, 337, 354
    rhetorical figure, 345
rhyme, 5, 41, 112, 113, 115–132, 148, 240, 241, 245, 246, 277–281, 325, 326, 447, 473, 474–477, 484, 490, 498, 623, 636–637, 638, 640 see also *grouping effect of rhymes*
    equi-rhyme, 324
    anti-grammatical rhyme, 14, 440–441, 442, 446, 447, 448, 473, 474, 477, 481, 639
    grammatical and anti-grammatical rhymes, 277–281, 473, 632–636 see also *tame and vigorous rhyme*
    rhyme pattern, 440, 482, 498, 499, 607, 608, 609
    rhymed couplets, 624, 626
    rhymed prose, 325
    rhyming system, 324
rhythm, 38–39, 41, 108, 123, 126, 132–154, 155–180, 181–208, 213, 377
    rhythmic shape, 87–89, 101–103, 155–180, 181–208
    rhythmical performance of poetry, 38, 155–180, 181–208 see also *performance*
Richards, 14, 28, 213, 501, 578, 582, 584–585, 592
riddles, 67–75
ridiculous, 304
Riffaterre, 28

rigidity, 9, 344, 353, 354
Rimbaud, 65, 510
Ritual Drama, 360, 362, 367
Robbe-Grillet, 518
Rohwer, 111
Romain, 289–290
Romanticism, 299, 315–322, 432,
    452, 609
    romantic, 20, 21, 22, 23, 24, 93,
    296, 326, 330–335, 550, 616
    romantic drama/tragedy, 361, 362,
    381, 622, 630
    romantic nature imagery, 500
    romantic nature poetry, 613
    romantic poem, 64, 314, 505
    romantic poetry, 283, 286, 297–
    308, 327, 405, 411, 412, 445,
    453, 469, 485, 537, 555, 609
    romantic poets, 469
    romantic view of the universe,
    536–538
Ronsard, 35
Rorschach, 113, 114, 393
Rosch, 258–259, 319
Ross, 139
Rostand, 531, 623–640
Rubáiyáth, 34–35, 123–126
Rückert, 212
rule of significance, 43, 69–75, 406
    see also literary competence
Rumelhart, 258, 263–266
Ruskin, 545
Russian Formalism, 4, 68, 93, 398

Samson's riddle, 69
sarcasm, 433
satire, 554
saturation, 123–126
saving of mental energy, 407
Schachtel, 113
Schank, 7, 11, 13, 14, 15, 245, 258,
    263–266, 586, 604
Scheerer, 354

schema, 18, 19, 24, 258, 263–271,
    329, 355, 363, 385, 397, 406,
    412, 413, 419, 421, 438, 536,
    537, 538
scheme, 344
Schirmann, 340, 433–434, 438
Schlegel, 318
Schneider, 31, 32–33, 274–275, 472
Scholem, 452
Schramm, 176, 182
Schroder, 530–538
script, 10–11, 24, 258, 263–271
Scrutiny group, 533
Searle, 74, 586, 588, 591–592
second-order language, 15
seeing as, 628
SEEING IS KNOWING, 585 see also
    conceptual metaphor
segmental discontinuation, 179, 191
selection restriction features, 15, 395
self-reference, 573–574
self-specifying information, 386,
    392, 411, 412
semantic features, 7, 12, 14, 214,
    245–281, 498, 612
semantic memory, 19, 258, 259–263
semantic primitives, 245–281
semantic representation, 6, 7, 12–15,
    245–281, 319
semantic transformation, 43, 406
semiotic, 5
semiotic code, 73, 75
sense datum, 463–465
sense impression, 283
sensory information, 112
sensuous metaphor, 73, 248–249,
    405–411, 452
sentence fragment, 195
sentence meaning, 267 see also
    utterer's meaning
sequential processing, 396–399, 612
sestet, 130–132, 502, 505
shading, 87, 90, 113, 114, 146, 147

Shakespeare, 137, 139, 145–146, 158, 164, 171, 187–200, 211, 274, 275, 276–277, 327, 329, 334–335, 355, 356–360, 453, 511, 513, 550, 607
Shakespearean sonnet, 607
Shankweiler, 17
shape perception, 385, 386–387, 389, 392–393, 401–402, 438
Sheen, Michael, 186–187
Shelley, 136–137, 139, 141–142, 147–154, 158, 164, 167–168, 207, 331–332, 392, 452, 499, 506, 545, 548, 595, 602–609, 638, 639
Shelley, Mary, 601
Shen, 286
shift mental sets
shift of mental set, 11, 12, 24, 25, 26, 27, 43, 44, 55, 56, 95, 251, 269, 273, 352, 353, 405, 421, 524–526, 529, 559, 574, 584
Shklovsky, 4, 13, 46, 295, 414, 555
Shlonsky, 140, 262, 405–409, 423, 610–611
Shmuel Hannagid, 72–73
short–term memory, 6, 102, 172, 462, 608
sibilants, 210
    sibilants, double–edgedness of, 222
Sibley, 80, 83–84, 103, 206, 541
Sidney, 523
sign, 281
    sign vehicle, 111, 112
    sign-using animal, 111–112
    signifiant and signifié, 5, 41, 71, 73, 93, 111–112, 555–556, 564
    signifier, 149
significant variation, 350
Silberschlag, 323
Silberstein, 408

similarity, 113, 116, 117, 166, 317, 366
simile, 89, 249, 271, 281, 285, 433, 490, 497, 498
singular terms vs. general terms, 251–257
situation appraisal, 56–57, 58, 365
Sitwell, 290–291
skepticism, 133
Slobin, 134
Smart, 82
Smith, James 94, 95, 331, 335, 499
Smith, Horace, 604–605, 606
Snyder, 471–479
Socrates, 274
sonnet, 126–132, 211, 325, 499, 500, 501, 503, 504, 505, 506, 523, 547, 548
sonnet form, 608, 609
sonorants, 214, 242
sonority, 215, 223
Sophocles, 381
sound gestures, 235, 239, 242
sound patterns, , 562–564
sound stratum, 39, 41, 111–154, 155–180, 181–208, 284, 295, 483, 484, 502, 558
sound symbolism, 41, 209–243
sound-recorders, 182
space perception, 302, 385–403, 438, 453, 469, 470, 477
spatial imagery, 364, 366, 577, 581–583, 585, 587
spatial processing, 396–399
spatio-temporal continuity, 107, 251–257, 303, 463, 465, 610, 615
SPECT camera brain-imaging, 613–615
spectrogram, 216–231
spectrograph, 216
speech code, 6–10, 541

speech mode, 9, 10, 16, 176, 216–234, 478see also *nonspeech mode*
speech reception, 459
speech sounds, 209–243, 477–481, 498
spell-weaving, 471 see also *hypnotic*; *trance-inductive*
Spencer, 17
Spenser, 85–91, 104, 136–137, 139, 509
spiritual space, 276–277
Spitzer, 501, 543–544, 546, 575
St. Bernard de Clairvaux, 434, 443
St. Ignatius, 467, 611, 613
stable world, 43–76, 272, 294, 361, 529
Stanford, 283, 288–291
stanza, 41, 115–132, 442, 446, 447, 448, 449, 472, 473, 481–484, 488, 493, 505, 509
Steen, Gerard, 595
Stekel, Wilhelm, 578
Stevens, Wallace 559, 562–564, 569, 574
stock response, 578, 582, 584–585, 592
Stockwell, 595–622
stop release, 183
stops, 9, 10
Stopwatch,592–593
storage, 6, 8, 260
strange loopiness, 573
stratified system of norms, 39–41, 85, 297, 313–315, 319–326, 339, 473, 557
Strawson, 23, 252–257, , 462–463, 541, 610–611, 616
stress, 155, 173–180, 181–208, 474, 477, 560, 561
    stress group, 159–164, 173
    stress maximum, 157–180, 208, 560–561

stress maximum in a weak position, 181
stress pattern, 157–180, 560
stress valley, 160–169
lexical stress, 157
Streufert, 530–538
Stroop test, 111
Structuralism, 213, 219, 235, 599
structuralist criticism, 1
structure, 1
style, 63–64, 90, 97, 469, 527, 569
    style as diagnosis, 343–354, 356
    style as hypothesis, 343–354, 356
    stylistic syndrome, 343–354
subject vs. predicate, 253–257
sublime, 24, 40, 92, 93, 94, 95, 96, 97, 98, 99, 303, 304, 324, 381, 388–391, 426, 448, 449, 489, 565, 566, 601, 614, 618
    sublime poetry, 105, 106
    dynamic sublime, 390
substantive level, 401, 499
superordinate, 13, 48, 539, 563
surface structure, 6, 10, 11, 460, 473
    see also *deep structure*
sweet-talk, 237
Sweetser, 623–640
Syllabic meter, 155
Syllabotonic (syllabic accentual) meter, 155, 180
syllepsis, 345
symbol, 19, 44, 45, 251, 272–276, 281, 316, 320, 382, 399–403, , 501, 512, 515
    symbolic meaning, 55
    symbolic processes, 577
    Symbolism, 46, 47, 77, 209, 240–241, 283, 402–403, 515
    symbolist, 20, 21, 439
    symbolist poetry, 293, 503, 508
    symbolization, 43, 272–276

symmetry, 111–154, 160, 278, 411, 440, 447, 448, 481, 483, 488, 505, 627
synaesthesia, 21, 283–294
syncopation, 163
syndeton, 349 see also *asyndeton*
synecdoche, 250
synonym, 13, 22, 246, 407, 437, 483, 486, 487, 514, 542
syntactic inversion, 120–122, 127, 150, 151
syntactic rhymes, 170
syntagmatic, 236, 237, 238, 279, 563
Sypher, 336, 413, 419
ˇǝkhina, 310

tacit knowledge, 324, 325, 420
Talmud, 266–270, 310
Tamburlaine, 22
tame and vigorous rhyme, 632–636 see also grammatical and anti-grammatical rhyme
Tartakovsky, 624
Taylor, 306
Tchernikhovsky, 302–305, 494
teleological transcendence, 300–301, 305
telling and showing, 149, 152, 397, 453, 464, 468, 470, 485
Tennyson, 144, 329, 545
tenor, 408, 555, 556 see also *vehicle*
tercet, 132, 504
terms of exclusion, 320
terzina, 142, 147, 148, 440
tetrameter, 122, 123, 136, 137, 144
Theatre of the Absurd, 55
thematic transformation, 43
thematized predicate, 461–468, 545, 574, 610–616 see also *ABSTRACT of the CONCRETE*; *GERUND of the CONCRETE*;
theology, 297

Theophrastus, 497
thing destruction, 20, 293, 500, 505, 544, 545, 546
thing-free, 19, 20, 21, 22, 23, 92, 96, 99, 114, 236, 241, 278, 284, 287, 290, 291, 292, 303, 364, 380, 393, 395, 396, 397, 400, 445, 453–466, 498, 500, 501, 502, 503, 504, 505, 542, 544, 545, 546, 615 see also *gestalt-free*
Thomson, 24, 409–411, 413, 427–433, 445, 553–559, 565, 566–567
tip-of-the-tongue (TOT) phenomenon, 5, 14, 19
Todorov, 416
tolerance of ambiguity, 424
    tolerance of uncertainty, 513, 578
    tolerance vs. intolerance of ambiguity, 514, 528 see also *intolerance of ambiguity*
Tolstoy, 295, 598
tone-group, 183–184, 194
Tonic (accentual) meter, 155
top-down, 329
top-down vs. bottom-up, 82–83
topic, 541
topicalized attribute, , 461–468, 574, 610–616 see also *ABSTRACT of the CONCRETE*; *GERUND of the CONCRETE*; *thematized predicate*
topographia, 92
topoi, 356, 382
Tóth, 140, 293
Tragedy of Man, The 604–606
tragic, 324, 328
tragic rhythm of life, 360
tragicomedy, 64, 427
trance-inductive, 471 see also *hypnotic*; *spell-weaving*
transcendence, 375
transfer features, 15
transferred epithet, 288
transformational grammar, 462

Treisman, 467
Trilling, 511
trimeter, 122, 123
triple-encodedness, 203, 206
trochaic, 123, 471
trochaic inversion, 166, 175
trope, 555
Tsur, 21, 28, 31, 34, 35, 116, 122,
    126, 132, 135, 136, 139, 144,
    155, 158, 165, 169, 174, 180,
    181, 209, 241, 277, 294, 307,
    390, 394, 398, 400, 407, 408,
    434, 452, 453, 456, 461, 470,
    471, 472, 474, 478, 479, 480,
    503, 506, 508, 510, 529, 542,
    545, 568, 611, 613, 637
Turner, 637
twenty questions, 50–52, 53
types of style, 313

Ullmann, 285–289, 291, 292
uncanny, 484
unconscious, 521
underarticulation, 191–192, 193
undifferentiated, 394, 400, 402, 455,
    459, 466, 468, 470, 480, 485,
    498, 503, 537
undifferentiation, 304, 362, 395
unique conscious quality, 8, 10, 11,
    12, 19, 24, 25
units of meaning, 245–281, 283–294
units of meaning stratum, 39, 41,
    483, 558
unity, 206, 355 see also *canons of
    evaluation*
unity-in-variety, 630, 632
universal, 107
utterer's meaning, 267 see also
    sentence meaning

values, 8, 19, 297, 328, 358, 406,
    412, 539–540

vehicle, 335, 406, 419, 420, 555,
    556, 564 see also *tenor*
Veiling and Revealing in Language,
    46
verbal vs. nominal style, 41, 147 see
    also *phrasal vs. clausal style*
Verlaine, 209, 212–216, 239, 240,
    241, 403, 603, 633, 636
vers libre, 174, 175
versatile reader, 313–341, 343, 495
versification, 8, 623–640
vibrato, 337
Villon, 35, 140, 415–418
Virgil, 5, 559
visual proprioception, 386
voiced fricatives, 215
voiced sibilant, 563
voiced stops, 214, 215, 217
voiceless fricatives, 215
voiceless stops, 214, 215, 222

Waisman, 572–574
Waiting for Godot, 302, 309, 355,
    384, 517–527
Wallin, 176
War and Peace, 598
Warren, Austin 29, 38, 39–41, 78,
    157, 158, 182, 183, 207, 295,
    311, 313, 324, 339, 344, 426,
    538–540, 548–550, 557, 624,
    638, 639
Warren, Robert Penn, 31, 581
Warton, 318
Wason, 52–54, 519
Watson, 274–275
Waugh, 219, 229, 235
wave plot, 177–179, 186–205
Weinreich, 15, 463
Weisstein, 403, 513
Weitz, Morris, 32–33, 207, 317–
    319, 425, 432, 513, 587, 640
Wellek, 29, 38, 39–41, 78, 85, 157,
    158, 182, 183, 207, 295, 311,

313, 316–322, 324, 339, 344,
356, 382, 533, 538–540, 548–
550, 557, 603, 624, 638, 639
Wells, 107–108
Werner, 611
Wernicke's area, 593
Wertheimer, 113
Whitman, 37, 334, 456–468, 470,
616
Wilde, 289
Wimsatt, 182, 277, 328–329, 400,
500, 501, 548, 560, 633
Winner, 408, 604
Winnicott, 361
wit, 10, 11, 12, 24, 25, 27, 56, 92–
95, 121, 145, 249, 250, 265, 273,
278, 284, 292, 405, 554, 562,
584, 627
witty, 41, 84, 101, 102, 103,
112, 117, 121, 122, 145, 146,
147, 148, 236, 249, 253, 262,
283, 290, 291, 294, 304, 305,
393, 398, 415, 471, 476, 503,
508, 574
witty effect, 251, 269, 271, 407,
555, 627, 630, 631, 636
witty quality, 283, 284, 486, 496,
628, 639
Wittgenstein, 33, 64, 194, 206, 229,
315–322, 339, 628

womb as representative anecdote,
309–311
Woodring, 489
Woolf, 317
word acquisition, 13
word association, 14, 245, 246
word order, 498
Wordsworth, 129, 170, 261, 322,
329, 394–396, 397, 452, 453,
486, 487–492, 505, 506, 544–
545, 616, 633
world knowledge, 10, 245, 255, 257–
271
world stratum, 39, 41, 284, 295–
312, 397, 483, 484, 558, 639
Wuthering Heights, 596–597, 601
Wyatt, 35, 69

Yeats, 155, 156, 158, 171, 329
Yehoshua, 75, 529
Yehuda Halevy, 49, 70, 332–333
Youmans, 198

Zeitgeist, 314
Zemach, 71, 72, 73, 206
Zenon, 571
zeugma, 121, 345